THE
MORMON
DELUSION

Volume 5

Doctrine and Covenants
– Deception and Concoctions

Jim Whitefield

The Mormon Delusion. Volume 5.
Doctrine and Covenants
– Deception and Concoctions

Paperback Edition

First published in February 2012 by
Lulu Press Inc. Raleigh, North Carolina, USA.

First Edition – February 2012

Copyright © Jim Whitefield 2012

ISBN 13: 978-1-4710-4770-0

British Library Catalogue System Number: 015497834

Lulu ID: 12416652

All rights reserved. No part of this publication may
be reproduced, stored in a retrieval system, or
transmitted in any form or by any means,
electronic, mechanical photocopying, recording,
or otherwise, without the prior permission
of the author.

www.themormondelusion.com

Email the author: jim@themormondelusion.com

Dedication

For Catriona –
who gave me the time, the space
and the encouragement to write.

Jim Whitefield 2012

Also by this author

The Mormon Delusion. Volume 1.
The Truth Behind Polygamy
and Secret Polyandry

First Edition – Feb 2009
Second Edition – Aug 2009
Third Edition – Sept 2010

The Mormon Delusion. Volume 2.
The Secret Truth Withheld
From 13 Million Mormons

First Edition – May 2009
Second Edition – Sept 2010

The Mormon Delusion. Volume 3.
Discarded Doctrines and
Nonsense Revelations

First Edition – July 2009
Second Edition – Sept 2010

The Mormon Delusion. Volume 4.
The Mormon Missionary Lessons
– A Conspiracy to Deceive

First Edition – January 2011

The First Vision – The Joseph Smith Story. (Booklet).

First Edition – August 2011
Second Edition – October 2011

The TMD series is available in hardcover, paperback and e-Book format.
Bookstore: http://www.lulu.com/spotlight/themormondelusion
Visit www.themormondelusion.com for more information.

**I spent 43 years believing in a false religion.
Now I want my 43 years as an atheist.
God owes me that.**
Jim Whitefield

Acknowledgements

My thanks, as ever, to my wife Catriona, for freely allowing me the time and space to write yet another volume in which she has no real personal interest. This time, when I mentioned the idea for the book, she actually encouraged me to set to and write it. In the beginning, Cat knew that writing was my therapy but now I no longer need the relief writing once brought, she understands it is a subject I know well and can write about. She also appreciates the fact that my work seems to have helped many others come to an understanding of the truth behind the Mormon Church, judging by the feedback received. Cat's continued unconditional support has allowed me once again to spend each day working uninterrupted. I previously mentioned that I retired when I turned sixty in February of 2006 and my journey to the truth began the following month when, quite accidentally, I discovered early Mormon polyandry. I was sixty-five in February of 2011, the month following publication of volume four. After five years full time research and writing, with no word of complaint from my wife, I thought that any further writing may be greeted with at least a frown. Just the opposite has been the case and with Cat's love and encouragement I have once again put pen to paper – well, these days, of course, that really means fingers to keyboard – for the fifth time. It is now February of 2012 and six years since I discovered the truth about Mormonism. It is still unbelievably devastating.

Jean Bodie and John Bleazard have again kindly been of invaluable help with proof reading and editing suggestions. Their tireless efforts have helped to hone my work into a format which sits far better than the original final draft – even after my own numerous rewrites. The meticulous work of my two good friends will undoubtedly once again make the journey through this book more flowing and enjoyable than would otherwise have been the case. I am deeply grateful to them both for their help and advice – and their ongoing friendship and support.

My grateful thanks also again go to my good friends and fellow authors, Arza Evans, Simon Southerton, Pamela McCreary, Lyndon Lamborn and to Richard Packham (founder and first President of the Exmormon Foundation) for kindly reviewing and enthusiastically endorsing the final draft of volume five. I am most grateful to them for their kind comments and continued encouragement.

Unsurprisingly, I have to again report that to date, I have still not received the promised response from Mormon Church leaders concerning my research and questions regarding polyandry and other issues that I submitted (as requested by the Church) in 2006. As mentioned in volumes 1-4:

I can only assume that the Church *(still)* has no answers…

Guidance Notes

This work is an exposé regarding the book 'Doctrine and Covenants' published by The Church of Jesus Christ of Latter Day Saints. Early members were more commonly known as 'Mormonites'. In later years, the terms 'Mormons' and 'The Mormon Church' were in common use both inside and outside of the Church. Then Church leaders spent several decades trying to remove what they appeared to consider a stigma regarding 'Mormonism' which had followed the Church from the beginning. The following paragraph appeared in volumes 1-3 of my work for that very reason:

> "This work is an exposé regarding the Church of Jesus Christ of Latter Day Saints. Today, the Church prefers the nickname 'LDS' (Latter Day Saints) rather than 'Mormon' which was previously the case, both inside and outside the religion. As the term 'Mormon' is actually still more widely recognised, particularly in the United Kingdom, that is the term I have used throughout this work."

Now, it transpires the Church has changed its view and has once again decided to embrace terms which it once found offensive. Church related web sites are now replete with references to 'Mormons' and 'Mormonism'. It seems that my comment that 'the only thing consistent about Mormonism is its inconsistency' applies to even more aspects than I imagined. Perhaps the continued lacklustre growth experienced by the Church over recent years has made Mormon public relations advisers clutch at straws in order to try to make Mormonism more familiar and acceptable to the general public; who knows?

Where quotes are included, original spellings and grammar have been retained. Unless otherwise stated, any emphasis was in original quotes. D&C references extracted into the body of the text are denoted by "double" speech marks.

The word 'Church', with a capital 'C', is used throughout this book. Where it occurs without further explanation, it always refers to the Mormon Church. The expression 'the Church' *specifically* refers to the controlling leaders of the organisation or to the organisation itself. The context in each case should be self-evident. In other contexts, 'church' in the lower case is used as normal. I also capitalise 'Section(s)' when referring to Sections of the D&C – for clarity.

Internet addresses are notorious for changing or even disappearing altogether. Nevertheless, my books include a number of them, as so much information is now available on the internet, allowing readers access to further research with relative ease. If sources cannot be located, just use a search engine, referencing the topic or related words, to locate the required information.

Many and some rare, historical books are now available to read or research online. Some such works that I recommend are listed in the bibliography. In addition to those listed, *Google Book Search* is building an online collection very quickly. Before purchasing a book, it is always worth first checking to see if it is available to read or download free online at: http://books.google.com/

Online copies of all the Mormon Scriptures – *Book of Mormon, Doctrine and Covenants, Pearl of Great Price* – are available to research and review along with the *King James Version* of the Bible. All these are made available online by the Mormon Church and their web site is useful for researching anything you may need to review or compare. This is the link: http://scriptures.lds.org/

The above site was recently updated, when yet again the Mormon Church made some changes. In this volume, when I refer to the 2010 version of the D&C, it means the recently updated internet version. The online introduction to the *Book of Mormon* now incorporates the 'Doubleday' 2006 edition change regarding the so-called Lamanites, from the original claim found in *older copies of the book*, "…they are the principal ancestors of the American Indians", to read "…*among* the ancestors of the American Indians", watering down something that all Mormons accepted as a known *fact* until irrefutable DNA evidence proved otherwise. The Church would never accept the idea that Smith could be *entirely* wrong, so whilst being effectively forced to accept conclusive evidence that Smith was absolutely *not correct*, it has to settle on suggesting that residual Lamanites must still be out there – *somewhere*.

Reference works available for copies of the 1833 *Book of Commandments* and also the 1835 *Doctrine and Covenants* include the following, further details of which appear in the bibliography.

Joseph Smith Begins His Work. Vol. 2.
450 pages. (Product Code XB072).
Published by Wilford C. Wood.
Available from UTLM.
Paperback. 2011 price $17.50 (currently discounted to $16).

Includes:
Book of Commandments 1833.
Doctrine and Covenants 1835.
The Lectures on Faith.
Fourteen Articles of Faith.

http://www.utlm.org/booklist/titles/josephsmithbeginshisworkvol2_xb072.htm

Joseph Smith Papers: Revelations and Translations, Vol. 2: Published Revelation.
770 pages. (Product code SKU 5055258).
Published by Deseret Book. 2011.
Hardcover. 2011 price $69.95 (currently discounted to $59.46).

Includes:
Book of Commandments 1833.
Doctrine and Covenants 1835.
Other printed versions of Smith's revelations published (or in the process) during his lifetime.
Lectures on Faith.
Additional texts added to the D&C in 1844.
Revelation texts published in the church newspaper *The Evening and the Morning Star* (1832-1833) and its later, reprinted version, *Evening and Morning Star* (1835-1836).

http://deseretbook.com/Joseph-Smith-Papers-Revelations-Translations-Vol-2-Published-Dean-C-Jessee/i/5055258 This should not be confused with 'Joseph Smith Papers: **Journals**', Vols. 1 & 2. See www.josephsmithpapers.org In this work, JSP Vol. 2 always refers to the 'Revelations and Translations' Volume 2.

Rather than just take each Section of the *D&C* in the order they are now listed in modern editions, this work deals with each section in chronological sequence in order to give a better perspective of the way the 'behind the scenes' history was developing. Smith's revelatory skills, or rather, ability to dream up ideas, also evolved. There was a definite developmental curve in Smith's writing as his experience and confidence grew. Section 107 is a classic example, deriving its content from multiple texts which were 'revealed' in entirely different years.

From the list below, we see a few (14) in 1829, the year in which the *Book of Mormon* was being written. More were recorded in 1830 (20), the year when the Church was formally established, and Smith's most prolific year was 1831 when no less than thirty-seven (and a half) of his revelations were recorded.

At the time, Smith was having some trouble retaining control of his Church. Was the Lord getting better at expressing himself, or was Smith just becoming more practiced in his ability to write, whilst pretending the Lord was the voice for his ideas? The answer to that will become clear and obvious as we journey through Smith's 'Covenants'.

Fewer revelations were recorded in each of the years following 1832 and in some years there were none at all. Did the Lord have less to say, or couldn't Smith think of any more new ideas?

The reader can be the judge of that at the end of our journey.

Chronological Order of Contents of the Doctrine and Covenants

Date		Place	Section Sequence
1823	September	Manchester, New York	2
1828	July	Harmony, Pennsylvania	3
	Summer	Harmony, Pennsylvania (misdated)*	10 (now April 1829)
1829	February	Harmony, Pennsylvania	4
	March	Harmony, Pennsylvania	5
	April	Harmony, Pennsylvania	6, 8, 7, 9 (10*)
	May	Harmony, Pennsylvania	11, 12, 13
	June	Fayette, New York	14, 18, 15, 16, 17
1830	March	Manchester, New York	19
	April	Fayette, New York	21, 23, 20**
	April	Manchester, New York	22
	July	Harmony, Pennsylvania	24, 26, 25
	August	Harmony, Pennsylvania (orig. 4th Sept)	27
	September	Fayette, New York	29, 28, 30, 31
	October	Fayette, New York	32**, 33
	November	Fayette, New York	34
	December	Fayette, New York	74***, 35, 36, 37
1831	January	Fayette, New York	38, 39, 40
	February	Kirtland, Ohio	41, 42, 43, 44
	March	Kirtland, Ohio	45, 46, 47, 48, 49
	May	Kirtland, Ohio	50
	May	Thompson, Ohio	51
	June	Kirtland, Ohio	52, 53, 54, 55, 56
	July	Zion, Jackson County, Missouri	57
	August	Zion, Jackson County, Missouri	58, 59, 60
	August	By Missouri River, Missouri	61, 62
	August	Kirtland, Ohio	63
	September	Kirtland, Ohio	64
	October	Orange, Ohio	66
	October	Hiram, Ohio	65
	November	Hiram, Ohio	68, 1, 67, 133, 69
	November	Hiram, Ohio (Part of 107–Mar 1835)	Part of 107
	November	Kirtland, Ohio	70
	December	Hiram, Ohio	71
	December	Kirtland, Ohio	72
1832	January	Hiram, Ohio (74 re-dated to Dec 1830)	73, (74***)
	January	Amherst, Ohio	75
	February	Hiram, Ohio	76
	March	Hiram, Ohio	77, 78, 80, 79, 81
	April	Jackson County, Missouri	82
	April	Independence, Missouri	83

1832	August	Hiram, Ohio	99
	September	Kirtland, Ohio	84
	November	Kirtland, Ohio	85
	December	Kirtland, Ohio	86, 87**, 88
1833	February	Kirtland, Ohio	89
	March	Kirtland, Ohio	90, 91, 92
	May	Kirtland, Ohio	93
	June	Kirtland, Ohio	95, 96
	August	Kirtland, Ohio	97, 94, 98
	October	Perrysburg, New York	100
	December	Kirtland, Ohio	101
1834	February	Kirtland, Ohio	102, 103
	April	Kirtland, Ohio	104**
	June	Fishing River, Missouri	105
	November	Kirtland, Ohio	106
1835	March	Kirtland, Ohio (Part of 107–Nov 1831)	Part of 107
	August	Kirtland, Ohio (17 Aug–Gen Assy del)	(Old 101 del), 134
	December	Kirtland, Ohio	108
1836	January	Kirtland, Ohio	137
	March	Kirtland, Ohio	109
	April	Kirtland, Ohio	110
	August	Salem, Massachusetts	111
1837	July	Kirtland, Ohio	112
1838	March	Far West, Missouri	113**
	April	Far West, Missouri	114, 115
	May	Spring Hill, Daviess County, Missouri	116
	July	Far West, Missouri	117, 118, 119, 120
1839	March	Liberty Jail, Clay County, Missouri	121, 122, 123
1841	January	Nauvoo, Illinois	124
	March	Nauvoo, Illinois	125
	July	Nauvoo, Illinois	126
1842	September	Nauvoo, Illinois	127, 128
1843	February	Nauvoo, Illinois	129
	April	Ramus, Illinois	130
	May	Ramus, Illinois	131
	July	Nauvoo, Illinois	132
1844	June	Nauvoo, Illinois	135
1847	January	Winter Quarters (now Nebraska)	136
1890	October	Salt Lake City, Utah	Official Dec. – 1
1918	October	Salt Lake City, Utah	138
1978	June	Salt Lake City, Utah	Official Dec. – 2

del = deleted. * Re-dated in JS Papers Vol. 2:473 & 720. ** At or near that location. *** Re-dated in JS Papers Vol. 2:512 & 721 to December 1830. *(See p. 165)*.

Several details at http://lds.org/scriptures remain incorrect at time of this publication.

x

BOC / D&C – Comparative Section Numbers

1833 Book of Commandments CHAPTER	1835 *(1844 additions)* Doctrine & Covenants SECTION	2010 Internet Version Doctrine & Covenants SECTION
—	**Lectures of Faith** Included from 1835-1921	—
—	Preface	Introduction
I 'A Preface'	I	1
—	—	2 (added in 1876).
II	XXX	3
III	XXXI	4
IV	XXXII	5
V	VIII	6
VI	XXXIII	7
VII	XXXIV	8
VIII	XXXV	9
IX	XXXVI	10
X	XXXVII	11
XI	XXXVIII	12
—	—	13 (added in 1876)
XII	XXXIX	14
XIII	XL	15
XIV	XLI	16
—	XLII	17
XV	XLIII	18
XVI	XLIV	19
XXIV	II	20
XXII	XLVI	21
XXIII	XLVII	22
XVII to XXI	XLV	23
XXV	IX	24
XXVI	XLVIII	25
XXVII	XLIX	26
XXVIII	L	27
XXX	LI	28
XXIX	X	29
XXXI to XXXIII	LII	30
XXXIV	LIII	31
—	LIV	32
XXXV	LV	33
XXXVI	LVI	34
XXXVII	XI	35

XXXVIII	LVII	36
XXXIX	LVIII	37
XL	XII	38
XLI	LIX	39
XLII	LX	40
XLIII	LXI	41
XLIV, XLVII	XIII	42
XLV	XIV	43
XLVI	LXII	44
XLVIII	XV	45
XLIX	XVI	46
L	LXIII	47
LI	LXIV	48
LII	LXV	49
LIII	XVII	50
—	XXIII	51
LIV	LXVI	52
LV	LXVI (numbering error)*	53
LVI	LXVII	54
LVII	LXVIII	55
LVIII	LXIX	56
—	XXVII	57
LIX	XVIII	58
LX	XIX	59
LXI	LXX	60
LXII	LXXI	61
LXIII	LXXII	62
LXIV	XX	63
LXV (incomplete)	XXI (complete)	64 (BOC ended mid v.36)
LXVII (unpublished)	XXIV	65
LXVI (unpublished)	LXXIV	66
LXIX (unpublished)	XXV	67
LXVIII (unpublished)	XXII	68
LXX (unpublished)	XXVIII	69
LXXII (unpublished)	XXVI	70
LXXIII (unpublished)	XC	71
LXXIV (unpublished)	LXXXIX	72
LXXV (unpublished)	XXIX	73
—	LXXIII	74
LXXVI (unpublished)	LXXXVII	75
—	XCI	76
—	—	77 (added in 1876)
—	LXXV	78
—	LXXVI	79

—	LXXVII	80
—	LXXIX	81
—	LXXXVI	82
—	LXXXVIII	83
—	IV	84
—	—	85 (added in 1876)
—	VI	86
—	—	87 (added in 1876)
—	VII	88
—	LXXX	89
—	LXXXIV	90
—	XCII	91
—	XCIII	92
—	LXXXII	93
—	LXXXIII	94
—	XCV	95
—	XCVI	96
—	LXXXI	97
—	LXXXV	98
—	LXXVIII	99
—	XCIV	100
—	XCVII	101
—	V	102
—	*1844 – CI*	103
—	XCVIII	104
—	*1844 – CII*	105
—	XCIX	106
LXXI (unpublished)	III (major additions 1835)	107
—	—	108 (added in 1876)
—	—	109 (added in 1876)
—	—	110 (added in 1876)
—	—	111 (added in 1876)
—	*1844 – CIV*	112
—	—	113 (added in 1876)
—	—	114 (added in 1876)
—	—	115 (added in 1876)
—	—	116 (added in 1876)
—	—	117 (added in 1876)
—	—	118 (added in 1876)
—	*1844 – CVII*	119
—	—	120 (added in 1876)
—	—	121 (added in 1876)
—	—	122 (added in 1876)
—	—	123 (added in 1876)

—	*1844 - CIII (unnumbered)*	124
—	—	125 (added in 1876)
—	—	126 (added in 1876)
—	*1844 – CV*	127
—	*1844 – CVI*	128
—	—	129 (added in 1876)
—	—	130 (added in 1876)
—	—	131 (added in 1876)
—	—	132 (added in 1876)
LXXVII (unpublished)	C Appendix *(1844-CVIII)*	133
—	CII *(1844-CX)*	134
—	*1844 – CXI (John Taylor)*	135
—	*— (Brigham Young)*	136 (added in 1876)
—	—	137 (added in 1981)
—	*— (Joseph Fielding Smith)*	138 (added in 1981)
—	*— (Wilford Woodruff)*	OD 1 (added in 1908)
—	*— (Spencer W. Kimball)*	OD 2 (added in 1981)
—	CI *(1844-CIX)*	Discarded in 1876
—	17 Aug 1835 Gen Asmbly	Discarded after 1835 ed.

*The 1835 D&C has two Sections '66'. In 1844, the 2nd Sec. 66 became 67, moving everything else through to Sec. 102 along one, becoming Sections 68-103 respectively.

The *Doctrine and Covenants* was dictated by Joseph Smith, other than Sections 135, 136, 138 and Official Declarations 1 and 2. No other canonised revelation or prophesy given to latter-day Mormon prophets exists in Mormonism. In fact, Mormon prophet, Gordon B. Hinckley, publicly declared that the Lord doesn't provide communication the way He used to. It now comes through 'feelings'…

> **Q:** And this belief in contemporary revelation and prophecy? As the prophet, tell us how that works. ***How do you receive divine revelation? What does it feel like?***
> **A:** Let me say first that we have a great body of revelation, the vast majority of which came from the prophet Joseph Smith. ***We don't need much revelation.*** We need to pay more attention to the revelation we've already received. Now, ***if a problem should arise on which we don't have an answer, we pray about it, we may fast about it, and it comes. Quietly.*** Usually no voice of any kind, but ***just a perception in the mind.*** I liken it to Elijah's experience. When he sought the Lord, there was a great wind, and the Lord was not in the wind. And there was an earthquake, and the Lord was not in the earthquake. And a fire, and the Lord was not in the fire. But in ***a still, small voice. Now that's the way it works.*** *(San Francisco Chronicle. Don Lattin interview with Gordon B. Hinckley. 13 Mar 1997.* (Emphasis added).

The Mormon Church always claimed a *need* for continuing revelation. It seems that this is no longer the case. Hinckley: "We don't need much revelation."

Published Editions

As we proceed to review the 'Doctrine' and the 'Covenants' of the Mormon Church, the following publication summary will assist in understanding the sequence taken into account when reviewing each section. The 'Lectures of Faith' (later to become known as 'Lectures *on* Faith') were included in every edition from 1835, until being discarded in 1921. Referencing scans of original documents, I have retained the original title 'Lectures of Faith' in this book.

1833   Book of Commandments – containing 65 'Chapters'. The printing press was destroyed and the surviving part of the book ended in Ch. 65, mid v.36. A further twelve chapters were intended for publication but consequently did not get included.

1835   Doctrine and Covenants – containing the Lectures and 103 'Sections'. 38 had been added, but as two were numbered 'Section 66', the last of the 103 was numbered 102. This error was corrected in 1844 when the second Section 66 became 67 and the remainder moved forward one.

1844   New edition. 8 Sections were added.

1845   British Edition.

1846   Reprint (same plates used in 1844, 1845 & 1846).

The printing plates subsequently became lost and the British Editions were imported to Utah from 1854 on. Further editions were published in Britain in 1849, 1852, 1854, 1866, and 1869. From 1852-1869, 'stereotype plates' were used. Most of the 1854 edition was shipped from Britain to Utah.

1876   New edition. 26 Sections were added and one (CI) was deleted.

1879   New edition published in Britain, including an index and footnotes for the first time. 'Electrotype' plates were used.

1880   The 1879 electrotype plates, British version, first published in Utah.

1882-1920. 28 editions published, most using the electrotype plates from 1879.

1908   This edition included Wilford Woodruff's Manifesto which explained the claimed discontinuation of plural marriage. It was a 'glued-in' extra page but not included in all versions, such as the then new 'vest-pocket' edition.

1921   This was a major revision. The footnotes were rewritten, introductory statements at the beginning of revelations expanded, and the text was divided into two columns on each page. The "Lectures of Faith" were **deleted** without reference. Changes and deletions were ***not*** voted on or approved by the general membership of the Church. The title 'Doctrine' and Covenants was retained.

1981   New edition with major revisions. It included Joseph Smith's Vision of the Celestial Kingdom and Joseph F. Smith's Vision of the Redemption of the Dead, transferred from the Pearl of Great Price and becoming Sections 137 and 138 respectively. The statement concerning giving the priesthood to 'all worthy male members of the Church', issued on 9 June 1978, was added as Official Declaration 2. Woodruff's 1890 manifesto remained as Official Declaration 1 along with his 'explanation' for issuing the manifesto. Footnotes were revised to match the format of the footnotes in the Mormon edition of the *King James Version* of the Bible. These revised footnotes included cross-references to the Topical Guide in the Bible. Introductory statements at the start of each section were yet again revised and a gazetteer was included.

2010   For the last few years, an internet version of all the 'Standard Works' of the Mormon Church has been provided online. In late 2010, a new web site replaced the old version and certain updates were incorporated into the content, such as in the *Book of Mormon*, in order for it to match the recent 'Doubleday' alterations – which some would term 'falsifications' – but the content of *D&C* Sections appears the same as the 1981 edition. This work uses the 2010 edition.

During the 1800s, further editions were published in the following languages:

1851   Welsh
1852   Danish
1876   German
1888   Swedish

At least one Swedish edition included John Taylor's revelations on Priesthood organisation but they were never canonised and became obscure after that.

During the twentieth century, many further language editions were published and today the D&C is available in close to one-hundred different languages.

The above information was collated from a variety of sources and included as a general guide to the early publication sequence. It may well be incomplete.

Important publications being compared are the 1833 *Book of Commandments*, 1835, 1844, 1876, and 1981 (2010 internet version) *Doctrine and Covenants*. Some *exact* Section dates have been derived from *Joseph Smith Papers, Vol 2*.

Contents

Chapter		Page
	Acknowledgements	v
	Guidance Notes	vi
	Chronological Order of Contents of the Doctrine and Covenants	ix
	BOC/D&C – Comparative Chapter and Section Numbers for 1833, 1835, 1844, 1876, 1981 (2010 Internet) Editions	xi
	D&C Published Editions	xv
	D&C Sections – Page Locations	xix
	Preface	1
1.	Doctrine and Covenants – Introduction	7

Doctrine:

2.	Lecture First of Faith	15
3.	Lecture Second of Faith	29
4.	Lecture Third of Faith	43
5.	Lecture Fourth of Faith	55
6.	Lecture Fifth of Faith	61
7.	Lecture Sixth of Faith	71
8.	Lecture Seventh of Faith	77

Covenants:

9.	D&C Section 2. (Claimed as) September 1823	87
10.	D&C Sections 3 & 10. Summer 1828	97
11.	D&C Sections 4–9. Spring 1829	105
12.	D&C Sections 11–18. May – June 1829	123
13.	D&C Sections 19–29. March – September 1830	135
14.	D&C Sections 30–37, 74. September – December 1830	159
15.	D&C Sections 38–50. January – May 1831	171
16.	D&C Sections 51–64. May – September 1831	211
17.	D&C Sections 1, 65–73, part 107, 133. Oct 1831 – Jan 1832	241
18.	D&C Sections 75–86, 99. January – December 1832	265
19.	D&C Sections 87–98. December 1832 – August 1833	307

20.	D&C Sections 100–108, 'old 101' (marriage), 134, General Assembly. October 1833 – December 1835	339
21.	D&C Sections 109–120, 137. January 1836 – July 1838	381
22.	D&C Sections 121–131. March 1839 – May 1843	415
23.	D&C Sections 132, 135-6, OD 1 & 2. July 1843 on	455

The Final Analysis

Part 1. Joseph Smith's Prophecies	471
Part 2. Pet Phrases used by Smith's God/Jesus	483
Part 3. The Mormon God says the Strangest of Things	493
Part 4. Who am I; God, Jesus, or Both?	497
Part 5. Smith and his Lamanites	503

Appendix A:	Extracts – Ezra Booth's Letters	507
Appendix B:	Extracts – Mormonism Unvailed [sic], E. D. Howe	515
Appendix C:	Extracts – Early Temple Experience	519
Bibliography and Recommended Books		527
Index		537

Supplementary Material

I reviewed some short Sections of the D&C, almost at random, in *TMD Volume 3, Section 6*; including Sections 1, 7, 9, 28, 39, 40, 81, 111, 87, 8 – in that order and Section 132 in *TMD Vols. 1 & 4*. I somewhat covered Section 138 (Joseph F. Smith's 1918 vision) in *TMD Vol. 4, Ch. 10*. Therefore, these and one or two other aspects previously covered have not been fully analysed in this book, in the interest of space, undue repetition, increased cost to the purchaser, and as most readers will no doubt already own the earlier volumes.

However, I am making them available as a *free* 146 page PDF supplement for readers who may not own earlier volumes. Even if you do have them and would still like a handy PDF file of related material, which can also be printed out for ease of reference, please feel free to request one. Indirect references are not included, but direct references available in the supplement are *highlighted* thus throughout the book, followed by supplement page numbers; e.g. *(S3-6)*. If any references and *(S)* numbers appear a second time, they are not highlighted.

I cannot guarantee how long this offer will be available, but I will continue as long as I reasonably can. If you would like a free PDF file containing all the additional Sections and notes referenced from earlier TMD volumes which are not included in this book, please email me at: jim@themormondelusion.com

There is no need to add a message unless you wish to do so. Just put **'Volume 5 Supplement'** in the subject line to be sent a free copy of the file.

D&C Sections – Page Locations

Section	Page	Section	Page	Section	Page
1	246	37	168	73	264
2	87	38	171	74	165
3	97	39	172	75	265
4	105	40	172	76	267
5	106	41	174	77	278
6	112	42	175	78	290
7	116	43	187	79	293
8	117	44	193	80	292
9	120	45	193	81	294
10	97	46	202	82	295
11	123	47	203	83	297
12	125	48	204	84	299
13	126	49	204	85	304
14	125	50	206	86	305
15	125	51	211	87	307
16	125	52	212	88	310
17	132	53	217	89	321
18	127	54	218	90	322
19	135	55	221	91	325
20	141	56	222	92	326
21	139	57	224	93	326
22	144	58	228	94	332
23	140	59	231	95	328
24	145	60	232	96	330
25	147	61	233	97	330
26	146	62	234	98	334
27	148	63	235	99	298
28	157	64	237	100	339
29	152	65	242	101	340
30	159	66	241	102	350
31	161	67	247	103	352
32	162	68	243	104	356
33	163	69	255	105	361
34	163	70	258	106	367
35	166	71	261	107	255 & 368
36	167	72	263	108	379

109	383	123	426	137	381
110	385	124	427	138	465
111	389	125	439	OD 1	462
112	393	126	440	OD 2	467
113	397	127	441	CI (101) [1]	374
114	398	128	443	Gen Assy [2]	378
115	400	129	444	HC1:315-6	319
116	404	130	446	HC2:145	366
117	410	131	451	HC4:550-1	444
118	412	132	455	HC5:1-2	
119	413	133	248	HC5:336	451
120	414	134	377	HC5:394	452
121	418	135	459	HC6:116	
122	424	136	461	KSSB [3]	391

1. Section CI "Marriage", known as 'Old Section 101', was discarded in 1876.

2. The "General Assembly" of 17 August 1835 was added to the 1835 D&C but not included after that edition. No 'Section' number was allocated.

3. The Kirtland Safety Society Bank becomes The Kirtland Safety Society *Anti* Bank*ing Co.*

**Santa Claus, the Easter Bunny and the Tooth Fairy
are creatures in which every child has absolute faith
until it is utterly destroyed by adults
who burst the bubble and explain the truth.**

**God is the one imaginary friend that many never grow out of;
and all because no one tells them the truth before it is too
late and the delusion becomes their reality.**

~ Jim Whitefield, 2012

(See p. 27).

You *cannot* work science
around a predetermined belief system;
you can *only* work (or rework) a belief system
around science, current knowledge, and new *evidence*.

If you are not willing to do that,
you *believe* in the fanciful
instead of *understanding* the factual
– and *that* is delusional.

~ Jim Whitefield, 2012.

(See p.282).

Preface

As an active and faithful Mormon, I tried hard not to question the Church and I would avoid anything that seemed to be anti-Mormon in any way, knowing that I already had the assurances of General Authorities of the Church that we had the truth and anything 'offending' that supposed truth, or my testimony of it, would stem from Satan or his servants – the so-called 'enemies of the Church'.

I had intended to stop writing after Volume 3 of this work as I thought I had covered all major issues of any significance. Then, one day, I came across the Mormon missionary lesson manual online and Volume 4 was born. This fifth volume has arisen, equally as unexpectedly, as the result of reflecting on what actually bothered me most when I was a member; the things I most often had to 'shelve' and try to avoid as they were very uncomfortable for me. Cognitive dissonance was something I had never heard of and was yet to learn about – long after leaving the Church. I did answer the question somewhere, regarding one thing that bothered me constantly; it was the *Doctrine and Covenants*.

Although I did once read it all the way through, much of it was very strange to me and it seemed bizarre that any God would ever say many of those things, or that He would express them in the way Joseph Smith recorded them. They were always extremely difficult to accept and believe in. So it was that I ended up not reading the book unless directed to specific common passages used in classes, in order to substantiate a fundamental Mormon teaching. Now, I look back and realise what was happening and how a delusional state of mind can train the brain to block out and avoid uncomfortable truths.

Recently, I decided to review a few aspects of the Doctrine and Covenants (D&C) in order to identify what it was that had once bothered my otherwise faithful mind. It led me, once again, on a journey of new discovery and some interesting conclusions. Almost all the D&C is supposedly the Lord speaking to or through Joseph Smith, apart from a handful of Sections recorded on behalf of later supposed prophets. The Church claims they are direct *revelations* and *prophecies* and asserts Joseph Smith can be identified as a true prophet because many (I don't think they dare say *all*) of his *prophecies* came to pass.

However, as with many such things Mormon, these bold statements are made without offering proof or further explanation concerning all the things Smith said that did *not* materialise.

THE MORMON DELUSION

A journey through the D&C reveals Joseph Smith did not get *anything* right at all. In fact, he made such a mess of all his predictions and prophecies that *none* of them have any merit whatsoever. It turns out that there aren't very many real 'prophecies' to be found in the D&C at all and none of them have ever materialised, despite Mormon Church claims to the contrary. When such a statement is made, invariably someone defending Smith will blurt "What about Section 87 and the Civil War?" Members today have little idea that in 1832 *everyone* expected the war, and had done so for many years. At that time, it was actually expected by the following year and was in the newspapers almost daily. It was not an idea unique to Smith at all; it was a general expectation by everyone. Smith's 'prophecy' was far from a personal communication from God; it was in the newspapers. The question never asked, is why God would have had Smith 'prophesy' of such an event anyway; did God give Smith any instruction or advice as to how to avoid the conflict? Did Smith have any idea as to what God's 'desires' about it were? No, none whatsoever. In the context of *prophecy*, it was a pointless exercise of no help or merit to *anyone*.

The problem was that it did *not* happen as and when expected and it was some three decades later when the war finally started. Smith incorporated ideas into the event which turned out not even close to what ultimately transpired and they prove he had no communication with deity about it. He also referred to it in Section 130 where he adds that a voice told him about it – and also that the Saviour would return when he would have been eighty-five years old (1891). I have reviewed Section 87 in *TMD Volume 3:309-12*.

In the D&C, Joseph Smith's version of the *manner* in which God, or the Lord (Jesus Christ), speaks and reveals His will is positively appalling, and unrecognisable when compared to correctly structured early modern English language – which is more than evident where Smith includes New Testament verses in his work.

I reviewed some Sections of the D&C in earlier volumes. These have not been fully repeated in this book in the interest of space, added cost, and as most readers will already have the earlier volumes. However, they are available as a free PDF supplement for readers who may not own earlier volumes – and those who do, but who would also like them in one file. Please see p. xviii for details.

Whenever we come to a previously reviewed Section, there will be a very short summary in line with details specifically analysed for the purpose of this volume, along with a location reference back to the earlier treatment of that Section. References included in the supplement are *highlighted*. Everything appearing in this volume should therefore pretty much be new to the reader.

As we review each Section, we will be looking for anything of possible *merit*. It will be discovered a high proportion of verses are simply repetition or meaningless filler and the extent of such material in each Section soon becomes

PREFACE

apparent. There is a great deal of it and clearly no God would waste time with such nonsense that has no theological or educational value.

Many verses contain material already stated, reworded and repeated. Smith had a habit of having the Lord use the phrase "in other words", which he also used in his *Inspired Revision*. (The Mormon Church uses the term 'Joseph Smith Translation' or JST, but I use the original title *'Inspired Revision'* in my work because it is published by that title – *An Inspired Revision of the Authorised Version*, by the Reorganised [RLDS] Church – now Community of Christ).

Smith used the expression "in other words" more than once in his *Inspired Revision* but it *never* appears in the *KJV* – or any other version of the Bible for that matter. Smith used it several times in the *Book of Mormon* and also several times in the *D&C*. Does it not strike you as odd that the Lord would *ever* need to rephrase and then repeat what he had just said in order for us to understand what he meant, and that he *only* did so in material that Smith recorded?

We will look at the *way* the Lord supposedly spoke and what he had to *say* and consider whether or not the sayings were meaningful or came to pass. We will separate the provably false from what may be true and see what remains.

It is quite amazing to me now, just how many things there were that I had to subconsciously rationalise as a faithful member, into a form of acceptable plausibility, in order for it to fit with what we *believed* to be the truth. Much that the Church proffers as so-called scripture simply does not make any sense whatsoever. If something does not logically 'compute', we somehow *ignore* the problem and *make* it fit with our overall perception of the 'truth' of the Church.

Once again, I am compelled to state that these works are *not* intended to be read by faithful Mormons who would rather not know the truth and who wish to remain in their delusional state. If the reader is in that category, I suggest not proceeding further. Should such a person decide to continue, please remember you proceed on your own volition. Please don't blame me for the consequences of your journey or the possible resulting destruction of a presently perceived testimony. Please understand if you decide to proceed, that you do so entirely at your own risk.

I am not about trying to convince the faithful that their Church is not true; I am a facilitator of facts and the truth, supported by concrete evidence, for those seeking it; for those already questioning and looking for answers to questions based on evidence and substantiated facts – rather than Mormon fiction. This warning is further expanded upon in earlier volumes of my work.

It is only from the outside looking in, especially at the D&C, that we can see just how much of it is sheer nonsense, which could and would never have come from the lips of any God. That which eluded us as members, now stares right back at us when we read such material. It will become more than evident, page after page in this work. Why? Because we can now look at it *objectively*, rather than subjectively – when a programmed mind would reject, exclude or rationalise away absolute *facts* and *evidence* that conflict with *belief*. There is no longer a preconceived subconscious notion that we must manipulate what we read to 'fit' our beliefs. It is what it is – and it will stand or fall on *evidence*.

Those who remain faithful and able to rationalise all the absurdity will naturally claim Satan is deceiving us. Those who have come to understand the truth, realise this is far from the case and in fact all that has happened is that we have learned to accept evidence over fiction in order to arrive at conclusions that require common sense and reason to understand; something unavailable to the faithful, unless and until they have the courage to question things which bother them and yet they have previously feared to face and deal with.

I also want to reiterate the fact that it is impossible to debate or counter the nonsense apologists continue to churn out when they attack those who expose the truth. I will never respond if they ever criticise my work, as they first attack the messenger and try to discredit him or her, and then reel off more nonsense than ever, in the end satisfying only themselves that they are correct.

Some apologetic notes that I recently came across when researching for this volume demonstrated how they chop and change with the prevailing wind – or rather, in the light of further *evidence* they become obliged to face and explain. Once, it would have been *impossible* to argue that Smith did *not* tell anyone about a First Vision in the 1820-1830 decade. It was a given that Smith told all and sundry – and was persecuted for it. Now, apologists seem to embrace the facts but are then stuck with Smith's multiple claims of persecution between 1820 and 1823, which did *not* happen. They now accept Smith did not even tell his own mother about his First Vision experience, but still maintain he did tell a Methodist minister and that it led to persecution – yet there was *none* recorded. *(See 'The First Vision' on the TMD website or Whitefield 2011b).*

They also now try to 'excuse' the fact that there were no newspaper reports of Smith's vision or his persecution, by asking why a newspaper would bother to report such a claim by a mere fourteen-year-old boy. The problem with such tactics is that, assuming they have actually bothered to study the history and what was happening in the era, they would know very well that the newspapers did indeed take an interest in such things as similar claims were commonplace.

Many such vision claims were published long before Smith ever made his own claim public. In Smith's case, whilst he claimed a vision *of* 1820, unlike some other recorded 'visions', Smith didn't make the claim *in* the year of his claim. He made his 'official version' claim for the first time in 1838 and didn't publish it until 1842. It was *backdated* to 1820, so it's no wonder no one knew.

Visions were extremely popular stories in those days. Apologists generally don't mention that there were similar 'vision' stories published that Smith had access to, such as those of Benjamin Abbott, Norris Stearns and eleven-year-old Billy Hibbard, who had ecstatic visions and saw God and Jesus. *(Quinn*

PREFACE

1998:15). Out of interest – and for the benefit of those who think Smith was unique, this is an extract from *Early Mormonism and the Magic World View:*

> Billy Hibbard wrote about an ecstatic vision at age eleven. "When I came to the place of prayer, had kneeled down, and closed my eyes, with my hands uplifted toward the heavens, I saw Jesus Christ at the right hand of God, looking down upon me, and God the Father looking upon him." Hibbard added that as a young married man in the 1790s, "as I looked up I saw heaven open, and Jesus at the right hand of God, and the heavenly hosts surrounding the throne, adoring the Father and Son in the most sublime strains." This second vision occurred at Norway, New York (120 miles east of Palmyra), and Hibbard's conversion narrative went through two editions at its initial 1825 publication. *(Quinn 1998:15).*

Does that not sound familiar? Smith's 'official version' of his 1820 vision was not considered or written until over a decade after Billy Hibbbard's was published. Had Smith had a real experience even close to his eventual official account, actually *in* 1820, he would most certainly have said so and he would have *published* it. It would have been the very basis of Mormonism from day one and the natural foundation of the Church when it was organised in 1830. It is unthinkable that Smith just didn't mention it in all those years. He actually *claimed* that he told everyone who would listen, yet no one ever knew about it.

This is a little more from Quinn concerning similar stories:

> Far better known and more frequently published in the early 1800s was Benjamin Abbott's narrative of a theophany in which both the Father and Son spoke to him. Concerning a 1772 vision just before dawn, Abbott remembered: "and at that instant I awoke, and saw, by faith, the Lord Jesus Christ standing by me, with his arms extended wide, saying to me, *'I died for you.'* I then looked up, and by faith I saw the Ancient of Days, and he said to me, *'I freely forgive you for what Christ has done.'*" (emphasis in original). Abbott's narrative went through thirteen printings from 1801 to 1844, with New York editions in 1805, 1813, 1830, 1832, 1833, and 1836. In the early nineteenth century, New Yorkers obviously liked reading about youthful visions of the Father and Son.

> In 1815 Norris Sterns published his vision in which "there appeared a small gleam of light in the room, above the brightness of the sun..." The young man then saw two beings. "One was God, my Maker, almost in bodily shape like a man. His face was, as it were a flame of fire ... Below him stood Jesus Christ my Redeemer, in perfect shape like a man – His face was not ablaze, but had the countenance of fire, being bright and shining."

THE MORMON DELUSION

Lorenzo Dow's narrative of his theophany had an even closer connection with those who later became leaders of Mormonism. "When past the age of thirteen," this evangelist dreamed he "was taken up by a whirlwind" into heaven. Dow's journal said he saw "a throne of ivory overlaid with gold, and God sitting upon it, and Jesus Christ at his right hand..." Brigham Young's brother Lorenzo Dow was named after this preacher who had seen the Father and the Son, and in 1820 Dow's published journal was on sale nine miles from Joseph Smith's home. *(Quinn 1998:15-16).*

I am not quite sure what modern-day readers would think of God sitting on a throne of *ivory*, unless He didn't care about endangered species. Joseph Smith didn't have to look far for ideas about starting and developing a religion. The fact that his backdated First Vision account was put together so long after the time of the claimed event, reveals not just a conspiracy to deceive but also just how much material was available from which he may have drawn his ideas. *(See 'The First Vision' on the TMD website or Whitefield 2011b).*

Apologists also fail to mention that a local newspaper actually confirmed in 1831 that Smith had **not** made any claim to visions before 1827. *(See TMD Vol. 2:16-17)*. Apologists cannot be trusted with the truth – they manipulate it. It never ceases to amaze me that apologists continue to take a stand which is forever being eroded until they clutch at flimsy straws in final attempts to hold that Mormonism is still true. Once, I would have said that it is futile when there is a shed-load of evidence against the Church. Now, the evidence against even the remotest possibility of a God ever being involved with Smith and Young et al affects every imaginable aspect of Mormonism. The evidence now fills more sheds than we could ever have imagined. Nothing is left which can support the idea of the Mormon Church being even close to true. Yet Mormon apologists still keep on, chopping and changing their positions, writing more and more nonsense in order to defend the indefensible, all to no avail. No matter what they argue; no matter how many times they move the goal posts; no matter that having first argued, they later accept some things, regroup and take a different stand; no matter how much they *want* it all to be true, or at least what is left for them to try to *make* true, it simply *isn't* – and that's all there is to it.

That is not my opinion; it is the only possible conclusion any sane person could reach, based solely on the evidence. As several so-called prophets have declared, the Church stands or falls on the First Vision and it stands or falls on the Book of Mormon. Smith demonstrably lied about every aspect *surrounding* the vision, making the actual event completely unsustainable, and the Book of Mormon has been proven entirely fraudulent in every way. That's before even considering the hoax Book of Abraham plus the impossible stories contained in it. And it is also before we consider Smith's so-called prophecies in the D&C.

So, let's do that now and see how we get on.

Chapter 1

Doctrine and Covenants

Introduction

In deciding on a suitable sub-title for this volume, I eventually settled on the Doctrine and Covenants (*hereafter D&C*) being nothing but deception and 'concoctions'. It turns out that the word (*concoction*) first took on the sense of 'a made-up story' in 1823, which is coincidentally the same year in which Smith's first D&C entry (Section 2) was set, describing a claimed angelic visitation. Perhaps someone knew Smith was about to embark on the biggest hoax of the 19th century and invented the new connotation in honour of the occasion.

It is doubtful that Smith actually invented his angelic vision *in* 1823, any more than his First Vision *in* 1820. All evidence suggests that it was late 1827 before he came up with the 1823 (or any other) ideas and 1832 before his first attempt at an earlier vision of any form of deity. Nevertheless, the year 1823 is when the storyline was first *set*, long before his First Vision ideas evolved; so it seems quite appropriate that the word used to describe what Smith wrote in the D&C took on its new meaning in the same year as the first recorded revelation *in* the D&C. Smith's 'Section 2' is dated to September 1823, the year in which 'concoctions' started to mean "a made-up story"; fitting the D&C perfectly.

The 1835 D&C had a Preface which introduced the *Lectures of Faith* as 'doctrine' and then stated the "second part contains items or principles for the regulation of the church, as taken from the revelations which have been given..."

The modern day 'Introduction' claims that it is "...a collection of divine revelations and inspired declarations..." and although written primarily for Mormons, "...the messages, warnings, and exhortations are for the benefit of all mankind..."

It claims the D&C is unique among the Mormon 'Standard Works', which comprise the *King James Version* of the Bible, the *Book of Mormon* and the *Pearl of Great Price* in addition to the D&C, as it is not a translation of ancient documents, but rather, direct communication from God to modern day prophets who were chosen to 'restore' His one true gospel.

With knowledge of what the D&C actually contains, it is difficult not to raise an eyebrow at the claim that in these revelations "...one hears the tender but firm voice of the Lord Jesus Christ...", as much of it is anything *but* tender and it is often way beyond just *firm*. Indeed, one could say that at times it is more reminiscent of the malicious God of the *Old Testament (OT)* rather than the generally loving nature of Christ as portrayed in the *New Testament (NT)*.

The introduction continues with a short explanation about how it all began:

> Joseph Smith, Jr., was born 23 December 1805, in Sharon, Windsor County, Vermont. During his early life, he moved with his family to Manchester, in western New York. It was while he was living near Manchester in the spring of 1820, when he was fourteen years of age, that he experienced his first vision, in which he was visited in person by God, the Eternal Father, and his Son Jesus Christ. He was told in this vision that the true Church of Jesus Christ that had been established in New Testament times, and which had administered the fulness of the gospel, was no longer on the earth. Other divine manifestations followed in which he was taught by many angels; it was shown to him that God had a special work for him to do on the earth and that through him the Church of Jesus Christ would be restored to the earth.

The question has to be asked, and it is fully answered in *TMD Volume 4*, and also in 'The First Vision' article which can be located on the TMD website at http://themormondelusion.com, why, if the above is true, did Joseph Smith's claimed glorious 'First Vision' of 1820 *not* appear as the first revelation in the Book of Commandments (*hereafter BOC*) in 1833, or in the 1835 D&C, or even in the 1844 edition?

A study of the history, origins and evolution of the first vision story as it appears in Smith's own journals will more than answer that question. Had what

DOCTRINE & COVENANTS – INTRODUCTION

has become known as the 'official version' of the First Vision, actually been a one-time true and original account of such an experience recorded *in* 1820 as most Mormons assume, it would assuredly have appeared *somewhere*, as Smith was forever dreaming up revelations for his followers who were always thirsty for new information. It did not, and the reason is that Smith did not dream up the idea until the early 1830s and it didn't finally settle into its ultimate and now well known storyline until 1838 – and that was not published until 1842, when it appeared for the very first time – twenty-two years after the claimed event and twelve years after the official establishment of the Mormon Church.

I have approached British members of the Mormon Church regarding this subject and without exception they thought there was only one 'version' of the First Vision and that it was recorded shortly after the event *in* 1820. No one has ever told them otherwise and their testimonies are invariably based on that false premise, as that is the inference given in the Mormon missionary lessons.

Any kind of 'First Vision' was almost completely unknown before the 1842 *Times and Seasons* publication. Even Smith's own mother, Lucy, remained completely unaware of such a thing until long after her son's death, when the official version was *inserted* into her own book – without her permission or her knowledge when it was published. *(See TMD Vol. 4:106).*

The 'Introduction' also lists some of the prophets who supposedly appeared or spoke to Joseph Smith – including 'Elias'. "Other ordinations followed in which priesthood keys were conferred upon them by Moses, Elijah, Elias, and many ancient prophets…" The Church is stuck with a problem that members simply do not see; accepting that *Elias* was a real person. They have to, as Joseph Smith, and later, Joseph F. Smith, both claimed to *see* him. Therefore a new fictional character has been 'created' in the Mormon mindset. The fact that 'Elias' is actually 'Elijah' and that they are one and the same biblical character, is firmly established throughout all Christianity and yet whilst the Mormon Church does agree on that, another 'Elias' also has to be considered *as* an OT character in his own right – or it would mean the two 'Smiths' got it all wrong. *(See TMD Vol. 4:200, 201, 218, 248). Elias* is just the *NT* Greek form of the *OT* Hebrew *Elijah*. It is as simple as that – but both of the Smith's mistakes are not at all just simple – they are utterly *condemning*.

The Church claims that "These sacred revelations were received in answer to prayer, in times of need, and came out of real-life situations involving real people. The Prophet and his associates sought for divine guidance, and these revelations certify that they received it." They don't "certify" anything of the sort. If anything, they actually certify that God wasn't involved at all as, if He was, He would have surely spoken more eloquently – about more important issues. That will become more than clear as we journey though each Section.

When you read some of the things the Lord is claimed to have actually *said* in the D&C, the reasoning behind the above statement becomes clear, but at the same time, it makes us realise the Lord would never have bothered with all the trivia that is included when so much more of real importance to his 'saints' and also to the rest of the world was never said. Clearly, if God really were to speak to humankind, He would say something *useful* – and in the D&C He *doesn't*.

Additionally, the actual wording that is sometimes attributed to the Lord is positively abysmal by any standard of language you care to entertain, and could only be from the mind of the less than educated Joseph Smith rather than any deity. Judge for yourself as we review what the Lord supposedly said in each claimed revelation.

The Introduction goes on to say "In the revelations one sees the restoration and unfolding of the gospel of Jesus Christ and the ushering in of the dispensation of the fulness of times". Well, we shall see.

We are informed that some Sections refer to the publication of the Book of Mormon (3, 5, 10, 17 and 19) and some to Smith's 'inspired' translation of the Bible (37, 45, 73, 76, 77, 81, 91 and 132), each of which "has some direct relationship to the Bible translation". We will be looking closely at these ideas (but only where they *do* have relevance) when we get to each of those Sections.

The statement that "…the gradual unfolding of the administrative structure of the Church is shown with the calling of bishops, the First Presidency, the Council of the Twelve, and the Seventy and the establishment of other presiding offices and quorums" is claimed to stem from continuing revelation; but it could be argued that these offices should have been instituted from the beginning, when the Church was first established, as it looks more like Smith just making things up as he went along rather than the Lord 'revealing' new ideas 'line upon line' as the Church claims. Smith started with just a 'First' and 'Second Elder' of the Church – but that idea was not to last very long.

Smith had to constantly fight to retain his overall position of power and control at the top, something that was regularly questioned and challenged. If the Lord was establishing His one true Church on earth, the overall structure should have been clear and specific from the beginning, even if many of the offices were filled later as time went by and the Church grew. The fact that the whole structure of the Church along with Smith's other ideas, for example the huge difference between the Kirtland endowment and the Nauvoo endowment, kept changing completely as he dreamt up new concepts, tends towards human determination rather than being the Lord's original, perfect, *unchanging* ideas.

It mentions that the early revelations were incorporated into "A Book of Commandments for the Government of the **Church of Christ**" in 1833 (emphasis added). Note that the Lord couldn't even make up His mind what He wanted to call His Church in the early days *(See Section 115, p. 400)*. It was eight years, and there were several alternatives used, before the final name was selected, by which time several schisms had broken off and formed their own sects. I have stated elsewhere that if there is a God, He isn't very good at

DOCTRINE & COVENANTS – INTRODUCTION

religion. I can most certainly state that if the Mormon version of God is real, He is absolutely hopeless at Mormonism.

As was the custom of the day, several 'witnesses' (eighteen), attested to the work of 1833. That testimony was written in 1831 *(see: Joseph Smith Papers: Revelations and Translations, Vol. 2:193)*. The fact that a statement did not appear in the BOC was due only to it not being completed because the press was destroyed. It ends in the middle of Chapter 65 but should have included a total of 77 chapters plus the witness statement. In the 1835 D&C, a written 'testimony' of the twelve apostles was attached. Only six of the original names remained but the wording was almost *identical*, clearly indicating that it was pre-prepared and that the signatories just added their names to the document. It appears in the Introduction today and simply claims the Holy Ghost bore record to each of them that the revelations were true. As with many early 'witnesses' not all of the original eighteen or quorum of twelve remained faithful to the Church.

In any event, it has already been firmly established that Smith's witnesses were completely unreliable and several are known to have lied outright for him in published sworn affidavits *(See: TMD Vol. 1:33-4)*.

The Introduction goes on to explain there were originally seven 'theological lessons' included in the 1835 edition of the D&C. It says they became known as 'Lectures **on** Faith'. In fact, they were entitled 'Lectures *of* Faith' and that is how I refer to them in this work. A need to cover the fact that the lectures no longer appear in the D&C is evident from the following explanation:

> These had been prepared for use in the School of the Prophets in Kirtland, Ohio, from 1834 to 1835. Although profitable for doctrine and instruction, these lectures have been omitted from the Doctrine and Covenants since the 1921 edition **because they were not given or presented as revelations to the whole Church.** (Emphasis added).

The above statement is an utter lie, inasmuch as the 1835 D&C was indeed *presented* to the Church; it was voted on; it was accepted and canonised on 17 August 1835. It became canonised scripture, before rank and file members had even seen the manuscript as it had not then been published. The fact that they really had no idea what they were voting *on* for canonisation is beside the point. It may be argued that the consent of the members was simply based on faith. The Church members *were* asked to vote and they *did*, thus the statement that it was *not* presented to the 'whole Church', which then meant a 'general assembly' of the membership, for a vote – is a *false* one. The Church *recorded* the vote in extensive detail its own history *(HC. V.2:243-6)*.

I find it extremely arrogant and deliberately deceptive for Church leaders to now claim such a thing in the introduction to canonised scripture. The notion will invariably be accepted as read by modern day Mormons. In point of fact, the lectures had indeed been accepted as canonised scripture, along with the rest of the D&C, by vote of the Church, not just once – but *twice*.

The fact that members generally had yet to actually *see* a copy, applied just as much to the rest of the D&C as it did to the lectures. They were originally considered important enough not only to include, but to form part of the very title of the work. The seven lectures actually comprised the 'doctrine', and the revelation Sections were the 'covenants' in the original work. The title remains, but most modern-day Mormons have no idea how it originated.

The later deletion of the lectures was rationalised to be because they were *not* voted upon as **revelation** – but the very fact they were included, specifically as **doctrine** of the Church had clearly amounted to the same thing for prophets and followers alike from 1835-1921. Whatever the case, despite the fact that no one had seen the book, it was nevertheless voted upon in 1835 – in its entirety, including the lectures – and accepted as canonised *scripture*, whether direct revelation or not. Whatever the Church claims, it must apply to the entire work and not just the lectures. The vote *was* taken, it *was* recorded, and they *were* canonised as *scripture*. Once canonised, how can such action be challenged?

As if that were not enough, at the October 1880 General Conference, when the latest revised version of the D&C was published, President George Q. Cannon held up copies of the *Doctrine and Covenants* (which still faithfully included the Lectures of Faith) and the *Pearl of Great Price* and said, "As there have been additions made … by the publishing of revelations which were not contained in the original edition, it has been deemed wise to submit these books **with their contents** to the Conference, to see whether the Conference will vote to accept the books and their **contents as from God**, and **binding upon us** as a people and **as a Church**." (Emphasis added). President Joseph F. Smith so moved; it was seconded, and the congregation voted affirmatively. (*Deseret Evening News, 11 Oct. 1880, p. 2, col. 4.*) Thus, for a **second** time, the Church voted to sustain the 'doctrine' section of the D&C "as from God" and it was retained as scripture. The modern day *lie* is thus even further reinforced.

The real reason that the seven lectures were deleted was due to the theology they contained becoming diametrically opposite to that which the Church *later* came to believe after they were published and Smith's concepts evolved and changed. In order to escape the now unpleasant facts, the Church resorts to **lies**.

When the *Book of Mormon* was written; when the *Inspired Revision* of the Bible was written; and when the lectures were used, Smith and his followers were entirely monotheistic. Only later did his polytheism evolve, when the first vision then became what it is today and the lectures became less than usable.

The fact is that when the seven lectures were written, taught and included in the D&C, they represented the doctrine of the day in the Church. We will of course review each of the lectures in this work.

DOCTRINE & COVENANTS – INTRODUCTION

The 2010 online version of the D&C includes the 1981 statement "…in the current edition of the Doctrine and Covenants, three documents have been included for the first time. These are sections 137 and 138, setting forth the fundamentals of salvation for the dead; and Official Declaration—2, announcing that all worthy male members of the Church may be ordained to the priesthood without regard for race or color." We will be reviewing these in their turn, along with all the other Sections.

Admission of errors being perpetuated in past editions is included, along with the fact that several have been corrected in this edition; but not the fact that some Sections had been completely altered or later added to, or one even designated for an entirely different person, since first being published.

> Consequently, this edition contains corrections of dates and place-names and also a few other minor corrections when it seemed appropriate (such as discontinuing the unusual names beginning with section 78). These changes have been made so as to bring the material into conformity with the historical documents. Other special features of this latest edition include maps showing the major geographical locations in which the revelations were received, plus improvements in cross-references, section headings, and subject-matter summaries, all of which are designed to help readers to understand and rejoice in the message of the Lord as given in the Doctrine and Covenants.

It is perfectly understandable that such updates would be required and those aspects will be ignored in this work. There have been arguments put forward that people just don't 'understand' that revelations *can* be added to *(see p.111)*.

I simply cannot see that, as any additional *later* communication from deity surely forms new and separate revelation. In any event, what is *not* acceptable, if you are inclined to consider the idea that the Lord revealed these things to Smith, is where they were arbitrarily *altered* later, often changing not just the earlier text but also original ideas and meanings. At times, new material added after the event was in order to back up things that had already happened.

It is not always clear that such additional material was *not* included the first time around, in effect creating a lie. Claiming things from God *after* they have happened, and backdating them to show that they would happen, is not exactly difficult – and certainly not convincing. And it is *not* prophecy. Nevertheless, it occurred and some instances will be revealed as we go along.

We are going to commence with a review of the *Lectures of Faith* as they appeared at the start of the original D&C. When reviewing the D&C Sections, they are listed in the original date sequence rather than the current numbering system. This gives a clearer picture of what was happening. It also allows us to

THE MORMON DELUSION

take a look on occasion behind the scenes and consider what was going on in the background and which sometimes gave rise to Smith's revelations.

It turns out that there were not many actual prophecies at all. Any that are discovered are summarised at the end of each Section and also at the end of the book in 'The Final Analysis' *(Part 1)*. In addition, there are summary notes of a few 'non-prophetic revelations' that I felt worth mentioning. You may spot others that I have not included. With many sections, there was no summary required.

I have commented on things that seemed interesting and I have ignored many that some readers may feel would have been worth mentioning. The reason for this is there is only so much you can include and I have tried to pick out some interesting, informative and important aspects that will entertain as well as inform readers. For this reason, at times, we stop to review individuals mentioned in revelations and also what was happening at the time.

Chapter 2

Lectures of Faith

Since the mid-late 1800s, these lectures have been referred to as the 'Lectures *on* Faith' but in the spirit of accuracy, I use the originally published wording in this work. They were first published in 1835 as the "Lectures *of* Faith".

When the 1835 first edition of the *Doctrine and Covenants* was published, the Mormon Church was called "The Church of the Latter-Day Saints" and the book is addressed to the members of that Church. It was not the first name the Mormon Church was called and it was certainly not to be the last.

Apologists have long tried to 'excuse' the fact that the now somewhat embarrassing lectures ever appeared in the D&C at all, despite the fact that they remained there for over eight decades before being unceremoniously dropped from the book without so much as a mention to members, let alone a vote for their agreement. Whilst Joseph Smith was not in attendance when they were canonised, he was heavily involved with their construction and teaching.

From *HC Vol. 2. Ch. XVIII:*

> Wherefore, Oliver Cowdery and Sidney Rigdon, members of the First Presidency, (Presidents Joseph Smith, Jun., and Frederick G. Williams being absent on a visit to the Saints in Michigan,) appointed Thomas Burdick, Warren Parrish, and Sylvester Smith clerks, and proceeded to organize the whole assembly...

An explanatory statement that appears just before the above paragraph, tells us that Smith had headed the committee that put the first D&C together.

> A general assembly of the Church of Latter-day Saints was held at Kirtland on the 17th of August, 1835, to take into consideration the labors of a committee appointed by a general assembly of the Church on the 24th of September 1834, for the purpose of arranging the items of the doctrine of Jesus Christ for the government of the Church. The names of the committee were: Joseph Smith, Jun., Sidney Rigdon, Oliver Cowdery and Frederick G. Williams, who, having finished said book according to the instructions given them, deem it necessary to call a general assembly of the Church to see whether the book be approved or not by the authorities of the Church: that it may, if approved, become a law and a rule of faith and practice to the Church.

Joseph Smith headed up the committee which had just finished its work, so what was presented to the Church was the completed *Doctrine and Covenants*. Considering Smith taught the lectures in his 'School of the Prophets' and had people commit them to memory, we can safely say that he knew something, if not everything, about them. He definitely approved of the content which he had worked on. These are Smith's own words, again from *HC Vol. 2. Ch. XVIII.*

> 1 December 1834. Our school for the Elders was now well attended, and with the lectures on theology, which were regularly delivered, absorbed for the time being everything else of a temporal nature.
>
> January, 1835--During the month of January, I was engaged in the school of the Elders, and in preparing the lectures on theology for publication in the book of Doctrine and Covenants, which the committee appointed last September were now compiling.

Smith was a member of that committee and he worked on the lectures for inclusion in the D&C; he certainly never objected to them, nor did he remove them from the D&C. They appeared in the next edition and subsequent ones. They are a fair account of the theology of early Mormonism which existed for several years prior to Smith dreaming up his ideas on plural gods. Smith's hand in things is clearly in evidence in the preface to the 1835 D&C:

> The first part of the book will be found to contain a series of Lectures as delivered before a Theological class in this place, and in consequence of their embracing the ***important doctrine of salvation***, we have arranged them into the following work. *(1835 D&C Preface – Joseph Smith, Oliver Cowdery, Sidney Rigdon and F. G. Williams).* (Emphasis added).

LECTURE FIRST OF FAITH

Smith most certainly would have been party to the choice of a title for the book. The 'doctrine' referred specifically to the lectures and the 'covenants' to the revelation 'sections'. We deal with the lectures first, as they appeared at the start of the D&C. They were written after the 1833 *Book of Commandments* was published and of course no longer appear in modern day editions of the D&C as they were dropped in 1921. We will consider each lecture and measure the content against what the Church now teaches. It will become increasingly clear as to why the Church now effectively pretends they just don't exist. Well, the Church will admit to them if pressed, but you won't readily find a copy lying around. They are not exactly 'promoted' any longer in the Church.

The lectures are too lengthy to include in their entirety in this work but they are available to read online. This is one current link: http://solomonspalding.com/docs/1835DnC2.htm#pg001

Theology

Lecture First

ON THE DOCTRINE OF THE CHURCH OF THE LATTER DAY SAINTS.

Of Faith.

SECTION I.

This lecture starts out by affirming that faith is the first principle in revealed religion. It promises to address 'what faith is', the 'object on which it rests' and the 'effects which flow from it'.

Hebrews 11:1 is quoted in this manner. "Now faith is the substance [assurance] of things hoped for, the evidence of things not seen." The word 'assurance' does not appear in the *KJV* but does now appear in the *American Standard Version* instead of 'substance', and it also has 'conviction' rather than 'evidence'. This seems logical, as there can be no 'evidence' of things *not* seen.

That surely is the whole point of faith – it exists only as long as there is no evidence to support (or refute) the thing you have faith *in*. Once evidence (of either persuasion) is available, faith in the matter is rendered redundant. This will become an extremely important point throughout this work and should be remembered at each stage. In the final analysis, only ***evidence*** counts.

THE MORMON DELUSION

The lecture continues with a strange statement which really cannot be taken seriously, but it is easy to see how the conclusion was reached in the early nineteenth century. In paragraph 10 (hereafter 'para'), it indicates that if men (initially it was *only* men who heard these lectures) thought about it, they would discover that "...it is faith, and faith only, which is the moving cause of all action in them; that without it, both mind and body would be in a state of inactivity, and all their exertions would cease, both physical and mental."

Obviously, this very first assertion is scientifically flawed, as most human actions that keep us alive are completely subconscious and involve nothing remotely close to *faith* that we will keep going. Much of what we do as humans takes place entirely naturally. In the main, we are not even conscious of what goes on. This is the result of evolutionary determination over millions of years – the inbuilt instinct for survival, not just for or by us, but also the trillions of bacteria on and in our bodies that we rely upon to keep us alive and that in turn rely on us for their own survival. So, the very first aspect in the 1835 D&C is shown to be sheer nonsense – and it goes downhill with the wind after that.

The rationale for the claim follows. The 'class' is asked, from their first recollections, what "principle excited them to action... Would it not be that it was the assurance which we had of the existence of things which we had not seen as yet?" A whole diatribe about 'faith' or 'belief' in the results of actions follows, but again it is based on a completely flawed supposition. "Would you have ever sown if you had not believed that you would reap? Would you have ever planted if you had not believed that you would gather? ...Are not all your exertions, of every kind, dependent on your faith? Or may we not ask, what have you, or what do you possess, which you have not obtained by reason of your faith? Your food, your raiment, your lodgings, are they not all by reason of your faith? Reflect, and ask yourselves if these things are not so."

Well, I have reflected, as everyone should have who originally heard this nonsense. The things mentioned have *nothing* whatsoever to do with *faith*.

Each action may well be taken with an *expectation* of naturally anticipated results but not because of faith; rather it is because of an abundance of *evidence* which supports anticipated results. They have happened countless times before and can thus be *expected* to happen again. We sow, because whenever people have previously done so (notwithstanding complications resulting from weather conditions), they have in turn usually been able to reap. It involves science and nature – not faith at all. Experience teaches us what we can expect when certain actions are undertaken. I remember a similar argument in Church – you have 'faith' that the sun will rise in the morning. No, you really do *not*. It is a logical *expectation* which we *know* for a *fact* will happen – through *evidence* to date – and a very modest understanding of astrophysics. If it were *not* to do so, then the Earth would have ceased to exist, as something very dramatic which would mean the end of our solar system must have occurred. This is *not* related to

LECTURE FIRST OF FAITH

faith; it is simple science, and to relate such things to religious 'faith' is a very cruel manipulation intended to persuade people toward religious 'thinking'.

The faith 'trick' is used to dupe people into believing they can 'expect' similar results with 'faith' in religion, with absolutely no *evidence* whatsoever, in just the same way as they do from normal daily activity; the results for which are supported by more *evidence* than we would ever need. When we do sow, we really can *expect* to reap. Experience and evidence are the control factors. Man has not only learned to do so from experience (not faith), but has also experimented and developed many new species of animals and crops that never existed before. This again has nothing to do with 'faith' in the outcome, but rather it is just the result of extensive experimentation.

Faith is not an applicable term in relation to such things. Religion tries to accommodate its needs through any means possible. If people are gullible enough to accept that their belief in an expected result, based on experience and scientific knowledge, is the same as faith in something for which there is zero evidence, then they are severely mistaken – and that is the start of the road to a full-blown delusional state. It is subtle and clever – and it is very, very wrong.

The explained rationale is that "as faith is the moving cause of all action in temporal concerns" (which it is ***not***) "so it is in spiritual…" – and people accept that, without ***thinking.*** Once someone accepts it, there is little hope for them.

Para 13 goes on to explain "as we receive by faith, all temporal blessings that we do receive, so we, in like manner, receive by faith all spiritual blessings, that we do receive." This again is simply *not* the case. Whether someone *feels* they are exercising faith or not, the same result (or *reaction*) will apply to each and every *action* and there will *never* be a measurable difference, no matter what someone believes 'faith' can achieve. If a real God exists and actually does 'bless' such people, then He stands accountable for neglecting those of this world that really deserve His help and have never received any 'blessings' whatsoever. The Mormon God is more than culpable. His system is fundamentally flawed and unconscionable.

We then have the argument that "through faith we understand the worlds were framed by the word of God". Unfortunately, 'faith' in what Mormonism, and many other religions, for that matter, tell us about such things, completely undermines science and reason – and a lot of logic and common sense as well these days, when we know so much more than they did all those years ago when such superstitions were first created. That they still prevail is testament to the fact that delusion is still alive and well in the modern world and people do not keep up with scientific advances and understanding. We now know how the worlds were 'framed' and a believer should fit their version of God into the scientific *evidence* for the evolution of the universe and life upon the Earth. To have faith that something scientifically proven is *not* the case, is to *decide* on a delusional state rather than accept the known *reality*. Religion should adapt to accept known reality and then fit God into it. To abandon scientific knowledge in favour of faith in provable fiction is not at all healthy. However, to be a Mormon, that is what you now have to do – with almost every aspect of the religion.

Apparently (para 16-17), God framed the worlds by faith, and faith is His principle *power*. Thus it is ours also. Passages from the Bible and Book of Mormon are referenced to support the supposition, which only works once you are suckered into the overall concept. Para 21 cites Joshua (10:12) making the sun and moon stand still, as if it were a true account of something that really happened. How do we *know* that it did *not*? Not through faith, but simple science. It was not 'done', as the verse states; it was simply a *story*, and it was a completely scientifically impossible one at that.

If you understand the simple mechanics of our solar system and the interdependent inter-planetary forces of space–time curvature that we call gravity, and you are then still actually capable of believing that the sun and moon really did 'stand still', without an adverse effect on everything existing within our solar system – then there is no hope for you whatsoever. You will just believe anything, without the use of common sense, let alone reason. Such an event would instantly destroy our entire solar system. Faith that it *did* happen, just because the Bible claims it, is based on delusion rather than common sense, reason, or evidence of what the result would have been if it did. Faith may start where reason ends, but it is delusional to think that it overrides common sense and scientific laws which, if you believe in Him, were set by God Himself.

The reality is that if God's works really are determined by His own faith, they are also determined by scientific laws which He must also abide by – after all, He supposedly set them in place to make the universe work the way it does.

No amount of faith *by* this God could or would ever override scientific laws of His own making. No amount of faith, even by a God, could ever make the sun and moon stand still without killing us all. That is an absolute *fact* that even the simplest human mind should be able to grasp and clearly understand.

Just as much as faith is *not* required in order to expect the sun to rise every day, as it is a perfectly natural occurrence, so it is not required to understand that God could not make it stand still. To a believer, God has *set* the very laws that make it impossible, and to argue that God can do anything, including changing those laws, invites only cosmic confusion, and although humans may yet not understand everything, they most certainly understand the 'laws' of the universe well enough to know that.

It is not something that any amount of faith will ever make real. The reality of Santa Claus is as plausible as the sun and moon actually standing still. The consequences of such a reality would have initiated an immediate extinction of all life on this planet, among other things. Belief in such nonsense is something that must be **overcome** in order to 'see the light' as it were. The truth is entirely

LECTURE FIRST OF FAITH

different from any such silly stories. No, it was *not* done by faith, they were just myths, invented to make Israel and their God look good in the eyes of the local tribes people compared with the rest of their known world.

The lecture concludes that faith is the first governing power and without faith even God cannot function. The lecture then moves on to answer questions on theology which is apparently "revealed science". That should be interesting – God revealing *science* to Joseph Smith.

OF THEOLOGY

Question. -- What is theology?

Answer. -- It is that revealed science which treats of the being and attributes of God -- his relations to us -- the dispensations of his providence -- his will with respect to our actions -- and his purposes with respect to our end (Buck's Theological Dictionary, page 582).

As previously stated, it really does go downhill with the wind now. The idea that theology is "revealed science" is about as silly as it gets. Although many Mormons now seem to accept evolution as individuals, the Mormon Church itself is obliged to accept the concept of Adam and Eve – and in a timeframe consistent with the Bible, as Smith firmly integrated it into his theology. He claimed to locate 'Adam's altar', thus further supporting the Adam and Eve story. He used the flood mythology extensively in his *Book of Abraham* where Egyptus 'discovered' Egypt following the flood. The Earth has a mere seven thousand years of temporal existence, according to the 'revelation' in *D&C 77*.

The Church remains quiet about evolution and takes no stand on it. This is quite strange considering evolution is now a well established scientific ***fact.***

We know how old the Earth is; we know how humans evolved and how long it took; we know that whilst there have been five mass extinctions, there was *not* a global flood during biblical times and that the story cannot be true by any and every scientific measure you consider – and also every engineering measure for the equally impossible ark. So much for theology having anything remotely to do with 'revealed science'. It clearly points to the ideas of men, and not very clever ones at that, purported to have come from an ethereal source. Proof of fraudulent claims is inherent at every stage of each assertion that is made. *Nothing* stands up to scrutiny at all. Faith doesn't help.

Having stated that 'theology is revealed science', the lecture then quantifies the principles involved – or rather, it really doesn't, despite the claim.

Q. What is the first principle in this revealed science?

A. Faith.

THE MORMON DELUSION

How faith can be the first principle of 'revealed science' only the Mormon God knows. Religious 'faith' has no place in science which relies on evidence alone in pursuit of truth. Science admits it can be wrong and is ever searching for truth through further evidence. Faith, in contrast, may continue to be placed in things which have long been proven false through conclusive evidence.

Q. Why is faith the first principle in this revealed science?

A. Because it is the foundation of all righteousness: Heb. 11:6, Without faith it is impossible to please God. 1st John 3:7. Little children, let no man deceive you: he that doeth righteousness, is righteous, even as he (God) is righteous.

How ludicrous to claim that faith is the first principle in revealed science. If you have faith, you are righteous – but you cannot 'please' God without faith.

Q. What arrangement should be followed in presenting the subject of faith?

A. First, Should be shown what faith is.
Secondly, the object upon which it rests; and
Thirdly, The effects which flow from it.

The above question is then further answered in those three stages:

Q. What is faith?

A. It is the assurance of things hoped for, the evidence of things not seen: Heb. 11:1. That is, it is the assurance we have of the existence of unseen things. And being the assurance which we have of the existence of unseen things, must be the principle of action in all intelligent beings. Heb. 11:3. Through faith we understand that the worlds were framed by the word of God.

See the second paragraph under 'Section 1' on p.17. When you consider the concept of 'faith' in the religious sense, it most certainly is *not* what Hebrews 11:1 implies any more than it is what the lecture extends that premise to include. Faith is definitely not the 'substance' of things hoped for, or even the 'assurance' claimed above. Any such perceived assurance is purely imaginary, experienced as an internal *emotion* not remotely connected to reality.

I have personally experienced what it is supposed to feel like and to mean to an individual, many times, and whilst such emotional states can seem real at the time, they cannot actually be *quantified* as anything other than wishful thinking. No outside influence is involved, nor can they remotely be considered 'evidence' of things not seen (Heb 11:1).

LECTURE FIRST OF FAITH

The reality is that faith is not related to either 'substance' or 'evidence'; indeed it is the very *lack* of such that makes faith what it really is. Faith has *no* substance. In the secular sense, 'faith' is just a term used to describe *confidence* or trust in a person or thing. In the religious sense, it is purely *belief* that is specifically *not* based on proof but rather a complete and utter *lack* of any.

Likewise, faith cannot possibly be equated to 'evidence' regarding anything whatsoever, as once evidence *exists*, faith in that thing becomes superseded and completely *obsolete*. Knowledge and understanding of evidence *replaces* faith or belief – with *fact*. Therefore, to support Hebrews 11:1, no matter how nice it sounds, as plausible supposition is completely ludicrous. It is a contradictory statement which makes the faithful feel vindicated and the sane scratch their heads.

I think Hebrews 11:1 might more appropriately be rephrased this way:

> "Faith is the unquantified anticipation of things hoped for, the unsubstantiated conviction of things not seen." *(Jim Whitefield)*.

Faith, or belief, is without substance *or* evidence; else it is no longer just faith or belief. Substance, in support of something when it is, at least in part, substantiated, and evidence, when it becomes more firmly established, or even identified as known fact, *removes* faith from the equation entirely. Expressions used in the above Q&A such as "…the 'assurance' we have of the existence of unseen things…" started to lead people down the path of a belief system for which no such assurance actually existed. It was a confidence trick perpetrated by the unscrupulous Joseph Smith and his close cohorts. Most of Smith's early followers probably believed such things and were just gullible converts rather than deliberate perpetrators of the hoax. There is no such thing in reality as an 'assurance' of *anything* beyond the known universe and this life.

Anything *religious* is conjecture and completely unsubstantiated. When the response to a question is that something is 'a matter of faith' that means *exactly* what it says; faith stands alone, with no support or tangible evidence at all.

Belief in ethereal matters is simply that, personal belief, based on nothing substantive. When evidence exists, belief and faith give way to *knowledge*.

> Q. How do you prove that faith is the principle of action in all intelligent beings?

> A. First, By duly considering the operations of my own mind; and secondly, by the direct declaration of scripture. -- Heb. 11:7. By faith Noah, being warned of things not seen as yet, moved with fear, prepared an ark to the saving of his house; by the which he condemned the world, and became heir of the righteousness which is by faith. Heb. 11:8, By faith, Abraham, when he was called to go out

> into a place which he should after receive for an inheritance, obeyed; and he went out, not knowing whither he went. Heb. 11:9, By faith he sojourned in the land of promise, as in a strange country, dwelling in tabernacles with Isaac and Jacob, the heirs with him of the same promise. Heb. 11:27. By faith, Moses forsook Egypt, not fearing the wrath of the king; for he endured, as seeing him who is invisible.

The above answer completely fails to properly address the question "how do you 'prove' that faith is the principle of action in all intelligent beings." The answer suggests first considering our own minds. Faith is not an applicable aspect unless you are religious and you replace other more suitable expressions with the idea that it is 'faith' being used. Most things are achieved through self belief, personal drive or normal everyday experiences and expectations. The concept of faith in oneself is far removed from any religious connotation.

The answer actually claims that Noah was initially moved with fear rather than faith. Abraham going to a place that he didn't 'know', was not unusual and regardless, once again it is not 'proof' of faith.

Likewise, Moses 'forsaking' Egypt is also bereft of such proof of faith. The fact that the flood, much of the Abraham story, and Moses leaving Egypt with millions of Israelites, are all Jewish mythology is also neglected in the lecture. At the time the lectures were written, the stories would have seemed plausible enough simply because they were in the Bible. Today, scientific evidence has proven much of the Bible to be handed down mythology rather than reality. The Israelites never were in Egypt in significant numbers, they did not cross the Red Sea, they did not dwell in the wilderness for forty years, and faith is not required to know these things. Evidence proves the case through extensive archaeology in the Sinai and very detailed Egyptian history.

> Q. Is not faith the principle of action in spiritual things as well as in temporal?
>
> A. It is.

Having failed to properly address proof of faith in the temporal sense, we move on to faith being the principle of action in the spiritual sense. That should be a lot easier – as it clearly is.

> Q. How do you prove it?

My question here is why is there any *need* to prove it? It is surely a given that faith, invariably combined with fear, is a prime motivator in any religion. If someone does not have 'faith' in something for which there is no proof, they will not believe in it and are thus not religious at all. It is actually such 'faith'

LECTURE FIRST OF FAITH

that drags people into the delusional world that religion creates. Nevertheless, an answer, of sorts, is given.

> A. Heb. 11:6. Without faith it is impossible to please God. Mark 16:16 He that believeth and is baptized shall be saved. Rom. 4:16. Therefore, it is of faith, that it might be by grace; to the end the promise might be sure to all the seed; not to that only which is of the law, but to that also which is of the faith of Abraham, who is the father of us all.

So, we cannot please God without faith. But then the lecture claims that whoever believes and is baptised shall be saved and it is through faith they will be *saved* by *grace*. That is *now* interpreted by the Church to mean all will be *resurrected* by grace but any reward beyond that must be *earned*.

> Q. Is faith any thing else beside the principle of action?
>
> A. It is.
>
> Q. What is it?
>
> A. It is the principle of power, also.

Faith is apparently the principle of power to do things, according to the above, but...

> Q. How do you prove it?
>
> A. First, it is the principle of power in the Deity, as well as in man. Heb. 11:3. Through faith we understand that the worlds were framed by the word of God, so that things which are seen were not made of things which do appear.

Of course, as there is no proof of deity, there can be no proof of faith being the principle of power *in* such deity. It is another unanswerable question, yet answered it is. Apparently, God could only frame the worlds through His faith. That is a very strange concept indeed. The real question is, whilst it is quite understandable that humans must have faith if they are to believe in something for which there is zero proof, why would a supreme, all powerful, all knowing God need faith regarding *anything*? He would be the ultimate scientist and already know the end result of any action or creation He ever undertook. Faith, surely, would never enter into it. Why would it? It is a purely human concept, created to bridge the gap between reality and the supernatural, which in turn keeps followers shackled to whatever they have been enticed to have faith in.

THE MORMON DELUSION

Billions of people express faith in tens of thousands of sects all claiming their God to be the one true deity. Some even have multiple Gods which are just as plausible as the one Mormon God. There is no more, or less, evidence for any one of them. Individual faith confirms a particular God to be real. Thus we see that faith is a fundamentally flawed and unreliable concept, and one which an all knowing deity would never rely on as it can deceive us. It must do, or there would be just one Church and one God and everyone would express identical faith in a singular concept of that deity. Humans can be deceived, but theologically deity cannot, thus the unreliable concept of faith cannot apply to God. The same is true for prayer, another completely unreliable concept.

> Second, it is the principle of power in man also. Book of Mormon, page 264, Alma and Amulek are delivered from prison. Do. page 421. Nephi and Lehi, with the Lamanites, are immersed with the Spirit. Do. page 565. The mountain Zerin, by the faith of the Brother of Jared, is removed. Josh. 10:12. Then spake Joshua to the Lord in the day when the Lord delivered up the Amorites before the children of Israel, and he said in the sight of Israel, Sun, stand thou still upon Gibeon; and thou, Moon, in the valley of Ajalon. Josh. 10:13. And the sun stood still, and the moon stayed, until the people had avenged themselves upon their enemies. Is not this written in the book of Jasher? So the sun stood still in the midst of heaven, and hasted not to go down about a whole day. Mat. 17:19. Then came the disciples to Jesus apart, and said, Why could not we cast him out? Mat. 17:20. And Jesus said unto them, Because of your unbelief: for verily I say unto you, If ye have faith as a grain of mustard-seed, ye shall say unto this mountain, Remove hence to yonder place; and it shall remove; and nothing shall be impossible unto you. -- Heb. 11:32. And what shall I say more? for the time would fail me to tell of Gideon, and of Barak, and of Samson, and of Jephthah, of David also, and Samuel, and of the prophets. Heb. 11:33. Who through faith subdued kingdoms, wrought righteousness, obtained promises, stopped the mouths of lions, Heb. 11:34. Quenched the violence of fire, escaped the edge of the sword, out of weakness were made strong, waxed valiant in fight, turned to flight the armies of the aliens. Heb. 11:35. Women received their dead raised to life again: and others were tortured, not accepting deliverance; that they might obtain a better resurrection.

Here, the idea that faith is "the principle power in man" is expounded. The fact is that it is not a *power* at all; it is just a word used to describe a feeling that improbable and unprovable things are real. It is a dangerous position to take. Without *evidence*, no one really knows where they are. The rest of the above consists of *Book of Mormon* and biblical nonsense, including the sun

LECTURE FIRST OF FAITH

and moon standing still – which, as previously stated, would of course destroy our entire solar system in an instant.

I will just say this. If God really did stop the sun and moon, if He did stop the mouth of lions and all the other nonsensical things attributed to faith in Him, why has He *never* answered the many supplications made with the utmost faith, to save millions of people from starvation, disease, natural disaster and death? If the pointless stories are true and yet He simultaneously ignores those in real need, He is not very good at being a God and not at all worthy of being followed. Faith in such a being is entirely misplaced. He is just not worth it.

> Q. How would you define faith in its most unlimited sense?
>
> A. It is the first great governing principle which has power, dominion, and authority over all things.
>
> Q. How do you convey to the understanding more clearly, that faith is the first great governing principle, which has power, dominion, and authority over all things?
>
> A. By it they exist, by it they are upheld, by it they are changed, or by it they remain, agreeably to the will of God; and without it there is no power; and without power there could be no creation, nor existence!

The definition of faith is claimed as the "first great governing principle" having "power, dominion and authority" over all things. The *fact* is that it is *not*, and it does *not*. Faith is just a fanciful expression of belief in abstract things that are no more substantiated than Santa Claus, the Easter Bunny or the Tooth Fairy, all of which every child has absolute 'faith' in, if you will, until it is utterly destroyed by adults who burst the bubble and explain the truth. God is the one imaginary friend that many never grow out of, and all because no one tells them the truth before it is too late and the delusion becomes their reality.

As for conveying the idea more clearly, saying that everything is held in place "agreeably to the will of God" is just an extension of belief in the concept and has no merit regarding the burden of *proof*. If, when a child asked about God, they got a similar answer to their question about Santa Claus, they would immediately stop believing in God and the world would become filled with a new adult generation holding as rational an approach to the idea of deity as this one does about Santa Claus.

From this first lecture, we learn the supposed answers to the early questions that Joseph Smith's followers were taught to pose. In it, the concept of faith is manipulated to cover everything the followers are to be taught, which they must accept *on* faith and without question – it's all down to 'revealed science'

– from God to Smith. None of this is remotely *science* and none is from any God. It is that simple.

Chapter 3

Lectures of Faith
Lecture 2

LECTURE SECOND.
Of Faith.

SECTION II.

As we review the rest of the lectures, paragraphs that contain meaningless filler and are of no significance will be omitted in the interest of space. Occasionally, something may be included just to emphasise how silly some things really are. The full lectures can be read online if the reader is so inclined and are located at the link provided near the start of Chapter 2.

This lecture promises to show "the object on which it [faith] rests".

> 2 We here observe that God is the only supreme governor, and independent being, in whom all fulness and perfection dwells; who is omnipotent, omnipresent, and omniscient; without beginning of days or end of life; and that in him every good gift, and every good principle dwells; and that he is the Father of lights: In him the principle of faith dwells independently; and he is the object in whom the faith of all other rational and accountable beings centers, for life and salvation.

THE MORMON DELUSION

At the time the lectures were taught, Joseph Smith and his followers were still entirely monotheistic in their outlook. The concepts of God having a body and of there being plural Gods had yet to evolve. This is one reason why the Church now makes excuses for the lectures and largely ignores them. In para 2 we learn that the Mormon God is a traditional being – "omnipotent" (infinite, unlimited power and authority), "omnipresent" (present *everywhere* at the same time), "omniscient" (with complete or unlimited knowledge, awareness, or understanding; perceiving all things), and "without beginning of days" (he has *always* been there). Faith dwells *in* Him.

Whilst the Church started out with these concepts which mirror mainstream Christianity, they were not all to last and it is one reason why the lectures were later abandoned. The idea of an *omnipresent* God who dwells everywhere at once is now decried in Mormonism and was even the object of ridicule in the temple ceremony when I was a member. A minister, complete with dog collar, explained his teachings about God who was "so large He fills the universe and yet so small he can dwell in your heart". In 1835 that was equally a Mormon belief. Today, in Mormonism, God has a body and dwells in one place at a time. He gets nowhere near your heart. That is the Holy Ghost's job, as he is a spirit being. In 1835, the Mormon God was still considered a spirit without a body and the Holy Spirit was the *mind* of God. That was all to change *after* the lectures were written. The "without beginning of days" idea also became very awkward when Smith developed his plural Gods idea along with the concept that our God was once a man like us who 'progressed' to become a God.

Thus His Godhood *did* have a 'beginning of days'. Despite press interviews in which Gordon B. Hinckley, a recent Mormon prophet, claimed he didn't know much about it, that concept is still a core fundamental Mormon doctrine.

All faithful Mormon men aspire to become Gods, just as our own God did. The Mormon Church doesn't seem to find the idea an easy sell these days so clearly it would rather that sort of thing be 'discovered' later when people are 'ready' for such details. The habit of withholding deeper and often somewhat less believable doctrine is termed 'milk before meat'. In reality, that invariably means something is so bizarre and unbelievable, a certain level of delusion must be achieved before someone would be gullible enough to accept it.

That may sound harsh, but I apply it as equally to myself as to anyone else for I certainly experienced times when I troubled over accepting things I hadn't heard before. Had I been told *everything* from the beginning, I would quickly have seen through the obvious hoax and never converted in the first place.

From para 3 on, much of the creation as detailed in Genesis is visited, but *not*, it is declared, "…evidences … manifested by the works of the creation, which we daily behold…" giving the impression that we already *know* God did all that as we 'see' it every day. There is of course no actual evidence for such a notion whatsoever. References are taken from what is termed the 'New

LECTURE SECOND OF FAITH

Translation', which means Smith's *Inspired Revision* of the Bible, in which he added more detail to the *KJV*. As with everything else religious, the validity of what Smith changed and added is also a matter of 'faith'.

Para 11 reiterates the concept that *every* creature was brought to Adam and that he named "every living creature", except of course fish are not mentioned. It is quite obvious why, when you think about it. God could have shown Adam all the fish if He wanted to, but humans, who wrote this, did not even think about them. "Adam gave names to *all* cattle, and to the fowl of the air, and to every beast of the field." I mentioned in *TMD Volume 4:199* that as this would amount to countless millions of species, it is yet another absolute reason why this was a completely silly and utterly impossible idea. Other than a handful of local beasts and birds in any given location, no one ever knew what most things were called before they were later discovered, catalogued and named. What would have been the point?

Try thinking up twenty names for pictures of animals and birds you are unfamiliar with and then imagine thinking of *millions*. Also, they would have needed drawing and cataloguing, in the absence of photography, if anyone else was to benefit from the long list. Of the twenty names for pictures of animals you have named, try shuffling the drawings and then remembering what you called them. You will get, on average, between five and nine correct – if you are lucky. So, how were they recorded, later re-identified and learned of by the following generations? *Where* were they ever recorded, and unless local to them, why would they even need to know anything about them? Couple this with the fact that this was long before the written word was ever developed.

A further problem for the Mormon Church is that according to Smith, everything was supposedly spoken and written in a pure 'Adamic' language, yet all we now have was written in Hebrew a few centuries BCE. Nevertheless, this absurd legend is incorporated into the lecture as if it were true. It is further evidence that Smith and company were as taken in by early legends as every other Christian of the day. Instead of showing that he was a true prophet by explaining what was *behind* the legends, Smith just perpetuated the myths within the lectures – because he *believed* them. God didn't correct matters.

It is abundantly clear that it is all no more than mythology. The 'creatures' known locally, at the time Genesis as we now read it was first written, a few centuries BCE, would have amounted to few by comparison to the now known possible total. Naturally, they already had names for them which they attributed to the fictional character Adam; a logical assumption for the day – but not now.

The Israelites took no account of their own pre-historical position when creating the myths, any more than they had any idea how many species actually existed. Even at the time Genesis was penned as we now read it, the animals named in Hebrew didn't amount to the millions that are now known to exist. Why would they be? Genesis claims Adam named them *all* – and Smith agrees.

THE MORMON DELUSION

From para 13 we move on to the fall and that story is retold as if it were a true account of a series of real events. The misogyny of the Mormon God is clearly identified in para 16, which is taken from Moses 4:22, where He says:

> I will greatly multiply your sorrow, and your conception: in sorrow you shall bring forth children, and your desire shall be to your husband, and he shall rule over you.

How cruel can you get, unnecessarily multiplying the pain and suffering of childbirth for the many billions of women yet to be born, and declaring men should "rule over" them. These are clearly just the silly thoughts of controlling and dominating men and not of any kind of loving deity. Women did not have a voice in early Judaism and not a lot has changed. Well, they did finally get a very small section of their own at the 'Wailing Wall' in Jerusalem. I have seen first hand how things still work there and not much else has changed. I have mentioned in earlier work that Smith and Young followed suit. Women were dominated by men and even today in Mormonism women have no voice.

Paras 18-19 claim two important items are shown from the quotations. First, man retained his earlier intelligence after the fall and God spoke with him face to face; second, that his transgressions did not deprive man of previous knowledge relative to the existence of his creator. The fact that we now know the real history of human beings is entirely lost among this fiction.

Para 22 claims "after Adam had been driven out of the garden, he began to till the earth... have dominion over all the beats of the field" and "...eat his bread by the sweat of his brow" confirming Joseph Smith's clear belief that *domesticated* animals were around from the beginning of human existence, regardless of how long ago that was, along with agricultural farming and a knowledge of how to harvest, grind and prepare kernels into flour and how to use and control fire, along with an understanding of cooking.

The fact is that humans existed without the use of fire for eons before it was tamed and then used for warmth and cooking. Hunter-gatherers did not 'till the earth' and there were no domesticated forms of any animals *or* crops as we know them today. Before the transition from wild grasses to domesticated cereals, humans did not have a diet which included such things – as they simply did not exist. Evidence against the Adam and Eve story is **conclusive**.

God did not *create* the range of cereals humans now rely on for sustenance. This fact is another evidence for evolution. In theological terms, God 'created' every living thing (animal and vegetable) as they *now* are, on day one; well, on days three, five and six to be precise. He stopped to make the sun, moon and stars on day four – but you will know what I mean. We know for an absolute fact that this is *not* the case. The evidence for evolution in every single variety of life on this planet is now so vast you could never study it all in a lifetime.

LECTURE SECOND OF FAITH

Even a cursory glace at just a few examples of 'life' will prove the point to anyone who cares to take a little time to look at some of the many millions of examples available.

Modern cereals were once grasses, domesticated and developed by humans over time, just as were many vegetables that we have today. There are many strange stories surrounding what we now eat. Most of our modern foods didn't always exist and the diets of our ancestors would be impossible for our evolved modern stomachs and digestive systems to process. Likewise, early humans were not adapted to milk from animals or many other processed foods that our systems are now able to accommodate. Those today who are lactose intolerant should take comfort from the fact that humans were once all that way.

When considering evolution, many people still only consider the human element and forget that absolutely *everything* evolved over time. For example, carrots originated in Afghanistan about five-thousand years ago. That's about a thousand years *after* the supposed time of Adam, so Adam did not eat carrots. Earlier wild carrots were small, bitter and inedible. The first edible carrots were purple or yellow. Were it not for the preference of the Dutch, modern-day carrots would not be orange; but then that is yet another quite long, albeit interesting, story for another day.

Grasses were first tamed and domesticated for many cereal crops now used for human consumption, in the 'fertile crescent' which is a region in Western Asia, eight or nine-thousand years ago, following the first farming practices some twelve-thousand years ago. For those interested in this area, the link below is to a very interesting paper on the "Origin and Domestication of the Fungal Wheat Pathogen Mycosphaerella graminicola via Sympatric Speciation" which appears in the 'Molecular Biology and Evolution' series of Oxford Journals. http://mbe.oxfordjournals.org/content/24/2/398.full.pdf Don't let the title put you off. It is easily readable and a good example of the stories behind pretty much everything we now eat (or drink, for that matter). God did *not* provide these things for Adam. Humans cultivated and developed them.

How would Adam ever have even known what 'bread' was, let alone how to make it? And what would he have made it with? Sacrifices were burnt, according to biblical legend, and yet man did not tame fire for a very long time in human evolutionary terms. Adam was a creature well out of any plausible historical time frame. The biblical claims are provably completely erroneous.

That's not to even mention the scientific impossibility of the creation story itself. It doesn't form part of the lectures but precedes everything biblical so it is important. If the Genesis account was revealed from God, He *lied* about it. Genesis 1 is scientifically impossible. First the heaven and earth are created and it is permanently dark. Then (v.3) God created *light* and yet the sun and moon do not exist until v.14-18. Before that, He created grass, herbs and trees. Only then do the sun, moon and stars get created. No matter that the solar system could not exist in that format; and where did the light come from *before* there was a local sun? Only minds of men, sitting around camp fires dreaming up such things, would create such a silly story. If you study creation myths and legends of Native Americans, it is easy to see they are mythological. Why? Because we were not raised to *believe* they are true. *(See TMD Vol 2:179-183 for an example).* Had we been, they would be equally accepted, just as other cultures believe in their legends regarding the creation. 'Adam' is scientifically utterly impossible, generated from very limited understanding. Today, the real 'creation story' includes all the science we know – and of course evolution.

We know humans have existed for a very long time, so if an 'Adam' ever existed, it was long ago and he would not have had fire or cereals, he would not have tilled the earth, as there was nothing to till, or to till *with* for that matter, and animals were hunted rather than domesticated for a very long time. Every single aspect of the Genesis 'story' – and therefore Smith's expanded *'Book of Moses'* – is provably *fictional*. Unfortunately, Smith wove it so well into his theology that the Mormon Church is still stuck with the concepts. They don't generally comment of course but when pressed, leaders will just say we don't know the overall story, it will all be made clear in the hereafter and meanwhile it won't affect your eternal salvation – just continue to pay, pray and obey (as Steve Benson would quip). However, when you attend a Mormon endowment session, the 'Garden of Eden' story is still played out in intricate detail.

Para 22 claims Adam and Eve were to offer the firstlings of their 'flocks' as sacrifices to God. Just as when early humans inhabited the Earth there were no cereals or root vegetables that we see today, equally, there were no 'flocks' of domesticated animals for hundreds of thousands of years of hominid existence. Thus it becomes more and more abundantly clear, when compared with what we now know concerning human history, that these stories were invented by people who had daily experience of such things as making bread themselves and just assumed they had always been that way. They were very wrong – but had a God really 'revealed' such things to them, He would surely *not* have just made up silly fairy stories which these things provably constitute; He would have revealed the truth – whatever that may be.

We move on in para 23-24 to that part of Smith's *Book of Moses* which should make every Mormon stop and think long enough to conclude that it is sheer nonsense, but we all seem capable of *not* doing so, as long as we *want* to believe in the Church. It is only when common sense and reason find a voice, or are at least allowed the room for us to think clearly, that it all makes sense.

The following verses are incorporated into the lecture from Moses 5:6-7.

> 23 And after many days an angel of the Lord appeared unto Adam, saying, why do you offer sacrifices unto the Lord? And Adam said

LECTURE SECOND OF FAITH

> unto him, I know not; save the Lord commanded me to offer sacrifices.
> 24 And the angel said unto him, This thing is a similitude of the sacrifice of the Only Begotten of the Father, who is full of grace and truth. And you shall do all that you do in the name of the Son: and you shall repent and call upon God in his name forever. In that day, the Holy Spirit fell upon Adam, and bore record of the Father and the Son.

Adam had no idea *why* he was making sacrifices of the firstlings of his flocks – that could not possibly have even existed at the time. But what comes next never even registered properly with me as a member – and it should have; it should have hit me like a brick. God introduces to Adam the idea that it is in similitude of the sacrifice of His son which would happen thousands of years later, and from that very moment, Jesus Christ is known about and prayed through... The *Book of Mormon* also confirms that *all* the prophets from the time of Adam did so (Jacob 4:4). Jacob claims in 544-521 BCE, that he and *all* the prophets before him *knew* of Christ.

The now obvious and very clear point that should be made is the original scriptures were of course Hebrew. Jews have *never* believed in such things because neither did their prophets who wrote the *Tanakh*, or *Old Testament*, in the first place. They were subsequently hijacked into Christianity much later and thus essentially became 'Christian' prophets; then on into Mormonism, where of course they became 'Mormon' *OT* prophets with all the biases Smith heaped upon them. They all prayed to God in the name of Jesus, throughout the BCE period. Somehow, after Lehi and his family left Jerusalem, all traces of such worship not only evaporated completely but all records of such things mysteriously disappeared. If I say that if you believe that, you will believe anything... it is absolutely true. I somehow managed to, and yet it is clearly a preposterous idea. We just don't *think* as faithful Mormons; in fact, when something just doesn't sit right, we often consciously try ***not*** to think about it.

Para 25 includes a claim that the 'Holy Spirit' bore record of the Father and Son.

> ...And further, that no sooner was the plan of redemption revealed to man, and he began to call upon God, than the Holy Spirit was given, bearing record of the Father and Son.

Unfortunately, this is also completely impossible, as Jews did not believe in the Son. Also, to them, the Holy Spirit was and is the mind or will of God, in a now truly monotheistic religion. The fact Judaism was a polytheistic religion, including at least one feminine god, until just a few centuries BCE seems to also escape the Mormon Church. To consider that somehow these supposedly 'true' teachings that Smith inserted into the story were believed and *taught* by *all* the prophets, so that *everyone* prayed to God in the 'name of the Son' who later came to Earth and in whom Jews do not believe but Lehi and his sons continued the concepts in the Americas – is ridiculous. Not *one* of the prophets who had lived or later lived in the Holy Land, or anyone they taught, even once alluded to such nonsense and no one ever remembered or recorded praying that way. That should tell us something, if not everything about this ludicrously impossible idea. To then suggest that it is all a matter of faith, which is the only avenue that I can imagine left to the Church, is sheer insanity to be frank. The same is true of every 'residual' Native American tribal legend – no God of Israel and no Jesus Christ remotely appear in any single one of them.

Cain and Abel are mentioned next, and of course fruit is offered by Cain but God doesn't care for that. Did Cain have any idea that his 'offering' would offend God? Abel offers the firstlings of his flocks – which pleases God immensely. The fact that there could not have *been* any 'flocks' to offer is missed by anyone who just accepts the story as written without thinking things through. It is obviously sheer nonsense. Six thousand years ago, there were indeed flocks – but then there were also about five million humans living around the globe. If Adam existed as a first being, it was long before any 'flocks' of domesticated animals ever did, and Abel would not have been in a position to offer any. A 'first family' would have been hunter gatherers with no domesticated animals around for a very long time after they had lived.

Satan is happy though; another fictional character introduced at this stage. Jews never believed in such a creature either and he does not appear in the *Old Testament* at all. I have covered this in earlier work. *(See TMD Vol. 2 starting p.323; Vol. 4 starting p.40 & p.251).* Cain ends up killing Abel and that's when black skin starts to appear as a curse to some humans. No one in Mormonism ever explains how or *why* it is that there are some very black people from some islands, nor why they were never denied the Priesthood. From where did their black skin come, theologically speaking? Many black Africans are nowhere near as black yet they were 'cursed' with a black skin when the islanders were not. The 'tree of life' – the evolutionary one, not the mythological Garden of Eden version – explains the true story of course and it has nothing to do with Cain and Abel who are another part of the fictional story. A lot of mythology is now rejected by modern humans and yet this conclusively proven fairy tale is accepted as if it is real in the face of conclusive evidence to the contrary which corroborates the facts from more sources than we could ever have imagined.

Paras 32-33 claim that God condescended to talk with Cain after his 'great transgression, in slaying his brother' so he carried with him a 'knowledge' of God. It is claimed that from this we see "the whole human family ... in all their different branches, had this knowledge..." Clearly, if this were the case, it

LECTURE SECOND OF FAITH

would have been carefully taught and recorded for all generations; there would be only one Church and everyone would have the same understanding.

Research the known history of various cultures around the world which *predate* these ideas and compare their religious systems and ideas. There is no comparison with the Bible, let alone Smith's crazy ideas. The claim that the "whole human family" had an identical concept of God is not just implausible, it is utterly *impossible*. History proves that to be the case beyond question.

This is followed by a lengthy genealogy, derived from the Bible, of people who lived and died, from the supposed time of Adam through to Abraham, in order to show that some people were alive at overlapping times. The objective is to prove some were alive during the life of Adam and still alive when Noah was around, and likewise, some were around at the time of Noah's post-ark life and still alive when Abraham was around. The purpose (para 53) is to show:

> beyond the power of controversy, that there was no difficulty in preserving the knowledge of God in the world, from the creation of Adam, and the manifestation made to his immediate descendants, as set forth in the former part of this lecture, so that the students in this class need not have any dubiety resting on their minds on this subject; for they can easily see that it is impossible for it to be otherwise; but that the knowledge of the existence of a God, must have continued from father to son, as a matter of tradition, at least. For we cannot suppose, that a knowledge of this important fact, could have existed in the mind of any of the before-mentioned individuals, without their having made it known to their posterity.

If we were to suppose this to be true, then again, it would indeed be the case that they *would* all have prayed in the name of the 'Son' and *would* have had knowledge of Him and also the Mormon concept of the Holy Spirit, just as Smith here claims and also had prophets claim in his *Book of Mormon*. The fact is that these early biblical prophets were all Jews; no matter that they did indeed hand down the 'traditions of their fathers', they most certainly did *not* teach, record or hand down in any way the things that Smith claims. According to Smith "we cannot suppose, that a knowledge of this important fact, could have existed in the mind of any of the before-mentioned individuals, without their having made it known to their posterity." He is of course quite right – and they ***didn't***; thus Smith, by his own reasoning, is hoisted on his own petard – yet again. The things he proposes are absolutely absurd and did *not* happen.

Para 56 confirms the idea that "God became an object of faith for rational beings" but does not venture to explain why it was that well *before* 4000 BCE, which is his own confirmed and admitted concept of the 'time' of Adam and Eve, which Smith of course cannot now change his mind about, there were already many concepts of all sorts of gods in cultures around the globe.

THE MORMON DELUSION

Leaving aside concepts of any gods they may have had, the following are some early cultures that all existed long before the time Joseph Smith claims Adam and Eve appeared on the scene. Smith does not venture to explain where these cultures came from, why they existed or what they believed – which was *not* the much later Hebrew concept of God, let alone Smith's version of events.

Remember, Joseph Smith confirmed his belief that the Earth has a temporal existence of seven thousand years *(D&C 77)* and that Adam and Eve existed some four thousand years BCE. *(Book of Moses and Lecture of Faith 2)*.

c.7000 BCE.	Beginning of the Peiligang culture in China.
c.7000 BCE.	Neolithic settlement at Mehrgarh, modern-day Baluchistan, Pakistan.
c.7000 BCE.	Agriculture developed among Papuan peoples of New Guinea.
c.7000 BCE.	Elam becomes a farming region.
c.7000 BCE.	A figure from Ain Ghazal, Jordan was made and now appears in the National Museum, Amman, Jordan.
c.6850 BCE	Sesklo culture, Thessaly, Greece (advanced agriculture and pottery).
c.6500 BCE	Palaeolithic period ended. Neolithic period started in China.
c.6500 BCE	Beginning of the Houli culture in China.
c.6500 BCE	Çatalhöyük, Turkey. Inhabitants traded obsidian.
c.6200 BCE	Start of the Xinglongwa culture in China.
c.6000 BCE	Beginning of the Cishan culture in China.
c.6000 BCE	Traces of habitation of the Syarthola cave in Norway.

People inhabited many areas of the world tens of thousands of years before the claimed time of Adam and Eve. Human dispersal extended right across the globe including the Bonian culture, China, Cucuteni-Trypillian, Europe, Korea, Malta, Mehrgarh, Pre-Colombian Americas, Sesklo Culture, South Asia, Varna Culture, Vinča culture and the Vučedol culture.

With millions of people already following many different paths, the world was already multicultural. If you follow the history of any of these cultures, there was no biblical timescale 'flood gap' in *any* of them, thus dispelling any notion of a global flood just a couple of thousand years BCE. I have mentioned in earlier work, the extensive history of the Egyptians in this regard. Trace the Egyptian culture back twelve thousand years and you transcend the time of the flood and Adam and Eve. There was no 'beginning' and no flood after which the land was repopulated by Egypt and her posterity as Smith claimed in his *Book of Abraham. (See TMD Vol 2:300-3)*. There were localised flood stories when the sea rose following the last ice age 10,000 years ago. These formed the basis of mythology that evolved into a story of Noah and the flood in the Bible.

LECTURE SECOND OF FAITH

The rest of the lecture consists of a lengthy set of questions and answers which are completely meaningless. The first question confirms God has 'faith' in Himself, which was a ludicrous notion even for Smith at the time, especially given the second question, which yet again confirms the traditional Christian concept that God is "omnipresent", meaning He dwells everywhere at once.

That notion later became defunct in Mormon theology when Smith decided God has a body and dwells in only one place at a time. Before that theology evolved, Smith had already written the *Book of Mormon* and his *Inspired Revision* of the Bible and penned many revelations that appeared in the 1833 *Book of Commandments* in addition to the 1834-5 *Lectures of Faith*. Without exception, they each retained a monotheistic God who was singularly a spirit *without* a body. The lecture also confirms God was without beginning of days, so He *always* existed *as* the one and only God. Later, and still current, Mormon theology claims God was once a man who *progressed* to become a God. Men in the Mormon Church aspire to exactly the same thing today. Of course, this is considered a heresy in mainstream Christianity.

> *Question.* -- Is there a being who has faith in himself independently?
>
> *Answer.* -- There is. Q. Who is it? A. It is God.
>
> Q. How do you prove that God has faith in himself independently?
>
> A. Because he is omnipotent, omnipresent, and omniscient; without beginning of days or end of life, and in him all fulness dwells. Eph. 1:23. Which is his body, the fulness of him that filleth all in all. Col. 1:19. For it pleased the Father, that in him should all fulness dwell.

To give such an answer as 'proof' of anything is just silly. The answer also confirms God is **omnipresent.** The nonsense continues...

> Q. Is he the object in whom the faith of all other rational and accountable beings centers, for life and salvation?
>
> A. He is.
>
> Q. How do you prove it?
>
> A. Isa. 45:22. Look unto me, and be ye saved, all the ends of the earth: for I am God, and there is none else. Rom. 11:34, 35, 36. For who hath known the mind of the Lord? or who hath been his counsellor? or who hath first given to him, and it shall be recompensed unto him again? For of him, and through him, and to him, are all things: to whom be glory forever. Amen. Isa. 40: from the 8th to the 18th. O Zion that bringest good tidings (Or, O thou that

tellest good tidings to Zion,) get thee up into the high mountain: O Jerusalem, that bringest good tidings (Or, O thou that tellest good tidings to Jerusalem,) lift up thy voice with strength; lift it up, be not afraid; say unto the cities of Judah, Behold your God! Behold, the Lord your God will come with strong hand (Or, against the strong,) and his arm shall rule for him: behold, his reward is with him, and his work before him (Or, recompense for his work.) He shall feed his flock like a shepherd: he shall gather the lambs with his arms, and carry them in his bosom, and shall gently lead those that are with young. Who hath measured the waters in the hollow of his hand, and meted out heaven with the span, and comprehended the dust of the earth in a measure, and weighed the mountains in scales, and the hills in a balance? Who hath directed the Spirit of the Lord, or being his counsellor, hath taught him? With whom took he counsel, and who instructed him, and taught him in the path of judgment, and taught him knowledge, and shewed to him the way of understanding? Behold, the nations are as a drop of a bucket, and are counted as the small dust of the balance: behold, he taketh up the isles as a very little thing. And Lebanon is not sufficient to burn, nor the beasts thereof sufficient for a burnt offering. All nations before him are as nothing; and they are counted to him less than nothing, and vanity! Jer. 51:15,16. He (the Lord) hath made the earth by his power, he hath established the world by his wisdom, and hath stretched out the heaven by his understanding. When he uttereth his voice there is a multitude of waters in the heavens; and he causeth the vapors to ascend from the ends of the earth: he maketh lightnings with rain, and bringeth forth the wind out of his treasures.1st Cor. 8:6. But to us there is but one God, the Father, of whom are all things, and we in him; and one Lord Jesus Christ, by whom are all things, and we by him.

The above question and answer are of course unrelated to *proof* of anything of any description whatsoever. It gets worse...

Q. How did men first come to the knowledge of the existence of a God, so as to exercise faith in him?

A. In order to answer this question, it will be necessary to go back and examine man at his creation; the circumstances in which he was placed, and the knowledge which he had of God.

First, When man was created he stood in the presence of God. Gen. 1:27,28. From this we learn that man, at his creation, stood in the presence of his God, and had most perfect knowledge of his existence.

LECTURE SECOND OF FAITH

Secondly, God conversed with him after his transgression. Gen. 3: from the 8th to the 22nd. From this we learn, that, though man did transgress, he was not deprived of the previous knowledge which he had of the existence of God.

Thirdly, God conversed with man after he cast him out of the garden.

Fourthly, God also conversed with Cain after he had slain Abel. Gen. 4: from the 4th to the 6th.

Q. What is the object of the foregoing quotation?

A. It is that it may be clearly seen how it was that the first thoughts were suggested to the minds of men, of the existence of God, and how extensively this knowledge was spread among the immediate descendants of Adam.

Following the above recap on how man came to be aware of God, the lecture moves on to confirm that every generation had this knowledge passed on to them. To 'prove' all the prophets knew of God and prayed in the name of the Son, this is how it explains the transfer of knowledge must have occurred.

Q. What testimony had the immediate descendants of Adam, in proof of the existence of a God?

A. The testimony of their father. And after they were made acquainted with his existence, by the testimony of their father, they were dependent upon the exercise of their own faith for a knowledge of his character, perfections and attributes.

Q. Had any others of the human family, beside Adam, a knowledge of the existence of God, in the first instance, by any other means than human testimony?

A. They had not. For previous to the time that they could have power to obtain a manifestation for themselves, the all-important fact had been communicated to them by their common father; and so, from father to child, the knowledge was communicated as extensively, as the knowledge of his existence was known; for it was by this means, in the first instance, that men had a knowledge of his existence.

Q. How do you know that the knowledge of the existence of God was communicated in this manner, throughout the different ages of the world?

A. By the chronology obtained thro' the revelations of God.

Q. How would you divide that chronology in order to convey it to the understanding clearly?

A. Into two parts: First, by embracing that period of the world from Adam to Noah; and secondly, from Noah to Abraham; from which period the knowledge of the existence of God has been so general, that it is a matter of no dispute in what manner the idea of his existence has been retained in the world.

Q. How many noted righteous men lived from Adam to Noah?

A. Nine; which includes Abel, who was slain by his brother.

Q. What are their names?

A. Abel, Seth, Enos, Cainan, Mahalaleel, Jared, Enoch, Methuselah, and Lamech.

Q. How old was Adam when Seth was born?

A. One hundred and thirty years. Gen. 5:3.

Q. How many years did Adam live after Seth was born?

A. Eight hundred. Gen. 5:4.

Q. How old was Adam when he died?

A. Nine hundred and thirty years. Gen. 5:5.

The reader will no doubt not want to read more questions and answers in this series which covers who was alive and when. It extends for several pages and is comprised of over one-hundred-and-forty more questions and answers. The final few recap on early human testimony and knowledge of God.

This lengthy attempt to show that a testimony of God and how to approach Him in prayer through 'the Son' must surely have occurred by word of mouth, serves only to confirm that if the age spans are accurate, the Jews *did* have the *opportunity* to faithfully record and pass on exactly what *was* taught from their 'beginning', but it was most certainly not even close to the claims made here, because we have the actual record. It is called the *Tanakh* or *Old Testament*.

Chapter 4

Lectures of Faith
Lecture 3

LECTURE THIRD
Of Faith.

SECTION III

Recapping on the first two lectures, the start of the third lecture includes this:

> For faith could not center in a being of whose existence we had no idea; because the idea of his existence in the first instance is essential to the exercise of faith in him. Rom. 10:14 "How then shall they call on him in whom they have not believed? And how shall they believe in him of whom they have not heard? And how shall they hear without a preacher?" (or one sent to tell them?). So then faith comes by hearing the word of God. (New Translation.) *[Inspired Revision]*.

The next few paragraphs reiterate three aspects covered in lectures one and two.

> 3. First, the idea that he actually exists.
> 4. Secondly, A *correct* idea of his character, perfections and attributes.
> 5. Thirdly, An actual knowledge that the course of life which he is pursuing, is according to his will.

Para 6 confirms the next stage of the lecture, which includes:

> "...we shall proceed to examine his character, perfections, and attributes..."

Para 7:

> "...we are indebted to the revelations which he has given to us for a correct understanding of his character, perfections, and attributes; because without the revelations which he has given to us, no man by searching could find out God."

In support of the idea of 'finding out God', *Old Testament* scriptures are quoted which claim God reveals Himself through His spirit. The lecture says it will then "proceed to examine the character which the revelations have given of God". So, with no other evidence whatsoever, God's 'character' is to be explained by using biblical verses to suit early Mormon claims.

> 7. Cor. 2:9,10,11: "But as it is written, eye has not seen, nor ear heard, neither have entered into the heart of man, the things which God has prepared for them that love him; but God has revealed them unto us by his Spirit: for the Spirit searcheth all things, yea, the deep things of God. For what man knows the things of a man, save the spirit of man which is in him? Even so, the things of God no man knows but by the Spirit of God."

This is followed by several other Bible verses which define God in the way most Christians accept to be the case. Such writings are of course historically written by *men* and contain *no* empirical evidence of the involvement of a God. The oft repeated line "God spoke to Moses" found in the *Old Testament* is *not* a compelling argument. It then moves on to extracts from the Mormon *Book of Commandments* which has even less credibility than the *Old Testament*.

> 10. Book of Commandments, chapt, 2nd, commencing in the third line of the first paragraph: "For God doth not walk in crooked paths, neither does he turn to the right hand or the left; or he vary from that which he hath said, therefore his paths are strait and his course is one eternal round:" Book of Commandments, chapt. 37:1. "Listen to the voice of the Lord your God, even Alpha and Omega, the beginning and the end, whose course is one eternal round, the same today as yesterday and forever."

The above 'characteristics' are similar to any and every description of any gods ever invented by man and again it contains no *evidence* of the existence of such a being, let alone a reliable understanding of what He is like if He does

LECTURE THIRD OF FAITH

exist. Claiming that God does not change direction or change His mind is a joke when considering Mormonism. The 'unchanging' Mormon God *promised* never to take polygamy (meaning *polygyny* in Mormonism) from the earth. It is long gone. The temple endowment was claimed to have been the same as at the time of Adam and also Solomon and eternal in nature, never to be *altered* in any way. It has changed beyond recognition. The Priesthood was never to be given to anyone of black African descent until the millennium, when every 'white' person would first have been given the opportunity. In 1978, Smith's unchanging God changed his mind and now everyone can hold the Priesthood. In light of the above, the following in para 11 needs some serious explanation.

> 11. Numbers 23:19. "God is not a man, that he should lie; neither the son of man, that he should repent." First John 4:8, "He that loves not, knows not God; for God is love." Acts 10:34: "Then Peter opened his mouth, and said, Of a truth I perceive that God is no respecter of persons, but in every nation he that fears him, and works righteousness is accepted with him."

Clearly, evidence contained in Mormon history, such as noted in the above paragraph, confirms that *if* He is real, the Mormon God *does* lie; He does 'repent' of what He promised; He *is* a respecter of persons and He does *not* work righteousness. In fact, you never know where you are with the Mormon God as He is always chopping and changing Mormon doctrine.

The Mormon God was not exactly a 'God of love' in the early Mormon Church either. He seemed to want vengeance for a lot of things which resulted in a culture of murder and destruction and introduction of 'blood atonement' which was meted out to people whether or not the unfortunate recipients even believed in it. *(See TMD Vol. 3. Section 4).*

The lecture then affirms that from the "foregoing testimonies" we learn:

> 13. **First**, that he was God before the world was created, and the same God that he was, after it was created.
> 14. **Secondly**, That he is merciful, and gracious, slow to anger, abundant in goodness, and that he was so from everlasting, and will be to everlasting.
> 15. **Thirdly**, That he changes not, neither is there variableness with him; but that he is the same from everlasting to everlasting, being the same yesterday to-day and forever; and that his course is one eternal round, without variation.
> 16. **Fourthly**, That he is a God of truth and cannot lie.
> 17. **Fifthly**, That he is no respecter of persons, but in every nation he that fears God and works righteousness is accepted of him.
> 18. **Sixthly**, that he is love. (Bold added for ease of location in relation to the six points as covered on the following two pages).

THE MORMON DELUSION

At the time of these lectures, it is understandable that such characteristics were taught as correct. How ironic it is that every one of them quickly changed and evolved beyond recognition within Smith's ever changing doctrine.

First, at that time, God may well have been considered to have been God long before the world was created, but later, in Mormon theology, He became considered as having originally been just a man who then 'progressed' until He 'became' a God. Thus He was not an *eternal* God at all but just one in a long succession of Gods who had achieved the same thing.

Secondly, the Mormon God was not at all merciful – or gracious. He was quick to anger and many people were murdered in His name. Incidentally, I question why a God would *ever* get angry at all? Personally, I do not have a temper and have *never* felt anger as such; I get saddened and upset rather than angry – and I am not even close to being a 'god'. When people get angry they lose control. God is depicted as meting out vengeance on people who had no idea why they were being treated that way. For many biblical characters, the way they lived was just the way they were raised. Mormon 'enemies' who God was apparently going to take vengeance on (including the US government) had every reason to fear Mormons at the time as Smith wanted to take over the territory and then the country – and eventually the world. God therefore has a lot to answer for and needed to learn to *control* his anger – wouldn't you say?

If people did not carry a 'safe conduct pass' when travelling through Utah territory in the mid-late 1800s they would have been highly unlikely to leave the valley alive. A culture of killing travellers suspected of being spies for the army, and of indiscriminate robbery and murder, was firmly established under Brigham Young. It culminated in the Mountain Meadows massacre which the Church tried to deny for decades, only admitting the truth in very recent years.

Apologists still try to 'excuse' Young by claiming he knew nothing of the massacre until after the event. Such an approach is an insult to those who were brutally murdered in cold blood – as well as to their descendants.

No one seems to ever face and answer the only real question that needs to be asked, the answer to which is so obvious it cannot be escaped. The wagon train passed through Salt Lake City and they were *directed* to that trail. Some refused, preferring the northern route, and they survived. Why were they *not* all given a safe conduct pass, if Young wanted them to remain alive? More importantly, why would anyone even *need* such a thing to be sure of survival?

The Church was founded on a culture where not only those opposed to the Church but also claimed apostates could very well find themselves "used up (in the pocket of the Lord)", or once they were in the valley "taken over the rim of the basin", both of which expressions meant *murdered* by the Danites, or later, Brigham Young's 'destroying angels'. Don't be fooled by claims it was all just rhetoric. It was 'blood atonement' in *practice*. It was very real and it happened many times during Brigham Young's tenure and beyond.

LECTURE THIRD OF FAITH

The Mountain Meadows massacre was so dastardly and reprehensible as to be an impossible crime, unless the very culture which lead to such action was not already firmly established and embedded in the hearts and minds of the perpetrators. The action was premeditated – and was spearheaded by two Stake Presidents, William H. Dane and Isaac C. Haight, assisted by Bishop John D. Lee, who claimed he never killed anyone personally and yet years later was the only person ever brought to justice for the crime. He became the fall-guy for Young and did not even present a proper defence at the retrial which convicted him and then had him shot to death for his part in the massacre.

Young was culpable, whether he was aware in advance or not. It was not the first such abomination but it was most certainly the worst. To murder over one-hundred-and-thirty unarmed men, women and children in cold blood when they thought they were being led to safety would have led any God – had such a being even been involved with such a cruel people – to immediately abandon them. If they had *ever* been a chosen people of God, they had long gone astray under such tyrannical and cruel concepts and He would not have remained associated with such things. But then, as much of early Mormonism was based on the God of the *Old Testament*, perhaps they felt justified in actions that resulted in such blood baths. In *any* age, any such action is an ***abomination***.

The fact is that such attitudes *were* embedded in the very culture of early Mormonism. They believed God delivered such people into their hands and that all things belonged to *them*; and they could just take them if and when the opportunity arose. Life, unless you were Mormon, was of very little value and everyone passing through the valley was treated with suspicion. The Mormon God supposedly 'inspired' Young in such matters. *(See TMD Vol. 3, Sec. 4).*

Thirdly, as previously stated, the Mormon God *does* change. He changes all the time. I have stated elsewhere, the most consistent thing in Mormonism is the inconsistency.

Fourthly, the Mormon God is not a God of truth. He is full of lies. If He dictated the *Book of Mormon* into Smith's hat, He lied about everything in it – and provably so. He lied about people, places, animals, agriculture, technology, currency and much more. God obviously had no idea about DNA and forgot to account for humans becoming a little more advanced than He apparently is. He lied about polygyny continuing; He lied about the unchangeable endowment; and He lied about who would be eligible to hold the Priesthood and when.

Fifthly, there is no evidence anywhere that God has treated any 'people' differently to other people. If God exists, all people are 'respected' (or not) in exactly the same manner – without exception. He does nothing for anyone.

Sixthly, the Mormon God was anything but *love* in the early years. He hated anyone who came from places such as Illinois, Ohio or Arkansas (where Parley P. Pratt was murdered by an irate husband after Pratt stole his wife, see *TMD Vol. 1. Ch. 13)*, and who was unfortunate enough to enter the Salt Lake valley. He was thoroughly misogynistic and made women covenant to *obey* their husbands. He gave the 'Law of Sarah' *(D&C 132)* which dictated that if a woman objected to her husband taking a further wife, she was *always* in the wrong and even in danger of losing her salvation, which itself was at the express 'discretion' of her 'Lord and husband', and the husband could, and generally would, marry again regardless of what his wife wanted. *(See TMD Vol. 1:27-29).*

All in all, the early Mormon God turned out to be exactly the *opposite* of all the attributes portrayed in the lecture and the scriptures used to support the description of His character. Taking all that into account, para 20 actually claims that if God was *not* that way, then faith would not exist and men would doubt…

> 20 But secondly: Unless he was merciful, and gracious, slow to anger, long suffering, and full of goodness, such is the weakness of human nature, and so great the frailties and imperfections of men, that unless they believed that these excellencies existed in the divine character, the faith necessary to salvation could not exist; for doubt would take the place of faith, and those who know their weakness and liability to sin, would be in constant doubt of salvation, if it were not for the idea which they have of the excellency of the character of God, that he is slow to anger, and long suffering, and of a forgiving disposition, and does forgive iniquity, transgression and sin. An idea of these facts does away doubt, and makes faith exceedingly strong.

An "idea of these facts" does *not* do away with any doubt and neither does it make "faith strong", for they are proven not to *be* facts at all but just fanciful ideas of 1834-5 which were soon to be overridden in a reality which was as dark and deplorable as in any cult that has ever existed.

Everything is, as ever, then reiterated and para 21 asserts "faith lays hold upon the excellencies in his character with unshaken confidence, believing he is the same yesterday, today, and forever, and that his course is one eternal round." We have already discussed the fact that the Mormon God is anything *but* the same from one day to the next. After all the reiteration, comes the now familiar sequence of questions and answers in order to reaffirm everything in the lecture. Most are of no significance whatsoever.

The first is:

> Question. What was shown in the second lecture?
>
> Answer. It was shown how the knowledge of the existence of God came into the world.

LECTURE THIRD OF FAITH

The rest are equally as silly and there is an obsession to 'prove' everything, despite the fact that such things cannot actually *be* proven.

> Q. What is the effect of the idea of his existence among men?
>
> A. It lays the foundation for the exercise of faith in him.
>
> Q. Is the idea of his existence, in the first instance, necessary in order for the exercise of faith in him?
>
> A. It is.
>
> Q. How do you prove it?
>
> A. By the 16th chapter to Romans and 14th verse.

This is typically the extent of any 'proof' of the concepts. The fact Romans was purportedly written by Paul, a man who never even met or knew Jesus, is of course missed. In fact, there is nothing that has ever been recorded by anyone who actually met or knew Jesus; therefore, there is no direct evidence he ever even existed as one individual being. Many scholars consider the Christ to be a caricature created from the lives of several different local itinerant preachers of the era. The reference to Romans 16:14 is an obvious error, as it says "Salute Asyncritus, Phlegon, Hermes, Patrobas, Hermas, and the brethren that are with them." Clearly, no one ever checked that reference or corrected it. Questions and answers continue to repeat everything already covered.

Within them is the following sequence:

> Q. How are we to be made acquainted with the before mentioned things respecting the Deity, and respecting ourselves?
>
> A. By revelation.
>
> Q. Could these things be found out by any other means than by revelation?
>
> A. They could not.
>
> Q. How do you prove it?
>
> A. By the scriptures: Job 11:7,8,9. 1 Corinthians 2:9,10,11.

Once again, the burden of proof is ignored in real terms, as clearly Job and Corinthians are as unreliable as anything else written by men who themselves had no idea about such things, other than from what others had written and from their own imagination. It is not proof of anything just because someone writes something down that you would *like* to believe. Out of interest, this is Job 11:7-9 and 1 Corinthians 2:9-11.

> **Job 11:7.** Canst thou by searching find out God? canst thou find out the Almighty unto perfection?
> **8.** *It is* as high as heaven; what canst thou do? deeper than hell; what canst thou know?
> **9.** The measure thereof *is* longer than the earth, and broader than the sea.

> **1 Cor 2:9.** But as it is written, Eye hath not seen, nor ear heard, neither have entered into the heart of man, the things which God hath prepared for them that love him.
> **10.** But God hath revealed them unto us by his Spirit: for the Spirit searcheth all things, yea, the deep things of God.
> **11.** For what man knoweth the things of a man, save the spirit of man which is in him? even so the things of God knoweth no man, but the Spirit of God.

These are taken as "revelations of God respecting his character" when the real question is, what *proof* is there that such is the case? There is *none*. That really is 'a matter of faith' rather than proof of anything at all. The questions culminate in asking "could a man exercise faith in God so as to obtain eternal life unless he believed that" followed in turn by each of the six 'attributes' previously noted in the lecture. Each is answered in the same way. For example, the one on God being love is answered thus:

> A. He could not; because man could not love God unless he has an idea that God was love, and if he did not love God, he could not have faith in him.

We have already discovered that the early Mormon God was not exactly *love* by any stretch of the imagination. Finally, this question is asked and an answer given, which doesn't even deserve comment.

> Q. Is the character which God has given of himself uniform?

> A. It is; in all his revelations whether to the Former Day Saints, or to the Latter day saints, so that they all have the authority to exercise faith in him, and to expect by the exercise of their faith, to enjoy the same blessings.

LECTURE THIRD OF FAITH

Taking into account the fact that the idea of this lecture was to 'prove' God, it recapped that lectures one and two were to show "he actually exists", give "a *correct* idea of his character, perfections and attributes" and "an actual knowledge that the course of life which he is pursuing, is according to his will". This lecture then promised to "examine his character, perfections, and attributes…"

Having shown that the Mormon God is anything *but* as first claimed, we should perhaps add a few other *Old Testament* statements on what God *was* like and 'required' in those days. If Smith and his pals want to reference the *Old Testament* as proof of God's character, we should perhaps refer back to para 7:

> "…we are indebted to the revelations which he has given to us for a correct understanding of his character, perfections, and attributes; because without the revelations which he has given to us, no man by searching could find out God."

You cannot 'find out God' by selecting *extracts* from a book supposedly containing 'Holy Scripture' that appear at first glance to support what you want it to 'prove'; you must also consider the *rest* of it. God 'spoke' to Moses about these things in Lev 19:1; 21:16; 23:1, 23, 26; 24:13 for example. There are many more references to God speaking with Moses, so the point is regularly made that it is supposedly God rather than man making the rules. So, this, as they say, is how the God of the *Old Testament* rolled:

> **Lev 20:9.** For every one that curseth his father or his mother shall be surely put to death: he hath cursed his father or his mother; his blood *shall be* upon him.
> **10.** And the man that committeth adultery with *another* man's wife, *even he* that committeth adultery with his neighbour's wife, the adulterer and the adultress shall surely be put to death.
> **11.** And the man that lieth with his father's wife hath uncovered his father's nakedness: both of them shall surely be put to death; their blood *shall be* upon them.
> **12.** And if a man lie with his daughter in law, both of them shall surely be put to death: they have wrought confusion; their blood *shall be* upon them.
> **13.** If a man also lie with mankind, as he lieth with a woman, both of them have committed an abomination: they shall surely be put to death; their blood *shall be* upon them.

14. And if a man take a wife and her mother, it *is* wickedness: they shall be burnt with fire, both he and they; that there be no wickedness among you.

15. And if a man lie with a beast, he shall surely be put to death: and ye shall slay the beast.

16. And if a woman approach unto any beast, and lie down thereto, thou shalt kill the woman, and the beast: they shall surely be put to death; their blood *shall be* upon them.

It will immediately be argued that these were strict laws given in a different time and place for a race of people who needed such discipline. In v.13, God's homophobia is disclosed. Today, we may ask why He devised a system which sometimes hard wires the 'wrong' sexual orientation into the human brain from birth. He didn't do a very good job of human (or several other species for that matter) creation in six to nine percent of his male and female population who are homosexual and then blamed humans for His own mistakes. Apart from the question, why would God 'choose' such a depraved people in the first instance and wouldn't He have been far better off choosing a different and much better behaved people as his supposed 'chosen race' somewhere else in the already well populated world, the point is that we are not judging that; we are looking at God's 'attributes' and His 'character' of the day – and it was positively *evil*.

In respect of v.14, "if a man take a wife and her mother, it *is* wickedness: they shall be burnt with fire"; Joseph Smith took a wife and her mother; Sylvia and Patty Sessions *(TMD Vol. 1:139)*. God says they should have been burnt.

There is of course a lot more that could be added but I will just mention this. God was not very caring. If someone blasphemed, they were to be stoned to death by the congregation (Lev 24:16). God approved of slavery – so he had no respect for some of His own children and was clearly far less humane than many modern day mere mortals (Lev 25:44). He should have forbidden slavery completely to be the 'consistent' God preached about by Joseph Smith. These were God's own children that He permitted taken as slaves. Why? If anyone worked on the Sabbath day, they were put to death (Exodus 35:2). I could go on, but having made the point I will stop there.

Remember the question and answer mentioned on page 50:

Q. Is the character which God has given of himself uniform?

A. It is...

No, according to God's own 'record' it really is **not**. It is perfectly clear that the Hebrew account of their God's requirements was just in the imagination of men who wanted to maintain tight control over their people through fear.

LECTURE THIRD OF FAITH

Likewise, the rationale in the lectures was the 'take' on things, convenient for the day. That they were soon superseded by other teachings and doctrine regarding God clearly shows that at every stage, no God was ever *involved* with any of it. The notion that deity would require such nonsense as is included in the *Old Testament*, any more than He would 'reveal' what Smith claimed He did through him, is perfectly ludicrous to anyone who takes a moment to **think**.

THE MORMON DELUSION

Chapter 5

**Lectures of Faith
Lecture 4**

LECTURE FOURTH
Of Faith.

SECTION IV

The now familiar review of earlier lectures is followed by an account in paras 4-10 of God's 'attributes' supposedly supported by various scriptures that are referenced. There are six categories; knowledge, faith, justice, judgment, mercy and truth. To take just one aspect and comment on it; para 9 concerns mercy and includes this, "Exodus 34:6. And the Lord passed by before him, and proclaimed, The Lord, the Lord God, merciful and gracious. Neh. 9:17. -- But thou art a God ready to pardon, gracious and merciful." God didn't seem ready to pardon anyone who 'blasphemed' or who 'cursed' their parents in Leviticus, which is conveniently not referenced – he wanted them stoned to death. The God of the Old Testament appears as contradictory as the God of Mormonism – and far from merciful.

Para 11 then informs us that "the idea of the existence of these attributes in the Deity, is necessary to enable any rational being to exercise faith in him. For without the idea of the existence of these attributes in the Deity, men could not exercise faith in him for life and salvation." Such attributes are of course assumed, even claimed, by all Christians, despite the fact that biblically He did not actually display them as such. Getting to grips with the real 'attributes' of the God of the Old Testament leads to the conclusion that Richard Dawkins was absolutely correct in his description of that being, which does not exactly coincide with the next statement in the lecture "…that enables him to give that understanding to his creatures, by which they are made partakers of eternal life." In contrast, I was, although at first reluctantly, ultimately obliged to agree with Dawkins, as mentioned in the Preface to *TMD Volume 1*, who accurately described God thus:

> The God of the Old Testament is arguably the most unpleasant character in all fiction: jealous and proud of it; a petty, unjust, unforgiving control-freak; a vindictive, bloodthirsty ethnic cleanser; a misogynistic, homophobic, racist, infanticidal, genocidal, filicidal, pestilential, megalomaniacal, sadomasochistic, capriciously malevolent bully. *(Dawkins 2006:31)*.

There is no defence against the above claims – they are indeed all in the Old Testament and either God is entirely responsible for His attributes, or He is just a fictional character. The lectures ignore them all in favour of the fanciful ideas presented, which are needed in order to justify the concepts being taught.

Next, para 12 says men cannot be saved unless they put their "trust in God", believing He has "power to save all who come to him, to the very uttermost". Note the monotheistic tone of the writing which still prevailed. At the time, God and Jesus were still one and the same being. No differentiation is made anywhere in the lectures or any of Smith's other writing before 1836. It is also consistent, once again, with the mainstream Christian concept of God.

Para 14 is strange in that it claims:

> …if God were not to come out in swift judgment against the workers of iniquity and the power of darkness, his saints could not be saved; for it is by judgment that the Lord delivers his saints out of the hands of all their enemies, and those who reject the gospel of our Lord Jesus Christ.

And yet God was never recorded as delivering "his saints out of the hands of all their enemies" in regard to early Mormons, despite the fact that Smith's God continually mentions retribution in the D&C. He never took any at all and it was only the saints who really suffered. Sooner or later, they were driven out

LECTURE FOURTH OF FAITH

of every location selected for settlement. The lecture then appears to 'realise' and admit to this by further explaining that this really means they have to put up with all the persecution and have faith that God will take care of their enemies "in due time", which to date has been – *never* in all of recorded history, apart from some fairy tales in the Bible which count for nothing as they never actually happened in the way they were much later depicted.

> But no sooner is the idea of the existence of this attribute, planted in the minds of men, than it gives power to the mind for the exercise of faith and confidence in God, and they are enabled, by faith, to lay hold on the promises which are set before them, and wade through all the tribulations and afflictions to which they are subjected by reason of the persecution from those who know not God, and obey not the gospel of our Lord Jesus Christ: believing, that in due time the Lord will come out in swift judgment against their enemies.

Here we see a complete back-tracking of the initial promise "if God were *not* to come out in *swift* judgment" to an admission that He really doesn't – and never has to date. As always, it comes down to 'suffer in silence' and one day, God will get 'swift' about things. It was a false promise made by men who were never in a position to make it. The Mormon God was to be swift in destroying their enemies and that later included a promise to overthrow the United States government, an oath about which was included in the Mormon temple endowment for several decades. The Mormon God never did fulfil that either and it is now far too late for such a thing to transpire relative to Mormon prophecy. *(See TMD Vol. 3:167-168).*

Likewise, para 15 claims God's attribute of 'mercy' will be "poured out upon them in the midst of their afflictions, and that he will compassionate [sic] them in their sufferings" but it never was 'poured out', irrespective of the odd supposed 'faith promoting' stories that still abound. Several thousands of those who crossed the plains died along the way and what awaited the early saints at first when they reached the valley wasn't much better than the experience of their journey. Many people later suffered and died needlessly. God didn't even begin to help them. *(See: Ensign, July, 1998, 'I have a Question').*

Had better thought and consideration been given to their welfare by Young, who supposedly acted on behalf of this benevolent God of "knowledge, faith, justice, judgment, mercy and truth", thousands could have been saved from such a fate as death on the journey. The idea that "the mercy of God will lay hold of them and secure them in the arms of his love, so that they will receive a full reward for all their sufferings" must presumably be claimed as something that awaited them in the hereafter, as there was none shown to them during the 1800s when anything and everything was going wrong for them.

Lastly, claims para 16, is the idea of the existence of truth in God.

> ...with the idea of the existence of this attribute in the Deity, in the mind, all the teachings, instructions, promises and blessings become realities, and the mind is enabled to lay hold of them with certainty and confidence: believing that these things, and all that the Lord has said, shall be fulfilled in their time; and that all the cursings, denunciations and judgments, pronounced upon the heads of the unrighteous will also be executed in due time of the Lord:

Here we have unsubstantiated confirmation that God will indeed not only be true to His word and bless them, but that He will also fulfil all "cursings, denunciations and judgments" pronounced. But all the pronouncements came from Smith and Young and others and not from any God. The fact that to date absolutely none have been authenticated as having been fulfilled leaves a gaping hole in the claim that God has kept His supposed word about any such things. There is no evidence of this 'truth' or 'mercy' existing in the Mormon God. In fact, there is no evidence that He ever helped early Mormons at all.

Not that it is related to God avenging enemies, but regarding giving help to the saints, Mormons today will immediately reference the 'seagulls' experience of 1848 in Salt Lake for which they even have a monument. But, they won't mention similar problems in other years when seagulls did not arrive and many crops were destroyed by crickets. They may also refer to the claimed miracle of rain appearing some months after it was prayed for in St. George. If God was involved, why did it not rain before the very last minute? These were natural occurrences and weather conditions which have happened before and since. They had nothing to do with deity.

The next para continues the theme of God subduing their enemies – which of course never happened. There has never been any deliverance or victory. US law subdued the Church, seized its assets and forced an end to polygyny.

> ...his saints can have the most unshaken confidence, that they will, in due time, obtain a perfect deliverance out of the hands of all their enemies, and a complete victory over all those who have sought their hurt and destruction.

The same promises continue to be made, this time referencing 'judgment'.

> And as judgment is an attribute of the Deity also, his saints can have the most unshaken confidence, that they will, in due time, obtain a perfect deliverance out of the hands of all their enemies, and a complete victory over all those who have sought their hurt and destruction.

As always, by now we have heard it all before and we have the same things repeated over and over again. No matter how many ways these things were

LECTURE FOURTH OF FAITH

written or taught, the end result was ultimately the same. The Mormon God never lived up to the attributes ascribed in the way the lectures claimed and promised He would. The idea of the Lord's 'due time' came and went with the 1800s. It is far too late for the early 'saints' now. That is a historical *fact* which cannot be denied and is one very good reason why the lectures may have been deleted from the D&C. They later became a complete embarrassment to the Church in so many ways.

The idea in para 17 that there would be...

> a complete victory over all those who have sought their hurt and destruction. And as mercy is also an attribute of the Deity, his saints can have confidence that it will be exercised toward them; and through the exercise of that attribute toward them, comfort and consolation will be administered unto them abundantly, amid all their afflictions and tribulations.

...amounted to nothing. There was no deliverance from 'all their enemies', there was no 'victory' over *anyone*, and no 'mercy' was shown by God to anyone amid their 'afflictions and tribulations'. If there was anything perceived as such, it had to be purely imaginary as it certainly wasn't real – or recorded.

The questions and answers follow a similar pattern to earlier lectures.

Question. What was shown in the third lecture?

Answer. It was shown that the correct ideas of the character of God are necessary in order to exercise faith in him unto life and salvation; and that without correct ideas of his character, men could not have power to exercise faith in him unto life and salvation, but that correct ideas of his character, as far as his character is concerned in the exercise of faith in him, lay a sure foundation for the exercise of it.

Q. What object had the God of heaven in revealing his attributes to men?

A. That through an acquaintance with his attributes they might be enabled to exercise faith in him so as to obtain eternal life.

Q. Could men exercise faith in God without an acquaintance with his attributes, so as to be enabled to lay hold of eternal life?

A.   They could not.

Q. What account is given of the attributes of God in his revelations?

A. First, Knowledge, secondly, Faith, or power, thirdly, Justice, fourthly, Judgment, fifthly, Mercy, and sixthly truth.

Q. Where are the revelations to be found which give this relation of the attributes of God?

A. In the Old and New Testaments, and they are quoted in the fourth lecture, fifth, sixth, seventh, eighth, ninth, and tenth paragraphs.

Q. Is the idea of the existence of those attributes, in the Deity, necessary in order to enable any rational being to exercise faith in him unto life and salvation?

A. It is.

Q. How do you prove it?

A. By the eleventh, twelfth, thirteenth fourteenth, fifteenth and sixteenth paragraphs in this lecture.

Q. Does the idea of the existence of these attributes in the Deity, as far as his attributes are concerned, enable a rational being to exercise faith in him unto life and salvation?

A. It does.

Q. How do you prove it?

A. By the seventeenth and eighteenth paragraphs.

Q. Have the Latter Day Saints as much authority given them, through the revelation of the attributes of God, to exercise faith in him as the Former Day Saints had?

A. They have.

Q. How do you prove it?

A. By the nineteenth paragraph of this lecture.

Note. Let the student turn and commit those paragraphs to memory.

These are all the questions and answers relating to lecture four. As the sequence is short, it is included in full in order to give an idea of the absurdity surrounding the concepts and also the constant reiteration of the same things. It is strange that those attending the lecture were instructed to memorise it.

Chapter 6

**Lectures of Faith
Lecture 5**

LECTURE FIFTH
Of Faith.

SECTION V

Lecture five deals with the Godhead – "we mean the Father, Son and Holy Spirit."

Immediately, the then current Mormon theology is set out in no uncertain terms. Para 2 confirms doctrine which was later to dramatically change when Smith invented new and radical ideas on the Godhead. Those who believe that the idea of God having a body was a theology set in stone from the very time of the claimed First Vision *in* 1820 are sadly mistaken. The First Vision was not invented in its currently published format until 1838; the 1830 *Book of Mormon* was monotheistic throughout *(TMD Vol. 2. Ch. 8)*; the *Inspired Revision* of the Bible was *altered* to *clarify* monotheism where it may have been ambiguous *(TMD Vol. 2:114;127-8)*; none of over one-hundred Smith revelations included in the 'Covenants' section of the 1835 D&C contained the notion that God has a body; the alleged *Book of Abraham* was also partly 'translated' during 1835, in which God still had no physical body. Everything remained consistent.

THE MORMON DELUSION

All that Smith wrote which *preceded* the lectures was consistent with the concepts taught *in* them. The fifth lecture in particular became controversial later on, but it is no good apologists arguing that Smith may not have written the lectures as it makes no difference whatsoever. Whoever actually wrote the lectures, they were consistent with all of Smith's teachings to that point.

Para 2 gets straight to the point which is made in a manner that leaves no room for doubt – which is why apologists can only postulate that Smith may not have actually written them. But then apologists haven't got their heads around the rest of the facts; the First Vision was a later invention and Smith himself was entirely monotheistic at the time. The lectures could not have been written any other way, no matter who put pen to paper. Additionally, apologists ignore the fact that Smith kept tight control over everything and would have been hardly likely to allow such lectures to be taught in the School of the Prophets and included as 'Doctrine' in his Doctrine and Covenants had they not represented his own theology. The very notion is completely absurd. The seven lectures remained canonised as *scripture* for well over eight decades.

From para 2:

> There are two personages who constitute the great matchless, governing and supreme power over all things -- by whom all things were created and made, that are created and made, whether visible or invisible: whether in heaven, on earth, or in the earth, under the earth, or throughout the immensity of space -- They are the Father and the Son: **The Father being a personage of spirit**, glory and power: possessing all perfection and fulness: (Emphasis added).

Immediately and without equivocation we learn the Mormon theology of 1835. There are only *two* personages in the Godhead, the Father and the Son. The father is distinctly "a personage of spirit" and the Holy Spirit (Holy Ghost) is *not* a member of the Godhead.

Para 2 continues:

> The Son, who was in the bosom of the Father, a personage of tabernacle, made, or fashioned like unto man, or being in the form and likeness of man, or, rather, man was formed after his likeness, and in his image; -- he is also the express image and likeness of the personage of the Father: possessing all the fulness of the Father, or, the same fulness with the Father; being begotten of him, and was ordained from before the foundation of the world to be a propitiation for the sins of all those who should believe in his name, and is called the Son because of the flesh…

LECTURE FIFTH OF FAITH

The expression "who was in the bosom of the Father" is a monotheistic one, meaning that Jesus was and is God Himself, manifest in the flesh when He came to Earth. The Son is expressly "a personage of tabernacle" which is entirely different to the above description of the Father, who is singularly a "personage of spirit". Lecture 2 already confirmed this, along with the concept that He is *omnipresent*, which of course only a spirit could be. The son is in the "express image and likeness of the personage of the Father" but this does not indicate that the Father possesses a body. The Father is expressly defined as a spirit, and the Son, who is *also* the Father and in His likeness, *has* a body. Note that He "is called the Son *because* of the flesh". That should be perfectly clear in context of the theology of the day, both inside and outside of Mormonism.

You will find many similar descriptions in Smith's other writings; the *Book of Mormon* (1830) and *D&C 93* (1833) for example, confirm this theology.

> **Mosiah 15:2.** And because he dwelleth in flesh he shall be called the Son of God, and having subjected the flesh to the will of the Father, being the Father and the Son—
> **3.** The Father, because he was conceived by the power of God; and the Son, because of the flesh; thus becoming the Father and Son—
> **4.** And they are one God, yea, the very Eternal Father of heaven and of earth.
>
> **D&C 93:4.** The Father because he gave me of his fulness, and the Son because I was in the world and made flesh my tabernacle, and dwelt among the sons of men.

We have ample confirmation from Smith himself *(see TMD Vol. 2. Ch. 8)* that the theology in the lectures was entirely consistent with his earlier work. Para 2 continues with further confirmation of the Father and Son possessing the same *mind* as follows:

> And he being the only begotten of the Father, full of grace and truth, and having overcome, received a fulness of the glory of the Father -- ***possessing the same mind with the Father, which mind is the Holy Spirit***, that bears record of the Father and the Son, and ***these three are one***, or in other words, these three constitute the great, matchless, governing and supreme power over all things: by whom all things were created and made, that were created and made: and these three constitute the Godhead, and are one: ... ***The Father and the Son possessing the same mind***, the same wisdom, glory, power and fulness: (Emphasis added).

The 'mind' of God is here defined as the Holy Spirit, just as Judaism taught – and still teaches. Only later, actually in the *twentieth century*, was the Holy Ghost to become doctrinally confirmed as an entirely separate 'personage' of spirit in Mormon theology. Before then, there was constant confusion over several Mormon beliefs...

> Yet, between 1890 and 1925 these doctrines were reconstructed principally on the basis of works by three European immigrants, James E. Talmage, Brigham H. Roberts, and John A. Widtsoe ... **Talmage reconsidered and reconstructed the doctrine of the Holy Ghost.** In response to questions raised by Talmage's lectures, George Q. Cannon, "commenting on the ambiguity existing in our printed works concerning the nature or character of the Holy Ghost, expressed his **opinion** that the Holy Ghost was in reality a person, in the image of the other members of the Godhead--a man in form and figure; and that what we often speak of as the Holy Ghost is in reality but the power or influence of the spirit." The First Presidency on that occasion, however, "deemed it wise to say as little as possible on this as on other disputed subjects." (Emphasis added).
>
> In 1894 Talmage published an article in the *Juvenile Instructor* elaborating on his and Cannon's views. He incorporated the article almost verbatim into his manuscript for the *Articles of Faith,* and the Presidency approved the article virtually without change in 1898. The impact of the *Articles of Faith* on doctrinal exposition within the Church seems to have been enormous. Some doctrinal works like B. H. Roberts's 1888 volume *The Gospel* were quite allegorical on the nature of God, Christ, and the Holy Ghost. In the 1901 edition, after the publication of the *Articles of Faith,* Roberts explicitly revised his view of the Godhead, modifying his discussion and incorporating Talmage's more literal interpretation of the Holy Ghost. *(From Joseph Smith to Progressive Theology. Thomas G. Alexander. Sunstone Magazine. July/Aug 1980:24-33).* Currently available at the following link:

https://www.sunstonemagazine.com/wp-content/uploads/sbi/articles/022-24-33.pdf

Here we see that modern Mormon theology on the Holy Ghost came from no more than the minds of men who considered their *opinions* on the matter to be logical and worthy of consideration. The First Presidency hadn't a clue as to what the Holy Ghost really was and "deemed it wise to say as little as possible on this as on other disputed subjects." Later it was to become official *doctrine.* Additionally, the above referenced article covers some other twentieth-century Mormon inventions, such as the doctrine of our 'pre-existence', again from the

LECTURE FIFTH OF FAITH

minds of men, put to the First Presidency for consideration. I have never met a Mormon who does *not* believe such doctrines originated with Joseph Smith.

Mormon theology matched mainstream Christianity in 1835; God and Jesus were one and the same being and the Holy Spirit was without question the *mind of God*; monotheism; trinitarianism; three *in* one.

Questions and answers follow, in order to firm up the idea that there were only *two* 'personages' in the Mormon Godhead; this is then supposedly *proven*.

If we were to accept the so-called 'proof' as real evidence, then Smith's and also later Mormon Church leaders' ideas – were 'provably' *incorrect* – and thus modern Mormonism has it all wrong. Smith's definitive position was later *altered*.

> Q. How many personages are there in the Godhead?
>
> A. Two: the Father and the Son.
>
> Q. How do you prove that there are two personages in the Godhead?
>
> A. By the Scriptures. Gen. 1:26. And **the Lord** God said **unto the Only Begotten, who was with him from the beginning**, Let us make man in our image, after our likeness:-- and it was done. Gen. 3:22. And **the Lord** God said **unto the Only Begotten**, Behold, the man is become as one of us: to know good and evil. John, 17:5. And now, O Father, glorify thou me with thine own self with the glory which I had with thee before the world was. (Emphasis added).

The only problem with the above is that the scriptures are quite different from the KJV; they are actually from Smith's 'Inspired Revision', altering the detail completely. Unsurprisingly, even today's IR is now somewhat different.

For comparison, these are the KJV and IR versions compared with the above. Note, in the IR, Genesis 1:26 becomes v.27 and Genesis 3:22 becomes v.28; also, they are written in the first person. John 17:5 remains the same.

> **KJV. Gen 1:26.** And God said, Let us make man in our image, after our likeness...
>
> **IR. Gen. 1:27.** And I, God, said unto mine Only Begotten, which was with me from the beginning, Let us make man in our image, after our likeness; and it was so. *(This also matches Smith's Moses 2:26).*
>
> **KJV Gen 3:22.** And the LORD God said, Behold, the man is become as one of us, to know good and evil...

IR Gen 3:28 And I, the Lord God, said unto mine Only Begotten, Behold, the man is become as one of us, to know good and evil... *(This also matches Smith's Moses 4:28).*

Next, the sequence establishes God as a personage of 'glory' and 'power' with any idea of a physical body completely excluded from the description and from the subsequent 'proof'.

Q. What is the Father?

A. He is a personage of glory and power.

Q. How do you prove that the Father is a personage of glory and of power?

A. Isaiah 60:19. The Sun shall be no more thy light by day, neither for brightness shall the moon give light unto thee: but the Lord shall be unto thee an everlasting light, and thy God thy glory. 1 Chron. 29:11. Thine, O Lord, is the greatness, and the power, and the glory. Ps. 29:3. The voice of the Lord is upon the waters: the God of glory thunders. Ps. 79:9. Help us, O God of our salvation, for the glory of thy name. Romans 1:23. And changed the glory of the incorruptible God into an image made like to corruptible men.

Secondly, of power. I Chron. 29:4. Thine, O Lord, is the greatness and the power, and the glory. Jer. 32:17. Ah! Lord God, behold thou hast made the earth and the heavens by thy great power, and stretched-out arm; and there is nothing too hard for thee. Deut. 4:37. And because he loved thy fathers therefore he chose their seed after them, and bro't them out in his sight with his mighty power. 2. Samuel 22:33. God is my strength and power. Job 26. commenceing [sic] with the 7 verse, to the end of the chapter. He stretches out the north over the empty place, and hangs the earth upon nothing. He binds up the waters in his thick clouds; and the cloud is not rent under them. He holds back the face of his throne, and spreads his cloud upon it. He has compassed the waters with bounds, until the day and night come to an end. The pillars of heaven tremble, and are astonished at his reproof. He divides the sea with his power, and by his understanding he smites through the proud. By his Spirit he has garnished the heavens; his hand has formed the crooked serpent. Lo, these are parts of his ways: but how little a portion is heard of him? But the thunder of his power who can understand?

As an aside, it is interesting that Smith includes verses which claim God "hangs the earth upon nothing" as if it is suspended in space by God, and that

LECTURE FIFTH OF FAITH

the clouds hold so much water without being "rent" under the weight of it. Modern scientific laws explain things the ancients believed were mystical acts of God. Smith seems to follow the old ideas to a large degree. God never took the time to explain the truth to Smith.

In contrast to the description of God, the Son is *immediately* established as having a 'tabernacle' which God does *not* have.

Q. What is the Son?

A. First, he is a personage of tabernacle.

Q. How do you prove it?

A. John 14:9,10,11, Jesus says unto him, Have I been so long time with you, and yet have you not known me, Philip? He that has seen me has seen the Father; and how do you say then, Show us the Father? Do you not believe, that I am in the Father, and the Father in me? The words that I speak unto you, I speak not of myself: but the Father that dwells in me, he does the works. Believe me that I am in the Father, and the Father in me.

Secondly, and being a personage of tabernacle, was made or fashioned like unto man, or being in the form and likeness of man.
Philip. 2. Let this mind be in you, which was also in Christ Jesus; who being in the form of God, thought it not robbery to be equal with God; but made himself of no reputation, and took upon him the form of a servant, and was made in the likeness of man, and, being found in fashion as a man, he humbled himself, and became obedient unto death, even the death of the cross. Heb. 2:14, 16. Forasmuch then as the children are partakers of flesh and blood, he also himself likewise took part of the same. For verily he took not on him the nature of angels: but he took on him the seed of Abraham.

Thirdly, he is also in the likeness of the personage of the Father.
Heb. 1:1, 2, 3. God, who at sundry times, and in divers manners, spake in time past to the fathers, by the prophets, has in these last days spoken unto us by his Son, whom he has appointed heir of all things, by whom also he made the worlds; who, being the brightness of his glory, and the express image of his person. Again, Philip. 2:5,6. Let this mind be in you, which was also in Christ Jesus; who being in the form of God, thought it not robbery to be equal with God.

Q. Was it by the Father and the Son that all things were created and made, that were created and made?

A. It was. Col. 1:15,16,17. Who is the *image of the invisible God*, the first born of every creature; for by him were all things created that are in heaven, and that are in earth, visible and invisible, whether they be thrones or dominions, principalities or powers; all things were created by him and for him; and he is before all things, and by him all things consist. Gen. 1:1. In the beginning God created the heavens and the earth. Heb. 1:2. (God) Has in these last days spoken unto us by his Son, whom he has appointed heir of all things, by whom also he made the worlds. (Emphasis added).

Note the inclusion of a scripture which claims God is *invisible*. So, God is first confirmed a *spirit* with no body; now he is confirmed an *invisible spirit*.

The Son is firstly a tabernacle of flesh. Secondly it was fashioned in the physical form of a man. Thirdly, He was in the likeness of the 'personage' of the Father, which has already been firmly established as one of spirit without any physical attributes. Next, the Son 'possesses' the fullness of the Father.

Q. Does he possess the fulness of the Father?

A. He does. Col. 1:19. 2:9. For it pleased the Father that in him should all fulness dwell. For in him dwells all the fulness of the Godhead *bodily*. Eph. 1:23. Which is *his (Christ's) body*, the fulness of him that fills all in all. (Emphasis added).

The above explicitly states that in the *Son* dwells the "fulness of the Godhead *bodily*" which is "his (Christ's) body..." Next is affirmation that *God* is *called* the *Son* "because of the flesh" *(below)*; unlike God the Father, he had a body.

Q. Why was he called the Son?

A. **Because of the flesh.** Luke 1:33. That holy thing which shall be born of thee, shall be called the Son of God. -- Math. 3:16, 17. And Jesus, when he was baptized, went up straitway out of the water: and lo, the heavens were opened unto him, and he [John] saw the Spirit of God descending like a dove and lighting upon him: and lo, a voice from heaven, saying, This is my beloved Son, in whom I am well pleased. (Emphasis added).

Following a question and answer about Christ being ordained before the foundation of the world, we move on to confirmation that indeed the Holy Spirit is the *mind* of God rather than a spirit 'person' in his own right as now believed in Mormonism.

LECTURE FIFTH OF FAITH

Q. *Do the Father and the Son possess the same mind?*

A. **They do.** John 5:30. I (Christ) can of my own self do nothing: as I hear, I judge, and my judgment is just; because I seek not my own will, but the will of the Father who sent me. John 6:38. For I (Christ) came down from heaven, not to do my own will, but the will of him that sent me. John 10:30. I (Christ) and my Father are one.

Q. *What is this mind?*

A. **The Holy Spirit.** John 15:26. But when the Comforter is come, whom I will send unto you from the Father, even the Spirit of truth, which proceeds from the Father, he shall testify of me. (Christ.) Gal. 4:6. And because you are sons, God has sent forth the Spirit of his Son into your hearts. (Emphasis added to all the above).

The summary question and answer reaffirms the Trinitarian concept; God the Father, God the Son, and God the Holy Spirit. God is a spirit, Christ is God manifest in the flesh, and the Holy Spirit is the mind of God.

Q. Do the Father, Son and Holy Spirit constitute the Godhead?

A. They do.

Let the student commit this paragraph to memory.

Q. Does the believer in Christ Jesus, through the gift of the Spirit, become one with the Father and the Son, as the Father and the Son are one?

A. They do. John 17:20, 21. Neither pray I for these (the apostles) alone, but for them also shall believe on me through their word; that they all may be one; as thou, Father, art in me, and I in thee, that they also may be one in us, that the world may believe that thou hast sent me.

Q. Does the foregoing account of the Godhead lay a sure foundation for the exercise of faith in him unto life and salvation?

A. It does.

Q. How do you prove it?

A. By the third paragraph of this lecture.

Let the student commit this also.

THE MORMON DELUSION

The logical question, which no Mormon ever seems to pose, is why would a God leave mankind in such ignorance, believing He was a spirit rather than a being with a physical body for thousands of years and yet chat to Moses about killing people who blasphemed or abused their parents? Surely, His very *first* obligation was to explain that He actually had a body – and also *why* and *how* He came by it. It simply doesn't make sense and yet those who want to believe the modern Mormon story will block out any rational thought to protect the delusion that it is somehow true and that we only learned of it (much later than this of course) through Smith when he changed his mind about the Godhead. Smith then made up a whole new theology which inherently allowed Smith to ultimately become what he wanted to be himself – a god.

There is nothing ambiguous about lecture five. It completely contradicts later theology that Joseph Smith invented. When that happened, Smith altered some of the *Book of Mormon (TMD Vol. 2. Ch. 8)*, he reverted to the original KJV of Revelation 1:6, despite the fact that he had 'corrected' it in his earlier *Inspired Revision*, and he also completely ignored all of his earlier so-called revelations *(TMD Vol. 2:135-9)* and rewrote the First Vision story for at least the third time *(TMD Vol. 2. Ch. 2)*. If God does have a body, He would have declared Himself correctly – and without confusion, from the beginning – that is, in Genesis 1, rather than to Smith, thousands of years later. He didn't, and Smith went along with traditional thinking until about 1836. Thus we can be certain that no God was ever involved with Smith's ever changing theology.

Failing that – and there is no excuse for such failure – if God *has* a body, if the Holy Ghost is *not* the mind of God, but rather a 'personage' (male of course) in his own right, if we *were* pre-existent spirits, and if God wanted us to understand such things, they would have formed an *essential* part of the very *first* revelations given to Smith, if not on day one in his claimed First Vision, and certainly by the time his Church was established in 1830. (God would still have to explain why He didn't say all that in Genesis of course). They weren't, and when Smith died, he had *still* never even heard of some such ideas. Thus the Mormon Church was founded on (God's?) *deception* regarding the Holy Ghost, as well as other important doctrines such as pre-existence, formulated from *opinions* at the beginning of the following century.

Mormons are now obliged to accept the *fact* that major Mormon doctrine, such as the official Godhead theology as it now stands, simply came about as the result of *opinions* of Talmage, Roberts and Widtsoe, none of whom were even apostles when they first wrote about those opinions *(See p.64)*. The problem is, the Church doesn't tell members about such things, so the rank and file have absolutely no idea when or how such doctrine surfaced and *changed*. They continued to make things up as they went along and hid the facts from members – and they still do.

Chapter 7

Lectures of Faith
Lecture 6

LECTURE SIXTH
Of Faith.

SECTION VI

'Lecture Sixth' moves on to reveal the supposed knowledge that people must acquire if they are to live a life according to the will of God. Para 2 actually confirms the *invisibility* of God, as described in scriptures referenced in 'Lecture Fifth' *(see p.66)*.

> 2. This knowledge supplies an important place in revealed religion; for it was by reason of it that the ancients were enabled to endure *as seeing him who is invisible.*

The text continues:

> An actual knowledge to any person that the course of life which he pursues is according to the will of God, is essentially necessary to enable him to have that confidence in God, without which no person can obtain eternal life.

THE MORMON DELUSION

Fair enough, assuming there is a God and that He can communicate an idea of how we should live. So, what does the lecture claim our pattern of life should be like and from where does it derive proof that it is the case? Speaking again of the ancients, the lecture first tries to establish the idea that it didn't much matter if people had a terrible life and a 'horrid' death; all would be well hereafter.

> 3. Having the assurance that they were pursuing a course which was agreeable to the will of God, they were enabled to take, not only the spoiling of their goods, and the wasting of their substance, joyfully, but also to suffer death in its most horrid forms; knowing, (not merely believing,) that when this earthly house of their tabernacle was dissolved, they had a building of God, a house not made with hands, eternal in the heavens. Second Cor. 5:1.

It is actually typical of religious leaders to teach such nonsense. Put up with grief now and don't worry about it because the next life will be better. If God *is* real, He would surely want His children to enjoy a good life in the here and now. We can all try to live good lives, but why the constant need for suffering?

Is it not just an excuse for the fact that historically so many humans have suffered so badly at the hands of other humans – and often in the name of God; or through epidemics, illnesses or natural disasters, all of which are of God's creation or invention and under His control? He created this unstable planet, tornadoes, earthquakes and volcanoes – and *all* life, including harmful bacteria.

Humans gradually developed a much better world in which to live. All God appears to have done is to destroy what humans created, as the planet is a very unstable place to live in so many ways. There have been five mass extinctions, all before humans ever evolved. We are due for a further one in the foreseeable future (within a few million years). God won't stop it. Our species will become as extinct as almost all have before us, and other species will inherit the Earth.

To emphasise the idea that nothing matters in this life and all expectations should be reserved for the next life – thus conveniently nothing has to be accounted for by religious leaders in the here and now, so whatever mess they get us into doesn't matter, it's all part of the test – the following is posed:

> 5. For a man to lay down his all, his character and reputation, his honor and applause, his good name among men, his houses, his lands, his brothers and sisters, his wife and children, and even his own life also, counting all things but filth and dross for the excellency of the knowledge of Jesus Christ, requires more than mere belief, or supposition that he is doing the will of God, but actual knowledge: realizing, that when these sufferings are ended he will enter into eternal rest; and be a partaker of the glory of God.

LECTURE SIXTH OF FAITH

Unless the reader can see what this amounts to in the cold light of day, there is little hope for them. It is clear that this is a confidence trick. To suggest a man's character, reputation, good name, honour, brothers, sisters, wife and children and even his own life are "but filth and dross" is scandalous. If Smith wanted your wife or daughter for himself, here is a mandate to allow him to ask for them, and ask for them and take them he did – and he even took some without asking. When the sufferings have ended, "he will enter into eternal rest; and be a partaker of the glory of God." That's the con. Suffer now, and be rewarded *after* you are dead. Nothing whatsoever is *ever* promised in *this* life.

In Smith's view, unless a person was not only willing to give up everything but proved it by physically doing so – usually to him, then they were not living the laws of God. Under Smith's theology, a religion that did not make people suffer was not worth having.

> 7 Let us here observe, that a religion that does not require the sacrifice of all things, never has power sufficient to produce the faith necessary unto life and salvation; for from the first existence of man, the faith necessary unto the enjoyment of life and salvation never could be obtained without the sacrifice of all earthly things: it was through this sacrifice, and this only, that God has ordained that men should enjoy eternal life; and it is through the medium of the sacrifice of all earthly things, that men do actually know that they are doing the things that are well pleasing in the sight of God. When a man has offered in sacrifice all that he has, for the truth's sake, not even withholding his life, and believing before God that he has been called to make this sacrifice, because he seeks to do his will, he does know most assuredly, that God does and will accept his sacrifice & offering, & that he has not nor will not seek his face in vain. Under these circumstances, then, he can obtain the faith necessary for him to lay hold on eternal life.

It should be remembered that the lectures were written at a time when Smith's actions were inviting so-called 'persecution' on the saints. The leaders considered local residents their enemies. They became so, not because of any hatred they had for a group of law abiding devoutly religious citizens, as many were religious themselves, but rather, through fear and intimidation which was a constant worry for anyone in areas where Mormons tried to settle, take over, and then control. The things Mormons did to their neighbours inevitably led to mayhem and murder on both sides. Inciting people to such action came under the command of Joseph Smith – not as a meek prophet of God, but ultimately a self-styled 'General' complete with an elegant uniform and troops he created into an imposing army the local and state officials became seriously concerned about, eventually sufficiently to reluctantly issue an extermination order. No prophet or members of a true Church of God would have ever behaved in a manner, so as to invoke such a response. A study of the history of events that took place reveals the arrogance and constant illegal activities, plundering and murder organised and approved by Smith and his close associates, but that is a matter that the Church now hides and denies and it is also one for another time.

Why would God actually require people to sacrifice so much in an era when life in the 'New World' could have been so good; when immigrants and settlers were making lives for themselves in relative peace in Ohio and Illinois?

If Smith had integrated his people peacefully and in a 'Christ-like' manner into the local society, things would have turned out far differently. Ultimately, Smith spent most of his short adult life either in jail or on the run from the law with a price on his head – he was an outlaw who lived, just as Brigham Young later openly declared he and the rest of the saints did, above the law.

Para 8 describes the concept that those who don't sacrifice heavily needn't think they qualify for the same rewards as those who sacrifice everything, thus gearing people up to virtually expect to have to do so, or the desired rewards may not be achieved. This is emphasised by reference to the fictional character Abel who supposedly offered sacrifice before there were 'flocks' *to* sacrifice, as previously discussed. Abel is described as the first 'martyr' in para 9. The description of the Mormon God is pretty scary and nothing like the loving Christian God of many other sects.

> And from the days of righteous Abel to the present time, the knowledge that men have that they are accepted in the sight of God, is obtained by offering sacrifice: and in the last days, before the Lord comes, he is to gather together his saints who have made a covenant with him by sacrifice. Ps. 50:3,4,5. Our God shall come, and shall not keep silence: a fire shall devour before him, and it shall be very tempestuous round about him. He shall call to the heavens from above, and to the earth, that he may judge his people. Gather my saints together unto me; those that have made a covenant unto me by sacrifice.
>
> 10 ...But those who do not make the sacrifice cannot enjoy this faith, because men are dependent upon this sacrifice in order to obtain this faith; therefore, they cannot lay hold upon eternal life, because the revelations of God do not guarantee unto them the authority so to do; and without this guarantee faith could not exist.

The lecture continues to next affirm that "all the saints of whom we have account in all revelations" obtained their knowledge through sacrifice and we must do the same. The fact is that had Smith not exposed his followers to such retribution that occurred due to the way *he* behaved, they would never have had to sacrifice much of anything at all and would not have been driven out.

LECTURE SIXTH OF FAITH

Through sacrifice:

> 11 ...their faith became sufficiently strong to lay hold upon the promise of eternal life, and to endure us seeing him who is invisible; and were enabled, through faith, to combat the powers of darkness, contend against the wiles of the adversary, overcome the world, and obtain the end of their faith, even the salvation of their souls.

The final paragraph is a pathetic last attempt to coerce people into the notion that painful sacrifice is essential to avoid doubt. "Doubt and faith cannot exist in the same person at the same time."

I have to thank my proof reader, Jean Bodie, for pointing out that of course doubt and faith can in exist in the same person at the same time. Because faith is *not* evidence, doubt often does exist simultaneously. You can doubt the story of young Joseph in a grove of trees but *hope* that it is true. In fact, this is the position of many church members today as evidenced by the numerous posts on Mormon websites.

> 12 ...here faith is weak, the persons will not be able to contend against all the opposition, tribulations and afflictions which they will have to encounter in order to be heirs of God, and joint heirs with Christ Jesus; and they will grow weary in their minds, and the adversary will have power over them and destroy them.

An end note claims that "This lecture is so plain, and the facts set forth so self-evident, that it is deemed unnecessary to form a catechism upon it: the student is therefore instructed to commit the whole to memory."

I wonder if anyone ever bothered to do that – and why?

Chapter 8

Lectures of Faith
Lecture 7

LECTURE SEVENTH
Of Faith.

SECTION VII

Having established "agreeably to our plan", a treatment of what faith is, the final lecture sets out to show the *effects* of faith. Para 2 reminds us that "faith was the principle of action and of power in all intelligent beings, both in heaven and on earth". It then tells us that an attempt will not be made to cover everything applicable because:

> 2. ...it would embrace all things in heaven and on earth, and encompass all the creations of God, with all their endless varieties: for no world has yet been framed that was not framed by faith; neither has there been an intelligent being on any of God's creations who did not get there by reason of faith, as it existed in himself or in some other being; nor has there been a change or a revolution in any of the creations of God but it has been effected by faith: neither will there be a change or a revolution unless it is effected in the same way, in any of the vast creations of the Almighty; for it is by faith that the Deity works.

This paves the way for selective teaching designed to entice those being taught, to do whatever they are told as it will show evidence of their faith – and of course it is all God's will. Faith seems to work like magic according to the lecture, through words rather than actions:

> 3. ...We understand that when a man works by faith he works by mental exertion instead of physical force: it is by words instead of exerting his physical powers, with which every being works when he works by faith -- God said, Let there be light, and there was light -- Joshua spake and the great lights which God had created stood still -- Elijah commanded and the heavens were stayed for the space of three years and six months, so that it did not rain: He again commanded, and the heavens gave forth rain, -- all this was done by faith; and the Savior says, If you have faith as a grain of mustard seed, say to this mountain, remove, and it will remove; or say to that sycamine tree, Be ye plucked up and planted in the midst of the sea, and it shall obey you. Faith, then, works by words; and with these its mightiest works have been, and will be performed.

Having set out their stall by claiming faith works by words, the fourth para says "It surely will not be required of us to prove" that is the case. Clearly Smith and his friends did not have the 'faith' to put their money where their mouths were, so to speak, and to prove they had the faith to do similar things.

"...every reflecting mind must know..." will have to be enough evidence for the saints. Smith didn't need to prove it; people just had to believe it. Dare we say they just had to have 'faith' in it? It is claimed (para 5) that the "whole visible creation, as it now exists, is the effect of faith". I personally take issue with that concept, but we are talking of things ethereal, so the reader can draw his or her own conclusion about such things.

> 5. ...It was by faith which it was framed, and it is by the power of faith that it continues in its organized form, and by which the planets move round their orbits and sparkle forth their glory: So, then, faith is truly the first principle in the science of THEOLOGY, and when understood, leads the mind back to the beginning and carries it forward to the end; or in other words from eternity to eternity.

The idea that "science is theology" is as nonsensical as anything else Smith taught. Science is no more theology than theology is "revealed science", which Smith also claimed in 'Lecture First' *(see p21)*. Planets do not move by faith, they move according to combined gravitational forces that we now understand sufficiently to be able to know 'faith' has nothing to do with it, regardless of who or what set them in motion. Everything is governed by scientific laws

LECTURE SEVENTH OF FAITH

which have absolutely nothing to do with 'faith' or 'theology'. Those laws are *set*; they work independently, regardless of faith, and cannot be altered.

Para 6 explains that we should expect to find confirmation of this "set forth in a revelation from God" but throughout the rest of the text, one isn't actually provided. Para 7 reaffirms that without faith it is impossible to please God. We could ask why – and indeed that question is posed:

> If it should be asked, Why is it impossible to please God without faith? the answer would be, because, without faith it is impossible for men to be saved; and as God desires the salvation of man he must of course desire that they should have faith, and he could not be pleased unless they had, or else he could be pleased with their destruction.

It is quite amazing that such nonsense passed for *theology*. Para 8 goes on to explain what we learn from this. Fair enough that in theological terms faith brings a person nearer to God, but being saved because *He* is saved? Strange.

> 8. ...without it there was no salvation, neither in this world nor in that which is to come. When men begin to live by faith they begin to draw near to God; and when faith is perfected they are like him; and because he is saved they are saved also; for they will be in the same situation he is in, because they have come to him; and when he appears they shall be like him, for they will see him as he is.

Discussion then moves on to an explanation of salvation, the question of who is to be saved, and what the difference is between someone who has been saved and someone who has not been saved.

> As all the visible creation is an effect of faith, so is salvation, also. (We mean salvation in its most extensive latitude of interpretation, whether it is temporal or spiritual.) In order to have this subject clearly set before the mind, let us ask what situation must a person be in, in order to be saved? or what is the difference between a saved man and one who is not saved?

The question, having been asked, is answered thus:

> 9. We answer from what we have before seen of the heavenly worlds, they must be persons who can work by faith, and who are able, by faith to be ministering spirits to them who shall be heirs of salvation. And they must have faith to enable them to act in the presence of the Lord, otherwise they can not be saved.

This is followed by a long and dreary statement which could easily put a reader to sleep, but it is important enough to include. Imagine being asked to memorise this. Luckily – you won't be.

> 9. ...what constitutes **the real difference between a saved person and one not saved, is the difference in the degree of their faith**: one's faith has become perfect enough to lay hold upon eternal life, and the other's has not. But to be a little more particular, let us ask, where shall we find a prototype into whose likeness we may be assimilated, in order that we may be made partakers of life and salvation? or **in other words**, where shall we find a saved being? for if we can find a saved being, we may ascertain, without much difficulty, what all others must be, in order to be saved -- they must be like that individual or they cannot be saved: we think, that it will not be a matter of dispute, that **two beings, who are unlike each other, cannot both be saved**; for whatever constitutes the salvation of one, will constitute the salvation of every creature which will be saved: and if we find one saved being in all existance, we may see what all others must be, or else not be saved. We ask, then, where is the prototype? or where is the saved being? We conclude as to the answer of this question there will be no dispute among those who believe the bible, that it is Christ: all will agree in this that he is the prototype or standard of salvation, or in other words, that he is a saved being. And if we should continue our interogation, and ask how it is that he is saved, the answer would be, because he is a just and holy being; and **if he were any thing different from what he is he would not be saved**; for **his salvation depends on his being precisely what he is** and nothing else; for if it were possible for him to change in the least degree, so sure he would fail of salvation and lose all his dominion, power, authority and glory, which constitutes salvation; for salvation consists in the glory, authority, majesty, power and dominion which Jehovah possesses, and in nothing else; and no being can possess it but himself or one like him: Thus says John, in his first epistle, 3:2 and 3: Behold, now we are the sons of God, and it doth not appear what we shall be; but we know, that when he shall appear we shall be like him; for we shall see him as he is. And any man that has this hope in him purifies himself, even as he is pure. -- Why purify himself as he is pure? because, if they do not they cannot be like him. (Emphasis added).

It is a strange concept that the difference between a 'saved' and 'not saved' person is "the difference in the *degree* of their faith", as Christianity does not tend to *measure* faith in that respect. In mainstream Christianity, faith is all that is required to be saved. There is no 'degree'; you either have faith to believe or you do not. Faith saves. A lack of faith may often be blamed for something not happening by way of an answer to prayer or a miracle, but not regarding being 'saved' as it is not measurable or even quantifiable. It is yet another aspect of religion which is a theoretical supposition based on nothing more or less than the philosophies of men presented as scripture and supposed by Christians to be true, despite the fact that there is *no* evidence to support it.

The idea "two beings, who are unlike each other, cannot both be saved" is claimed without any consideration for many millions of faithful non-Mormons who truly believe they have faith – and behave far better than Smith and many early Mormons did. The lecture creates an exclusive 'club' based on Smith's philosophies and theology which were ever changing. The underlying message was, have faith in what we say and follow us blindly; be like us or you will not be saved. Smith and company clearly considered themselves examples of what it took to be saved – otherwise who would their followers have to follow? The recorded example of Joseph Smith is more than enough for anyone who studies it to realise he was anything *but* a man of faith who was duly saved.

Christ is set up as the 'prototype', despite the fact that most of Smith's life was spent doing anything but the things Christ did or taught. 'Christ is a saved being so we must become like him'. That is logical enough, but the strange thing is that that conclusion is followed by the statement "if he were any thing different from what he is he would not be saved" which is a bizarre thing to consider in theological terms. It gets even sillier in the following statement "his salvation depends on his being precisely what he is". Think about all that.

In Christianity, including Mormonism, if Christ was not perfect, *none* of us would be saved. He was part of the plan, and God, who knows everything, past, present and future, knew full well that Christ *would* achieve what he did before the show even started. That is common theology which Smith here misses, or rather mis*uses*, entirely. The supposition that the lecture poses is not exactly convincing but at the time, no doubt followers just accepted anything they were taught; after all, Smith was their prophet.

For anyone who may remember my comments in *TMD Volume 4 (p. 288)* about Smith having God use the expression "in other words" several times in the *Book of Mormon* and also in the *D&C*, you may recognise the same style of wording here, suggesting that Smith was very much involved with writing the lectures. I can't think of a reason why he would not be, or why they would not reflect his personal theology; anything else doesn't make any sense at all.

The lecture moves on to review the idea of Christ being one with the Father and that we can also be one with Him. There is nothing new in the concept being taught. The essence of the lengthy ramble is captured in this short extract from para 10. So, what's new? This is what all Christians believe, is it not? It hardly needs such lengthy explanation which goes on for pages.

Matthew, 15:48: Be ye perfect, even as your Father who is in heaven is perfect. If any should ask, why all these sayings? the answer is to be found from what is before quoted from John's epistle, that when he (the Lord) shall appear, the saints will be like him: and if they are not holy, as he is holy, and perfect as he is perfect, they cannot be like him; for no being can enjoy his glory without possessing his perfections and holiness, no more than they could reign in his kingdom without his power.

Emphasis is given to John 17:20-24 including the following in para 12:

And the glory which thou gavest me, I have given them, that they may be one, even as we are one; I in them, and thou in me, that they may be made perfect in one; and that the world may know that thou hast sent me, and hast loved them as thou hast loved me. Father, I will that they also whom thou hast given me be with me where I am...

As ever, Joseph Smith's interpretation of such standard Christian concepts stretches them beyond recognition. More is required from Smith's followers than simple belief and faith in the Saviour that he will keep his word that they will be saved through his grace. The language is as always sloppy and includes such words as "The works that Jesus done they were to do, and greater works than those which he done among them should they do..."

Just as it seems the lecture is meandering towards its conclusion, as it says in para 15, "It is scarcely necessary here to observe what we have previously noticed", it then continues and does just that in another lengthy and completely unnecessary dialogue, repeating everything again. It reminds me of the temple endowment as it was when I first attended the temple. It then lasted for two-and-a-half hours and much of it was sheer repetition. If there were new people attending, a twenty minute 'lecture' followed the endowment, recapping yet again on all that had gone on. Prior to the lecture being played as a recording, I remember it being memorised and repeated by a temple worker. I have no idea how they managed to do that. Most long-time members simply slept through it. Just as these seven lectures have been dropped, so have the temple lecture and about an hour of the endowment which today runs for about ninety minutes.

It finally gets round to saying "Who cannot see, then, that salvation is the effect of faith?" in para 17 which is pretty much all that needed saying in the first place. But still it goes on – and on. More examples of faith are given from the Bible. Finally, after several lengthy paragraphs of (vain?) repetition, almost at the end, we get this:

LECTURE SEVENTH OF FAITH

> ...when faith comes, it brings its train of attendants with it--apostles, prophets, evangelists, pastors, teachers, gifts, wisdom, knowledge, miracles, healings, tongues, interpretation of tongues, &c. All these appear when faith appears on the earth, and disappear when it disappears from the earth...

A couple of things are of interest in this statement. Firstly, the 'attendants' include evangelists and pastors, which were, and still are, conspicuous by their complete absence in Mormonism, despite the fact that the sixth Article of Faith still mentions both of them. They are apparently the equivalent of Patriarch and Bishop respectively, but that is a modern-day Mormon excuse for the missing positions and historically they had nothing to do with either. I have covered this elsewhere *(TMD Vol. 4:378-80)* showing the absurdity of such a claim.

Secondly, when faith appears on the Earth, among the other things we see are 'tongues' and 'interpretation of tongues'. Without these, faith "disappears from the earth..."

In modern-day Mormonism, this is rationalised to mean that sometimes people are 'miraculously' able to communicate far better in a foreign language than their meagre training in the Mission Language Training Centre has been able to accommodate, or that a listener may be able to understand what is being said when such inadequacy prevails. This is the spirit prompting the speaker in what to say or what the listener is hearing respectively. There is certainly no impromptu speaking in foreign tongues by someone who has no idea what they are saying, in any language, known or unknown, and no interpretation of such.

At the time of the lectures, and right through until the late 1800s, 'speaking in tongues' meant something *entirely* different in the Mormon Church. Prolific in meetings, and particularly popular with the women, was 'glossolalia' and that is what the definition referred to when the lectures were written. Someone would stand and speak gobbledegook and someone else would then stand and 'interpret' what had been said. There were even regular glossolalia meetings among the women for that purpose. Revelations were received and prophecies given concerning the Church and kingdom in this manner. This was more than accompanied by faith in such people and their ability to do these things. This lecture confirms faith *disappears* from the earth in the absence of such gifts. Ergo, faith no longer exists on Earth as glossolalia has gone from Mormonism.

> All these appear when faith appears on the earth, and disappear when it disappears from the earth. For **these are the effects of faith and always have, and always will attend it.** (Emphasis added).

That does say "always" does it not? As ever, it doesn't much matter to the Mormon Church – they have deleted the lectures, so the faithful won't even notice any of this unless they develop enquiring minds and search for the truth.

THE MORMON DELUSION

It is easy to understand why the Church dropped the lectures from the D&C, just from all the nonsense included in the last lecture alone.

Notwithstanding the later very awkward problems created by the inclusion of concepts of an omnipresent God, God being a spirit with no body, only two personages in the Godhead and the Holy Spirit being the mind of God rather than an independent spirit personage, the seven lectures remained canonised scripture; they were the 'doctrine' in the *Doctrine and Covenants* throughout the rest of Smith's life. There they remained throughout the administration of the next *five* prophets; Brigham Young, John Taylor, Wilford Woodruff, Lorenzo Snow and Joseph F. Smith. *None* of them ever seemed to consider the lectures anything other than canonised *scripture*. They were not discarded until 1921 when Heber J. Grant was President of the Church and Mormon theology on the 'Godhead' was settling into a twentieth century perception.

The question must be asked, if all those so-called prophets were content with the lectures, did any of them really have a clue as to what was supposed to actually be believed? Did they even care? After Brigham Young, of course they were all contending with the concept that Adam was God as well, and that survived right though until Joseph F. Smith's time *(see TMD Vol 3. Sec 2)*, so I expect they had enough to deal with without reconsidering the lectures.

Perhaps it was only when someone took a more serious interest and noticed what was actually *in* the lectures, compared with the later evolved teachings of the Church, that they became so awkward all that could be done was to pretend they didn't exist and just drop them. Excuses would follow. As ever, that job would be left to apologists who do not represent God and have no authority to speak on His behalf. Meanwhile, Mormon leaders just kept quiet following their 'explanation' of the de-canonisation of the lectures which *still* appears in the D&C introduction, as mentioned on pages 10-11. To remind the reader:

> These had been prepared for use in the School of the Prophets in Kirtland, Ohio, from 1834 to 1835. Although profitable for doctrine and instruction, these lectures have been omitted from the Doctrine and Covenants since the 1921 edition **because they were not given or presented as revelations to the whole Church.** (Emphasis added).

The above *current* statement is one of the most outrageous of *lies* in modern Mormon print, as Church leaders are fully aware this was *not* the case at all.

They **were** presented, accepted, and canonised, on 17 August 1835.

The Church **recorded** the voting in its own history. *(HC. V.2:243-6)*.

They were presented and accepted yet **again** at the October 1880 General Conference. These are the records that modern-day leaders completely ignore:

LECTURE SEVENTH OF FAITH
CHAPTER XVIII.

THE BOOK OF DOCTRINE AND COVENANTS PRESENTED TO THE GENERAL ASSEMBLY OF THE PRIESTHOOD AND THE CHURCH.

...A general assembly of the Church of Latter-day Saints was held at Kirtland on the 17th of August, 1835, to take into consideration the labors of a committee appointed by a general assembly of the Church on the 24th of September, 1834, for the purpose of arranging the items of the doctrine of Jesus Christ for the government of the Church.

After recording a long series of unanimous votes from the various quorums, then "the whole congregation, accepted and acknowledged it as the doctrine and covenants of their faith, by a unanimous vote." The Church subsequently voted a *second* time at Conference in 1880 *(see pp. 11-12)*. You can't argue with that. But then, perhaps we don't need to. Mormon apostle, Bruce R. McConkie seemed quite content to accept the lectures as "eternal scripture" written by "the power of the Holy Ghost".

> Now these statements that I now read were in part written by the Prophet and in whole approved by him and taught by him in the school of the prophets. They're taken from the Lectures on Faith... this in effect is a creed announcing what Deity is. And in my judgment, it is the most comprehensive, intelligent, inspired utterance that now exists in the English language—that exists in one place defining, interpreting, expounding, announcing, and testifying what kind of a being God is. It was written by the power of the Holy Ghost, by the spirit of inspiration. And it is, in effect, eternal scripture, it's true. *(Apostle Bruce R. McConkie. 4 January 1972. Cited in 'The Mormon Handbook' at this link:*
> http://www.mormonhandbook.com/home/lectures-on-faith.html

An audio version of McConkie's speech is available from BYU here:
http://speeches.byu.edu/?act=viewitem&id=607&tid=2).

It is extremely difficult to imagine how the Church can possibly deal with this conflict of facts and fiction. The current doctrine in Mormonism regarding the Godhead and the nature of God, which is *supposed* to date from 1820, is perfectly clear. The Church *now* claims Smith saw God and Jesus, determining *immediately* that they were two separate and distinct beings with bodies *in* 1820. The truth is that Smith did no such thing. Following his earlier attempts at an 1820 'First Vision' story in 1832 and 1835, he only arrived at his final official version, which was to include this *new* idea, in 1838. Smith made no such claim to *any* kind of an 1820 vision before 1832, and his 1835 version included only angels, as was the case with his other visionary claims.

Therefore, in 1835, these lectures were entirely in concert with Smith's monotheistic thinking of the time. How the Mormon Church can rationalise the lectures and McConkie's comparatively recent and powerful endorsement of them, with such opposing later beliefs remains a mystery. Clearly, there is *no* comparison, and it only goes to show that there is no real argument here. The lectures did indeed fully embrace Joseph Smith's early traditional monotheistic thinking which he later discarded in favour of new ideas on polytheism. The Church eventually 'overcame' the resulting contradictions by simply deleting the lectures from the *D&C*, but the problems will *not* go away.

Once again – God does not change – but Smith's doctrines constantly ***did***.

Chapter 9

COVENANTS

Doctrine and Covenants Section 2

21 September 1823. Manchester, New York.

History.

Added in 1876. 2010 D&C Sec. 29.

Despite the claimed date (1823) of this supposed revelation, Section 2 did *not* appear in the 1833 *Book of Commandments (BOC)* or the 1835, or even the 1844 *Doctrine and Covenants (D&C)*, and for very good reason – which will soon be discovered. D&C Section 2 actually appeared for the very first time in the 1876 edition.

In chronological order, this section bears the earliest date of any section in the D&C. In fact, it was not *recorded* until 1838 but the Church goes with the claim that the revelation was given in 1823, although, outside Smith's *later* claim in 1838, that he told his father about the vision the following day, there is no extant evidence to support this. The earliest accounts of *anything* related to Smith's visions that I could locate were from 1827 or later, following his claim to locate the gold plates *(See TMD Vol. 2:76-7)*. As it is short and also quite important, Section 2 is included here in entirety, along with the introduction.

THE MORMON DELUSION

Section 2

An extract from the words of the angel Moroni to Joseph Smith the Prophet, while in the house of the Prophet's father at Manchester, New York, on the evening of 21 September 1823 (see History of the Church, 1:12). Moroni was the last of a long line of historians who had made the record that is now before the world as the Book of Mormon. (Compare Malachi 4:5–6; also sections 27:9; 110:13–16; and 128:18.)

1, Elijah is to reveal the priesthood; 2–3, The promises of the fathers are planted in the hearts of the children.

1. Behold, I will reveal unto you the Priesthood, by the hand of Elijah the prophet, before the coming of the great and dreadful day of the Lord.
2. And he shall plant in the hearts of the children the promises made to the fathers, and the hearts of the children shall turn to their fathers.
3. If it were not so, the whole earth would be utterly wasted at his coming.

I have not referred to Section 2 in earlier work, but I have dealt extensively with Smith's claim that Moroni appeared in 1823 and delivered what amounted to a sermon to Smith which included the above – and a lot more. *(See TMD Vol. 2: Ch.6)*. Smith claimed that Moroni (whom he called *Nephi* at the time) rehearsed part of Malachi 3 to him and all of Malachi 4, followed by Isaiah 11, Acts 3:22-23 and Joel 2:28-32. One of the problems with accepting Smith's claim, which the Mormon Church *never* draws the attention of its members to – is that whilst Smith pretended to have seen and heard all this in 1823, he didn't **say so in** 1823. Smith only claimed and wrote down such a detailed account of what happened, from *memory*, some fifteen years later – in **1838**.

In citing other D&C Sections where Smith mentions similar wording, the header avoids including *Section 98*. I suspect this is due to Smith's misuse of Malachi in Section 98 where it conflicts with the Bible and even with Smith's own alternate claims about it *(See p. 335)*.

The three verses that comprise D&C Section 2 are quite meaningless really in the overall scheme of things, but by them being published as Section 2, they condemn Smith utterly and completely – and this is why.

When Joseph Smith wrote down Moroni's version of Malachi 4:5-6, which comprises the above text, he claimed that Moroni *altered* some of the words from those we now see in the King James Version *(KJV)* of the Bible. Moroni's changes also altered the *meaning* entirely, as no 'Priesthood' is mentioned in these verses in the Bible at all. An analysis of all the differences appears in

DOCTRINE & COVENANTS – SECTION 2

TMD Vol. 2:80. (S3). In itself, that should not be a problem for Smith. He could simply claim that as a prophet, Moroni just 'clarified' the text.

Smith's problems arise through his own bad memory – or possibly lack of caring what was really true, as he seemed to make things up as he went along, often without regard for what he had previously claimed. In the interim (1831-1834), when Smith wrote his 'Inspired Revision' *(IR)* of the Bible, he left Malachi 4:5-6 alone – and it still reads the *same* as the KJV, despite Moroni supposedly 'correcting' it several years *earlier*, in 1823. If Smith remembered word for word, what Moroni had said in 1823 sufficiently to record it *perfectly* in 1838, there is *no* excuse for forgetting about it when he wrote his Bible revision in 1831-1834, yet he did *not* 'correct' it in line with his Moroni claim.

It gets worse, as it was not the only time Smith made his 'Malachi' mistake. Smith's memory was not only bad enough to forget what he had written in his IR in 1831-1834 when he wrote down Moroni's version in 1838; he had clearly suffered from the same problem when writing his Book of Mormon in 1828-9.

It contains the very same problem and ***Jesus*** is the one to expose it. Smith had Jesus tell the Nephites about Malachi's words, which he claims they "never knew before". *(See TMD Vol. 2. Ch. 11. Fundamental Flaws in the Book of Mormon: More 'Old Testament' in The Book of Mormon)*. Despite the fact that Moroni supposedly *altered* the text when talking to Smith in 1823, Smith had Jesus *quote* it in the Book of Mormon in 1828-9 (or in 34 CE if you must), *just* as it appears in the KJV – something which, in and of itself, was impossible.

The question is how Jesus managed to do that, long before it had ever been written in Jacobean (Early Modern) English. Why did *Jesus* not also 'correct' the words when speaking to the Nephites in 34 CE? Why would Jesus recite words recorded incorrectly in a book not to be written for hundreds of years?

In D&C 128:17-18, Smith claims that turning "the heart of the children to their fathers", actually refers to baptism for the dead – so why were there no baptisms for the dead in the Book of Mormon if Jesus went to all the trouble of quoting Malachi?

But even *that* is not the end of Smith's problems regarding these verses. Later, in his infamous King Follett sermon of 7 April 1844, Smith once again quoted the *original* KJV text when referring to Malachi 4:5-6. Despite claiming that Moroni changed Malachi, Smith did *not use* it in a direct quotation in this major sermon to a claimed 20,000 Saints, years later. It would have been a glorious occasion for Smith to have reminded his followers about the *correct* words given to him by Moroni.

Questions I pose in *TMD Vol. 2, Ch. 6*, include the following. If the original was so *wrong*, why did Jesus (meaning Smith) 'quote' it in 34 CE, *literally* from the KJV, in the Book of Mormon? Why did Smith not 'correct' it, in line with Moroni's version, in his Inspired Revision? Why use the KJV in his 1844 sermon as if it were correct, and not use Moroni's words instead? How could

Smith have ever remembered word for word what Moroni actually said on the morning following the claimed vision in 1823, let alone some fifteen years later? Why did Smith *not* record it at the time in 1823? The questions continue in *TMD Vol. 2*. Smith's changes make absolutely no sense and certainly don't sit at all well with a literal translation *(See TMD Vol. 2:83-4)*. Once again, Smith is caught in his duplicity; not just once, it happened over and over again.

The introduction to this Section gives a clue as to why it is included in the D&C, as the reason is not at first all that clear. It suggests cross referencing Malachi 4:5-6 in order to see the alterations. As mentioned above, I show the differences in *TMD Vol. 2:80*. It also suggests Sections 27:9 (1830); 110:13–16 (1836); and 128:18 (1842). This is because there is very little relating to *any* restoration of Priesthood recorded in the D&C and they add grist to the mill.

Section 27:9 just mentions "**And also** Elijah, unto whom I have committed the keys of the power of turning the hearts of the fathers to the children..." *(Emphasis added. See 'And also' below)*, with no mention of Priesthood. Other connected verses *not* referenced, include v.6 which talks of *Elias* "to whom I have committed the keys of bringing to pass the restoration of all things spoken by the mouth of all the holy prophets since the world began, concerning the last days;" – despite the fact there was no such person as Elias. *(See pp. 148-9 to discover who the Mormon Church claims this version of 'Elias' was)*.

The verses following v.9 additionally mention "And also" Joseph, Jacob, Isaac, Abraham and Michael, or Adam. About these 'and also's', Jesus says "I will drink of the fruit of the vine with you on the earth" (v.5). It is a strange thing to say and an odd group to consider getting together for a drink – which the header claims means the *sacrament*. But, does it? Smith's inference is that they will have a social drink together. Either way, the idea is absurd.

The previous verses (7-8), tell of John the Baptist ordaining Smith and Cowdery to the Aaronic Priesthood and v.12 mentions Peter, James and John had also ordained them as apostles, so the Priesthood was supposedly given to Smith *before* August 1830 – long before the Elijah claim of Section 110 in 1836, reviewed below. We will come back to that and more when reviewing Section 27 in detail; the *date* of that supposed revelation was later falsified and backdated from the one given in the 1833 BOC *(see p. 148 on)*.

"I will reveal unto you the Priesthood, by the hand of Elijah the prophet" claims Section 2:1, recorded in 1838 and backdated to 1823. It is certainly *not* what the Bible says.

A search among the online Mormon scriptures for 'Elijah' and 'Priesthood' brings up, among other things, this statement under the title of 'Moses – The Guide to the Scriptures':

> Moses' ministry extended beyond the limits of his own mortal lifetime. **Joseph Smith taught that, in company with Elijah, he**

DOCTRINE & COVENANTS – SECTION 2

came to the Mount of Transfiguration and bestowed priesthood keys upon Peter, James, and John. (Matt. 17:3–4; Mark 9:4–9 etc. are referenced for this). (Emphasis added).

It is ironic that it claims Smith *taught* that Moses "in company with *Elijah*" appeared on the mount. The scripture references are of course to the New Testament and as we have already discovered, in the NT, it is **Elias** who is spoken of rather than Elijah. This shows that Smith, and of course modern-day Mormon Church leaders, must have been aware that Elias is the Greek form of the Hebrew name Elijah. Indeed, it is evidence that Smith et al *did* realise that at some point. And yet Smith separately claims that 'Elias' *appeared* to him, in *addition* to Elijah, thus falling foul of pretending a character appeared to him who never actually existed.

Section 110:13-16 just repeats the idea that Elijah will come, much in the same way as previously stated, but this time Elijah *does* come when a "great and glorious vision" bursts forth wherein Elijah talks about what Malachi says. It is followed by Elijah saying (v.16): "Therefore, the keys of this dispensation are committed into your hands; and by this ye may know that the great and dreadful day of the Lord is near, even at the doors." This will be claimed by the Mormon Church as prophecy 'fulfilled'. Notwithstanding the fact that both the Aaronic and Melchizedek Priesthoods were supposedly given to Smith by 1830 and that over one-hundred-and-eighty years later, that 'day' still remains "at the doors" and we are *still* waiting, we need to look more closely at the sequence of real 'events' to arrive at the truth; not just *claimed* historical events – but the *dated sequence* of Smith's claims.

1. Section 110 **claims** Elijah handed over Priesthood keys.
   Date recorded: **3 April 1836.**
2. Joseph Smith *recorded* Moroni altering Malachi 4:5-6 (D&C 2).
   Date recorded: **1838.**
3. Smith backdated his idea of **1838**, claiming it *happened* in **1823**.

It is very easy to make a prophecy a couple of years *after* you have claimed it fulfilled and then backdate the claim to a period before the 'prophecy' was supposedly fulfilled. However, that does not constitute prophecy. In any event, there is no evidence to support the 1836 claim, regardless of when Smith wrote what he did. The reference doesn't include the previous verse (110:12) which claims *Elias also* appeared in a separate vision, thus meaning the Church has to somehow 'make' an impossible *character* 'Elias' fit into the *Old Testament*.

Section 128:18 was written 6 September 1842, some years later, in a letter, when Smith obviously did not have immediate access to the alterations he had made in Malachi. The reason was that Smith was in hiding, on the run from the law. There was a warrant issued for his arrest as a suspected accomplice in the failed assassination attempt of Missouri Governor Lilburn Boggs. Joseph Smith claimed to remember his supposed 1823 vision, word for word, in 1838, but now cannot recall the changes he made to Malachi. It was probably the same in 1844 when Smith gave his King Follett sermon, although on that occasion he didn't even bother to mention the changes at all.

In Section 128:18 Smith says he could have given a 'plainer' translation but the KJV will do. This time he relates it to the Earth being smitten with a curse unless they do baptisms for the dead, rather than mentioning Priesthood, none of which of course is in the KJV at all.

Let's just see what the Mormon Church says in their Bible Dictionary about Elias:

> **Elias.** There are several uses of this word in the scriptures. (1) It is the N.T. (Greek) form of Elijah (Hebrew), as in Luke 4:25–26, James 5:17, and Matt. 17:1–4. Elias in these instances can only be the ancient prophet Elijah whose ministry is recorded in 1 and 2 Kings. ***The curious wording of JST Mark 9:3 does not imply that the Elias at the Transfiguration was John the Baptist, but that in addition to Elijah the prophet, John the Baptist was present.*** (2) Elias is also a title for one who is a forerunner, for example, John the Baptist, as in JST Matt. 11:13–14, JST Matt. 17:10–13, and JST John 1:19–28. These passages are sufficiently clarified to show that anciently two Eliases were spoken of, one as a *preparer* and the other a *restorer*. John was sent to prepare the way for Jesus, Jesus himself being the Restorer who brought back the gospel and the Melchizedek Priesthood to the Jews in his day (see JST John 1:20–28, in the Appendix). In this particular instance there is reflected also the comparative functions of the Aaronic and Melchizedek priesthoods. (3) The title Elias has also been applied to many others for specific missions or restorative functions that they are to fulfill, for example, John the Revelator (D&C 77:14); and Noah or Gabriel (D&C 27:6–7, cf.Luke 1:11–20). (Emphasis added).

I would say, so far, so good – but it really isn't. So, let's just deal with the above before we get to the final Bible Dictionary comments. First, the Church admits to Elias being the Greek form of Elijah – but can't just leave it at that.

Note the next claim. "The curious wording of JST Mark 9:3 does not imply that the Elias at the Transfiguration was John the Baptist, but that in addition to Elijah the prophet, John the Baptist was present." The wording is *not* curious at all. It is not even ambiguous; it is crazy though. It is specific and it *declares*, rather than implies, that Elias *was* John the Baptist. For comparison, the *KJV*, in which it is actually v.4, reads thus:

DOCTRINE & COVENANTS – SECTION 2

KJV. **Mark 9:4.** And there appeared unto them Elias with Moses: and they were talking with Jesus. [This is *NT* – read Elijah for Elias].

IR. **Mark 9:3.** And there appeared unto them Elias with Moses, *or in other words, John the Baptist* and Moses; and they were talking with Jesus. (Emphasis added).

Here we also see Smith having the Lord use one of his favourite phrases, "in other words" which *only* appears in 'scripture' Smith was involved with; the *D&C*, *Inspired Revision* and *Book of Mormon*. The words in the *IR* are clear and precise. The Church just has to *pretend* that it does *not* imply Elias was John the Baptist on that occasion because it is indeed a silly idea, despite the fact that Smith's translation makes it perfectly clear that *he* thought it was. The dictionary claim is a blatant contradiction of Smith's very clear 'revision'.

Smith has the Lord rephrase, or sometimes even *repeat* the exact same thing, using the phrase "in other words" on no less than **twenty-two** occasions in the D&C (10:17; 42:37,69,74; 58:20; 59:13,14; 61:23; 63:42; 78:9; 82:9,17; 83:5; 88:127; 93:36,45; 95:17; 101:12; 104:5,69; 107:66; 128:8).

In addition, Smith has several different characters use "in other words" a ***dozen*** times in the Book of Mormon, where it appears ***three times by Nephi*** (1 Nephi 8:2, 10:4; 19:7) some 600 years BCE; ***once by Mosiah*** (7:27) 121 BCE; ***six times by Alma, the Son of Alma*** (Alma 13:7; 32:16; 40:2,19; 46:21; 48:15) 82-72 BCE; ***once by Nephi, son of Nephi the son of Helaman*** (3 Nephi 6:20); CE 26-30); and also once by him quoting a ***letter from Gaddianhi*** (leader of the Gadianton robbers), to Lachonius, asking him to surrender:

> **3 Nephi 3:6.** …desiring that ye would *yield up unto this my people*, your cities, your lands, and your possessions, rather than that they should visit you with the sword and that destruction should come upon you.
> **7.** *Or in other words, yield yourselves up unto us*… (16-18 CE).

Note that the use of "in other words" does not even introduce a clarification in this, or in many of the other instances where Smith has his characters use it; it repeats *exactly* the same thing again – on gold plates, which were supposedly difficult to write on, in addition to the fact it would be a very unlikely thing for anyone to *write* in the first place. What are the chances of so many characters, including God and Jesus, using *that* phrase so many times, *never* in the Bible and *only ever* from words ascribed – one way or another, to Joseph Smith?

"In other words" was not the only pet phrase that Smith had God, Jesus and his Book of Mormon characters *exclusively* use; there were several others and we will pick up on some more of them along our journey through the D&C. *(See: The Final Analysis, Part 2).*

THE MORMON DELUSION

The reader may wonder why v.4 in the *KJV* becomes v.3 in Smith's *IR*. This is because Smith leaves out v.1 entirely. It was a supposed prophecy made by Christ that did not materialise:

> **Mark 9:1.** And he said unto them, Verily I say unto you, That there be some of them that stand here, which shall not taste of death, till they have seen the kingdom of God come with power.

We can't blame Jesus for actually making this clearly unfulfilled prophecy. It should be remembered that the Gospels were written long after Christ lived and died, by people who never knew or met him and wrote at least second or third hand accounts of what other people thought they remembered him saying. There is no telling what, if anything, the Lord actually said about that at all.

However, Smith seemed to think the same thing in his era and thus many people were promised, particularly in patriarchal blessings, that they would *live* to see the second coming. Everyone from both eras is long since dead.

Within the scriptures referenced, Smith changed the meaning of John 1:21 completely, making John say the *opposite* of what the KJV records.

> **KJV. John 1:21.** And they asked him, What then? Art thou Elias? And he saith, I am not. Art thou that prophet? And he answered, No.

> **IR. John 1:21.** And he confessed, and denied not that he was Elias; but confessed, saying; I am not the Christ.

Finally, the Church has to bite the bullet and go with the claim that *Elias* was an actual *man* in *OT* times – despite the fact it is a complete impossibility that anyone in the *OT* timeframe could have had a name recorded in the Tanakh in *Greek*. Elias remains simply the Greek transliteration of Elijah. If you want to work backwards and say 'Elias' in Hebrew you can *only* end up with 'Elijah'. (Elias – Hebrew *'Eliahu*, "Yahveh is God"; also called Elijah). *Elias* is a completely ***impossible*** *separate* Hebrew *name*; it just *cannot* exist.

Nevertheless, and getting back to the Mormon Bible Dictionary definitions we started to look at on page 92, the Church jumps in with both feet...

> (4) A man called Elias apparently lived in mortality in the days of Abraham, who committed the dispensation of the gospel of Abraham to Joseph Smith and Oliver Cowdery in the Kirtland (Ohio) Temple on April 3, 1836 (D&C 110:12). We have no specific information as to the details of his mortal life or ministry.

Even the way that is written sounds a little coy, "apparently lived", but they have to say *something* of course because they can't get away from Smith's

DOCTRINE & COVENANTS – SECTION 2

unfortunate but telling mistake. Naturally we don't know anything *about* a man named 'Elias' *in* the *Old Testament*. It is quite impossible; he was a fictional character straight out of Joseph Smith's vivid imagination. Had such a second person really existed, he could only ever have been known as another *Elijah*.

A final Mormon Bible Dictionary statement appearing below the above admits the problem thus:

> …the fragmentary information in our current Bibles is not sufficient to give an adequate understanding of what was involved in use of the term. Only by divine revelation to the Prophet Joseph Smith is this topic brought into focus for us who live in the last days.

– Or not, as the case may be.

At the end of the coverage of each 'Section' there will be a summary analysis of any prophecy located. Many sections contain no prophecy at all and in such cases no summary will appear. Prophecies simply copied from the Bible, such as Section 2 and the 'hearts of the children', will be ignored as they are not original Joseph Smith prophecies; not that there is any more merit or evidence of fulfilment of those than Smith's. Repetition or meaningless filler make up a significant part of the D&C and will largely be ignored. Some non-prophetic revelation is included and summarised out of general interest.

Section 2 – Summary Analysis

Prophecies made: 2
Prophecies fulfilled: 0

Pr. 1. "I will reveal unto you the Priesthood, by the hand of Elijah."

Pr. 2. "…before the coming of the great and dreadful day of the Lord", which according to the referenced D&C 110:16, was "at the doors".

Results:

Pr. 1. The prophecy was written (1838) *after* the supposed, but completely unquantifiable fulfilment (in 1836).

Pr. 2. Smith claimed in the D&C that a voice told him the Saviour would return by 1891. One-hundred-and-twenty years after Smith's deadline, we find ourselves still waiting.

> **D&C 130:14.** I was once praying very earnestly to know the time of the coming of the Son of Man, when I heard a voice repeat the following:
> **15.** Joseph, my son, if thou livest until thou art eighty-five years old, thou shalt see the face of the Son of Man; therefore let this suffice, and trouble me no more on this matter.

For the Church to claim the Saviour did not return just because Smith died before then doesn't explain why billions of people have been born since 1891. The Mormon Church believes that *all* spirits still in their 'pre-existent' state and awaiting their mortal birth will have the opportunity to come to Earth before the 'end'. Some apologists appear to realise this and instead claim it only meant Smith would have *seen* the Saviour again rather than he would actually return by then. When you think about it, what else *can* they say?

This makes a liar of the Lord and the question should be as perfectly clear to apologists as the answer is in the D&C. This fact creates a major problem which cannot be resolved other than by an admission that Smith was wrong about the voice and the message. That of course brings into question everything else Smith claimed to ever hear and see. However, it will be seen that this was not the only time Smith was wrong. He was actually wrong all the time. Smith even confirmed his understanding of the timing of the Saviour's return when he recorded, on 14 February 1835, that they should:

> go forth to prune the vineyard for the last times, or the coming of the Lord which was nigh, even fifty six years should wind up the scene. (Joseph Smith: Kirtland Council Minutes). *(Collier & Harwell 2002:70).*

Both of Smith's confirming prophecies, one of them canonised, stipulate 1891 as the latest year in which the Saviour would *return*. This was believed and later spoken of by some of the apostles who seemed to accept the idea.

It never happened.

Chapter 10

Doctrine and Covenants
Sections 3 & 10

Section 3: July 1828. Harmony, Pennsylvania.
Section 10: April 1829. Harmony, Pennsylvania.

As we review the rest of the D&C, each chapter or subsection will start with the history of the Section being covered. Section 10 is attributed to the summer of *1828* in the modern D&C but the 1835 edition dates it **May 1829**. It has now been admitted as **April 1829**, as above *(JS Papers, Vol. 2:473)*. Despite the re-dating, I am breaking my 'sequence' rule for Section 10 and dealing with it together with Section 3 as they concern Joseph Smith losing the first 116 pages of the *Book of Mormon*, otherwise known as the 'Book of Lehi'. Additionally, they concern the concept of residual 'Lamanites' being converted to the Church through the *Book of Mormon*.

History.

1833 BOC Ch. II. 1835 D&C Sec. XXX. 2010 D&C Sec. 3.
1833 BOC Ch. IX. 1835 D&C Sec. XXXVI. 2010 D&C Sec. 10.

Alterations:

Section 10:1 now reads:

> 1. Now, behold, I say unto you, that because you delivered up those writings which you had power given unto you to translate **by the means of the Urim and Thummim**, into the hands of a wicked man, you have lost them. (Emphasis added).

The emphasised words did not appear in the 1833 version but were added in 1835, presumably to clarify the fact that Joseph Smith used the 'Urim and Thummim' during his initial claimed translation of the gold plates, rather than his old money-digging seer-stone which was used during his 'translation' of the remainder of the Book of Mormon. *(See TMD Vol. 3: Ch. 7)*. I would not have a problem with the added explanation, except for the fact that the words are attributed to the Lord who could not possibly have spoken them, only to have them inadvertently left out of his revelation and then later inserted. It is clear evidence of Smith making it all up – yet again. See *TMD Vol. 2:96-7* regarding the loss of the 116 pages and also for an explanation of the original meaning of 'Urim and Thummim'. Far from Smith's claims, they had an entirely different purpose anciently. There is no evidence that Martin Harris (the person that v.1 refers to) was a 'wicked' man at all; he was just extremely gullible.

Moving on to locate *prophecy* within the two sections, of course we encounter a lot of meaningless filler that anyone could write and which tells us nothing.

Words ascribed to the Lord provide absolutely no worthwhile information at all. Throughout the remainder of this book there may be notes of a number of such 'filler' verses, but they will not all be shown as they really are pointless.

Not everyone will agree that they are all just filler of course, but at the end of the day, claimed rants and recaps by the Lord do *nothing* to educate or illuminate. In just one example, at the start of Section 3, the Lord (apparently) takes the time to personally inform us that:

> 1. The works, and the designs, and the purposes of God cannot be frustrated, neither can they come to naught.
> 2. For God doth not walk in crooked paths, neither doth he turn to the right hand nor to the left, neither doth he vary from that which he hath said, therefore his paths are straight, and his course is one eternal round.
> 3. Remember, remember that it is not the work of God that is frustrated, but the work of men;

DOCTRINE & COVENANTS – SECTIONS 3 & 10

> 4. For although a man may have many revelations, and have power to do many mighty works, yet if he boasts in his own strength, and sets at naught the counsels of God, and follows after the dictates of his own will and carnal desires, he must fall and incur the vengeance of a just God upon him.

If you think carefully about any plausible communication from deity to humans, would it really contain a series of such meaningless statements? If He exists, of course God cannot be frustrated; of course His path is straight; of course He can take His vengeance; it is all in the Bible. What is the need to repeat such things over and again to Smith throughout his writings? Is it meant to frighten people who should instead feel loved? Was that really God's voice or was it just Smith excusing his silly mistake? Such statements are typically written in the third person. Does God speak in the third person, referring to Himself, or was Smith just taking his lead from the *Old Testament* which also contains some third person statements, which equally were written by *men* pretending God was speaking?

The story behind Smith's loss of the 116 pages began with Harris pestering Smith for them in order to convince his unbelieving wife about the book. Smith asked the Lord who twice said no, and then finally, on the third occasion – by which time you would think Smith would have got the message – the Lord said do what you like. The Lord didn't bother to tell Smith to keep a *copy*, despite the fact that he apparently already *knew* very well what would happen. Instead, He supposedly predicted the whole thing and provided for it on the gold plates.

Was that a clever ploy by the Lord, or was it yet another Smith concoction? The answer becomes clear and obvious when we look at Smith's rationale for the solution and how it was formulated and executed. For a full review of the Martin Harris story see *TMD Vol. 1:96-97*. We could ask why God bothered with the idea of having everything repeated elsewhere on the plates considering Smith didn't actually look at them during his 'translation' process. God could just as well have dictated it to Smith in his hat without the need for the ancients to have repeated the same story in different words on the gold plates.

In Section 3, the Lord tells Smith off for giving the 116 pages to a wicked man. The *way* the Lord does this is both strange and unlikely. As Smith knew very well who he was, why does God tell him his name is Joseph, unless Smith just wanted it to *sound* biblical? Can you imagine a God *really* saying this?

> 9. Behold, thou art Joseph, and thou wast chosen to do the work of the Lord, but because of transgression, if thou art not aware thou wilt fall.

10. But remember, God is merciful; therefore, repent of that which thou hast done which is contrary to the commandment which I gave you, and thou art still chosen, and art again called to the work;

11. Except thou do this, thou shalt be delivered up and become as other men, and have no more gift.

12. And when thou deliveredst up that which God had given thee sight and power to translate, thou deliveredst up that which was sacred into the hands of a wicked man,

What awful wording – from God no less. Harris was not wicked; rather, he was an enthusiastic believer who wanted to convince his wife about Smith's book. It was clearly not the Lord saying this. Would He really say such a thing as "but because of transgression, if thou art not aware thou wilt fall". I have often commented that if the Lord really did speak to anyone, it would surely be eloquent and noteworthy. *Nothing* in the D&C that Smith claimed came from the Lord is *either*.

The result of Smith's mistake was that he claimed evil men would alter the words of the manuscript and if he retranslated the same material, they would then claim he was a false prophet because it would be different. The fact is the 'evil men' would have had to present the original pages in order to substantiate any such claim. Since they were hand written, it would be very easy to spot any alterations. If Joseph Smith retranslated an exact match, it would have been compelling evidence that in fact he *was* a prophet. Clearly, Smith knew he could *not* do it, so he had to make up an alternate solution, and for that he needed to invent further input from the Lord. Any new text would invariably be very different, but the story had to be similar as it covered Lehi and his family leaving Jerusalem and going to the Americas.

As an aside, Smith seemed unable to remember many of the names he had used in the lost pages, particularly the female names, which is why the books of Nephi are somewhat bereft of them. Very few of the women are named.

Section 10 was invented to cover Smith's mistake. Firstly, the Lord again accuses Martin Harris of being a wicked man and v.6 goes so far as to claim Harris tried to 'destroy' Smith. The Lord got that very wrong indeed and Harris remained a staunch supporter until 1837 when, along with many others, he left the fold following Smith's Kirtland bank fraud. At the time of the Lord's accusations, Harris was faithfully trying to raise money for publication of the book – for which he was promised a share in the profits. What then did the Lord really know? At the time, Smith hoped to make his fortune from sales of the Book of Mormon.

DOCTRINE & COVENANTS – SECTIONS 3 & 10

In a complex plan to overturn the wicked plot against Smith, the Lord had already prepared a way to solve the problem. This he did millennia before the event. The problem is that the idea simply doesn't work and instead it becomes yet another nail in the coffin for Smith. This is what Smith claimed happened – and what really did happen.

In Section 10:10-14 Smith has the Lord claim evil men had *already* altered the words, ready to say they "have caught you in the words which you have pretended to translate". Of course, Smith *had* only pretended to translate them, so here we have at least one correct statement in the D&C, despite the fact it is not intended to be taken as such. Satan, with a "cunning plan" put the thought into their minds. The Lord is not going to allow Satan to get away with that.

In v.16-19 the Lord even explains what the evil men are *thinking*, in what is essentially a pointless repeat of what is claimed in Section 3. All will be well as the Lord has a plan even more cunning that Satan's – and that plan was hatched some six-hundred years BCE.

> **Section 10:38.** And now, verily I say unto you, that an account of those things that you have written, which have gone out of your hands, is engraven upon the plates of Nephi;
> **39.** Yea, and you remember it was said in those writings that a more particular account was given of these things upon the plates of Nephi.
> **40.** And now, because the account which is engraven upon the plates of Nephi is more particular concerning the things which, in my wisdom, I would bring to the knowledge of the people in this account—
> **41.** Therefore, you shall translate the engravings which are on the plates of Nephi, down even till you come to the reign of king Benjamin, or until you come to that which you have translated, which you have retained;
> **42.** And behold, you shall publish it as the record of Nephi; and thus I will confound those who have altered my words.

Smith sometimes forgets himself and exposes the hoax through his choice of words. Note that having had the Lord explain that He had the same details recorded a second time, notwithstanding the fact that in the Book of Mormon Smith has those making the record claim they could write 'but little', Smith then inadvertently slips up in v.42, by adding "you shall publish it *as* the record of Nephi". This may not immediately strike the reader as an error, but when we consider the fact that Smith had lost the pages and needed an excuse for an obviously different and yet suitably *similar* account, he could only write about the same things he had written in his Lehi account and this time publish it – *as* the record of Nephi instead of Lehi. In real life, surely the Lord would have said, publish the record of Nephi *instead* of the Lehi account. It was obviously Nephi's account. "…publish it *as*" is a small but significant error by Smith.

Smith also had the Lord say "thus I will confound those who have altered my words" yet no one ever did. Remember, Smith was yet to write the Book of Mormon, so he could include whatever he wanted in it. All the subterfuge could have been avoided if Smith had not given Harris the 116 pages, or at least had had the sense to make a copy first. He could even have then pretended to retranslate it; something that would have been right up Smith's alley. But he didn't think to make a copy. Smith was clever, but still naïve. The idea that the Lord would go to all the trouble of preparing a second account of the very same details because He knew Smith would lose the pages is taught, and readily accepted, as a 'faith-promoting' story within Mormonism. In the cold light of day, it is an absolute absurdity. He would have told Smith to make a copy. Yet Smith has the Lord confirm a second account in Section 10:38 (above).

The funny thing is that Smith needn't have worried, as it appears there were no evil designing men at all and Harris's wife probably just burned the pages. Certainly nothing was ever heard of them again. The simple fact is that Smith could not remember what he had written and had to start again from scratch; the Lord was never involved at all. If He had been, Smith would have rewritten the *same* account, word for word, and exposed any evil men for what they were, as any alterations to his original manuscript would have been clear and easily discernable. Thus Smith would have been proven to be a prophet and his problem simultaneously solved. The fact that he didn't even consider that and invented a complex excuse for such inability is further proof of Smith's hoax.

There is a second 'prophetic' aspect in these two sections. It concerns the Book of Mormon and residual Lamanites. During the early years of the Church and right through until the time when I was a member, everyone *knew* the Lamanites constituted Native North Americans – and many islanders as well. Mormon prophet, Spencer W. Kimball, spoke extensively about it when he was an apostle, and he did *not* recant any of his words when he later became the President and prophet of the Church. *(See TMD Vol. 2:176-78)*.

In Sections 3 and 10, we find specific *prophecies* that the *Book of Mormon* will convert Lamanites, and Smith sent men on missions to various tribes who once fitted the bill but which are now discounted as DNA evidence has proven them not to be of Israelite descent after all. Yet Smith had the *Lord* explain very clearly that they *were* indeed residual Lamanites. Therefore, if you believe the Lord was actually speaking, He deliberately *lied* in the following verses taken from Section 3:

DOCTRINE & COVENANTS – SECTIONS 3 & 10

3:16. Nevertheless, *my work shall go forth*, for inasmuch as the knowledge of a Savior has come unto the world, through the testimony of the Jews, even so shall the knowledge of a Savior come unto my people—

17. And *to the Nephites, and the Jacobites, and the Josephites, and the Zoramites, through the testimony of their fathers*—

18. And *this testimony shall come to the knowledge of the Lamanites, and the Lemuelites, and the Ishmaelites, who dwindled in unbelief because of the iniquity of their fathers,* whom the Lord has suffered to destroy their brethren the Nephites, because of their iniquities and their abominations.

19. And for this very purpose are these plates preserved, which contain these records — that the promises of the Lord might be fulfilled, which he made to his people;

20. And *that the Lamanites might come to the knowledge of their fathers*, and that they might know the promises of the Lord, and that they may believe the gospel and rely upon the merits of Jesus Christ, and be glorified through faith in his name, and that through their repentance they might be saved. Amen. (Emphasis added).

The lies continue to be expounded by the Lord Himself in Section 10:

10:64. Therefore, I will unfold unto them this great mystery;
65. For, behold, *I will gather them as a hen gathereth her chickens under her wings,* if they will not harden their hearts; (Emphasis added). *(See pp. 188-9 for more on hens, chickens and Lamanites).*

See TMD Vol. 4:424-5; 436-7. (S3-6), regarding above sections and details of missions to the Lamanites.

It is interesting that Section 10:46 claims the Book of Mormon contains "all those parts of my gospel" which were to be shared with residual Lamanites.

46. And, behold, all the remainder of this work does contain all those parts of my gospel which my holy prophets, yea, and also my disciples, desired in their prayers should come forth unto this people.

No, it really does not; in reality, the Book of Mormon contains very little of anything concerning the gospel. Most of Smith's and later Mormon leaders' ideas on doctrine came about long *after* the Book of Mormon had been written.

THE MORMON DELUSION

Sections 3 & 10 – Summary

	Section 3	Section 10
Prophecies made:	2	2
Prophecies fulfilled:	0	0

Prophecies made: (The same two prophecies were made in both sections).

Pr. 3 & 5. God knew Smith would lose the 116 pages and provided an alternative BCE version on the gold plates in order to resolve the problem.

Pr. 4 & 6. Residual Lamanites are Native North Americans whom the Book of Mormon will convert. Missionaries were sent *to* the 'Lamanites'.

Results:

Pr. 3 & 5. Smith wrote Sections 3 and 10 in 1828 *before* he wrote the Book of Mormon in which he then included the required prophecy and story.

Pr. 4 & 6. DNA evidence has conclusively proven Native North Americans are *not* of Israelite descent and Mormon apologists are still searching in vain to find such people – *somewhere*.

In the following verses ***God is speaking:***

> **D&C 28:8.** And now, behold, I say unto you [Oliver Cowdery] that you shall ***go unto the Lamanites*** and preach my gospel unto them;

> **D&C 32:3.** And that which I have appointed unto him is that he [Parley P. Pratt] shall go with my servants Oliver Cowdery and Peter Whitmer, Jun., ***into the wilderness among the Lamanites.***

> **D&C 54:8.** …take your journey into the regions westward, unto ***the land of Missouri, unto the borders of the Lamanites.***

In case there is any further doubt, records were kept of those missions and we know where the men all went. Without exception, it was to tribes of Native North Americans who were taught that they were indeed Lamanites. *(See: The Final Analysis; Part Five. Smith and his Lamanites).*

Chapter 11

Doctrine and Covenants
Sections 4 – 9

Section 4
February 1829. Harmony, Pennsylvania.

History.

1833 BOC Ch. III. 1835 D&C Sec. XXXI. 2010 D&C Sec. 4.

Section 4 consists of just seven verses in which God is supposedly addressing Smith's father; Joseph Smith Sr. It has no revelatory or prophetic statements in it whatsoever. This early Smith 'revelation' contains the idea that something great is going to happen, phrased as "a marvellous work" – stolen from Isaiah 29:14, which Smith later also used twice in his Book of Mormon in 2 Nephi. It says to serve God; if you want to do the work, you are called to it; "the field is white already to harvest" – which was also plagiarised, this time from John 4:35. Following this is a list of suggested attributes. This revelation serves no purpose and is entirely meaningless filler. Smith was learning how to construct material that *sounded* like God speaking. The only question is, *why* would a God 'reveal' this to anyone – rather than saying something *important* or *useful*?

Section 5
March 1829. Harmony, Pennsylvania.

History.

1833 BOC Ch. IV. 1835 D&C Sec. XXXII. 2010 D&C Sec. 5.

Alterations:

The purpose of this book is not to list or analyse all of the alterations that have been made to the D&C over the years. Alterations included will be limited to those relevant to prophecy or other aspects significant to this work. Section 5, which was Ch. IV in the BOC, has in fact had a huge amount of reconstruction. For those requiring more details of all the alterations, the following link is to an excellent analysis at the 2think.org web site:

http://www.2think.org/hundredsheep/boc/boc_main.shtml

Section 5:4 (originally part of BOC Ch. IV:2) now reads:

> And you have a gift to translate the plates; *and this is the first gift that I bestowed upon you;* and I have commanded that you should pretend to no other gift *until my purpose is fulfilled in this;* for I will grant unto you no other gift *until it is finished.* (Emphasis added).

Emphasised words were *added* by Smith *after* he had completed the Book of Mormon and started work on his Inspired Revision of the Bible. He needed to somehow retract the idea that he had only *one* gift, so Smith simply changed the words originally attributed to the Lord by adding in further text. It is easier to gain a clearer understanding of the originally intended idea if we see it as it was first recorded and then compare it with the later version above.

> **BOC** **IV:2.** ...and he has a gift to translate the book, and I have commanded him that he shall pretend to no other gift, for I will grant him no other gift.

Obviously the original wording of BOC Ch. IV:2 would no longer do at all once Smith changed his mind about what 'gifts' he wanted to claim and use. Don't forget, once again, the original – *and* the alterations – are attributed to *God*. It says the Lord God is *speaking*. Note the above emphasised text which covers the additions is not the end of the matter. Several other words were altered in that verse, some changing the entire conversation from it being *about* Smith to directly speaking *to* him. For this to be a real revelation, the *context* of the speech – never mind the actual message – should have remained consistent, and once again identifies a clear and obvious hoax by Smith. God could not possibly have said what was in BOC IV:2 *and also* what it became in D&C 5:4 by any stretch of the imagination. It could only ever have been one thing or the other, thus it could *only* be Smith tidying up after himself when he decided to do more than he had allowed for in the initial pretended 'revelation'.

It would defy all credibility to go from just being commanded to 'pretend to no other gift' and 'no other gift will be granted' – to effectively rescinding that and allowing Smith to have whatever gifts he liked in a *further* revelation; but it is absolutely absurd to completely **change** what God said in the first place, in a claimed original revelatory text. God *cannot* say two opposing things and He cannot **lie**. Ergo, Smith did. Smith first pretended that God said translating the Book of Mormon was his **only** gift. Later Smith changed the text to read "first gift". Originally Smith was to "pretend to no other gift, for I will grant him no other gift". Then he claims God really said "pretend to no other gift *until my purpose is fulfilled in this,* for I will grant unto you no other gift *until it is finished.*" Cleverly situated additional text changed the meaning completely.

Modern-day Mormons have no idea about such changes, unless they search and compare currently published versions with the originals. Unless someone is suspicious and already questioning, they will never be likely to do so. Such falsifications are tricks a con artist might decide to undertake but are definitely not something a God could or would ever do. It is far from 'clarification'.

When Smith wrote BOC IV, he was trying to reassure Martin Harris that he had the gold plates and that the Book of Mormon was being translated at the behest of God. He was not thinking ahead and at that time had obviously not considered anything else he may end up doing. When Smith started to have problems with his position of leadership and needed to establish himself more firmly in the Church, he had revelations confirming him a prophet – and more.

On the occasion of the organisation of the Church at Fayette, New York, 6 April 1830:

> **Section 21:1.** Behold, there shall be a record kept among you; and in it thou shalt be called *a seer, a translator, a prophet, an apostle of Jesus Christ, an elder of the church through the will of God* the Father, and the grace of your Lord Jesus Christ, (Emphasis added).

Smith was involved with his Inspired Revision of the Bible in Kirtland, Ohio, and on 8 March 1833, he penned a revelation reinforcing his continued leadership and control:

> **Section 90:13.** And when you have finished the translation of the prophets, you shall from thenceforth preside over the affairs of the church and the school;

Two years later, again in Kirtland, on 28 March 1835, Smith recorded:

> **Section 107:92.** Behold, here is wisdom; yea, to be a seer, a revelator, a translator, and a prophet, having **all the gifts of God which he bestows upon the head of the church.** (Emphasis added).

It must be remembered that in 1829 when Sec. 5 *(BOC IV)* was pronounced, no one knew of any 'First Vision' as it was yet to be invented. Even the Moroni story had not yet been fully padded out and all most people knew was that in September 1827, an angel had led Smith to gold plates which were then being translated. Joseph Smith seemed to aspire to no more than being the translator and making money from the resulting book. It didn't seem to occur to Smith that the Church evolving out of his exploits would be complex both to run and to control. Others wanted in on the act and his leadership was constantly under threat for various reasons after 1830, with schisms breaking off almost from the start. Further revelations became required in order to bolster Smith's authority and leadership during the turbulent times that followed.

The 'Pure Church of Christ' was the first known Mormon schism, founded in 1831 by Wycam Clark, Northrop Sweet and four others, who liked Mormon concepts but became more than dissatisfied with Smith and concluded that he was a false prophet. The 'Church of Christ' was established in 1837 by Warren Parrish for similar reasons – but by then Smith's true colours had more than surfaced and many were leaving the fold due to his lifestyle and deceptions, not least of which was his Kirtland Bank fraud. Further revelations confirming authority for Smith were always needed. God reminded everyone in 1841.

> **D&C 124:125.** I give unto you my servant Joseph to be a presiding elder over all my church, to be a translator, a revelator, a seer, and prophet.

The Lord confirmed there would only be *three* witnesses to the Book of Mormon:

> **BOC IV:4.** ...yea and the testimony of three of my servants shall go forth with my words unto this generation; yea, three shall know of a surety that these things are true, ... And the testimony of three witnesses will I send forth...

Between the time of writing BOC IV in 1829 and it appearing as D&C XXXII in 1835 (now D&C 5), the Book of Mormon was published and Smith had managed to persuade eight more people to witness the book. Yet Smith had already had God declare there would be only *three*. In order to accommodate the possibility of more witnesses, Smith altered the text of the Section so it became unclear enough to allow for the extra witnesses. Once again, Smith was playing around with words God was recorded as having categorically stated.

Nevertheless, Section 5 still confirms that only three witnesses will be granted and "to none else will I grant this power". The emphasised text below identifies the later alterations.

> **5:11.** *And in addition to your testimony,* the testimony of three of my servants, *whom I shall call and ordain, unto whom I will show these things, and they* shall go forth with my words *that are given through you.*
> **12.** Yea, they shall know of a surety that these things are true, for *from heaven will I declare it unto them.*
> **13.** I will give them power that they may behold and view these things as they are;
> **14.** And to none else will I grant this power, (Emphasis added).

As ever, the Lord's anger is kindled against the people.

> **BOC IV:3** And verily I say unto you, that *wo shall come unto the inhabitants of the earth, if they will not hearken my words*, for behold, if they will not believe my words, they would not believe my servant Joseph, if it were possible that he show them all things. O ye unbelieving, *ye stiffnecked generation, mine anger is kindled against you!* (Emphasis added).

This became v.5-8 in the D&C, when it was somewhat expanded. Emphasis below identifies alterations and additions to the original text.

> **5:5.** Verily, I say unto you, that *woe* shall come unto the inhabitants of the earth if they will not hearken unto my words;
> **6.** *For hereafter you shall be ordained and go forth and deliver my words unto the children of men.*
> **7.** Behold, if they will not believe my words, they *will* not believe *you*, my servant Joseph, if it were possible that *you should* show them all *these* things *which I have committed unto you.*
> **8.** Oh, *this* unbelieving *and* stiffnecked generation—mine anger is kindled against *them*. (Emphasis added).

Verse 19 emphasises that God means what He says:

5.19. For a desolating scourge shall go forth among the inhabitants of the earth, and shall continue to be poured out from time to time, if they repent not, until the earth is empty, and the inhabitants thereof are consumed away and utterly destroyed by the brightness of my coming.

In contrast, what God originally supposedly said, which was later adapted to become v.19 above, cannot readily be even recognised as the same message. How could Smith have got it so wrong the first time? The above was originally v.5-6 in the BOC and it read like this:

BOC IV:5. And thus, if the people of this generation harden not their hearts, I will work a reformation among them, and I will put down all lyings, and deceivings, and priestcrafts, and envyings, and strifes, and idolatries, and sorceries, and all manner of iniquities, and I will establish my church, like unto the church which was taught by my disciples in the days of old.
6. And now if this generation do harden their hearts against my word, behold I will deliver them up unto Satan, for he reigneth and hath power at this time, for he hath got great hold upon the hearts of the people of this generation: and not far from the iniquities of Sodom and Gomorrah, do they come at this time: and behold the sword of justice hangeth over their heads, and if they persist in the hardness of their hearts, the time cometh that it must fall upon them.

The latter part of v.5 in the BOC becomes v.20 in the D&C and remains as it was:

5:20. Behold, I tell you these things, even as I also told the people of the destruction of Jerusalem; and my word shall be verified at this time as it hath hitherto been verified.

Whether it was locally, nationally, or globally, God's anger was 'kindled' against those who would not listen to Smith. Woe was going to come, and originally they were to be delivered up to Satan; they were close in their iniquities to Sodom and Gomorrah no less; and the sword of justice would fall on them, just like the destruction of Jerusalem.

When I write my own work, the number of times I review, correct, change, update, rethink and rewrite material, before even bothering my proof readers and editors with it, amounts to dozens. Exchanges with my proof readers lead to even more corrections and considerations before I actually publish. That is quite normal for a human to do, thus ensuring one presents one's thoughts as well as possible. However, **God** *cannot* do the same thing and must get *His* words right first time – after all, He is *God*. Smith *cannot* be a prophet if he

DOCTRINE & COVENANTS – SECTIONS 4-9.

even *once* alters (or has to 'clarify') words claimed to have come *directly* from God. Smith and subsequent leaders of the Mormon Church have altered many first hand words that Smith attributed to God, in the D&C and Book of Mormon – and that is evidence of nothing but *fraud*.

As an aside, the fact that Jerusalem was destroyed by the Babylonians and had nothing to do with God whatsoever seems to escape those involved with believing such prophecies. The Jews considered it to be a result of them being unworthy but in reality it was just another conquest by those currently powerful enough to overrun their neighbours. It had happened many times before and it has since, all around the world, and doesn't look like stopping any time soon. Look at the history of such things and try to define where God stands in it all. His own supposed *chosen* people have never fared very well at all and yet the prophecies continue unabated – this time through Joseph Smith.

The original text claimed it was in "this generation" such destruction would come but there is no validated record anywhere of any such woe coming to anyone, or in fact of God doing *anything* to, or about, any people anywhere who would not listen to Smith's message, regardless of who presented it to them, or for that matter when they received it – from that day to this.

An Ensign article once claimed that people don't realise you *can* edit and *change* revelations. I doubt many Mormons 'realise' that either. What a silly claim this is.

> Because the originals contained spelling and grammar errors, a Church conference moved that Joseph Smith should make the necessary corrections. (Far West Record, p.16.) This was the beginning of controversies and charges made by persons who do not know or understand that the text of recorded revelation can be edited and "changed." *(The Story of the Doctrine and Covenants. Robert J. Woodford. Ensign, Dec 1984, p.32).*

Editing badly recorded words from God is one thing, notwithstanding the fact that Smith should have spoken them perfectly correctly the first time, as he reportedly always spoke them 'slowly and deliberately' so they could easily be recorded by someone in longhand; but to then change them completely, so they meant just the opposite of the original revelation is quite another matter, for which there is *no* plausible explanation and certainly no excuse.

Much of the 'filler' in this section concerns Smith's supposed revelation about Martin Harris which was really just a ploy to get Harris to accept that God had given Smith the plates and that he (Harris) was to witness that he had actually *seen* them – or else. The fact that Harris and the other two of the three witnesses only ever imagined seeing the plates in their minds explains a great deal. All three were later excommunicated from the Church. After leaving the

Church, Harris later confirmed his testimony of Shakerism was actually *greater* than his testimony of Mormonism. People were full of ecstatic imaginings at the time. Despite any claims that have been made and witness statements given, no one ever *physically* saw any gold plates. *(See TMD Vol. 2. Ch. 11)*.

Sections 5 – Summary

Prophecies made:	3
Prophecies fulfilled:	0

Prophecies made:

Pr. 7. Joseph Smith was to have one and only one gift and that was to translate the *Book of Mormon*. He was explicitly to have *no* other gift.

Pr. 8. There would be three witnesses to the *Book of Mormon*. No one else would be granted that power.

Pr. 9. If that generation did not accept Smith's words they would be destroyed.

Results:

Pr. 7. Smith later falsified the original account to make it read that translation was just the first of his gifts, making a liar of God.

Pr. 8. Smith managed to convince eight close family and friends to be further witnesses to the *Book of Mormon* in direct contradiction of words claimed to have come from God.

Pr. 9. A very small percentage of people approached ever joined the Mormon Church. No verifiable evidence exists to confirm God has ever done anything about those who rejected it – either then or now.

Section 6
April 1829. Harmony, Pennsylvania.

History.

1833 BOC Ch. V. 1835 D&C Sec. VIII. 2010 D&C Sec. 6.

DOCTRINE & COVENANTS – SECTIONS 4-9.

Section 6 was a revelation supposedly given to both Joseph Smith and Oliver Cowdery. It was of course a matter of Smith dictating it and Cowdery having to accept what was said. Cowdery had entered Smith's life just a few days earlier and almost immediately started to help Smith with his 'translation' of the Book of Mormon by becoming Smith's scribe. The twenty-two year old was keen and also wanted to do some translating *(see also Sections 8 and 9)*. Cowdery came from a background which included money-digging and using a divining rod. He attended a Congregational church where the Pastor, Ethan Smith, was writing his book *View of the Hebrews*. Ethan's book speculated that Native Americans were of Hebrew origin and the number of similarities that ended up in the Book of Mormon is quite remarkable.

Smith received this revelation in answer to Cowdery's request that the Lord should grant him the gift of translation. Smith may well have liked Cowdery's input regarding Ethan Smith's ideas but wasn't going to let him actually write the manuscript for the Book of Mormon. This revelation plus two later ones gave Smith his 'out' and put Cowdery off with promises that were never kept.

The first few verses of Section 6 may seem strangely familiar. Compare them with Section 4 and you will see what I mean. Here we find God repeating Himself – and as usual, for no worthwhile reason. In addition, we later discover that the first five verses of D&C 6 are the very same as the first five verses of Sections 11, 12 and 14. Minor word variations are shown below **[thus]**.

Sections 6; 11; 12; 14. v.1-5   Section 4. v.1,4,3,7

Sections 6; 11; 12; 14. v.1-5	Section 4. v.1,4,3,7
1. A great and marvelous work is about to come forth unto **[Sec 11, 12 – among]** the children of men.	1. Now behold, a marvelous work is about to come forth among the children of men.
2. Behold, I am God; * give heed unto **[Sec 14 – to]** my word, which is quick and powerful, sharper than a two-edged sword, to the dividing asunder of both joints and marrow; therefore give heed unto my words **[Sec 11, 12, 14 – word]**.	[Section 4 was dictated in February of 1828, before Smith started using the 'two edged sword' idea in revelations. Having invented it, naturally it appears in Sections 11, 12 and 14. If God *did* say all this, why then is it *not* in Sec. 4?]
3. Behold, the field is white already to harvest; therefore, whoso desireth to reap, let him thrust in his sickle with his might, and reap while the day lasts, that he may treasure up for his soul everlasting salvation in the kingdom of God.	4. For behold the field is white already to harvest; and lo, he that thrusteth in his sickle with his might, the same layeth up in store that he perisheth not, but bringeth salvation to his soul;
4. Yea, whosoever will thrust in his sickle and reap, the same is called of God.	3. Therefore, if ye have desires to serve God ye are called to the work;

5. Therefore, if you will ask of me you shall receive; if you will knock it shall be opened unto you.	7. Ask, and ye shall receive; knock, and it shall be opened unto you. Amen.

* In the 1833 BOC and also in the 1835 D&C, the word 'and' appears here in what are now Sections 6, 11, 12 and 14. It is no good apologists arguing that they must have been printer's errors four consecutive times, and it is equally no good claiming God *said* it that way four separate times; it is awful as speech and also written grammar. The word was included on four separate occasions by Smith who claimed *God* was speaking. Subsequently, it has been *removed*. Only Smith could have made up the phrase and then used it continuously; God would have got it right and spoken correctly, the first time – and every time.

God is talking of "two edged swords" and "dividing asunder both joints and marrow". Does that not also sound familiar? It should, as it comes straight from Hebrews 4:12. You could argue that the Lord might have said that if he wanted to, but in Hebrews it was Paul's *description* for the 'word of God' and certainly not something God actually said Himself. In Smith's 'revelation' it is God who is *speaking*. Why would *God* talk about swords and cutting people asunder?

Men would, but it is a bizarre thing to attribute to a God who is supposed to love his children. It is archaic to us but two-thousand years ago it may have had more impact. Smith used fear in his theology from the beginning. He wanted people to believe his revelations were real and to be frightened of not obeying whatever he had God say. At first, many revelations were addressed to specific individuals and were a form of control.

It is only when we analyse what Smith has God *saying* that we can clearly see who was behind the words. Smith has **God** use these words in D&C 6:2.

> **6:2.** Behold, I am God; give heed unto my word, which is quick and powerful, sharper than a two-edged sword, to the dividing asunder of both joints and marrow; therefore give heed unto my word.

Once is bad enough to have God Himself speak in such a manner, but it doesn't end there. Smith wrote Section 6 in April of 1829. He then has God use the *exact* same words again, except the first 'unto' becomes just 'to' in the later versions – in Sections 11:2; 12:2 and 14:2, in May and June of the same year. Smith later also used similar words in Section 33:1, in October of 1830, but had obviously forgotten the exact phrase by then as it became somewhat altered.

After that, he doesn't use it again. If one is considering God actually saying such nonsense, why would he use the phrase a few times and then never again? Once again, it also begs the question why He wouldn't say something a little more worthwhile, not to mention a little less graphic – or so utterly pointless.

DOCTRINE & COVENANTS – SECTIONS 4-9.

God tells Cowdery that he has a sacred gift (v.10) but not to tell anyone who is not a believer. God explains to Cowdery that he will be saved in the kingdom of God (v.13), "If thou wilt do good, yea and hold out faithful to the end". You just need to decide whether you can accept that God would use such a turn of phrase or if it was just Smith making it up as he went along. I can only reiterate that if a God ever did deign to speak to humans, surely he would speak more eloquently – and say something actually useful.

Verse after verse contains meaningless filler intended to placate Cowdery and make him feel reassured and important – God witnesses the work is true and Cowdery is faithfully to 'stand by' Smith – but he *isn't* going to translate.

Note in v.2, we have "Behold, I am God." And in v.21 we have "Behold, I am Jesus Christ, the Son of God." Did the speakers *change* in Smith's head or was it because until the mid 1830s Smith and his followers were monotheistic, meaning God and Jesus were in fact considered to be one and the same being? There is certainly no indication of a change in speaker throughout the Section.

In fact, the concept that they are one and the same is clearly identified by God Himself within the space of three verses.

> **21. Behold, *I am Jesus Christ, the Son of God*.** I am the same that came unto mine own, and mine own received me not. I am the light which shineth in darkness, and the darkness comprehendeth it not.
> **22.** Verily, verily, I say unto you, if you desire a further witness, cast your mind upon the night that you cried unto me in your heart, that you might know concerning the truth of these things.
> **23. *Did I not speak peace to your mind*** concerning the matter? What greater witness can you have than ***from God***? (Emphasis added).

Now, we finally come to some prophecy; God has held back some records "because of the wickedness of the people" which Cowdery will one day translate, but we don't learn which people were actually wicked. The only later records Smith did claim to translate formed the *Book of Abraham*. If they really did get 'held back', if you read the book, you may well wonder why it ever was brought to light, as rather than help matters it completely contradicts known documented Egyptian history and scientific fact by having Egyptus 'discover' Egypt following a fictional flood. Even then, Cowdery did not get to translate.

> **25.** And, behold, ***I grant unto you a gift***, if you desire of me, ***to translate***, even as my servant Joseph.
> **26.** Verily, verily, I say unto you, that there are ***records*** which contain much of my gospel, which have been ***kept back*** because of the wickedness of the people;

27. *... then shall you assist* in bringing to light, **with your gift**, those parts of my scriptures which have been hidden because of iniquity.

The rest of the section is meaningless filler containing the usual warnings and promises of rewards for obedience.

Sections 6 – Summary

Prophecies made: 1
Prophecies fulfilled: 0

Prophecies made:

Pr. 10. Oliver Cowdery was promised he would translate records that had thus far been kept back because of the wickedness of the people.

Results:

Pr. 10. No records of any kind were ever translated by Oliver Cowdery.

Section 7
April 1829. Harmony, Pennsylvania.

History.

1833 BOC Ch. VI. 1835 D&C Sec. XXXIII. 2010 D&C Sec. 7.

This section is dealt with in *TMD Vol. 3:287-292 (S7-12)* and is also mentioned in *Vol 4:119*. Considering it was supposedly written on parchment by the apostle John himself, it is amazing that the original 1833 BOC text was altered significantly in the 1835 D&C and also that further words were added even later. How could something that someone personally wrote down *ever* change? The text does contain a prophecy of sorts, so it is included here; not because there is any reason to believe John actually recorded such nonsense but because Smith *claimed* he did and therefore Smith is *responsible* for the outcome.

Smith saw this, according to the modern D&C header, via the Urim and Thummim, although the original BOC version makes no such claim.

2. ...give unto me power over death, that I may live and bring souls unto thee.

DOCTRINE & COVENANTS – SECTIONS 4-9.

3. And the Lord said unto me: Verily, verily, I say unto thee, because thou desirest this thou shalt tarry until I come in my glory, and shalt prophesy before nations, kindreds, tongues and people.

Obviously John could not have been actively 'bringing souls' to God before the time of Joseph Smith, theologically speaking, as according to Mormon doctrine, the gospel was absent from the Earth due to apostasy and a restoration was required – hence Smith's calling. Thus we need to see evidence of John's involvement in such things *after* 1829 when Smith made the claim. Did John ever bring anyone to God? Did he ever "prophesy before nations, kindreds, tongues and people"? No, he did not. The fact is that *if* John lived, then he died almost two thousand years ago. The concept of John living until the Saviour returns is actually a misunderstanding of the New Testament text which meant something else entirely. Smith just capitalised on the idea and used it for effect.

Sections 7 – Summary

Total number of verses:	8 (Originally only three).

Prophecies made:	1
Prophecies fulfilled:	0

Prophecies made:

Pr. 11. Apostle John would live until Christ returns, bring souls to him and would prophesy before nations, kindreds, tongues and people.

Results:

Pr. 11. The apostle, John, has never been recorded and evidenced as having survived beyond his own time period nor has he prophesied before anyone, anywhere, ever.

Section 8
April 1829. Harmony, Pennsylvania.

History.

1833 BOC Ch. VII. 1835 D&C Sec. XXXIV. 2010 D&C Sec. 8.

THE MORMON DELUSION

Section 8 is more fully analysed in *TMD 3:314-17 (S12-16)* and also mentioned in *Vol. 4:273*. Once again, this is God, through Smith to Oliver Cowdery and of course, as Mormons, we just accepted that this is the way God *speaks*:

> **1.** …you shall receive a knowledge concerning the engravings of old records, which are ancient, which contain those parts of my scripture of which has been spoken…

Why would a *God* say "old records, which are ancient?" Obviously, He wouldn't. Thus we immediately know what is going on here. Smith actually has the Lord explain to Cowdery how revelation is given. This is frightening, as it shows how the minds of men can concoct anything they like and actually come to believe, or at least convince others to believe, that it was God who was responsible for their *thoughts*. Revelation from God – is formed in the *mind*. But then, that is exactly what the recent Mormon prophet, Gordon B. Hinckley confirmed, so we should not be too surprised *(see p. xiv)*.

> **2.** Yea, behold, I will tell you in your mind and in your heart, by the Holy Ghost, which shall come upon you and which shall dwell in your heart.
> **3.** Now, behold, this is the spirit of revelation;

The technique that Smith used to achieve his 'translation' is very disturbing indeed. The 'method' is further elaborated on and explained in the next Section *(9:8)* below.

Smith continues by telling Cowdery that this is the spirit of revelation, just as with Moses and the Red Sea. Smith was fond of that story and he repeated it several times in the *Book of Mormon* – despite the fact that extremely detailed Egyptian history and extensive archaeology in the Sinai has long proven the whole concept to be just a fable; the Israelite nation never was in Egypt and did not cross the Red Sea or wander in the wilderness of the Sinai for forty years.

Cowdery had used a divining rod before his association with Smith. Both Smith and Cowdery were very familiar with and practitioners of occult or folk magic techniques and both firmly believed in them. Thus the Mormon God was also obliged to do so, and next, Smith has the Lord endorse Cowdery's use of his divining rod. Incidentally, for those who may have missed the point in my earlier work, on 28 July 1847, Brigham Young chose the location of the Salt Lake temple by using Oliver Cowdery's divining rod. They don't teach that in Mormon Sunday School lessons.

Naturally, as time passed and human intelligence evolved, the era of folk magic became not only a thing of the past but also one of embarrassment to the Church. It would be obvious to modern day Mormons that God would not have embraced the occult in any of his revelatory processes, yet in Smith's day God had no choice in the matter.

After telling Cowdery that he has the gift of translation and that for some reason, that gift "shall deliver you out of the hands of your enemies" (v.4) and without it they would "slay" him – and I am still not sure how that works – God tells Cowdery that he has another gift. It is the gift of being able to use his divining rod. Such rods are used to give yes-no answers to questions, or they will supposedly 'dip' when locating something underground, such as water or treasure. Originally, the revelation was straight forward and Cowdery was told that his gift was "working with the rod" and God calls it "this rod of nature", referring to a common forked witch-hazel twig, and "therefore whatsoever you shall ask me to tell you by that means, that will I grant unto you". *(BOC 7:3).*

Today, this will not do at all for the Church and the Mormon God cannot possibly be associated with the occult. They can't change history of course but they can obfuscate the truth of it. The *D&C* today mentions "the gift of Aaron" – twice, in order that members will *assume* it to be a simple straight rod or staff and not associate it with the occult. All references to "the rod" and "gift of nature" have been **deleted**. God's own words have been *falsified*. However, they neglect to advise us how "whatsoever you shall ask me to tell you by that means, that will I grant unto you" can ever be associated with a straight staff. Cowdery is not recorded anywhere as ever having used one of those.

The final verse gets back to Cowdery's first gift and reinforces the promise.

> **11.** Ask that you may know the mysteries of God, and that *you may translate and receive knowledge from all those ancient records* which have been hid up, that are sacred; and according to your faith shall it be done unto you. (Emphasis added).

Apart from the Book of Abraham, we never learn what the rest of "all those ancient records" are, and Cowdery never did get to translate anything at all.

Sections 8 – Summary

Prophecies made:	1
Prophecies fulfilled:	0
Other non-prophetic revelation:	1.

Prophecies made:

Pr. 12. Cowdery is again promised that he will "translate and receive knowledge from all those ancient records which have been hid up."

Results:

Pr. 12. No records of any kind were ever translated by Oliver Cowdery.

Non-prophetic revelation: 1

1. Divining rods were approved by the Lord.

Section 9
April 1829. Harmony, Pennsylvania.

History.

1833 BOC Ch. VIII. 1835 D&C Sec. XXXV. 2010 D&C Sec. 9.

Section 9 is analysed in *TMD Vol. 3:293-5. (S16-18)* in terms of translation and technique. It is also mentioned in *Vol. 4:59-60*. I will deal here with Smith's *third* repetition of the Cowdery 'prophecy'. It becomes obvious from the start of this section that Cowdery had been pestering Joseph Smith all month as he wanted to do some translating himself. Sections 6-9 were all 'received' in April of 1829, the very month in which Smith first met Cowdery, who just two days after their first encounter started working as Smith's scribe.

It becomes clear in the very first verse that Smith was fed up with being asked and he wanted to write the Book of Mormon manuscript himself. Smith had obviously got to a stage where he just told Cowdery to try translating so he could then inform him the translation was entirely erroneous and thus keep him in his place. After all, how would Cowdery know if his ideas were correct or not? Only Smith could decide the matter and clearly he was having none it.

> **1.** Behold, I say unto you, my son, that because you did not translate according to that which you desired of me, and did commence again to write for my servant, Joseph Smith, Jun., even so I would that ye should continue until you have finished this record, which I have entrusted unto him.
> **2.** And then, behold, *other records have I, that I will give unto you power that you may assist to translate.*
> **3.** Be patient, my son, for it is wisdom in me, and *it is not expedient that you should translate at this present time.*
> **4.** Behold, the work which you are called to do is to write for my servant Joseph.

DOCTRINE & COVENANTS – SECTIONS 4-9.

> **5.** And, behold, it is *because that you did not continue as you commenced, when you began to translate, that I have taken away this privilege from you.*
> **6.** Do not murmur, my son, for it is wisdom in me that I have dealt with you after this manner. (Emphasis added).

Smith thus convinced Cowdery to keep going as scribe, yet again promising him that later he would be given other records to translate. Of course, it never happened. There was little that Cowdery could say or do, unless he questioned Smith's own revelatory powers, as Smith had God Himself tell Cowdery not to complain about it in v.6 – Clever!

Smith then has God describe the process of translation; you make it up in your head and then if you get excited about it, you ask God – and if it is right God will make you 'feel' that it is. It is that simple. If the idea is not so good, you lose interest and forget about it, and then it was wrong. The clincher is that had Cowdery known all this *before* he tried to translate, he would have been able to do it, but unfortunately for him neither God nor Smith bothered to tell him.

> **8.** But, behold, I say unto you, that *you must study it out in your mind*; then you must *ask me if it be right*, and if it is right I will cause that *your bosom shall burn* within you; therefore, you shall *feel that it is right.*
> **9.** But if it be not right you shall have no such feelings, but you shall have *a stupor of thought that shall cause you to forget* the thing which is wrong; *therefore, you cannot write that which is sacred save it be given you from me.*
> **10.** Now, *if you had known this you could have translated*; nevertheless, it is not expedient that you should translate now.
> **11.** Behold, it was expedient when you commenced; but you feared, and the time is past, and it is not expedient now;

Incidentally, the Mormon Church uses this so-called scripture entirely out of context today to convince Church members that they need to use the same technique when asking God for anything. What is the point in having a God who knows everything if our finite minds have to figure things out anyway?

God concludes his chastisement of Cowdery by explaining it *was* expedient that he translated but now it *isn't*. He doesn't explain why, and Smith is of no help either. The entire episode between Sections 6 through 9 had covered less than four weeks. Cowdery gave up asking and continued to be scribe. Verse 12 goes on to say "For, do you not behold that I have given unto my servant

Joseph sufficient strength, whereby it is made up?" Certainly, Smith must have meant he had sufficient strength to make up any shortfall caused by Cowdery's inability, but it is ironic that it can also be read as if to say Smith had enough strength to make up the story all by himself – which he obviously did.

Section 9 – Summary

Prophecies made: 1
Prophecies fulfilled: 0

Prophecies made:

Pr. 13. Cowdery is promised for the third time "other records have I, that I will give unto you power that you may assist to translate "

Results:

Pr. 13. No records of any kind were ever translated by Oliver Cowdery.

****

As ever, this Section is full of obvious early modern English errors. Several appear in the verses appearing on *pp. 120-21* above. I am not a linguist and will not try to explain them but would instead refer the reader to Richard Packham's excellent work in this area. A link to his web site appears below.

> The English of 1611 had its grammatical rules, many of which were quite different from the grammatical rules of modern English. Although they were not always as strictly observed by the English of that time, there was not a lot of latitude. Many usages we now consider "correct English" were barely coming into use then, and were thus "incorrect." For example, "thou" "thee," "thy," and "thine" were used to refer only to the single (singular) person being addressed; "ye," "you," "your" and "yours" were used only when addressing more than one person, or a person to whom great respect was due. ("Ye" was the subject form, "you" the object form.) They were not interchangeable, any more than "I" and "we" are interchangeable in modern English. Nor were "ye" and "you" interchangeable, any more than "they" and "them." *(Richard Packham. See:* http://packham.n4m.org/linguist.htm *).*

See also *The Final Analysis. Part 3 (particularly p. 496).*

Chapter 12

**Doctrine and Covenants
Sections 11 – 18**

Section 11
May 1829. Harmony, Pennsylvania.

History.

1833 BOC Ch. X. 1835 D&C Sec. XXXVII. 2010 D&C Sec. 11.

This revelation was 'received' for Joseph Smith's brother Hyrum. The first few verses in which *God* declares *He* is speaking were discussed on pp. 113-4 as they are the same as several other sections. Following them are several verses of filler, intended to sound like *Jesus* is actually speaking to Hyrum. I will summarise them in order to give an idea of just what Smith claimed the Lord spoke about. There are many similar chunks of filler in other Sections that will not always be covered as they serve no purpose whatsoever. Hyrum is told to keep the commandments, not to seek for riches but rather for wisdom; desires will be granted; teach repentance; two more mentions of keeping commandments; he has a gift – or at least he will have if he asks; trust, do justly, walk humbly, judge righteously – and that is "my spirit".

Next, God/Jesus is going to enlighten Hyrum's mind – which will fill his soul with joy; he is not to suppose that he is called to preach until he is called, so wait a little longer; a *fourth* 'keep the commandments' – as if he needed reminding yet again; hold his peace; appeal to God's spirit and cleave unto Him with his heart that he may assist with the translation. It doesn't say exactly *how* he will assist in that. Perhaps Joseph was lining Hyrum up to be another scribe, as he certainly never allowed him to try translating anything. Yet God did apparently say regarding "…the translation of my work; be patient until **you** shall accomplish it" but I am not counting that as a *prophecy* as such, as the context is too ambiguous. Either way, it remained unfulfilled.

Hyrum is to keep the commandments – for a *fifth* time – but this time with all his "might mind and strength". Perhaps God/Jesus forgot to mention that on the four earlier occasions. He must seek God's word before he declares it, hold his peace, and study.

Then Hyrum is reminded what his name is, "Behold, thou art Hyrum" – as if he didn't already know that; he is Jesus' son; seek the kingdom of God and "all things will be added". Note the carrot – and then wait for the stick. He is to build the gospel, not deny the spirit of revelation or prophecy, for "wo unto him that denieth these things". There's the inevitable stick. There is always a stick following the carrot in Smith's revelations.

Finally, Hyrum is to treasure up in his heart… but it doesn't say *what* he is to treasure up, until Jesus decides it is time for Hyrum to 'go forth'. The text then confirms it is Jesus speaking and that when he came to his own they didn't receive him, but now those who believe can become sons of God. That's it; nothing of any merit; no revelation and no prophecy. It is just the same type of rambling that today appears in many patriarchal blessings, when the speaker makes up things in his head that could be applied to almost anyone. It is a pointless exercise and there are many other D&C 'revelations' just like it. It was however, good practice for Smith whose revelatory 'skills' were still being honed. He soon learned to expand and amplify 'revelations' into more complex and prophetic material. Such excursions would be his undoing in terms of exposing him as a fraud. Uncannily, as a believer, you simply don't see it. You first have to step outside the box and look in, when it all becomes perfectly clear.

You also don't notice Smith constantly changing between God and Jesus as the 'voice'. Sometimes, Smith even confirms they are one and the same being. It didn't seem to occur to Smith that individual identification might one day be needed. His theology was yet to evolve and change into polytheism. *(See: The Final Analysis. Part 4: Who Am I; God, Jesus – Or Both?).*

No summary is needed for this section; it contains nothing but meaningless filler.

DOCTRINE & COVENANTS – SECTIONS 11-18

Section 12. May, 1829. Harmony, Pennsylvania.
Sections 14, 15 & 16. June, 1829. Harmony, Pennsylvania.

History.

1833 BOC Ch. XI. 1835 D&C Sec. XXXVIII. 2010 D&C Sec. 12.
1833 BOC Ch. XII. 1835 D&C Sec. XXXIX. 2010 D&C Sec. 14.
1833 BOC Ch. XIII. 1835 D&C Sec. XL. 2010 D&C Sec. 15.
1833 BOC Ch. XIV. 1835 D&C Sec. XLI. 2010 D&C Sec. 16.

Section 12 is directed to Joseph Knight Sr. The reason it was given was that Knight believed Smith had the gold plates and was actually translating them. This led him to help so Smith could look after his family and continue the work and then Knight asked for his own revelation. He didn't get much of anything compared with Hyrum's Section 11. Once again, the first five verses were dealt with on pp. 113-4. There are only four further verses. This time, Smith seems in a hurry to oblige and doesn't bother to say much.

Naturally, just as Hyrum was reminded no less than five times, Knight is told "as you have asked" – he is to keep the commandments. He is to help bring forth the cause of Zion; in other words, to keep giving Smith money. No one can assist unless they are humble, full of love, faith, hope and charity, and temperate. The final verse (9) says it all really, both in terms of the way Jesus is claimed to have spoken – and what he says. Pointless – and very obviously not remotely close to any words that would ever emanate from deity.

> **9.** Behold, I am the light and the life of the world, that speak these words, therefore give heed with your might, and then you are called. Amen.

Needless to say, there is no comment or summary needed for this non-revelation.

Likewise, Section 14 to David Whitmer – which is similar to Section 12. *(See also TMD Vol. 4:220).* Section 15, to John Whitmer and 16, to Peter Whitmer Jr., are *identical*, with the exception of one word (unto) added into the latter. All were 'received' during May and June of 1829 and contain nothing but filler that anyone could make up. It is interesting to note that here Smith gives two separate yet identical revelations to two different people. Later we will review a more important revelation where, when the person to whom it was directed did not do as predicted, a year later the name was *removed* and replaced with someone else's name instead. *New* revelation was required – but *not* provided.

125

As faithful members, Melchizedek Priesthood holders will often give 'blessings' by laying on of hands, and leaders also 'set apart' people for new callings and pronounce blessings, in modern-day terms, containing very similar nonsense that could apply to anyone, and consider the Lord is prompting them in what to say. I know; I did such things myself hundreds of times. Inside, you always knew you were trying to think of suitable things to say and convince yourself that the Lord was inspiring you with the right words. The faithful will invariably state that is not the case and that an apostate would naturally have to claim such a thing in order to justify his lack of faith.

However, when promises are made so many times that remain unfulfilled and when people die rather than live as promised, and even live, when they are told they are actually going to die – something my own mother experienced when she was ill, more than two decades before she actually did pass on – then you start to put together the underlying reality. My family was extremely upset to think my mother would not survive what was essentially a bad case of flu. Of course, our prayers saved her, theologically speaking, but the person who was 'voice' proclaimed to the family, following the blessing, that the Lord had revealed to him she would not survive her illness. Imagination is a marvellous, often meaningless and sometimes even very distressing thing.

Section 13
15 May 1829. Harmony, Pennsylvania.

History.

This Section was first added to the D&C in 1876. 2010 D&C Sec. 13.

Section 13 is more fully dealt with in *TMD Vol. 4:111-17. (S18-24)*. It contains just one verse and is essentially an afterthought, written many years after the claimed event and backdated to 1829. It is reminiscent of Smith's treatment of the First Vision, written in 1838 and backdated to 1820.

In summary, this is the underlying story. In order to set the scene, the 'Introduction' to the *D&C* explains that the Aaronic Priesthood was conferred by John the Baptist in May [15th] 1829 and refers the reader directly to Section 13. It then states that the Melchizedek Priesthood was later conferred by Peter, James and John *(see D&C 27:12)*. It goes on to claim that other 'ordinations' followed, in which priesthood 'keys' were conferred by Moses, Elijah, Elias, and 'many ancient prophets'. These are mentioned in the Introduction because you will be very hard pressed to find any specific evidence of dates or details concerning restoration of priesthood anywhere else in the D&C. It references Sections 110; 128:18 & 21, which we looked at when considering Section 2 in

Chapter 9. We will discover an astounding discrepancy regarding the Peter, James and John claim when we review Section 27.

Meanwhile, just to remind the reader, this is all that Section 13 contains.

> **1.** Upon you my fellow servants, in the name of Messiah I confer the Priesthood of Aaron, which holds the keys of the ministering of angels, and of the gospel of repentance, and of baptism by immersion for the remission of sins; and this shall never be taken again from the earth, until the sons of Levi do offer again an offering unto the Lord in righteousness.

The introduction to this Section is actually longer than the verse. There is no prophecy as such, but out of interest I will just mention that not included in *TMD Vol. 4* is the fact that the first time this ordination was even mentioned was when it was published in the Times and Seasons in 1842, thirteen years after the supposed event. It was in fact *exactly* the same scenario as with the First Vision. It just *appeared* many years later and was conveniently backdated for effect.

Section 18
June 1829. Fayette, New York.

History.

1833 BOC Ch. XV. 1835 D&C Sec. XLIII. 2010 D&C Sec. 18.

This section extends to forty-seven verses and is designated for Joseph Smith, Oliver Cowdery and David Whitmer. Jesus is speaking and once again, in the final verse, confirms that he is "Jesus Christ, your **Lord and your God, and your Redeemer**..." as Smith is still of course in full early monotheistic mode.

Jesus first speaks to Oliver Cowdery; the things he has written are true and Cowdery is to rely on them. Jesus goes on to claim (v.4) "in them are all things written concerning the foundation of my church, my gospel, and my rock." In fact, there is little of anything in the Book of Mormon remotely related to the Mormon 'gospel' at all, let alone "all things" as Smith has Jesus himself here declare. Cowdery is to build up the Church and not 'marvel' that Joseph has been called – then at the end of v.8, Jesus tells Oliver that "his name is Joseph" (referring to Smith), but he already said that it was Joseph in v.7 so it is really a stretch to accept that Jesus was speaking these words and repeating himself for no reason. There is nothing but filler here but just to review what Smith claims the Saviour is actually saying:

7. Wherefore, as thou hast been baptized by the hands of my servant Joseph Smith, Jun., according to that which I have commanded him, he hath fulfilled the thing which I commanded him.
8. And now, marvel not that I have called him unto mine own purpose, which purpose is known in me; wherefore, if he shall be diligent in keeping my commandments he shall be blessed unto eternal life; and his name is Joseph.

Of all the things you could think of that Jesus could or would bother to reveal to humans, if he actually did decide to communicate… is this the best he can do? We have to step back from the delusion and look at what Joseph Smith is claiming Jesus Christ himself is actually *saying*. Jesus' purpose is known to himself and Joseph's name is Joseph. The *manner* of speech is also appalling.

The Section continues with a message, which from this point on is for Cowdery and also for Whitmer. They are both to 'cry repentance' and endure to the end, among many other things that are now a common theme in these so-called revelations – all of which are meaningless and could be applied to anyone who wishes to believe Jesus is actually instructing them as individuals. Verse 9 states "I speak unto you, even as unto Paul mine apostle, for you are called even with that same calling with which he was called" yet there is no record that either man was ever ordained as an apostle.

There is no specific detail worthy of further consideration until we reach v.25 where it says "Behold, Jesus Christ is the name which is given of the Father…" In fact, it really isn't, and Jesus would *not* have claimed that. The name 'Jesus' and also the title 'Christ' are English words derived from Greek constructs that were *invented* by humans *after* the Christ had lived. If he lived, Jesus' actual name was 'Yeshua', the original Aramaic proper name for 'Jesus the Nazarene'. The word 'Jesus' is actually a mis-transliteration of a Greek mis-transliteration. The Emperor Constantine even mistook Jesus for Apollo, the son of the Greek god Zeus. In Hebrew, Yeshua means Salvation while the name Jesus has no intrinsic meaning in English at all. See this link for more information. http://www.thenazareneway.com/yeshua_jesus_real_name.htm

God did *not* give the name 'Jesus' – ever. There were other names and titles for a Messiah used in the Old Testament – but not those, and they were not *given* by God – they were the invention (and mistranslations) of *men*. Christ would of course know that, but Smith did not think it through.

Cowdery and Whitmer are charged with the task of *finding* twelve apostles who will go into all the world to preach the gospel. In v.31, Jesus then actually speaks *to* the twelve – who have yet to be located and converted. At first, it appears quite strange that Jesus didn't wait until he had twelve men to talk to directly. Then we discover that Smith wanted Cowdery and Whitmer to use this 'revelation' in order to show and convince twelve men to take up the cause and in v.39 he confirms his ploy. "And when you have *found* them you shall show these things unto them." Smith has Jesus commit to this and as such it can be considered a prophecy. Jesus should have known whether or not the two were going to fulfil his requirement to find and convert twelve future apostles.

There isn't space here to provide a complete analysis of who was called and when or what became of them all and it is not the main subject matter of this volume, but as this is effectively a prophecy, a short summary is provided on page 131. Suffice it to say at this point that it was June of 1829 and the Church was organised in April 1830. Ten apostles were eventually *called* in February 1835 but whilst they may have been then *ordained* by the three witnesses, they had certainly not been 'found' or *converted* by Cowdery or Whitmer. A further apostle was called in April and then Thomas B. Marsh was called in May. He was thought to have been the oldest and thus he presided.

These days, the last apostle to be called would never preside. It is always the longest serving apostle who presides and then, assuming he remains alive, he becomes the next president of the Church by default; something that has become known as the 'law of apostolic succession'; although that is technically not set in stone and someone outside the quorum could theoretically be called, although no one ever has been. Thus the Church is always headed by aged men who often become incapable of running the show long before they die.

By 1838, several apostles started to be excommunicated and new ones called. *(See TMD Vol. 1. Appendix N, for calls, releases and excommunications of early apostles and other leaders).*

When Smith's Kirtland Safety Society bank predictably collapsed, he and Sidney Rigdon fled to Far West as they were being chased down by creditors and writs were issued for tens of thousands of dollars in compensation and interest by non-Mormons *(see pp. 391-3).* Members would not dare to go to law over such things – they were dealt with by the High Council but no one ever complained against Smith to one of those as they would never have survived if they did.

Smith's departure left many Mormons bereft of everything they had owned when the bank went under. Whitmer was presiding over the Church in Kirtland at the time and he and his counsellors (his brother John Whitmer and W.W. Phelps) were involved in a leadership struggle and excommunicated – along with Oliver Cowdery, Martin Harris and many others.

The Whitmers and others who became branded 'dissenters' owned a lot of property in Caldwell County but the 'Danites' (a secret band, organised to take care of such dissenters) acted under a public call from the presidency to expel them from the county. Having been warned to "depart or a more fatal calamity shall befall you" the Whitmers fled to Richmond in fear of their lives. *(See TMD Vol. 3:42-44 for more details of Smith's Kirtland bank fraud and how the Mormon Church lied about it in their 2008 Priesthood Manual).*

Verse 33 confirms – for the umpteenth time, that Jesus *is* God. "And I, Jesus Christ, your Lord and your God, have spoken it." Smith then follows this monotheistic statement with an incredible piece of psychology. It is difficult to believe that anyone fell for this when you read it and *think* about it.

> **34.** These words are not of men nor of man, but of me; wherefore, you shall testify they are of me and not of man;
> **35.** For it is my voice which speaketh them unto you; for they are given by my Spirit unto you, and by my power you can read them one to another; and save it were by my power you could not have them;
> **36.** Wherefore, you can testify that you have heard my voice, and know my words.

Smith is trying to convince the twelve before they have even been located, and also Cowdery and Whitmer of course, that because they can *read* the words that he (Smith) has written down, which he *claims* were directly from Jesus – they can 'testify' that they have actually *heard* the voice of the Lord. What a confidence trick this is. It goes hand in hand with Smith's earlier promise, which was again supposedly from Jesus, that the three witnesses would 'see' the gold plates with their *eyes* when ultimately they only ever imagined such a thing in their minds. No one ever really saw or heard anything as there was nothing to see or hear. Clearly, no God was involved with any of this.

There is more repetition of the same things yet again before the final verse (47) reconfirms who Jesus is: "Behold, I, Jesus Christ, your Lord and your God, and your Redeemer, by the power of my Spirit have spoken it. Amen." So, Jesus *is* **God and** *the redeemer*, and yet for some reason needs the 'power' of his own spirit in order to speak about it. It confirms Smith's monotheism once again, but this is supposedly Jesus *speaking* and yet the sentence makes little if any sense.

Sections 18 – Summary

Prophecies made:	1
Prophecies fulfilled:	0
Other non-prophetic revelation:	1

Prophecies made:

Pr. 14. June 1829: "Oliver Cowdery, and also ... David Whitmer ... you shall search out the Twelve ... And when you have found them you shall show these things unto them."

DOCTRINE & COVENANTS – SECTIONS 11-18

Results:

Pr. 14. Oliver Cowdery and David Whitmer did not search out, show, or convert a single one of the original twelve apostles.

1. Brigham Young – baptised 14 April 1832 by Eleazer Miller.
2. Heber C. Kimball – baptised April 1832 by Alpheus Gifford.
3. Lyman E. Johnson – on 12 Sept 1831, Joseph and Emma Smith moved in with the Johnson's. A month later Lyman was ordained an elder and then a high priest.
4. David W. Patten – baptised by his brother John. Killed 25 Oct 1838 at the battle of Crooked River.
5. Orson Hyde – baptised by his former minister, Sidney Rigdon, 30 October 1831.
6. Luke S. Johnson – baptised 10 May 1831 by Joseph Smith.
7. William E. McLellin – baptised in 1831 by Hyrum Smith.
8. William B. Smith – Joseph Smith's brother - baptised 9 June 1830 by David Whitmer, but it could hardly be claimed Whitmer 'found and converted' William who was involved with his brother's religion long before Whitmer came along.
9. John F. Boynton – baptised Sept 1832 by Joseph Smith.
10. Parley P. Pratt – baptised about 1 Sept 1830 by Oliver Cowdery, but not found or Converted by him. Parley had read a copy of the Book of Mormon owned by a Baptist deacon; he travelled to Palmyra and spoke with Hyrum Smith. Cowdery just happened to be the one to baptise Parley.
11. Orson Pratt – baptised 19 September 1830 by his brother Parley.
12. Thomas B. Marsh – baptized by David Whitmer but not found or converted by him. A woman had told Marsh about the gold plates and Marsh went to Palmyra and met Martin Harris. After obtaining a copy of the first sixteen pages of the printer's proof of the Book of Mormon, Marsh corresponded with Smith and Cowdery. Far from discovering and converting Marsh, Whitmer just happened to be the one to baptise him.

Non-prophetic revelation.   1.

1. Referring to the pages of the Book of Mormon, Smith has Jesus claim (v.4) "in them are **all things** written concerning the foundation of my church, my gospel, and my rock." (Emphasis added).

In fact, there is little of *anything* in the *Book of Mormon* remotely related to the Mormon 'gospel' at all, let alone "all things" as Smith has Jesus himself here declare. This is a *false* revelation.

Section 17
June 1829. Fayette, New York.

History.

Not in the 1833 BOC. 1835 D&C Sec. XLII. 2010 D&C Sec. 17.

This was to be the last revelation of 1829; the next was given some nine months later, in March of 1830, just before the Church was formally organised.

The heading to Section 17 says it all really. This is a 'revelation' given to Oliver Cowdery, David Whitmer and Martin Harris. As with several other revelations, before the Lord apparently confiscated Smith's seer stones, this is 'given' via the Urim and Thummim, which means that Smith did not hear the Lord's voice, he saw the words in his hat. Later, such revelations were received through the same 'pebble in the hat' method when Smith reverted to the stone he had found in the Chase family well in his money digging days. There is no record of Smith ever translating using the so-called 'spectacles' type frame which is described as being far too wide for human use. Why then did it exist? God confiscated the Urim and Thummim following Smith's loss of 116 pages containing the Book of Lehi. Why would he do that?

We are informed that Joseph Smith and Oliver Cowdery had 'learned' from the translation of the *Book of Mormon* that three special witnesses would be designated. It is not surprising that once Smith had set the scene, Cowdery, Whitmer and the ever gullible Harris, all effectively acted like excited school children raising their hands and calling out 'pick me, pick me'. Smith asks Jesus if they can be the three witnesses and Section 17 is the response.

First, they are informed (v.1) that they must "rely upon my word" and then they will be shown the gold plates, the breastplate, the sword of Laban, the Urim and Thummim and the "miraculous directors" (Liahona) given to Lehi.

Clearly, they had so far not actually seen the Urim and Thummim Smith was using to translate or to receive this divine communication. Next, they are informed that when their faith is strong enough such that they have seen these things, they will then testify about them. They are to do this: "that my servant Joseph Smith, Jun., may not be destroyed" (v.4). This the three dutifully did; the "Testimony of Three Witnesses" is recorded in the Book of Mormon – and yet Smith *was* destroyed, despite the fact that Jesus himself declared that if they so testified, he would *not* be. At least, that's what Smith claimed Jesus said.

They are instructed that after they "have seen them **with your eyes**" (v.3), "ye shall testify that you have seen them, even as my servant Joseph Smith, Jun., has seen them" (v.5) and yet ultimately the three witnesses only ever 'saw' the plates in their imaginations and never did view, let alone handle, any physical plates. If the plates actually existed, then Joseph Smith clearly did see and handle them as claimed, thus that prophecy did *not* come to pass.

All three Book of Mormon witnesses, including his *ordained* successor, David Whitmer, were considered (just eight years later) by Joseph Smith as "…too mean to mention, and we had liked to have forgotten them." *(HC Vol. 3:332).* All three of them were excommunicated from the Church and all three confirmed that they did *not* physically see any plates at all. It was all a matter of vivid (and desired) imagination. In other words, it was just wishful thinking on their part. *(See Appendix A: Letter III extract; also TMD Vol. 2:168-172).*

Once again they are reminded that they must have faith – the same as Smith – and are told the gates of hell will not prevail against them if they "do these last commandments of mine" (v.8) – but there are no "last commandments" given. Today, that is cross referenced to *D&C 19:13* which just says to repent and keep the commandments. Finally, once again, Smith in full monotheistic mode (as this was 1829) has Jesus confirm "I, Jesus Christ, your Lord and **your God**, have spoken it unto you…"

Sections 17 – Summary

Prophecies made:	2
Prophecies fulfilled:	0
Other non-prophetic revelation:	1

Prophecies made:

Pr. 15. The three witnesses were promised that they would physically *see* the gold plates, even as Joseph Smith had seen them.

Pr. 16. Joseph Smith was not to be destroyed if the three witnesses had faith and testified that they had *seen* the gold plates.

Results:

Pr. 15. If the gold plates existed, Smith physically saw and handled them. The three witnesses only ever *imagined* them in their minds.

Pr. 16. In spite of the witnesses dutifully testifying, Joseph Smith *was* destroyed. He was shot dead in June 1844, leaving the Church in disarray and confusion, creating a succession crisis which resulted in several schisms.

THE MORMON DELUSION

Non-prophetic revelation.

17:6. And he has translated the book, even that part which I have commanded him, and *as your Lord and your God liveth it is true.* (Emphasis added).

Here, Joseph Smith is having Jesus Christ *personally* claim the Book of Mormon to be true. Conclusive evidence concerning every imaginable aspect of the book confirms that it most certainly is *not* true by any stretch of the imagination. It remains true only for those embracing and choosing to remain in a deep seated delusional state. *(See: TMD Vol. 2: Chs. 9, 11-13, 15-16).*

This was the last revelation of 1829 – given in June; the next one was to be in March of 1830.

Chapter 13

Doctrine and Covenants
Sections 19 – 29

Section 19
March 1830. Manchester, New York.

History.

1833 BOC Ch. XVI. 1835 D&C Sec. XLIV. 2010 D&C Sec. 19.

Section 19 is introduced in *History of the Church* as "a commandment of **God** and not of man, to Martin Harris, given by him who is Eternal" *(HC 1:72)*. Christ once again is speaking and immediately says so:

> **1.** I am Alpha and Omega, Christ the Lord; yea, even I am he, the beginning and the end, the Redeemer of the world.

In v.4, Jesus confirms two things; men must repent or suffer and that ***he* IS God**.

> **4.** And surely every man must repent or suffer, for I, God, am endless.

I think that what follows is one of the reasons why I shied away from the D&C as a Mormon. It is completely unbelievable that any God would provide such a tenuous link (if indeed there is any at all) as 'feelings' in confirmation of His existence and expectations and yet promise torment (endless or not) for anyone who does not repent and follow someone who claims to represent Him.

Reading the next few verses slowly and carefully does not support the concept that they came as a direct revelation from the God of this planet – they smack purely and simply of one man's attempt to frighten people into doing what he claimed God wanted them to do. Smith tries once again to look clever by 'explaining' *endless*.

> **5.** Wherefore, I revoke not the judgments which I shall pass, but woes shall go forth, weeping, wailing and gnashing of teeth, yea, to those who are found on my left hand.
> **6.** Nevertheless, it is not written that there shall be no end to this torment, but it is written *endless torment*.
> **7.** Again, it is written *eternal damnation;* wherefore it is more express than other scriptures, that it might work upon the hearts of the children of men, altogether for my name's glory.
> **8.** Wherefore, I will explain unto you this mystery, for it is meet unto you to know even as mine apostles.
> **9.** I speak unto you that are chosen in this thing, even as one, that you may enter into my rest.
> **10.** For, behold, the mystery of godliness, how great is it! For, behold, I am endless, and the punishment which is given from my hand is endless punishment, for Endless is my name. Wherefore—
> **11.** *Eternal punishment is God's punishment.*
> **12.** *Endless punishment is God's punishment.*
> **13.** Wherefore, I command you to repent, and keep the commandments which you have received by the hand of my servant Joseph Smith, Jun., in my name;
> **14.** And it is by my almighty power that you have received them;
> (Italics in original.)

'Endless' or 'eternal' or not, judgments will *not* be revoked and there will be woes, weeping, wailing and gnashing of teeth. I never considered how cruel and unkind this God was; I suppose I just thought it would not apply to me personally. Now, doctrinally it most certainly will apply to me and yet I simply follow my conscience for the sake of truth and integrity. Therefore, there is something alarmingly wrong with the whole concept as described by Smith. It is clearly yet another confidence trick.

DOCTRINE & COVENANTS – SECTIONS 19-29

Smith explains in v.6 "Nevertheless, it is not written that there shall be no end to this torment, but it is written *endless torment*." He says that damnation is *termed* 'eternal' because God is eternal and it is his punishment being meted out but that doesn't mean it will necessarily last forever. This raises a serious question concerning the corollary.

In Mormonism, the concept of '*eternal* life' means that for those who earn it, they will dwell with God forever. Yet those who do not make it will have *eternal* damnation – which may *not* last forever. On the basis that 'eternal' damnation may not last very long for many people who were not as bad as others, surely 'eternal' *life* – given by God, who is eternal, must not be *forever* for everyone either. Many will only just have made the cut and not be nearly as deserving as others who may have earned more permanent 'eternal life' status.

To *balance* Smith's claim, some people would have to enjoy eternal life for a period which they earned and then revert back to a lower status or there is no compatibility. This concept, as described by Smith is inconsistent and the problem is not solved by suggesting that is what the lower kingdoms are for.

We are talking of eternal damnation, which until this point meant forever, and eternal life, which meant, and still means, living with God forever. If God's punishment is not eternal for everyone, then living with God in an eternal life equally cannot be permanent for everyone. The concept, supposedly 'revealed' by Smith, creates complete disparity.

The heading claims the revelation was for Martin Harris and yet v.8 speaks of "mine apostles". Harris was not an apostle – in fact in March 1830, when this was recorded, no one was. In Section 20:2-3, written the following month, Smith declares that he and Oliver Cowdery were ordained apostles and first and second elder of the Church respectively but there is no record of this actually happening. *(See Section 27 on pp.148-52 for more details).* The first recorded apostle to be ordained was Brigham Young on 14 February 1835, almost five years later. If this was real revelation, Jesus may have called them disciples as followers, but not apostles, as that is an 'office' defined in Mormonism as requiring Priesthood ordination. Any account of such a thing happening should have been properly recorded long before this.

Verse 8 (above) is ambiguous enough that the Church may claim it refers to the apostles of old in order to escape the problem. If it really did then the Lord should have made it clear – and he didn't. The context suggests the very people he is talking to are being addressed as apostles. *(The verses that follow, D&C 19:15-19, are reviewed in* TMD 4:177-8). (S24-5)*.*

Just to mention – v.18 has Smith once again confirm his monotheism. It states quite categorically that "Which suffering caused ***myself, even God***, the greatest of all, to tremble because of pain, and to bleed at every pore…"

From v.20 on, Jesus continues his rant about repenting or suffering the consequences. They are only to preach repentance and not share 'these' things yet, as the world is not ready and must have milk before meat – yet there is nothing in this Section anyone would have been the least troubled by. Smith has Jesus actually claim in v.22 "they must not know these things, lest they perish." Can you see anything in Section 19 to merit that? To everyone not convinced by Smith's so-called revelation, it would all be considered nonsense – both then and now, so why would Jesus need to say don't show anyone yet? Clearly he would not have done, as it would have made no difference to anyone whatsoever. Outside Smith's convinced circle – no one cared.

Perhaps the following are things that people outside Smith's group would not have been ready for. Verse 25 is a classic Smith statement which he later personally violated over and over again.

> **25.** And again, I command thee that thou shalt not covet thy neighbor's wife; nor seek thy neighbor's life.

Smith went on not only to covet, but also *marry* up to eleven 'other men's wives' *(see TMD Vol. 1:122-3)* and he was ultimately responsible for countless murders carried out by his followers who attacked other settlers. In addition, his secret Danite band took revenge on any 'dissenters' and drove them out, threatening their lives if people did not leave.

At this point, Smith seems to remember that he is supposed to be talking to Harris so he says not to covet your own property – but to freely give it to Smith for the publication of the Book of Mormon. Jesus moves on to repeat the usual things and says the last commandment is to carry on teaching repentance for the rest of their lives. Verse 30 says they must not revile against the revilers, but that idea was not to last long; Jesus was later completely ignored in that respect.

Following Smith's traditional carrot and stick routine, v.31 says: "misery thou shalt receive if thou wilt slight these counsels, yea, even the destruction of thyself and property." That threat from Jesus was no doubt partly to convince Harris that Jesus would not be pleased if he (Harris) did not come up with the goods. It was to become the way of early Mormonism though and such action was carried out in reality on anyone who dissented and tried to leave the fold or expose the truth about polygyny. Jesus wasn't personally going to take revenge on dissenters, but Smith's loyal followers certainly did.

Harris is to pay his 'debt' to the printer for the Book of Mormon and yet he is also to leave his house and farm to go off and preach, only returning when he wants to see his family. It is difficult to see how he would support himself by selling off land and then not working on what was left. The Mormon God (or Jesus in this case) moved in very mysterious ways. This section contains a lot of meaningless filler that Harris was supposed to swallow but there is nothing that could be considered prophecy or worthwhile revelation.

Reminder: Sections reviewed in date order. Section 20 is dated 10 April 1830.

Section 21
6 April 1830. Fayette, New York.

History.

1833 BOC Ch. XXII. 1835 D&C Sec. XLVI. 2010 D&C Sec. 21.

Section 21 was recorded the day the Mormon Church was formally organised. Smith immediately establishes his leadership position by including in the very first verse: "Behold, there shall be a record kept among you; and in it thou shalt be called a seer, a translator, a prophet, an *apostle* of Jesus Christ, an elder of the church..." *(as mentioned on p.107)*. This is apparently directed *to* Smith (a clever ploy by Smith) who claimed to *be* those things but there is no evidence that he actually was. He most certainly never gave any details of how he *became* an apostle; he just claimed that he was one.

In v.5, Smith's words are to be received as if they are the Lord's words. This put Smith in a very commanding position with those who were inclined to believe that it was indeed the Lord speaking. As ever, the 'gates of hell' will not prevail against them if they do what Smith says. The Lord will do more; he will "disperse the powers of darkness" and "cause the heavens to *shake* for your good, and for his name's glory" (v.6). Think about that statement for a moment and ask yourself if that sounds like a rational thing for deity to say.

Why would 'the heavens' shake for their *good* and why was Jesus concerned for his *own* name's 'glory'? Smith is trying to make it *sound* like a powerful God who is on their side of things. He stole the idea of the heavens and Earth shaking from the Bible – but there, the heavens do not shake for the *good* of anyone on Earth; God was always angry *(See 2 Samuel 22:8; Hebrews 12:26; Isaiah 13:13; Hagai 2:6 for example)*. Smith and Cowdery are to ordain each other as elders and Cowdery is also mentioned as already being an apostle – before he was even ordained an elder. There is no record of that either.

An even more strange (and very telling) thing is Jesus' statement in v.11 "...unto this **church of Christ**, bearing my name–" Here Jesus confirms the name of the Church as the "church of Christ" which is how it started out, and yet over the next few years that name was to evolve and change several times before ultimately becoming 'The Church of Jesus Christ of Latter-day Saints'. We should question why Jesus didn't 'reveal' that name to Smith in the first instance. The reason is all too obvious. The 'revealed' name was yet another *false* revelation *(see below)*.

In the last verse, Jesus uses a very strange turn of phrase which once again is more akin to Smith's early attempts at making up revelation than it is to a plausible manner of speech for deity. They are to preach "before the world, yea, before the gentiles; yea, and thus saith the Lord God, lo, lo! To the Jews also. Amen." The 'To the Jews also' end statement became typical of the style of Joseph Smith afterthoughts in many of his revelations – he often added things at the end that he appeared to have almost forgotten to include. Deity would of course not have had such a bad memory. There are no prophecies that require summarising. There is one false revelation.

Section 21 – Summary

Non-prophetic revelation.   1.

1. Smith has the Lord himself declare that the name of the Church is the 'Church of Christ' ("bearing my name"). That idea did not last very long.

It was informally known as the Church of Christ during 1829 and legally instituted with that same name on 6 April 1830. It became the 'Church of the Latter Day Saints' in 1834. Note that it then no longer bore Christ's name. Later it was to change to the 'Church of Jesus Christ' and then the 'Church of God', once again losing the name of Christ, before the Lord eventually got round to giving a further revelation in 1838, stating that it should be called "The Church of Jesus Christ of Latter-day Saints" *(D&C 115:3)*. If it had really been the Lord speaking the first time, he would have given that name in the first instance. Had it been the Lord speaking the second time, he would *not* have contradicted his first revelation. Ergo, it does not take a genius to work out where all five names came from.

Section 23
April 1830. Manchester, New York.

History.

1833 BOC Ch. XVII to XXI inc. 1835 D&C Sec. XLV. 2010 D&C Sec. 23.

The *JS Papers Vol. 2* places this between Sections 21 and 20, meaning it may have been 'received' in (or near) Fayette, rather than Manchester.

This little Section originally consisted of five separate *Chapters* in the 1833 Book of Commandments. It stems from five men asking Smith to find out from the Lord what their "respective duties" were. They were keen to help. Do we imagine the Lord revealing various different and interesting callings and duties for them to get individually involved with and achieve? Of course not. Smith was hard pushed to think of anything they could actually *do* at all, let alone outline different and interesting 'duties' for them. Later, he got better at this, but it was early days and Smith (or if you prefer, the Lord) was still learning how to construct better ideas.

The five enquiring were Oliver Cowdery; Hyrum Smith; Samuel H. Smith; Joseph Smith, Sr.; and Joseph Knight, Sr. Each received his own individual response, supposedly from the Lord.

Cowdery is blessed; he is under no condemnation but is to beware of pride. He is not actually given any duties, yet he is told to make his calling known to the church and the world and his heart will be opened to preach forever. That's it for him.

Hyrum, Joseph Smith's brother, doesn't fare much better. He isn't told he is 'blessed' but he is under no condemnation; his heart is opened and tongue loosed; his calling is to exhortation and to strengthen the church. This is his duty forever "because of thy family" but we are left to guess why that is.

Samuel, another Smith brother, who is also 'not under condemnation', gets the same deal as Hyrum, except in his case he is not yet called to preach to the world. Samuel was twenty-two years old.

Joseph Sr., Smith's father, gets exactly the same words as Hyrum, except he doesn't get his heart opened or tongue loosed as Hyrum did, so it is unclear what difference that made.

Finally, Knight must take up his cross and pray vocally before the world and in secret, in his family, with friends and in all places. He is also called to 'exhortation continually'.

This complete lack of any worthwhile information for these men will no doubt be explained by the Church today as them each simply being encouraged by the Lord to teach and preach continually in order to build the kingdom. However, in context of the question asked and it being the Lord supposedly responding, the result is pretty pathetic for all of them really.

Section 20

10 April 1830. At or near Fayette, New York.

History.

1833 BOC Ch. XXIV. 1835 D&C Sec. II. 2010 D&C Sec. 20.

THE MORMON DELUSION

It is v.2 of Section 20 that the Church relies on to support the idea Smith was given priesthood authority. You would think something more than this single unquantified verse would have been recorded.

> **2.** Which commandments were given to Joseph Smith, Jun., who was called of God, and ordained an apostle of Jesus Christ, to be the first elder of this church;

Section 20 starts off with a statement that it was "one thousand eight hundred and thirty years since the coming of our Lord and Savior Jesus Christ..." – something that historians generally agree was *not* the case at all.

Varying analysis dates Christ's birth (assuming he lived at all), to either between 3 and 5 BCE or possibly 6 CE, although the latter argument is not strong. Not that it much matters, but considering Joseph Smith was supposedly 'revealing' such things, he got it *very* wrong indeed. Christ's birth was also no more on 6th April of that year (as the Church proclaims), any more than it was 25th December, a date which most people accept as entirely inaccurate. There are various possibilities rendered regarding the date. None of them agree with Smith's statement which was made out of ignorance rather than knowledge or revelation.

The gospels, if you are inclined to believe what they say, confirm Christ was born shortly before Herod the Great died. Herod's death can be fixed because Josephus recorded an eclipse of the moon just before Herod died. That eclipse occurred 12th-13th March in 4 BCE. Josephus also mentions that Herod died just before the Passover which was 11th April that year. In fact, going by the most logical analysis that I located from other details provided by Josephus, Herod's demise occurred between 29th March and 4th April in 4 BCE, which means Christ was born some time 'shortly' *before* then.

It may sound strange that Christ was born BC (which means *before* Christ) but the modern calendar we now use, which splits time between BC and AD, Anno Domini – Latin for 'The Year Of Our Lord' and is used in the Gregorian Calendar to refer to the current era, was not invented until AD 525. Note that in my work, I usually use BCE (Before Common Era) and CE (Common Era), terms preferred by those who are not Christian. Dionysis (a monk), was asked by Pope John I to prepare a standardised calendar for the western world and he missed the BCE/CE split by about four or five years. His guess was close but the world was then stuck with it – right or wrong. The point here is that Smith 'revealed' something that he *assumed* was taken for granted – but if it was a revelation, it was a *false* revelation as it is demonstrably historically inaccurate.

Smith then goes on to recap on his calling and ability to translate. In v.9 Smith claims once again that the Book of Mormon contains the fullness of the gospel, which it clearly does not, and then says in v.10 that the translation was given by 'inspiration'. This is interesting, as the Church accepts that Smith translated with his face in a hat whilst looking at his old money-digging seer stone, yet they appear to consider the idea of words 'appearing' one at a time as being the result of that method. Smith talks about the method he used, in Section 9:8 – as studying the translation out in his mind and then 'feeling' that it was right, which of course means you make it up as you go along and if you like the ideas then they must be correct. *(See pp. 120-1 and also TMD 3:293-5, already referenced from p. 120 to S16-18).*

That is hardly a sensible or likely successful method of communication from the Lord to humans. Moreover, to ***accept*** the idea that so many people went to so much trouble to make a difficult record on gold plates and then hide it – only for it to be tied in a bundle or buried outside while Smith 'translated' by making up the Book of Mormon in his head and then accepting the resulting 'translation' as correct if he felt good about it – is beyond ludicrous. It is *insane* and if the Church were obliged to make such detail known to its investigators before they considered associating themselves with Mormonism, no one would *ever* join the Church. If I had been privy to such information even as a fourteen year old, I most certainly would have been far too sensible to have remotely considered that any God would ever have been involved with such nonsense.

Nevertheless, Smith rambles on in his usual way – the book was confirmed to others by the ministering of angels (they saw it in their minds). Yet if they were real, would not God have at least allowed some actually to see and handle physically the gold plates? They must teach, and people with faith will obtain a 'crown' of eternal life. Anyone who rejects the message will naturally suffer condemnation. It is the same story every time. I have had more than one active Mormon email to tell me that Jesus loves me and wants me to repent – or I will be condemned. Nothing changes. The thing I want to know is how you 'repent' of an absolute *knowledge* of the truth which cannot be denied because it is substantiated by conclusive and irrefutable evidence rather than mere faith?

There is more 'filler' where Smith repeats information about the creation, basically as described in the Bible, following which yet again his then current monotheism is confirmed.

> **28.** Which Father, Son, and Holy Ghost are one God, infinite and eternal, without end. Amen.

After more filler, Smith determines baptism should be by full immersion, a traditional and preferred concept among many of his converts. It then moves on to priesthood and the now bizarre notion that an apostle is an elder and is called to baptise. At the time I am sure it made sense. The rest of the Section concerns priesthood and sacrament prayer details – the latter lifted from the Book of Mormon as Smith had also included it there. Considering the fact that such exact words were supposedly used by Nephites centuries ago and all surviving cavitations retain many old traditions, why is there not a single solitary culture anywhere in the Americas that has a remotely connected language or culture let alone knowledge of Jesus or a 'sacramental' ceremony within it? Anything and everything is represented in cultures discovered throughout the Americas, one way or another, with the notable absence of anything remotely connected to Judaism or Christianly.

Some details not appearing in the original 1833 Book of Commandments were added to this section in the 1835 edition of the D&C. The 1833 BOC Chapter XXIV: v.44 concludes with the word 'calling'. This verse became v.15 in 1835 and had the words "– or he may receive it from a conference" added. This is now v.64. What are now v.65-67 were also added into the 1835 D&C. More of Section 20 is discussed in TMD Vol. 4. *(See TMD 4:132, 249-50, 358-59) (S25-30)*.

Section 20 – Summary

Non-prophetic revelation: 1

1. Smith 'revealed' the birth of Christ to an incorrect day, month and year. The Mormon Church believes it was organised on Christ's birthday, 6th April 1830, and Smith declared Christ to have been born in the year 1 CE.

Whatever analysis is referred to, none of them date Christ's birth to that day, month or even year. Smith's claim remains entirely impossible by any and every plausible calculation.

Section 22
16 April 1830. Manchester, New York.

History.

1833 BOC Ch. XXIII. 1835 D&C Sec. XLVII. 2010 D&C Sec. 22.

This consists of four short verses declaring that prior baptisms into other churches are not valid in Smith's new Church. All must be baptised again. Just to make sure people get the message, Smith has the Lord tell them to do as he has commanded and "seek not to counsel your God" for good measure.

Section 24
July 1830. Harmony, Pennsylvania.

History.

1833 BOC Ch. XXV. 1835 D&C Sec. IX. 2010 D&C Sec. 24.

Jesus is apparently speaking once again in this revelation as he mentions it in v.5. In v.1, Smith was chosen to "write" the Book of Mormon, rather than *translate* it; a Freudian slip there by God – or Smith?

It then goes on to say in v.2 that Smith's sins are not excusable and he is to sin no more. Smith is to go to the Church in Colesville, Fayette and Manchester and they are to support him, both spiritually and temporally. If they don't, the Lord will curse them instead of blessing them. Smith's God was very fond of cursing people, even his own, and this idea was to rub off on Smith, and later Brigham Young, who cursed the *nation* and included that curse in the temple ceremony *(see TMD Vol. 3:167-8)*. Leaders of the United States were not at all impressed and they considered it treason. Ultimately, it was removed from the temple ceremony.

Smith is told to keep on speaking and writing, as 'given' by the comforter. It will be given to him in the very moment, what to speak or write, and if people don't listen they will be cursed. So Smith would just blurt out whatever things came into his head. This is the very same thing that members do today when blessing others; it is what Mormon patriarchs do when giving patriarchal blessings; and from evidence of things unfulfilled and completely contrary to the ultimate reality that people experience, it is a highly unreliable technique and does not come from a God.

In v.9, Smith slips in the concept that he is not strong enough for temporal labour and that is not his calling. Smith didn't seem to like hard work at all. As a money-digging 'seer', his role was to locate where to dig for treasure but the seer wasn't there to dig, just to ward off any spirits guarding the loot, in case it should slip away into the bowels of the earth – which it generally did; or at least that was the excuse given when nothing was discovered.

There is a lot of filler, including the Lord apparently saying (v.13) "Require not miracles, except I shall command you, except casting out devils, healing the sick, and against poisonous serpents, and against deadly poisons;" which does seem rather odd. As ever, it smacks of the mind of man rather than deity.

They must leave cursings rather than blessings when people reject them and cast the dust from their feet as a testimony against them. Smith stole that idea from Matthew 10:14, Mark 6:11, Luke 9:5 and Acts 13:51. Smith used it again several times, in Sections 60:15, 75:20, 84:92 and 99:4, sometimes including the idea of 'washing' their feet as well. In the Bible, there is no mention of the washing of feet being associated with the symbolic shaking of dust from feet. It was a Smith addition. The question is: why would God reintroduce the idea?

In Jesus' time they wore sandals and they always had to wipe the dust or sand from their feet so they used the idea symbolically. In Smith's day, they had socks and shoes or boots and there would rarely be any dust in them as such to deal with. A quaint idea, but not one the Lord would have been likely to bother with in Joseph Smith's day. Do Mormon missionaries shake the dust from their feet today when people reject them and their message? Of course not; almost everyone rejects them; their shoes would be more off than on if they were required to do that. If symbolically shaking the dust from (and also sometimes washing) feet was reinstituted in Smith's time, when, and more importantly, *why* did the Church subsequently discontinue the practice? Why did people in Smith's day need to be cursed for rejecting the gospel when today they don't? The Mormon God is illogical and inconsistent in His requirements.

If anyone sets about them with violence, they are to command them to be smitten in the Lord's name and he *will* smite them – in his own due time, which by all accounts was never. The same is true for the next promise which was that if anyone took them to law, they would be *cursed by* the law. The fact is there is no evidence that I could locate of that happening, but there is every evidence of Smith being taken to law by countless people to whom he owed money, especially following the Kirtland bank fraud and subsequent collapse.

Smith was arrested several times on polygamy charges, he went on the run from the law when charged with accessory to attempted murder, and ultimately he was killed while in jail awaiting trial for treason. Those who took Smith to law generally won their cases and many thousands of dollars in compensation and interest was stumped up by Smith's followers as Smith put all his assets in his first wife Emma's name and he could never pay his own debts. *(See: TMD Vol. 3:42-44) (S30-32).*

We could conclude that the failure of the Lord to 'smite' anyone and the failure of the law to 'curse' anyone were failures of *prophecy* but the details are too ambiguous to include in a summary analysis. Nevertheless, they were said and did *not* materialise.

Section 26
July 1830. Harmony, Pennsylvania.

History.

1833 BOC Ch. XXVII. 1835 D&C Sec. XLIX. 2010 D&C Sec. 26.

DOCTRINE & COVENANTS – SECTIONS 19-29

This Section consists of just two verses which are as meaningless and pointless as anything Smith ever wrote and deserve no comment. They are included here purely so show the reason why nothing needs to be said. Much of the D&C is similar to this and will not be covered for the same reason. Following our closer look, up to this point, at some of Smith's early attempts at 'revelations', such close analysis of his later Sections will only be considered where there is something deserving of further comment.

> **1.** Behold, I say unto you that you shall let your time be devoted to the studying of the scriptures, and to preaching, and to confirming the church at Colesville, and to performing your labors on the land, such as is required, until after you shall go to the west to hold the next conference; and then it shall be made known what you shall do.
> **2.** And all things shall be done by common consent in the church, by much prayer and faith, for all things you shall receive by faith. Amen.

Section 25
July 1830. Harmony, Pennsylvania.

History.

1833 BOC Ch. XXVI. 1835 D&C Sec. XLVIII. 2010 D&C Sec. 25.

This is a message from "the Lord your God" – which could have meant God or Jesus, as they were one and the same to Smith at the time – to Smith's wife Emma, although at the end the Lord says it applies to everyone. Essentially, it appears that it is to get Emma on board with her husband's ideas. Her life is to be preserved "if thou art faithful", implying that if were it not for that promise she would have died earlier in life than she eventually did. So, why did she *not* die earlier, considering the fact that following her husband's demise, Emma rejected Brigham Young as the new leader and was essentially estranged from any Mormon schism for a long time, eventually aligning herself with the reorganised version of the Church when Joseph III was eventually persuaded to run it many years later? If the Mormon Church was true and Emma's life was to be 'preserved' *if* she was *faithful*, why did the Lord let her live to be seventy-four years of age? Emma died 30 April 1879 in Nauvoo. She was a member of the RLDS Church, now known as the Community of Christ.

It makes no more sense than the things that follow; the usual – sins are forgiven, despite the fact that Emma may have wondered what her sins actually were; she was to comfort her husband in his 'afflictions', with meekness; she was to be a scribe, and unusually, also to be "ordained" under her husband's hand to expound scriptures, and to exhort the church. There is no record of that ever happening and any idea of women being 'ordained' to anything in the Church quickly disappeared, never to resurface. In the early Mormon Church women gave blessings but were not 'ordained' to do so. The practice did not survive into the twentieth century. Emma was also told to make a collection of hymns which she dutifully did.

Emma had clearly wanted to at least look at the gold plates or perhaps even see an angel as this is addressed. God tells Emma not to 'murmur' because of things she has *not* seen, as they are to be kept from the world – including her. God says that it "is wisdom in me in a time to come." But the time clearly never came. One may question why Emma was refused sight of the plates. As the wife of a supposed prophet, Emma at least deserved tangible confirmation, which was readily available, if she was to be expected to support her husband in his venture.

But then, Emma would have been deemed as *only* a woman, which in those days did not amount to much in the scheme of priestly things. Women were not involved with such aspects at all. As it happens, not much has changed over the years in the Mormon Church in that respect and women still have to keep their peace and mind their place.

Section 27

4 September 1830. (Later *falsified* to August 1830). Harmony, Pennsylvania.

History.

1833 BOC Ch. XXVIII. 1835 D&C Sec. L. 2010 D&C Sec. 27.

This section was originally specifically dated to a *day*, 4 September 1830. When the 'chapter' entered the Book of Commandments in 1833, it consisted of just *seven* verses; those which now comprise v.1-4 and part of v.5, ending with the word 'earth'. What follows that in modern versions was added in 1835, with the last part of the original BOC text of v. 6-7 (now v.5) then continuing as v.14 and part of v.15. What now comprises most of v.5, through to and including v.13, plus the latter part of v.15 through to the end (v.18), comprises *later* additional text.

It is impossible for all the added words to have been part of an original revelation which somehow got missed out. Had they been true words revealed from the Lord somewhat later, clearly they should and would have become another separate revelation dated to when they were actually given. There is a good reason why that was not the case – and it had nothing to do with deity.

DOCTRINE & COVENANTS – SECTIONS 19-29

The original seven verses related *only* to the sacrament, with an instruction not to buy wine from their enemies but rather to make it themselves.

Considering the fact that later the sacrament was to become *water* rather than wine in Mormonism, we should question why Jesus didn't simply suggest that idea in this Section. Traditionally, it is not just wine used for sacramental purposes; it is specifically red wine, representing the blood of Christ. Mormon departure from this tradition is a strange one, as the Saviour himself supposedly instituted the original concept at the last supper.

Jesus says he will come back and drink "the fruit of the vine" with Smith – yet for Mormons, alcohol is now forbidden, even for the sacrament so that isn't going to happen. You could call that a failed prophecy – straight from Jesus, but I will not include it as such as no doubt the Church would claim that when Jesus does return, he will drink some grape juice with Smith and his fictional friends. In the later added verses, Smith included names of several other men whom Jesus would drink with, including the fictitious 'Elias' *(see p. 90)*. The Mormon Bible Dictionary tries to explain each instance of the appearance of the name 'Elias', and this mention is claimed to be a pseudonym for Noah – or the angel Gabriel, who Mormons believe became Noah. You won't get that notion from reading the text of v.6-7.

This is a very strange claim. The surrounding verses additionally mention drinking with Moroni and also "John the son of Zacharias, which Zacharias he (Elias) visited and gave promise that he should have a son, and his name should be John." So, it was *Noah* who visited Zacharias, yet John the Baptist is also referred to as an 'Elias' in Mormonism, making it all very confusing.

The excuses needed to cover Smith's error in his incorrect use of 'Elias' make for complete confusion among Mormons. Apologists have had to concoct quite an array of explanations to get Smith off the hook. None of them make any theological sense.

Drinking with Jesus will also involve Joseph, Jacob, Isaac, Abraham and Michael, or Adam, Peter, James and John. So, rather than confuse everyone with the name 'Elias' in v.6-7, why did it not simply say 'Noah or Gabriel' just as it said 'Michael or Adam' in v.11? If you point out v.6-7 to almost any Mormon, they will *not* know it supposedly refers to Noah.

The words added to this section in 1835 are not just tagged on at the end; they are inserted into the original text and have nothing whatsoever to do with the original subject matter. Most of it is of no consequence but amongst the filler that Smith added is v.12 which, out of nowhere, allows for his authority to hold the ancient priesthood, given at the hands of Peter, James and John. *(See also pp. 126-7)*.

> **12.** And also with Peter, and James, and John, whom I have sent unto you, by whom I have ordained you and confirmed you to be apostles,

and especial witnesses of my name, and bear the keys of your ministry and of the same things which I revealed unto them;

There never was a record of Joseph Smith and Oliver Cowdery receiving the Melchizedek Priesthood. In fact, whilst this so-called revelation was later both manipulated to include such an idea as if it had happened years earlier, and then falsified by backdating it to the preceding month in order to make it fit with Church organisation, when Oliver Cowdery *did* mention the idea himself, it entirely contradicted this version of events.

> "...there is no definite account of the event in the history of the Prophet Joseph, or, for matter of that, in any of our annals," *(History of the Church 1:40).*

This 'revelation' (v.12 above) claims that Peter, James and John ordained Joseph Smith and Oliver Cowdery at some undetermined previous date which Smith apparently did not even bother to record. Cowdery's 'memory' was that 'the angel' performed the ordinance. You would think that two men having had the very same experience would at least get the number, if not the names, of the participants correct.

Cowdery mentioned only an *angel* in connection with the restoration of the priesthood. For it to have been a real experience, he would have to confirm that Peter, James and John restored the Melchizedek Priesthood. Alternatively, Smith would have needed to corroborate the idea that it was an angel. Cowdery doesn't even mention the first angel being John the Baptist as claimed by Smith in *JS–H 68:72*. He doesn't appear to know who it was.

Cowdery declared:

> I was present with Joseph when **an holy angel** from God came down from heaven and conferred on us, or restored, the lesser or Aaronic Priesthood, and said to us, at the same time, that it should remain upon the earth while the earth stands. I was also present with Joseph when **the higher or Melchizedek Priesthood was conferred by the holy angel from on high. This Priesthood, we then conferred on each other** by the will and commandment of God. *(History of the Church, Vol. 1, p. 40 footnote).* (Emphasis added).

Cowdery says a "holy **angel** from on high" conferred the *higher* priesthood. Smith claims Peter, James and John performed the ordinance. Was it just one unidentified angel – or three named apostles? The contradictory claims confirm just one thing; the whole episode was a complete *lie*. It should be remembered that in Mormonism, John is supposedly still alive and not a spirit. He would

DOCTRINE & COVENANTS – SECTIONS 19-29

have appeared in *person*. There are claims that Cowdery saw three apostles but they are not substantiated and contradict his own record from Church history.

The two accounts are far too contradictory to remotely be regarded as confirmation of the truth, reflecting only wishful thinking of the moment by Smith who was trying to fill the gaps in his story. *(See also TMD Vol. 4:117-9).*

La Mar Petersen concluded that important details are missing from Church history:

> The important details that are missing from the 'full history' of 1834 are likewise missing from the Book of Commandments in 1833. The student would expect to find all the particulars of the Restoration in this first treasured set of 65 revelations, the dates of which encompassed the bestowals of the two Priesthoods, but they are conspicuously absent... The notable revelations on Priesthood in the Doctrine and Covenants before referred to, Sections 2 and 13, are missing, and Chapter 28 gives no hint of the Restoration which, if actual, had been known for four years. More than four hundred words were added to this revelation of August, 1829 in Section 27 of the Doctrine and Covenants, the additions made to include the names of heavenly visitors and two separate ordinations. The Book of Commandments gives the duties of Elders, Priests, Teachers, and Deacons and refers to Joseph's apostolic calling but there is no mention of Melchezedek Priesthood, High Priesthood, Seventies, High Priests, nor High Councilors. These words were later inserted into the revelation on Church organization and government of April, 1830, making it appear that they were known at that date, but they do not appear in the original, Chapter 24 of the Book of Commandments three years later. Similar interpolations were made in the revelations known as Sections 42 and 68. *(La Mar Petersen; Problems in Mormon Text 1957:7-8).*

If you consider the additional notes on Priesthood restoration, added in 1835, and the blatant backdating of this section, to be '*claimed* revelation' then of course we clearly have a false claim to note.

Section 27 – Summary

Non-prophetic revelation: 1

1. Whatever it is thought to be, a definite second false claim is the ordination to the Melchizedek Priesthood. Smith here claims it was given by Peter, James and John but obviously forgot to tell Cowdery what he was to say he had seen and experienced. Cowdery claimed the angel (who Smith identified as John the Baptist) came back and ordained them. No one knows when. This complete

contradiction, coupled with the interpolation of scant detail, inserted into a previous revelation and then backdated from 4 September 1830 in the 1833 version to August 1830 in the 1835 edition, confirms one and only one thing. The whole thing was a complete and utter lie that was manufactured in order to accommodate the need for a priesthood restoration which never happened.

Section 29
September 1830. Fayette, New York.

History.

1833 BOC Ch. XXIX. 1835 D&C Sec. X. 2010 D&C Sec. 29.

This Section starts out with something mainstream Christians might consider a most unusual and arrogant thing for Jesus to actually say about himself.

> **1.** Listen to the voice of Jesus Christ, your Redeemer, the Great I AM, whose arm of Mercy hath atoned for your sins;

This is something never before recorded in scripture. God and Jesus are not known for having to glorify their own position – but Smith certainly was, and using such phraseology was clearly meant to more firmly establish himself as the spokesman for 'the Great I AM'.

In the Bible, such references are generally *about* God rather than *by* Him. Examples such as Psalm 147:5 and Jeremiah 10:6 establish how such things were usually mentioned in the Bible.

> **Psalm 147:5.** Great is our Lord, and of great power: his understanding is infinite.

> **Jeremiah 10:6.** Forasmuch as there is none like unto thee, O Lord; thou art great, and thy name is great in might.

These are statements of worship *toward* God and certainly not *by* God telling us how great He is. Why would He need to do that? Yet here Smith uses language attributed directly to Jesus Christ which is anything but humble and everything arrogant – and completely out of character. It gets worse, as he uses the exact same language again. The above was in September of 1830 and then on 2nd and also 5th January 1831, Smith has Jesus at it again.

DOCTRINE & COVENANTS – SECTIONS 19-29

2 Jan 1831. D&C 38:1. Thus saith *the Lord your God, even Jesus Christ*, the *Great I Am,* Alpha and Omega, the beginning and the end, the same which looked upon the wide expanse of eternity, and all the seraphic hosts of heaven, before the world was made;

5 Jan 1831. D&C 39:1. Hearken and listen to the voice of *him who is from all eternity to all eternity*, *the Great I Am*, even Jesus Christ—

Note that yet again, on 2 January, Jesus also confirms that *he is God.* On 5 January, he uses the expression "him who is from all eternity to all eternity" which means exactly the same thing – Jesus *is* God. It is more than suspicious that Smith would claim Jesus said such a thing, but even more so that Jesus had never used that expression before September 1830 and he never used it again after 5 January 1831.

This Section was given in the presence of six unidentified 'elders' of the Church. Naturally, Jesus almost immediately confirms their sins are forgiven and begins to ramble about gathering them as a hen does and that they are to preach. He goes on to confirm how he will treat everyone who does not listen and believe – including the usual weeping and wailing; adding hailstorms, flies and maggots "and their flesh shall fall from off their bones, and their eyes from their sockets" (v.19). The traditionally benevolent Jesus of the New Testament exclaims in v.17: "I will take *vengeance* upon the wicked, for they will not repent; for the cup of mine indignation is full; for behold, my blood shall not cleanse them if they hear me not." Jesus sounds more and more like his dad in the Old Testament in Smith's writings; but then Mormons believe Jesus *was* the God of the Old Testament; they have to, to cover anomalies left by Smith.

In reality, that concept is the *only* way the Church can rationalise away an otherwise all too obvious entirely monotheistic Bible. A belief that God and Jesus are two separate and distinct beings *and* that Jesus was **not** the same God as in the Old Testament simply doesn't work for a myriad of reasons, so they *have* to conclude it was Jesus speaking in the Old Testament – *representing* his Father. To accommodate that, you have to virtually ignore the fact that he often states that he *is* God. Quite a feat of theological manipulation is required to achieve that concept, along with rank and file Mormons being willing to adapt their thinking to the supposition sufficiently to blindly accept it without further consideration. Further independent *thought* would inevitably lead to an entirely different conclusion and understanding of the truth, which in Mormonism will not do at all. Obedience and an absolute acceptance of *doctrine* are mandatory.

Smith includes some details of what will happen when the Saviour returns, drawing on several biblical references to achieve this. He has Jesus saying that the sun will be darkened and the moon will be turned into blood; stolen from Joel 2:31, which was also used by Peter in the New Testament (Acts 2:20). Joel and Acts are identical and say "the sun shall be turned into darkness". In D&C 29:14, Smith has Jesus say "the sun shall be darkened" and repeats *exactly* the same words again in D&C 34:9 and 45:42. It may be a small point, but the two biblical references are the same and Smith has Jesus change it and repeat the same change three separate times word for word. Such inconsistency would not be so much associated with deity but it very often is with Smith.

> **8.** Wherefore the decree hath gone forth from the Father that ***they shall be gathered in unto one place upon the face of this land***, to prepare their hearts and ***be prepared*** in all things ***against the day when tribulation and desolation are sent forth upon the wicked***.
> **9.** For the ***hour is nigh and the day soon at hand*** when the earth is ripe; and all the proud and ***they that do wickedly shall be as stubble; and I will burn them up***, saith the Lord of Hosts, that wickedness shall not be upon the earth; (Emphasis added).

Part of v.9 is of course from one of Smith's favourite scriptures that he had Moroni use when he first supposedly appeared to Smith, taken from Malachi 4:1. In Smith's account of Moroni's *alterations* to Malachi 4 Smith changes the original words from "and the day that cometh shall burn them up" to read "for they that come shall burn them" which is *not* how it is translated in any other work. Here, Smith has Jesus go even further and say: "*I* will burn them up."

Joseph Smith made some huge mistakes when making his 'Moroni' claims regarding this scripture, not just with the changes he made but also in using the *original* KJV words in his Book of Mormon, written *after* Moroni supposedly visited and changed the words, but *before* he recorded what he claimed Moroni said. It was *after* this D&C 29 'revelation' was written that Smith wrote his 'Inspired Revision' of the Bible but in it he did *not* alter Malachi 4. Smith had a terrible memory and for that reason was often caught in his duplicity. This area is a classic example of multiple errors by Smith. *(See TMD Vol. 2:80-6 for a full review of Smith's claims and mistakes regarding Moroni and Malachi 4).*

In v.8, we have what is essentially a prophecy. We haven't seen one for a while, but here Jesus explicitly states "the decree hath gone forth from the Father that they shall be "gathered in unto *one place* on the face of this land". This was September 1830 and the 'one place' turned out to be Kirtland, Ohio, where Smith resided from 1831-1837 and where they built a temple. Smith also started talking about Zion being established at Independence, Missouri, as early as 1831. Then, in 1834, Smith led 'Zion's Camp' on a march to redeem Zion

DOCTRINE & COVENANTS – SECTIONS 19-29

(Independence) but they were unsuccessful. Dejected, they returned home, with many suffering from malaria along the way.

Following Smith's temporary stay in Far West during 1838, in 1839 they settled in Nauvoo, Illinois, but by the time they had almost completed a temple there, Smith was killed (1844), they were driven out and started heading west.

Had Section 29 been a real revelation and instruction from God via Jesus – would he not have been better off saying that they should immediately travel across the plains to Utah in order to save all the trouble and bloodshed? Despite revelation and prophecy on gathering and building a temple in Independence, and Brigham Young even talking about possibly still doing so many years later when in Salt Lake City, to this day no such gathering and no such temple have materialised. In the 1860s, Brigham Young prophesied the Civil War would *continue* until the land was *emptied* so the Mormons could return to Missouri. *(See: Tanner 1987:190-192).* It did not – and they did not.

Verse 8 is explicit, in that they must gather in order to "be prepared in all things against the day when tribulation and desolation are sent forth upon the wicked". The "tribulation and desolation" – if it ever was "sent forth", seems to have affected only early Mormons when hundreds died from illnesses including cholera, malaria and dysentery, some of which could largely have been avoided had there had been just *one* **real** revelation about sanitation and clean water before they were driven out *(See TMD Vol. 4:290-1)*.

Thousands died crossing the plains, many travelling at entirely the wrong time of year, using cheaply constructed handcarts instead of sturdy wagons drawn by oxen. Brigham Young did not provide either the right vehicles or advice and this led to countless deaths, many of which could and should have been avoided. Many more suffered and died from the effects of their journey after arriving in the valley *(see p. 57; also: Ensign, July, 1998, 'I have a Question')*. Since Jesus told the saints in 1830 to gather to one place to await his return, that entire generation has long since died, as have their children, their grandchildren – and their great-grand-children.

Verse 10 confirms the saints should gather in one place because "the hour is nigh", and yet that was over one-hundred-and-eighty years ago, since when the Church has 'gathered' to several different places. A little while before I joined the Mormon Church in 1960, leaders specifically asked members to *stop* gathering to Utah and to 'build the kingdom' where they lived, in complete contradiction to Jesus' instruction and prophecy given in 1830. The Church never has gathered (and I venture to suggest never will) to "one place" to await Jesus coming as he commanded in Section 29.

The "great and abominable church, which is the whore of all the earth, shall be cast down by devouring fire" in v.21. Early Mormons, including my own young generation, understood this to refer explicitly to the Roman Catholic Church. This idea ultimately became so politically incorrect that it was watered down and explained to mean *everything* outside of Mormonism; but when you think about it, that's even worse.

In v.34, Jesus confirms that *he* created Adam. Smith firmly believed in Adam and Eve, even 'discovering' Adam's altar which the saints would then travel to see. *(See TMD Vol. 2:186-7; Vol. 4:282-3)*. It is not surprising that Smith has Jesus confirm such a belief. The problem is that fewer people today (even within the Mormon Church) accept the Adam and Eve story as a version of reality, because scientific evidence of the truth discredits any possibility of the story being anything other than fictional. Many religious organisations today understand it to be just a construct to 'explain' a beginning, and many people, including the Pope, accept evolution as a fact and therefore the method by which God populated the world.

The Mormon Church does not take an official stand on evolution. It would be difficult for it to do so as on the one hand, if they reject it, they are rejecting what has long been accepted as proven scientific *fact* and no longer just a hypothesis, and on the other hand, if they accept it, they have to explain how Smith had Jesus get it so wrong about Adam. I had Jehovah's Witnesses visit me recently and I tried to explain evolution is now a known fact supported by several scientific disciplines, rendering the fossil record a kind of bonus. They asked "then why is it called a theory". I had to explain everything in science is labelled 'theory'; a word which has two meanings. Something is proposed as a hypothesis; some 'theories' get overturned whilst others become proven. They remain 'theories' whether proven or not, and that confuses some people.

The Church is thus stuck with the concept, along with Smith's increasingly embarrassing 'seven thousand years' of the Earth's existence *(See pp. 285-6)* which may not have been such a problem were it not a canonised 'explanation' of some of the book of Revelation – a book considered by many scholars to have been written by a madman.

It is also interesting that in describing Adam being cast out of the garden and hell being prepared for Satan, that **Jesus, who is speaking**, once again confirms that he is indeed **God**. Verse 41 clearly states: "Wherefore, **I, the Lord God**, caused that he should be cast out from the Garden of Eden." The same words are repeated in v.42 and then again in v.43.

Verses 43-44 are covered in *TMD Vol. 4* where the Mormon concept of the difference between immortality and eternal life is discussed. Biblically, it is the same thing. In 1830, that's what Smith also believed and these verses confirm it. Only later did Smith's new concept, differentiating between immortality and eternal life arise. *(See TMD Vol. 4:219-20) (S32-33)*.

After all the filler, this Section concludes by confirming that little children cannot sin. That is hardly a revelation and should be obvious to anyone who believes in sin – and of course it is more than obvious to the rest of the world who do not believe sin actually exists, except in the minds of believers in gods.

DOCTRINE & COVENANTS – SECTIONS 19-29

This is to be achieved "through mine Only Begotten;" (v.46) showing Smith has been moving between statements supposedly from Jesus and also from God – with no differentiation between speakers, thus again confirming his belief of the day that they were one and the same being.

Section 29 – Summary

Prophecies made: 1
Prophecies fulfilled: 0
Other non-prophetic revelation: 1

Prophecies made:

Pr. 17. The saints shall be "gathered in unto *one place* on the face of this land" and are to "be prepared in all things against the day when tribulation and desolation are sent forth upon the wicked".

Results:

Pr. 17. They 'gathered' at Kirtland; they 'gathered' in Nauvoo; they 'gathered' to Salt Lake; later the Church instructed members to *stop* gathering and build the kingdom where they lived.

Non-prophetic revelation. 1.

1, Verses 46-7. Little children are redeemed and without sin. This is similar to the beliefs of many other religions and not exactly a unique 'revelation' exclusive to Mormonism.

Section 28
September 1830. Fayette, New York.

History.

1833 BOC Ch. XXX. 1835 D&C Sec. LI. 2010 D&C Sec. 28.

Section 28 is discussed in *TMD Vol. 3:295-7. (S34-36)*. It concerns Hiram Page claiming to receive revelations through a seer stone and Oliver Cowdery being inclined to believe him. Unfortunately, Page's revelations concerned the "upbuilding of Zion and order of the Church" which wouldn't do for Joseph Smith at all. Smith, having to stamp his authority on matters and not wanting anyone else to get in on his act, quickly had a revelation wherein the Lord confirmed that only Smith's seer stone worked and Page had been deceived by Satan.

This is actually quite comical, as Smith got some of his own revelations wrong – such as the failed Canada trip to sell the Book of Mormon copyright – a trip confirmed by looking at his old money-digging seer stone in his hat.

Following the complete and utter failure of the trip, Smith repeated the same manner of seeking revelation, to discover *why* it failed – through the stone in his hat, for a second time, despite the fact that he had got it wrong with that method the first time. Smith himself declared that he could not be sure of his revelations stating that "Some revelations are of God: some revelations are of man: some revelations are of the devil." He had been deceived. *(Whitmer 1887:30-31; see also TMD Vol. 3:30)*. Smith later declined to add those two revelations to the D&C, declaring that he had been deceived and they were not from God. That says it all really.

What is also humorous is that Smith did not want to personally face Page about the issue. He sent Cowdery to do his dirty work for him and it was Cowdery who had to explain to Page that the devil had deceived him and only Smith had the Lord's ear. Smith just wrote down what he wanted the Lord to say for him and gave it to Cowdery.

Hiram Page obediently gave up his stone and agreed to follow only Smith's revelations. For good measure, his stone was ground down and his revelations were burned. Notwithstanding his faithfulness at that time, a few years later Page was excommunicated as a 'dissenter', along with several members of the Whitmer family, Oliver Cowdery and W. W. Phelps, during an 1838 power struggle. It happened when Smith and Rigdon fled Kirtland in fear of their lives and unexpectedly arrived in Far West. There had been a scandal over Smith's failed illegal Kirtland Bank. Mormons (including several apostles) who had lost everything were after Smith's blood. Ensuing law suits from gentiles later amounted to tens of thousands of dollars which characteristically, Smith never did pay. The money was eventually raised by members in order to keep Smith out of jail *(See TMD Vol. 3:42-44)*.

When Smith and Rigdon arrived in Far West, they immediately took over operations there. The existing leaders were none too pleased about Smith and Rigdon hijacking local authority. The outcome was that Smith simply had them all excommunicated. Page, along with some of the Whitmers, Oliver Cowdery, Martin Harris and others joined William McLellin's new 'Church of Christ' in 1847.

This section also tells Cowdery to go and preach to the Lamanites – and they all knew *exactly* who and where the Lamanites were; they also knew where the 'borders' of the Lamanites were (v.9), and yet today, Church leaders and their apologists haven't a clue where any Lamanites are.

Chapter 14

**Doctrine and Covenants
Sections 30–37 & 74**

Section 30
September 1830. Fayette, New York.

History.

1833 BOC Ch. XXXI-XXXIII. 1835 D&C Sec. LII. 2010 D&C Sec. 30.

This Section was originally three separate meaningless 'revelations' given to David Whitmer, Peter Whitmer Jr., and John Whitmer. In 1835, Smith combined them into one Section, adding 'Smith Jr.,' after 'Joseph' to more readily identify himself in v.7. They are all called to preach – and Peter is to preach to the *Lamanites*; once again providing evidence that they all had a clear understanding of exactly who the Lamanites were. Today, Mormon leaders and apologists have no idea who or where any Lamanites are – except that now, due to extensive DNA profiling of all the tribes, they know for sure who they are *not*. They *cannot* be any of the Native North American tribes; something that was undisputedly considered to be the case in Smith's day – and for that matter, in ***my*** day, as confirmed in no uncertain terms by Apostle Spencer W.

Kimball, who later became prophet of the Mormon Church – never to change his mind about whom the Lamanites were. If he and Joseph Smith were so wrong, then why didn't the Mormon God put them right? *(See also Section 32)*.

> With pride I tell those who come to my office that *a Lamanite is a descendant of one Lehi who left Jerusalem six hundred years before Christ* and with his family crossed the mighty deep and landed in America. And Lehi and his family became the *ancestors of all of the Indian and Mestizo tribes in North and South and Central America and in the islands of the sea,* for in the middle of their history there were those who left America in ships of their making and went to the islands of the sea. Not until the revelations of Joseph Smith, bringing forth the Book of Mormon, did anyone know of these migrants. It was not known before, but *now the question is fully answered.* Now *the Lamanites number about sixty million; they are in all of the states of America from Tierra del Fuego all the way up to Point Barrows, and they are in nearly all the islands of the sea from Hawaii South to New Zealand ... The descendants of this mighty people were called Indians by Columbus in 1492* when he found them here. *The term Lamanite includes all Indians and Indian mixtures, such as Polynesians, the Guatemalans, the Peruvians, as well as the Sioux, the Apache, the Mohawk, the Navajo, and others.* It is a large group of great people. *(Spencer W. Kimball. Of Royal Blood. Ensign: July 1971:7)*. (Emphasis added)

Kimball includes all and sundry as descendants of Lehi. Kimball's remarks were preceded by an introduction entitled "Lamanites". That introduction included this statement:

> Most members of the Church *know* that *the Lamanites, who consist of the Indians of all the Americas as well as the islanders of the Pacific*, are a people with a special heritage. (Emphasis added).

So, *direct* descendants of Lehi (then sixty million of them) are *everywhere*. Kimball claimed **ALL** the Native American Indian and Mestizo tribes covering the Americas *and* islands had descended from Lehi. That idea is now proven as entirely *false*; something that today appears to be accepted by the Church. Two years later, Kimball became prophet. As early as 1954, when Kimball was an apostle, he was already convinced as to who the Lamanites were:

> ...the Indian or Lamanite, with a background of twenty-five centuries of superstition, degradation, idolatry, and indolence... a people who, according to prophecies, have been scattered and driven, defrauded and deprived, who are a "branch of the tree of Israel - lost from its body - wanderers in a strange land" - their own land...

They may be Navajos or Cherokees… Mayas or Pimas… Piutes or Mohicans… these living descendants… will be redeemed, will rise and will become a blessed people. God has said it. *(Spencer W. Kimball, Conference Report, Apr. 1954:106-108).*

Kimball later made similar remarks, in 1975, when he was actually the *prophet* of the Church. He then stated: "When the Navajos returned from Fort Sumner after a shameful and devastating captivity, there were only 9,000 of them left; now there are more than 100,000. There are nearly 130 million Lamanites worldwide." He also said that: "There are now more than 350,000 Lamanite members of the Church." *(See more in TMD Vol. 2:176-83).*

In 1975, when I first read this, I was a twenty-nine year old firm believer in Mormonism and blindly accepted Kimball's assurances about the Lamanites. They were a further confirmation of my 'testimony' of the Book of Mormon. After all, he was my prophet and he knew all about such things.

I am sure that suggesting the Mormon Church perform its own DNA testing on its Lamanite members in order to prove their case would be met with stony silence today. Just because DNA evidence emerged only two or three decades after Kimball's claim makes him no less culpable or responsible for it. He was the Mormon prophet and here proves himself to be yet another *false* prophet. It is no good the Church claiming he wasn't speaking *as* prophet or that he didn't say "thus saith the Lord"; he was speaking in General Conference and members are taught that such remarks are to be held as *scripture. (See also pp. 189-92).*

Section 31
September 1830. Fayette, New York.

History.

1833 BOC Ch. XXXIV. 1835 D&C Sec. LIII. 2010 D&C Sec. 31.

This Section was specifically designated for Thomas B. Marsh, a man who had been baptised earlier the same month and was later called to preside over the Quorum of Twelve Apostles. Great things were in store for him. The words are apparently from Jesus and not of man. However, Jesus doesn't say much of anything other than Marsh is called to preach wherever takes his fancy. As ever, his sins are of course forgiven. This short Section is further padded out by the field being white, but strangely, on this occasion not 'ready to harvest', but rather, "already to be burned" (v.4). Marsh is nevertheless to thrust in his sickle and so forth. Smith often had trouble dreaming up new ideas. Jesus adds, in v.5 "Wherefore, your family shall live" – as if they may not have lived if he did not serve. That's all there is to the Section.

Marsh became President of the Quorum of Twelve Apostles on 2 May 1835 but during 1838, along with a number of other prominent members, he became disaffected due to Smith's aggressive stance taken against some non-Mormons.

In October of that year, Marsh prepared and co-signed an affidavit about Mormon attacks at Gallatin on Missourians. The document was used in the Missouri courts against Joseph Smith regarding charges of treason. *(See Quinn 1994:62; TMD 1:147)*. Marsh and others had turned state's evidence in the November 1838 trial. In March of 1839, in retaliation, Smith excommunicated Marsh (in absentia), along with Sampson Avard, George M. Hinckle; John Corrill; Reed Peck; Wm. W. Phelps; Frederick G. Williams; Burr Riggs and several others, for leaving the Church "in the time of our perils, persecutions and dangers, and were acting against the interests of the Church". *(Conference Minutes, 17 March 1839. See Times and Seasons V.1:15)*.

Incidentally, quite a number of Mormon writers and historians have, in modern times, been excommunicated for writings which were also considered "against the interests of the Church". Nothing changes. However, they were telling the truth and simply would not 'lie for the Lord'. All these 1839 excommunications were publicly made in absentia. The men had found out the truth about Smith. The Danites had burned Gallatin, stolen all the goods from the store and deposited them in the Bishop's storehouse at "Adam-on-diahmon". (The original spelling varied – now 'Adam-ondi-Ahman').

For those who still believe the 'milk strippings' saga attached to Thomas B. Marsh, it was just a false story invented to cover the fact that yet another apostle (he was President of the Twelve) had discovered the truth and left the Church. Even if the underlying story did have any merit, High Council records contain no such court details and Marsh certainly did not take the matter there or leave the Church for that reason. *(See TMD Vol. 3:175, 304, 320 n.6)*.

Section 32
October 1830. Fayette, New York.

History.

Not in 1833 BOC. 1835 D&C Sec. LIV. 2010 D&C Sec. 32.

This must now be a real embarrassment for the Church. The header, which was added *after* the 1835 edition but which has since *not* been changed, makes matters even worse. It states: *"Great interest and desires were felt by the elders respecting the Lamanites, of whose predicted blessings the Church had learned from the Book of Mormon. In consequence, supplication was made that the*

Lord would indicate his will as to whether elders should be sent at that time to the Indian tribes in the West." (Italics in original).

This Section is a response from Jesus who says "as I live I will that..." Parley P. Pratt, Oliver Cowdery, Peter Whitmer Jr., and Ziba Peterson should go "into the wilderness among the Lamanites ... and I myself will go with them and be in their midst." So, wherever they went – ***that*** is where the Lamanites are; just in case Mormon leaders and apologists want to know. And it was ***Jesus*** himself who said so – and he went with these men to teach them.

Section 33
October 1830. Fayette, New York.

History.

1833 BOC Ch. XXXV. 1835 D&C Sec. LV. 2010 D&C Sec. 33.

This is directed to Ezra Thayre and Northrop Sweet. It is *God* speaking. Smith is back for a fifth and final time to having God say His "word is quick and powerful, sharper than a two-edged sword, to the dividing asunder of the joints and marrow..." *(See pp. 112-14).* As usual, they are to preach with voices like the sound of a trump, and the field is white – which God mentions twice. It is the eleventh hour and the 'vineyard' is corrupt. They are to cry repentance but not told where to actually do so. The Church is built upon the rock of the gospel and the Book of Mormon and the Holy Scriptures are given for their instruction. Once again, He is going to come quickly – an expression usually attributed to Jesus, except God said He was speaking here. No matter whom it really meant was coming 'quickly', in the timeframe that everyone of the day expected, no one showed up. The Mormon Missionary Lesson Manual includes v.8-11, so missionaries are to say "Repent, repent, and prepare ye the way of the Lord, and make his paths straight; for the kingdom of heaven is at hand; Yea, repent and be baptized, every one of you," It turns out that it wasn't 'at hand' after all – and good luck with saying that kind of thing these days.

Section 34
4 November 1830. Fayette, New York.

History.

1833 BOC Ch. XXXVI. 1835 D&C Sec. LVI. 2010 D&C Sec. 34.

This is specifically for Orson Pratt. Jesus is speaking and he personally claims (v.2) that he is the light and life of the world. Then he declares in v.3 that he "so loved the world that he gave his own life, that as many as would believe might become the sons of God". Smith has *Jesus* declare it was *he* who loved the world so much that he gave himself. This is a strange departure from the traditional famous declaration *about* (not by) **God** giving His son, in John 3:16.

> **John 3:16.** For God so loved the world, that he gave his only begotten Son, that whosoever believeth in him should not perish, but have everlasting life.

Then we have the ever familiar things – Orson is his son; he is blessed because he believed Smith; he is to have a voice like a trump; cry repentance, preparing the way for the second coming which is "soon at hand" and he will "come in a cloud with power and great glory" – something Jesus only ever says *himself* through the mouth of Joseph Smith. Apart from the absurdity of Jesus declaring that he will come with power and great glory, an entirely pointless comment from an all powerful supreme being, why ever would he say he will come in a cloud? Nations will tremble, and v.9 mentions the sun and moon, covered in Section 29 *(see p. 154)*.

Orson is to prophesy about this, and once again Jesus will "come quickly" – but he didn't. He is actually coming more slowly by the century, thus making complete liars out of those he supposedly told, in 1830, to tell everyone that he would be there very soon, leading them to believe it would be well before the end of the nineteenth century. If any of that was real revelation and prophecy, Jesus was making complete fools of everyone and not giving them accurate or entirely understandable information regarding an anticipated timescale for his return. Getting on for two centuries later, no one can remotely suggest that 'any time soon' can still apply to the 1830 prophesy. Jesus lied – if Smith didn't.

Although I perhaps should, I am not including that as a prophecy, as the Church would no doubt fall back on the 'no man knows when' idea. However, for that to apply to Section 34, as well as several other sections, Jesus would have been better not saying anything about it at all. The Church today makes a big deal about giving a *false impression* being a form of lying.

Honest people love truth and justice.
They are honest in their words and actions.
Lying is intentionally deceiving others.
We can also intentionally deceive others by a gesture or a look,
by silence, or by telling only part of the truth.
Whenever we lead people in any way to believe something that is not true,
we are not being honest. (Emphasis added).
(Mormon Church Lesson Manual 'Gospel Principles' 1979. Chapter 31. Honesty).

DOCTRINE & COVENANTS – SECTIONS 30-37 & 74

If Joseph Smith is to be believed, giving an entirely *false* impression is *exactly* what Jesus did which is immoral, unfair – even devious. It should also be noted that whilst Jesus talks of so loving the world, through Smith's words, he also promises vengeance and retribution which will apparently affect a large proportion of humans who deserve better treatment. There is no good reason to believe Smith's version of God or Jesus, and to expect such severe and brutal punishment as predicted through Smith is unworthy of humans let alone deity. Would such words as these really come from an honest and loving Saviour?

Section 74
January 1832 (Re-dated December 1830). Hiram, Ohio.

History.

Not in 1833 BOC. 1835 D&C Sec. LXXIII. 2010 D&C Sec. 74.

Section 74 is dated to January 1832 at Hiram, Ohio, in the current D&C. The *JS Papers, Vol. 2:512 & 721* re-date it to circa December 1830, and that calls into question the location, as Smith was in Fayette, New York at that period, some three-hundred miles from Hiram.

The header refers to a conference to be held on 25 January. *"Upon the reception of the foregoing word of the Lord [D&C 73], I recommended the translation of the Scriptures, and labored diligently until just before the conference, which was to convene on the 25th of January. During this period I also received the following, as an explanation of the First Epistle to the Corinthians, 7th chapter, 14th verse."* (History of the Church,1:242). (Italics in original).

'History of the Church' does indeed read that way, following the record of what is now Section 73 which *JS Papers Vol. 2* dates, the same as the current D&C, to 10 January 1832. There is no mention of such a conference in January of *1831* in the Sections surrounding that period *(Sections 35 to 40)*, so I am confused about the new dating in the JS Papers. However, as my current work concerns what is actually *in* the so-called revelations, rather than exactly when they were written, I will leave it at placing Sec. 74 where the Church currently, albeit illogically, suggests it belongs, according to *JS Papers Vol. 2*.

In this section, Smith claims the Lord revealed to him that 1 Corinthians 7:14 means that circumcision was done away with and not required for children in the Church. However, in his *Inspired Revision* of the Bible, Smith left that verse exactly as it was in the KJV and repeated it as v.1 in D&C 74. Smith's note on it was pointless really, regardless of when it was written; especially as the Lord didn't 'inspire' Smith to clarify it in his Inspired Revision.

THE MORMON DELUSION
Section 35
7 December 1830. Fayette, New York.

History.

1833 BOC Ch. XXXVII. 1835 D&C Sec. XI. 2010 D&C Sec. 35.

This Section is yet another in which Smith immediately confirms that God and Jesus are one and the same being. Smith is *not* having God speak about Himself, with God and Jesus just being one in purpose. Firstly, the speaker is identified *as* God and then *as* Jesus, establishing the concept of a single being.

There is *no* change of speaker indicated. "Listen to the voice of God" – so we expect to hear God speak, and next he confirms "I am Jesus Christ, the Son of God." He says all can become one – as they are one. That means something else entirely in the Mormon Church today, but it certainly didn't in 1830. For those who may think God spoke and then Jesus spoke, v.8 confirms that God is *still* speaking.

> **1.** Listen to the voice of the Lord your God, even Alpha and Omega, the beginning and the end, whose course is one eternal round, the same today as yesterday, and forever.
> **2.** I am Jesus Christ, the Son of God, who was crucified for the sins of the world, even as many as will believe on my name, that they may become the sons of God, even one in me as I am one in the Father, as the Father is one in me, that we may be one...
>
> **8.** For I am God, and mine arm is not shortened...

Sidney Rigdon is called to be scribe for Smith during Smith's retranslation of the Bible after Oliver Cowdery and John Whitmer, who had been helping out, were given other assignments. Smith seemed to feel the need for God to tell Rigdon this rather than just ask him personally. It gave Smith the chance for God (as God, and simultaneously Jesus) to promise Rigdon all sorts of things which could never be materially quantified but as a believer would have sounded good to him. Does v.14 give the measure of God, or just Smith's ability to story tell? Speaking of Smith's followers, this is God speaking; v.14: "...and their enemies shall be under their feet; and I will let fall the sword in their behalf, and by the fire of mine indignation will I preserve them." Is it God or Smith who has an obsession with swords?

Verse 15 talks about the poor and meek having the gospel preached to them "and they shall be looking forth for the time of my coming, for it is nigh at hand—" yet not *once* does God ever tell them that it won't be for *centuries* –

causing everyone much confusion and complete misunderstanding; their logical expectations were never fulfilled. Essentially, if this was real revelation, you could now state quite categorically that God (as God and as Jesus), in several instances already covered, lied completely about this matter, giving more than just the wrong impression.

Verse 20 once again confirms Rigdon is to write for Smith and then God adds "and the scriptures shall be given, even as they are in mine own bosom" which is quite strange in that Smith's revision did not exactly change anything of significance – other than confirming God and Jesus *are* one and the same being where it could have been taken that they were separate *(see: KJV Luke 10:22 vs. IR Luke 10:23)* and providing a whole new 'Book of Moses' with *dozens* of references to 'God' in the singular, completely contradicting his later pretended translation of papyri into the 'Book of Abraham' which has the very same acts being carried out in dozens of references to 'Gods' in the plural – where God still does *not* have a body of course as it was written pre-1836. Whatever all that was doing 'in God's bosom' when Smith played around with the KJV, only He knows.

Once again, the heavens are going to "shake for your good" (v.24) but we still don't learn what good they will shake *for*. Satan will tremble for an equally undisclosed reason and Zion will rejoice and flourish. This was of course 1830, and it really didn't flourish, not for a very long time. God does add the caveat that "Israel shall be saved in mine own due time" but even then, something is now running more than just a little late, however you look at it.

Section 36
9 December 1830. Fayette, New York.

History.

1833 BOC Ch. XXXVIII. 1835 D&C Sec. LVII. 2010 D&C Sec. 36.

This 'revelation' incorporates much of what Smith had by now got used to proclaiming about someone. It is for Edward Partridge and is effectively a 'blessing' from God. There are no prizes for guessing what he is told. He is blessed; his sins are forgiven; he is called to preach "as with the voice of a trump" because God – or at least Smith, seemed to like trumps. Sidney Rigdon is to lay his hands on Partridge to give him the Holy Ghost and then Partridge is to "declare it" with a loud voice saying "Hosanna, blessed be the name of the most high God." I am not sure who would have listened if he ever did that.

Next, anyone willing to do so is to be ordained and called to go out and preach repentance. As in some other instances, both God *and* Jesus claim to be speaking, reemphasising Smith's monotheistic theology of the day. There are only seven verses and in the first verse "the Lord God, the Mighty One of Israel" announces Himself, and the last verse concludes with "I am Jesus Christ, the Son of God" – one and the same being with no announced change in speaker.

Jesus continues "wherefore, gird up your loins and I will suddenly come to my temple. Even so. Amen." Even so – he suddenly *didn't* – and to this day he still hasn't. Smith claimed Jesus appeared in the Kirtland Temple in 1836 but of course that cannot be substantiated. In any event, it was a claimed 'visit' and not the second coming; something which is always inferred from such claims.

Section 37
30 December 1830. Fayette, New York.

History.

1833 BOC Ch. XXXIX. 1835 D&C Sec. LVIII. 2010 D&C Sec. 37.

This little section was given about the time Smith was starting to create his 'Inspired Revision' of the Bible. The Lord excuses Smith from continuing for the time being. The header states that it is the *first* mention of a 'gathering'.

Whoever wrote that clearly hadn't read Section 29:8, reviewed earlier. "…the decree hath gone forth from the Father that they shall be gathered in unto one place upon the face of this land…" so this is *not* the first time they have been commanded to gather – unless the writer thinks a 'decree' from the Lord does not constitute a commandment. The Mormon Church can be quite pedantic when it suits, yet also liberal with excuses when needs must. I am including Section 37 below as it is short and the reader can then quickly see what it leads up to:

Section 37.

Revelation given to Joseph Smith the Prophet and Sidney Rigdon, near Fayette, New York, December 1830 (see History of the Church, *1:139). Herein is given the first commandment concerning a gathering in this dispensation. 1–4, The Saints are called to gather at the Ohio.*

DOCTRINE & COVENANTS – SECTIONS 30-37 & 74

1. Behold, I say unto you that it is not expedient in me that ye should translate any more until ye shall go to the Ohio, and this because of the enemy and for your sakes.
2. And again, I say unto you that ye shall not go until ye have preached my gospel in those parts, and have strengthened up the church whithersoever it is found, and more especially in Colesville; for, behold, they pray unto me in much faith.
3. And again, a commandment I give unto the church, that it is expedient in me that they should assemble together at the Ohio, against the time that my servant Oliver Cowdery shall return unto them.
4. Behold, here is wisdom, and let every man choose for himself until I come. Even so. Amen.

What these verses lead up to is the concept that the saints should gather, albeit each man (not *person*, and as ever, no mention of *women*) can choose for himself – "until I come", with the clear implication that the second coming would be within the lifetime of those being addressed. If the Church claims that this is not explicit, because obviously it didn't happen, then the statement is misleading and deceitful, as anyone hearing it at the time would have expected to have been alive when Jesus returned. The implication was clear. The Church didn't exactly permanently gather at the Ohio any more than the other locations they later selected. At the end of the day, this Section amounted to nothing.

Chapter 15

**Doctrine and Covenants
Sections 38 – 50**

Section 38
January 1831. Fayette, New York.

History.

1833 BOC Ch. XL. 1835 D&C Sec. XII. 2010 D&C Sec. 38.

This Section commences with yet another unequivocal declaration by the 'voice' Smith claims to be hearing, that God and Jesus comprise one and the same being. There can be *no* debate about this absolutely specific statement.

> Thus saith **the Lord your God, even Jesus Christ, the Great I AM, Alpha and Omega, the beginning and the end,** the same which looked upon the wide expanse of eternity, and all the seraphic hosts of heaven, before the world was made; (Emphasis added).

God is keeping the wicked in chains of darkness to await the judgment which will come at the end of the earth when those who "will not hear my voice but harden their hearts, and wo, wo, wo, is their doom" (v.6). Yet again, I have to question whether that really sounds like a sequence of words one would reasonably expect from deity. In v.8, Jesus claims that the saints are *soon* going to see him. Despite the fact that many such statements led the saints to firmly believe they would indeed live to see his return, of course no one ever did.

Next, God is going to reveal a mystery (v.13), which turns out to be that they will receive great riches and also a 'land of promise' flowing with milk and honey; something which is of course far from an original idea. The fact is they 'gathered' to different places, at least one of which was considered to be where they would stay, before ultimately traversing the plains to Utah several years later, and they suffered enormously over the intervening years.

Assuming the Church claims the Salt Lake area to now actually be the land of promise, they didn't exactly get the right direction from the Lord in this revelation of 1831. They are also to possess their land of promise again in eternity, according to v.20, but that doesn't account for scientific calculations concerning the eventual fate of not just the Earth, but the universe, which will not actually last for all eternity. Due to the ongoing effects of entropy, the entire universe will likely consist only of photons in about 10^{100} years time. Not that such a notion will concern the Church at the moment, as that of course is a very long time into the future.

In v.22, the Lord says "ye shall have no laws but my laws when I come" and then in v.32 he says "I gave unto you the commandment that ye should go to the Ohio; and there I will give unto you my law". Section 42, written just a few weeks later, has a modern-day heading claiming it includes the 'law' that the Lord was referring to. We will be reviewing that idea shortly.

Sections 39 & 40
5 January and 6 January 1831. Fayette, New York.

History.

1833 BOC Ch. XLI. 1835 D&C Sec. LIX. 2010 D&C Sec. 39.
1833 BOC Ch. XLII. 1835 D&C Sec. LX. 2010 D&C Sec. 40.

These two sections are thoroughly dealt with in *TMD Vol. 3:298-301. (S36-40)*. In brief, they concern Jesus giving a very flowery revelation (Section 39) concerning Smith's latest protégé, one James Covill, a Baptist minister who offered to join the Church. He never was baptised and when he ignored Smith's revelatory direction to go to the Ohio, as he wanted to go 'back east' and preach, Smith was left in a very embarrassing situation. This he quickly tried to overcome by recording Section 40.

DOCTRINE & COVENANTS – SECTIONS 38-50

Something I had not been aware of when writing *TMD Vol. 3*, that we now learn from the Church published *Joseph Smith Papers: Revelations and Translations, Volume 2*, is that D&C 40 was 'received' the very *next day* in order to explain things away. *(JS Papers, Vol. 2:497-8)*.

In Section 39, dated 5th January, Jesus says he 'knows' Covill and proceeds to give him all kinds of blessings and promises, but then makes his mistake by telling Covill that he is called to go to the Ohio. Covill doesn't go. On the very next day, 6th January, Jesus admits he didn't get Covill right after all and Satan got to him, apparently *overnight*. I previously assumed there were several days or even weeks between the two 'revelations' to allow time for Covill to refuse the assignment and decide not to join the Church after all. The fact that Section 40 was penned the very next day strongly suggests that Covill had no intention of joining the Church and just wanted to see what Smith would come up with if he pretended to have a serious interest. He was after all, a Baptist minister of some forty years standing.

Whatever the case, Smith was then stuck with Section 39 which he claimed was from Jesus. In order to somehow accommodate the awkward situation this left for Smith, he not only dictated Section 40, wherein Jesus had to explain his mistake, he also *falsified* the original 1833 BOC account of what is now Section 39, in the 1835 D&C version by adding the words "*if* thou wilt hearken to my voice, which saith unto thee" to v.10, thus implying that the Lord knew he may yet *not* be baptised. A supposed prophet cannot add words at a *later* date, *pretending* they were *originally* spoken but for some reason omitted, just because things did not go the way he predicted, yet this was a typical Smith ploy. The words weren't even added the following day when Section 40 was dictated; they were added *years* after the 1833 publication.

The Lord also prophesies 'a great blessing' for them.

> **15.** And inasmuch as my people shall assemble themselves at the Ohio, I have kept in store a blessing such as is not known among the children of men, and it shall be poured forth upon their heads.

As it turned out, there was not much of a blessing awaiting the saints at all, whichever way you look at things. However, I have not included that promise as an unfulfilled prophecy as it is a meaningless and unquantifiable prediction.

As ever, the vineyard is going to be 'pruned' for the last time and it is such statements that led the saints to firmly believe they would be the ones to conclude matters before the Saviour returned – in their own lifetimes.

In Section 40, Jesus' excuse for getting Covill so wrong is that Satan immediately got to Covill – but he never explains why he, the Lord, who supposedly knows *everything*, did not know that would happen *prior* to making Covill such an abundance of promises just twenty-four hours earlier and thus making such a fool of himself. It is certainly evidence of an entirely false revelation – if not of false prophecy; moreover it is evidence of a false prophet.

Sections 39 & 40 – Summary

Non-prophetic revelation: 1

1. Jesus is recorded as pronouncing an abundance of blessings and promises on James Covill, a man he says he 'knows'. Covill is called to the Ohio.

Almost immediately, Jesus is obliged to somehow excuse the fact that Covill took no notice of his supposed call to the Ohio and didn't even so much as get baptised. Covill returned east and notwithstanding Jesus saying he would "do with him as seemeth me good", Covill lived until he was eighty-eight years of age and continued to serve as a Baptist minister. Jesus' excuse was that Satan got to Covill *(Sec. 40)* and yet Jesus should have known what would happen the previous day and not have made such embarrassing promises and predictions in the first instance. It serves only to prove once again that Jesus was certainly not involved with the claimed revelation *(Sec. 39)* at all.

Section 41
4 February 1831. Kirtland, Ohio.

History.

1833 BOC Ch. XLIII. 1835 D&C Sec. LXI. 2010 D&C Sec. 41.

This little Section appears to have come about primarily because there was some disagreement between members of the fledgling group as to what the Church was about and some 'strange notions' had crept in, according to the header. The Lord doesn't take the time to set out his own stall and actually explain any of his requirements; rather, in v.2, he tells them to agree what his word is – among themselves.

> **2.** Hearken, O ye elders of my church whom I have called, behold I give unto you a commandment, that ye shall assemble yourselves together to agree upon my word;

Those who do as they are told – "receiveth my law and doeth it", will be fine, but those who don't like it – "receiveth it and doeth it not", are to be thrown out – "cast out from among you", and that is *exactly* what happened.

Anyone who did not like what Smith said they should do, or indeed what Smith himself did, was branded a 'dissenter' and invariably driven out – unless they very quickly 'repented'.

The Lord explains that "prayer of your faith" will do to ascertain what is right and from God. For a *committee* to agree on the Lord's "word" on such a basis reminds me of the early Christian Church which did exactly the same thing at the Council of Nicaea in 325 CE. Just as Constantine didn't much care what the committee decided, so Smith did not appear to care how they ran their local Church or meetings and left them to it. Perhaps he had run out of ideas.

This is followed by the Lord saying something more or less the same as is found in the Sermon on the Mount in Matthew 7:6, although the phraseology used in the D&C version leaves a lot to be desired and is clearly not 'Christ-like'.

> **D&C 41:6.** For it is not meet that the things which belong to the children of the kingdom should be given to them that are not worthy, or to dogs, or the pearls to also be cast before swine.

Not that there is the remotest chance of any original words that may or may not have been spoken by the Saviour being accurately recorded decades later in the Gospels, through at least second or third hand memories – this is what is recorded in Matthew in comparison to what Smith has Jesus say in D&C 41:6. Whether it really reflects words of Jesus or not, there is no denying the quality.

> **Matt. 7:6.** Give not that which is holy unto the dogs, neither cast ye your pearls before swine, lest they trample them under their feet, and turn again and rend you.

Having got the local problem out of the way by telling the elders to decide between themselves what is right, in the very next verse Smith has the Lord say that Smith should have a house built for him so he can translate there. Nice move. Next, Sidney Rigdon should 'live as seemeth him good' whatever that means, and Edward Partridge is to be the Bishop of the Church in that area. Although not specifically mentioned in this Section, such early leaders were to be financially supported by members, a tradition that ended in the late 1800s.

Section 42
9 & 23 February 1831. Kirtland, Ohio.

History.

1833 BOC Ch. XLIV & XLVII. 1835 D&C Sec. XIII. 2010 D&C Sec. 42.

When BOC XLIV and XLVII were first recorded, they were worded somewhat differently to what ended up in the D&C in 1835, where they were combined; adding extra verses (74-77) in what became Section XIII. For those who would like to compare the extensive changes, additions and deletions made to this Section, the following is a direct link to the correct page at 2think.org where there is an analysis: http://www.2think.org/hundredsheep/boc/boc44.shtml.

Alterations from v.78 on (previously BOC XLVII) have *not* been noted at 2think.org. My comments on that have been kindly added at the bottom of the above web page. There are several changes to the original text, but none that are of material significance. They just demonstrate yet again that God could not have spoken the original words as recorded, or for that matter the later changes.

The heading to the original BOC Chapter XLIV says "A revelation given to *twelve* elders assembled in Kirtland, Ohio; and also the law for the government of the Church, given in the presence of the same, February, 1831." The original BOC Chapter XLVII header says "A revelation given to *seven* elders of the church, assembled in Kirtland, Ohio, given February 1831". The 1835 D&C *combination* of the two chapters which then became Section XIII simply says "Revelation given February 1831". The two intermediate revelations (now Sections 43 & 44) were to "the elders" and "Joseph and Sidney" respectively.

Today, most rank and file Mormons will have no idea that Section 42 consists of two distinct revelations, separated by two weeks and two other revelations, later combined and significantly altered *without* reference. They will think the Lord revealed it all at the same time and to the same twelve people. You may ask if that really matters. If only in the interest of honesty and integrity, of course it matters. This kind of subterfuge was endemic in Smith's work and still continues in the Mormon Church today. As such evidence is discovered, it is rarely explained or corrected by the Church; it is just ignored.

The modern-day D&C 42 header states *"Revelation given through Joseph Smith the Prophet, at Kirtland, Ohio, 9 February 1831"* and that it was *"received in the presence of twelve elders and in fulfillment of the Lord's promise previously made that the "law" would be given in Ohio (see section 38:32). The Prophet specifies this revelation as "embracing the law of the Church."* (Italics in original). Members are thus somewhat misinformed, as only the first part of it relates to 9 February; v.78 onwards comprises what was originally BOC XLVII, given on 23 February to just *seven* elders, and we don't even know if they were some of the original twelve or seven different elders.

If information is to be inserted, surely it is important that it be historically *accurate* and properly *annotated*. In effect, this creates entirely unnecessary lies and deception. Add to that the fact that the text has undergone multiple changes, additions and deletions, and then it once again brings into question the very idea that these were the Lord's words in the first instance. Words claimed to come directly from the Lord almost always seemed to need later alteration or 'clarification' (as the Mormon Church would have it) in order to tidy up the mess Smith made of recording them.

In this Section, all the elders are to go out in twos and preach, except Smith and Rigdon who don't have to go. The pairs are to go westward and build up the church in each area until the New Jerusalem is prepared and the Lord gathers them together. Elders, priests and teachers are to teach "the principles of my gospel, which are in the Bible and the Book of Mormon, in the which is the fulness of the gospel" (v.12) – which as discussed elsewhere, "in the which the fulness of the gospel" is absolutely *not*.

Then we have the commandments that everyone has been waiting for, as promised in Section 38. There is nothing surprising here. They are not to kill, and anyone who does will not be forgiven in this life *or* the next (v.18). I am not sure how they excused all the later murders perpetrated by Mormons who theologically will never be forgiven – the Aitkin party murders and Mountain Meadows massacre for example. *(See TMD 3, Section 4 for more examples).*

A number of years ago, a son of some friends of mine committed a double premeditated murder (homicide) when he stabbed a young man and woman to death and received two life sentences for his crime. As the years passed, his parents, a strong Mormon couple, were struggling with the absolute knowledge that doctrinally their son could *never* be forgiven for his actions. His mother was particularly grief stricken and it seemed to be affecting her health.

As I had a friend in the Quorum of Twelve Apostles, I wrote asking him if perhaps the prophet of the day could take a moment to write to the couple and offer them some words of consolation. He responded that the prophet was too busy and it was not the sort of thing that could reasonably be asked of him. I didn't ask why. However, he himself wrote a very kind letter to the couple and enclosed a copy for me. It was indeed very consoling, which is all I had asked of him; but I was stunned to read his words to them which went far beyond any consolation. He actually stated that there was hope for their son and that one day, in the eternities, it was possible that he may be forgiven for what he had done. He didn't so much as promise it *would* happen, but he gave them *hope* for something that up to that point I *knew* was doctrinally impossible.

I was amazed and at the time, although my wife and I were happy that our friends were comforted, we had a lot of trouble getting our heads around how doctrinally such a thing could ever be so. We did not mention our concern to anyone. Now I understand completely. Mormon doctrines are made up as people think they should apply to the generation of the day and often change as time goes by. This is evidenced in so many areas; not least of which is the ever changing but doctrinally unalterable temple endowment ceremony.

THE MORMON DELUSION

The Mormon Church ultimately, albeit usually somewhat later than might be more appreciated (as was the case with those of black African descent and the Priesthood), generally moves with the times and the tide of popular public opinion rather than stick rigidly to the Lord's claimed original and supposedly unchangeable doctrines.

What was once doctrinally sound is often later not considered in the same way at all. It is more evidence that God was and is *not* involved in Mormonism. God needs to be *seen* to be consistent and unchanging; the same yesterday, today and forever; the Mormon God is anything *but* that. 1831 – murder *cannot* be forgiven in this life *or* the next *(The Lord)*. Late twentieth century – double premeditated murder *might* be forgiven one day *(letter on file from Elder Jeffery R. Holland, Mormon Apostle)*.

Next, we learn that they are not to steal or lie – as if they didn't already know and understand that, and then we get this:

> **22.** Thou shalt love thy wife with all thy heart, and shalt cleave unto her and none else.
> **23.** And he that looketh upon a woman to lust after her shall deny the faith, and shall not have the Spirit; and if he repents not he shall be cast out.
> **24.** Thou shalt not commit adultery; and he that committeth adultery, and repenteth not, shall be cast out.
> **25.** But he that has committed adultery and repents with all his heart, and forsaketh it, and doeth it no more, thou shalt forgive;
> **26.** But if he doeth it again, he shall not be forgiven, but shall be cast out.

This was of course during Smith's monogamous period, before he had his first recorded adulterous affair with Fanny Alger. It is interesting how times change. We learn, directly from the Lord, that if someone commits adultery and earnestly repents, they may be forgiven – but if they do it *again*, then "he shall not be forgiven, but shall be cast out". I wonder how it came about that a few years ago, I sat on a High Council disciplinary hearing in respect of a Melchizedek Priesthood holder who was then readmitted to the Church for a *third* time following his repeated adultery – in direct violation of the above revelation.

They are not to speak evil of their neighbours or to do them harm. I wonder if they *ever* considered non-Mormon locals to be 'neighbours' in that sense. If so, they developed a funny way of showing it by plundering and looting instead of honouring the Lord's mandate. Smith then seems to realise there is nothing new here and has the Lord say they know his laws as they are in the scriptures. The question is – why did he bother to repeat them. If anyone sins and doesn't repent they are to be cast out, repeating what was said in earlier revelations.

They are to look after the poor, and property consecrated to the Church can never be taken back from the Church. Each person was to have a 'stewardship' according to their needs. That meant that if anyone did decide to leave or they got 'cast out', they then left with *nothing*. After more filler, there is yet another reminder that if members got things wrong they would be cast out, allowing for confirmation that if that happened they would indeed leave with nothing: "and shall not receive again that which he has consecrated unto the poor and the needy of my church, or in other words, unto me—" (v.37). Or in other words, unto Smith & co—.

I mention v.39 in *TMD Vol. 3*. The comment is short and worth repeating here:

> **BOC 44:32** had read "...for I will consecrate the *riches of the gentiles* unto the poor of my people which are of the house of Israel." They really believed God gave them the right to just *take* things. Whitmer was against publishing the revelations (especially ones like this) in case they provoked hostility from the gentiles. Smith and Rigdon would not listen and they sent the book to Independence for publishing. The destruction of the press during printing and the resulting hostilities are recorded history.
>
> The same verse, when printed (as **D&C 42:39**) in 1835 was *altered* to read "...for I will consecrate of the *riches of those who embrace my gospel among the gentiles* unto the poor of my people who are of the house of Israel." If ever a 'clarification' was more of a *falsification* in order to soften a position previously taken, I have yet to see one. Theologically, everything the gentiles had, belonged to the saints and when they could, members just stole them. *(TMD 3:321-2)*.

Clearly, the original words of 1831, as published in 1833, were not from the Lord any more than the rehashed version of 1835. Would God really say the riches of the gentiles were for the poor saints, when the only way they ever got their hands on such things was by theft? Equally, if it is claimed the Lord did actually say that, then why was it altered to soften the meaning, including only those who were rich *and* converted?

Back to the 'laws'; they are not to be proud, they are to dress plainly, keep clean and not be idle. They are to look after the sick and the Elders can bless them. Whether the sick then live or die, they do so "unto me" says the Lord. If the sick are "not appointed unto death" and have faith, they will live – a statement that makes little sense at all, as inherent within that concept is the possibility that someone who is *not* "appointed unto death" but does *not* have the faith to be healed could die anyway. Those who have faith to 'see', 'hear' or 'leap' will do so, but there is no documented historical medical evidence provided to substantiate such miracles actually happening during the early period of the Mormon Church. They are not to take things that don't belong to them ('thy brother's garment') and anything they don't need is to be given to the storehouse.

Smith's "nation, kindred, tongue and people" fetish.

We move on to the scriptures (from v.56) and the gospel is to be preached to "all nations, kindreds, tongues and people" (v.58). This is a very familiar expression within Mormonism because Smith used it at the beginning of his 'Testimony of Three Witnesses' and also the 'Eight Witnesses' for his Book of Mormon. It is a particularly interesting expression – and this is why. Smith used it in that *exact* sequence, sometimes singular and sometimes plural, no less than *nine* times in the D&C, once in JS–History, and *fifteen* times, by *eight* different characters in his Book of Mormon, in *addition* to several other quite *similar* expressions.

In D&C 7:3, Smith claims the apostle *John* wrote that exact sequence on parchment that Smith saw, presumably in his imagination, and translated. In addition to this Section (42:58), in Sections 10:51; 88:103; 98:33; 112:1 and 133:37 the **Lord** is repeating the sequence. In D&C 77 verses 8 and 11, Smith in explaining Revelation 7:1-2 uses the exact expression twice.

In addition to my own count, in speaking of locals going to war against the saints, in D&C 98:34-36 Smith has the Lord use it twice more, just omitting the word 'kindred', as clearly the saints would not go to war against their own.

In JS–History 1:33, *Moroni* is speaking. Smith has him say "...my name should be had for good and evil among all **nations**, **kindreds**, and **tongues**, or that it should be both good and evil spoken of among all **people**" – in the same sequence.

From the Book of Mormon, we have exactly the same sequence of words from **Lehi** *(1 Nephi 5:18)*, **Nephi** *(1 Nephi 11:36; 14:11; 22:28; 2 Nephi 26:13; 30:8)* **Zenos** *(1 Nephi 19:17)* **King Benjamin** *(Mosiah 3:20)*, **Abinadi** *(Mosiah 15:28; 16:1)*, **Alma the son of Alma** *(Alma 9:20; 37:4; 45:16)*, Alma the Younger, quoting **the Lord** *(Mosiah 27:25)*, and **Mormon** *(3 Nephi 28:29)*. Additionally, in the Book of Mormon we get several other *similar* occurrences; for example: "...all people, and all kindreds, and all nations and tongues" *(3 Nephi 26:4)* and "...every kindred, nation, and tongue" *(Mosiah 3:13)*; similar phrases to other examples found in the book of Revelation (see below). Smith used quite a number of other quite similar phrases, but he clearly remembered "nations, kindreds, tongues, and people" best.

DOCTRINE & COVENANTS – SECTIONS 38-50

The 'Testimony of Three Witnesses' and 'Testimony of Eight Witnesses' in the Book of Mormon both start with: "Be it known unto all nations, kindreds, tongues, and people…" so it doesn't take a genius to work out who wrote that for the witnesses to sign.

Smith plagiarised the sequence of words from Revelation 14:6 which reads "every nation, kindred, tongue and people." Ignoring for a moment the fact that many historians consider Revelation to have been written by a lunatic, and that originally it wasn't going to be included in the Bible at all, it most certainly was *not* written by the apostle John and was of course penned many decades after Christ lived. Those words, in that sequence, had never before that moment ever been recorded *anywhere* at all – other that is, than if you believe Smith's multiple Book of Mormon claims where it is used at least fifteen times by eight different characters.

In chronological order, the first person to have ever said those words would have been Smith's fictional Old Testament prophet 'Zenos' whom Nephi claims said it some time before 600 BCE. The Book of Mormon was written in 1829 and instances of use of that phrase were backdated to anything from over 600 BCE through to the early CE period.

Smith simply used the expression he located in the KJV of Revelation 14:6 on no less than *twenty-six separate occasions*, attributing the words to several different characters and also many times to the Lord, who was not recorded in the Bible as having ever used such an expression at all. Smith also failed to spot the fact that whoever wrote Revelation also used the words at least four different times but **not once** in the same sequence…

Rev. 5:9.	kindred, and tongue, and people, and nation;
Rev. 7:9.	nations, and kindreds, and people, and tongues
Rev. 11:9.	people and kindreds and tongues and nations
Rev. 14:6.	nation, and kindred, and tongue, and people

Revelation also contains some other similar expressions, such as 10:11, "…peoples, and nations, and tongues, and kings" and 13:7 "…all kindreds, and tongues, and nations". There are expressions as far back as Genesis, showing how somewhat similar expressions were used and how the words and context varied – and were also used in more realistic settings than Smith's. Genesis 10:20 says "…after their tongues, in their countries, and in their nations" and 10:31 has "….after their families, after their tongues, in their lands, after their nations". The significance of biblical scriptures, when compared with Smith's evidenced fiction, shines through in these as well as other instances where explanations are *not* consistently identical. Smith's are more than suspicious.

I had never considered it previously, but what is the probability of so many different characters from varying periods of history, with some on different continents, using those *exact* words in that *exact* sequence *so many times*? I can tell you it is so close to zero that it is *impossible* rather than merely improbable.

Smith found the phrase and used it numerous times by multiple characters in his Book of Mormon. He had the Lord use it several times in his D&C revelations between 1828 and 1837, yet the Lord *never* used it before or since then. He liked it so much that Smith also used it for testimonies of 'three' and 'eight' witnesses, and in 1838 Smith recorded Moroni using it during his claimed visit, which Smith then backdated to 1823. ***Every*** reference that Smith made, from his Moroni claim, the Book of Mormon, for the witness statements, and D&C revelations, was *written* between 1828 and 1837 – all twenty-six, plus several others which I have not included, that closely match the sequence.

Imagine someone trying to express the idea that everyone in the world should be told something, or that something would affect everyone. They may say to tell all of your family (kindred); they may mention all nations; they may say no matter what language people speak, they must somehow be told; they may even add the idea that it encompasses all 'people'; but so many different characters using the very same words in *exactly* the same sequence? *Never*.

We would expect *original* statements which may on occasion have been somewhat similar but significantly different enough to allow for them *not* to have been plagiarised. For that *exact* sequence of words to appear even once or twice in ancient America in the same format as used in Revelation, it could be considered very suspicious and more than just mere coincidence. It appears *twenty-six* times, used by many different characters in various locations over a huge timescale, including several times by the Lord who was not even the originator of the phrase. There is *no* other explanation for this other than the obvious. These are not divine words. Smith and his helpers had to be the ones to concoct every single instance of the use of that expression outside the book of Revelation, along with inventing every single character who ever used it – including Smith's version of the Lord.

We move on in v.61 to something that may not look remarkable at first glance but which is actually quite interesting. It says "If thou shalt ask, thou shalt receive revelation upon revelation, knowledge upon knowledge, that thou mayest know the mysteries" – but *why* is that so interesting? For two reasons; firstly there is nothing Smith later 'revealed' that is remotely a real revelation giving any worthwhile information or knowledge and there are certainly no real mysteries revealed in his works of fiction. Secondly, as discussed elsewhere, when recent Mormon prophet Hinckley was asked how he received revelation, he said he didn't get any and that the Lord no longer provided it the way he once did. He only ever got *feelings* – and even then he had to think of questions to ask first. No mysteries are being revealed any more, but then there weren't actually any in Smith's day either, regardless of Mormon claims. *(See p. xiv)*.

In v.62 the Lord explains that "...it shall be revealed unto you in mine own due time where the New Jerusalem shall be built". In the book of Revelation, which the Mormon Church accepts as scripture, the writer, who claims to be 'John', explains that he knew "the name of the city of my God, which is new Jerusalem, which cometh down out of heaven from my God" *(Rev 3:12)* and that he "saw the holy city, new Jerusalem, coming down from God out of heaven..." *(Rev. 21:2)*, but that is not exactly the Mormon take on their New Jerusalem.

It should be noted that 'new Jerusalem' does not appear *anywhere* in the Bible at all, other than the two references in Revelation mentioned above. 'Jerusalem' is mentioned 626 times in the Old Testament, the first occasion being in the book of Joshua, a person who dates to around 1440 BCE – give or take. Original source material for the book of Joshua dates from the mid 900s BCE; it was rewritten in the 600s BCE and again around 500 BCE. This gives us a clear idea of the unreliability of ancient records, as the first known written material is dated several hundred years *after* Joshua actually lived and is derived from handed down stories; although Joshua's mention of Jerusalem is accurate.

Out of interest, 'Zion' is mentioned 153 times in the Old Testament, the first occasion being in 2 Samuel where it says Zion is the City of David – the timescale for Samuel was not that long before 1000 BCE. First and Second Samuel originally formed one book, compiled of material written during two, or possibly three, periods; the oldest from 961-922 BCE; the most recent from 750-650 BCE, and a possible third source from the period in between.

From this, we can again glean an idea of how stories and legends were first handed down orally from generation to generation and then written and rewritten, translated and retranslated, until we have what eventually became the Old Testament, which may, or in many instances most definitely may not, be representative of what actually transpired all those years ago.

Although the concept appears *nowhere* in the Old Testament at all, the idea of a 'new Jerusalem' is mentioned several times in the Book of Mormon, including Ether, which also mentions it coming down from heaven. "And that it was the place of the New Jerusalem, which should come down out of heaven, and the holy sanctuary of the Lord." *(Ether 13:3)*. In 3 Nephi 20 and 21, it claims a New Jerusalem will be 'built' in fulfilment of the promise made to Jacob. However, you won't find any promise made to Jacob in the Bible concerning a New Jerusalem to be built thousands of years later. What you will find is what Smith manipulated to accommodate his own ideas in his D&C revelations, the Book of Mormon and his *rewrite* of the Bible.

In Smith's version of Genesis 50, he has the Lord make a promise that he will deliver Jacob's progeny from Egypt. "...for the Lord hath visited me, and I have obtained a promise of the Lord, that out of the fruit of my loins, the Lord God will raise up a righteous branch out of my loins; and unto thee, whom my father Jacob hath named Israel, a prophet; (not the Messiah who is called Shilo;) and this prophet shall deliver my people out of Egypt in the days of thy bondage." *(IR Gen. 50:24)*. Not only is that typical of Smith's extraordinarily bad grammar compared with the Bible but it typifies his lack of ability as a so-called prophet. 'Shilo' was never a biblical name for the Messiah. 'Shiloh' did mistakenly become *used* as a name but was really a *place*. Smith was not the only one to get that wrong but God could have explained it to Smith to correct matters, then Smith would have looked as though he knew what he was doing. [1]

Although more readily accepted in Joseph Smith's era, today many Hebrew scholars and historians know and accept the Israelite nation was never *in* Egypt and thus were not 'delivered' *out* of Egypt. There is no mention of Israelites in such numbers in very detailed Egyptian history, nor is there any archaeological evidence of them ever being in the Sinai. It was all just a story to elevate the credibility of small Israelite tribes and of course their God. If Smith had been a real prophet, his God would surely have mentioned that to him. How wise he might have seemed today had Smith debunked the 'Israelites in Egypt' story along with the fable of the plagues. See this article from the New York Times: http://www.nytimes.com/2002/03/09/books/new-torah-for-modern-minds.html?pagewanted=1

In December of 1830, Smith was rewriting some of the Bible and in his new 'Book of Moses' Smith has Enoch *see* the "New Jerusalem" well before 3000 BCE, "...to gather out mine elect from the four quarters of the earth, unto a place which I shall prepare, an Holy City, that my people may gird up their loins, and be looking forth for the time of my coming; for there shall be my tabernacle, and it shall be called **Zion, a New Jerusalem**." (Emphasis added). This is quite important in terms of determining whether or not Joseph Smith had the least idea about what he was saying.

What would Enoch have ever known about *old* Jerusalem let alone a *new* one? If he did, why wasn't it *ever* mentioned in the Old Testament? Whilst pottery discoveries indicate there was a small settlement, some three-thousand-five-hundred years ago, at the location that later *became* Jerusalem, it was not *called* Jerusalem then and the earliest structures date from the early Bronze Age, 3100-2800 BCE. The earliest 'houses' discovered date from about 2500 BCE, long after the time of Enoch but, as it happens, well before the biblical date of the global flood, for which there is *no* geological evidence at Jerusalem – or anywhere else for that matter.

None of the cultures from around the globe, nor any of the archaeology which traces evidence of their history, contain any geological evidence of a 'flood gap' or of their civilisations 'restarting' at some post-flood stage when Noah's descendants eventually turned up and rekindled human life in each area of the world. Following a study of the history of each known civilisation, I do not see how it would be possible for anyone to retain any belief in a biblical 'global flood'. If anyone reading this actually does still believe there was such a thing, I urge them to study the recorded history of every known civilisation, along with the biological and evolutionary progress of each area of the world over the last ten-thousand years or so and then rethink their reality.

Biblically, of course Enoch lived *before* the flood when everything was annihilated and they started from scratch. What became the Tanakh or Old Testament was handed down by oral legend from about 1100 BCE and only written during the last few centuries BCE. If he actually lived as a person, it is *impossible* that Enoch knew the first thing about a 'Jerusalem' of *any* era, yet Smith makes him very knowledgeable indeed.

Smith mentions the 'New Jerusalem' several more times in Section 42 and then again the following month (March 1831) in Section 45. In Section 57 (July 1831), the *exact* location is specified, and there are further mentions in Sections 133 (November 1831) and 84 (September 1832).

The concept was also incorporated into the 'Articles of Faith'. Article 10 states "We believe in the literal gathering of Israel and in the restoration of the Ten Tribes; that Zion (the New Jerusalem) will be built upon the American continent; that Christ will reign personally upon the earth; and, that the earth will be renewed and receive its paradisiacal glory." When I was young, it said "upon 'this' the American continent" but subsequently the Church altered it as it considers itself a global operation and doesn't want to offend those who are not American.

All Mormons will be very familiar with the Articles of Faith and most just assume they originated when Smith penned his 'Wentworth letter' in 1842, but their history actually dates back to as early as 1834 when Oliver Cowdery had a go at writing some. *(See TMD Vol. 1. Apx. H)*.

The saints anticipated building their Zion there and then; they expected to complete it and for the Saviour to return during their lifetime. Today, almost two centuries later, the city of Zion – the New Jerusalem, along with its temple still don't exist and Jesus remains conspicuous by his absence, despite Smith's countless revelations, prophecies and promises that it would all happen in *that* generation.

Patriarchal blessings were replete with prophetic statements about what the recipient would experience. For example, what B. F. Johnson was promised by Joseph Smith Sr., in his blessing certainly didn't come from God, unless God is a prankster. "Thou shalt see the Temple of God reared in Zion and the glory of God resting upon it. Thou shalt see the Ten Tribes return from the North with St. John at their head and shall strike hands with him and call him Brother. See: http://www.vibrationdata.com/BFJohnson.htm So much for patriarchs.

We will come back to Smith's 'Zion, the New Jerusalem' prophecies, when reviewing Section 57 *(p. 224 on)*. Meanwhile, suffice it to say that it remains prophecy unfulfilled to this day. The Church claims there are many definitions of 'Zion', one of which is that it can mean wherever anyone lives. However, none of the definitions explain Joseph Smith's prophecies concerning building a New Jerusalem at a specific location which has never materialised.

In v.71-73, we learn that in addition to the Bishop, his counsellors and their families are also to be financially supported "out of property consecrated to the Bishop, for the good of the poor, and for other purposes, as before mentioned;"

Today, there is no paid Mormon ministry below the level of General Authority but resources donated expressly to benefit the poor and needy are often hived off to support ventures that members have no idea their donations are used to support. *(See TMD Vol. 2:338-346).*

In v.75 we learn that adulterers are to be cast out, but that didn't stop Smith embarking on all his extra-marital affairs which were to commence shortly.

From v.78 on we have the old BOC XLVII which recaps on Church laws concerning killing, adultery, stealing, lying and disputes. Remember, this was originally given two weeks after the preceding verses were recorded.

Section 42 – Summary

Prophecies made:	1
Prophecy fulfilled:	0
Non-prophetic revelation:	3

Prophecies made:

Pr. 18. In v.62 the Lord explains that "...it shall be revealed unto you in mine own due time where the New Jerusalem shall be built".

Results:

Pr. 18. The location for Zion, the New Jerusalem, and the temple "to which all nations should come" was explicitly to be Independence, Jackson County, Missouri *(Sec. 57)*. It has never been built.

Non-prophetic revelation: 3

1.   **D&C 42:12**. "...the principles of my gospel, which are in the Bible and the Book of Mormon, in the which is the fulness of the gospel."

DOCTRINE & COVENANTS – SECTIONS 38-50

As discussed extensively elsewhere, the fullness of the gospel is absolutely *not* remotely recorded in the Book of Mormon.

2. **D&C 42:18.** "And now, behold, I speak unto the church. Thou shalt not kill; and he that kills shall not have forgiveness in this world, nor in the world to come." *(The Lord – 19th Century).*

Someone who commits a violent premeditated double murder has hope for possible forgiveness at some stage in the eternities. *(Apostle Jeffery R. Holland – 20th Century).*

3. **D&C 42:22.** Thou shalt love thy wife with all thy heart, and shalt cleave unto her and none else.
   23. And he that looketh upon a woman to lust after her shall deny the faith, and shall not have the Spirit; and if he repents not he shall be cast out.
   24. Thou shalt not commit adultery; and he that committeth adultery, and repenteth not, shall be cast out.

Joseph Smith had his first documented adulterous affair with Fanny Alger two years after this 'revelation'. Smith managed not to get 'cast out' although eventually Smith's first wife, Emma, threw Fanny down the stairs and out of the house when she was noticeably pregnant; an act which may have led to Fanny losing her baby. There is no evidence of a polygynous marriage of any description between Smith and Fanny. The Church *assumes* one because the affair is so well documented. *(See TMD Vol. 1. Ch. 4).* This led on to dozens of relationships; some just appear adulterous, some were polygynous and yet others were polyandrous in nature. All were entirely illegal and everything Smith did directly violated the above words that he had attributed to the Lord.

Section 43
February 1831. Kirtland, Ohio.

History.

1833 BOC Ch. XLV. 1835 D&C Sec. XIV. 2010 D&C Sec. 43.

This Section is primarily in response to yet more problems with enthusiastic members having revelations which undermined Smith's own authority and also his own ideas which he wanted endorsed and accepted without question. The

Lord immediately confirms Smith is the *only* one chosen and able to actually hear and speak for the Lord. No one else's ideas count and Smith's exclusivity is determined to be so the saints won't be deceived. If they want "the glories of the kingdom, appoint ye my servant Joseph Smith, Jun., and uphold him before me" (v.12). But Smith doesn't stop there. "...if ye desire the mysteries of the kingdom, provide for him food and raiment, and whatsoever thing he needeth to accomplish the work wherewith I have commanded him;" (v.13). So, look after Smith financially and he will tell you what you would like to hear.

They are to go out and preach because the Lord is coming soon, when trumps and Earth shaking will be the order of the day. We have of course heard all this before. Thunder and lightening are mentioned and somehow lightening "shall streak forth from the east unto the west, and shall utter forth their voices unto all that live, and make the ears of all tingle that hear, saying these words—Repent ye, for the great day of the Lord is come?" (v.22). In days when humans did not understand lightening and became frightened, such an idea as it being the 'voice' of a god might have been plausible to them, but even in Smith's day they knew better than that. It is just another scare tactic that no longer works.

The Lord says he is going to speak from heaven and talks about gathering them as hens gather their chickens: "O, ye nations of the earth, how often would I have gathered you together as a hen gathereth her chickens under her wings, but ye would not!" (v.24). Sound familiar? It should because Smith plagiarised it from Matthew.

> **Matthew 23:37.** O Jerusalem, Jerusalem, thou that killest the prophets, and stonest them which are sent unto thee, how often would I have gathered thy children together, even as a hen gathereth her chickens under her wings, and ye would not!

Smith, being Smith, of course couldn't just leave it at that. He had to go overboard and add a plethora of further impossible ways the Lord had been trying to get through to people yet they wouldn't listen. Would anyone today ever seriously consider any of the following to be the Lord actually trying to tell people something they would not listen to?

> **D&C 43:25**. How oft have I called upon you by the mouth of my servants, and by the ministering of angels, and by mine own voice, and by the voice of thunderings, and by the voice of lightnings, and by the voice of tempests, and by the voice of earthquakes, and great hailstorms, and by the voice of famines and pestilences of every kind, and by the great sound of a trump, and by the voice of judgment, and

DOCTRINE & COVENANTS – SECTIONS 38-50

by the voice of mercy all the day long, and by the voice of glory and honor and the riches of eternal life, and would have saved you with an everlasting salvation, but ye would not!

Apparently, in addition to his servants, angels, and his own voice – which is strange as Smith claimed he was the only one actually allowed to hear it – the Lord also used the 'voice' of thunderings, lightnings, tempests, earthquakes, hailstorms, famines, pestilences, a trump – and then strangely, also judgment, mercy, glory, honour, riches of eternal life and everlasting salvation, to 'speak' to people but still they wouldn't listen. How we ever get from all the bad stuff, invariably caused by natural disasters and/or adverse weather conditions, to enticements that don't all make much if any sense, remains unclear. Smith was obviously one of the many religionists to believe natural calamities really are acts of God – trying to get our attention. That is a dangerous supposition.

Luke 13:34 records a similar phrase about hens but uses the word 'brood' rather than chickens. Smith used it again in *Section 29:2*. He also had Christ say it *four times* within just three verses in his Book of Mormon, supposedly in 34-35 CE. Read the following very carefully and seriously consider the probability that Jesus would have repeated himself so many times in such a short speech – and more importantly, why? There is nothing that can be said to even begin to explain such nonsense as this away...

> **3 Nephi 10:4.** O ye people of these great cities which have fallen, who are descendants of Jacob, yea, who are of the house of Israel, ***how oft have I gathered you as a hen gathereth her chickens under her wings***, and have nourished you.
> **5.** And again, ***how oft would I have gathered you as a hen gathereth her chickens under her wings***, yea, O ye people of the house of Israel, who have fallen; yea, O ye people of the house of Israel, ye that dwell at Jerusalem, as ye that have fallen; yea, ***how oft would I have gathered you as a hen gathereth her chickens***, and ye would not.
> **6.** O ye house of Israel whom I have spared, ***how oft will I gather you as a hen gathereth her chickens under her wings***, if ye will repent and return unto me with full purpose of heart. (Emphasis added).

Smith had the Lord use this same material in *Section 10:65 (see p. 103)* when referring to gathering the Lamanites "as a hen gathereth her chickens"; something else which was once thought to be happening through the Church's 'Lamanite placement programme' of the twentieth century which was finally abandoned in 1996. In one Mormon 'Ensign' magazine, published in July 1971, a series of articles unequivocally confirmed the *absolute* belief that *every* culture of the Americas and most of the Islands was of **Lamanite** origin. The series starts with acting President of the Quorum of Twelve Apostles, Spencer W. Kimball: "Of Royal Blood". *(See also TMD Vol. 2:248-49 which discusses Kimball's 1960 'New Era' article confirming the same beliefs).*

> It pleased me to hear Mr. MacDonald [non-Mormon chairman of the Navajo Tribal Council] say that he was a "Lamanite." We knew it all the time, but we didn't know that he did ... Not until the revelations of Joseph Smith, bringing forth the Book of Mormon, did any one know of these migrants. It was not known before, but now *the question is fully answered*. Now *the Lamanites number about sixty million*; they are *in all of the states of America* from Tierra del Fuego all the way up to Point Barrows, and they are *in nearly all the islands of the sea* from Hawaii south to southern New Zealand.
>
> The term *Lamanite includes all Indians and Indian mixtures*, such as the Polynesians, the Guatemalans, the Peruvians, as well as the Sioux, the Apache, the Mohawk, the Navajo, and others. *It is a large group of great people…*
>
> Today we have many **Lamanite leaders in the Church**. For example, in Tonga, where 20 percent of all the people in the islands belong to the Church, we have three large stakes. Two of them are **presided over wholly by Lamanites** and the other almost wholly by them. There are three stakes in Samoa and another is to be organized in those small Samoan islands. Four more stakes **with Lamanite leaders!**
>
> There are three stakes of Zion in Mexico City with **Mexican leaders—Lamanite leaders.** The stake presidencies, the bishops, the high council, the auxiliary leaders—**everybody, with one or two exceptions—are Lamanites**. In Monterrey, Mexico, in Guatemala, in Lima, in New Zealand, and elsewhere we have stakes of Zion with all their appropriate leaders.
>
> That is in **direct fulfillment of the prophecies** that were made, and it is a great change. **A dozen years ago there was not a single Lamanite stake in the world**. There were no Lamanite bishops; there were no Lamanite stake presidents. In a period of a few years all of this has come about. **Christ said, as he looked down through the stream of time**, "And thus we see that the commandments of God must be fulfilled. And if it so be that the children of men keep the commandments of God he doth nourish them, and strengthen them, and provide means whereby they can accomplish the thing which he has commanded them; wherefore, he did provide means for us while we did sojourn in the wilderness." (1 Ne. 17:3.) (Emphasis added).
>
> See: http://lds.org/ensign/1971/07/of-royal-blood?lang=eng

DOCTRINE & COVENANTS – SECTIONS 38-50

Kimball is convinced they are not only *all* Lamanites, but also that Christ "looked down through the stream of time" and saw this would happen. Today, conclusive scientific DNA evidence precludes the remotest possibility, proving that not only were Kimball and company entirely wrong, but also that Christ most certainly did *not* "look down through the stream of time" and see any such thing – showing Kimball's Book of Mormon claim to be entirely fanciful.

The next article is entitled "Lamanites and the Church" where reference is made to the concept that 'Indians' are Lamanites.

> Nine Indian youngsters were taken into Latter-day Saint homes the next fall. It was an informal beginning that has grown into the **Indian Student Placement** program, touching the lives of more than **five thousand Lamanite students** during the past school year. And it could further be identified as a new awakening on the part of members of the Church to **the Lamanite and his prophetic destiny**.
>
> The Church of Jesus Christ of Latter-day Saints is unique in its theological and philosophical understanding of the peoples in the Americas known as **Indians and of the inhabitants of the Pacific islands**. These people are a remnant of the House of Jacob and **descendants of Lehi, an Israelite who left Jerusalem** and came to the Americas around 600 B.C. Found in the Book of Mormon, a record of revelations received by these ancient peoples, are great promises for **the Lamanites**.
>
> These prophetic promises prompted Joseph Smith, who translated and published the Book of Mormon in 1830, to **carry the gospel to the Lamanites** in the very early days of the Church's existence. And from that day until this the gospel has been preached to **those who are identified as Lamanites**...
>
> **Today, as never before, the Church is carrying the gospel to the Lamanites**, providing secular and religious training, and attempting to be a catalyst for the economic emergence of this great people...
>
> Elder Marvin J. Ashton, Assistant to the Council of the Twelve, is managing director of the Social Services Department. Within that department Stewart A. Durrant serves as **coordinator of Lamanite and other cultures**...
>
> Possibly the most important thing that could be said about the **Lamanite programs** of the Church is that they are developing leadership and strength **among the Lamanites.** The gospel of Jesus Christ brings men and women to a greater measure of their potential,

and nowhere is this more evident than *among the Lamanite members* of the Church. (Emphasis added).

See: http://lds.org/ensign/1971/07/lamanites-and-the-church?lang=eng

Every Mormon *knew* who the Lamanites were and the Church even had a *department* assigned to them. God never told any of the leaders they had got it all wrong. In the article which follows the above, which is entitled "Hope for the American Indian?" they are also referred to as 'Lamanites'.

> There is a very special responsibility for Latter-day Saints to be sensitive to the needs of *the Lamanites (Indians)* wherever they are in the world. The role of the Lamanite in the program of the restoration is significant, and his ability to play that role is in part related to his opportunity to be an intelligent contributor to society. (Emphasis added).

See: http://lds.org/ensign/1971/07/hope-for-the-american-indian?lang=eng

Even the article after that, "The Vanished American", refers to Lamanites several times: http://lds.org/ensign/1971/07/the-vanished-american?lang=eng

As if that wasn't enough, the next article "Awakening Guatemala" refers to the people there as Lamanites too. As the first article says, and as Spencer W. Kimball also declared as far back as 1960, Lamanites comprised *everyone* in the Americas and most of the Islands – without question. Now the Church and its apologists haven't a clue where *any* Lamanites are. *(See also pp. 159-61).*

> Prophecy concerning *the Lamanite people* states that the gospel will be restored to them and that the scales of darkness will fall from their eyes so that *they will become a white and delightsome people.* (See 2 Ne. 30:5–6.) A few of *the Lamanites in Guatemala*, so long numbed by poverty and misery, are beginning to stir because of the efforts of a white brother and his family whose fondest hope is that love, patience, hard work, and sacrifice will continue to awaken more of God's chosen people in the years ahead.
> (*See:* http://lds.org/ensign/1971/07/awakening-guatemala?lang=eng)

The "white and delightsome" issue is discussed in *TMD Vol.2. Ch. 13.*

Finally, amid filler and nonsense, Jesus is having another rant; "…the cup of the wrath of mine indignation is full" (v.26). I don't know why he gets so upset; most people are doing their best in the world; they just don't listen to such nonsense as this, and Jesus should readily understand *why* if he really is

DOCTRINE & COVENANTS – SECTIONS 38-50

deity. Jesus confirms these are *his* words and reminds them they are to labour in the vineyard for the last time; he will come (as ever – in his 'own due time') in judgment when his people will be redeemed and reign with him. I expect some like the idea of reigning over others. Smith certainly did. The millennium will arrive, Satan will be bound and then loosed, and then the end will come. The righteous will be changed in the twinkling of an eye and the rest will "pass away so as by fire" (v.32) in a change to Smith's previous revelatory claim that *Jesus* will *burn* them. *(Sec. 29:9. See p. 154)*. The wicked will go away into unquenchable fire. The saints are to be 'sober'. There is nothing new here.

Section 44
Late February 1831. Kirtland, Ohio.

History.

1833 BOC Ch. XLVI. 1835 D&C Sec. LXII. 2010 D&C Sec. 44.

This short meaningless revelation calls the elders home for a conference, after which they are to go off preaching once again. The Lord even suggests sending letters to call them home; can you imagine the Lord really saying that? Many will be converted. They will obtain 'power' to organise themselves "according to the laws of man" although again, we may wonder why the Lord would say such a thing. Their enemies will not have power over them, and they must look after the poor. Had Smith and his followers acted differently and been less aggressive, they wouldn't have had enemies to worry about. Had they worked *with*, instead of trying to take over, every community they tried to settle in or near, they could have become a force (for good) to be reckoned with, but that wasn't Smith's style at all. He wanted power and control – and that had a price.

Section 45
7 March 1831. Kirtland, Ohio.

History.

1833 BOC Ch. XLVIII. 1835 D&C Sec. XV. 2010 D&C Sec. 45.

Several verses from this Section are referred to in the Mormon missionary lesson manual and I comment on them (v.3-5, 8, 44, 72-75) in *TMD Vol. 4:220, 230-32 (S40-43)*.

Smith has Jesus start off by establishing that *he* is speaking and "by whom all things were made which live, and move, and have a being". Smith clearly did not consider evolution and assumed everything was 'made' as it appears today – and thus has Jesus say so. With our modern-day understanding of the fact of evolution, at least some credibility would have been gained had Jesus said he set life on earth in motion and from that evolved all species, including humans – but of course he didn't; instead we have evidence that Jesus wasn't actually speaking at all.

In v.2, Jesus goes on to say that they should listen to him "lest death shall overtake you; in an hour when ye think not the summer shall be past, and the harvest ended, and your souls not saved", indicating, and not for the first time, that the end would come at some stage *during* that generation; possibly sooner than they might think.

For the next few verses Jesus is talking about himself and how great he is; only when *Smith* pretends Jesus is speaking does that happen. Then Jesus says *he* is Alpha and Omega – again.

In v.11-12, Smith has Jesus talk about Enoch and his city which was taken up into heaven. Many Mormons do not fully appreciate the fact that this is just another Smith fairy tale, woven into his own 'translation' of Genesis and his 'Book of Moses' which was supposedly a 'revealed' development of further information not included in the Bible. You will not find any city of Enoch in the Bible at all, other than the one built by a different Enoch (the son of Cain), let alone one that was taken up into heaven. Smith has Enoch and everyone in his righteous city, not taste of death but become 'translated' into some kind of immortal state when the entire city (also known as Zion) is lifted from Earth – to who knows where. Very little is known of Enoch and some scholars question whether he, along with several other biblical characters, ever even existed.

In v.15, Jesus says he is going to prophesy "as unto men in days of old" which is a strange thing to say. So, what gems does Jesus have in store for us? It turns out that Jesus meant he was going to repeat what he *told* men "in days of old" before Jerusalem fell to the Babylonians, and for the next few verses we get a pointless history lesson; not a difficult task for Smith really. The temple at Jerusalem will be destroyed so "there shall not be left one stone upon another" (v.20). The Israelites will be scattered but will be gathered again. A 'light' will come, which is Smith and his restored gospel of course. People will not receive it because they do not 'perceive' the light apparently; in which case one could argue that the light was not exactly convincing. It should have been better formulated and presented in order to have the remotest credibility with anyone other than the gullible few such as I, out of the billions of 'God's children' who simply laugh at the concepts of Mormonism – if they even hear of them.

DOCTRINE & COVENANTS – SECTIONS 38-50

29. But they receiveth it not; for they perceive not the light, and they turn their hearts from me because of the precepts of men.
30. And in that generation shall the times of the Gentiles be fulfilled.
31. And there shall be men standing in that generation, that shall not pass until they shall see an overflowing scourge; for a desolating sickness shall cover the land.

Verse 31 claims *in* the generation when the gospel is restored, a desolating sickness will cover the land. Well beyond that generation and several that have followed, that prophecy remains unfulfilled. It is far too late to consider any sickness that may one day 'cover the land' to be a fulfilment of that prophesy.

It was specifically for *that* generation. If the Mormon Church wants to argue, which it now must as there is no alternative, that 'generation' can mean *any* time after Joseph Smith came along, then it does not explain why Smith's followers firmly believed that it applied to *their* generation and exposes Jesus, or rather Smith, as being deceptive, or at least not specific enough for people of the day to grasp the true meaning of the prophesy. It might have been kinder to say not to worry, it would not happen in their lifetime – but then the ever essential 'fear factor' that is used in religion would have been somewhat lost.

With nothing new to add, Jesus then starts yet again to talk of earthquakes and men taking up the sword against each other. It would have been more convincing, well, probably not, if Jesus had said they would take up guns or other weapons such as rifles and cannons which had been developed long before Smith's time. Swords were spoken of biblically as that was a weapon of the day. In Smith's time, the gun was in use and would soon replace the sword in terms of military encounters. Soon – in the sense that if the Church wants to claim it meant much *later* than Smith's time – Jesus should then have said they would use guns, because the yet to be fulfilled prophecy would hardly include swords these days. The Church may then naturally counter that it was probably metaphorical. There is always another goal post to be moved – even though they have long run out of goalposts in reality. Today, 'moves', such as Book of Mormon geography and Lamanite location, have gone from the sublime to the ridiculous. In efforts to make up new 'theories', apologists forget that in my young day, *everyone* from the prophet down to the likes of me, a fourteen-year-old, knew for a *fact* that the Lamanites covered the Americas and most Islands.

Jesus then says that when he told his disciples these things, they were troubled; he told them not to be, and when they saw these things come to pass they would know the promises that had been made to them would be fulfilled. But, if that really was for his disciples, way back when, it was equally *not* fulfilled at that time and they didn't see any of it – and it still hasn't happened.

Following a weak 'parable' wherein Jesus says signs of his coming, in a cloud of course, are like the new shoots on a fig tree, then you know summer is coming, we have the following, which, as v.39 explains, are apparently the 'signs' of the coming of the "Son of Man".

> **40.** And they shall see signs and wonders, for they shall be shown forth in the heavens above, and in the earth beneath.
> **41.** And they shall behold blood, and fire, and vapors of smoke.
> **42.** And before the day of the Lord shall come, the sun shall be darkened, and the moon be turned into blood, and the stars fall from heaven.

Verse 43 goes on to say "And the remnant shall be gathered unto this place;" but they never have been. I have not counted that as a prophecy as no doubt the Church will claim it can happen *after* the moon turns to blood, despite Smith's other mentions of a more immediate 'gathering'. We discussed v.42 earlier, in conjunction with some other sections *(see p.154)*.

Something about the above verses that I have not mentioned before is quite interesting – and Smith would not have had a clue about the origins of such prophecies. As previously discussed, Smith just stole these ideas from Joel 2:30-31. As ever, Smith didn't just have Jesus talk about someone else's words, he had Jesus plagiarise them directly from the KJV, almost identically – an impossible feat.

Compare Joel 2:30-31 below, with D&C 42:40-42 above.

> **Joel 2:30.** And I will shew wonders in the heavens and in the earth, blood, and fire, and pillars of smoke.
> **31.** The sun shall be turned into darkness, and the moon into blood, before the great and the terrible day of the LORD come.

Joel doesn't mention the stars falling from heaven but it is mentioned several times in the New Testament, particularly Revelation which Smith was fond of. Matthew 14:29 also gives us the rest of Smith's 'Jesus' quote: "...the sun be darkened, and the moon shall not give her light, and the stars shall fall from heaven…"

But, where did Joel, a minor and virtually unknown prophet of the Old Testament, get his ideas from? The original concepts actually form part of most if not all known religions in one way or another and all appear to stem from the very same source, countless thousands of years ago.

My friend and scientist, Bill Lauritzen, in his new book, 'The Invention of God; The Natural Origins of Mythology and Religion', describes in detail, how early humans first observed volcanoes and came to believe some power under the earth was a 'creator' through lava flow eventually breaking down from rock into fertile soil, seemingly creating life out of nothing when it really came from seeds dropped by birds or floating debris from the sea, as observed from 1963 on when the volcanic island Surtsey raised out of the sea. I was seventeen years old then and I remember it well; I followed its progress for quite a time. Life quickly arrived and spread there through quite natural means.

Over tens if not hundreds of thousands of years, early humans observed magma coming from inside the earth; the fire, smoke columns, volcanic lightening without a cloud in the sky, which eventually became 'fiery darts', 'spears' or 'swords' in later early 'religion'. The lava flows that looked like fiery snakes to the ancients were later incorporated into Greek, Egyptian and other religions. The sky, and therefore the sun and moon, turned red. Erupting volcanoes would throw hot lava bombs and ash high into the sky, which looked like the stars falling as they rained down upon the earth. Every single aspect of volcanic activity and cycles became contained in early mythology when the first 'gods' were invented, and much has remained, becoming incorporated in some way into all religion that humans embrace today.

The Supreme Deity of the volcanic island of Bali is depicted encased in flames, and large lava bombs were also to become the first 'angels' in ancient religions for the same reason. In early Egyptian hieroglyphs, and regularly in the 'Book of the Dead' – which Lauritzen informs us is actually slang for the real name of "…the book of "going forth by day" (per em hru) in other words, the book of being reborn" *(Lauritzen 2011:21)* – we find plentiful evidence of many such beliefs that eventually found their way into the Hebrew religion and subsequently into Christianity – and thus quite naturally, into Mormonism.

Volcanoes would sink into the sea, soon to be replaced by another – hence the concept of resurrection, which was further enhanced by other natural and misunderstood occurrences regarding breathing, death and the effects of fire. *(See: Lauritzen 2011)*. The sun often turned red in appearance as it set into the earth, to be rejuvenated by magma in order to rise again the following day.

Humans passed on the legends that formed, possibly before they could even speak a real language, and over tens of thousands of years, as eruptions would recur – some at fairly regular intervals, future expectations would be conveyed to following generations.

Therefore, there arose 'predictions' that what had transpired previously would inevitably happen again in the future. Ancestors had experienced the phenomena – more than once. Thousands of years later, in environments where many humans had never even experienced volcanoes, the myths and legends and the 'prophecies' took on a different guise and the once obvious became obscure – in one instance out of many, re-emerging as Jesus and his return, but the original ideas still prevailed in the new religions. A full perspective will be gained from a reading of Bill Lauritzen's book.

Verse 45 tells of an angel and the sound of a trump – which concept may have originated in large lava bombs and the sound of an erupting volcano. Read the above verses again in the context of volcanoes and all will become clear; in fact, read any apocalyptic biblical prophecy or even a few of the later verses of this Section in light of the volcanic experiences of early humans who told and retold tales of the events, and everything is readily explained. For example:

> **48.** And then shall the Lord set his foot upon this mount, and it shall cleave in twain, and the earth shall tremble, and reel to and fro, and the heavens also shall shake.
> **49.** And the Lord shall utter his voice, and all the ends of the earth shall hear it; and the nations of the earth shall mourn, and they that have laughed shall see their folly.
> **50.** And calamity shall cover the mocker, and the scorner shall be consumed; and they that have watched for iniquity shall be hewn down and cast into the fire.

Further along, Smith is told that the Lord isn't going to say any more but will do so in Smith's 'translation' of the New Testament which he can now get on with.

> **60.** And now, behold, I say unto you, it shall not be given unto you to know any further concerning this chapter, until the New Testament be translated, and in it all these things shall be made known;
> **61.** Wherefore I give unto you that ye may now translate it, that ye may be prepared for the things to come.
> **62.** For verily I say unto you, that great things await you;

The subheading for this Section regarding v.60-62 claims: *"The Prophet is instructed to begin the translation of the New Testament, through which important information will be made known;"* The thing is that alterations and additions found in Joseph Smith's version of the New Testament are anything but "important information". Most of it is meaningless and all of it is pointless.

Regarding v.63-75, the subheading claims *"The Saints are commanded to gather and build the New Jerusalem, to which people from all nations will come."* Quite detailed instructions are given for them to achieve this. They are to 'gather' riches in order to build the New Jerusalem; the wicked will not dare to battle with them. It never happened. In fact, in Missouri, serious Mormon conflicts ultimately resulted in an 'Extermination Order'.

DOCTRINE & COVENANTS – SECTIONS 38-50

Section 45 – Summary

Prophecies made:	3
Prophecies fulfilled:	0
Other non-prophetic revelation:	1

Prophecies made:

Pr. 19. Verse 2, "…when ye think not the summer shall be past, and the harvest ended, and your souls not saved." It was ***their*** souls being considered and Jesus was expected to return in their generation.

Pr. 20. Verse 31 claims that *in* the generation when the gospel is restored, a desolating sickness will cover the land.

Pr. 21. The saints are commanded to gather riches and people from across the world and build the New Jerusalem where no one will dare do battle with them.

Results:

Pr. 19. Almost two centuries have passed and Jesus still hasn't returned. If he wasn't going to return, he should have ensured *they* didn't *expect* him.

Pr. 20. In that generation and several that followed, the prophecy remained unfulfilled. No *desolating* sickness occurred that *covered the land*. Locally, they experienced extensive cholera from 1832, most probably taken to the United States by European immigrants. It did not cover the land; it may have been considered devastating in the areas that were affected, but it was not national or desolating. Well *after* that generation, in the 20th Century, there was a world Spanish flu pandemic *(see p. 284)*, far too late to relate to Smith's idea.

Pr. 21. Zion, the New Jerusalem, never was built and Mormon conflicts in Missouri resulted in an Extermination Order which ultimately drove the Mormons out.

Non-prophetic revelation.   1

> **60.** And now, behold, I say unto you, it shall not be given unto you to know any further concerning this chapter, until the New Testament be translated, and in it all these things shall be made known;

THE MORMON DELUSION

It would perhaps be correct to claim this as unfulfilled prophecy as nothing special is 'made known' in Smith's attempts at altering the New Testament. However, as he did make many changes and additions, some of which were actually extremely silly, it could be argued that these constitute the Lord's extra information – for what it is worth; so, let's just call this a non-prophetic revelation and leave it at that.

Smith's alterations to the New Testament are not an integral part of this work. Suffice it to say that they don't amount to anything of significance – other than proving Smith hadn't a clue about anything that may or may not have been accurate in the Bible. Smith's work on the Bible is largely ignored by the Mormon Church, as firstly, the copyright is owned by the Reorganised Church (now Community of Christ) and secondly, there is nothing much that is worthy of note. There are a few selected 'JST' (Joseph Smith Translation – or Inspired Revision) footnotes in the Mormon edition of the KJV but Smith's Inspired Revision as such is not in general use within the Mormon Church. The KJV is used in preference.

When the gospels were eventually written, many decades to well over a century after the Christ purportedly lived, they were then assigned, 'according to' people who did *not* have anything remotely to do with writing them. The Gospel 'according' to St. Matthew is called 'The **Testimony** of St. Matthew' by Smith, showing that he clearly believed it was actually written *by* the apostle Matthew. It is now generally accepted that it most certainly was *not*. It goes downhill from there for Smith. As I feel obligated to at least say something about Smith's painful efforts, here is a short example of his 'development' of the New Testament. In D&C 45:60 (above) Smith had Jesus affirm that "…in it all these things shall be made known".

Let's just start from the beginning of the New Testament; this is the result of Smith's review of Matthew chapter 1. He twice spells each biblical name 'Naasson' as 'Naason' and 'Zorobabel' as 'Zorobable'. Matthew 1, says David begat Solomon "of her **that had been the wife** of Urias" which Smith changed to read "of her **whom David had taken** of Urias" for what that was worth. To the statement that "…Mary, of whom was born Jesus, * who is called Christ", Smith inserted * "as the prophets have written" – as if people didn't know that.

There is a verse reflecting the generations from Abraham to David, from David to the Babylonian captivity, and from then to Christ. Each comprises fourteen generations. Each says they 'are' fourteen generations. Smith alters the text *three times* to read 'were' fourteen generations, which does nothing to enlighten us and pointlessly changes what was quite acceptable biblical text.

Smith split Matthew 1 into two chapters. Matt 1:22. "Now all this **was done**, that **it** might be fulfilled which **was** spoken of the Lord by the **prophet**, saying," becomes Smith's IR Matt 2:5 "Now this **took place**, that **all things** might be fulfilled, which **were** spoken of the Lord, by the **prophets**, saying…"

200

DOCTRINE & COVENANTS – SECTIONS 38-50

What was a straightforward explanation is widened by Smith to encompass who knows what "all things" as there is no further explanation, leaving another pointless change. Remember, this is supposedly Jesus himself helping Smith to properly restore the original text and meaning as well as add "great things" into the New Testament. *(D&C 45:62 above)*. Matt 1:24. "Then Joseph being raised from *sleep...*" becomes IR Matt 2:7. "Then Joseph, *awaking out of his vision*," Matt 1:25 "...and *he* called his name JESUS" becomes IR Matt 2:8. "...*they* called his name Jesus." That is the extent of the Lord's added text and wisdom in Smith's version of Matthew chapter 1. There was no point to any of the changes. I could go on – but that would take yet another volume.

We know the Lord was not involved with Smith's ideas on the Bible simply because of the way Smith used and abused Revelation 1:6. *TMD Vol. 4:103-4* explains that Smith altered the text of Revelation 1:6 from the KJV in his IR because it appeared to read God had a father and in Smith's early monotheistic mode that would not do at all. The KJV reads "And hath made us kings and priests unto **God and His Father**; to him be glory and dominion forever and ever. Amen." (Emphasis added). Smith altered that verse to explicitly confirm that God does *not* have a father. Smith's IR version reads: "...and hath made us kings and priests unto **God his Father**. To him be glory and dominion, forever and ever. Amen." (Emphasis added). As it happens, that is actually a better translation of the original text. It may well be the *only* thing that Smith (quite accidentally) got right; not that he stuck with the idea very long.

Some years later, Smith developed his plural Gods theology and claimed God was once human just like us and therefore he *did* have a father after all. It was far too late to change his Inspired Revision so in his infamous King Follett Sermon, Smith abandoned his 'Jesus revealed' version of Revelation 1:6 and reverted to the KJV as it then suited his new purpose better than his previous 'translation'.

Smith then boldly pronounced the KJV of Revelation 1:6 was "altogether correct" – thus admitting that he *lied* in his Inspired Revision, nullifying any and all claims to any earlier inspiration and according to the biblical 'tests' of a prophet, also nullifying any and all claims to being a true prophet. Any Bible scholar will confirm that the KJV of Revelation 1:6 is not 'altogether correct' but is in fact mistranslated. Almost every other version of the Bible available today correctly translates it the way Smith guessed it should have read when he penned his so-called Inspired Revision of the Bible. *(See also: TMD Vol 2:136-7 & Whitefield 2011b:22-23).*

THE MORMON DELUSION

Section 46
8 March 1831. Kirtland, Ohio.

History.

1833 BOC Ch. XLIX. 1835 D&C Sec. XVI. 2010 D&C Sec. 46.

This Section, which was given almost a year after the Church was formally organised, finally gets around to (claiming to) specify how meetings should be run. It seems strange (if you believe God was involved) that He didn't reveal His ideas on this before, or even on the day the Church was organised. The header suggests the Section includes *"...the will of the Lord relative to governing and conducting meetings."* (Italics in original).

They are not to cast anyone out who wants to attend meetings and those who have sinned can still attend but should not partake of the sacrament. After some now familiar waffle, we get something that I always found strange:

> **11.** For all have not every gift given unto them; for there are many gifts, and to every man is given a gift by the Spirit of God.
> **12.** To some is given one, and to some is given another, that all may be profited thereby.
> **13.** To some it is given by the Holy Ghost to know that Jesus Christ is the Son of God, and that he was crucified for the sins of the world.
> **14.** To others it is given to believe on their words, that they also might have eternal life if they continue faithful.

My perception was always that *everyone* was entitled to a witness by the Holy Ghost that the Church was true. No one need rely on, or just have faith in, the words of others. The above still makes no sense to me in terms of what the Church proclaims to potential converts. I have heard it explained as holding to the faith of experienced leaders and believing their words on faith until you 'develop' a testimony of your own. In other words, that really means, until the delusion becomes so deeply entrenched that your brain accepts the impossible as the truth. It is the religious equivalent of Stockholm syndrome.

Some other 'gifts' that are listed, include "the differences of administration, as it will be pleasing unto the same Lord" (v.15). To me, it means that when Smith didn't have any new ideas, if anyone came up with something he liked, then that was evidence of a gift from God; yet another clever ploy by Smith.

I suspect that for the same reason, some will "know the diversities of operations, whether they be of God," (v.16). Some will know the 'word of wisdom' (not to be confused with the later 'Word of Wisdom' health code), the 'word of knowledge', to 'be healed', to 'heal', to 'do miracles', 'prophesy' –although Smith didn't really care for other people actually claiming that one very much – 'discerning spirits', 'speaking in tongues', 'interpreting tongues', which, as discussed elsewhere, specifically referred to glossolalia. Some are to be given *all* those gifts so they can head up the Church. The closest we get to "governing or conducting meetings" is in v.2 where the elders are "to conduct all meetings as they are directed and guided by the Holy Spirit" and that's about it.

If I declare the Section to be a complete waste of time, no doubt that would outrage the faithful, but in the rational world – of what *use* is it to anyone?

Section 47
8 March 1831. Kirtland, Ohio.

History.

1833 BOC Ch. L. 1835 D&C Sec. LXIII. 2010 D&C Sec. 47.

This entirely pointless four verse Section records John Whitmer being asked to keep the history of the Church instead of Oliver Cowdery who had been doing that but is now "appointed to another office" but we don't learn what that may have been. Smith has the Lord explain that to the two men – thus they can hardly say no.

The Mormon Church claims that Cowdery (along with Smith) received the Melchizedek priesthood (were ordained apostles), May-June 1829, via Peter, James and John (citing D&C 20:2 & 27:12) – despite the fact Cowdery himself claimed it was the *angel* who returned and did that *(see pp. 142 & 149-50)*.

Sustained as Second Elder to Smith at the formation of the Church on 6 April 1830, Cowdery was ultimately ordained a high priest by Sidney Rigdon (who had started to somewhat replace Cowdery during 1831), on 28 August 1831, several months after this 'revelation' was given. On 5 December 1834 Cowdery was sustained as assistant counsellor to the First Presidency. He was excommunicated 11 April 1838, along with several other 'dissenters' including John Whitmer, following a leadership struggle at Far West where Smith and Sidney Rigdon had fled after the Kirtland Bank scandal. Following Rigdon's famous 'salt sermon', Cowdery and Whitmer fled the county in fear of their lives. Nevertheless, Cowdery was eventually rebaptised on 12 November 1848; he died 3 March 1850 *(Church Almanac, 2007)*.

Section 48
10 March 1831. Kirtland, Ohio.

History.

1833 BOC Ch. LI. 1835 D&C Sec. LXIV. 2010 D&C Sec. 48.

Originally, this Section (as BOC Chapter LI) was headed *"A Revelation to the bishop, and the church in Kirtland..."* In the 1835 D&C LXIV, it became *"Revelation given March, 1831"* and today it reads *"Revelation given through Joseph Smith the Prophet, at Kirtland, Ohio, March 1831..."* (Italics in originals). The changes reflect the fact that the original BOC v.6, which says "and as is appointed to him by the bishop **and elders of the church**, according to the laws and commandments," was altered in the 1835 D&C LXIV (now part of v.2) to read "and as is appointed to him by **the presidency and** the bishop of the church, according to the laws and commandments" (emphasis added), incorporating a term heretofore unseen in recorded scripture. This late introduction of a new 'presidency' status reflects the fact that the Lord most certainly did not 'reveal' it – or add it years later. Currently, it appears as part of v.6.

In this Section, we see Smith attempting to get members to 'impart' land to the Church, to purchase land for temporary use, but also to save, ready to buy land for their inheritance in the 'city' (yet to be revealed) where they would finally settle.

Section 49
March 1831 *(per 1833 BOC, 1835 D&C & 2010 D&C)*. Kirtland, Ohio.
Actual date: 7 May 1831. *(Joseph Smith Papers, Vol. 2:501)*.

History.

1833 BOC Ch. LII. 1835 D&C Sec. LXV. 2010 D&C Sec. 49.

Smith's recurring problems where other people had their own ideas about the Church once again surface in this section due to the conversion of one Leman Copley who had previously been a 'Shaker'. Leman Copley was still somewhat entrenched in some of the Shaker ideas and so as ever, Smith conveniently had this revelation confirming Shaker traditions to be incorrect. But, he goes further than that and boldly produces this as a revelation to be read to the entire Shaker congregation. Sidney Rigdon, Parley P. Pratt and Leman Copley were charged

DOCTRINE & COVENANTS – SECTIONS 38-50

with that task. Apparently, the Shakers "know the truth in part" but are not "right" before the Lord and they must repent.

According to v.5, God is speaking. They are to teach the Shakers that no one knows exactly when the Saviour will return. The Shakers believed he had already returned, in the form of a woman – Ann Lee. Marriage is of God, but interestingly, only *one* wife is allowed, but then it was only 1831, a couple of years before Smith started getting into extramarital relationships which started with his teenage housemaid, Fanny Alger, in 1833. *(See: TMD Vol. 1. Ch. 4).*

The shakers deemed celibacy higher than marriage. The three were also to tell the Shakers, who did not believe in eating pork, that anyone who forbids the eating of meat is not ordained of God. In less than two years, the Mormon Word of Wisdom was to appear, when that idea changed radically and meat was to be used "sparingly" and "only in times of winter, or of cold, or famine", not that anyone took any notice of it, then or now. The Church owns the largest cattle ranch in the USA *(See Section 89, pp. 321-22 and TMD Vol. 2, Ch. 10).*

When the Saviour does return, he most certainly won't take the form of a woman (v.22). Naturally, that concept would not do at all in Smith's male dominated Church. They are not to be deceived but wait for "the heavens to shake", the "earth to tremble" and "reel to and fro", valleys to rise up and mountains to be made low, and for an angel to sound a trumpet. Smith is once again regurgitating old myths and legends that made a more recent appearance in the Bible, the origins of which predate history; unwittingly describing the effects of volcanic eruption which evolved into religion. *(See: Lauritzen 2011).*

The Lamanites are going to blossom "as the rose", not that the Shakers would understand that idea when they heard it of course. Zion will flourish – and they are to repent, which essentially meant they should drop their beliefs and follow Smith.

So, the three men, Rigdon, Pratt and Copley took the revelation and read the entire thing to the Shaker congregation which was situated near Cleveland, Ohio. Unless already aware, I wonder what the reader thinks the outcome was? That's right; it was 'rejected', which really means that the three were thrown out on their ears; the Shakers were having none of Joseph Smith's nonsense.

Finally, the speaker, who previously identified himself *as* God, "…for I am God" in v.5, now declares, in v.28, that he is also "Jesus Christ, and I come quickly". You would have thought God would know of the Shakers reaction in advance and not bothered with the revelation. Obviously, the Mormon God did not know everything yesterday, today and forever; He didn't know what would happen tomorrow. The Church would dream up an excuse for failure of course. In this case, no doubt it would be a 'testimony' against the Shakers as they had been given the chance to accept Smith's 'truth'. If God expected them to accept it, He clearly didn't pick the right words or surely they would have listened.

Section 49 – Summary

Non-prophetic revelation.   1

1. This revelation was given specifically to be read to the Shaker congregation in order to set them straight (and, I suspect, to keep Copley in his place) and have them follow Smith.

Considering the Shakers rejected the revelation, and the Lord is supposedly 'all knowing', perhaps we should question why he bothered with the revelation at all as he should clearly have been able to anticipate the ultimate outcome.

Section 50
9 May 1831. Kirtland, Ohio.

History.

1833 BOC Ch. LIII. 1835 D&C Sec. XVII. 2010 D&C Sec. 50.

The modern-day header to this Section includes *"...some of the elders did not understand the manifestations of different spirits abroad in the earth and that this revelation was given in response to his special inquiry on the matter. So-called spiritual phenomena were not uncommon among the members, some of whom claimed to be receiving visions and revelations."* (Italics in original).

In v.1, God announces that *He* is speaking and is going to give them "words of wisdom" concerning "the spirits which have gone abroad in the earth".

Many are false spirits, sent from Satan to deceive them. This all came about because once again some saints were claiming to have seen and heard things; some of which could, if accepted, have had an affect on the very basis of the beliefs, doctrines and systems of Smith's Church; not to mention completely undermining his autonomy which was essential to retain control of the group.

It is not surprising to learn that God immediately informs them that some spirits are false spirits and that Satan is trying to deceive them. How are they supposed to know that? Well, God is about to explain, through Smith of course. But first, there is naturally the mandatory 'filler', so Smith has God waffle on about seeing abominations in churches that profess His name; if the faithful endure (in life or death) they will inherit eternal life; He will bring deceivers and hypocrites (some of whom are among them) to judgment.

Finally, God gets around to saying "...let us reason together, that ye may understand." A slightly strange turn of phrase coming from God, don't you think? Even stranger is God's next statement, "Let us reason even as a man reasoneth one with another face to face" (v.11), but of course God does not follow through, or appear to them, or actually talk – face to face. God then asks them a question – to what were they ordained? He then answers it for them: "To preach my gospel by the Spirit, even the Comforter which was sent forth to teach the truth." That is D&C 50:14, the reference which today appears on the front cover of the Mormon missionary lesson manual, 'A Guide to Missionary Service – Preach My Gospel'.

God finally seems to (but really doesn't) get round to some explanations. He says they have seen spirits they couldn't understand and have assumed them to be from God; in this are they justified? God then says they can answer that for themselves; so much for God 'reasoning face to face'. In v.23, we learn "that which doth not edify is not of God, and is darkness" which is not exactly startling news. Conversely, in v.24, "that which is of God is light" – more not so enlightening information. Smith should have considered the fact that the many millions of good people who then believed in God, also believed that to be the case; and yet Smith (and his God) decried anyone and everyone who did not follow *his* teachings. One must question why God would allow so many people to be so wrong for so long and then have them obliged to accept the word of a man renowned for being a con artist, who presented strangely worded and unsustainable concepts claimed to be from God, which almost everyone was invariably going to reject out of hand.

If this really was a *plan* devised by *God*, it was a hopeless plan and it did not work – actually making a fool of God. The Mormon Church considers itself successful, but if after almost a couple of centuries it can only boast somewhat less than five million active participants out of fewer than fourteen million claimed members, then it really is not.

The closest God gets to helping them discern spirits in this Section is in v.31 where it says that if they behold a spirit they can't understand, to ask the Father in the name of Jesus so they can know. If "he give not unto you that spirit" they will know it is not of God and they will be given power to shout at it that "it is not of God"; not exactly a convincing storyline really. Especially as God adds that they should not do that with "railing accusation" so they are not "overcome", "neither with boasting nor rejoicing" in case they are "seized". There are no words...

Considering Smith's ideas on discerning spirits are nonexistent, I am drawn to ask why the Lord didn't have Smith reveal the more precise detail contained in Section 129 which Smith succinctly covers in just six verses *(see pp. 445-6)*.

Whatever the initial problem with people seeing spirits was, it appears (v.39) to have involved Edward Partridge, as out of nowhere we get this.

> **39.** Wherefore, in this thing my servant Edward Partridge is not justified; nevertheless let him repent and he shall be forgiven.

It is strange, that is, if anyone today actually accepts this as remotely true, that no such things ever happen *now*. On the rare occasion someone does claim such manifestations, they are usually declared delusional, schizophrenic or mentally ill and treated accordingly. Charlatans do still manage to create new religions out of such claims from time to time but the incidence of such claims in Smith's day was prolific by comparison. It was essentially almost considered a normal part of society within the class of people that included the Smith family and many of the followers of local religious groups. Damage limitation was all that could be considered by Smith.

They are ordained to preach the "word of truth" by the Comforter and receive His word in the same way. "If it be some other way it is not of God" (v.20). It is interesting to note that following God's announcement in v.1 that it is He who is speaking, which he reaffirms in other verses through to v.13, He then seems to quickly revert to speaking *of* God, *of* the Father, Jesus Christ, and the Son. By v.27 Smith has God speaking in the third person, "the will of the Father through Jesus Christ, his Son". There is no consistency at all. It is not until v.36 that God gets back to speaking in the first person, "blessed are you who are now hearing these words of mine from the mouth of my servant," And why are they blessed? You can guess – "for your sins are forgiven you" – always a feel-good explanation to give people.

God is pleased with John Wakefield; he and Parley P. Pratt are to go off and preach together. John Corrill and anyone else who wants to can also go.

From v.40, God calls His people children; but wait, it isn't God any more, it is Jesus speaking about "my father" and through to the end, Jesus is the voice with no noted *change* of speaker anywhere. Perhaps this is because he confirms "the Father and I are one. I am in the Father and the Father in me". Verse 42 claims "And none of them that my Father hath given me shall be lost". I thought in Mormonism, that that was Satan's plan – which God rejected. Jesus got the job based on humans having free agency so they could choose – and change their minds, in which case some are bound to be lost – unless they are here *predestined* to be saved; something that cuts across Mormon doctrine entirely. Smith's comment from Jesus is doctrinally unsustainable.

It gets worse for Smith, as he then has God, now in the persona of Jesus, specifically declare that he will return *before they die.*

> **45.** And the day cometh that you shall hear my voice and see me, and know that I am.

DOCTRINE & COVENANTS – SECTIONS 38-50

46. Watch, therefore, that ye may be ready. Even so. Amen.

This is not some old biblical text which may have lost an original meaning in translation; these are the first hand words of God/Jesus to the saints at that time. He states *categorically* that the day will come when *they* will *hear* his voice and *see* him, so *they* are to **watch** for it and be ready. That is explicit – he wasn't speaking to future generations, he was speaking to *them*, in concert with discerning spirits – something we no longer seem to have the need for. It meant before those who heard it died – and it remains prophecy unfulfilled.

If Jesus had returned, the Mormon Church would immediately declare these verses to have meant *exactly* what they say. If the Church claims (as it must do, because Jesus didn't turn up) that it does *not* mean what it clearly *says*, then they make a liar out of Jesus, who should have been clearer in what he meant. Theologically, God/Jesus cannot lie; therefore, either he/they are illiterate and incapable of explaining themselves – or Smith was an utter liar.

There is always an escape route in Mormonism, and no 'excuse' is beyond consideration, so nothing surprises me any more. And, it is why I will never respond to apologists who do not represent God and are just the 'puppets of the prophets', hired to explain the inexplicable by manipulating truth even further than the Church has already indiscriminately falsified it.

It reminds me very much of Samuel Katich and his article on polyandry. *(See: TMD Vol 1:113-20 for full discussion)*. He explains that polyandry means a woman who has more than one husband. He accepts such a relationship is altogether contrary to Mormon doctrine. Then he *proves* several polyandrous relationships that Smith, Young and Kimball entered into. A way out of the hole he has dug may at first seem entirely impossible. However, Katich clearly had "a plan so cunning that you could put a tail on it and call it a weasel" to quote one of my favourite TV characters *(Blackadder Ser. 3.1.)* – and to lighten the moment. Katich says something even more bizarre and his 'escape' crashes from the sublime to more than the ridiculous. Katich absurdly concludes that as polyandry can *only* mean a woman with more than one husband, and as that *is* contrary to doctrine, and as Smith and others definitely *did* participate in it… we must just call it something else. (www.fairlds.org/pubs/polyandry.pdf).

Deciding to write his own dictionary, Katich protests that "Applying the definition of polyandry to describe these marriages is misleading, as its compatibility deviates from LDS marital theology." I was speechless the first time I read that – and I am just as speechless when I see it again now. It is not misleading at all – it correctly defines the exact situation – Smith and others married women who already had husbands; that was polyandry and contrary to established doctrine; end of story. You can't just make up a new *name* for it in order to make the insurmountable problem go away; it was still polyandry.

Regarding the 'discerning' of spirits, Smith was obviously still new to the game in 1831 and the details he provided regarding supposedly discerning spirits in this revelation were, to say the least, more than just pathetic. With experience, and over a decade to think about it, Smith eventually came up with what at first glance may seem a much better idea – but which was really just as silly when you think about it. They are contained in Section 129 (1843) briefly mentioned above, which we will discuss in its turn *(see pp. 445-6)*.

****

Notes

1. **Shiloh:** Generally understood as denoting the Messiah, "the peaceful one," as the word signifies (Gen. 49:10). The Vulgate Version translates the word, "he who is to be sent," in allusion to the Messiah; the Revised Version, margin, "till he come to Shiloh;" and the LXX., "until that which is his shall come to Shiloh." It is most simple and natural to render the expression, as in the Authorized Version, "till Shiloh come," interpreting it as a proper name (comp. Isa. 9:6). Shiloh, a place of rest, a city of Ephraim, "on the north side of Bethel," from which it is distant 10 miles (Judg. 21:19); the modern Seilun (the Arabic for Shiloh), a "mass of shapeless ruins." Here the tabernacle was set up after the Conquest (Josh. 18:1-10), where it remained during all the period of the judges till the ark fell into the hands of the Philistines. "No spot in Central Palestine could be more secluded than this early sanctuary, nothing more featureless than the landscape around; so featureless, indeed, the landscape and so secluded the spot that from the time of St. Jerome till its re-discovery by Dr. Robinson in 1838 the very site was forgotten and unknown." It is referred to by Jeremiah (7:12, 14; 26:4-9) five hundred years after its destruction. *(Easton's 1897 Bible Dictionary).*

Chapter 16

**Doctrine and Covenants
Sections 51 – 64**

Section 51
May 1831. Thompson, Ohio.

History.

Not in 1833 BOC. 1835 D&C Sec. XXIII. 2010 D&C Sec. 51.

Members arriving from the east were temporarily gathering in Ohio. Edward Partridge was the Bishop and he asked Smith how to organise the new people. Smith asked God and God is once again the 'voice' for this revelation – at least to start with, but as we have observed in many earlier Sections, God soon ends up also describing himself as Jesus Christ. "Hearken unto me, saith the Lord your God" (v.1); "I, the Lord" (v.16); "Verily, I say unto you, I am Jesus Christ" (v.20). Interestingly, he ends with "who cometh quickly, in an hour you think not. Even so", inferring it may be sooner than they think. They expected him during their generation, and certainly by 1891, according to everything they had heard and were yet to hear about it. *(See TMD Vol. 1:188-9, 202).* Now Smith adds further pressure by having the Lord say it may be sooner.

In this Section God/Jesus is explaining to Partridge how he should handle matters. The people must be organised according to *God's* laws. Everyone is to be given their "portion" equal to the "wants and needs" of their family. Prior to that allocation, everyone had to hand over everything they had to the Church. What they got back, whether more or less in value to that which they had given up, was to be their 'inheritance'. But, there was always a catch with Smith.

This one was in a document they had to sign which held their 'inheritance' to be theirs "until he transgresses and is not accounted worthy by the voice of the church", upon which they had absolutely no claim on anything they had consecrated to the Church and they left with nothing but the small 'inheritance' given them which would not amount to much of anything in real terms. All that they had previously owned now belonged exclusively to the Church.

The system was to be worked in the local Church community and not shared with other 'churches', which meant the other branches of the Mormon Church which should have their own similar arrangements. If other branches ask for help, they must arrange repayment. The idea was tried a couple of times in early Mormonism but never lasted long. The Bishop of course could also have everything he needed for his own family, including food and clothing. He was to be fully supported. As the Bishop, he was "employed" in that role (v.14).

> **51:5.** And if he shall transgress and is not accounted worthy to belong to the church, he shall not have power to claim that portion which he has consecrated unto the bishop for the poor and needy of my church; therefore, he shall not retain the gift, but shall only have claim on that portion that is deeded unto him.

The Lord says they won't be there very long but "let them act upon this land as for years, and this shall turn unto them for their good" (v.17). History does not paint a very rosy picture of anything ultimately turning "unto them for their good" in any area where they resided. Something always went wrong as Smith immediately tried to take control of the local community, and eventually they had to move on. Ultimately, they would be driven out of Nauvoo, Illinois.

Section 52
6 June 1831. Kirtland, Ohio.

History.

1833 BOC Ch. LIV. 1835 D&C Sec. LXVI. 2010 D&C Sec. 52.

DOCTRINE & COVENANTS – SECTIONS 51-64

The Section header dates this to 7 June 1831 but the *Joseph Smith Papers* date it to 6 June 1831, the day on which the conference concluded. Whenever it was actually written, the Lord declares that he is going to explain what they are to do between then and the next conference, which is designated to be held in Missouri. This, the Lord declares in v.2, is the "land which I consecrate unto my people which are a remnant of the house of Jacob, and those who are heirs according to the covenant". This is a direct reference to the so-called Lamanites (Native North Americans). Just a few weeks later, Independence, Missouri, is confirmed (in Section 57) as being the location for Zion – the New Jerusalem, something which has never materialised. Native North Americans have *not* inherited Independence – or anywhere else in Missouri in general.

Smith and Rigdon are to go to Missouri as soon as they can arrange to do so. The rest of this Section is essentially a catalogue of who should go and preach where, all ending up in Missouri in time for the next conference. This is the detailed extent to which the Lord was apparently 'directing' the Church. If Smith and Rigdon are faithful, they will know what to do and they will also be informed where the land of inheritance is. If they are *not* faithful "they shall be cut off, even as I will, as seemeth me good" (v.6). Not only is that statement slightly nonsensical and unnecessarily repetitive, the last phrase, "as seemeth me good" seems quite a strange turn of phrase for the Lord to use about Smith – or about anyone else for that matter. It smacks of being a human term used to *sound* like the Lord; moreover Smith often has the Lord use it. Does that really sound like something a God would say even once, let alone quite a number of times?

Taking into account that "as seemeth me good" is not a phrase attributed to the Lord **anywhere**, other than in Smith's own writings, this is another very suspicious aspect regarding Smith; even more so because he doesn't *only* have the Lord use the phrase, he also has Moroni use it in the Book of Mormon where Moroni (10:1) says he will "…write somewhat *as seemeth me good*".

In the D&C, it appears several times in addition to the above. Section 40:3 "…it remaineth with me to do with him *as seemeth me good*"; 42:16 "…ye shall speak and prophesy *as seemeth me good*"; 56:4 "I the Lord, command and revoke, *as it seemeth me good*"; 84:103 the "Lord shall direct them, for thus *it seemeth me good*". In D&C 60:5 and also 62:5 the Lord says "…*as seemeth you good*, it mattereth not unto me"; in 100:1 the Lord says to "…my friends Sidney and Joseph" that their families are well "and I will do with them *as seemeth me good*". In 124:72 and also 124:77 Hyrum can put stock into a house "*as seemeth him good*". God had **never** said it before Smith put the words into His mouth – numerous times. In Smith's Moses 6:32, he has God

213

say *"I will do as seemeth me good"* to Enoch. In **eleven** instances, Smith has the Lord introduce a phrase *never* seen elsewhere.

When Joseph Smith wrote his 'Inspired Revision' of the Bible, in his version of Genesis 19:11-13, Smith has some men say *"We will have the men, and thy daughters also; we will do with them as seemeth us good."* Smith has Lot say "...ye shall *not do unto them as seemeth good* in your eyes" – once again using similar wording. The story, as recorded in the Bible, does not read that way at all; in fact, that part of the story is entirely different in the Bible.

The closest it gets to Smith's "as seemeth me good" in the Bible, is in Judges 19:24, in the horrific story of a Levite traveller invited to stay at a house in Gibeah. Some local men, the 'sons of Belial', surround the house and bang on the door, demanding the man be sent out as they want to gang rape him. The host, believing this to be an abomination, offers them his daughter and the traveller's concubine instead, saying "...do with them *what seemeth good unto you*: but to this man do not so vile a thing", which even then is not quite the same as Smith's wording. The women are repeatedly raped and the concubine ultimately dies on the doorstep of the house. The Levite cuts her into twelve pieces and sends her "into all the coasts of Israel". It is actually a strange and disturbing story to include in the Bible and the chapter ends: "...consider of it, take advice, and speak your minds." I have, and will; I would have left it out. In this instance, as with a few other similar remarks in the Bible – which are not actually the same as Smith's line, it is part of the storyline and never the Lord speaking.

Smith also seems to have the Lord say "in mine own due time" quite a lot, often when something has gone wrong and someone hasn't performed in the way Smith had the Lord predict they would. Smith then has the Lord say that he is going to deal with that person – in his own due time. My research into such instances reveals *no* recorded retribution coming upon anyone in that category. "In mine own due time" appears twelve times in the D&C; 24:16; 35:25; 42:62; 43:29; 56:3; 67:14; 71:10; 82:13; 90:29; 90:32; 117:16; 136:18. All were written by Smith, except Section 136, which was recorded in 1847 by Brigham Young who copied Smith's style. The expression also appears three times in the Book of Mormon (2 Nephi 27:21; 3 Nephi 20:29; Ether 3:27). The Lord is speaking on every occasion. As with "as seemeth me good", the Lord was *never* recorded as saying "in mine own due time" *other* than in material written by Joseph Smith – and once by Brigham Young. These 'Smith created' phrases, attributed to the Lord, are reminiscent of his "nation, kindred, tongue and people" fetish *(See pp. 180-82)*. Smith created several 'pet phrases' for the Lord to use. *(See: The Final Analysis, Part 2).*

The Lord then gets into discussion regarding the proposed journeys. There is no such detailed revelation these days for apostles regarding their travels.

Even missionaries, who in my young day were given to understand that individual destinations were considered in the Holy of Holies of the temple and when call and release letters were personally signed by the First Presidency of the Church (as indeed were my own), today get their destination selected by computer and letters signed by a machine. The Mormon God is 'progressive' in at least some areas it seems. The 'brethren' are self admitted as no longer receiving revelation about important issues, let alone mundane details such as recorded in this Section *(See p. xiv).*

The Lord says Lyman Wight (who is to beware of Satan) and John Corrill should go 'speedily' to Missouri; John Murdock and Hyrum Smith, via Detroit.

From v.14 through v.18, the Lord says he is providing a "pattern" so they won't be deceived; Satan is in the land. It is no pattern at all really. It just says those who pray and are contrite are accepted – if they obey the ordinances. If they speak, and their language is meek and it edifies people, they are of God – but once again, only if "he obey mine ordinances". If they tremble they shall be made strong, bringing forth fruits of "praise and wisdom". However, he that is overcome and "bringeth not forth fruits" according to "this pattern" is *not* of me. In other words, convert people and you are acceptable; fail to do so, and Satan got to you. It is such nonsense that it becomes impossible to consider the idea that the Lord would say such things; but it is exactly what we have come to expect of Smith, who was constantly trying to more firmly establish himself.

The next verse supposedly explains what all that means: "Wherefore, by this pattern ye shall know the spirits in all cases under the whole heavens" (v.19). Are these eloquent, meaningful and divine words directly from God, or just pathetic nonsense from the not so divine imagination of Joseph Smith?

The list continues, the Lord apparently pairing off individuals on behalf of Smith. Quite a number of pairings are listed and all are to take (unspecified) separate routes, ending up in Missouri. If they are faithful, they will end up with "much fruit". Apparently, one man, Heman Basset, has done something to displease the Lord and "that which was bestowed upon him" is to be given to Simonds Ryder instead (v.37). Clearly the Lord got yet another person wrong.

Verse 39 is a classic example of Smith getting words mixed up. It will be argued by the Church that these are indeed the Lord's words and therefore they must be correct, but there appears no reasonable explanation for the Lord to say such a thing. He would surely *not* have used the word 'idolatry' in this sentence. When had they ever resorted to worshiping idols?

See what you think.

> **39.** Let the residue of the elders watch over the churches, and declare the word in the regions round about them; and let them labor with their own hands that there be no idolatry nor wickedness practised.

It seems fairly obvious that Smith meant to say they should labour so they didn't become *idle* and thus wicked. He undoubtedly meant 'idleness' rather than idolatry. There is no record of anything close to idolatry being practiced among the saints when left to their own devices. The notion that the Lord would say *any* of this, let alone specifically refer to 'idolatry' is more than just bewildering, it is incomprehensible. Apologists would no doubt resort to claims that it must have referred to a love of money or some other such nonsense.

Some filler now takes over, and they are to remember the poor and needy, the sick and afflicted, because if they don't, they are not the Lord's disciples.

Finally, the Lord says the land of Missouri is the land of their inheritance, which is now "the land of your enemies". Here Smith is categorising – or rather having the Lord categorise, innocent, peaceful (and many devoutly Christian), residents of Missouri as their *enemies* before the saints even arrived in the area. Smith has come to *expect* resistance.

At the end of this Section, the Lord expresses himself in a most strange manner.

> **43.** But, behold, I, the Lord, will hasten the city in its time, and will crown the faithful with joy and with rejoicing.
> **44.** Behold, I am Jesus Christ, the Son of God, and I will lift them up at the last day. Even so. Amen.

This appears to indicate that the Lord is going to speed up the construction of the city, but it is a little unclear. Whatever it was supposed to mean, the city never materialised and they were eventually forced to 'hasten' *out* of the area.

The faithful did not get crowned with joy or rejoicing, they fled the state and many of them died crossing the plains following their expulsion. Whether any of them ever will be lifted up at a 'last day' of some description remains to be seen, but I for one suspect not.

Section 52 – Summary

Prophecies made: 1
Prophecies fulfilled: 0

Prophecies made:

DOCTRINE & COVENANTS – SECTIONS 51-64

Pr. 22. Verse 2: …Missouri, upon the land which I will consecrate unto my people, which are a remnant of Jacob, and those who are heirs according to the covenant.

Results:

Pr. 22. This prophecy referred to the Native North Americans – Lamanites, inheriting the land. These 'Lamanites' not only did *not* inherit the land; the question now is: where are those Lamanites?

Section 53
8 June 1831. Kirtland, Ohio.

History.

BOC Ch. LV. 1835 D&C Sec. LXVI (numbering error). 2010 D&C Sec. 53.

Modern-day Sections 52 and 53 were both erroneously numbered LXVI in the 1835 D&C. This error was rectified in 1844 *(see pp. xii & xiv)*. It could be said that this section, as with many similar ones, really could have been left out altogether as it contains nothing of merit whatsoever. One 'Algernon Sidney Gilbert' wants to know what his calling is to be in the Church. The Lord himself takes the time to tell him – virtually nothing dissimilar to several other earlier so-called revelations where people had asked Smith the same question.

Apart from being told he can be an agent for the Church, as designated by the Bishop, the Lord pads things out to all of seven short verses by first including a note that he was crucified for the sins of the world – just in case they didn't know that – and then saying Gilbert can be ordained an elder and preach, and he can go with Smith and Rigdon to Missouri. And then, as there is nothing more the Lord (or Smith) can think of – he will be told more later on.

He must naturally "endure to the end". This is not a real revelation from the Lord by any standard other than the Mormon one which demands we accept on faith the idea that this really was the way the Lord operated. Once again, if it actually *was* the Lord, then why didn't he at least say something *useful*? Not once have we ever discovered a beautifully worded viable example of the Lord conveying some marvellous new, worthwhile convincing information through Smith. Not once. Gilbert was one of the unlucky ones to die in agony from cholera in 'Zion's Camp', so his 'enduring to the end' was mercifully brief.

THE MORMON DELUSION

Section 54
10 June 1831. Kirtland, Ohio.

History.

BOC Ch. LVI. 1835 D&C Sec. LXVII. 2010 D&C Sec. 54.

The whole concept of consecrating everything to the Church and receiving back enough for a family's needs may have sounded wonderful to poor saints arriving in the area, but some were businessmen who were quite wealthy and they considered the need for their assets to sustain them and their businesses in the future to be more important than giving everything away in return for just enough to manage on. For some, whilst they may initially have been taken with the idea of consecration, the reality soon set in and many changed their minds.

Leman Copley was one such person. Smith wanted Copley's seven-hundred to one-thousand acre farm to accommodate the saints arriving from Colesville. At first, Copley had gone along with the idea, allowing many to stay on his farm. It was supposed to be 'consecrated' for their inheritance. When he fell out with Smith, Copley forced the saints to leave and that presented the Church with a major problem. Smith was in real a quandary. He first had this short revelation and then a few days later, once he had taken more time to think things over, Smith continued his rant in Section 56 which we will pick up on in its turn. Copley was excommunicated but readmitted in October of 1832 and he also served a mission. Following Smith's death, Copley did not follow Young; he joined two Mormon schisms in succession.

Newel Knight and some of the Elders had gone to Smith to ask how to handle the situation when Copley pulled out. The Lord is naturally displeased, but before getting into anything, he takes time to remind them (once again) that he is Alpha and Omega, the beginning and the end, and moreover – that he was crucified. Why does he always repeat things that they already know? He should have *first* 'revealed' where the evicted saints should go. Ultimately, they travel to Jackson County, Missouri to settle, arriving in late July.

If their 'brethren' want to escape their enemies, they must repent and "become truly humble before me" – and contrite, which is tagged on at the end of the sentence in what has become the classic Smith 'oh, and I almost forgot' style of writing on behalf of deity. Because the covenant has been broken, the Lord declares it is now "void". Did he have a choice? More importantly, *why* did he not see this coming? Could he not have warned them? The Lord says "wo" to him who committed the offence and it would have been better had he drowned in the depths of the sea. Conversely, those who *kept* the covenant and commandment are blessed and shall have "mercy", but we do not learn what it was that required *mercy* to be extended to them as they *had* kept the covenant.

DOCTRINE & COVENANTS – SECTIONS 51-64

Newel Knight is clearly in some sort of trouble over the affair, as Smith has the Lord instruct him to "flee the land" in case his enemies get to him. They are to go west to the "borders of the Lamanites" (v.8), evidencing once again that they knew *exactly* where and who the Lamanites were *(see pp. 102-4)*. Once in Missouri, Knight is to take a job and (v.10) be *"patient in tribulation until I come; and, behold, I come quickly, and my reward is with me"* (emphasis added). Here, the Lord confirms in no uncertain terms that he will return *during the lifetime of Newel Knight*. Knight died on 11 January 1847. If Jesus had no intention of returning during Knight's lifetime, he had no cause to pretend that he would in such a specific statement directed exclusively to him.

"...behold, I come quickly, and my reward is with me" is direct plagiarism from the book of Revelation (22:12). "I come quickly" – "and my reward is with me" – "to give to every man according as his work shall be" are all stolen from verses in Revelation.

"I come quickly" appears 11 times in the D&C. The Lord is not personally recorded as having said that *anywhere* else at all. 'Revelation' is a record of the ramblings of someone claiming they saw and heard all these things in visions.

On two occasions, Smith also adds "and my reward is with me" for good measure and even paraphrases "to give every man according as his work shall be" – all from Revelation, and clearly identifying unadulterated plagiarism.

The book of Revelation only just scraped into the Bible, well into the CE period and is considered by many scholars and theologians to have been written by a lunatic. The Eastern Church does not use Revelation for readings. Even if the author was not mad, it most certainly was not written by the 'John' with whom many people associate it. At best, it consists of handed down stories, or memories combined with imagination or dreams rather than any exact words ever spoken by the Saviour. The exact sequence of translated words in the KJV is *impossible* for Jesus to ever have spoken in the first person in his own day, let alone to Smith in the 1800s. Compare these:

> **D&C 54:10.** And again, be patient in tribulation until I come; and, behold, ***I come quickly, and my reward is with me***, and they who have sought me early shall find rest to their souls. Even so. Amen.

> **D&C 112:34.** Be faithful until I come, for ***I come quickly; and my reward is with me to recompense every man according as his work shall be.*** I am Alpha and Omega. Amen.

> **Revelation 22:12.** And, behold, ***I come quickly; and my reward is with me, to give every man according as his work shall be.***

The above sequence of *nineteen words* in D&C 112 and Revelation 22 is *identical* with the exception of one word Smith replaced (give = recompense).

THE MORMON DELUSION

The chances of that sequence happening twice are in reality so infinitesimal as to be rendered not just implausible but entirely *impossible*. That is especially the case with translated works such as the KJV which cannot possibly contain a perfect rendition, word for word, of something originally spoken and recorded in another language. Add to that the fact that it is at least second hand hearsay concerning something that *might* have been said, and you can start to see the scale of Smith's problem. Smith's *pretended* words of the Lord were quoted *verbatim* from the KJV. If Smith had access to some other translation in his own time, say a copy of J. B. Phillips New Testament for example, he would undoubtedly have had the Lord say:

> See, *I come quickly*! I carry **my reward with me**, and repay **every man according** to his deeds. (Emphasis added to identify any exact words included in the KJV rendition of Revelation 22:12).

In the above example, only *eleven* words out of nineteen remain the same, and yet they represent a translation of the *same* original text. Which words are correct, the KJV, or J. B. Phillips'? The answer is there is no 'correct' version.

The New International Version presents the idea in a more modern manner; one in which the Lord may actually be more likely to speak in the modern (or even Smith's) day, were He actually going to speak at all. Instead of using such archaic speech, had he really been speaking, perhaps he would have said this.

> Look, I am coming soon! **My reward is with me**, and I will **give** to each person *according* to what they have done. (Emphasis added).

Here, we are down to only seven words being the same. Every translation can vary slightly and it quickly becomes clear the KJV is not representative of a one and only clear and perfect sequence of words originally spoken or even written. There are numerous variations in interpretation. Smith simply *copied* the version that he had access to and then pretended the Lord repeated those exact words.

Obviously, this was just Smith up to his old tricks, but it created yet another unfulfilled prophecy in this category; a regular feature in the way Smith had the Lord conclude a lot of his so-called revelations. He was always 'coming soon', and early Mormons came to believe that he really would – in *their* generation.

Section 54 – Summary

Prophecies made:	1
Prophecies fulfilled:	0

DOCTRINE & COVENANTS – SECTIONS 51-64

Prophecies made:

Pr. 23. Newel Knight is told he must be *"patient* in tribulation *until I come*; and, behold, I come quickly, and my reward is with me."

Results:

Pr. 23. Newel Knight died 11 January 1847 at age 46. Jesus did not return as promised during the lifetime of Knight. One-hundred-and-eighty years have passed since then.

Section 55
14 June 1831. Kirtland, Ohio.

History.

BOC Ch. LVII. 1835 D&C Sec. LXVIII. 2010 D&C Sec. 55.

William Phelps and family arrived in Kirtland. He was a printer, so naturally Smith has the Lord immediately call him to print materials for the Church. The Lord is talking directly to Phelps. He is to be baptised, to be ordained an Elder, and also to preach. He is to assist Oliver Cowdery with printing; selecting and writing books for children in the Church. He can go with Smith and Rigdon to be 'planted' in the land of his inheritance to do this work. The Lord takes quite an interest in small details and yet completely ignores major world issues that would have been more deserving of the attention of the God of the universe. Such mundane and finite detail is completely unbecoming of an all powerful infinite God who should have had much better things to do.

Joseph Coe can go with them and "the residue" (whatever the residue was supposed to be) "will be made known later". As a member, your mind glosses over Sections such as this one and you just move on, looking for more spiritual enlightenment. With a questioning mind, you are drawn to stop and question why God would ever become involved in such trivia, at the expense of giving the world at large a clue about *anything* of real significance. Was that all he had? It is no wonder that not many people joined the Mormon Church, and there is little wonder why so few do today, or why so many are now leaving the Church. We will later be reviewing some other Sections where the Lord takes an even closer interest in things so mundane that it is hard to believe people (including myself) could ever have just blindly accepted them as true, instead of employing rational thinking and questioning everything more closely.

Section 56
15 June 1831. Kirtland, Ohio.

History.

BOC Ch. LVIII. 1835 D&C Sec. LXIX. 2010 D&C Sec. 56.

This Section picks up the storyline from Sections 52 and 54. We could ask why God did not foresee the 'problem' *(see below)* with Ezra Thayre and make different arrangements in the first instance. Smith has to resort to having God say he 'commands' and 'revokes', as well as make other excuses for things not going as planned *and* directed, by *Him*.

God confirms that His anger is still 'kindled'. Creating fear always helps – at least in Smith's mind. You would think a God would learn to control His temper and act rationally. God says His anger is against the rebellious; in other words, in this instance, against those who won't give everything they have to the Church; also, for no stated reason "they shall know mine arm and mine indignation, in the day of visitation and of wrath upon the nations". That is just meant to *sound* scary and cannot actually be God *speaking*, as surely 'the nations' in general did not deserve such 'indignation' from God. If they were not following Him as He wished, God had already had several thousands of years to explain Himself to the world. To date, if no one had got things right at all – until Smith came along to correct matters, then who was to blame? Surely not most humans who thought they *were* obeying God – in one way or another.

If Smith and his nonsense were all God could come up with, there was and is no hope for the world ever knowing what He really wants, because the majority of people are simply not going to accept for one moment, in this (or even back in Smith's) day and age, that God really would behave like that or ask of them the sorts of things that Smith dreamt up.

Once again, those who won't obey will be cut off – and as ever, "in mine own due time". Amid the selected pairings that God Himself dictated, He had 'revealed' this in Section 52:

> **D&C 52:22.** And again, verily I say unto you, let my servant Thomas B. Marsh and my servant Ezra Thayre take their journey also, preaching the word by the way unto this same land.

When it came to it, Thayre was just not ready to go and he deferred. Smith, as observed on several other occasions, was once again in a real pickle, as *God* had dictated the pairing and He should have known full well that this would happen and not put the two together in the first place. To get out of the mess this then created, Smith now has to have God cover the mistake by having His commandment to Thayre 'revoked'; He had only given it five days earlier.

> **D&C 56:5.** Wherefore, I revoke the commandment which was given unto my servants Thomas B. Marsh and Ezra Thayre, and give a new commandment unto my servant Thomas, that he shall take up his journey speedily to the land of Missouri, and my servant Selah J. Griffin shall also go with him.

The next problem was that God had previously paired Griffin with Newel Knight, so He now has to 'revoke' that as well and tell Knight that instead of accompanying Griffin, he is to remain and later accompany as many others as want to go "to the land which I have appointed". Thayre is either to repent or have his money back and be cut off from the Church.

Thayre must have eventually chosen to repent as he was not 'cut off' and he did serve a mission to New York with Marsh the following year. Thayre later became a member of the Stake High Council at Adam-Ondi-Ahman. He was among a select group of men, including Brigham Young and Wilford Woodruff (both then apostles and future Church Presidents), George A. Smith (apostle), and Jedediah M. Grant (a future apostle and father of Heber J. Grant, another later Church President), to campaign for Joseph Smith to become President of the United States. Thayre also became a member of the 'Council of Fifty'.

Following the death of Joseph Smith in June 1844, Thayre was one of the saints who would not follow Brigham Young. Remaining in Nauvoo, he moved to Michigan in 1849 where he joined the Reorganised Church of Jesus Christ of Latter Day Saints (now Community of Christ) on 24 August 1860.

Meanwhile, God assures Smith that if *he* has to repay Thayre's money, He (God) will pay Smith back when they are in Nauvoo; God does not explain exactly *how* He intends to do that (v.12). People will receive according to that which they do. They have much to repent of and are not pardoned because they seek to counsel in their own ways. They don't obey the truth and they "have pleasure in unrighteousness". I suspect each member thought that must apply to anyone *but* them, as surely, in reality, no one who joined the Church actually did take *pleasure* in being unrighteous. Smith was always portraying God as angry and somewhat unforgiving. People do their best, but Smith's God never seemed to cut anyone any slack.

Back to the money problem, Smith has God yet again say "wo" unto the rich who won't give their money to the poor. Then he adds, "wo unto the poor" who are lazy and won't do any work. Finally, the poor will be fine if they are pure in heart (v.18). This verse is referenced in the Mormon missionary lesson manual *(See also TMD 4:234)*.

> **56:18.** ...blessed are the poor who are pure in heart, whose hearts are broken, and whose spirits are contrite, for they shall see the kingdom of God coming **in power and great glory** unto their deliverance; for the fatness of the earth shall be theirs. (Emphasis added).

Smith uses the phrase "in power and great glory" several times in the D&C; Smith is the *only* one to ever put those words *directly* into the mouth of *deity*.

Section 57
20 July 1831. Zion, Jackson County, Missouri.

History.

Not in 1833 BOC. 1835 D&C Sec. XXVII. 2010 D&C Sec. 57.

When reviewing Section 42, I mentioned that we would come back to Smith's 'Zion – the New Jerusalem' in this Section. Section 52:5 informed us that God will reveal the *exact* location, and now Smith has God personally do so, in very clear and specific detail.

> **D&C 57:1.** Hearken, O ye elders of my church, saith the Lord your God, who have assembled yourselves together, according to my commandments, in this land, which is the land of **Missouri**, which is the land which I have appointed and **consecrated for the gathering of the saints.**
> **2.** Wherefore, *this is the land of promise*, and the place *for the city of Zion.*
> **3.** And *thus saith the Lord your God*, if you will receive wisdom here is wisdom. Behold, the place which is now called **Independence is the center place**; and *a spot for the temple is lying westward*, upon a lot which is not far from the courthouse.
> **4.** Wherefore, it is wisdom that the land should be purchased by the saints, and also every tract lying westward, even unto the line running directly between Jew and Gentile;
> **5.** And also every tract bordering by the prairies, inasmuch as my disciples are enabled to buy lands. Behold, this is wisdom, that they may obtain it *for an everlasting inheritance.* (Emphasis added).

DOCTRINE & COVENANTS – SECTIONS 51-64

In using the term 'Jew' in v.4, Smith has *God* referring to Native North Americans whom Smith considered were *all* 'Lamanites' and thus of Jewish origin. Note how specific God is about Zion being an *everlasting* inheritance. Unfortunately, it was never to be and it left Smith with yet another monumental 'prophecy problem'. A couple of years after the prophecy, in June 1833, Joseph Smith drew up 'plans' for the layout of Zion at Independence, Missouri. Smith even laid a cornerstone for the temple on 3 August 1831, but that was about as far as things ever went. This was Smith's idea of a 'plan' for the city of Zion.

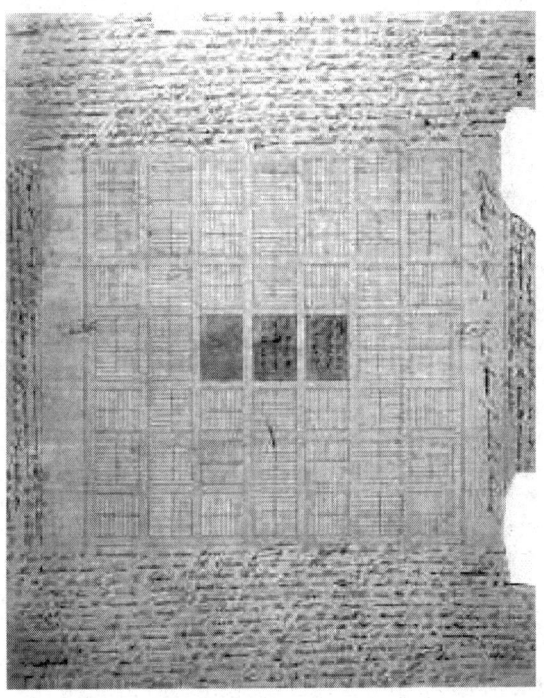

The city plan, which was based on Mormon principles of agrarianism order and community, included twenty-four temples at the centre of the city – and they were not just for worship. Other proposed uses included education and administration, as well as cultural events. The layout accommodated 15,000-20,000 saints in the one mile square city which also had agricultural land surrounding it. Further 'cities' were to be built along similar lines once the first one was full "and so fill up the world".

See article at: http://en.wikipedia.org/wiki/Zion_(Latter_Day_Saints)

Notwithstanding the fact that less than a couple of centuries later, such a plan would be so out of date as to be virtually unworkable in the modern world, at the time it was Smith's dream – and apparently, just what God wanted.

By 1841, it had become clear that there was a major problem in having this prophecy fulfilled and Smith was obliged to have God further explain Himself. After all the promises that had been made, what could God say? Section 124 was recorded on 19 January 1841. Today, in respect of v.45-55, it includes this in the Section heading: *The Saints are excused from building the temple in Jackson County because of the oppression of their enemies;* (Italics in original). Note the Church explains that they were 'excused' from building the temple at Independence – yet it had been *promised* to them as part of the bigger promise; Zion – the New Jerusalem.

> **D&C 124:49.** Verily, verily, I say unto you, that when I give a commandment to any of the sons of men to do a work unto my name, and those sons of men go with all their might and with all they have to perform that work, and cease not their diligence, and their enemies come upon them and hinder them from performing that work, behold, it behooveth me to require that work no more at the hands of those sons of men, but to accept of their offerings.
>
> **50.** And the iniquity and transgression of my holy laws and commandments I will visit upon the heads of those who hindered my work, unto the third and fourth generation, so long as they repent not, and hate me, saith the Lord God.
>
> **51.** Therefore, for this cause have I accepted the offerings of those whom I commanded to build up a city and a house unto my name, in Jackson county, Missouri, and were hindered by their enemies, saith the Lord your God.

It turns out that when God made his 'promised land' promises, He was in no position to do so; it was never going to happen, due to strong opposition against Smith and his ways. Yet Smith had his God make the promises, despite the fact that God should have already known this would happen. It calls God into question, but if we accept the idea that God could and would *never* make such an error, that only leaves Smith to answer for the mistake.

On 20 July 1831, verses 1-5 *(see p. 224)* confirmed the City of Zion would be for "an everlasting inheritance" and on 19 January 1841, they are 'excused' from building it. Something in there just doesn't sit right and as ever, there is only one remotely possible explanation. Today, the main Mormon Church still doesn't occupy the area; two schisms, the Church of Christ (Temple Lot) and the Reorganised Church (Community of Christ) have churches in that location.

Section 57 continues (from v.6) by confirming Sidney Gilbert is to stand in his place as an agent for the Church, buying up tracts of land. Edward Partridge was responsible for splitting up the land and assigning it to members as their 'inheritance', in exchange for all they had, by way of consecration. Gilbert is also to open a store and "sell goods *without fraud*, that he may obtain money to buy lands for the good of the saints, and that he may obtain whatsoever things the disciples may need to plant them in their inheritance". I wonder just what circumstances would have determined that Gilbert could sell 'with fraud', as the very mention of it suggests that selling *without* defrauding people was not always the case for Smith and his crew.

William W. Phelps is confirmed as the printer for the Church (v.11) and Cowdery is to help him. People are to gather there and as ever, they will be told more 'later'. For once, God signs off in v.16 without turning into Jesus. He doesn't say who He is at the end but it still seems to be God. He concludes by saying "Even so. Amen."

In yet another, 'hang on a minute' moment, is not "Even so. Amen" also starting to sound a little too familiar? It turns out that this was yet another favourite phrase that Joseph Smith picked up. It only appears *once* in the Bible, in Revelation 1:7 and it is *not* the Lord speaking. The writer of Revelation says "Amen. Even so, come, Lord Jesus" in Rev. 22:20 – if that counts for anything.

By comparison, Smith has God and/or Jesus say "Even so. Amen" a total of *fifty-five* times in his D&C and he also uses it in Moses 1:42. 'Suspicious' has long become an entirely inadequate word for such habits as these, that Smith had God *and* Jesus getting into. Joseph F. Smith also ended his 1918 vision (in which he saw people such as Elias who didn't actually exist), by personally adding "even so. Amen", copying his namesake's long standing 'sign-off' that he had so often put directly into the mouth of God/Jesus *(see Section 138)*.

Section 57 – Summary

Prophecies made: 1
Prophecies fulfilled: 0

Prophecies made:

Pr. 24. v2-5. "Wherefore, this is the land of promise, and the place for the city of Zion. And thus saith the Lord your God ... Independence is the center place; and a spot for the temple is lying westward ... for an everlasting inheritance."

Results:

Pr. 24. The Church never did build the City of Zion – the New Jerusalem, or a temple at Independence, Missouri. Two Mormon schisms now occupy some of that area.

Section 58
1 August 1831. Zion, Jackson County, Missouri.

History.

BOC Ch. LIX. 1835 D&C Sec. XVIII. 2010 D&C Sec. 58.

Much of this section contains filler designed to look as though the Lord is closely directing the Church and its future. Detailed instructions are given to a few named individuals, always including the idea that they are still unbelieving and sinful; they must repent, confess their sins and be forgiven, then they will be blessed if they keep the commandments. It is always that way, time after time. After the tribulation come the blessings, says the Lord. Only in a religious setting does that seem to be the order of things. In real life, there doesn't need to be tribulation – or blessings for that matter. Life can be good without such notions. Sometimes things go wrong and sometimes they go well.

There are not tribulations or blessings at all – unless you think that God is involved. It is just the way life is and if God exists, He would almost certainly not be involved in such trivia as Smith describes. Such concepts are designed by religious leaders like Smith in order to control the flock. Amid the nonsense that a real God would clearly *not* concern Himself with, we get a couple of things that dig deep holes for Smith, compared with the reality that followed.

The Lord has sent them there, to Zion, Jackson County, Missouri, "that you might be obedient, and that your hearts might be prepared to bear testimony of the things which are to come;" (v.6). The Lord quantifies his requirement in v.7. "And also that you might be honored in laying the foundation, and in bearing record of the land upon which the Zion of God shall stand." Here we have Smith having the *Lord confirm* that they are to testify in his (the Lord's) name that Jackson County is indeed where **"the Zion of God shall stand."** It didn't – and still doesn't. According to Smith's revelation, the Lord *instructed* them to testify of something that God promised and never fulfilled. Verse 12 confirms: "Behold, I, the Lord, have spoken it." And then, "Who am I, saith the Lord, that have promised and have not fulfilled?" (v.31). Who indeed? Smith had God make promises and even had Him confirm that He had made them. If the buck doesn't stop with God, then it most certainly stops with Smith.

The Lord also instructs them to obey the laws of the land. You would think that to be a sensible thing for anyone to do without being instructed on it by the Lord. So, why did Smith include it?

> **58:21.** Let no man break the laws of the land, for he that keepeth the laws of God hath no need to break the laws of the land.

22. Wherefore, be subject to the powers that be, until he reigns whose right it is to reign, and subdues all enemies under his feet.

Apart from the fact that there always seemed to be 'enemies' that it would take the returning Lord to subdue, the passage seems innocuous enough and is easily glossed over – until you start to consider the facts. It starts with *"Let no man break the laws..."* which is just common sense really, but of course that includes Smith and his closest associates. Yet Smith's record on law breaking goes almost beyond anything imaginable. From adultery and illegal marriages, polygyny and polyandry, to looting and plundering and conspiracy to murder; from exacting assets from people (consecration) and then cutting them off with nothing if they became 'dissenters', to opening an illegal bank and printing countless worthless bank notes, taking out what he could and then absconding when it all went wrong; from having people lie under oath in legal documents regarding polygamy to destroying the printing press owned by William Law; such was Smith's idea of personally *obeying* the law.

Smith was in and out of jail or the run from the law with a price on his head during much of his short adult life. Charges ranged from at first being a con artist to later more serious offences including conspiring to attempted murder. Smith died in jail awaiting trial on charges of treason. If anyone ever ignored a commandment from the Lord, it was Smith himself deliberately violating his own so-called revelations over and over again. Events in Smith's personal life are evidence enough that he did not believe God was actually dictating these revelations. If he had done, he would surely have obeyed at least some of them.

Among more directions about who should go where and do what, Smith seems to realise that the Lord hasn't been getting everything right, as discussed in the last couple of Sections. The excuses start to appear.

32. I command and men obey not; I revoke and they receive not the blessing.
33. Then they say in their hearts: This is not the work of the Lord, for his promises are not fulfilled. But wo unto such, for their reward lurketh beneath, and not from above.

Smith is obviously trying to recover from a succession of people *not* doing what he has had God say they will do, or at least *should* do. Why was the Lord getting so many people so very wrong? Smith then goes on to push his luck once again with Martin Harris from whom he is still trying to extract money.

34. And now I give unto you further directions concerning this land.

> 35. It is wisdom in me that my servant Martin Harris should be an example unto the church, in laying his moneys before the bishop of the church.

Then Smith has the Lord say that also applies to everyone else as well, but he can't help but return to Harris yet again before he finishes. He really does want Harris's money.

> 36. And also, this is a law unto every man that cometh unto this land to receive an inheritance; and he shall do with his moneys according as the law directs.
> 37. And it is wisdom also that there should be lands purchased in Independence, for the place of the storehouse, and also for the house of the printing.
> 38. And other directions concerning my servant Martin Harris shall be given him of the Spirit, that he may receive his inheritance as seemeth him good;
> 39. And let him repent of his sins, for he seeketh the praise of the world.

The same applies to William W. Phelps who the Lord is not at all pleased with. Phelps also needs to repent. It is the same old story for everyone who Smith wants to control. The idea of confessing sins and forsaking them clearly includes handing over their money and obtaining an 'inheritance' in place of what they previously owned. If they don't do what the Lord says, they may receive "none inheritance, save it be by the shedding of blood" (v.53). Is that Smith saying they may well end up fighting for the land?

Ziba Peterson is named by the Lord as yet another person who he isn't pleased with; he is to have what he has been given taken away again until he is chastened and repents of sins he has been trying to hide. The Lord gets into detail about individuals when it affects what Smith wants them to do for him.

The Section concludes by informing us once again "And behold the Son of Man cometh. Amen" (v.65). All that can be said to that, as ever, is *no*, in reality he did not 'cometh' at all, despite the fact that so many such statements led the saints firmly to expect him to return during their own lifetimes.

Section 58 – Summary

Prophecies made:	1
Prophecies fulfilled:	0
Other non-prophetic revelation:	1

DOCTRINE & COVENANTS – SECTIONS 51-64

Prophecies made:

Pr. 25. v.7. "…that you might be honored in laying the foundation, and in *bearing record of the land upon which the Zion of God shall stand.*" v.12, "Behold, I, the Lord, have spoken it." (Italics added).

Results:

Pr. 25. It didn't – and still doesn't stand there. According to Smith's revelation "Who am I, saith the Lord, that have promised and have not fulfilled?" (v.31).

Non-prophetic revelation: 1.

1. Joseph Smith had the Lord declare in D&C 58:21 "Let no man break the laws of the land, for he that keepeth the laws of God hath no need to break the laws of the land."

Smith's own track record, as detailed on p.229, was anything but law abiding. He persuaded people to lie under oath in legal documents regarding polygamy; he even destroyed the printing press owned by William Law in order to stop a second edition of the Nauvoo Expositor being published and exposing more of his crimes. This was Smith's final act that landed him in jail on charges of high treason – but he did not live to face the charges.

Joseph Smith spent much of his life in and out of jail or the run from the law – with a price on his head. The earliest charges against Smith related to him being a money-digging con artist but later more serious offences including polygyny and attempted murder were levelled at him. Ultimately, he died in jail awaiting trail for treason. If anyone ever ignored a commandment from the Lord, it was Smith himself deliberately violating his own so-called revelations over and over again. Smith's personal life is evidence enough that he did not believe God was actually dictating these revelations. *(Evidence of all the above can be found throughout TMD Vols. 1-4).*

Section 59
7 August 1831. Zion, Jackson County, Missouri.

History.

BOC Ch. LX. 1835 D&C Sec. XIX. 2010 D&C Sec. 59.

Section 59:9-24 is further discussed in *TMD Vol. 4:296-8. (S43-45)*. The verses cover commandments that appear to have been mainly extracted from the Ten Commandments in the Bible and suggests how the Sabbath should be observed. Verse 12 instructs that they must spend their time "confessing thy sins unto thy brethren, and before the Lord". At that time in the very young Church, people would stand in turn and make confessions in front of everyone. That idea was not to last. In v.15, we learn that things on Sunday should be done "not with much laughter, for this is sin", but it is acceptable to be cheerful and smile. The Mormon God's idea of 'sin' is quite strange, to say the least.

In the earlier verses not discussed in *TMD Vol. 4*, we learn that those who stand in Zion will be very blessed. Those who live shall inherit the earth (which they most certainly did not) and those who die will rest from all their labours and receive 'crowns' in 'mansions'. However, they did not 'stand' there long and history shows they were anything but blessed. The continuous aggressive nature and actions of Smith, which upset the locals as well as state authorities, ensured they were constantly hounded and eventually driven out from wherever they tried to settle.

Section 60
8 August 1831. Zion, Jackson County, Missouri.

History.

BOC Ch. LXI. 1835 D&C Sec. LXX. 2010 D&C Sec. 60.

As with many other Sections, this one came about because Smith was asked some questions. Following the conference, some Elders who were assigned to travel back east, ask Smith how they should travel and by what route. Smith has the Lord decide. Of course we can now easily predict what will be added by the Lord. Let's see who has pleased the Lord (if anyone) and who has not.

The Lord immediately says he is not pleased with some of them because they didn't "open your mouths" because of "the fear of men" and guess what… "Wo unto such, for mine anger is kindled against them." And that's just as far as v.2. If they are not more faithful, even what they have (such as it is) will be taken away. The Lord gets a little strange in v.4, saying that he not only rules "in the heavens above" but also "among the armies of the earth" which makes me wonder which ones; whose 'side' was the Lord on? According to Smith, everyone outside Mormonism was as bad as each other, so who was the Lord showing preference to? We remain uninformed. Instead, the Lord just adds "…and in the day when I shall make up my jewels, all men shall know what it is that bespeaketh the power of God." Make of that what you will.

On to the proposed journeys – and the Lord says they can make a craft – or buy one, "as seemeth you good". Remember that pet phrase? *(See Section 52 pp. 213-14)*; "it mattereth not unto me." They are to go to St. Louis. Smith, Rigdon and Cowdery are to go to Cincinnati and preach. They failed to do that when they got there and they just went home *(See Apx. A: Part 1)*. For good measure, their sins are forgiven (again). I am not sure how many sins they could have committed since the Lord last forgave them, just a week earlier, in Section 58:42, as they had all been at the conference, but the Lord seemed to quite like saying that – as much as saying his anger was kindled against them. It became an established part of the carrot and stick routine in Smith's revelations.

Edward Partridge is to give the travellers some of the money that he has been given by the Lord, although the Lord doesn't explain exactly how he came to personally give Partridge any money. It was undoubtedly a reference to consecrated funds. Everyone is to preach, whether they have come 'up' to Zion or are returning east. They must not idle away their time. Verse 15 speaks of shaking dust from feet and this time 'washing them' *(as discussed on pp. 145-6)*.

Section 61

12 August 1831. By the Missouri River, Missouri.

History.

1833 BOC Ch. LXII. 1835 D&C Sec. LXXI. 2010 D&C Sec. 61.

Section 61 is fully discussed in *TMD Vol. 4:284-92. (S45-53)* and it is a classic example of the absurdity of the whole idea of the Lord getting involved in trivia. In a nutshell, William W. Phelps thought he saw 'the destroyer' riding on the waters of the Mississippi in broad daylight. On this occasion, Smith doesn't correct Phelps, telling him he saw no such thing; instead, he embraces the idea and spouts off a whole revelation which includes more nonsense than you could ever imagine. Smith really gets into the idea that the waters are cursed. "For I, the Lord, have decreed in mine anger many destructions upon the waters; yea, and especially upon these waters" (v.5).

Among other things, the apostle John had apparently cursed the waters for the Lord, but who knows when – or even why? This is the section where the Lord gets involved in who should take what clothes where. It contains so much detailed trivia that it is laughable. They are to "take their journey in haste" (v.21) but first, the Lord wants to chastise them. At the end, they are to be "watchful and be sober, looking forth for the coming of the Son of Man, for he cometh in an hour you think not." Such statements led the saints to firmly believe the Lord would return while they were still alive, when of course he did not. I will leave the reader to review full details of this Section in *TMD Vol. 4:284-92 (or S45-53)*. Having done so, please see Section 71 *(pp. 260-62, and Apx A: Part 1)* and link to Ezra Booth's letters to learn what *really* happened on the river.

Section 62
13 August 1831. By Missouri River, Missouri.

History.

BOC Ch. LXIII. 1835 D&C Sec. LXXII. 2010 D&C Sec. 62.

This revelation was recorded the day after Section 61 above. I hardly need mention that yet again God confirms He is *also* Jesus, "…saith the Lord your God, even Jesus Christ"; such statements have become quite a habit in Smith's early revelations. They constantly appear during Smith's monotheistic years. God/Jesus is one and the same being, and one or the other, and often both, are referenced as speaking, but not once are they differentiated between.

Smith and his group have come across another group of Elders who are on their way up to Zion. Smith tells them to travel on, hold a meeting when they get there, and then travel back and testify about Zion, not that there was much of anything there to testify about of course. It is just the *concept* of Zion and the Lord's promises that they are to testify about. They can travel back "even altogether, or two by two", in a now extremely familiar comment by the Lord "as seemeth you good, it mattereth not unto me" *(see Sec 52. pp. 213-14)*. If it didn't matter to the Lord, then why did he even bother to mention it?

The Lord says that he has brought them "together that the promise might be fulfilled, that the faithful among you should be preserved and rejoice together in the land of Missouri. I, the Lord, promise the faithful and cannot lie". Yet he seemed to mange to lie well enough about Independence, where Zion – the New Jerusalem did *not* get established as promised.

The Lord includes another strange comment to those travelling up to Zion, yet none of them had any money – they generally just walked. Chariots?

> 7. I, the Lord, am willing, if any among you desire to ride upon horses, or upon mules, or in chariots, he shall receive this blessing…"

Section 63
30 August 1831. Kirtland, Ohio.

History.

BOC Ch. LXIV. 1835 D&C Sec. XX. 2010 D&C Sec. 63.

Smith claimed this was received in response to people asking about Zion and related aspects. Naturally, the Lord's first response is that his anger is kindled against the wicked and rebellious. Isn't it always? Such people need to take heed and tremble because "the day of wrath shall come upon them as a whirlwind, and all flesh shall know that I am God".

In the next few verses the Lord rambles about not seeking signs, before getting to a verse confirming an obvious Christian principle regarding morality. After mentioning that some of them have been adulterous, we get this verse:

> **16.** And verily I say unto you, as I have said before, he that looketh on a woman to lust after her, or if any shall commit adultery in their hearts, they shall not have the Spirit, but shall deny the faith and shall fear.

Notwithstanding the fact that Smith may have intended to adhere to that idea at the time, some eighteen months later he had his first documented affair with the family housemaid, the sixteen-year-old Fanny Alger. That adulterous liaison, which itself lasted for quite some time, ultimately led to other affairs, opening the door to polygyny and polyandry which became Smith's excuse for all of his extramarital excursions. *(See TMD Vol. 1, Apx. A & B for full list and details).*

In the following verses, the Lord gets very specific about what will happen to anyone who does the sort of things Smith was soon getting up to. Was this really the Lord speaking and did Smith completely ignore him, or was it just Smith making it all up in the first instance, knowing the Lord was not involved at all? If it *was* the Lord, then Smith is well and truly done for.

> **17.** Wherefore, I, the Lord, have said that the fearful, and the unbelieving, and all liars, and whosoever loveth and maketh a lie, and the whoremonger, and the sorcerer, shall have their part in that lake which burneth with fire and brimstone, which is the second death.
>
> **18.** Verily I say, that they shall not have part in the first resurrection.

THE MORMON DELUSION

Anyone who keeps the commandments will have mysteries revealed to them (v.23), the expected incentive following the "fire and brimstone" message above. Once again, the Lord commands them to assemble in "the land of Zion, not in haste, lest there should be confusion, which bringeth forth pestilence." Pestilence? I am not sure that *confusion* would bring forth pestilence but the Lord certainly never instructed Smith on how to avoid or even deal with such pestilence (defined in the dictionary as a deadly or virulent epidemic disease) as they did get caught up with diseases such as malaria and cholera. Smith buying up cheap land in mosquito infested swamp areas to sell on at much inflated prices to incoming saints didn't exactly help matters. As previously mentioned, some simple instruction on that could have helped avoid countless deaths and many serious illnesses; nevertheless, the Lord kept quiet about simple hygiene and not living in the swamps, preferring instead to constantly chastise – and forgive sins.

In v.25, the Lord declares that he is holding Zion in his hands and then goes on to say something about rendering unto Caesar the things which are Caesars in v.26. Of course, that is biblical where it refers to taxes; not a good analogy, but he was talking about having to buy the land rather than just *take* it. If they pay for the land they will fare well but if they take it by shedding blood, people will be angry with them. Really?

The Lord is still angry with the wicked (v.32) and so in v.33 he declares "I have sworn in my wrath, and decreed wars upon the face of the earth, and the wicked shall slay the wicked, and fear shall come upon *every man*;" (Emphasis added). Considering the Lord declared in Section 60 that he rules "among the armies of the earth" *(see p. 232)*, surely "fear" should *not* come upon "every man" as he has to be on *someone's* side. Then, in v.34 he goes on to say that "the saints shall hardly escape" which really seems pretty mean of the Lord, considering he was the one to "decree war" on everyone in the first place. What kind of a Lord is this? He is going to "consume the wicked with unquenchable fire" – "not yet, but by and by."

In v.36, the Lord finally gets back to Zion by saying "I will that my saints should be assembled upon the land of Zion;" Everyone is to warn people that desolation shall come upon the wicked. Mundane details follow about who should do and sell what, including a statement by the Lord "...let all the moneys which can be spared, it mattereth not unto me whether it be little or much, be sent up unto the land of Zion, unto them whom I have appointed to receive" (v.40). Again, if it doesn't matter – why bother to mention it at all. The Lord says Smith can discern who should go and who should stay.

There is more talk of the end coming, wise and foolish virgins, people being burned with unquenchable fire, and they are to repent – again. Amid all this, suddenly the Lord is not pleased with Sidney Rigdon. Smith obviously wants to tighten the reins on Rigdon for some unstated reason. The Lord says "…he exalteth himself in his heart, and received not counsel, but grieved the Spirit;" In v.56 he adds "Wherefore his writing is not acceptable unto the Lord, and he shall make another; and if the Lord receive it not, behold he standeth no longer in the office to which I have appointed him." A very good way to get someone out of a position and another person in is to have the Lord take care of it for you. If the people believed Smith to be a prophet, they had to obey what he had the Lord declare. If they didn't believe him, they were cut off from the Church as dissenters. Either way, Smith couldn't lose.

The Lord reminds them he is "from above" (v.59) although in scientific terms we could question what that actually means, as there is no such thing as "above" for him to come from. The Church would claim that to be metaphoric I expect. Most of the section is quite meaningless with no revelation or prophecy worthy of note. I expect the deluded will find all sorts of wonderful things in there, which to those who can see through it all are quite meaningless.

Section 64
11 September 1831. Kirtland, Ohio.

History.

BOC Ch. LXV (incomplete). 1835 D&C Sec. XXI (complete).
2010 D&C Sec. 64.

Section 64 was the last of the BOC Chapters (LXV) to be published and it ended mid-verse 36. In the 1835 D&C, the full section was included as it would have appeared had the BOC been fully published as originally planned. The Sections now numbered 65-73, 75, 107 and 133 were also originally intended for inclusion in the 1833 BOC *(see pp. xii-xiv)*.

As always, sins and forgiveness are mentioned and they are also to forgive each other. Smith is declared 'safe' from the Lord taking away the mysteries of the kingdom from him – as long as he is obedient of course. This leads into the Lord saying that some people have gone against Smith without good cause. One was Ezra Booth, mentioned in v.15-16 *(See Section 71, pp. 260-62 for more details)*. It's nice to have the Lord on your side, and then you can have him say anything you like. Even so, this time, Smith has also sinned – but naturally he is forgiven.

The Lord then names all those he is angry with and says they must repent. He instructs individuals what to do, which in the main means sell up, give their money to the Church, and go to Zion where an inheritance awaits them, such as with Isaac Morley (v.20). Frederick G, Williams should not sell, as the Lord wants to maintain a presence in Kirtland for a further five years (v.21). They must pay tithing so they won't be burned when the Lord returns. This verse (23) led to tithing being termed 'fire insurance' when I was a young member. In v.24, the Lord reminds us once again that he will *personally* burn the people up when he comes.

The Lord confirms the land of Zion is for their inheritance:

> **34.** Behold, the Lord requireth the heart and a willing mind; and the willing and obedient and shall eat the good of the land of Zion in these last days.
> **35.** And the rebellious shall be cut off out of the land of Zion, and shall be sent away, and shall not inherit the land.

It should hardly need repeating yet again that the Lord entirely reneged on this promise and the saints never did occupy the land of Zion any more than they built a New Jerusalem there – but for the fact that this time the Lord goes even further. He declares Mormon Church leaders will *judge everyone*, from Zion. People from every nation will go there, and the nations will "tremble because of her".

So, indeed we must reiterate that it never happened, as there is no Zion; no people there to judge anyone; there is nowhere to go *to*, and nothing to tremble about. Smith concludes this section by adding a definite responsibility: "The Lord hath spoken it. Amen." It is supposedly the Lord actually speaking, so you can put an "I" in front of that statement. Amen, of course interprets as 'so be it', so it is the *Lord* declaring, and then confirming – established **lies**.

> **38.** For it shall come to pass that **the inhabitants of Zion shall judge all things** pertaining to Zion.
> **39.** And **liars and hypocrites shall be proved by them**, and they who are not apostles and prophets shall be known.
> **40.** And even the bishop, who is a judge, and his counselors, if they are not faithful in their stewardships shall be condemned, and others shall be planted in their stead.
> **41.** For, behold, I say unto you that **Zion shall flourish**, and the glory of the Lord shall be upon her;
> **42.** And she shall be an ensign unto the people, and **there shall come unto her out of every nation under heaven.**
> **43.** And the day shall come when **the nations of the earth shall tremble because of her**, and shall fear because of her terrible ones. **The Lord hath spoken it. Amen.** (Emphasis added).

Section 64 – Summary

Prophecies made: 1
Prophecies fulfilled: 0

Prophecies made:

Pr. 26. v.38-43. "the inhabitants of Zion shall judge all things pertaining to Zion ... Zion shall flourish ... there shall come unto her out of every nation under heaven ... the nations of the earth shall tremble because of her ... The Lord hath spoken it. Amen."

Results:

Pr. 26. Zion did not "flourish"; it was never built and the Church still does not have a viable presence in the location repeatedly specified by the Lord. This remains unfulfilled prophecy and "[I] The Lord hath spoken it. Amen."

Chapter 17

**Doctrine and Covenants
Sections 1, 65–73, part 107 & 133**

Section 66
29 October 1831. Orange, Ohio.

History.

BOC Ch. LXVI (unpublished). 1835 D&C Sec. LXXIV. 2010 D&C Sec. 66.

Whilst Section 66 is dated 25 October 1831 in the current D&C, the *JS Papers, Vol. 2:513 & 722* date it to 29 October 1831. In any event, it was written before Section 65, so in order to maintain the chronological sequence, it appears here first. In this chapter we also find Sections 1 and 133 appearing in their original date order.

In Section 66, William E. McLellin has asked Smith what the Lord wants of him. McLellin is blessed for receiving the 'everlasting covenant' or fullness of the gospel. As ever, he still has some repenting to do and the Lord will show him where he is going wrong.

Naturally, McLellin is called to go and preach rather than go to Zion "but inasmuch as you can send, send; otherwise, think not of thy property" (v.6). That means give everything you can, send your money, then go off and preach.

Samuel H. Smith (Joseph's brother) is to accompany McLellin. They can lay hands on the sick and they will be healed. McLellin is told not to commit adultery, something with which God apparently thinks he has been troubled.

Smith is still not worrying too much about whether it is God or Jesus Christ speaking and intermixes the two as if they are one and the same being; but then of course, at the time, he still considered they were.

13. Verily, thus saith the Lord your God, your Redeemer, even Jesus Christ. Amen.

Other than having the Lord tell McLellin not to think of his property and to send it to Zion while he goes off preaching, there is nothing much of anything in this Section at all. There are a number of occasions where Smith gets people to part with money and go out preaching by having the Lord personally instruct them. To disobey would mean not accepting Smith as a prophet and becoming a dissenter. Such people were thrown out of the Church and left with nothing.

Section 65
30 October 1831. Hiram, Ohio.

History.

BOC Ch. LXVII (unpublished). 1835 D&C Sec. XXIV. 2010 D&C Sec. 65.

Joseph Smith designated Section 65 as a prayer, but it is also still claimed as a revelation. However, the phraseology is quite strange for a prayer and Smith seems to have trouble making up his mind who is actually speaking at times, him or the Lord. Verse 1 doesn't seem at all like a prayer: "Hearken, and lo, a voice as of one sent down from on high, who is mighty and powerful, whose going forth is unto the ends of the earth, yea, whose voice is unto men—Prepare ye the way of the Lord, make his paths straight." Whatever that is meant to convey, and no matter who actually said it, the wording is atrocious.

There are just six verses, and other than the idea of spreading the gospel and preparing the way of the Lord – who once again personally proclaims that he will come clothed in glory – we don't get much of anything other than the notion that the kingdom of heaven will come down and meet the kingdom of God which is to be set up on the earth. There is nothing new in that idea.

It is yet another one of those Sections that make you wonder why they ever bothered to include it in the D&C; it is as meaningless as it is pointless. This Section gives nothing of merit to the world whatsoever. It is just Smith hype.

Section 68
1 November 1831. Hiram, Ohio.

History.

BOC Ch. LXVIII (unpublished). 1835 D&C Sec. XXII. 2010 D&C Sec. 68.

Orson Hyde, Luke S. Johnson, Lyman E. Johnson, and William E. McLellin asked Smith for a revelation regarding them and as ever Smith complied, but then 'revealed' more detail applicable to the whole Church. They are told that anything they say, as moved upon by the Holy Ghost, shall be scripture, and moreover, it shall be "the will of the Lord, shall be the mind of the Lord, shall be the word of the Lord, shall be the voice of the Lord, and the power of God unto salvation" (v.5) – and that's a *promise* says the Lord.

That is indeed a very powerful statement and quite a promise for the Lord to make. It is somewhat strange that *nothing* they subsequently preached was ever recorded and then included in the 1835 D&C if that was the case. Surely any such "scripture" should have been properly recorded and published for the benefit of posterity.

There are no prizes for guessing what the Lord tells them to do; they are of course to go "into all the world and preach" – and baptise (v.8).

Smith has the Lord quickly move on to other things, as his words addressed to the four men are so short that they were hardly worth mentioning on their own. Had he stopped there, it is easy to imagine the four wondering why that was all there was for them. Smith gets into things that would ensure discussion followed the revelation, which in turn would distract them from the 'short and sweet', and somewhat pointless, message the four men had been given.

They are to have more Bishops, who should be High Priests, unless they are direct and firstborn descendants of Aaron, who would then have the automatic lineal right to be a Bishop. It is interesting that they never discovered a direct descendant of Aaron and as far as I am aware (and I could be wrong of course), the Church has yet to afford that lineal right to *anyone*; so it raises the question, why did the Lord ever bother to mention it if there was no way of discerning such a person at that time? The modern day problem would of course be that if such a person were discovered and verified, they would have the absolute right to be a Bishop, without counsellors, in an *autonomous* roll. *(See D&C 107:76)*.

What would happen if they took advantage of their position? Would the Church ever put itself in such an invidious and uncontrollable situation? I doubt it very much. It is something that is 'known' of course, as it is in the D&C, but it is something that is never actually mentioned these days and I doubt that anyone is trying to research any such descendants through DNA profiling. Can

243

we imagine the Church *wanting* to locate such people these days? It seems that they would rather not even try.

In v.20, Smith has the Lord add the following:

> **20.** And a literal descendant of Aaron, also, must be designated by this Presidency, and found worthy, and anointed, and ordained under the hands of this Presidency, otherwise they are not legally authorized to officiate in their priesthood.

Did the Lord expect them to actually find a direct descendant of Aaron? It seems to imply so, as he instructs them what to do when they do find such a person. *This Presidency* is to take care of the ordinance. Where then is there any evidence that it ever happened? There is none. Therefore, either the Lord did *not* convey that message – or he needn't have bothered to. It is hard to see the Lord talking about something that was never going to happen. That leaves Joseph Smith and his imaginative ideas responsible for the concept. Invariably, a firstborn descendant of Aaron would be a native Israelite – or at least a Jew.

I am sure the Mormon Church will shout about it if ever they find and confirm such a person – who then of course would also have to be (or then become) a member of the Church before being called to the office of Bishop. If the Church wishes to maintain the idea that the Lord did indeed 'reveal' this then it was incumbent upon the Lord to reveal, from time to time, such persons who were actually eligible, otherwise it was pointless exercise. As far as I have been able to determine, it still remains a pointless and unfulfilled revelation.

Verses 25 and 27 are mentioned in *TMD Vol. 4:182* as they are referenced in the Mormon missionary lessons. The verses concern baptism, which in the Mormon Church takes place for a child no earlier than the age of eight.

Baptism at age eight is *not* scriptural. No age for baptism is specified in the Bible at all. In *Luke 2:41-50*, Jesus was twelve years old when he was found in the temple talking with the 'doctors' and he was thirty years old before he became a preacher for three short years. When Jesus was baptised, he was in fact already preaching and was about thirty years old. Jesus never did define any suitable baptismal age – or much of anything else doctrinal for that matter; he just said 'believe and be saved'. The Mormon Church derived its concept that age eight is the appropriate age for baptism from Smith who pretended it was the Lord's idea:

> **D&C 68:25.** And again, inasmuch as parents have children in Zion, or in any of her stakes which are organized, that teach them not to understand the doctrine of repentance, faith in Christ the Son of the living God, and of baptism and the gift of the Holy Ghost by the

laying on of the hands, when eight years old, the sin be upon the heads of the parents.

68:27. And their children shall be baptized for the remission of their sins when eight years old, and receive the laying on of the hands.

The fact is that an eight-year-old knows absolutely *nothing* upon which he or she could ever base such a pivotal decision as being baptised and generally goes along with what his or her parents arrange for them. A child that is born into Mormonism is groomed for the event from birth and accepts it as normal. It is a perfect age to manipulate a child ready for their Mormon future, and a terrible age at which to suggest any child actually knows what they are doing.

So, having added enough material to detract from there not being much of anything new for the four enquiring men, has the Lord forgotten anything? Of course; he is not very pleased with the members; there are 'idlers' among them and children are growing up in wickedness. The Lord signs off once again by saying he is coming quickly. The pattern has become highly predictable.

Section 68 – Summary

Non-prophetic revelation: 3.

1. Anything that Orson Hyde, Luke S. Johnson, Lyman E. Johnson, and William E. McLellin preach when moved upon by the Holy Ghost is to be considered "scripture"; it shall be "the will of the Lord, shall be the mind of the Lord, shall be the word of the Lord, shall be the voice of the Lord, and the power of God unto salvation" (v.5) – and that's a promise, says the Lord.

There is no record in Mormon scripture of *anything* that any of these four men ever preached to anyone. Thus the "scripture", designated by the Lord himself as his "will", his "mind", his "word" and his "voice" was clearly not worth recording.

2. Joseph Smith declares the age of baptism for children is to be eight years of age or over.

There is no scriptural basis for this determination. Even in Smith's Book of Mormon, written in 1829, which has about one-hundred-and-fifteen references to baptism and a whole chapter on not baptising 'little children' (Moroni 8), there is no confirmation of a minimum age. In 3 Nephi 12:1, Jesus supposedly calls 'twelve' to baptise but neglects to tell them not to baptise anyone under the age of eight. The 'age of baptism' was a Smith concoction of 1831. If he had thought of it earlier, it would have invariably appeared in his Book of Mormon.

3. Firstborn direct descendants of Aaron have the automatic right to become an autonomous Bishop without counsellors.

To the best of my knowledge, no one has ever been made a Bishop by right.

Section 1
1 November 1831. Hiram, Ohio.

History.

BOC Ch. 1 (A Preface). 1835 D&C Sec. 1. 2010 D&C Sec. 1.

The first part of the D&C which introduces the Lectures of Faith under the title of 'Theology' says that it is "On the ***Doctrine*** of the Church of the Latter Day Saints". 'Part Second', which contains the D&C 'Sections', states "***Covenants*** and Commandments of the Lord to his servants of the church of the Latter Day Saints"; hence the title "Doctrine and Covenants". As discussed in earlier chapters covering the lectures, they were considered absolute ***doctrine*** in their day. Many modern-day converts will not even be aware that they ever existed.

Section 1, which formed an introduction to the D&C, was written on 1 November 1831 and is fully covered in TMD Vol. 3:282-7 & Apx. N. (S54-61), where subsequent alterations have been noted. As stated in TMD Volume 3, Section 1 is mainly meaningless filler and of no real consequence at all. The verse 'summary' at the start says it all really; there is a warning to everyone; apostasy and wickedness will precede the second coming; Smith has been called to restore the gospel; the Book of Mormon has been "brought forth" and the Church has been established; peace will be taken from the earth; and they are to search the commandments.

I am not quite sure exactly why peace will be *taken* from the earth; it would be better to leave some here for us to enjoy. It is a typical religious take on the world; it is always an evil place and peace is replaced by war. Nowhere does Smith, any more than any other religious leader, stop to think and realise that the majority of wars and battles that have ever been entered into had a religious foundation of one sort or another, from the earliest of times.

I will just make mention of v.37-8 which are relevant to the subject matter of this volume:

37. Search these commandments, for they are true and faithful, and the ***prophecies and promises*** which are in them ***shall all be fulfilled.***
38. What I the Lord have spoken, I have spoken, and ***I excuse not myself***; and though the heavens and earth pass away, my word shall not pass away, but shall be fulfilled, whether by mine own voice or by the voice of my servants, it is the same. (Emphasis added).

Here we have a claimed statement from the Lord that there are *no excuses* and the prophecies and promises made by Joseph Smith on his behalf will *all* be fulfilled. So far, *none* that we have encountered have remotely come to pass; and it will come as no surprise, I am sure, to discover that none that we have yet to review have ever been fulfilled either. I hope that statement will not be regarded as a 'spoiler' for the rest of this book; I am sure by now the reader does not really expect anything Smith ever claimed as a prophecy actually to end up being reliably documented as having been fulfilled. If so, I regret they will be disappointed.

Section 67
2 November 1831. Hiram, Ohio.

History.

BOC Ch. LXIX (unpublished). 1835 D&C Sec. XXV. 2010 D&C Sec. 67.

It turns out that it is not just people of the modern day who have problems with the language structure Smith used in his revelations. The header to Section 67 confirms that following the dictation of what became Sec. 1 (discussed above), some "negative conversation was had concerning the language used in the revelations", which is hardly surprising as it was, as usual, positively awful.

There were the odd word changes made later to tidy it up a little but it still reads pretty much as it originally did. *See TMD Vol. 3. Apx. N. (S59-61).* Smith has the Lord say that if they don't like the way the commandments are written, to try to write some themselves but "if ye cannot make one like unto it, ye are under condemnation if ye do not bear record that they are true" (v.8).

The fact is that anyone could have made up the things Smith came up with and many would probably have made a somewhat better job of much of the language structure. However, at the time, doubters seemed to run scared of that so Smith (appeared) to win the day. But then the history of all this was written by Smith and the Church, so who knows what else went on in the early days.

Smith has the Lord say that despite his (Smith's) problems with language structure and usage, "and his language you have known, and his imperfections you have known" (v.5), there is no unrighteousness in Smith's revelations and "that which is righteous cometh down from above, from the Father of lights" (v.9). Smith stole "Father of lights" from James 1:17, but in Smith's case he has the Lord himself say it. There is no mention of the fact that these are supposedly words *dictated* directly by the Lord – they are all in the first person. Is this effectively an admission that the Lord is *not* actually speaking at all, but just supposedly putting *ideas* into Smith's head that Smith then formulates into attempted Jacobean speech attributed directly to deity? That's called making it up as you go along – and hoping for the best. But in reality, that's all it can be.

Smith has the Lord promise if they will "strip yourselves from jealousies and fears, and humble yourselves before me, for ye are not sufficiently humble, the veil shall be rent and you shall see me and know that I am—not with the carnal neither natural mind, but with the spiritual" (v.10). Are they ever humble enough? The Lord says that when they are worthy, they will see him – with spiritual minds, which means in their imagination of course. And that will be "in mine own due time", which as previously discussed has become a well worn excuse for things that ultimately never transpired.

Section 133
3 November 1831. Hiram, Ohio.

History.

BOC Ch. LXXVII (unpublished). 1835 D&C Sec. C. (Appendix). 1844 D&C Sec. CVIII. 2010 D&C Sec. 133.

Section 133 was originally an appendix to the 1835 D&C. It dates between Sections 67 and 69. The header is important – and for a very good reason. It declares that the Prophet himself wrote *"At this time there were many things which the Elders desired to know relative to preaching the Gospel to the inhabitants of the earth, and concerning the gathering; and in order to walk by the true light, and be instructed from on high, on the 3rd of November, 1831, I inquired of the Lord and received the following important revelation" (History of the Church, 1:229)*. (Italics in original).

You would think, regardless of what followed in this 'revelation', that the Lord would have told Joseph Smith to give everyone a fully detailed account of the 1820 First Vision story in order to assist in converting people. After all, it is almost the first thing presented to investigators today. Yet strangely, the Lord makes no mention of his first encounter with Smith and doesn't remind Smith about it at all. Why? Because this was late 1831 and Smith didn't even start to invent a Fist Vision concept of *any* description until the following year, and it didn't become the ultimate glorious experience now portrayed by the Church until 1838, when Smith then finalised his ideas and backdated the resulting claimed experience to 1820. Thus it was far too early for all that at this time, as Smith was yet to even think up the idea of a vision. Instead, Smith is given this "important" revelation. It is God speaking.

The Lord is going to come suddenly to his temple and "come down upon the world with a curse to judgment"; not very well worded, but that is just the start. The judgment will be "upon all the nations that forget God, and upon all the ungodly among you", which really doesn't leave many people at all.

It gets worse; in v.3, God declares He will *"make bare his holy arm* [does that mean He will roll up his sleeves to set about the wicked?] *in the eyes of all the nations, and all the ends of the earth shall see the salvation of their God"* which makes absolutely no sense at all for a God to say. Smith, who was really the 'voice' rather than any deity, perhaps meant they would see just who God would save, but it *reads* that God will be the one to have salvation, in a typical Smith style (and misuse) of early modern English language. It is no wonder that people were questioning Smith about his choice of words for the Lord to use in Section 67 (above). The language that Smith put into the mouth of deity was positively appalling and even Smith's followers could clearly see that.

Smith goes on to say some very strange things indeed, mixing up aspects entirely. They are to get out of Babylon and gather to Zion. Then the strange wording starts: "…gather ye out from among the nations, from the four winds, from one end of heaven to the other" (v.7). What do "the four winds" and "heaven" have to do with gathering "from?" Gathering to Zion, remember, is something that didn't actually happen. They are to go to "all nations"; first to the gentiles and then to the Jews. They never actually went to *most* nations of the Earth, let alone "all" of them and some nations were only just starting to be visited during the late twentieth century, yet the Lord sent them to *all* nations to teach the gentiles *before* going to teach the Jews. They were in the Holy Land teaching long before Smith died; Orson Hyde for one was on a 'mission' to Palestine by 1842; although he did a lot of sightseeing *(See TMD Vol. 1:100)*.

"And let them who be of Judah flee unto Jerusalem, unto the mountains of the Lord's house" (v.13). Notwithstanding that statement, there is no record of anyone in the early (or even later) Church *ever* enticing Jews to 'flee unto Jerusalem'. Many Jews had habitually returned to Jerusalem when they could after being conquered, many times, over thousands of years. A summary of the history of Jewish defeats, expulsions, exile and return is available here: http://www.jewishvirtuallibrary.org/jsource/vie/Jerusalem1.html

Following the conquest by Ottoman Turks at the beginning of the sixteenth century, extortionate taxes, oppression and neglect took huge toll on the Jewish community. The population had dwindled to no more than seven-thousand by the end of the 17th century. It wasn't until the nascent Zionist movement in Eastern Europe motivated Jews to return to Palestine that the first modern Jewish settlement was established – in Petah Tikvah in 1878. This had nothing to do with the Mormon Church whatsoever.

They are not to hurry, but when they do go, "he that goeth, let him not look back lest sudden destruction shall come upon him" (v.15). Perhaps they would have turned to pillars of salt if they did look back. They are to tell everyone to repent (as ever) and God reminds them that an angel (Nephi or Moroni – take your pick) came to prepare the way, but there is still no mention of God and Jesus appearing to Smith in a 'First Vision' in order to prepare the way as it is portrayed by the Mormon Church today.

Smith has God talk of "a hundred and forty-four thousand" standing with the Lamb of God on Mount Zion and his voice being heard from Jerusalem, which is drawn from the book of Revelation and which Smith 'explains' in Section 77 *(see p. 286)*.

There is then talk of the "great deep" being "driven back into the north countries" (v.23) and the land joining together "like as it was in the days before it was divided" (v.24). That will be some geological feat – if you are even a little familiar with currently available knowledge concerning movement and predictions of the continued movement of tectonic plates.

There is **no** going back and when land masses do converge again (which they ultimately will), they will not remotely be the *same* as they were before they started to diverge. Scientifically, the future situation regarding 'continental drift' is now fairly accurately predictable, both in the timescale and the ultimate geological position. At the following web site, http://www.scotese.com/, you will find world maps for every era, right from the Precambrain break-up of the supercontinent, Rodinia, http://www.scotese.com/precambr.htm, which formed 1100 million years ago, stage by stage, through time, to the future position, http://www.scotese.com/future2.htm, some 250 million years ahead – and that is a very long time away. By then, humans will undoubtedly have long become yet another extinct species and we won't be around to see it.

Proposing a return to the original position is as scientifically impossible as the biblical flood which Smith also believed in, as he had Egyptus impossibly 'discover' Egypt after the flood in his fictional Book of Abraham *(See TMD Vol. 2:296-303)*. If the geological evolution of the planet was set in motion quite naturally *or* even by a supernatural power, one thing is for certain, it is *not* reversible and can *only* continue its *natural* course; no amount of faith can ever change that; it goes against universal laws of science and nature, including space time curvature (gravity), regardless of who or what set them in motion.

Following more unquantifiable long term predictions and filler, Smith has God proclaim in v.37 that "this gospel shall be preached unto every nation, and kindred, and tongue, and people." We have heard *that* somewhere before *(See pp. 180-82)*.

From v.40-63, Smith has God list all the things people will say "Calling upon the name of the Lord day and night, saying..." and the list is quite amazing. In a nutshell, God will do many terrible things, but of course the righteous will ultimately be okay and be 'crowned'; something which God (or at least Smith) often seemed to think people would like.

I find it quite bewildering to see the inclusion of such statements as "...they shall mention the loving kindness of their Lord, and all that he has bestowed upon them according to his goodness, and according to his loving kindness, forever and ever" when I only see 'hellfire and damnation' in everything else that is spoken by the Lord through Smith. Even the saints can never do enough to please Him. He is anything but "loving" or "kind" in anything He *ever* really says through Smith. In fact, He comes across as very vindictive towards people and 'nations' who could never have ever known they were *not* pleasing Him, and that is not very kind at all. If people have not been properly *informed*, how then can they be fairly *judged*?

In v.64 Smith has God makes an unfortunate – and utterly condemning statement:

> **D&C 133:64.** And also that which was written by the prophet Malachi: For, behold, the day cometh that shall burn as an oven, and all the proud, yea, and all that do wickedness, shall be stubble; and the day that cometh shall burn them up, saith the Lord of hosts, that it shall leave them neither root nor branch.

It is unfortunate, not just because it accurately *quotes* the KJV of Malachi 4:1 just as it still appears...

> **Malachi 4:1.** For, behold, the day cometh, that shall burn as an oven; and all the proud, yea, and all that do wickedly, shall be stubble: and the day that cometh shall burn them up, saith the LORD of hosts, that it shall leave them neither root nor branch.

...but because Smith claimed Moroni *altered* that in 1823 when he visited Smith, so the KJV, according to Smith's own record, *cannot* be accurate. It is condemning because although in this instance Smith altered just one word – wickedly becomes wickedness – other than that meaningless change, it remains *exactly* as per the KJV which it definitely should *not* – if Moroni 'corrected' it.

I covered Smith's pretended changes to Malachi by Moroni extensively in TMD Volume 2 *(See Vol. 2:80-6; 193-5)*, although I did not mention *Section 133* which is yet another nail in the coffin for Smith. In *TMD Vol. 2*, I cover the fact that Smith had Moroni *alter* that verse, supposedly in 1823 but first *recorded* as altered text in 1838. This date is very important because –

In 1829 Joseph Smith (probably with the help of others) wrote the Book of Mormon. In it, words that appear in the KJV of Malachi 4:1 are recorded, long before they were even *written* by Malachi c.400 BCE. Smith put them in a part of his *Book of Mormon* supposedly written in 588-570 BCE but actually written in 1829 *(2 Nephi 22:15)*. He claimed the words were taken from brass plates that were engraved almost two-hundred years *earlier* than Malachi's time.

In 3 Nephi, Smith goes even further, providing even more evidence of his fraud. He has the audacity to have *Jesus* quote the entire verse of Malachi 4:1 almost *exactly* as it appears in the KJV with just two very minor word changes – to the Nephites in 34 CE. Jesus was *not* the author of the original Malachi quote and the KJV is not the only possible or even exactly correct translation. Smith *copied* the text exactly. Jesus would not have quoted an exact text from a book which was not to be written for another 1600 years, originally spoken and written in a language which, after several translations, would later come to be written in Jacobean English. Here, Joseph Smith uses the original KJV words throughout. He is also backdating it to CE 34 in America, having Jesus recite the words – even stating that the Nephites did not have them before that.

Perhaps Smith forgot that he had used some of the words before, in 1 Nephi 22:15, dated to BCE 588-570; so in fact (if they were a real people) they **did** have them before 34 CE *(See also 1 Nephi 22:23)*. This outrageous multiple plagiarism and bad memory, combine to evidence once again, the fraud and hoax Smith was perpetrating, giving no thought to consistency or viability.

Between 1831 and 1834, Smith wrote his 'Inspired Revision' of the Bible. In it, Malachi 4:1 remained *unchanged* from the KJV original text. The changes Smith attributed to Moroni in 1823 were first recorded in **1838**, long after all the plagiarism Smith had used which remained entirely faithful to the original KJV. The dates confirm the hoax and Smith's conspiracy to deceive. *(See TMD Vol. 2:80-6; 193-5 for a full review of this area)*.

Section 133 was of course written in November 1831 and it wasn't until 1838 that Smith decided Moroni had made alterations during his claimed 1823 visit. Had the 1838 claim of 1823 been *real*, Smith's 1831 account in D&C 133 should have been *corrected* by God to match Moroni's version. The fact that it matches the KJV word for word, is evidence that Smith did *not* hear Moroni correct Malachi – let alone remember what was said, word for word, fifteen years later when he wrote it down. It is also evidence that it would *not* have been related by God in Section 133 in 1831, just as recorded in the KJV. The KJV is just one translation out of several possibilities and *cannot* accurately reflect what may or may not have originally been spoken or recorded.

In v.65-74, God answers those who are supposedly saying the things listed in v.40-63 and within His now familiar rants God says "I make the rivers a wilderness; their fish stink, and die for thirst (v.68). Can you imagine God ever making such an oxymoronic statement as that? Of course not; it just goes to show how ignorant Smith was. Whilst salt water fish do take in some water through their mouths, freshwater fish absorb water as needed, by osmosis, and don't actually *drink*. With ocean and fresh water fish, water 'consumption' has to do with the balance of salt in the cells of their bodies compared with water surrounding them. Interestingly, ocean fish excrete salt though their gills to keep the salt in their bodies *down*, whereas in fresh water fish it is quite the opposite. Dried up rivers will not stink due to fish dying from 'thirst'. Water to a fish is as air to a human and freshwater fish no more drink water than we drink air. If a God exists, I think we can take it as read that He understands the nature of His creations and would never have made such a fundamental error as to say that.

A freshwater fish *cannot* die from 'thirst' as such. Any fish out of water would ultimately die from lack of oxygen (they would effectively suffocate). There are a few fish that can flop their way from one pond/hole to the next; e.g. walking catfish, mudskippers and snakeheads. Most of these fish will last until they dry out. Some lungfish survive when their lake dries up for the summer. God could have quite easily described such a concept much more accurately, using other just as easily understandable words. Why would *God* make Himself appear so ignorant? Whatever the case, it all sounds very fishy to me.

Finally, as always there comes the stick; people "...shall go away into outer darkness, where there is weeping, and wailing, and gnashing of teeth" (v.73). We know Smith is claiming that God said all this, as he concludes (in v.74) with "Behold the Lord your God hath spoken it. Amen." There are *no* excuses.

Smith picked up the idea of "weeping and wailing and gnashing of teeth" from the New Testament where there are several references to either, "weeping and gnashing of teeth", or "wailing and gnashing of teeth" – but as it happens, never "weeping *and* wailing and gnashing of teeth". Smith combined them and had characters use the new phrase a couple of times in his Book of Mormon; Abinadi, c.148 BCE *(Mosiah 16:2),* and Alma, son of Alma, c.74 BCE *(Alma 40:13)*, long before the expressions were used in the NT; and once in his Book of Moses, supposedly thousands of years ago *(Moses 1:22)*. It appears three times in the D&C *(19:5 and 101:91 in addition to 133:73)*.

Smith also used "wailing, and anguish, and gnashing of teeth" in D&C 124:52; "wailing and gnashing of teeth" in 85:9; and "gnashing of teeth" in 124:8. There are two or three instances of "weeping and wailing" in the Old Testament, but no gnashing of teeth in the same references, although that idea is found elsewhere in the OT. Smith also used "gnashing their teeth upon them" in Alma 14:21, which is stolen from Psalm 35:16 which says "they gnashed upon me with their teeth." Smith's work was anything but original. In the D&C, of course Smith is putting these highly unlikely words directly into the mouth of the Lord who is never recorded in the Bible as having personally spoken them at all.

Section 133 – Summary

Non-prophetic revelation: 2

1. "*...there were many things which the Elders desired to know relative to preaching the Gospel to the inhabitants of the earth...*" (Section header, extracted from HC 1:229).

This is actually a '*non-revelation*' which is inexcusable. The Lord makes no mention of his first encounter with Smith and doesn't remind Smith it could be taught in order to help convert people as is the case today. Why? Because this was late 1831 and Smith didn't even start to invent a Fist Vision concept of *any* description until the following year.

2. They are to go to "all nations", first to the gentiles and then to the Jews. This could be classified a prophecy, but as the Lord only confirmed that they *should* go rather than *would* go, which makes it more of a commandment rather than a prophecy, I will leave it at just mentioning the idea.

They never actually went to *most* nations of the Earth, let alone "all" of them and some nations were only just starting to be visited during the late twentieth century, yet the Lord sent them to *all* nations to teach the gentiles *before* going to teach the Jews. They were in the Holy Land teaching long before Smith died; Orson Hyde for one, was on a mission to Palestine by 1842 *(See TMD Vol. 1:100)*.

Section 69
11 November 1831. Hiram, Ohio.

History.

BOC Ch. LXX (unpublished). 1835 D&C Sec. XXVIII. 2010 D&C Sec. 69.

Once again, God is speaking. Oliver Cowdery is to take the 'commandments' and the money to pay for their publication, to Independence, Missouri for printing. John Whitmer is to go with him.

God also says in v.5 "And also, my servants who are abroad in the earth should send forth the accounts of their stewardships to the land of Zion;" so, we should ask how it is that all the preaching of Orson Hyde, Luke S. Johnson, Lyman E. Johnson, and William E. McLellin that the Lord declared should be considered "the will of the Lord, shall be the mind of the Lord, shall be the word of the Lord, shall be the voice of the Lord, and the power of God unto salvation", just ten days earlier in Section 68:5 *(see p. 243)*, never made it's way back to be recorded for posterity "to possess it from generation to generation, forever and ever. Amen." (v.8).

Section 107 (Part)
(v. 59-69, 71-72, 74-75, 78-87, 89, 91-92, 99-100)
11 November 1831. Hiram, Ohio.
(The balance of Section 107 was recorded circa April 1835 in Kirtland, Ohio).
(See pp. 368-73).

History.

BOC LXXI (Unpublished). 1835 D&C Sec. III. 2010 D&C Sec. 107.
(The 1835 D&C, 11 November 1831, equivalent verses: 31-33, 35-42 & 44).

Section 107 is dated to 28 March 1835 in the modern D&C and to circa April 1835 in *The JS Papers Vol. 2:392, 722-3*, where it also notes that the above verses were recorded on 11 November 1831. The modern D&C heading says *"that various parts were received at sundry times, some as early as November 1831"* (Italics in original), so it may be that some of the remaining verses were written earlier than April of 1835. This section is a classic example of different ideas being recorded some years apart and then combined as if they formed part of a singular event. From the current D&C heading, there is no telling which parts were received and when, as it just mentions "various parts" – but not *which* parts. Readers will have no idea that the very earliest parts of the Section don't start until they reach v.59.

Although I am tempted to do so, I will not include the full Section in this volume in the interest of space, but would suggest the serious reader should cut and paste Section 107: http://lds.org/scriptures/dc-testament/dc/107?lang=eng into a word document and then highlight the above verses which date to 1831. Then carefully read the entire Section through and note the difference in style and content of verses written earlier, compared with the later, more confident and dynamic material that Smith came up with in 1835, most of which appears *before* the 1831 material. You can also see several insertions between some of the earlier verses which add further detail to the passages. The Church will no doubt claim God was expanding and explaining the 'revelation' in more detail. No one explains why God didn't make a better job of it the first time around.

When Smith wrote the November 1831 verses, he was in his second year of making up such revelations and by the time he wrote the rest of this Section he had gained some three and a half years more experience – and it shows; there is a distinct and very noticeable difference and maturity of writing style; not that anything Smith ever wrote was actually *mature* in real terms, it was still awful.

Once again, you can discover the true author of the material in the D&C in several ways, and one is through Smith's growing experience. The combining of material from varying dates into one Section allows a unique opportunity to see the flow, at one point almost from verse to verse, of how Smith's ability and experience had developed and changed over the years. The Lord of course would have been more consistent in his style from the start; not to mention more eloquent and more sensible if he really had condescended to say anything to a mere mortal. Above all, he would surely have had something actually worth saying. This is clear evidence that it was not the Lord speaking at all.

In the original 1831 verses, Smith has the Lord establish the idea that there should be 'presiding' elders, priests, teachers and deacons for each group. "Then comes the High Priesthood which is the greatest of all" (v.64). A "President of the High Priesthood of the Church" (v.65) is to be called.

"Presidents" were introduced into Smith's new Church at every level and the concept is mentioned several *dozens* of times in the D&C. It was *not* a biblical office of the church. It was a term that was *known* in biblical times and it is mentioned several times in Daniel – but not in relation to any ministry; they were presidents of kingdoms. This was just another Smith concoction – after all, he aspired to become President of the United States and in February 1844 Smith set about an election campaign, with Sidney Rigdon running for the office of Vice President. Smith was killed four months later and that left Sidney Rigdon as the senior surviving member of the First Presidency.

Rigdon returned home in order to fight for the Presidency of the Church – which he then lost to Brigham Young and the quorum of twelve apostles. One problem was that Rigdon was strongly opposed to polygamy and the twelve all either participated in it, or at least supported it. When you study the succession debacle and resulting schisms – it is no wonder Young and his group won the lions share of followers – they stood together as a group, or a gang, against all comers in order to sustain their position in heading up the Church, whereas all the other contenders that Smith had 'appointed' at one time or another, stood virtually alone in their contests. Smith's wife Emma supported William Marks, President of the central stake (the presiding High Council) but unfortunately he supported Rigdon. When Rigdon's speech (which was somewhat bizarre, to say the least) was not well received by the congregation and Young won the day with his, it effectively put paid to several other contenders at the same time.

The reality was they stood no chance against Young who had no authority whatsoever personally to take the lead of the Church. The rest of the twelve thought they had equal status as a group and had no idea that ultimately Young would become so autonomous. This led to constant unrest and suspicion which permeated the quorum for several decades, resulting in long delays in calling new Presidents of the Church through several successive Presidents following Young's death.

Bishops are also to be chosen from the High Priesthood – unless a literal descendant of Aaron can be found *(See Section 68, pp. 243-5)*. Aaronic lineage is mentioned in the 1831 verses and further emphasis was then added into the text in the later 1835 version. The Bishop was to be a "common judge" (v.74) but his main roll of the day was to run the storehouse. Interestingly, the Bishop was not just to preside over a single unit of the Church at that time.

> **107:74.** Thus shall he be a judge, even a common judge among the inhabitants of Zion, or in a stake of Zion, or in any branch of the church where he shall be set apart unto this ministry, until the borders of Zion are enlarged and it becomes necessary to have other bishops or judges in Zion or elsewhere.

The Presidency of the High Priests can call twelve other High Priests and is to be the *highest* 'council' of the Church (v.80). No one is exempt from their (final) judgments and they will deal with the most important business of the Church and hear the most difficult 'cases' brought to them for consideration and judgment. This firmly establishes the High Council *above* the twelve apostles who were called to go out and preach, yet Young usurped this group following the death of Smith, claiming the twelve apostles had the right of succession to the Presidency. Perhaps this was because Smith later created an anomaly when he recorded the minutes of a meeting which became Section 102. In that, he contradicted the Lord's mandate as recorded here and said there *can* be an appeal from the high council but not from the Quorum of Twelve Apostles *(See pp. 350-51)*. Smith made up his ideas as he went along.

Over the years, Smith had made a record of, and even ordained, several different successors – the quorum of twelve was ***not*** one of them, something the Church would also no doubt argue, had Young *failed* in his take-over bid.

However, as Young did not fail, they will point to D&C 107:23-4 as his authority to do so. It really was not, as will be discovered when we review the rest of this section later on.

The Presidency of the High Priests will of course be headed up by Smith (v.91) who will be like Moses – "a seer, a revelator, a translator, and a prophet, having all the gifts of God which he bestows upon the head of the church" (v.92).

The final verses that appear in Section 107 were also part of the original verses recorded in 1831. Naturally, the Lord ends with the idea that everyone should learn his duty and anyone who is slothful or does not learn his duty "shall not be counted worthy to stand".

Section 107 (Part) – Summary

Non-prophetic revelation: 1

1. Joseph Smith had the Lord introduce 'Presidents' of various quorums and also for the leadership of the Church itself.

This was never a biblical office in the ministry of the Church in any era. It was in invention by Smith who saw being 'President' of *anything* as a powerful position and a worthwhile ambition. Smith himself aspired to be, and started to run for, the office of President of the United States. He would of course have failed miserably in his attempt – but such were his delusions of grandeur.

Section 70
12 November 1831. Kirtland, Ohio.

History.

BOC Ch. LXXII (unpublished). 1835 D&C Sec. XXVI. 2010 D&C Sec. 70.

DOCTRINE & COVENANTS – SECTIONS 1, 65-73, PART 107, 133

Following a series of four conferences held over several days, the Lord says he has something to say that the Church should listen to, via Smith, Martin Harris, Oliver Cowdery, John Whitmer, Sidney Rigdon and William W. Phelps, "by the way of commandment unto them". So, what does the Lord have to say that is so important? Are we at last to be favoured with some unique, beautifully phrased and inspiring words of wisdom and information worth mentioning?

Not really; it turns out they are to be 'stewards' over the revelations and commandments and the Lord will require an accounting from them regarding that at the day of judgment for some reason.

Next, the Lord reminds the five (it should be six, but Smith never included himself in such matters) that "inasmuch as they receive more than is needful for their necessities and their wants, it shall be given into my storehouse" (v.7). He reminds them that it is also required of everyone else and no one is exempt. In temporal things, they are all to be equal.

Should the Lord not have known that the idea could and would not possibly last? The Lord concludes by saying in v.18 "Behold, I, the Lord, am merciful and will bless them, and they shall enter into the joy of these things. Even so. Amen."

Unfortunately, the Lord didn't live up to his word and the system quickly broke down and was eventually abandoned – they did not enter into the *joy* of any such thing at all. The saints had to tough-out the next few years and once they arrived in the Salt Lake valley, Brigham Young was quickly to become a millionaire because he used tithing donations to fund his own ventures and then charged his 'services' back to the Church to cover hundreds of thousands of dollars at a time so he didn't have to repay it. Young rarely paid for goods or services either and many a supplier had the most unpleasant surprise of being given tithing 'script' (tithing credit) instead of their expected payment.

Young certainly never entertained the Lord's earlier idea of everyone being 'equal' in temporal things. Following his death, the Church had to sue Brigham Young's estate for over a million dollars in order to recoup just some of the tithing he had taken and used. We know he did so because the Church won the case. *(See TMD Vol. 2:347)*. This is what Young thought of the whole idea:

> Those who are in favour of an equality in property say that this is the doctrine taught in the New Testament. True, the Saviour said to the young man, 'Go and sell that thou hast, and give to the poor, and thou shalt have treasure in heaven, and come and follow me,' in order to try him and prove whether he had faith or not. In the days of the Apostles, the brethren sold their possessions and laid them at the Apostles' feet. And where did many of those brethren go to? To naught, to confusion and destruction. Could those Apostles keep the

Church together on those principles? No. Could they build up the kingdom on those principles? No, they never could. Many of those persons were good men, but they were filled with enthusiasm, insomuch that if they owned a little possession they would place it at the feet of the Apostles. Will such a course sustain the kingdom? No. Did it in the days of the Apostles? No. Such a policy would be the ruin of this people, and scatter them to the four winds. We are to be guided by superior knowledge—by a higher influence and power. *(Deseret News, 10 September 1856).*

When did the Lord change his mind about 'consecration', considering a new start in Salt Lake provided a unique opportunity to re-establish his way of doing things? Today, the whole concept which was supposed to be everlasting, has long since been forgotten – other that is than in a meaningless promise that is still made in the Mormon temple endowment ceremony when patrons covenant to: "…consecrate yourselves, your time, talents and everything with which the Lord has blessed you, or with which he may bless you, to the Church of Jesus Christ of Latter-day Saints, for the building up of the kingdom of God upon the earth and for the establishment of Zion."

Section 70 – Summary

Prophecies made:	1
Prophecies fulfilled:	0
Other non-prophetic revelation:	0

Prophecies made: 1

Pr. 27.

D&C 70:7. "Nevertheless, inasmuch as they receive more than is needful for their necessities and their wants, it shall be given into my storehouse;
8. And the benefits shall be consecrated unto the inhabitants of Zion, ***and unto their generations***, inasmuch as they become ***heirs according to the laws of the kingdom***.
9. Behold, this is what ***the Lord requires*** of every man in his stewardship, even as I, the Lord, have appointed or shall hereafter appoint unto any man.
10. And behold, ***none are exempt from this law*** who belong to the church of the living God;"

The Lord had already established the law of consecration and here he reemphasises it, confirming that *no one* is exempt. Then he makes a promise in v.18 "Behold, I, the Lord, am merciful and will bless them, and *they shall enter into the joy of these things*. Even so. Amen." (Emphasis added). This is a prophecy from the Lord that everyone must comply with and the *generations* will experience the joy of these things.

Results:

Pr. 27. The system quickly failed and rather than re-establish it and make it work, given a fresh opportunity and a new start in Salt Lake, instead, Young simply developed his personal empire using tithing for his own purposes. The last thing Young wanted was to be equal with everyone else. Many saints were in dire straits, especially many polygamous wives who were left destitute while husbands went off on missions, often bringing back new and younger wives when they returned.

Section 71
1 December 1831. Hiram, Ohio.

History.

BOC Ch. LXXIII (unpublished). 1835 D&C Sec. XC. 2010 D&C Sec. 71.

Joseph Smith was in the process of translating the Bible with Sidney Rigdon as his scribe. Suddenly, a 'revelation' was received, instructing the two to stop, in order to perform a "mission for a season", to 'proclaim' to the world in the regions round about them and also to the Church. They were to confound their enemies by asking to meet them in public and in private. If any man lifts his voice against them, the Lord will confound him "in mine own due time" – a now very familiar phrase – which really meant *never.*

That's all there is to this little Section, so why did the Lord suddenly need to reveal this to Smith? What was so important that it that prompted the Lord to have Smith stop the work and go off preaching? The 'problem' of the day was a man named Ezra Booth.

Booth, who had been a Methodist minister, was converted and baptised into the Mormon Church and also ordained an Elder in May of 1831. On 3 June, Booth was ordained a High Priest by Lyman Wight and three days later called to go to Missouri and preach along the way *(see Section 52:23).* The Lord had gleefully sent Ezra Booth along with Isaac Morley, off on a mission, but clearly did not have the foresight to tell Smith that things would ultimately go horribly wrong and Booth would turn against Smith and apostatise. That information would have assisted Smith enormously but as ever, the Mormon God was not very good at judging people and only ever seemed to realise their true colours after the event.

Booth did preach on the Book of Mormon, to a large audience, in Norton Township, Ohio, and he also attended a special conference with several other Elders, but Booth was soon to figure out what was really going on and he quickly fell from favour. On 6 September, Booth was stopped from preaching as an Elder by Smith. A few days later, Section 64 was received and Booth was mentioned in v.15-16 *(See p.237)*.

> **D&C 64:15.** Behold, I, the Lord, was angry with him who was my servant Ezra Booth, and also my servant Isaac Morley, for they kept not the law, neither the commandment;
> **16.** They sought evil in their hearts, and I, the Lord, withheld my Spirit. They condemned for evil that thing in which there was no evil; nevertheless I have forgiven my servant Isaac Morley.

Almost immediately, Booth renounced Mormonism and started writing a series of nine letters that were first published in the Ohio Star, disclosing things that Smith clearly did not want made public. Booth had only been a Mormon for about five months. He later organised the 'Church of Christ', claiming Smith a false prophet and the Book of Mormon not true. His new Church did not survive longer than the first few meetings.

Having got Ezra Booth entirely wrong, the Lord now has to give Smith a revelation telling him to go preaching the truth to the surrounding area and to members of the Church, due to Booth's untimely letters being published and raising all kinds of questions, both in and out of the Church. The Mormon God hadn't been a lot of help to Smith in avoiding the ensuing trouble.

For anyone interested in Ezra Booth's letters, they are included in the book 'Mormonism Unvailed' [sic] *(Howe, 1834)*, which is available to read online. Below, is a direct link to the Ezra Booth letters in which he confesses "I now know Mormonism to be a delusion; and this knowledge is built upon the testimony of my senses. In proclaiming it, I am aware I proclaim my own misfortune -- but in doing it, I remove a burden from my mind, and discharge a duty as humbling to myself, as it may be profitable to others."

I can only comment that that is ***exactly*** how I felt when I started writing.

http://www.truthnet.org/mormon/mormonismunveiled/15_1831Ezrabooth.htm

As some readers may be interested in what Ezra Booth had to say about his experiences without immediately reading all his letters online, I have included a few short and interesting extracts from some of his letters as *Appendix A*. However, reading the letters in their entirety will give the reader a very clear and extraordinary insight into some of the 'goings on' in the early Mormon Church during mid-late 1831 – providing contemporary reflections on some of the so-called revelations, actions and reactions of Smith; something rarely found elsewhere – and I would encourage you to take the time to read them in full at some stage. Before doing so, I recommend reading my analysis of *D&C Section 61* in *TMD Vol. 4:284-92. (S62-70).* A whole new perspective on that revelation, 'received' on the banks of the Missouri River, can be gained from Booth who was there and experienced it first hand. See *Appendix A, Part 1*, in respect of *D&C Section 61* and *Appendix A, Part 2* in respect of *D&C Section 71*.

Section 72
4 December 1831. Kirtland, Ohio.

History.
BOC Ch. LXXIV (unpublished). 1835 D&C Sec. LXXXIX.
2010 D&C Sec. 72.

This Section combines two revelations recorded on the same day. The first comprises v.1-8, and the second, v.9-26. As with many other revelations that we have encountered, this is yet another where several people came to Smith asking what their role is and to be 'instructed'.

Other than details concerning the Bishop and his storehouse procedures, no one gets anything concerning themselves as individuals. In this instance, the first part of the revelation relates to Newel K. Whitney being called as the Bishop.

In the second part we learn, not surprisingly, that the main duty of the Bishop is to keep the storehouse and receive money from everyone; v.15 "…according to the law every man that cometh up to Zion must lay all things before the bishop in Zion." Every Elder must give a proper accounting to the Bishop or they will receive nothing. One function of the storehouse money is to pay for the revelations to be published. Smith's 'revelation' was, as always, entirely self-serving.

Section 73
10 January 1832. Hiram, Ohio.

History.

BOC Ch. LXXV (unpublished). 1835 D&C Sec. XXIX. 2010 D&C Sec. 73.

Following the publication of Ezra Booth's letters, referred to in Section 71, Smith and Rigdon had spent several weeks preaching, effectively trying to fend off the adverse publicity, and as the header puts it *"by this means much was accomplished in diminishing the unfavorable feelings that had arisen against the Church"* – in what we would today call 'damage control'.

Having temporarily abandoned the project of 'translating' the Bible, now they are to continue to preach until conference and then, by the 'voice' of the conference, they will know their "several missions" – whatever that means.

After the conference, they are to "continue the work of translation until it be finished". The only problem is that it never was finished. This was the beginning of 1832 and when Smith died in 1844 he still hadn't completed it.

Chapter 18

Doctrine and Covenants
Sections 75–86 & 99

Section 75
25 January 1832. Amherst, Ohio.

History.

BOC Ch. LXXVI (unpublished). 1835 D&C Sec. LXXXVII. 2010 D&C Sec. 75.

"The Lord and your God" is speaking here, "even by the voice of my spirit" (v.1) – clearly Smith did not think of God as having a body at this time; that came later. Encouraging more people to go out and preach, Smith has the Lord God promise them that they "shall be laden with many sheaves, and crowned with honor, and glory, and immortality, and eternal life" (v.5). Even in Smith's day, why would God promise such an archaic concept as "many sheaves"?

Some of the men had been having trouble convincing people about their message and they came to Smith for advice. Does he now finally explain the

First Vision story and how that might assist in the conversion process? Of course not, because the concept was still years away from being invented. Even Smith's initial idea of a 'First Vision' where he had Jesus appear alone was still some months away.

God is not at all happy with William E. McLellin and "revokes" his commission to go to the eastern countries and instead, having told McLellin that he has sinned (but is forgiven), gives him a "new commission and a new commandment" to go to the south countries. Luke Johnson is to go with him. We could ask why God took such an interest in who went where – and why he would give a "commission". That is an odd word for God to use.

More importantly, we should perhaps also ask why God gave McLellin a command to go east in the first place if, as the all-knowing Creator, He knows *everything*, past, present and future? Why did He not just command him to go south in the first instance? As ever, everything points to human imagination rather than remotely providing plausible evidence of the involvement of deity.

God then dictates who else should go where. He starts with Orson Hyde and Samuel H. Smith who are to go east. Why didn't God just send them south instead of 'revoking' McLellin's "commission".

Well, McLellin had sinned; but after all, had he not been forgiven? It simply does not make sense when considered in context of the claimed involvement of deity. Lyman Johnson and Orson Pratt are also to go east; Asa Dodds and Calvers Wilson are to go west, as are Major N. Ashley and Burr Riggs. God says that if they are faithful, they will be "lifted up at the last day". Remember that earlier, Jesus confirmed he was *personally* going to burn everyone who was left *(see p.238)*, so being "lifted up" instead seems a good enough reason to be faithful.

In v.20, we once again see the 'shaking dust from feet' idea we discussed earlier *(see pp. 145-6)*. Such an act was supposed to "judge" the house and "condemn" them; which seems more than a little unkind towards people who may well have felt they already had a firm 'testimony' of something else they considered to have come from the very same God the Mormons represented.

Yet v.22 explains that "it shall be more tolerable for the heathen in the day of judgment, than for that house." As previously mentioned, "loving" is not a word readily associated with the Mormon God, regardless of His own supposed declaration of such to the Mormons in Smith's claimed revelations.

We learn that the Church is supposed to support the families of those who are away if they do not have the means to do so themselves. Then God lists several more pairs of men who are to be companions in preaching but He doesn't actually bother to tell them where to go.

DOCTRINE & COVENANTS – SECTIONS 75-86 & 99

The interesting, and by now, not surprising thing is that despite the Section header confirming *"Certain elders, who had encountered difficulty in bringing men to an understanding of their message, desired to learn more in detail as to their immediate duties"* (italics in original), they get absolutely *no* instruction whatsoever from God about their problem, just a general direction in which to travel; and in fact most of them don't even get that. If God is to be credited with such minutia – then He should be cross-examined about all the important issues that remained *un-helped* across the globe throughout the centuries, for surely He got His priorities entirely wrong – playing such foolish games with a con artist whist leaving the world at large to 'fend for itself' so to speak. There is so much that a real deity could and should, and I venture to suggest *would*, if He existed, have done for humanity rather than dictate who should preach and where for Smith. The Mormon God was anything *but* a 'humanitarian'.

Section 76
16 February 1832. Hiram, Ohio.

History.

1835 D&C Sec. XCI. 2010 D&C Sec. 76.

This contains a supposed 'vision' given to Joseph Smith and Sidney Rigdon. Before the vision commences, the first thing that God says, in clear and precise terms, confirms yet again that He is God *and* the Saviour: "the Lord is God, and beside him there is no Savior." God then provides several verses of filler before we get to the purported vision itself.

Smith claims he and Rigdon both saw and *conversed* with Jesus in the vision which was prompted by Smith coming across John 5:29 when 'revising' the Bible. Smith and Rigdon came up with a whole new theology on the afterlife from this single verse:

> **John 5:29** And shall come forth; they that have done good, unto the resurrection of life; and they that have done evil, unto the resurrection of ***damnation***. *(KJV)*. (Emphasis added).

To give some perspective to the possible meaning of that verse, here is another translation (or interpretation) of the original words, which remember, were written long after Christ lived, by someone *other* than John the apostle. There is of course a significant difference between 'damnation', the word used in the KJV, and 'judgment', the word used in *Young's Literal Translation* (YLT); not that it much matters in the context of Smith's claims.

267

THE MORMON DELUSION

> **John 5:29.** and they shall come forth; those who did the good things to a rising again of life, and those who practised the evil things to a rising again of ***judgment**. (YLT)*. (Emphasis added).

In v.11, Smith describes himself and Rigdon as "being in the spirit", which the Mormon Church would no doubt claim as being something akin to being 'carried away by the spirit' but which others may concluded to be a state of hallucination induced by anything from wishful thinking to marijuana or magic mushrooms. Of course, it could equally have just all been made up in order to suit Smith and Rigdon. Any truth (or otherwise) to the vision should become apparent in what the *claims* were. Verse 12 describes the experience thus: "By the power of the Spirit our eyes were opened and our understandings were enlightened, so as to see and understand the things of God—" In other words, whatever they were *influenced* by, it was all in the *imagination* rather than a real life experience beheld in the cold light of day.

The description of 'seeing' God and Jesus and many angels may have been the catalyst for Smith's later inventions which ultimately evolved many years later into the glorious First Vision experience which he ultimately recorded in 1838 and backdated to 1820.

Smith claims (v.13) that they saw things "from the beginning, before the world was" but he doesn't confirm, let alone describe *anything* they saw at all, providing not even anecdotal evidence that the vision could have been real.

Obviously, with all that we now understand about the fact of evolution, if Smith *really* saw things dating from before the world was, he could have provided a comprehensive evolution story for us – now that would have been impressive; very impressive indeed. Unfortunately, nothing Smith ever said (or did for that matter) was even close to being impressive.

Instead, all we get is a 'testimony' that "the record which we bear is the fulness of the gospel of Jesus Christ, who is the Son, whom we saw and with whom we conversed in the heavenly vision" – something which is completely meaningless and totally unsustainable as a fact. It is not helped by Smith's description of the event when (in v.19) he claims "the glory of the Lord shone round about". Sound familiar? It should do, Smith stole it from Luke 2:9 where "the glory of the Lord shone round about..." I am sure readers will remember what was going on at the time of that little story in Luke.

If this had truly been a real experience for Smith, would he not have written a first hand explanation and a comprehensive description of how it felt and appeared to *him*, rather than steal someone else's description of an ancient angelic event? Of course he would. Resorting to plagiarism in circumstances he should have been properly explaining to us reveals the truth behind Smith and

Rigdon's tall tale of conversation with God and Jesus. Smith had quite a good, albeit at times clearly limited, imagination and often stole things from the Bible to enhance his claimed revelations. He had learned to do that prolifically when he wrote the Book of Mormon. Nothing had changed.

The lack of explanation and use of biblical description are strong indicators of what the reality was in all Smith's writings. There is nothing provided that tends toward this being real at all. This 'vision' sounds a little like the eventual 'First Vision' in some ways, yet Smith, who made such a big deal about his 1838 invention, in this instance casually glosses over the experience. Had the First Vision been a real 1820 experience, Smith would undoubtedly have referred back to that as these details bear a marked similarity; but it was yet to be invented – so he didn't.

If the experience was *not* imaginary, it must of necessity be bolstered by something that at least affords some credibility. Later verifiable historical or evolutionary detail ("from the beginning" v.13) would have been a good start, but we get nothing of the sort. Specific and detailed verifiable prophecy would also have been good, but we get none of that either. All we do get is Smith's affirmation that they saw God, Jesus and angels – who between them didn't come up with anything verifiable whatsoever.

Instead, we just get Smith's ideas that we will come on to shortly, which as ever, cannot remotely be verified; they just have to be accepted on faith alone. Already deluded followers would of course have no trouble accepting whatever nonsense Smith dreamed up or more probably, looking at the historical position from the time Smith and Rigdon got together, what they dreamed up between them. However, that is something for the reader to decide and on which I will offer no further comment.

Apparently, they also 'saw' the fictional character 'Satan' (v.28); a CE creation placed into the Old Testament by early Christians in order to instil fear into followers of the new and still evolving religion. The Jews never believed in such a creature (and they still don't) and he does not appear at all in the Old Testament (Tanakh) other than by the mistaken inference of later Christians. I have mentioned in earlier work that 'HaSatan' of the Old Testament was in the employ of God. Do not confuse the Jewish HaSatan with the devil; he is a character who sits on God's council as an adversary working on behalf of God – and he is *not* evil. He could only act on God's instructions; a far cry from the autonomous creature depicted in Christianity. *(See TMD Vol. 2:323-9)*. Many Christians, including Mormons, think Isaiah 14:12 is about the devil (named Lucifer) rather than a fallen king of Babylon. The Mormon Church suggests a possible double or parallel meaning in order to overcome the problem. If Smith claimed to see one fictional character, there is no credence to any claim to have seen God or Jesus either, but to make matters worse, he also claimed to see other fictional characters, as we shall discover.

In claiming actually to have *seen* Satan, Smith doesn't give some kind of a useful description of him; perhaps height, colour of hair etc., such as he did regarding angels on page 214 in 'Teachings of the Prophet Joseph Smith' where he says that if an angel has sandy coloured hair, the angel is not from God. Instead, Smith uses these words to describe the experience:

> **D&C 76: 26** …he was Lucifer, a son of the morning.
> **27.** And we beheld, and lo, he is Fallen! is fallen, even a son of the morning!

Once again, considering the fact that Smith is claiming this is a first hand experience, which he does not remotely ***describe***, does that not also sound suspiciously familiar? Of course it does.

> **Isaiah 14:12.** How art thou fallen from heaven, O Lucifer, son of the morning! how art thou cut down to the ground, which didst weaken the nations!

If only people bothered to continue reading some passages instead of just accepting them out of context; it becomes perfectly clear in Isaiah that a *person* is being spoken of rather than Satan.

> **Isaiah 14:19.** But thou art cast out of thy grave like an abominable branch…
> **20.** Thou shalt not be joined with them in burial, because thou hast destroyed thy land, *and* slain thy people:

It can hardly be argued that Satan had a land he could destroy, people he could slay, or that he would (or would not) be buried in a grave.

The literal translation gives a better rendering of the meaning of Isaiah 14:12, although in the KJV, 'Lucifer' is accurate enough, if you understand the original meaning.

> **Isaiah 14:12.** How hast thou fallen from the heavens, O shining one, son of the dawn! Thou hast been cut down to earth, O weakener of nations. *(YLT)*.

In the original 1611 edition of the KJV, there is a marginal note for the words "O Lucifer". The marginal note reads "Or, O daystarre". The KJV translators themselves clearly understood the meaning of the Hebrew and

DOCTRINE & COVENANTS – SECTIONS 75-86 & 99

provided "daystarre" as additional translational meaning. Similarly, the marginal note in the 1672 edition of the KJV says "for the morning star that goeth before the sun is called Lucifer". "Morning star" is of course also one of Christ's titles.

In Moses 5:24, Smith introduces "the father of his lies; thou shalt be called Perdition." In D&C 76:26, "And he was called Perdition…" We learn that 'Sons of Perdition' are those who deny the Holy Spirit after having received it. For them, there is no forgiveness. The 'fire and brimstone' idea is still clearly in evidence; this time it is directed at such people. There are several verses *(31-38)* dedicated to explaining how bad that will be. The Mormon Church today claims hardly anyone will 'qualify' as they have to *know* and then deliberately follow Satan instead of Christ by choice; something that is highly unlikely.

However, this is what Smith originally had the Lord declare in v.31: "Thus saith the Lord concerning all those who know my power, and have been made partakers thereof, and suffered themselves through the power of the devil to be overcome, and to deny the truth and defy my power—".

In a nutshell, the concept was of course directed at new converts; having accepted Smith's claims, should you ever change your mind – there will be *no* forgiveness, in a psychology designed to ensure fear – and thus better retention, it was hoped. Verse 44 says it all in that respect "…he saves all except them—they shall go away into everlasting punishment, which is endless punishment, which is eternal punishment, to reign with the devil and his angels in eternity, where their worm dieth not, and the fire is not quenched, which is their torment—" Their "worm dieth not" – what kind of fear is that supposed to instil in people?

> Sec 76:36. These are they who shall go away into the ***lake of fire and brimstone***, with the devil and his angels—
> 37. And the only ones on whom the second death shall have any power; (Emphasis added).

As a member, I never really considered the fact that the Mormon 'Hell' will actually have more occupants than any of the other kingdoms Smith introduces in this Section. The Mormon Church teaches that only a very small handful of people who deny the Holy Ghost after receiving an absolute 'knowledge' of him will go Hell. Cain will rule over Satan, according to Mormon theology, because Cain has a body and Satan does not; another quaint Mormon idea. Bear with me for a moment, as I may appear to sidetrack – and all will become clear.

There are about seven billion people alive as of this year (late 2011). That's a billion more of us than there were in 1999. It is estimated there could be 10.1 billion people by the year 2100. Humans have been around for a long time and there were already about 10,000 of us in our early form some 200,000 years ago. At the supposed time of Adam and Eve (6,000 years ago) there were already some five million people around the globe (and historically provably so); by the time of Christ, about 300 million. The pace of population growth has continued to quicken. To cut a long story short, there have been about 75 billion humans to date (according to the BBC), and possibly up to 190 billion according to other sources, depending when 'human' became considered the correct term to use for 'us'.

If we assume an entire change in population, on average, every 100 years (which is generous, although we are living longer these days), even with *zero* assumed future growth (another considerably over-generous assumption), then if the end of the world (theologically speaking) transpires as early as say 2500, there would have been some 225 billion humans. As many religions these days seem to be expecting the 'return' of Jesus any minute (something by the way, that his followers in his own day expected during their own lifetimes) lets cut that short and say it will be very soon and assume a total of 210 billion humans to have lived by then. I will come back to that in a moment.

First, I really do want to digress, just to show the absurdity of belief in the legends of lengthy life-spans of the patriarchs and others who lived a few thousand years ago. The historical facts about human life-span become quite obvious when you consider the evolution of a species. We did not live that long at first, just as many of our cousins still don't. We have not only evolved as a species through natural selection, we have more recently learned how to live longer through the development (or evolution) of human intelligence. 200,000 years ago, the average life expectancy for humans was just fifteen years. That's right, *fifteen* years. Does that shock those who would consider 'underage sex' as bad historically as they do today? There were no 'rules' – just instincts for the survival of a species. By 20,000 BCE life expectancy had risen to all of twenty years. At the time of Christ (who was traditionally thirty-three when crucified) it was twenty-eight years on average. Bear in mind, these are average world-wide figures. By 1800 (CE) it had risen to thirty-five years.

Until very recently, life expectancy at birth hovered between 20 and 35 years, but in the past century it has risen to 67 years. It is highest in Monaco, at about 89 years, and lowest in Angola, where people on average still only live to be just 39 years old. As it happens, I used to be involved in the Life Insurance industry before I retired and was very familiar with mortality tables in the UK. Over the last three or four decades, we have been living, on average, three years longer per decade. It is now estimated that should this trend continue (and there is no reason to suppose that it won't), people being born today can *expect* to live to be one hundred, as that will be the new *average* life-span here.

Those facts are interesting – especially when you then have to incorporate God and a religion into the equation. You can do so if you must, but do *not* abandon scientific facts in the process. Those who wrote the Old Testament, just a few hundred years BCE, had no idea about all that and just repeated handed down myths and legends that had been around in one form or another for many thousands of years, so their old patriarchs traditionally lived for many hundreds of years – something humanly impossible at that time – just as it is today. That may change one day soon, thanks to science rather than God, but not so far. It was the same with giants – and the flood, as well as many other biblical claims – they were just repeated myths and legends handed down from even earlier myths and legends until they became part of Jewish tradition.

Now back to the point about Hell. In Mormon theology, there was a war in heaven and one third of the host of heaven 'sided' with Satan and were cast out as 'unembodied' spirits to roam the earth and tempt people – somehow all part of the 'plan'. If the remaining two thirds that made it to earth and gained a body amounted to some 210 billions, as very conservatively estimated above, then that means at least 105 billion more did *not* and are already consigned to Hell. It is assumed the Mormon 'Celestial kingdom' will accommodate many Mormons – and others who did not get the opportunity in this life but who will accept it in the spirit world. It contains three separate kingdoms in its own right, so who knows how many people will be there overall. Once upon a time, black Africans, who were not allowed the Priesthood or temple rights, could also get there – but only as *servants*; later (1978) that idea was abandoned completely as the very concept of human inequality ultimately (and quite rightly) became unacceptable. Recently, at least one Mormon apologist (Terryl Givens) has suggested that it could have been "an out and out mistake" from the start; quite an admission. *(See:* http://mormonstories.org/?p=2018 *and listen to part five, from 40:45–44.00 minutes in).* We should be above such things – yet the Mormon God clearly was not, for a very long time. That in itself should be a very clear indicator that no God was ever involved in such nonsense.

Wherever our example number of 210 billion people end up when spread between all the available kingdoms, a further 105 billion spirits, which will likely outnumber each of the other kingdoms, will be in Hell with Satan and Cain; they will therefore ultimately have control over many more spirits than God will have resurrected people in his Celestial kingdom.

If God started with, say 315 billion spirits in the Mormon pre-existence, and ends up with far fewer 'survivors' in his Celestial kingdom than Satan ends up with in his Hell, something was alarmingly wrong with God's 'plan' and he could and should have designed it differently. The complete absence of defined expectations for people on Earth which has led to many thousands of different religious concepts about many hundreds of different gods over the centuries represents a complete and utter failure on the part of a one true God to properly establish his position, His requirements, and to foster a 'correct' belief in Him.

THE MORMON DELUSION

We could ask, unless you really *wanted* a body – who really won the 'war in heaven'? It is also a good moment to reflect on the absurdity of the whole concept. Imagine – 200,000 years ago, there were about 10,000 of us on the planet and we lived on average for fifteen years. This is a historical *fact*. If (according to Mormon theology), say, some 105 billion spirits were around to 'tempt' us – not that we would have had a clue about what that even meant, as we could not properly reason let alone speak – there was a ratio of millions of such spirits to each living person. Even today, we are outnumbered by at least fifteen to one. No wonder people reject Mormonism with so many unembodied spirits 'tempting' them away from the truth. The very concept is absurd. As members, we don't think for ourselves, we simply accept what we are taught.

Consider this; if early humans could not communicate as we do today, how did they ever communicate intelligently as spirits prior to coming to the Earth? What was the point of a short lifespan on Earth, with no capacity to understand much of anything other than the instinct to survive and procreate? Evolution is a very difficult fact to fit into such theological thinking. Therefore, the religious notions are wrong and must be *reconsidered* in light of the scientific evidence.

Much of Section 76 deals with who will go to each of Smith's fictional kingdoms. The highest, Smith called 'Celestial' (a word which means heaven or the heavens), where the saints are to aspire to end up; and Smith provides as glowing a picture of the 'rewards' awaiting those who achieve that status as he does the punishments awaiting those who fail and fall to hell.

Then there is the Terrestrial kingdom which will accommodate many who were good but did not accept Mormonism, and the Telestial will house the rest – murderers, adulterers, bank robbers and other 'bad' people. 'Telestial' is a word that has no meaning at all and which Smith just made up.

Smith concocts some strange, and also conflicting, ideas about the Telestial kingdom, which in v.84 he confirms "These are they who are thrust down to hell." Smith was waxing biblical again in v.81: "…which glory is that of the lesser, even as the glory of the stars differs from that of the glory of the moon in the firmament." In v.85 "These are they who shall not be redeemed from the devil until the last resurrection, until the Lord, even Christ the Lamb, shall have finished his work." And yet in v.89 "And thus we saw, in the heavenly vision, the glory of the telestial, which surpasses all understanding;" So, after the constant hellfire and damnation, and God being so angry with everyone, even the worst of people will ultimately inherit a kingdom which "surpasses all understanding." It makes no sense whatsoever.

Then, for some reason Smith decides to put his foot in his mouth – ***twice***.

> **Sec 76:98.** And the glory of the telestial is one, even as the glory of the stars is one; for as one star differs from another star in glory, even so differs one from another in glory in the telestial world;

DOCTRINE & COVENANTS – SECTIONS 75-86 & 99

> 99. For these are they who are of **Paul**, and of **Apollos**, and of **Cephas**. (Emphasis added).

Smith mentions Paul, Apollos and Cephas. Fair enough, he had clearly been reading 1 Corinthians to get that idea and just inserted it. Not that they relate in any way to the three glories – but Smith seems to like the concept – which was once again plagiarised:

> **1 Cor. 3:22.** Whether Paul, or Apollos, or Cephas, or the world, or life, or death…

But then, in v.100, Smith goes on to list other names, including *Elias* and *Esaias*, who were none other than Elijah and Isaiah. Smith thinks that *Esaias* and *Isaiah* were two different people; "…some of Esaias, and some of Isaiah…" Smith's double mistake here is to include the names of two extra characters that never existed. If Smith claimed to *see* more nonexistent characters, his credibility (if ever there was any) is now completely shot to pieces and we cannot remotely accept that he actually saw anything (or anyone) he claimed to see at all.

The name of *Elias* is the Latin transliteration of the Greek name Ἠλίας. It is the Hellenised form of *Elijah*. *Elias* does *not* appear in the *Old Testament* for obvious reasons. The name only appears in the *Apocrypha* and the *New Testament*. Linguistically, *Elias* is derived from *Elijah* because the Hebrew suffix *-yahu*, rendered -iah or -jah in English is replaced with *-ias* in Greek, as in other names such as Jeremiah/Jeremias and Isaiah/Esaias.

> Therefore we know *Elijah* and *Elias* are one and the same person.
> Likewise, we know *Isaiah* and *Esaias* are one and the same person.

As the New Testament was translated from the Greek, such transliterations quite naturally occur. Everyone (other than Mormons of course) knows that Elijah of the OT becomes Elias in the NT and Isaiah of the OT becomes Esaias in the NT. It is that simple – but Smith didn't know that and thus created two additional *fictional* characters. However, his God should have known and told him before he made such a fool of himself – and Smith's God did *not.*

Having been firmly landed with such a monumental problem by Smith, from which there is seemingly no escape, what is the Mormon Church do?

Well, in this instance it simply bluffs its way through it. The Mormon *Bible Dictionary* **contradicts** the known indisputable facts, making the *impossible* claim that "Esaias was also a prophet who lived in the days of Abraham" referring to D&C 76:100 and to D&C 84:11 as 'evidence' of the claim.

The Mormon Church contradicts *itself*. It of course is an utterly impossible claim. A Greek name could *not* appear in ancient Hebrew scripture. If there really had been another person with that name in Abraham's time, he also would have been called **Isaiah** as the Hebrews did not speak or name people in Greek. The very notion is absurd.

Before leaving this Section, we should stop and consider for a moment *why* God did not see fit to reveal the nature of all these available kingdoms to the Jews or even to Lehi and his descendants in the Book of Mormon. There is nothing biblical about *multiple* kingdoms. That concept has absolutely nothing to do with Christianity or Judaism but is rooted in some other religious myths and legends. Considering Lehi and his family were chosen by the Lord to settle in the Americas, and further considering Smith's claim that the fullness of the gospel is to be found in the Book of Mormon, how is it that over their entire recorded history, the Lord left the Nephites and Lamanites in the dark concerning what they could and should have aspired to achieve – other than getting to 'heaven'? That neglect, if real, was unforgivable.

The Book of Mormon makes absolutely *no* mention whatsoever of any one of Smith's three new kingdoms; not one of them – *not once*; and yet it refers specifically to "heaven" or "the kingdom of heaven" many *dozens* of times. It also refers to "hell" a few dozen times for that matter, but *never* in the context that Smith here describes for 'sons of Perdition'. The biblical and Book of Mormon version of hell pretty much becomes the Telestial kingdom in Smith's *new* theology.

Think – why would God not only *not* reveal the truth about several eternal 'degrees of glory' to *anyone* for six thousand years; why would he *substitute* the whole system with one 'heaven' instead, misleading and effectively lying to everyone? If God exists, he is a God of truth, not lies; and 'heaven', as a singular place which everyone believed and accepted as the truth for so long, is turned on its head to become an outright lie by Smith in Section 76 *(See v.70-98)*.

If Smith's 'kingdoms' were real, isn't it obvious that God would have been morally obliged (He is moral after all, is He not?) to reveal the *truth* from the start, rather than give people not just the wrong impression, but entirely the wrong *information* about eternity? Smith makes God a liar by teaching his new ideas that he attributes directly to Him.

There is a lot of filler and then v.113 says "This is the end of the vision which we saw, which we were commanded to write while we were yet in the Spirit." In order to make it seem as though there was more that the Lord did not want anyone else to know about, Smith concludes with this:

76:114. But great and marvelous are the works of the Lord, and the mysteries of his kingdom which he showed unto us, which surpass all understanding in glory, *and in might, and in dominion;*

115. Which he commanded us *we should not write while we were yet in the Spirit*, and are *not lawful for man to utter*;

116. *Neither is man capable to make them known*, for they are only to be seen and understood by the power of the Holy Spirit, which God bestows on those who love him, and purify themselves before him; (Emphasis added).

Doesn't that sound very much like someone who can't think of anything to add but still wants to appear as though they have the ear God? Ask yourself why anyone describing such an event, would add the emphasised words in such a description – words which add nothing other than an attempted scriptural 'look' about it. Having 'seen' things from the 'beginning' of the world which are *not described*, and having invented *characters that don't exist* and at least one *name* and place *(the Telestial kingdom) that doesn't exist*, Smith quits while he thinks he is ahead. He is not; he is undone in every detail. Smith's record of the claimed 'vision' conclusively demonstrates that it is not possibly a true account of a real experience.

Section 76 – Summary

Non-prophetic revelation: 3

1. Smith claimed that he and Rigdon saw things "from the beginning, before the world was" (v.13)

Not a single detail is provided about anything they supposedly saw, making the revelation about seeing things from the beginning a pointless observation; it benefited no one.

2. Smith claims that he and Rigdon saw Satan.

There is no description of the character Smith claimed to see. There never was a Satan (a Devil or Lucifer), as a character who had fallen from heaven, ever recorded in the Tanakh. The Christian concept of Satan was a fictional CE invention supplanted into the canon of an earlier religion (Judaism), a religion which had never even entertained such an idea, in order to instil fear into followers of the evolving new religion.

3. Smith claims they saw *Elias* and *Esaias* in their vision, even mentioning both Esaias and Isaiah in the same sentence: v.100: "…some of Esaias, and some of Isaiah…".

Elias is the Greek transliteration of Elijah and Esaias is Greek for Isaiah. Smith invented two entirely new and fictitious people in his revelation in addition to Elijah/Elias and Isaiah/Esaias, in another Elias and another Esaias because he did not understand the language from which the names had been translated. God did not correct Smith. Ergo, God was not there and He was not involved. Smith's duplicity is exposed by his own ignorance.

Section 77
March 1832. Hiram, Ohio.

History.

First added to the D&C in 1876. 2010 D&C Sec. 77.

The book of Revelation was a Smith favourite and he came to rely heavily on some of the content, notwithstanding the fact that many scholars conclude it was probably written by a lunatic, or that it barely even scraped its way into the Bible in the first (well, actually second) instance. It was added by the narrowest of votes in 367 CE. The canonical Christian Bible was formally established by Bishop Cyril of Jerusalem in 350, but it had been generally accepted by the church previously. It was confirmed by the Council of Laodicea in 363 but still lacked the book of Revelation.

Smith abused Revelation, altering Chapter 1:6 in his Inspired Revision of the Bible, only to later revert to use of the original KJV text when it suited his later theology *(See TMD Vol. 2:135-9)*.

In this Section, Smith poses fifteen questions from Revelation, to which *"I received the following explanation"* (Italics in the D&C). We will deal with the first which actually leads into the next four, and then briefly review the others.

> **1. Q.** What is the sea of glass spoken of by John, 4th chapter, and 6th verse of the Revelation?
> **A.** It is the earth, in its **sanctified, immortal**, and eternal state. (Emphasis added).

There are of course suggested meanings throughout Christianity for this and other verses that Smith has his Mormon God explain. Although some are far more plausible than Smith's ideas, I will not be entertaining any of them as we are only considering whether or not Smith's *God* could have been revealing the answers *Joseph Smith* provides. In this instance, the Alexandrian copy, the Complutensian edition, the Vulgate Latin and Syriac versions, all read, "there was *as* a sea of glass". The word "glass" is left out in the Ethiopic version; but the description is apt, the colour of the sea being sometimes green like that of glass. Smith did not appreciate that 'glass' at the time Revelation was written was not 'clear' or like any 'crystal' that *he* may have been familiar with, despite the word 'crystal' appearing in the verse. A green colour "*as*" the sea, would have been the reasoning behind the description (regardless of what it was supposed to represent) – and *that* is the issue. This is how Revelation 4:6 reads:

> **KJV: Revelation 4:6.** And before the throne there was a sea of glass like unto crystal: and in the midst of the throne, and round about the throne, were four beasts full of eyes before and behind.

Question: did Smith clarify this – or any other verses he then questions – when he wrote his Inspired Revision of the Bible? He should have, as the Lord was supposedly inspiring his 'corrections' and Smith's Bible revision was going on during the time this 'revelation' was received. Details should therefore match, or at least offer consistency. Smith did not actually 'clarify' much of anything but he did add words to this verse, although not in relation to the "sea" idea. This is Smith's Inspired *Revision* of the same verse:

> **IR. Revelation 4:6.** And before the throne there was a sea of glass like unto crystal; and in the midst of the throne **were the four and twenty elders**; and round about the throne, were four beasts full of eyes before and behind. (Emphasis added to denote Smith's added words).

Given that Smith's 'answer' (which he claims came from the Lord) is that the sea is "the earth, in its ***sanctified, immortal***, and eternal state" what do the added twenty-four elders have to do with anything? Well, to answer that question, we must review the preceding verses, when it all becomes clear – and it will also beg yet another question.

> **KJV. Rev. 4:1.** After this I looked, and, behold, ***a door was opened in heaven***: and the first voice which I heard was as it were of a trumpet talking with me; which said, Come up hither, and I will **(shew)** [show] thee things which must be hereafter.
> **2.** And immediately I was in the spirit: and, behold, ***a throne was set in heaven***, and one sat on the throne.

3. And he that sat **[there]** was to look upon like a jasper and a sardine stone: and there was a rainbow round about the throne, in sight like unto an emerald.

4. And *(round about)* **[in the midst of]** *the throne were four and twenty seats*: and upon the seats I saw *four and twenty elders* sitting, clothed in white raiment; and they had on their heads crowns **(of) [like]** gold.

5. And out of the throne proceeded lightnings and thunderings and voices: and there were seven lamps of fire burning before the throne, **[which]** are the seven **(Spirits) [servants]** of God.

(Emphasis added, and Smith's IR 'corrections' are shown above **[thus]** and removed words **(thus)**.

Smith made a total of six alterations. Are they helpful or meaningless? Did Smith really 'clarify' any of the first five verses in his IR? In John 14:9, he had changed the word 'shew' to read 'show', and sure enough, he does the same thing here in v.1, for no useful purpose whatsoever. For some obscure reason Smith places the seats *in* the throne instead of around it.

Smith claims that the "sea of glass" surrounding the throne is the Earth in a future state. Why then did he quantify twenty-four elders sitting on the seats?

Follow the representation in the KJV. In v.1, John is invited through a door that opened into **heaven**. In v.2 he confirms a throne was set in **heaven**. Smith doesn't ask who "sat on the throne" who was "to look upon like a jasper and a sardine stone" (v.2-3), so we never discover who it was supposed to represent (although we can guess). In v.3, he mentions a rainbow, but doesn't say it was raining in heaven, which it must have been if he really did see a rainbow. However, we know it was all just a dream or simply made up by the writer who would have had no idea about such (now so simple) science. In v.4, we see the seats surrounding the throne and that's where the twenty-four elders come in.

When we get to verse 6, it confirms the sea surrounds the throne which has twice been established as being in **heaven**. Early Christians did not believe in the Earth being immortalised. They perceived heaven to be an entirely different place to the Earth. In their day, these verses could not have meant what Smith later claimed; either that or God did not give 'John' the correct information about them.

Joseph Smith's mind immediately considered the sea of glass to equate to *translucent* glass; it being to him 'crystal' *clear*, something which could not possibly have been in the mind of the author of Revelation. Smith had made a similar mistake some three years earlier when writing the Book of Mormon, regarding Jaredites and 'windows' not being suitable for their for their bronze age submarines – in yet another fantastical fairytale *(See TMD Vol. 2:215-20)*.

DOCTRINE & COVENANTS – SECTIONS 75-86 & 99

Smith reaffirmed his impression of a *crystal clear* Earth in its "sanctified, immortal" state *(in answer 1 above, p. 278)*, in D&C 130.

> **D&C 130:9.** This earth, in its ***sanctified and immortal state***, will be made ***like unto crystal*** and will be a Urim and Thummim to the inhabitants who dwell thereon, whereby all things pertaining to an inferior kingdom, or all kingdoms of a lower order, will be manifest to those who dwell on it; and this earth will be Christ's. (Emphasis added).

Smith's take on the Urim and Thummim was that they could be looked into, as they were 'seer stones'. He described them as: "…a curious instrument which the ancients called "Urim and Thummim," which consisted of two *transparent* stones set in the rim of a bow fastened to a breastplate." *(Times & Seasons Vol. 3. No. 9:706-10. 1 Mar 1842).* (Emphasis added). Smith also claimed that God lives *on* a great Urim and Thummim and that one day the earth itself will become one – hence his mistaken interpretation of Revelation 4:6 *(see p. 279)*.

Linguists indicate that Urim means 'light' or 'to give light' and Thummim means 'completeness', 'perfection', or 'innocence'. Anciently, the stones were 'lots' and were cast to provide answers (including innocence or guilt) to yes-no questions. *(See TMD Vol. 2:95-6).* Smith was obviously not aware of this and invented his own use for them – not that he really actually *had* any ancient stones that had been *preserved* for such a purpose. All stones are ancient.

Whatever Rev. 4:6 was originally meant to represent, suggested Christian possibilities do not remotely resemble Smith's idea, which was an *impossible* answer from God. Two thousand years ago, glass was not crystal *clear* and the description could not have meant that.

Even more importantly, we now know how and when the Earth (and our Solar System) was formed, how it is doing along its evolutionary path (for example, how long continental drift has been progressing), and ultimately how – and even *when*, it will cease to exist – that is, if a sizable comet doesn't destroy life first. It has happened before and is predicted as extremely likely to happen again, long before the sun burns itself out. Earth will not last that long, relatively speaking, and will certainly *never* become "immortal". The sun will come to the end of its life and Earth will be consumed by it as it expands and explodes. We have seen it all before with other suns and it is now not only all predictable, but so is the time scale. It is not possible for the Sun (or the Earth) to survive at all, let alone become immortal.

Scientifically, the inner workings of the sun do not allow for that, and even if God created the Sun, He also simultaneously initiated its ultimate destiny and its *inevitable* self-destruction, and that will also be the end of the Earth. In fact, Earth will burn to a crisp long before the sun ultimately explodes. The Earth never was 'mortal' as such in the first place and 'immortality' is an impossible future state for it. If a God created the science that dictates that, He is also *bound* by the laws He created. They *cannot* be changed. The future is already determined and is now highly predictable. Today, we have knowledge the ancients did not have when they wrote their myths, legends and religious fantasies. Smith didn't have a clue. Today, we *must* be guided by science.

The sun's 'life' will span about ten billion years, and when it dies – so will everything else in our Solar System. In Smith's day, the science that we now understand so well was far from being discovered and understood. If he had known what we now know as scientific *fact*, it is certain that he would not have made such a silly statement. There is insufficient space here to go into the life of the Universe, which we now understand quite well, but I will just include a paragraph from one of my heroes, Professor Brian Cox, and refer the reader to his recent work on the subject which is *not* subjective – it is factual. The lesson here is that you *cannot* work science around a predetermined belief system; you can *only* work (or rework) a belief system around science, current knowledge, and new *evidence*. If you are not willing to do that, you *believe* in the fanciful instead of *understanding* the factual – and *that* is delusional. The truth, as Professor Cox describes it, is fascinating and beautifully illustrated; the book is based on his four part BBC TV series of the same name, 'Wonders of the Universe'.

> The fact that the Sun will die, incinerating Earth and obliterating all life on our planet, and that eventually the rest of the stars in the Universe will follow suit to leave a vast, formless cosmos with no possibility of supporting any life or retaining any record of the living things that brought meaning to its past, might sound a bit depressing to you. You might legitimately ask questions about the way our universe is put together. Surely you could build a universe in a different way? Surely you build a universe such that it didn't have to descend from order into chaos? Well, the answer is 'no', you couldn't, if you wanted life to exist on it. *(Cox & Cohen 2011:240).*

The passage of time will eventually see the end of *everything*, regardless of religious concepts invented by Smith – or anyone else. One day, in about a trillion, trillion, trillion, trillion, trillion, trillion, trillion years, the effects of entropy will render everything in the Universe into an entirely different 'sea' than the one that Smith so imaginatively described; it will ultimately become a sea of nothing but photons (which are far too small to be seen with the naked eye). The Universe then, to all intents and purposes, will appear **empty**. And where will that leave Smith and his God? Mere mortals have successfully worked out and understood the science. If God exists, He created everything through the medium we call science. We already know the end result of God's creations – we have worked it all out. Thus, if God does exist – His plan has to be entirely different to anything Smith claimed, as Smith's ideas turn out to be *impossible*. A different, or even a new Universe? A different dimension? A different 'time' of existence – somewhere else? Whatever it may (or more probably may not) actually be, any 'future' for humans cannot remotely be as Smith imagined. It is scientifically *impossible*.

The next few questions relate to the same vision. First, Smith asks about the four beasts. The Lord explains that they are just figurative, "describing **heaven, the paradise of God**, the happiness of man, and of beasts, and of creeping things, and of the fowls of the air" (Q.2). (Emphasis added). Here Smith claims heaven *is* paradise; Modern Mormon theology teaches differently. It all makes me wonder, as this was supposed to be a vision *of* heaven, why God didn't just *show* a happy person or people, a selection of real 'beasts' and a few birds, instead of 'four beasts' to *represent* those things (including heaven) which they were *in*. Well, in part he actually did and Smith makes a meal out of the verses that explain these beasts in Revelation.

> **Rev. 4:7.** The first beast was like a lion, and the second beast like a calf, and the third beast had a face as a man, and the fourth beast was like a flying eagle.
> **8.** And the four beasts had each of them six wings about him; and they were full of eyes within: and they rest not day and night, saying, Holy, holy, holy, Lord God Almighty, which was, and is, and is to come.

Why does everything have to be 'interpreted'? Why didn't God just say what he meant in plain English (or plain Hebrew or Greek)? It would have been easy enough. As ever, the answer is clear and obvious, not just in Smith's silly 'interpretation', but in the writer of Revelation's equally silly vision. Having had an answer to what the four beasts are meant to 'represent', Smith's third question is bizarre, as he then asks if the four beasts are "limited to individual beasts, or do they represent classes or orders?" The Lord answers "They are limited to four individual beasts, which were shown to John, to represent the glory of the classes of beings in their destined order or sphere of creation, in the enjoyment of their eternal felicity." So, they *are* limited to four individual beasts, yet they *do* represent the glory of the classes. It is just nonsense.

Why ask that, having just been told that they represent heaven, people, beasts and birds? Smith then asks what the eyes and wings of the beasts mean. The eyes represent "light and knowledge"; the wings, "power to move, to act, etc". Smith does not obtain an answer as to why the four beasts were "full of eyes, before and behind" (Rev. 4:6) and "full of eyes within" (Rev. 4:8). Why would God make up such strange and absurd concepts anyway? Would He not be clear and specific in any detail he wanted to impart? Of course He would. It's no wonder Revelation almost missed the final cut to get into the Bible in the year 367. Revelation is no more reliable than Smith's silly interpretations.

Again, considering the first answer, it makes no sense at all. The thing God's answer does confirm is the Mormon belief that *every* living thing will be resurrected. There are some pretty nasty little inventions that God is going to resurrect, and only He knows their 'place' in eternity, as they have certainly not been welcome guests here in 'mortality'. I have mentioned elsewhere, some of God's more distasteful 'creations' for which I am yet to discover a satisfactory explanation. They of course include microscopic life, some of which is useful, even essential to our survival, but some of which is positively devastating for humans and responsible for the demise of billions of us over the years. Why create them God? Why?

Just one example of God's little viruses followed the First World War – an event that was devastating enough for humans without being followed by the Spanish influenza pandemic. It lasted from June 1918 until December of 1920 and infected some 500 million people; 27% of the world population, which was 1.86 billion at the time. Between 50 and 100 million people died – at least 3% of the world population – making it one of the deadliest natural disasters in human history.

If such devastating things are the unfortunate outcome of an unwanted and yet unavoidable evolutionary chain of events on the tree of life, fair enough; but if a God *created* them as they are, then He has a lot to answer for. It is interesting that there are no myths or legends surrounding microscopic life. Why is that? Because until relatively recently, no one knew they even existed.

If our ancestors had no idea about them, they could not invent myths and legends that no doubt would have otherwise surrounded them. That should tell us something about all the things they *did* know about but did not readily understand – all of which gave rise to myths and legends that ultimately formed – and still form the very basis of *all* belief systems.

The twenty-four seats and elders dressed in white with gold crowns come next, along with seven burning lamps, which Revelation explains are the seven 'Spirits' of God. Smith's God has other ideas and proclaims they are the seven

DOCTRINE & COVENANTS – SECTIONS 75-86 & 99

'servants' in an IR 'correction' *(see p. 280)*. In the D&C, Smith's God changes his ideas yet again and seven 'churches' are now in the 'paradise' of God.

> **77:5. Q.** What are we to understand by the four and twenty elders, spoken of by John?
> **A.** We are to understand that these elders whom John saw, were elders who had been faithful in the work of the ministry and were dead; who belonged to the ***seven churches***, and were then ***in the paradise of God.*** (Emphasis added).

There are no churches mentioned in the KJV of Revelation 4. Earlier Smith had declared *paradise* was *heaven*, the immortal state of Earth *(see p. 283)*. Paradise, in Mormonism, is *not* heaven; it is a place where the spirits of people reside between this life and the resurrection. Smith is mixing up concepts that affect later Mormon doctrine.

Smith moves on in Q.6 to Revelation Chapter 5. He asks what is meant by the book that has seven seals on the back. The answer he 'receives' is evidence of Smith's scientific ignorance which was not untypical of his time. Many people believed in creationism and many still do, simply because they either do not understand, or perhaps refuse to accept, conclusive scientific evidence to the contrary; and the idea that the Earth had a life span of just seven thousand years – is God's answer. That we now know for a ***fact*** that that is *not* the case does not call for an abandonment of science, it calls for an abandonment of myths from the past that no longer deserve a place in our more enlightened world. Science admits it can be wrong and will readily accept new evidence to clarify matters. It cannot be entirely wrong about some things that are firmly established as fact, such as the age of the planet, evolution, and the tree of life which is now fairly well constructed from several different disciplines which all correlate and support one another. The work is *done*; the *proof* exists; creationists were *wrong*; and that's a ***fact***. Many who claim to represent God and have their beliefs set in stone are in serious trouble. Yet millions ignore the science – and some I have spoken to still don't even know the science *exists*.

As I previously mentioned, religious beliefs *must* bend to scientific *truth*. The alternative is to choose to live in a state of voluntary delusion, and that's not a healthy state of affairs for anyone.

Smith claimed that his God then said the book contained "the hidden things of his economy concerning this earth during the seven thousand years of its continuance, or its temporal existence." That Smith claimed the Earth has a life span of just seven thousand years is absolute proof God did *not* reveal that. It is a demonstrably impossible claim; an absurd concept in light of reality and all known science; and there is *no* argument that Smith and his God were *wrong*.

Essentially, this was a prophecy that the Earth would end after seven thousand years. The fact that this planet has been around for some 4.54 billion years is *indisputable*. That's already a little over seven thousand; isn't it?

Next, naturally, the seven 'seals' each represent a thousand years. Smith asks about four angels in Rev. 7:1 and is told they are "given power over the four parts of the earth..." We don't learn what the 'four parts' are. Scripturally, in relation to the place where people lived they often referred to the four points of the compass, or sometimes the 'four corners' of the Earth; but in terms of the whole world, which by Joseph Smith's time was known to be spherical (or rather, oblique spheroid), the concept no longer worked. Smith always ignored such problems, but you would think that a God would keep up with human understanding and use clearer terminology. The fact that He doesn't is more to do with Smith's lack of understanding than the idea God actually was involved with all the nonsense he came up with, as previously mentioned. The angels have the everlasting gospel to take to – who? Yes, you've guessed it, every "nation, kindred, tongue and people"; this is Smith's source for what became one of his favourite sayings *(discussed on pp. 180-81)*.

In Q&A 9, we learn that "the angel ascending from the east" is given the seal of God over the twelve tribes of Israel. He cries out to the other four angels "Hurt not the earth, neither the sea, nor the trees, till we have sealed the servants of our God in their foreheads. And, if you will receive it, this is Elias which was to come to gather together the tribes of Israel and restore all things."

Smith speaks (once again) of Elias, a fictional character who never actually existed as a separate entity to Elijah. It is unlikely that God would make such a mistake – leaving only one suspect. Elias (Greek for Elijah) is mentioned thirty times in the NT but he is not mentioned in Revelation at all. This is a Smith introduction, but in Smith's case he doesn't equate Elias to Elijah which *every* NT reference does.

Q&A 10 confirms everything written will be "accomplished" in the sixth thousand years. That meant 'now' to Smith. If we accept Smith's timescale from Adam onwards, have we not now definitely entered the *seventh* thousand year period? Clearly, everything was *not* accomplished in the sixth.

Following the idea that the 144,000 represent 12,000 from each tribe, taken from "every nation, kindred, tongue and people" of course, and that the trumps that sound (Rev. Ch. 8) represent each 'day' of the creation and the seventh, the start of the seventh thousand years (no surprises there), we learn that the little book "eaten" by John (Rev. Ch. 10) "was a mission, and an ordinance, for him to gather the tribes of Israel; behold, this is Elias, who, as it is written, must come and restore all things." Yet again Smith's mythical extra character 'Elias' is mentioned by God who should, and of course really would, know better.

Finally, we are informed that two witnesses mentioned in Rev. 11 are two prophets to be raised up to the Jewish nation "at the time of the restoration" to prophesy to them "after they are gathered and have built the city of Jerusalem in the land of their fathers", for what all that is worth. No such thing happened "at the time of the restoration" although the Church has sent authorities more than once during the twentieth century to Israel in order to 'dedicate' the land for the gathering of the Jews. Wasn't once enough? Not that the Jews ever asked for it of course.

As a final note on this section, I just want to point out another error by Smith. There are more, but space does not permit a list of every Smith mistake. When comparing Revelation Chapter 5 with Smith's Inspired Revision of the Bible in order to identify any revelatory 'corrections' that would help people better understand Revelation (assuming that they do not take it as the puerile and delusional fiction that it really is), the following changes are noted.

In v.1 Smith alters "him who *sat*" to read "him who *sits*", despite the original text being written in the past tense – as what the writer 'saw'. In v.2, we get "And I saw a strong angel proclaiming with a loud voice..." and Smith adds the words "and heard him", thus: "And I saw a strong angel, *and heard him* proclaiming with a loud voice..." as if it was not clear that you would actually hear someone who proclaimed something with a loud voice, without God needing to clarify it. Does anyone really want to claim that God *needed* to have Smith insert that? Smith's fundamental error occurs in v.6. This is the original, followed by Smith's 'inspired' correction.

> KJV. Rev. 5:6. And I beheld, and, lo, in the midst of the throne and of the four beasts, and in the midst of the elders, stood a Lamb as it had been slain, having *seven* horns and *seven* eyes, which are the *seven Spirits* of God sent forth into all the earth. (Emphasis added).

In Revelation 4:5 *(see p. 280)* Smith had changed "seven Spirits" to read "seven servants". The original of Revelation 5:6 is in harmony with the earlier concept of seven Spirits, but on the first occasion Smith left the number as *seven* and on this, he changes it to *twelve*, as well as from spirits – but this time to 'servants' rather than 'churches' as he did in D&C 77:5 *(see pp. 284-5)*. There is no consistency in Smith's work.

> **I.R. Rev 5:6.** And I beheld, and, lo, in the midst of the throne and of the four beasts, and in the midst of the elders, stood a Lamb as it had been slain, having *twelve* horns and *twelve* eyes, which are the *twelve servants* of God, sent forth into all the earth. (Emphasis added).

It does not compute; it is not compatible; and it does not work in *either* context. There is no continuity, which at least there is in the original. Smith's memory was not that good but sometimes he didn't even appear to care about such things as consistency, he just kept on making things up and that was good enough; as long as it looked and sounded like scripture, some people would believe his revelations. Sometimes they did, and often times they actually didn't, although the Church hid this by calling those who saw through Smith 'dissenters'.

Nevertheless, many members did see through Smith and then voted with their feet. Smith introduced the law of consecration so at least he could keep their assets when such dissenters left the fold.

Section 77 – Summary

Prophecies made:	1
Prophecies fulfilled:	0
Other non-prophetic revelation:	3

Prophecies made:

Pr. 28: Smith claimed that God said the book contained "the hidden things of his economy concerning this earth during the seven thousand years of its continuance, or its temporal existence." This is a ***prophecy*** that the Earth would last for a seven thousand year period.

Results:

Pr. 28: That Smith claimed the Earth has an overall life span of just seven thousand years is absolute proof God did *not* reveal that. It is a demonstrably impossible claim; an absurd concept in light of reality and known science; and there is *no* argument that Smith and his God were *wrong*. Essentially, this was a prophecy that the Earth would end after seven thousand years. We know humans have existed for tens of thousands of years longer than that. The fact that the Earth has been around for some 4.54 billion years is *indisputable*.

Non-prophetic revelation.

1. Joseph Smith claimed the 'sea of glass' was translucent and it represented the future 'immortal' state of the Earth which would be like a giant Urim and Thummim – stones that are translucent and can be seen into. In Mormon terms, that equates to the Celestial kingdom.

DOCTRINE & COVENANTS – SECTIONS 75-86 & 99

In reality, the sea of glass would have equated to a sea of green, with 'glass' probably reflecting the idea of a shimmering surface. The author of Revelation equates this to heaven or God's 'paradise' which is an entirely different concept to the Mormon idea of paradise. The earth will one day be burned to a crisp and will not survive the death of our Sun. There is no mechanism that a God has put in place for it to survive beyond that event. Ultimately, the Universe will become a sea of nothing but photons which are far too small to be seen with the naked eye. The Universe, to all intents and purposes, will eventually appear *empty*.

2. Smith's take on the Urim and Thummim was that they could be looked into, as they were 'seer stones'. He described them thus: "…a curious instrument which the ancients called "Urim and Thummim," which consisted of two *transparent* stones set in the rim of a bow fastened to a breastplate."

Linguists indicate that Urim means 'light' or 'to give light' and Thummim means 'completeness', 'perfection', or 'innocence'. Anciently, the stones were 'lots' and were cast to provide answers (including innocence or guilt) to yes-no questions. Smith did not know this and invented his own ideas. It should have been obvious to Smith that they were never used to translate anything anciently – as there was nothing to translate. The idea that things could be *seen* in them was just in Smith's overactive imagination, as again, biblically this was never claimed at all. They were, as stated, simply related to decisions made by sheer chance.

3. Smith claimed, and the Mormon Church today teaches, that the Earth will become 'Celestial' – a giant 'Urim and Thummim' – like a sea of crystal which can be looked into. Although Smith was ignorant of their history, the Mormon Church today ignores the fact (above) that 'Urim and Thummim' were simply 'lot stones' used to obtain yes-no answers or to determine innocence or guilt – in an impossible prediction concerning future of the Earth.

The sun's 'life' will span about ten billion years, and when it dies – so will everything else in our Solar System. In Smith's day, the science that we now understand so well was yet to be fully discovered and understood. Far from becoming a celestial planet, the Earth will be obliterated – and that's a *fact*, whether God was involved in creating it or not.

THE MORMON DELUSION

Section 78
1 March 1832. Hiram, Ohio.

History.

1835 D&C Sec. LXXV. 2010 D&C Sec. 78.

This Section marks the commencement of the use of 'code names' for some people referred to in the verses. There was a fear that the use of real names could elicit anger and reprisals from those who by now had become Smith's firm enemies. For example, in this Section, Joseph Smith becomes 'Enoch' and also 'Gazelam'; Newel K. Whitney is called Ahasdah and Sidney Rigdon's name is changed to Pelagoram. Subsequent to the perceived need abating, they reverted to the use of the real names. Eventually, later editions of the D&C removed code names and inserted the real names recorded in the original manuscripts. Today, code names are excluded from these Sections altogether. Having mentioned the fact that they existed, as they are not important to this work, we will ignore the earlier use of such code names. If Smith hadn't made so many enemies, they would never have needed them.

It is God who is speaking to Smith and God says He is going to "speak in your ears, the words of wisdom". So, what wise words does God have for Smith this time? Well, they are to be organised in "regulating and establishing the affairs of the storehouse for the poor" (v.3), both there in Ohio and also in the land of Zion. God then adds (v.4) that it is "For a permanent and everlasting establishment and order unto my church, to advance the cause," God goes on to say that if they can't be equal in "earthly things", they cannot be equal in obtaining heavenly things. If they want a place in the Celestial world, they must prepare themselves by doing the things *commanded* and required of them. This amounts to a prophecy by Smith that it *will* be forever a part of God's Church on Earth.

The problem here is that as we have previously discussed, the whole idea collapsed and never did work at all. Yet God states categorically that they must live the law of consecration in order to obtain a place in the Celestial kingdom. Furthermore, God says that is to be "permanent and everlasting", and those words are far from ambiguous. What was God doing, commanding such a thing if He *knew* it wouldn't survive? Perhaps, unlike the Christian God, the Mormon version doesn't know everything, past, present and future, as so far along our journey of discovery, in the revelations He gave Smith in the D&C, He doesn't seem to know much of anything at all – that is, until *after* the event when He conveniently 'revokes' things.

God commanded them to build Zion and that never happened either, so His track record on commanding things that fell flat is consistent if nothing else.

Brigham Young would have been well aware of this "commandment" too, yet did he re-establish it in Salt Lake, when and where they could have done so without any opposition? No, he did not; he made himself a millionaire at the expense of tithing instead. God didn't say anything about *that* idea *(see p. 259)*.

Smith, Whitney and Rigdon are to "sit in council" with the saints in Zion in case they are led astray by Satan and they are also to make an unbreakable bond or 'everlasting covenant' between them. If any of them breaks it they will be turned over the "buffetings of Satan" until the day of redemption. That sort of idea didn't last long either. God goes on to call Himself the "Lord God, the Holy One of Zion, who hath established the foundations of Adam-ondi-Ahman;" (v.15). Establishing the 'foundation', if you can call it that, was about all he ever did though.

There are a few verses of filler in which God says they are like little children who don't know much, but He will lead them along and they will have the 'riches of eternity'. There were always promises for the next life; they will have "an hundred fold, yea, more" (v.19) and yet they got nothing in this life other than constant suffering which could have largely been avoided had they remotely stopped to think and consider their options.

Finally, in what I call 'wind down' verses that often appear at the end of a Section, Smith has God, who has been speaking throughout, now "saith your Redeemer, even the Son Ahman…" Smith had invented the Adam-ondi-Ahman name and now (and again in Section 95) he pretends Ahman means God and so Jesus is the "Son of Ahman". It is *not* a word and it has no real meaning at all. Well, that is apart from the fact that 'Google translate' thinks it means 'idiot' in Turkish. That seems quite an appropriate translation for Smith and his God.

Section 78 – Summary

Prophecies made:	1
Prophecies fulfilled:	0

Prophecies made:

Pr. 29: They are to be organised in "regulating and establishing the affairs of the storehouse for the poor … For a permanent and everlasting establishment and order unto my church, to advance the cause."

Results:

Pr. 29: The system failed completely and was ultimately abandoned. Once in Salt Lake where it could have been re-established, Brigham Young preferred to use tithing to make himself into a millionaire instead.

THE MORMON DELUSION

Section 80
7 March 1832. Hiram, Ohio.

History.

1835 D&C Sec. LXXVII. 2010 D&C Sec. 80.

This pointless little Section typifies why the D&C is so silly. I am including all five verses just to show how ridiculous such a concept as the Lord bothering with the mundane can really be. Here, he says Stephen Burnett and Eden Smith should go off preaching together to anyone who will listen. It doesn't matter where they go; they can't go wrong. And the point of this revelation from the Lord, instead of something actually *useful* – is?

Section 80

Revelation given through Joseph Smith the Prophet, at Hiram, Ohio, March 1832 (see History of the Church, 1:257*). 1–5, Stephen Burnett and Eden Smith are called to preach in whatever place they choose.*

1. Verily, thus saith the Lord unto you my servant Stephen Burnett: Go ye, go ye into the world and preach the gospel to every creature that cometh under the sound of your voice.
2. And inasmuch as you desire a companion, I will give unto you my servant Eden Smith.
3. Wherefore, go ye and preach my gospel, whether to the north or to the south, to the east or to the west, it mattereth not, for ye cannot go amiss.
4. Therefore, declare the things which ye have heard, and verily believe, and know to be true.
5. Behold, this is the will of him who hath called you, your Redeemer, even Jesus Christ. Amen.

Despite having his own 'revelation', Stephen Burnett later 'dissented' and left the Church. Burnett famously claimed in a letter that Martin Harris had told him that the eight 'witnesses' never saw the plates and hesitated to sign that instrument for that reason, but were *persuaded* to do it. *(Letter to Lyman E. Johnson, 15 April 1838. Joseph Smith Papers; Letter book, 20 April 1837 – 9 Feb 1843).*

Section 79
12 March 1832. Hiram, Ohio.

History.

1835 D&C Sec. LXXVI. 2010 D&C Sec. 79.

This Section is even shorter than the last one. It simply calls Jared Carter to go, once again, to the east – from "place to place and city to city" with no other instructions. The 'comforter' will guide him. If he is faithful "I will crown him again with sheaves" says the Lord. That's it. Crown – with sheaves? Really?

We have to question, yet again, why the Lord would ever bother with such mundane nonsense. In addition, considering more weighty matters, such as the establishment of Zion and the commanded permanent nature of the law of consecration, neither of which ever worked out, Smith's deity wasn't much use at getting anything right anyway. This was a complete waste of time.

Smith's God seemed a bit obsessed with 'sheaves', mentioning them as a *reward* four times in the D&C. Such a concept does not appear in the NT and where 'sheaves' appears in the OT, it is either descriptive or perhaps a 'wave offering' rather than ever being a reward of any kind.

Smith would no doubt have claimed the Lord was being symbolic. Smith referred to sheaves a couple of times in his Book of Mormon, and in Alma (26:5), where it is used as a metaphor, it also mentions thrusting in a sickle – and then, just look how many sheaves they have. That was supposedly in 90-77 BCE.

The problem there was that they did not have manufactured sickles in the Americas at that time and even if they did, they had no crops that would need one and no sheaves of *anything* could have existed. The people would not be familiar with the concept. So, despite it being a metaphor, what would they have known about such an implement – or gathering process?

The other reference to sheaves in the Book of Mormon is where Smith has Jesus himself declare that he will "…gather my people together as a man **gathereth his sheaves into the floor**" (emphasis added). Well, actually, they didn't. They couldn't, because as mentioned above, they had no crops that could be bound into sheaves. Smith stole that line from Micah 4:12, "…for he shall **gather them as the sheaves into the floor**" (emphasis added), and put it into the mouth of Jesus. Smith's plagiarism knew no bounds, but he was unaware that there were no such crops in the Americas, so his hoax is once again entirely exposed by the lack of sickles and crops and the copied words from Micah 4:12. *(See TMD Vol. 2:239-41).* It all comes apart for Smith, over and over again in his writings.

As for Jared Carter, he was to become one if the leaders of the Danite movement within the Mormon Church, a secret band of men Joseph Smith allegedly organised to control, instil fear into, drive out, and sometimes even kill dissenters in order to 'protect' the Church.

Section 81
15 March 1832. Hiram, Ohio.
History.

1835 D&C Sec. LXXIX. 2010 D&C Sec. 81.

Section 81 is fully reviewed in *TMD Vol. 3:302-5. (S70–74)*. In a nutshell, this is what it was all about. Although the header to D&C 81 now at least includes an added admission that it was originally intended to be for *Jesse Gause*, it is casually passed over by saying: "...when he failed to continue in a manner consistent with this appointment, the call was subsequently transferred to *Frederick G Williams*."

This revelation was to Jesse Gause *alone*, simply calling him to be a counsellor to Smith. Much later, his name was crossed through in the original and replaced with Frederick G. Williams. Until the 1980s no one even knew that Gause had ever been called, as the revelation had been *falsified* to read Frederick G. Williams, as if he had been called in 1832, when in reality he was called a full *year later*.

Even today, the Church openly lies about this in its own Almanac every year. As of the 2007 edition, under **Other** Counsellors in the First Presidency, the first one still listed is indeed Jesse Gause. However, each year the Almanac states "Set apart as counsellor to Joseph Smith March 8, 1832; sent on a mission Aug 1, 1832. Excommunicated Dec. 3, 1832. Died about 1836". There is no mention of him ever being given his own personal revelation – D&C 81.

Then, under **Second Counsellors** in the First Presidency, Frederick G Williams is the *first* one listed. It actually says: **"Called by revelation March 1832 to be a high priest and counsellor to President Joseph Smith (D&C 81:1)**; ordained a high priest by Miles H Jones; **set apart as second counsellor to President Smith March 18, 1833**, at age 45; rejected Nov 7, 1837; excommunicated Mar 17, 1839; restored to fellowship April 8, 1840; died Oct 10, 1842..." *(Church Almanac; 2007)* (Bold emphasis added).

Williams, called in *1833*, was *not* called by revelation in March *1832*, as the Church here claims, *Gause* was called then and just not credited with the revelation once he was excommunicated. This is an outright *lie* appearing in a current annual Church publication. The modern Church proclaims Williams was called by revelation a year *early*, citing D&C 81:1 and regarding Gause, relegates him to "Set Apart as a counsellor", ignoring the fact that D&C 81 was given as revelation for him *personally* in 1832.

Trying to cover up an embarrassing 'revelation' is lacking in honesty and integrity. No matter what the Church now tries to hide, it seems that both men then fell by the wayside in their callings, irrespective of who was called or when. The Church writes its own history, disregarding real facts and replacing them with convenient fiction.

As it happens, there was an *unpublished* revelation dated 6 January 1833 calling Williams "to be a counsellor and scribe unto my servant Joseph." Frederick G Williams (1787-1842), as cited at www.saintswithouthalos.com *(c. Frederick G. Williams collection. MS782, fd. 2, Church Archives //JS revelations, 231)*. You would think Smith would have just left Section 81 alone and issued the new revelation for Williams. At least the Church could have later published it and been honest about Section 81. Honesty and integrity have never been a strong suit within Mormonism. At the end of the day, what difference would it have made to have left the revelation just as it was and then issue the 6 January 1833 revelation for Williams. It certainly would not have been as much of an embarrassment as some of the other antics Smith got up to – such as issuing the Lord's response to Section 39 with Section 40 regarding James Covill.

Section 82
26 April 1832. Jackson County, Missouri.

History.

1835 D&C Sec. LXXXVI. 2010 D&C Sec. 82.

The reader should now be able to predict what is going to be said at the start of this slightly longer revelation comprising twenty-four verses, given at a general council where others were clearly involved. There are no prizes... The Lord declares that inasmuch as they have forgiven each other for their 'trespasses', he also forgives them. Can he leave it at that? Of course not; nevertheless, he continues, they have all sinned and they must stop, to avoid sore judgments that will fall on their heads. Who would have guessed the Lord would say that?

They have apparently asked for revelation and the Lord is going to respond. Naturally, he isn't very pleased with the world. In fact, he comes right out and exclaims he is angry. "...the anger of God kindleth against the inhabitants of the earth; and none doeth good, for all have gone out of the way." There is no pleasing the Mormon God at all. But really, if *none* doeth good, whose fault is that, considering the lack of proper information and direction the world had received over the centuries?

Couple that with the handed down myths and legends of the past, of course it's a complete mess. God needed a much better plan if He wanted everyone to clearly understand what it was He required of them. If there had been a proper communication with humans at an early point, once they had learned how to write, explaining in simple and understandable terms, the way forward and how to best please Him, surely He would have had a better following and a more cohesive world wide religious base and He needn't be so angry all the time. I can only suggest that if the Mormon God was not happy, then He only had Himself to blame. Look at His history.

Anyway, God says they should sin no more – but if they do, their former sins will also come back to bite them. Next, the Lord has a new commandment for them. In Smith's characteristic way, he incorporates his "in other words" habit *(see p. 93 and also: The Final Analysis, Part 2)* into the new instructions. Is it really 'new' and somewhat 'marvellous'? Of course not. The Lord says:

> **8.** ...I give unto you a new commandment, that you may understand my will concerning you;
> **9.** Or, *in other words*, I give unto you directions how you may act before me, that it may turn to you for your salvation. (Emphasis added).

As ever, Smith's idea of "in other words" does not exactly add any new understanding and he may as well not have bothered; verse nine is very poorly constructed. We must remember that this is not supposed to be Smith, but rather the Lord himself rephrasing things "in other words", in order to make it all clearer. He wasn't very good at it. There are more 'pet phrases' to follow in this section.

The Lord adds that he is bound when they do what he says but if they don't, they have no promise. That is a very well known and oft quoted 'Mormonism' that the saints apply to themselves today. It keeps them faithful – they want the promised blessings for their obedience.

Next, the revelation requires that Edward Partridge, Newel K. Whitney, A. Sidney Gilbert, Sidney Rigdon, Joseph Smith, John Whitmer, Oliver Cowdery, W. W. Phelps and Martin Harris be bound together by a *covenant* that cannot be broken. It isn't a new covenant. We have already seen it in a recent Section.

It is to "manage the affairs of the poor, and all things pertaining to the bishopric both in the land of Zion and in the land of Kirtland" (v.12). The Lord has consecrated the land of Kirtland "in mine own due time" for the benefit of the saints, using another pet phrase which has no relevance to the statement.

They are to enter the covenant spoken of and to all be equal in everything they have. As we know, that idea didn't last long, despite the fact that it now became an *unbreakable* covenant. It certainly got broken – and quite quickly too. The Lord could never see that far ahead. He still liked to repeat himself, "you are to be equal, *or in other words*, you are to have equal claims on the properties…" (Emphasis added). As usual, the 'other words' are similar to the first ones and do not add any clarity at all; but they are a distinguishing feature of Smith's hoax – unless we accept the idea that the Lord really is not capable of expressing himself adequately, even 'in *other* words'.

In v.20, the Lord again confirms the continuing nature of this requirement. "This order I have appointed to be *an everlasting order unto you, and unto your successors…*" (Emphasis added).

Finally, the Lord tells them to make friends with the locals and not upset them so they don't destroy the saints; the Lord will 'repay' them himself. That was yet another idea destined not to last. Smith was far too aggressive to avoid conflict which became almost inevitable.

Section 82 – Summary

Prophecies made:	1
Prophecies fulfilled:	0

Prophecies made:

Pr. 30: Results: The same details we found in Section 78 are repeated here. They are to enter the covenant (now termed the 'law of consecration') and have *equal* claims, and that is to be "an everlasting order".

Pr. 30: The system failed completely and was ultimately abandoned. Once in Salt Lake where it could have been re-established, Brigham Young preferred to use tithing to make himself into a millionaire instead. The "everlasting order" the Lord had insisted upon has long been forgotten.

Section 83
30 April 1832. Independence, Missouri.

History.

1835 D&C Sec. LXXXVIII. 2010 D&C Sec. 83.

Put simply, this Section 'reveals' (although it is not a word I would use), that widows and orphans as well as the poor have claim on the Church for their support if it is needed. Why it took the Lord to explain that – only he knows.

Section 99
29 August 1832. Hiram, Ohio.

History.

1835 D&C Sec. LXXVIII. 2010 D&C Sec. 99.

This is yet another one of those so-called revelations that calls someone to go off and preach. None of such Sections contain anything of value or merit and served only as a 'convincer' for the recipient to encourage him to go.

In this case it is directed to John Murdock, who, like many before him is just told to go (in this case) east, from house to house, village to village and city to city – as if that wasn't the obvious thing to do. Those who accept him will be blessed (and obtain mercy of course) and in respect of those who do not, Murdock is to 'cleanse his feet' in 'secret places by the way' – for a testimony against them. The Lord obviously thought Murdock wouldn't want anyone to see him with his boots off.

I have commented previously, how cruel and unkind an act this is against people who may have been God-fearing and good in all respects, but already convinced, with a testimony of their own, that they were following God the way he wanted them to. For them to reject such a conviction would, to them at least, seem equally as condemning as the Mormon concept of rejection of their new gospel message. God should never put people in such an invidious position and He has no cause to be condemning them in this way. It is morally wrong for humans to do such a thing – but for a God, it is unforgivable.

How did we respond as faithful Mormons, when someone of another faith would knock on our door to try to persuade us toward their faith? Mormons suppose they are the only ones to *know* the truth whilst those of other faiths can only 'believe' they have the truth – as clearly they do not, as far as Mormons are concerned. It is not only extremely arrogant to suppose such a thing, it is also incredibly naive. Many people firmly believe that they *know* their God and their 'truth' just as much as Mormons, and I suspect, sometimes even more so without the need to stand and make a formal declaration of such to other believers.

As ever, the Mormon God's true colours shine through; He is going to come quickly to judgment; something He was expected to do, in what now amounts to centuries ago, but He never came. Finally, Murdock actually (and unusually) gets some direction. He doesn't have to go away until his children are provided for (isn't that thoughtful) and then after a few *years*, if he wants to, he can himself "go up unto the goodly land" to possess his inheritance, otherwise keep on preaching until he is 'taken' – some choice.

John Murdock, then aged forty, was one of the men to remain faithful to the Church; he was later in Zion's Camp and became the first Mission President in Australia in 1851. He served as a Bishop in Nauvoo and also in Salt Lake. Murdock died in 1871 at age seventy-nine. It was his children, the Murdock twins (Joseph and Julia), that Joseph and Emma Smith had adopted the year before this Section was recorded, when John's first wife, Julia Clapp Murdock had died in childbirth on the same day (30 April 1831) that Emma Smith's own twins (Thaddeus and Louisa) were born and had died. A few months before this Section was recorded, on the night of 24 March 1832, Joseph Smith was caring for one of the adopted twin babies, both of whom had measles, while staying at the home of John Johnson and his family, when he was suddenly dragged out to the woods and tarred and feathered by a mob. The baby died, possibly from exposure, a few days later *(See TMD Vol. 1:146)*.

Section 84
22 & 23 September 1832. Kirtland, Ohio.

History.

1835 D&C Sec. IV. 2010 D&C Sec. 84.

Section 84 is a revelation from Jesus Christ to Joseph Smith. For reference, this section is cited for varying reasons in *TMD Vol. 2:19, 32; Vol. 3:312-3; Vol.4: 61, 111, 202-5, 366-7 (S74-80)*. I recommend readers to review references from Volumes 3 and 4, as much of it is not included here.

Jesus gets straight to confirmation of building Zion in v.2-3. "…the city of New Jerusalem …shall be built, beginning at the temple lot, which is appointed by the finger of the Lord, in the western boundaries of the State of Missouri, and dedicated by the hand of Joseph Smith, Jun., and others with whom the Lord was well pleased." There is no denying either the confirmation of the prophecy or the *exact* location. Jesus goes even further and confirms that it will be built "in this generation" (v.4). That undeniable prophecy was *not* fulfilled.

Following Smith's death and the legal battles that ensued between various schisms, the lot was eventually split between three organisations and the only temple standing there is owned by the RLDS (Community of Christ). All the Mormon (LDS) Church has there is a visitor's centre. Perhaps the Mormon

Church claims fulfilment of the prophecy and they don't mind who actually owns the temple? Whatever excuse they wish to give, a temple was *not* built in Smith's generation; it *was* a false prophecy and there is still *no* Mormon (LDS) temple there.

In v.6-16, Smith has *Jesus* recite an entirely **impossible** sequence of Old Testament priesthood holders who supposedly passed on the Melchizedek priesthood from generation to generation. This is fully analysed and discussed in TMD Volume 4, as referenced above. It naturally includes *Esaias* instead of *Isaiah*, a name that Jesus at least should have understood and used correctly, even if Smith didn't.

This is also the section where Jesus tells Smith that no *man* can see God and live – **unless** they hold the Melchizedek priesthood (v.22). Of course, there was no question of a **woman** ever seeing God at all; an idea that would not be as readily accepted today. In fact, if God was starting his 'true Church' now, He would be almost *obliged* to include women in His Priesthood hierarchy. The idea of being obliged to hold the Melchizedek Priesthood in order to actually see God was no problem at the time (September 1832), as that was the year Smith made his *first* attempt at writing his First Vision idea which was then of Jesus alone. It was to become extremely problematic later however, when in 1838 he decided a First Vision of *God* as well as Jesus was a good idea. Unfortunately for Smith, he then *backdated* that idea to 1820, over twelve years *before* this revelation in which Jesus Christ himself categorically states that could *not* happen without the Melchizedek Priesthood. The truth of the matter is clear – and very obvious.

Smith has Jesus go on to claim that Moses tried to teach this to the children of Israel so they could also see God but they would not listen (v.23-5). God got angry about that and took Moses away, leaving them with just Aaron and his lesser priesthood. This, claims Jesus, continued until John the Baptist, who was apparently "baptized while he was yet in his childhood, and was ordained by the angel of God at the time he was eight days old unto this power, to overthrow the kingdom of the Jews, and to make straight the way of the Lord before the face of his people, to prepare them for the coming of the Lord, in whose hand is given all power" (v.28).

Smith makes some very strange claims in the D&C, but to have Jesus state that John was ordained when eight days old to "overthrow the kingdom of the Jews" – who were supposedly God's chosen race, is about as bizarre as it gets. As John did no such thing as to overthrow the kingdom of the Jews, why did Smith pretend Jesus said such a thing? The presence of Jesus in the Holy Land actually had little if any effect on the kingdom of the Jews which continued as if he had never existed.

Following more filler about Moses and Aaron and the two priesthoods, which culminates in Jesus saying that if anyone breaks the covenant they make with the Lord, they will not be forgiven in this life or the next (a statement clearly designed by Smith to frighten people and keep them faithful), he moves on to explain for the umpteenth time (v.49-51) that the "whole world lieth in sin, and groaneth under darkness and under the bondage of sin. And by this you may know they are under the bondage of sin, because they come not unto me. For whoso cometh not unto me is under the bondage of sin."

The problem with *Jesus* saying that, quite naturally never occurs to us as members. Stepping outside the box (of the Mormon faith) and looking back in, it is actually a ridiculous thing for Jesus to say. There were, even at that time, millions upon millions of people who thought they were in fact being faithful to him and that they were indeed *avoiding* sin. It was all very well *Smith* claiming the world was in sin, but Jesus? If it really were the case, then when you think about it, it was actually *his* fault. The text then descends into more filler and a lot of repetition until Jesus clarifies in v.57 "And they shall remain under this condemnation until they repent and remember the new covenant, even the Book of Mormon and the former commandments which I have given them, not only to say, but to do according to that which I have written—"

That statement really doesn't even deserve comment. If that *was* Jesus, and not just Smith conning his followers into a deeper acceptance of his belief system, then Jesus has a lot to answer for. There follows a lot more filler and promises of ability to perform miracles and then Jesus says anyone who does not accept what the Mormons teach and get baptised, will be damned. The harshness of the Mormon God and his son are beyond compare and such a statement is nothing short of unforgivable.

Missionaries are to go out without purse or scrip – and not even bother with two coats. In v.82 Smith has Jesus say "consider the lilies of the field, how they grow, they toil not, neither do they spin" which Smith obviously supposed Jesus really said, word for word, just as recorded in Matthew 6:28 and Luke 12:27. Of course, we know those verses actually just record an *idea* of what Jesus *might* have said rather than anything he actually did say. Smith had had Jesus use that *exact* phrase before, in the Book of Mormon (3 Nephi 13:28).

Anyone who accepts the missionaries and feeds them will be rewarded and (v.94) "wo wo unto that house, or that village or city that rejecteth you, or your words, or your testimony concerning me". As if the message wasn't clear, it is repeated again, exactly, in v.95: "Wo, I say again, unto that house, or that village or city that rejecteth you, or your words, or your testimony of me." I was almost surprised that Smith didn't have the Lord say "in other words" between the two identical statements *(See pp. 90-91)*.

They are reminded, not just to shake the dust from their feet, in biblical tradition, but also to *wash* their feet against such people, and Jesus even goes so far as to say they should do so whether it is "in heat or cold". Why would Jesus include such a silly detail? Just for once, could he not just say *one* thing *useful*?

We are now well over half way through Smith's so-called revelations and if it is not perfectly clear to the reader by now where they all came from – there is no hope, and continuing in a delusional state has become personal choice rather than being sustained by a testimony based on tangible evidence of the truth.

Jesus now describes himself as "the Almighty" in yet another very telling monotheistic tone, once again confirming the view then held by Smith. He is of course upset again and going to scourge the nations for their wickedness by sending plagues (v.96-7). Moreover, they will not be removed until he has completed his work – which has now been cut short. This was clearly meant to indicate Jesus would return even sooner than they may have thought and they already expected him in their generation. As previously stated, nearly two centuries on – he is very, very late by any standard or measurement – or at least the *perception* of that time.

From v.99-102 Smith includes a new 'song'. Bearing in mind this was Jesus (or the Almighty) speaking through Smith, it isn't even very good prose; and it is certainly not a song (or hymn) as we would recognise one. It was probably never set to music in readiness to be sung, as is predicted in v.98, and I would be very surprised to learn that it has been. It really can't be; there is no rhythmic element (metre) and it doesn't even rhyme.

In order to teach people, wherever they go, the Almighty suggests they send the lesser priesthood (Priests) first to make appointments and also keep ones the Elders and Apostles cannot attend. The Teachers and Deacons are to stay and run the Church. At that time all Priesthood offices were held by adult males. Today, young boys hold the lesser or Aaronic Priesthood (deacons, teachers and priests). Although, in later years Brigham Young got into the habit of ordaining his teenage sons as apostles (four are recorded) even though they were not members of the Quorum of Twelve and the other apostles didn't know anything about it at the time. They were not at all happy when they eventually discovered what Young had done. *(See TMD Vol. 4:360).*

When we get to v.114-15, Smith is in full flow and cannot resist predicting more devastation. Bishop Whitney is to preach in New York, Albany and Boston. If those cities will not listen, there will be "desolation and utter abolishment" and "if they do reject these things the hour of their judgment is nigh, and their house shall be left unto them desolate." There are more to be destroyed as the Almighty isn't finished yet. The rest of them are to go off and preach, reproving everyone, and anywhere they go they are to let people know the Almighty will "rend their kingdoms" – something he is yet to fulfil.

DOCTRINE & COVENANTS – SECTIONS 75-86 & 99

Section 84 – Summary

Prophecies made:	2
Prophecies fulfilled:	0
Other non-prophetic revelation:	2

Prophecies made:

Pr. 31: v.2-3. "…the city of New Jerusalem … shall be built, beginning at the temple lot, which is appointed by the finger of the Lord, in the western boundaries of the State of Missouri, and dedicated by the hand of Joseph Smith, Jun., and others with whom the Lord was well pleased." There is no denying either the confirmation of the prophecy or the *exact* location. Jesus goes even further and confirms that it will be built "in this generation" (v.4).

Pr. 32: Bishop Whitney is to preach in New York, Albany and Boston. If those cities will not listen, there will be "desolation and utter abolishment" and "if they do reject these things the hour of their judgment is nigh, and their house shall be left unto them desolate."

Results:

Pr. 31: Following Smith's death and legal battles that ensued between various schisms, the lot was eventually split between three organisations and the only temple standing there is owned by the RLDS (Community of Christ). There is still ***no*** Mormon (LDS) temple there.

Pr. 32: Smith himself also preached in New York and Boston. The gospel was no more 'received' in those places than anywhere else, but no such judgment as Smith predicted has ever befallen any of the cities mentioned.

Non-prophetic revelation.

1. In v.6-16, Smith has *Jesus* recite a sequence of Old Testament priesthood holders who supposedly passed the Melchizedek priesthood from generation to generation.

The list contains an entirely ***impossible*** sequence. This is fully analysed and discussed in *TMD Vol. 4:202-5 (S76-9)*. It naturally includes *Esaias* instead of *Isaiah*, a name that Jesus at least should have understood and used correctly, even if Smith didn't.

2. Jesus tells Smith that no man can see God and live – **unless** they hold the Melchizedek priesthood (v.22). Of course, there was no question of a *woman* ever seeing God at all. None of that was a problem at the time (September 1832).

1832 was the year Smith made his *first* attempt at writing his First Vision idea which was then of Jesus alone. The idea that 'no man can see God and live – without the Melchizedek Priesthood' was to become extremely problematic later. In 1838 Smith decided that a First Vision of *God* as well as Jesus was a good idea. Unfortunately for Smith, he then *backdated* that concept to 1820, over twelve years *before* this revelation in which Jesus Christ himself categorically states that could *not* happen without holding the Melchizedek Priesthood. That this sequence of events constitutes firm evidence of an entirely false revelation is absolutely conclusive.

Section 85
27 November 1832. Kirtland, Ohio.

History.

First added to the D&C in 1876. 2010 D&C Sec. 85.

Joseph Smith had been sending people 'up to Zion' and when they arrived, they fully expected to receive their promised *"...inheritance according to the established order of the Church."* (Italics in original). Unfortunately, the whole idea of consecration was not exactly working very well. This Section is an extract from a letter (called a revelation) from Smith to W. W. Phelps.

The clerk is to keep a list of those who consecrate "properties" to the Church and also a list of those who apostatise afterwards. Those who don't comply at all are not to be recorded as members. The Lord is going to "send one mighty and strong" to sort things out. That doesn't need comment.

There is a repeat of the idea that people will be cut off if they don't play ball and finally Smith even has the *Lord refer* directly to Ezra 2:61-2 and we are left to look it up. The reference is about people not being found in the register of genealogy who had been put out of the Priesthood. Among all the strange ideas Smith came up with, having the Lord *cite* a chapter and the verse numbers of a scripture from the KJV of the Old Testament really takes the biscuit. Delusion knows absolutely *no* bounds.

DOCTRINE & COVENANTS – SECTIONS 75-86 & 99

Section 86
6 December 1832. Kirtland, Ohio.

History.

1835 D&C Sec. VI. 2010 D&C Sec. 86.

Smith claimed this revelation was *"received while reviewing and editing the manuscript of the translation of the Bible."* (Italics in original). I am wondering why it even needed reviewing and editing? Didn't the Lord 'inspire' *correct* revisions the first time around? Apparently not.

This is essentially Smith's 'explanation' of the parable of the wheat and the tares. Naturally, it is the Lord explaining it, and conveniently, it applies to Smith's own time. He mentions the idea again in Section 101 a year later when persecution was at it's height in Kirtland, when those people classified as 'tares' must be bound tightly so they can be "burned with unquenchable fire" (101:66). I would ask the reader if they know, or have even ever met, *anyone* who has rejected the gospel, or the Lord in *any* guise, who actually deserves such treatment? I have discussed elsewhere *(See TMD Vol. 3, Sec. 5)* the fear factor in religion. It is **the** prime motivator – and it works, but only on those who readily believe in it, and they are generally followers of the religions that teach what to fear.

The irony is that God's threats may strike the 'fear of God' (as they say) into followers, who then assume it will have the same effect on people they subsequently warn, but the fact is that it really doesn't. No one outside of the frame of reference (membership) takes a blind bit of notice and they generally consider people that teach such things as completely delusional.

Why does God, or at least those who purport to represent Him, always resort to threats of unbelievably cruel consequences in efforts to persuade people to follow Him? It is an archaic concept and one not worthy of modern intelligent humans, let alone any real God who should know we have outgrown such nonsense. He should (and I venture to suggest that if such a being existed, He would) talk to us rationally, not to mention on a scientific level, instead of relying on myths and legends of the past that He knows, just as well as we now do, are complete and utter nonsense and scientifically unsustainable.

He could start by explaining how evolution fits into His plan. Even the Pope, whom the majority of Christians believe represents God (and who also accepts evolution) isn't quite sure when spirits first started inhabiting human bodies. Perhaps God could start by telling the current Mormon prophet the answer to that, so at least there is some cohesion between God and science. It would at least be a start. We know it won't happen, and if we are entirely honest with ourselves, we also know *why*.

Chapter 19

Doctrine and Covenants
Sections 87 – 98

Section 87
25 December 1832. Kirtland, Ohio.

History.

Added in 1876. 2010 D&C Sec. 87.

Section 87 is thoroughly dealt with in TMD Vol. 3:309-12 (S80-83), and covers what is probably the best known of Smith's claimed prophecies. Most Mormons will invariably cite Section 87 if questioned about Joseph Smith and prophecy. It concerns the American Civil War. The fact that Smith wrote this Section almost three decades before the war occurred is enough to convince any 'believing' member that Smith was a prophet, without further research into the history surrounding the event.

In a nutshell, if this was from God, it was a pointless piece of information as it helped no one and it prevented nothing; if God really 'revealed' such a future event, then why did He not at least also reveal ways possibly to avoid so much death and destruction? The fact is that it was not *just* Joseph Smith who thought the war an eventual, if not even an *imminent* and inevitable event. The sequence of events that ultimately led to the war actually commenced long before Smith was even born – see *TMD 3:309-12 (S80-83)*.

In 1832, the year in which Smith had his 'revelation', a few months prior to it being given, in July, President Andrew Jackson had threatened to use force to end threats of secession in South Carolina caused by the Nullification process. *Everyone* suspected that there would be a war *and* that it would inevitably start in South Carolina. The only thing was, they expected it *shortly*, early in 1833, rather than some three decades later. The fact is the *anticipated* war that Smith 'prophesied' about did not actually happen at all.

As to the *reason* for the revelation; the heading states that the group were actually: "reflecting and reasoning upon African slavery on the American continent and the slavery of the children of men throughout the world." Why? Because *everyone* was constantly talking about it; it was the topic of the day. The possibility of a Civil War was tossed around regularly in the press and in circles such as Smith's during 1832 and in many other years. For details of how Smith may have even plagiarised what was *in* the press at the time, see *Tanner (1987:190-192)*. There you will also find evidence of prophecies by others, including Brigham Young, in the 1860s, that the Civil War would *continue* until the land was *emptied* so the Mormons could return to Missouri – another prophecy that has never been fulfilled.

Smith claimed the slaves would be marshalled and disciplined for *war*; the *remnants left* would also marshal themselves, be angry and "vex" the *Gentiles*; with *sword and bloodshed* the inhabitants of the earth would *mourn*; and with *famine, plague, earthquake, thunder* of heaven and fierce *lightning*, the inhabitants of the earth would be made to feel the *wrath and indignation of God*, "until the consumption decreed hath made a *full end of all nations*". **None** of that remotely happened and the nations are still here. *Why* would it affect all 'nations' if the slaves of America rose up? And what was God so upset about? He predicted war would occur and yet did nothing to help prevent it.

Then, Smith has the Lord declare that the South would call on *Great Britain* and other nations "in order to defend themselves against other nations; and then war shall be poured out upon all nations". This did **not** happen. It is prophecy *unfulfilled*. Naturally, backed into such a corner, apologists postulate that the Civil Ware was just the beginning of this prophecy and that the rest will have transpired by the time the Saviour returns. However, that is certainly not the way Smith's prophecy *reads*.

And what was it that God was so upset about? That the north outmanned the south two-to-one and that well over half a million people died as a result of the conflict seemed only to anger God. If God exists, then perhaps He would be better directing his supposed prophets to help *avoid* such meaningless conflict.

DOCTRINE & COVENANTS – SECTIONS 87-98

Better yet, He could have inspired the nation's leaders who actually did believe in Him, to talk, and work out peaceful solutions rather than fight.

There were always prophecies concerning the need for the blood of the saints to be avenged against anyone who got in the way of their objectives, so it was just arbitrarily added in to whatever else was the order of the day. This Section is no exception, and Smith has the Lord add that all these horrible things will happen "That the cry of the saints, and of the blood of the saints, shall cease to come up into the ears of the Lord of Sabaoth *(see pp. 328-9)*, from the earth, to be avenged of their enemies" (v.7). The only part of this so-called prophecy eventually to be 'fulfilled' was nothing more than a *prediction* of an inevitable event that everybody expected anyway, with or without Smith saying God had told him – and even then it was almost three decades late.

Section 87 – Summary

Prophecies made:	1
Prophecies fulfilled:	0

Prophecies made:

Pr. 33. Smith predicted an imminent Civil War. Slaves would be marshalled and disciplined for *war*; the *remnants left* would also marshal themselves, be angry and "vex" the *Gentiles*; with *sword and bloodshed* the inhabitants of the earth would *mourn*; and with *famine, plague, earthquake, thunder* of heaven and fierce *lightning*, the *inhabitants of the earth* would be made to feel the *wrath and indignation of God*, "until the consumption decreed hath made *a full end of all nations*". Smith has the Lord declare that the south would call on *Great Britain* and other nations "in order to defend themselves against other nations; and then war shall be poured out upon all nations".

Results:

Pr. 33. The predicted war did not occur as and when expected. Almost three decades later, Civil War eventually broke out. Slaves did not vex the gentiles with sword and bloodshed. There were no famines, plagues, or earthquakes associated with the war. Thunder and lightening continued in normal weather patterns. Other than those who believe such nonsense and look for natural disaster which can be attributed to the Lord, no one has suggested they have felt the wrath and indignation of God. The South did not call on Great Britain to help their side of the Civil War and there has certainly not been a full end to all nations.

Section 88
27-28 December 1832 (v.1-126); 3 January 1833 (v.127-141). Kirtland, Ohio.

History.

1835 D&C Sec. VII. 2010 D&C Sec. 88.

This Section effectively consists of three different texts written on different days. We do not learn where the 'break' comes between December 27th and 28th but *JS Papers Vol. 2* does confirm that the 3rd January 1833 part starts at v.127. It is actually an obvious break point as the subjects could not be more different. The latter verses are clearly not a continuation of the same revelation and it is unclear as to why they did not form an entirely new Section. The Lord is speaking.

Here, Smith has the Lord talk about the Celestial, Terrestrial and Telestial kingdoms once again, which he previously discussed in Section 76. The Lord is somewhat repeating himself. Before getting into that, he talks about *now* giving them "another comforter". This is the end of 1832 and they had been baptising and giving the gift of the Holy Ghost for quite some time at this point. So, what is this new comforter? The "Holy Spirit of Promise" (v.3) *is* the Holy Ghost in Mormonism and v.3 also confirms it is the same comforter promised to John – which again, in Mormonism, was also the Holy Ghost. Yet here, the Lord is sending it *again* by all accounts; but then, perhaps not, as this time Smith seems to be equating "the Holy Spirit of promise" directly to "eternal life" (v.4) which is not exactly the way things are portrayed in the Mormon Church today. The Encyclopaedia of Mormonism *(p.652)* confirms the ultimate *manifestation* of the Holy Spirit of Promise is in having one's calling and election made sure *(see p. 319 & TMD Vol. 3:126-30)*, but was that really what Smith was alluding to here?

> **3.** Wherefore, ***I now send upon you another Comforter***, even upon you my friends, that it may abide in your hearts, even ***the Holy Spirit of promise***; which other Comforter is the same that I promised unto my disciples, as is recorded in the testimony of John.
> **4.** This ***Comforter is the promise which I give unto you of eternal life***, even the glory of the celestial kingdom;
> **5.** Which glory is that of the church of the Firstborn, even of God, the holiest of all, through Jesus Christ his Son—
> **6.** He that ascended up on high, as also he descended below all things, in that he comprehended all things, that he might be in all and through all things, ***the light of truth;***

7. Which truth shineth. *This is the light of Christ*. As also *he is in the sun*, and the light of the sun, and the power thereof by which it was made.

8. As also *he is in the moon, and is the light of the moon*, and the power thereof by which it was made;

9. As *also the light of the stars*, and the power thereof by which they were made;

10. And the earth also, and the power thereof, even the earth upon which you stand.

11. And the light which shineth, which giveth you light, is through him who enlighteneth your eyes, which is the same light that quickeneth your understandings;

12. Which *light proceedeth forth from the presence of God to fill the immensity of space—* (Emphasis added).

Before commenting further on the other "comforter", it is worth noting a couple of things the Lord could have and yet did not explain to Smith in this revelation. Firstly, the moon has no light whatsoever (v.8) and when we look at it, all we see is the moon bathed in the light of the sun; not that it much matters if this was just metaphorical. However, if all "light proceedeth forth from the presence of God", then it may have been useful for Smith to have been told just how old everything is and when God started sending that light, as Smith clearly believed, and stated (in Section 77), that the Earth only has a seven thousand year span of existence. The Lord could have advised (and this would have been impressive in Smith's day) that the light we see today from the farthest observable 'star' in the universe (which of course is a *sun*), started it's journey to our eyes (not that we can actually see it with the naked eye, as it is too far away) at the beginning of what we term 'time', some 13.75 ± 0.13 billion years ago. When we look at the stars, we are looking back in time. That is one of the wonders of the universe which the Lord completely failed to explain to Smith.

The 'other comforter' promised to John (v.3) is explained in Mormonism as the 'Holy Ghost' which was sent to attend people in place of Christ after he was gone. Today the Mormon Church claims exclusive right to the Holy Ghost.

The 'light of Christ' is explained as something everyone, not just Mormons, can enjoy. In that context, the above verses are difficult to rationalise. Smith supposedly already had the gift of the Holy Ghost and they had been conferring it on people for well over two years. When the Church was organised in 1830, the Lord allegedly said the following, recorded in Section 20. There is a lot of confusion in Smith's imaginative ideas yet many, such as this, were not exactly cohesive – although I am sure Mormon Church apologists have already devised their excuses for such nonsense.

> **D&C 20:38.** An apostle is an elder, and it is his calling to baptize…
>
> **41.** And to confirm those who are baptized into the church, by the laying on of hands for the baptism of fire and the Holy Ghost, according to the scriptures;
> **42.** And to teach, expound, exhort, baptize, and watch over the church;
> **43.** And to confirm the church by the laying on of the hands, and the giving of the Holy Ghost;

In v.15, we find the Mormon concept that the spirit and the body *combine* to become "the soul of man", a concept which is different from mainstream Christianity in which the 'soul' and the 'spirit' are one and the same. Following repetition about three kingdoms, the Lord explains that the Earth "transgresseth not the law" so it will become celestial. He doesn't explain just how an object such as Earth could 'transgress' anything. Only religion contains such bizarre and meaningless assertions as this – and Mormonism isn't short of them.

As previously discussed, the Earth will be obliterated when our sun finally runs out of fuel in about five billion years time, if it is not destroyed by a comet or other disaster prior to that. The sun should actually implode, due to its own extreme gravitational pull, but thanks to quantum physics which will rescue it from such a fate, it will eventually become a 'white dwarf' instead. The Earth will be destroyed long before that final stage. Nuclear fusion, deep within the solar core, converts 600 million tonnes of hydrogen into helium every second. "Vast though our star is, burning fuel at such a ferocious rate must ultimately have consequences, and one day the sun's fuel source will run out." *(Cox & Forshaw 2011:25-6)*. Smith's God has yet to reveal just how He intends to invent science that will accommodate such adventurous plans as Smith claims he was informed about. Far from our planet becoming celestial and existing forever, a far shorter lifespan is scientifically *inevitable*. Smith's 'prophesy' about the Earth is not scientifically sustainable; however, I am not including it as an unfulfilled prophecy as the final evidence of that will occur long after humans have ceased to exist as a species.

As ever, there is a lot of repetition and filler, and then we get this statement:

> **37.** And there are many kingdoms; for there is no space in the which there is no kingdom; and there is no kingdom in which there is no space, either a greater or a lesser kingdom.

As Mormons, we simply do not 'see' what is written in so-called scripture and we certainly don't *think* for ourselves when something doesn't readily 'compute'. To say there is no space in which there is no kingdom is ridiculous, and it is even more ludicrous to suggest there is no kingdom in which there is no space. Neither statement makes any scientific sense at all.

Although space is far from truly empty as there is plenty of material flying around, and at a molecular level space is littered; that is all relative and to all intents and purposes space is mainly *empty*, with nary a kingdom in sight. So it is with every single atom that makes up each of us, the planets and stars and all the bits and pieces flying around out there, as almost all the space within each atom is *empty* space. We have yet to discover any 'kingdom' other than Earth. When and if we do, life will almost certainly not exactly mirror that of Earth.

To Smith, the sequence and reversal of the words sounded good and he probably felt clever but in reality it was, as usual, just meaningless nonsense.

Smith makes another grave scientific error – but to be fair, as he could not possibly have known the truth, we could forgive him – but for just one thing, he had the *Lord* make the following statement when talking about the universe in v.44: "And they give light to each other in their times and in their seasons, in their minutes, in their hours, in their days, in their weeks, in their months, in their years—all these are one year with God, but not with man."

How could all those different time spans be one year to the Lord? What Smith clearly misunderstood is that time does not exist at all in the sense he portrays it. The Lord would not be concerned with 'years' of *any* length, any more than our mere human concepts of other measurements of time that Smith had the Lord list. It is a form of measurement created by humans, relative to what happens in our solar system – and even then, only from the vantage point of our planet's surface. Leave that, and time changes entirely. One hour *on* the planet is not the same as one hour somewhere else, such as *above* the planet. Time actually moves at a different pace, depending where you are – and where you are going, and how fast, in space. Time is different in different places of the universe. What is 'now' here is not necessarily 'now' somewhere else.

Also, as we have observed, the most distant star we can see (with the right equipment) is not seen 'now'; it is *seen* at the beginning of 'time', 13.75 billion years ago. It could have ceased to exist billions of years ago, possibly long before our own solar system even came into being, yet we can see it as it once *was* – now.

Locally, the time we experience on Earth is *different* to the time we would experience if we were in orbit above the earth, which is why global positioning satellites (GPS) have to regularly 'compensate' for difference in time in respect of navigation systems. Time moves more slowly on the Earth than it does in orbit above the Earth. If they measured time at the same *rate* as on earth, such navigational satellites would soon be telling drivers they were somewhere they were not. (From memory, I think they would be 'out' by about twelve metres a day). Time, as we understand it, bends in space. Gravity affects everything in the universe; all stars, planets and moons and even the smallest of rocks being subject to it. Gravity is in fact 'space-time curvature'. Gravity may seem like a simple concept, but we really don't even begin to fully understand it.

To help us better appreciate the idea of 'time', Professor Brian Cox, in his wonderful BBC TV series on 'The Wonders of the Universe', explained that if you could create a train that could travel very fast around the Earth (say several times every second) and you boarded the train and travelled at that speed for a few days, you would end up a very long way into the future, yet very little time would have passed for you personally. The thing is that in that sense, time 'travel' *is* possible – not that we have the technology to achieve it – yet. You cannot go *back* in time – that is the science fiction part. Having said that, as discussed, we can and we do 'look' back in time, every time we look 'up' at the stars. But even that statement is incorrect, as there is actually no such thing as 'up' (or down). If we look *up* at the stars here in the UK, are people in New Zealand simultaneously looking *down* at stars they can see? They too look 'up'.

The point is that if the Lord really was talking to Smith about 'time' in the manner described, he did not know what he was talking about. Just imagine how magical it would have been, had the Lord explained quantum physics to Smith and described the real truth about the universe in a way we could all appreciate, years before science caught up with such knowledge of time, space and gravity as we now understand it. To have explained the Second Law of Thermodynamics (the law of entropy) would have been impressive; but as ever, nothing Smith ever said, or had the Lord, say was remotely impressive; it was utterly and completely worthless, and in this case – entirely wrong.

In the Mormon missionary lesson manual there is reference to *D&C 88:41-47* regarding *evidence* that God made everything and therefore He must exist. Essentially, all those verses say is – look around you; isn't it obvious there is a creator? That's not *evidence*; it's emotional reaction. Additionally, it depends entirely on what you are looking *at*. If God does exist, some of His creations are positively evil. I have mentioned a few of them elsewhere in my work. We could equally suggest – look at those, isn't it obvious there is *no* creator as He would surely never create such abominations just to discombobulate humans? *(See p. 345 for example).*

From v.51-61, Smith has the Lord tell a parable of twelve workers digging in a field for twelve hours, each of whom is promised, and in turn receives, one of those hours with the presence and the 'light' of the lord who owns the field.

Twelve hour days would not be so popular these days. This is supposed to explain the relevance of time and light and kingdoms thus: "…unto this parable

I will liken all these kingdoms, and the inhabitants thereof—every kingdom in its hour, and in its time, and in its season, even according to the decree which God hath made" (v.61). Once again, if that really was the Lord and that was the best he could do, there is no real hope of ever understanding anything he said via Smith. It is meaningless. Nevertheless, the Lord left his 'sayings' for them to 'ponder'. I doubt anyone ever made much sense of them at all and the Lord may as well not have bothered to say anything.

The Lord does go on to say they only have to 'knock' and 'ask' in his name and he will tell them what they want to know. Why on earth did Smith not ask something sensible? Why did he not ask for a revelation explaining something remotely *useful*? There is not a single solitary *worthwhile* revelation to be found anywhere in the D&C – there is *nothing* of *significance* or merit at all.

In v.73, the Lord says he is going to *hasten* his work. He already declared that he would come 'quickly' on a number of occasions and early Mormons firmly believed he would return during their generation. Recently, a Mormon apostle stated in a General Conference talk that the youth of today don't have to worry about the second coming as it won't be for a very long time yet. Where did he get that notion from, considering the Church had previously settled on the idea that *no* man knows the hour or day of his coming?

> Sometimes you might be tempted to think as I did from time to time in my youth: "The way things are going, the world's going to be over with. The end of the world is going to come before I get to where I should be." Not so! You can look forward to doing it right—getting married, having a family, seeing your children and grandchildren, maybe even great-grandchildren. *(Boyd K. Packer. Counsel to Youth. 181st Semiannual General Conference, 1 Oct 2011. See: Ensign, Nov 2011:19).*

Packer's words more than suggest no return is imminent. In fact, if youth of today can expect to see "grandchildren and maybe even great-grandchildren" then he is confirming *no* return for at least another fifty to seventy years – or more. Joseph Smith himself declared that *no one* will know such things until the Lord actually shows up – not even the angels. That means we do not know when he is *not* coming any more than when he *is* coming. Packer's assertion conflicts with the words spoken by the Lord God Himself to Mormonism's first prophet. He confirmed that the first thing anyone will ever know about when the Lord is coming will be in the very moment that it happens – and *not* before.

> **D&C 49:7.** I, the Lord God, have spoken it; but the hour and the day no man knoweth, neither the angels in heaven, nor shall they know until he comes.

If you are Mormon, you believe the Lord God spoke the above and that Jesus made the following statement to Smith. How does Packer think he knows the Saviour will *not* return until at least 2060 and possibly not before 2080 when Jesus himself said *no one* would have a clue as to when it would (or would not) be? Did Packer somehow work it out, just guess, or was it a direct revelation? Recent prophet Hinckley declared he never had any revelations, so it is unlikely that Packer will claim one. Yet it *has* to be revelation, as if it is just 'speculation', then he was obliged to say that was just his *opinion* – and he didn't; he was quite authoritative about it. He probably knows he is safe, as clearly Jesus is not coming back at all – so Packer can't really go wrong.

D&C 39:21. For the time is at hand; the day or the hour no man knoweth; but it surely shall come.

I mention v.77-79 in *TMD Vol. 4 (p. 378)*. It concerns what they used to teach in 1832, which was a lot more than just the doctrine of the kingdom. It included (v.79) "…things both *in heaven and in the earth*, and *under the earth*; things *which have been*, things *which are*, things which must *shortly come to pass*; things which are at *home*, things which are *abroad*; the *wars* and the *perplexities of the nations*, and the *judgments* which are on the land; and a knowledge also of *countries and of kingdoms*—". In *TMD Volume 4*, I mention that you won't hear any talk in Mormon Church classes these days about things in and under the earth from the past, or we would perhaps see discussion on the *fact of evolution*, about which the Church still remains entirely noncommittal.

Admitting to that will eventually have to come, but it will cause all sorts of theological problems, as discussed elsewhere, as Smith more or less set the Adam and Eve story in stone and he also 'discovered' Adam's altar. Still, the Pope accepts evolution, and three years ago the Church of England (Anglican Church) issued an apology to Charles Darwin for the way they treated him and misunderstood his work, although the apology didn't exactly impress anyone.

Darwin is actually buried in Westminster Abbey and contrary to popular belief the church never really did have a problem with his theories at all. They were quite happy if evolution turned out to be the way God developed His plan. Many stories we hear are not to be believed, both in and out of Mormonism. Science is readily accepted by many religions. Mormonism tends to just ignore much of it – evolution, the age of the Earth, DNA and Native Americans…

Also mentioned in *TMD Vol. 4* is v.81, for the reason that new converts are immediately taught in missionary lessons that once converted, they too must spread the word. The best time to get converts to do that is immediately they accept the 'gospel' while it is still exciting to them. Later, once the novelty wears off, there is less likelihood of enthusiastic conversation about the Church

DOCTRINE & COVENANTS – SECTIONS 87-98

with family and friends. At the teaching stage, if converted, new members will be persuaded to invite family and friends to their baptism. That is the objective. As it says in v.82, "...they are left without excuse, and their sins are upon their own heads." All you have to do is teach people that something is sin and they must then obey related 'rules' in order to avoid it. Upon becoming a Mormon, it immediately becomes a 'sin' *not* to tell others about it. And why? "That their souls may escape the wrath of God, the desolation of abomination which awaits the wicked, both in this world and in the world to come" (v.85). That's quite an incentive really. As always, the Mormon God uses fear – of failure this time.

Next, the Lord (or at least Smith) starts lying again about when the signs of the end of the world will occur.

> **87.** For not many days hence and the earth shall tremble and reel to and fro as a drunken man; and the sun shall hide his face, and shall refuse to give light; and the moon shall be bathed in blood; and the stars shall become exceedingly angry, and shall cast themselves down as a fig that falleth from off a fig tree.

The Lord talks about "not many days hence" and yet he doesn't relate such a designation to the way humans equate time. Here we are; not days, weeks, months, or even years or decades later; it is almost two *centuries* since Smith's God (or Jesus – whichever you prefer the Lord to be) made the pronouncement. At the time of writing, it has actually been well over 65,000 days since he said it would *not* be *many* days. But it has been many, *many* days; and Packer wants to push it back another 25,000 – or more. Even in the devious world of Mormonism, they teach that leading people to believe something that is not true, by not telling all the truth or telling only part of the truth, is in fact a *lie*. God is not supposed to do that. If you believe Smith, here God clearly does.

No one would have remotely taken "not many days hence" in 1832, to actually mean a couple of centuries or at *least* 65,000 days, with probably many thousands more to come. Smith had already taught, and thought he had been told at least twice, that the second coming would occur by 1891. That would have been about 21,500 days or so; "not [that] many days hence". Twice as long again since 1891, and there is still no sign of anything happening. Other that is than superstition and belief in the supernatural coming into question more than it once did and science becoming more understood and accepted.

One day, science (particularly quantum physics) will help us understand even more and religion will continue to help us understand less and less until it becomes completely obsolete. Religion may never have survived at all if people had learned about volcanoes, astronomy, thunder and weather patterns *before* inventing gods to represent such things.

THE MORMON DELUSION

Through to the end of the December 1832 segment of this Section, Smith continues to have the Lord explain the sequence of events that will apparently transpire before and during the apocalypse. It is more than reminiscent of the book of Revelation and is surely where Smith stole those ideas. It has no point, unless you are inclined toward a belief that God is (and will be) that vindictive. Fear is still His prime motivator, and that is certainly unbecoming of any deity. But that is just my opinion, and I have tried to steer clear of opinion and stick to the facts, so let us move on.

Next, we have the January 1833 verses where the subject matter completely changes. Smith has the Lord ramble on about his 'house' for the school of the prophets *(See Sec 94, pp. 332-3)*. The Lord has some very strange requirements for them. Naturally, Smith is to be 'first' in the house. This is what the Lord apparently said (v.127-41).

The house is to be prepared for the presidency to instruct all officers (only men) from high priests – on down to the deacons. Smith, as president, shall be 'first' teacher in the house of God which idea apparently is "beautiful, that he may be an example". Smith (the teacher) first has to pray on his knees in token of the everlasting covenant. Then, whoever enters next, the teacher is to get up and raise his hands to heaven and 'salute' the brother (it never was a sister and still isn't because women cannot hold the Priesthood – *yet*), with these words: "Art thou a brother or brethren? I salute you in the name of the Lord Jesus Christ, in token or remembrance of the everlasting covenant, in which covenant I receive you to fellowship, in a determination that is fixed, immovable, and unchangeable, to be your friend and brother through the grace of God in the bonds of love, to walk in all the commandments of God blameless, in thanksgiving, forever and ever. Amen."

If anyone isn't worthy of that 'salutation' they should be thrown out. If they are worthy, they must also raise their hands and say the same thing back to the teacher, or – short version, they can just say Amen "in token of the same". Why anyone would bother to repeat all that when they could just say 'Amen' and be done with it is beyond me. Equally, why would the Lord give them a choice?

But really, why would a God want anyone to speak such nonsense at all? The Lord says this is an 'ensample' for a salutation in the "house of God". This was not recorded as being spoken after that era and certainly does not appear in the Mormon temple ceremony, so having gone to all this trouble, the Lord didn't seem to feel the need for a continuance of this 'ensample' for very long, if it was ever used at all.

Incidentally, 'ensample' is Middle English (c.1300) from Old French and it survived due to its use in the New Testament. Smith's deity obviously liked archaic language. It simply means 'example' and you would think that the Lord would keep up to date with at least the most common parts of his speech – which was actually all over the place, containing a mixture of Middle and Early

Modern as well as Modern English. Smith had the Lord use 'ensample' several times in the D&C for no logical reason at all, other than the usual – to look clever. It is illogical for the Lord to use a Middle English word among his Early Modern English speech just because the KJV retained it in 1611. The fact that 'example' had long replaced it would not have been missed by a God.

They are also to perform the ordinance of washing of feet "for unto this end was the ordinance of washing of feet instituted." If that were true, perhaps we should ask why it soon fell by the wayside, along with the 'school'. Washing of feet is still used today, but not in connection with such things as schools of prophets, or even the temple endowment where Smith had introduced it in the Kirtland Temple on 21 January 1836. The later endowment that Smith invented in Nauvoo was entirely different to his Kirtland ideas and largely influenced by his recent exposure to Masonic ritual which he incorporated in large measure into the new endowment *(See TMD Vol. 3, Sec 3)*.

'Washing of feet' was then not part of the endowment ceremony – but it did become part of the 'Second Endowment'; something more prolific in the early Church. It had all but disappeared completely by the mid-twentieth century but is now alive and well, even disseminated down as far as some Stake Presidents. Indeed, most Mormons may never have even heard of its continued existence. Washing of feet is used during the 'Second Anointing' or 'Second Endowment' ceremony, now given to a select few who have their 'calling and election made sure'. It means that no matter what they may do next, they have already done enough to ensure their eternal salvation. *(See TMD Vol. 3:126-30)*.

Despite the Lord declaring 'washing of feet' was instituted for the school of the prophets, when they also had to partake of the sacrament, it is today used in an entirely different setting. The Lord takes the time to say the teacher should "gird himself according to the pattern given in the thirteenth chapter of John's testimony concerning me" (v.141). To save people looking that up, he could have just said, tie a towel around your waist and dry their feet with it, as that is all John 13 says. The ordinance was to be administered by the *president* of the Church. Today, first hand reports confirm that it is often performed by one of the apostles.

****

History of the Church Vol. 1:315-6.
4 January 1833.

History

Letter from Joseph Smith to N. E. Seaton, an editor – not included in the D&C.

> And now I am prepared to say by the authority of Jesus Christ, that not many years shall pass away before the United States shall present such a scene of bloodshed as has not a parallel in the history of our nation; pestilence, hail, famine, and earthquake will sweep the wicked of this generation from off the face of the land, to open and prepare the way for the return of the lost tribes of Israel from the north country. The people of the Lord, those who have complied with the requirements of the new covenant, have already commenced gathering together to Zion, which is in the state of Missouri, therefore I declare unto you the warning which the Lord has commanded to declare unto this generation, remembering that the eyes of my Maker are upon me and that to him I am accountable for every word I say wishing nothing worse to my fellow-men than their eternal salvation; therefore, "Fear God, and give glory to Him, for the hour of His judgment is come." Repent ye, repent ye, and embrace the everlasting covenant, and flee to Zion, before the overflowing scourge overtake you, for there are those now living upon the earth whose eyes shall not be closed in death until they see all these things, which I have spoken, fulfilled. Remember these things; call upon the Lord while He is near, and seek Him while He may be found, is the exhortation of your unworthy servant. [Signed] JOSEPH SMITH, JUN.

The day after concluding Section 88, which included such rhetoric as found in v.87 *(see p. 317)*, Smith wrote a lengthy letter to the editor of a newspaper, and the above prophecy was the final paragraph. It was not canonised, thus it is 'excused' by the Church and not considered a real prophecy. Considering later verses in Section 88 include the following, surely it reflected prophetic words.

> **89.** For after your testimony cometh the testimony of earthquakes, that shall cause groanings in the midst of her, and men shall fall upon the ground and shall not be able to stand.
> **90.** And also cometh the testimony of the voice of thunderings, and the voice of lightnings, and the voice of tempests, and the voice of the waves of the sea heaving themselves beyond their bounds.
> **91.** And all things shall be in commotion; and surely, men's hearts shall fail them; for fear shall come upon all people.

That seems like a prelude to the paragraph extracted from Smith's letter. However, it is included out of historical interest rather than listed as unfulfilled prophecy as it was not included in the D&C.

****

DOCTRINE & COVENANTS – SECTIONS 87-98

Section 89
27 February 1833. Kirtland, Ohio.

History.

1835 D&C Sec. LXXX. 2010 D&C Sec. 89.

This is a very well known Section within Mormonism and concerns the modern era health code. It is discussed in depth in *TMD Vol. 2:153-66. (S84-97)*. Much of what it contains was completely ignored in the early Church and for many decades after it was 'received'. This was partly due to the fact that many of Smith's closest associates knew very well that it was just the result of a joke. In the early twentieth century, it was decided for a time that German beer was alright to drink as it was less alcoholic than American beer.

The situation that arose to evoke the 'revelation' started with a combination of the efforts of the Kirtland Temperance Society (which was founded in 1830 and predominantly non-Mormon), who were opposed to alcohol, tobacco and eating too much meat, and Smith training men in his 'School of Elders' every day. They met in a small smoke-filled room above Emma's kitchen, tobacco juice being spit all over the floor. Emma had the job of cleaning up following the meetings. As ever, what resulted was not revealed from God to Smith; he just copied ideas regularly published by the Kirtland Temperance Society and added in tea and coffee. The situation and results are available from several sources. This is just one:

> Thus Emma, faced almost daily with "having to clean so filthy a floor" as was left by the men chewing tobacco, spoke to Joseph about the matter. David Whitmer's account supports Brigham Young's description. "Some of the men were excessive chewers of the filthy weed, and their disgusting slobbering and spitting caused **Mrs. Smith ...** to make the ironical remark that 'It **would be a good thing if a revelation could be had declaring the use of tobacco a sin, and commanding it's suppression.'** The matter was taken up and joked about, one of the brethren suggested that **the revelation should also provide for a total abstinence from tea and coffee** drinking, intending this **as a counter 'dig' at the sisters**." Sure enough the subject was afterward taken up in dead earnest, and the 'Word of Wisdom' was the result. *(David Whitmer).* (Des Moines Daily News, 16 Oct 1886:20 c. in: Newell & Avery 1994:47, also c: An Historical Analysis of the Word of Wisdom, Paul H. Peterson - Masters Thesis [no location provided]; also: c. in Tanner 1987:406. See also Tanner 1987: Ch. 26 for excellent coverage). (Emphasis added).

Section 89 of the D&C is one of many sections written to appear, not just as inspired words but rather, as if it came directly from the mouth of the Lord, as verse 4 includes "...thus saith the Lord unto you..." It prohibits the use of "wine" and "strong drinks", "tobacco" and "hot drinks". It also states that meat should be eaten sparingly, "only in times of winter, or of cold, or famine".

However, upon reading the 1835 text, we discover that there was originally *no* comma before "only". It *originally* read "Nevertheless, they are to be used sparingly; and it is pleasing unto me, that they should **not be used only** in times of winter or of cold, or famine." The context alters completely with the added comma. It appears today between 'used' and 'only' in the Mormon D&C and the comma makes all the difference. The RLDS (Community of Christ) does *not* include a comma and they accept (and promote) the idea that it means meat should be used sparingly (sensibly) but *not* only in times of winter.

The idea wasn't to last in the Mormon Church either, even *with* the added comma and whilst it still appears in black and white including the comma, as if directly from the mouth of the Lord, today it is completely ignored and never discussed. It seems that no one wants to pay homage to what the Lord required by actually adhering to the way that part of the revelation is accepted.

As this Section was published *without* the comma in *Times and Seasons Vol. 3 page 801; Vol. 5:736*; and is also contained in *Comprehensive History of the Church, Vol. 1:306* without the comma, it appears to be a late typographical error in the Mormon D&C, sometime *after* 1835. Thus the RLDS Doctrine and Covenants is shown to contain the correct rendition of this passage. Why hasn't the Mormon God told any of his Mormon prophets to get rid of the surplus comma so members can eat meat all year round without feeling guilty?

Would it not have been easier to do what the Community of Christ did and remove the comma, which did not originally appear, and thus clarify matters? As things stand, the Lord is depicted as saying *don't* eat meat unless it is a time of winter, cold or famine, and yet no one takes a blind bit of notice. Perhaps it would be too embarrassing to follow in the footsteps of a smaller organisation that Mormons consider to be a schism. Whatever the Community of Christ is, they have got this right and the mainstream Mormon Church has got it wrong.

I will leave the reader to review *TMD Vol. 2:153-66 (S84-97)* where there is comprehensive coverage of this Section (except the above details on meat).

Section 90
8 March 1833. Kirtland, Ohio.

History.

1835 D&C Sec. LXXXIV. 2010 D&C Sec. 90.

Here, we are back to "thus saith the Lord" and Smith's sins are forgiven – yet again; as are sins of Frederick G. Williams and Sidney Rigdon. Interestingly, the Lord specifically says Williams and Rigdon "are accounted as equal with thee in holding the keys of this last kingdom" so we should ask why neither of them took over the Church when Joseph Smith was killed.

Well, Williams was excommunicated in 1839 for apostasy, although he did rejoin the Church in 1840, but he was no longer eligible for the leadership.

Rigdon was the surviving member of the First Presidency and he did seek to run the Church. Smith and Rigdon had not been getting along very well in the year prior to Smith's death and Rigdon had also been suffering from poor health, although he was Smith's running mate in Smith's campaign to become President of the United States at the time of his demise.

In 1843, Smith had wanted to replace Rigdon with Amasa M. Lyman in the First Presidency but the congregation voted to keep Rigdon in place instead; something that would never happen now. In those days, members really did have a voice in such matters. Smith was clearly unimpressed at not getting his own way, which no doubt he claimed was the Lord's way, and Church history records that after the vote Smith stood up and said ""I have thrown him off my shoulders, and you have again put him on me. You may carry him, but I will not" *(HC Vol. 6:49)*.

During the succession crisis following Smith's death, Rigdon's 'pitch' for leadership was somewhat pathetic by comparison with Brigham Young's more dynamic presentation. I wonder what would have happened had Rigdon had the forethought and temerity to cite D&C 90:6 and remind members that the Lord himself had declared that he (Rigdon) was "accounted as *equal* with thee [Joseph Smith] in holding the keys of this last kingdom". What would people have said then? A more dynamic character (such as Young) would no doubt have made a real issue out of that in order to win the day had the situation been reversed. The stronger 'character' won the day – not the Lord's 'chosen'.

The result all came down to the persuasive powers of the individual and most certainly had nothing to do with the Lord. If it had, then the Lord would surely have made the succession process much clearer long before Smith died and all would have been well from the start. Instead, several schisms were founded and although Brigham Young retained the majority, the Church was somewhat decimated. There was no help from the Lord in avoiding the mess it created; he didn't exactly prepare the way for a smooth continuation of Church leadership; and that mistake stands to tell its own story in terms of the *truth*.

The process of succession was still in dispute decades later and infighting within the Quorum of Twelve saw long delays in the calling and sustaining of successive prophets; a sure sign that no God was ever involved in the process.

A lot of filler follows, amid which the Lord says they are to teach everyone. He will also say when it is time for specific properties, then occupied by named people, to be sold and they should wait for him to say when that should be. The Lord is still taking an interest in the detail and yet not helping them at all with anything worthwhile that would have helped in any practical way. We have yet to find a revelation that provided *useful* suggestions for the saints.

After saying that they should keep their families small, by not taking in too many others, Smith has the Lord specifically mention Vienna Jaques, saying she is to be given money to go to Zion and then "receive an inheritance from the hand of the bishop; That she may settle down in peace inasmuch as she is faithful, and not be idle in her days from thenceforth" (v.30-1). Other than the odd mention of Emma Smith, Joseph's first wife (once in Section 25 and three times in Section 132, when the Lord tells her she will be "destroyed" unless she accepts Smith's other wives), how often do we see a *woman* mentioned in this way in the D&C? *Never*. Why would the Lord take such an interest in just one woman out of the many who were in the same situation?

Perhaps, as some historians have claimed, she was one of Smith's plural wives. I didn't find enough evidence in my own research to conclude that for certain, so I have her listed among additional 'possible' wives of Joseph Smith in *TMD Vol. 1*. However, several other historians conclude she became a Smith wife around 1832-3 and in reviewing this statement, perhaps they are correct in their assertions, as there is really no other reason for her to be picked out for such special treatment. The Lord doesn't usually mention women at all.

Smith must have been having some trouble with people in "Zion" as the Lord suggests Smith write to them and say "I have called you also to preside over Zion in mine own due time" (v.32). Smith's God liked the phrase "in mine own due time" but sometimes, as in this case, it really makes no sense at all to use it. Therefore, says the Lord, let them stop bothering me about it. They must repent and angels will rejoice. The Lord is not exactly happy with everyone. (Is he ever?) In particular, His is "not well pleased" with William E. McLellin or Sidney Gilbert – and not for the first time. They must of course repent.

In signing off, the Lord makes a specific prophecy that remains unfulfilled.

> **36.** But verily I say unto you, that I, the Lord, will contend with Zion, and plead with her strong ones, and chasten her until she overcomes and is clean before me.
> **37.** For she shall not be removed out of her place. I, the Lord, have spoken it. Amen.

DOCTRINE & COVENANTS – SECTIONS 87-98

Here, the Lord says Zion will *not* be removed out of her place and yet the saints were driven out, never to return, just a few short years later.

Section 90 – Summary

Prophecies made: 1
Prophecies fulfilled: 0

Prophecies made:

Pr. 34. The Lord declared that "Zion will not be removed out of her place. I, the Lord, have spoken it." (v.37).

Results:

Pr. 34. A few short years later, having unsuccessfully tried to establish Zion, the saints were driven from the territory, never to return. The people of Zion were well and truly moved out of their place and went to reside in Utah. They have never returned to Independence and Zion does *not* exist there.

Section 91
9 March 1833. Kirtland, Ohio.

History.

1835 D&C Sec. XCII. 2010 D&C Sec. 91.

It seems that when Smith came across the Apocrypha, he really didn't want to bother with reviewing that in addition to the Bible. He had the Lord say that it was *"mostly* translated correctly" but that many things were not true. I doubt that it would have taken much for the Lord to simply list any minor corrections, but as Smith was making all this up, he would have had to have made some uncomfortable decisions about a book that is highly suspect in great part. If readers have read the Apocrypha, they will know what I mean. Smith clearly did not want to get involved with it. The Lord said not to bother, if anyone wants to understand it, they can do so by the spirit. Of course, He could have said that about the Bible. The Mormon Church does not use the Apocrypha or specifically recommend it. Members can read it if they want to.

Section 92
15 March 1833. Kirtland, Ohio.

History.

1835 D&C Sec. XCIII. 2010 D&C Sec. 92.

Two verses containing just over eighty words confirm Frederick G. Williams should be received into the 'united order' and be a 'lively member' in it – and then the Lord adds that everyone else should join too. That meant giving up everything the person owned to the Church and receiving back what they needed. Williams had been sustained a member of the First Presidency and Smith needed him on side regarding the order. We previously discussed that despite the fact the idea was tried more than once, it never worked and was soon abandoned. Yet the Lord had stated it was to last *forever*. He didn't seem to know human nature very well. *(See Sec. 70: Pr. 26; Sec. 78: Pr. 27; Sec 82: Pr. 28).*

Section 93
6 May 1833. Kirtland, Ohio.

History.

1835 D&C Sec. LXXXII. 2010 D&C Sec. 93.

Back to one of Smith's classic openings for this Section – the Lord, who claims he is in the Father and the Father is in him and that they are one, says those who repent and obey him will see his face. On this occasion, forgiveness is apparently taken as read. In v.6-18, the Lord is speaking first hand about John's testimony of him. It doesn't match anything biblical. Smith had made a few changes to John 1 in his *Inspired Revision* but even that isn't close to this D&C 'revelation'. Smith's monotheism shines through in these verses though. He has the Lord quote John as saying that the Lord, who is speaking as *Jesus* here, was before the world was, and that "he was the Word" (in the Bible the 'word' was of course *God*) and that he created everything; "The worlds were made by him; men were made by him; all things were made by him, and through him, and of him" (v.10).

There are several verses explaining that we were also there in the beginning as spirits and that "Intelligence, or the light of truth, was not created or made, neither indeed can be" (v.29). Naturally, men who reject the spirit of truth will be condemned. Those who thus defile their body or 'temple' will have their temple destroyed. It's the same old story, just as Smith had the Lord tell his own wife Emma regarding acceptance of his plural wives; do as you are told or you will be destroyed. I have mentioned before that if God needs to resort to such tactics, he is not very good at being a God. There are far better ways to encourage people to follow you – even humans can work that out. The fear factor of religion is as archaic as the gods that were first created to instil that fear on behalf of early tribal leaders. Nothing has changed – except human intelligence. The problem is that the majority of people just don't seem to use it to determine the facts and recognise what is clear and obvious fiction.

Frederick G. Williams is still in trouble with the Lord (v.41). As a member of the First Presidency, you would have thought the Lord would be pleased with him. If he was that bad, why did the Lord prompt Smith to call him as a counsellor? Was Smith just after Williams' assets?

Apparently the Lord doesn't feel Williams has taught his children properly; such detail for the Lord to get involved with. Likewise, Sidney Rigdon hasn't taught his children correctly and they must both set their houses in order.

Next, even Joseph Smith hasn't kept the commandments and must repent. Smith doesn't include that idea very often but it crops up occasionally for good measure. We quickly learn that although Smith must "stand rebuked", it isn't really his fault – it's his family: "Your family must needs repent and forsake some things, and give more earnest heed unto your sayings, or be removed out of their place" (v.48). Note that as ever, if they don't listen to Smith, even his own family will be "removed out of their place". Smith valued his autonomy.

The Lord is not finished yet and next turns on Bishop Newel K. Whitney who also must "be chastened, and set in order his family". His family must be more diligent or they will also be removed out of their place. The Lord is certainly not pleased with the leaders' families. Or was it just that the families were not fully supportive of some of the things that Smith wanted Williams, Rigdon and Whitney to do, and their objections caused Smith to dream up these ideas in order to more firmly control them. It is certain that Smith didn't talk to the families – that would have been left to the three men, if they even bothered.

Rigdon is to set off on his mission and Smith is to hurry up and finish his "translation" of the scriptures. That is a strange thing to say as there was no *translation* involved with the KJV that Smith was rewriting. The resulting work was called an 'Inspired Revision' rather than it being a retranslation.

They were also to "obtain a knowledge of history, and of countries, and of kingdoms, of laws of God and man, and all this for the salvation of Zion. Amen" v.53). All very commendable, except the last part – there never was any salvation for Zion.

Section 95
1 June 1833. Kirtland, Ohio.

History.

1835 D&C Sec. XCV. 2010 D&C Sec. 95.

The heading in modern editions of the D&C explains that this revelation *"is a continuation of divine directions to build houses for worship and instruction, especially the house of the Lord"* (italics in original), citing *Sec. 88:119-36 and Sec. 94*. The reader may note that we have skipped Section 94 and moved directly from Section 93 to 95. This is because Section 94 was not written on 6 May as stated in the current header but, according to *JS Papers Vol. 2:723*, was recorded on 2 August, placing it after Section 97; so, if anything, it is actually Section 94 that continues from this Section.

Naturally, the Lord loves them but still he needs to 'chasten' and 'rebuke' them because they have sinned (again), but they will of course be forgiven (again). This time, the problem the Lord seems to have is that they have not yet built his house. The Lord says many have been ordained who *he* has called, but few of them are *chosen*; which idea Smith stole from Matthew 20:16 and 22:14. Smith uses that phrase twice more, in Section 121:34 & 40 *(see p. 421)*.

On this occasion, the Lord claims that those who he himself called, and yet have not been 'chosen', have sinned and are "walking in darkness at noon-day" (v.6). A good question would be – why then did the Lord call them in the first place? He claims that he personally did so in v.5 and has no one to blame but himself if they are not also chosen.

The Lord says that "for this purpose" they must hold a solemn assembly. Their fasting and mourning can "come up into the ears of the Lord of Sabaoth" *(also mentioned in Sec. 87, 88 & 98)*, which the Lord then informs us is "by interpretation, the creator of the first day, the beginning and the end". In fact 'Sabaoth' does not mean that at all. It is the Hebrew plural form of 'host' or 'army', so 'by interpretation' Smith should have said that it meant 'Lord of Hosts' but he just made up an alternate and completely incorrect 'translation'. I am sure the Mormon Church would argue that if Smith's Lord claimed it meant that, then it did. The problem is that it really *didn't*; Smith's Lord was *wrong*.

Now they are commanded to get on with building the Lord's house – and he is not very happy about all the arguing that has been going on in the school of the prophets.

The Lord is going to show three of them (whom they must pick and ordain) how the temple should be built. He goes on to say how big it should be, so that was a start for them. However, the Lord's ideas on what should go on *in* the temple are a far cry from what happened in the later Nauvoo temple, to say nothing of what goes on in Mormon temples today. The temple was to be used for sacrament, preaching, fasting, prayer and offering up most holy desires. The higher inner part was to be used for the school of the apostles.

The Lord signs off in an unusual manner, as Son Ahman or "in other words" Alphus or Omegus – even Jesus Christ your Lord. 'Ahman' is not a real word, but Smith had used it previously in Section 78 *(see p. 291)*. 'Alphus' and 'Omegus' aren't real words either. It is easy to see what they are supposed to mean, but Smith's attempt at making them appear rather special and directly from the Lord fall foul of any real translation from the original. He could have simply used Alpha and Omega which, as most people know, are the first and last letters of the Greek alphabet and can symbolise 'the first and the last' in the religious sense.

Even Alphas or Omegas would have been better, but even then, not really because in translating from the Hebrew or Phoenician 'aleph', the Greeks added 'a' because Greek words cannot end in most consonants. The sense of "beginning of anything" is from the late 14th century and that of "first in a sequence" is from the 1620s. Omega, from c.1400, comes from Medieval Greek; and from classical Greek, O mega "big 'O' " (in contrast to omicron "little 'o' "), so called because the vowel was long in ancient Greek. In any format, even in Smith's strange attempt at being clever, the 's' would signify plural, which doesn't work either. Smith got it all wrong – again; unless you choose to accept the idea the Lord really did say it and that *he* got it wrong.

Section 95 – Summary

Non-prophetic revelation: 1

1. Their fasting and mourning can "come up into the ears of the Lord of Sabaoth" *(also mentioned in Sec. 87, 88 & 98)*, which the Lord then informs us is "by interpretation, the creator of the first day, the beginning and the end".

In fact 'Sabaoth' does not mean that at all. It is the Hebrew plural form of 'host' or 'army' so 'by interpretation' Smith should have said that it meant 'Lord of Hosts' but he just made up an alternate and completely incorrect 'translation', exposing yet again, the fact that the Lord was *not* speaking.

THE MORMON DELUSION

Section 96
4 June 1833. Kirtland, Ohio.

History.

1835 D&C Sec. XCVI. 2010 D&C Sec. 96.

Here, Smith has the Lord declare that Newel K. Whitney should take charge of the temple area and the surrounding lots which should be given to those who seek 'inheritances', which they can decide in council among themselves.

It is also 'expedient' that his work should go forth. The Lord also seems favourable towards 'John Johnson' and proclaims he is actually a descendant of 'Joseph'. Johnson will have eternal life – if he keeps the commandments of course. Naturally, Johnson should become a member of the *order* as he was prosperous and owned a large farm. John Johnson was the father of the Johnson family, which including Luke and Lyman *(Secs. 68 & 75)*, and it was his farm where the Smith's had been staying when Joseph got tarred and feathered on 24 March 1832 *(see p. 299)*. As with many of the early Mormon leaders, John Johnson did not stay the course and was later "dropped from the High Council and excommunicated". *(See: A House Divided: The John Johnson Family. Ensign, Feb 1979. c. HC Vol. 2:510 & Jenson, Vol. 5:32)*.

Section 97
2 August 1833. Kirtland, Ohio.

History.

1835 D&C Sec. LXXXI. 2010 D&C Sec. 97.

The Lord starts off this section by confirming that he is speaking – with his voice no less, "I speak unto you with my voice" which is a little bizarre. For once, he isn't angry and berating everyone for sinning. He actually seems in a good mood for a change and even complements one person for his faithfulness.

I would say that's a first, but I am sure he has done so before – somewhere. He is pleased with Parley P. Pratt for what he has done with the school. The 'residue' of the school will be shown mercy but they need to be chastened. The good mood didn't last long. Those willing to observe the covenants through 'sacrifice' will be accepted. Then the Lord quickly moves on to asking about his house again. It is to be built 'speedily' by tithing the people. It seems that is where the sacrifice mentioned comes in.

DOCTRINE & COVENANTS – SECTIONS 87-98

This concerns the proposed temple in Zion (Independence, Missouri). If they build it and don't defile it, then his "glory shall rest upon it" (v.15). In v.16 the 'Lord' now seems to become God. "Yea, and my presence shall be there, for I will come into it, and all the pure in heart that shall come into it shall see God". Then the promises (that were never fulfilled) just spill out: "...if Zion do these things she shall prosper, and spread herself and become very glorious, very great, and very terrible." Very great, and very *terrible*? This will be the result: "And the nations of the earth shall honor her, and shall say: Surely Zion is the city of our God, and surely Zion cannot fall, neither be moved out of her place, for God is there, and the hand of the Lord is there" (v.19). That was wishful thinking on the part of Smith. If that really was the Lord speaking, he couldn't have been more wrong; yet Smith claims they were the words of the Lord – he was after all "speaking – with his voice" as he declared in v.1.

Predictably, we then get the promise of vengeance if things don't go to plan. It will come 'speedily', but obviously the Lord's idea of speedily is yet to be determined as there hasn't been any measurable vengeance seen as yet.

"Who shall escape it" asks v.22? Everyone, it seems, unless natural disaster and adverse weather conditions really are the work of a truly vindictive God. Such a God is consequently not worth even considering following. The Lord's "scourge" is going to pass over "by night and by day" and won't stop until he returns. There is no evidence of "the report thereof shall vex all people" actually being reported or vexing anyone at all. As ever, the Lord's indignation is kindled against abominations and wicked works. Isn't it time Smith thought of something better for the Lord to say rather than always repeat the same old complaints?

Nevertheless, says the Lord, Zion will escape all that "if she observe to do all things whatsoever I have commanded her". If Zion doesn't do as she is told – God help them too. The Lord confirms that he will visit her "according to her works, with sore affliction, with pestilence, with plague, with sword, with vengeance, with devouring fire." Well, that's about as mean as you can get. A couple of months later, the saints were driven out never to return. Zion, along with its temple, was never built and it doesn't exist. *(See Sec. 101, p. 340 on).*

If Zion doesn't sin any more she will be blessed, but the Lord, who had just said he is coming again – which makes him Jesus, now becomes *God*, in an interchanging role consistent with Smith's monotheistic view of the time. God does use some strange phraseology for a God – "multiplying a multiplicity of blessings" upon them. *(See: The Final Analysis, Part 3).*

27. Nevertheless, let it be read this once to her ears, that I, the Lord, have accepted of her offering; and if she sin no more none of these things shall come upon her;

28. And I will bless her with blessings, and multiply a multiplicity of blessings upon her, and upon her generations forever and ever, saith the Lord your God. Amen.

Section 97 – Summary

Prophecies made:	1
Prophecies fulfilled:	0

Prophecies made:

Pr. 35. v.19: "And the nations of the earth shall honor her, and shall say: Surely Zion is the city of our God, and surely Zion cannot fall, neither be moved out of her place, for God is there, and the hand of the Lord is there."

Results:

Pr. 35. The saints never did build a temple in Zion as commanded. They were subsequently driven out of Missouri following the Extermination Order.

Section 94
2 August 1833. Kirtland, Ohio.

History.

1835 D&C Sec. LXXXIII. 2010 D&C Sec. 94.

The Section header dates this to 6 May 1833 but the *JS Papers, Vol. 2:723* corrects it to 2 August of that year. In early January 1833, Smith had recorded the latter part of Section 88 which included some instructions about the 'house' that the Lord wanted built. Now, Smith has the Lord reveal more detail; "ye shall commence a work of laying out and preparing a beginning and foundation of the city of the stake of Zion, here in the land of Kirtland, beginning at my house. And behold, it must be done according to the pattern which I have given unto you" (v.1-2).

The first 'lot', south of the temple, was to be a building for the presidency and some details about the size and interior are furnished. Construction was never even started. Then the Lord says that the second lot south of the temple should be for a printing house, which the Lord also then describes. It is exactly the same as the first house – fifty-five by sixty-five feet in the inner court, with a lower and a higher court *(v.4-5 & 11)*. That too was never built. The printing operation ended up being housed in the attic of the Kirtland temple.

Hyrum Smith was to have the next lot south, and then north of the temple, Reynolds Cahoon and Jared Carter were each to have lots, but they were not to be built until commanded. These three also formed a 'building committee'.

The Kirtland temple was dedicated on 7 March 1836 but within two years Kirtland had become virtually abandoned by the saints. Following the 'Kirtland Safety Society' banking scandal, Joseph and Hyrum Smith fled Kirtland in the night, in fear of retribution from countless angry saints, including several of the apostles, who had lost everything. Some new schisms emerged following the debacle. Warren Parrish formed 'The Church of Christ' and took control of the Kirtland temple and other Church assets. The new church was incorporated in 1838 and Martin Harris, led by Warren Parrish, excommunicated Joseph Smith and Sidney Rigdon who had relocated to Far West, Missouri. *(See TMD Vol. 2:58 & Vol. 3:42-44)*.

Confusion over who owned what went on for years following the death of Joseph Smith in 1844, with several factions laying claim to the Kirtland temple. At one point, it was used to house livestock during the winter, with milk cows in the basement and sheep on the ground floor. Eventually, a probate court in Ohio sold the temple, which had reportedly cost some $40,000 to build (that's about $967,000 in purchasing power today), to pay off some of the outstanding debts still owed by Joseph Smith's estate. Eventually, legal ownership ended up with the Reorganised Church, now Community of Christ, which owns and operates the Kirtland temple today.

The proposed buildings and extensive detail provided by the Lord did not materialise as directed or specified. That could amount to unfulfilled prophecy, or at least revelation that did not transpire as the Lord had stated. Undoubtedly, the Church would argue that it was not prophecy and not even revelation which *had* to be instigated. It was just a good idea at the time, but events overtook the plausibility of having it ultimately fully instigated. I am not including this debacle in either category. We have identified much more important issues than this. Suffice it for us to ask *why* the Lord went into all that detail and dictated those requirements when he must have *known* none of it would ever happen?

THE MORMON DELUSION
Section 98
6 August 1833. Kirtland, Ohio.

History.

1835 D&C Sec. LXXXV. 2010 D&C Sec. 98.

The Lord once again confirms that their "prayers have entered into the ears of the Lord of Sabaoth", an expression that also appears in Sections 87, 88 and 95 *(see pp. 328-9 for comments)*. There were problems in Missouri and Smith was several hundred miles away, so the header makes the 'faith promoting' but entirely unsustainable claim that *"Although some news of the problems in Missouri had no doubt reached the Prophet in Kirtland (nine hundred miles away), the seriousness of the situation could have been known to him at this date only by revelation."* (Italics in original). Only by revelation?

There is nothing in this Section to remotely justify such a claim. The Lord doesn't tell Smith that the troubles are extensive, any more than he gives him a lasting solution to the problems. The Lord just says the prayers are heard and makes promises that are not kept, before getting embroiled in not being happy with the local saints and then moving on to other nonsense that we will come on to. There is nothing to indicate what Smith did or did not know about what was going on in Missouri or just how much trouble was brewing. The Lord doesn't even mention Missouri and the claim in the header is pure speculation.

The prayers were apparently "recorded with this seal and testament—the Lord hath sworn and decreed that they shall be granted" (v.2). The Lord gives an "immutable covenant" that *will* be fulfilled; "all things wherewith you have been afflicted shall work together for your good, and to my name's glory, saith the Lord." Everything would be all right – but it wasn't, things turned out to be anything *but* alright. Just two months later, in October 1833, the saints were evicted from Jackson County, Missouri. This was failed prophecy which Smith claimed came straight from the lips of the Lord.

They are to obey the laws of the land. Verse 7 states "pertaining to law of man, whatsoever is more or less than this, cometh of evil", which is a bit rich, considering the things Smith and his cohorts later got up to, such as destroying the Law's printing press and getting arrested on charges of treason, to say nothing of the polygyny and polyandry that went on. None of that was exactly legal by any stretch of the imagination. Yet here, the Lord instructs them in no uncertain terms to *obey* the law, confirming anything *less* "cometh of evil" – ergo, Joseph Smith's illegal actions all came from his own *evil* designs. That conclusion, according to Smith, came straight to him from the mouth of the Lord. He had *no* excuses.

They are commanded to forsake evil and cleave to the good. If anyone lays down their life for the Lord they shall have eternal life. Verses 16-17 are a little strange in that they say the saints should "renounce war and proclaim peace, and seek diligently to turn the hearts of the children to their fathers, and the hearts of the fathers to the children; And again, the hearts of the Jews unto the prophets, and the prophets unto the Jews; lest I come and smite the whole earth with a curse, and all flesh be consumed before me". This is just filler, using words that have no place in such a setting. Smith used the 'hearts of the fathers' and the earth being 'smitten with a curse' idea (which he stole from Malachi 4:5-6), several times elsewhere in the D&C *(2:2; 27:9; 110:15; 128:17)*, but *never* in connection with such ideas as these.

Turning the hearts of the Jews to the prophets and the prophets to the Jews? Just where did Smith get the notion that Malachi's words could remotely relate to that idea? It was *Old Testament* scripture and Malachi *was* a Jew. *(See Chapter 9)*. There was never any *seeking* to turn hearts required in Malachi, or even in Moroni's supposed restructuring of the verses. If he really did 'receive' Moroni's version in 1823, Smith completely ignored it for years until recording the details in 1838. This was originally an OT prophecy that *Elijah* would turn the hearts, but Smith's use (or rather misuse) of the scripture here is not only out of harmony with the Bible, it is also out of harmony with other ideas that he concocted and used elsewhere, in addition to what he pretended Moroni did with the wording of Malachi in 1823 – or rather, 1838 *(See TMD Vol. 2: Ch. 6)*.

The Lord isn't pleased with many of the saints in Kirtland (v.19). Nothing changes. Apparently, not only haven't they forsaken their sins or their wicked ways, they have pride in their hearts, they are covetous and like 'detestable' things. If that really was the case, it seems the Church was attracting the worst rather than the best of humanity. Naturally, the Lord is going to chasten them – again. If they repent and do what he says, he will then turn all his wrath and indignation away from them and the gates of hell won't prevail against them (v.22). What *had* these poor people done in order to deserve God's wrath and indignation? They had joined the Church and tried to follow Smith, but nothing ever seemed good enough for Smith's God. He remained as grouchy and as vindictive as ever.

The Lord quickly moves on to talk about what should happen when men 'smite' them or any of their families. This is as close as it gets to revelation concerning problems in Jackson County. The first time it happens, they are to bear it 'patiently', not revile or seek revenge, and they will be rewarded. Early Mormon history does not show any evidence of reward for obedience to this idea. If they bear the burden for a second time, their reward will then be "an hundredfold" (v.25). If they bear it a third time, the reward will be four times that. In fact, the Lord is not exactly good with math as he says after the third time it will be "doubled unto you four-fold". That is either a non sequitur, or if literally doubled *and* four-fold, it equals eight-hundred. It is confusing and meaningless, and no one ever saw any such rewards anyway. If they don't bear it, then such as was meted out on them by their enemy will be considered a just reward. Heads they lose – and tails they lose even more. Three instances will stand as a testimony against the enemy if he doesn't repent.

Then the Lord says something even more strange; if the enemy 'escapes' the Lord's vengeance and is not brought into judgment before him, then it is up to the person to warn the enemy in the Lord's name that they should not come again upon them or their children or their children's children "unto the third and fourth generation." The question is, how or why could or would anyone ever *escape* the Lord's vengeance? Why would someone be warned to stay clear for four generations, when they would not live that long and the later generations may not have a clue about what previously happened.

It gets even stranger, as the Lord declares that if they do "come upon you or your children, or your children's children unto the third and fourth generation, I have delivered thine enemy into thine hands" (v.29). How it would be possible for that to ever happen, the Lord fails to explain.

If the person then decides to spare his enemy, he will be rewarded – also "unto the third and fourth generation". Nevertheless, it is all up to the injured party, as the enemy is in his hands and he is justified in whatever he decides to do. The Lord goes on to explain that this is the same law he gave to Nephi and to *all* the ancient "prophets and apostles" such as Joseph, Jacob, Isaac and Abraham. If an enemy is offered peace three times and refuses, only then can they go out to battle against that "nation, tongue or people" (sound familiar?)

It is not only a strange and *impossible* concept; it is also strange that throughout the Book of Mormon and the Bible, there is no mention of any such system. It should appear in the Book of Mormon if the Lord instructed Nephi on this. It should be recorded in the OT if the ancients named were instructed, and it should also appear in the NT if all the apostles were so instructed. The concepts appear *nowhere* at all. It is easy to understand why.

> **37.** And I, the Lord, would fight their battles, and their children's battles, and their children's children's, until they had avenged themselves on all their enemies, to the third and fourth generation.

There is no record of such vengeance going on (or even needing to) with the Lord being with them in battles that lasted for several generations; but it is undoubtedly in such concepts that later events, such as the Mountain Meadows massacre had their roots. Encouraged by Brigham Young's attitude to take revenge on the enemies of the saints, which meant anyone who came from the wrong state, many atrocities were committed in Utah in the name of the Lord. They were fulfilling prophecy by murdering people – which they termed being 'used up (in the pocket of the Lord)' or later, taken 'over the rim of the basin'.

Smith had the Lord call his ideas an "ensample" unto all the people. We have discussed the Lord's supposed use of that word already *(see p. 318)*. Then the Lord repeats himself. He goes to the trouble of explaining the 'three strikes and they are out' rules, that don't just apply now but also applied to Nephi and all the ancients – yet again. The fourth time enemies attack, you don't forgive, you fight back, and the Lord will be with you. But the Lord then says if the enemy is sorry and asks forgiveness, forgive your enemy the first time and then the second and third time; in fact, forgive seventy times seven, as long as he repents each time (v.39-40). We know where Smith got that idea from.

Then he says the same things spoken of earlier, all over again, in v.41-3, about someone who does not repent and on the fourth occasion you do not have to forgive them; you take the testimony of it to the Lord who will not blot out the transgression until the enemy repents and repays you four-fold – then you forgive him. If he doesn't repent the Lord "will avenge thee of thine enemy an hundred-fold" (v.45).

In the earlier verses the reward was *four times* an hundred fold – or even more (v.25-7). Whatever the case, it is a ludicrous sequence of statements. Repetition and inconsistency abound. The Lord will again avenge the enemy an hundred fold and of course – for four generations. Why do their children's, children's children deserve to be treated that way? If the children repent and repay 'fourfold', then whatever it was the parents or grandparents did, they will be forgiven and the Lord will leave them alone. It's not a very fair system. But then of course it was all Smith fantasy with no basis in reality.

Section 98 – Summary

Prophecies made: 1
Prophecies fulfilled: 0

Prophecies made:

Pr. 36. The Lord gives an "immutable covenant" that will be fulfilled; "all things wherewith you have been afflicted shall work together for your good, and to my name's glory, saith the Lord."

Results:

Pr. 36. The Lord promised that everything would be all right – but it wasn't; things turned out to be anything *but* all right. Two months later, in October 1833, the saints were evicted form Jackson County, Missouri. This was failed prophecy and according to Smith's record, was spoken by the Lord.

Chapter 20

**Doctrine and Covenants
Sections 100–108, Old 101–Marriage, 134 & General Assembly**

Section 100
12 October 1833. Perrysburg, New York.

History.

1835 D&C Sec. XCIV. 2010 D&C Sec. 100.

Joseph Smith and Sidney Rigdon had been away from their families for a few days and were worried about them – so the Lord, once again, rather than deal with anything important or of real use to the world, lets them know that their families are all well. In order to give them this message, instead of just saying something like 'don't worry, I will watch over them' the Lord uses some strange words that we have seen before – but only when Smith has him speak: "your families are well; they are in mine hands, and I will do with them as seemeth me good" (v.1). It simply is *not* an appropriate expression to suggest the Lord would ever use. *(See pp. 213-14; and The Final Analysis: Part 2, Pet Phrases).*

The Lord adds that he has sent them there (to Perrysburg) for a purpose; he has "much people in this place, in the regions round about; and an effectual door shall be opened in the regions round about in this eastern land" (v.3). Smith's Lord seems incapable of speaking in the plain and simple language we see in the Bible. Also, "effectual door" deserves investigation *(see pp. 393-6)*.

Joseph Smith's attempts at recreating the beauty of ancient scripture don't just fall short; they expose his fraud on every single page if you read the D&C objectively. It is not just that some of the things Smith's God says are bizarre; it is the way Smith's God presents them that also exposes the hoax. Smith has no understanding of Jacobean English. There is no beauty to the Lord's purported words and they are generally not good examples of a literate mind or voice. They appear to match Smith's level of education which was quite low.

They are to teach the people in that area. The rest of this Section just says Rigdon will be a "spokesman" to the people and also to Smith in "expounding all scriptures" and that Smith will be a "revelator" to Rigdon and will be able to explain things of the kingdom. Amid all that, the Lord claims that concerning Zion: "Zion shall be redeemed, although she is chastened for a little season" (v.13). This was October 1833, the very month the saints *in* Zion were forcibly evicted from the county. If that was the chastisement, it was more than severe and it didn't last for just "a little season" either. It continued, and they never returned to Zion – "she" never was redeemed.

Finally, the Lord says that Orson Hyde and John Gould are "in my hands" and as long as they "keep his commandments" (the Lord is now speaking in the third person – again) they "shall be saved" (v.17) but we don't learn what it is they are to be saved from. If it was just in the general sense, then it was a wasted revelation as they already knew that and the same promise applies to everyone. As ever, this Section contains nothing but unquantifiable rambling laced with meaningless and worthless ideas that amount to – nothing.

Section 101
16 & 17 December 1833. Kirtland, Ohio.

History.

1835 D&C Sec. XCVII. 2010 D&C Sec. 101.

Section 101 (coincidentally) has one-hundred-and-one verses and is therefore quite long; but that doesn't mean the content is any more compelling than some shorter Sections. It is just as unfulfilling in terms of discovering any prophecy

D&C - SECTIONS 100-108, OLD 101, 134 & GENERAL ASSEMBLY

or revelation of merit. There were major problems that now cut across Smith's earlier promises; that is to say, the promises that Smith had had the Lord utter when he instructed Smith's followers to 'go up to Zion' and gather there. The saints were now being evicted from Jackson County which was supposedly the land of their 'inheritance'. Some tried to relocate to Van Buren County and most went to Clay County but the persecution followed, such was the disquiet among the locals due to the way Mormonism was affecting their communities.

Smith promised block voting in order to influence who was in power and the Mormon community was growing too fast for the locals. They felt unsafe. Ultimately, less than five years later, on 27 October 1838, Governor Lilburn Boggs perceived the problem as coming entirely from within the Mormon community and issued 'Missouri Executive Order 44' which became more commonly known as the 'Mormon Extermination Order'.

The Lord doesn't give the saints any comfort concerning being driven from their homes, having their goods stolen and crops burned. He just says (v.2) that he has "suffered" (read 'allowed') it all to happen "in consequence of their transgressions". Therefore, they need to be "chastened and tried" – just like Abraham who was to sacrifice his son; but one day, "when I come to make up my jewels", he says he will "own them"; not much comfort there.

Smith had sent the saints there and had the Lord promise them it was their inheritance and that they would build Zion, a place which the world would revere. Almost immediately, they had overstayed their welcome and were driven out. Smith needed an excuse, and he needed it from the Lord; it had supposedly been the Lord who had given them the promise. What other excuse could Smith possibly produce other than 'unworthiness' being the cause of their afflictions?

Then, as Smith has to somehow cover himself, what he says next is more than predictable. Anyone not willing to "endure chastening, but deny me" cannot be sanctified. Apparently, the reason they got chased out of Jackson County was that there were "jarrings, and contentions, and envyings, and strifes, and lustful and covetous desires among them; therefore by these things they polluted their inheritances" (v.6).

As previously observed, it sounds as if Smith's converts were drawn from among the worst of humanity rather than from the best. Clearly, this could not possibly have been the case at all and Smith was just pretending the Lord was speaking, saying things the saints could not argue with without appearing to show the exact lack of faith the revelation was speaking about. The cleverly constructed but very unkind and most certainly untrue words supposedly came from the Lord. Religion contrives systems where leaders can never be wrong, because they 'represent' God. In Smith's case, he was clever enough to have the Lord himself speak the words for him. Anyone contending against them would be considered a 'dissenter' and thrown out. The culture was firmly established to protect the leaders, regardless of the mess they got their followers into. The problems in Missouri were certainly *not* due to the personal sins of the saints.

Nevertheless, says the Lord, he is filled with compassion (although it doesn't sound like it to me) and he will not "utterly cast them off". He says "in the day of wrath I will remember mercy". For now, he is full of "indignation" and as he apparently previously predicted, has let the sword of that indignation fall on them. Soon, it will also fall on all nations "when the cup of their iniquity is full" (v.11).

The saints were chased off their properties, their belongings stolen and crops burned. What did they have left? And this was to be the fate of all nations? When and where exactly has that or anything remotely like it ever been recorded? And, once again, I have to ask, why? If the nations were bereft of the truth, it was entirely the Lord's fault for allowing things to go so wrong after Christ lived and died. Only God knew of the early 'apostasy' until Smith came along and explained it all; until that moment, everyone was blissfully ignorant of that supposed historical fact. Surely, no just God would blame his children for following their God in the wrong manner if they had no idea they were doing so – because He hadn't bothered to tell them.

Ultimately, the saints will be saved, gathered, comforted, and importantly (to Smith anyway) 'crowned' (v.12-16); promises, promises. That is supposed to give them some comfort for their destitute state. It has to, it's all they have, and God is the one speaking – He declares it. Smith certainly knew how to squirm out of awkward situations of his own making. He had God make the excuses and it was others who suffered.

> **17.** Zion shall not be moved out of her place, notwithstanding her children are scattered.
> **18.** They that remain, and are pure in heart, shall return, and come to their inheritances, they and their children, with songs of everlasting joy, to build up the waste places of Zion—
> **19.** And all these things that the prophets might be fulfilled.

Zion will not be moved and the saints will return to their inheritances – along with their children. The promises made here have been repeated several times and were never fulfilled. All those people have long since departed this world – and so have all their children. Today, it is a new and different world where everyone who is now living was born long after that period. Almost two centuries later, no one has returned, Zion has not been built, and there is no (Mormon) temple there. It is no good the Church claiming Salt Lake became Zion or that Zion is in the heart or in any place where the saints live, because God got pretty specific about what *this* Zion meant:

> **20.** And, behold, *there is none other place appointed* than that which I have appointed; *neither shall there be* any other place appointed than that which I have appointed, for the work of the gathering of my saints—
> **21.** Until the day cometh *when there is found no more room* for them; and *then I have other places* which I will appoint unto them, and *they shall be called* stakes, for the curtains or the strength of Zion. (Emphasis added).

Zion was a specific place with "none other place appointed", and only when that was full would the Lord appoint "other places" for the saints which "shall be called stakes". Today, there are over two-thousand-seven-hundred stakes worldwide, none of which should have existed before Zion was built and fully occupied.

They are to gather together and then (v.23) the Lord says: "…the veil of the covering of my temple, in my tabernacle, which hideth the earth, shall be taken off, *and all flesh shall see me together.*" (Emphasis added). The saints of the day appeared to think *they* would be the ones to see him but the Church will no doubt claim that is still a future prophecy so I will not include it as unfulfilled. Anyone familiar with the beautiful oratorio 'Messiah' by the composer Handel, will recognize the words taken from Isaiah 40:5, *"and all flesh shall see it together."* Smith, the master of plagiarism *cleverly* disguises the phrase by changing the word 'it' to 'me'.

Whilst the Mormon Church appears to teach the idea that the 'burning' at the second coming, spoken of in the scriptures, will be a burning of conscience rather than literal, Smith's God seems to have other ideas.

> **24.** And every corruptible thing, both of man, or of the beasts of the field, or of the fowls of the heavens, or of the fish of the sea, that dwells upon all the face of the earth, shall be consumed;
> **25.** And also that of element shall melt with fervent heat; and all things shall become new, that my knowledge and glory may dwell upon all the earth.

The |Lord goes on to say something else strange:

> **26.** And in that day the enmity of man, and the enmity of beasts, yea, the enmity of all flesh, shall cease from before my face.

Enmity is a feeling or condition of hostility, hatred, ill will, animosity or antagonism. Most people don't feel that way at all. In studying Smith's life and works, it is perfectly clear that he often did, and in the modern idiom you could say he thought the world owed him a living. It was Smith's attitude and actions that caused most problems the saints had to endure but the Church writes its own history in a manner that leads members to conclude otherwise.

Considering "beasts" do not have intelligence or feelings such as humans enjoy, this is a play on words to suggest something like Isaiah 11:6 "The wolf also shall dwell with the lamb, and the leopard shall lie down with the kid; and the calf and the young lion and the fatling together; and a little child shall lead them" – typical biblical ideology with no basis in reality.

The real problem with these assertions is that if God created all life, he also *created* the food chain system such that almost all creatures, unless they are fortunate enough to be at the top of a particular food chain, live their entire lives on high instinctual alert and they are lucky if they survive long enough to rear the next generation before they are eaten.

God could have made all creatures vegetarian – but He didn't. It is not the 'choice' of creatures to eat each other, it is a natural instinct and the digestive systems of those that do so are usually completely incapable of accommodating a vegetarian diet. Evolution creates its own path along its way, which is why early humans could not drink cow's milk. Later, the human digestive system evolved that ability and so now we do. Many people have no idea that our ancestors could not do that, or more importantly, why.

The point is that animals do not understand 'enmity' and are not really 'hostile' towards each other in that (human) sense. There may be a perceived hostility within a species when males fight over females but even that is not 'hostility' as humans understand it; it is a kind of defence mechanism that is a natural instinct and has in fact become an essential part of natural selection for many species. It is an evolutionary result; animals do not experience enmity.

Creatures that fight when another of their own (or other) species 'invades' their territory are not being particularly hostile toward each other either; they are either defending their territory or trying to establishing their rights to it respectively – each for the sake of its 'family' or the survival of their species.

Enmity is a human emotion. A predator views its prey in the same way we see food when we are hungry, be it an apple or a steak. When was the last time you felt 'hostile' towards the animal that provided your dinner? Even if you are a farmer or hunter and kill animals for food, there is no hostility involved. Early humans hunted big game and risked their lives for food – there was no enmity involved. *Millions* of creatures die horrible and painful deaths *daily* as they are ripped apart for food in a continuing fight for survival of species.

God designed some small creatures to lay eggs inside other small creatures and when they hatch, they eat them from the inside out. What kind of a God would *design* that? You could write a book on all the ways life survives at the expense of other life, which goes way beyond a benevolent 'design'. If that is evolution and natural selection at work, then it is just the way things are; horrible to us perhaps, but of no consequence to nature which has no plan, no agenda and no 'design'. However, if a God 'created' such extreme cruelty in his *design* of these things, then He is solely responsible for more cruelty and suffering than humans are even capable of imagining and consequently He has a lot to answer for.

Humans alone, who dominate the planet (at this time) are responsible for the death of countless millions of creatures – *daily*. Figures that are now a few years old, suggested that here in Great Britain, over 900 million animals are killed for food each year. That includes 2.25 million cattle, 9.35 million pigs, almost 15 million sheep, 20 million ducks, 28 million turkeys and over 850 million chickens. That is equal to 2.4 million animals every day; 100,000 an hour, 1,600 a minute or 26 each second. And that is just here in Great Britain. Multiply that up world wide and the figures are staggering. Not that I have a problem with all that personally; I am not vegetarian and do not advocate being one. I am just repeating the facts and saying God Himself approved of us doing such things in the Bible. It is His *plan*.

Some of God's inventions are positively evil. He should be asked about many of them. Humans could not possibly have invented such an array of more horrid things if they tried. Why would a God create a whole range of parasitic worms (Helminths)? Flatworms – Flukes and Tapeworms; Roundworms – Ascaris, Hookworms, Trichinella, Filarial worms, and my all time (I won't say favourite) *loathed* creation by God – the Eye Worm. For details of these lovely parasites see: http://parasitology.com/worms/index.html

There are several verses of filler about what will happen during the second coming and how well it will be for those who have suffered persecution or laid down their lives. Promises that do not have to be fulfilled in this life are always a safe bet. The saints should not care about the body but rather the soul.

In v.41, the Lord confirms yet again, "…here is wisdom concerning the children of Zion, even many, but not all; they were found transgressors, therefore they must needs be chastened—". That excuses Smith and his God for the persecution and saints being driven from their homes. But now Smith needs to reinforce the reason.

From v.43-68 Smith has the Lord give a parable. It is not really a parable at all but it is the best Smith could come up with. The parable is given so they can understand the Lord's will concerning Zion. In reality, it just firms up Smith's already stated excuse for the problems, in that many saints were unworthy and needed chastising. In essence, the 'parable' concerns a 'nobleman' who had a choice 'spot of land'; a *vineyard* into which the nobleman sends his servants to plant twelve *olive trees*. Yes, that's right; a vineyard comprised of olive trees.

A vineyard contains only grapes – which grow on vines. Planting olive trees would make it an olive grove. Smith was quite adept at getting such things entirely wrong and this was not the first time he had made that mistake. Smith had got entirely confused over vineyards and olive groves when he wrote the Book of Mormon too. This is from TMD Volume 4.

> Jacob 5 contains material from *Isaiah 5* which is about a 'vineyard' and also from *Romans 11*, where Paul is speaking to the Romans about an 'olive tree'. In *Jacob 5*, Smith refers to *olives* **nine** times and yet throughout, he is talking about 'vineyards', with no less than **ninety** references. Vineyards produce *one* thing and one thing *only* – and that is **grapes**, which grow on **vines**. Olives grow on the branches of **trees**, not on vines *or* in a vineyard. *(See TMD Vol. 4:361-6 for complete coverage of this).*

In this parable of a 'vineyard' which somehow has twelve 'olive trees' in it, a hedge is placed around it and watchmen are to be set in a tower to watch over it. While they were still building the foundation for the tower, the workers started to question the need for the tower. It was a time of peace and they thought the money could be better spent. So, they ignored their master and did not complete the tower. Enemies broke down the hedges and olive trees in the night, causing the servants to run away in fright. The workers are of course called to account.

Chastising his men, the lord explains that if they had built the tower they would have seen the enemy approaching and could have called for support before all was lost. Now, the "lord of the vineyard" (which had somehow been full of olive trees) sends them, along with his warriors, to redeem his vineyard. They are to break down the walls of the enemy and throw down their tower and scatter the watchmen. This they do and all is well again.

There is no point to this so-called parable where Smith confuses vineyards and olive groves. Nevertheless, Smith tries to relate it to the local churches. Metaphorically, they have been driven out because they didn't build the tower and later they will regain their inheritance when there are more of them and they can go up in force and take their land back. It was not a very good parallel, in addition to which, they never did get to go back and reclaim anything.

Smith has the Lord say the work of gathering should continue, ready for the time of harvest. Therefore, he says "I must gather together my people, according to the parable of the wheat and the tares, that the wheat may be secured in the garners to possess eternal life, and be crowned with celestial glory, when I shall come in the kingdom of my Father to reward every man according as his work shall be; While the tares shall be bound in bundles, and their bands made strong, that they may be burned with unquenchable fire" (v.65-6). Carry on gathering says the Lord, but as he has said before, "not in haste, or by flight" (v.68).

What the parable of wheat and tares had to do with the above parable of a vineyard and olive trees, goodness only knows. Smith had made his huge 'vineyard and olive trees' mistake in the Book of Mormon in 1829 when he wrote that. Now, four years later, he still hasn't learned the difference and repeats the same mistake again. That is, unless you want to accept the idea that the Lord was responsible for both stories and it is he who doesn't know the difference between grapes and olives. With such evidence of Smith's hoax before us, we can clearly see that this is no more from the Lord than the Book of Mormon error and Smith is entirely exposed in his fraudulent claims. And that is in addition to the so-called parable being meaningless, regardless of what it contained.

Now they are to get money together to purchase land "in the region round about the land which I have appointed to be the land of Zion" (v.70). "Wise men" should take care of that and the churches in the eastern counties should be ready to move there when they are built up. Verse 75 confirms that there is already sufficient in store to redeem Zion and she will no more be thrown down. How do they expect to get reinstated? Easy: "…those who have been scattered by their enemies, it is my will that they should continue to importune for redress, and redemption, by the hands of those who are placed as rulers and are in authority over you—" (v.76). Nice idea, but it didn't work. Smith has the Lord prattle on for several more verses about their rights, but it never amounted to anything. He then even has the Lord say that *he* suffered the laws *and* the constitution to be established – for that very purpose. That was of course a completely ridiculous claim and it didn't do any good; they never did return.

Smith, clearly impressed with himself and his parables, ventures into yet another one from v.81-95. He would have been better off calling it a day, as he wasn't very good at it – and it shows. "Now", Smith has the Lord say, "unto what shall I liken the children of Zion?" It is to be a parable about a woman and an unjust judge. There was a judge, a man who did not 'fear' God, neither 'regarded' man. A widow went to him asking him to avenge her adversary. At first he could not be bothered with her but then decided to do something for her to stop her coming to him and wearying him.

That, apparently, is likened to Zion. They should importune the judge and if he will not listen go to the governor, then to the President, and if that doesn't work – the Lord will come out of his hiding place and 'vex' the nation. It is not exactly a very good parable and again, Smith should have quit while he was ahead; not that he actually was ever ahead; everything he said just seemed to make matters worse. The 'parable' is dreadful and not compatible with what he suggests next.

Look at what the Lord says he will do if the President doesn't listen to the saints:

> **90.** And in his hot displeasure, and in his fierce anger, in his time, will cut off those wicked, unfaithful, and unjust stewards, and appoint them their portion among hypocrites, and unbelievers;
> **91.** Even in outer darkness, where there is weeping, and wailing, and gnashing of teeth.
> **92.** Pray ye, therefore, that their ears may be opened unto your cries, that I may be merciful unto them, that these things may not come upon them.

By 1838, things were so bad that the Extermination Order was issued. The perception was that were it not for the Mormons, everything would have been alright. In 1839, Joseph Smith himself visited President Van Buren to plead for the government to help around 20,000 Mormon settlers who had been forced from the state during the 1838 so-called 'Mormon War'. The reason for such pleading is clear in the above verses, written some five years earlier, and the Lord goes on to describe what will happen in what must rank as one of the oddest verses in all of Mormon 'scripture'.

> **95.** That I may proceed to bring to pass my act, my strange act, and perform my work, my strange work, that men may discern between the righteous and the wicked, saith your God.

Strange indeed. The Mormon God did not actually do anything to anyone in regard to the expulsion of His saints. Things went from bad to worse for them and following Smith's death in 1844, it was only a matter of time before they started to travel west and away from the trouble zone which had once promised to be their Zion – forever. The Lord constantly confirmed they would inherit Independence which would become the New Jerusalem – but they never did.

The Lord tags on a couple of things to this revelation. Apparently the Lord wants Sidney Gilbert to hang on to the storehouse until he (the Lord) decides it is time to sell it. His people should lay claim to areas they have been forced to leave, even if they cannot live there. He adds "Nevertheless, I do not say they shall not dwell thereon; for inasmuch as they bring forth fruit and works meet for my kingdom they shall dwell thereon. They shall build, and another shall not inherit it; they shall plant vineyards, and they shall eat the fruit thereof. Even so. Amen" (v.100-1).

The fact is that they never built anything there and even if they ever had regained the area and done so, I doubt that many vineyards would have been planted. If they had, undoubtedly they would have contained olive trees.

Section 101 – Summary

Prophecies made:	4
Prophecies fulfilled:	0

Prophecies made:

Pr. 37. v.17-18. "Zion shall not be moved out of her place, notwithstanding her children are scattered. They that remain, and are pure in heart, shall return, and come to their inheritances, they and their children, with songs of everlasting joy, to build up the waste places of Zion—"

Pr. 38. v.20-21. "And, behold, there is none other place appointed than that which I have appointed; neither shall there be any other place appointed than that which I have appointed, for the work of the gathering of my saints— Until the day cometh when there is found no more room for them; and then I have other places which I will appoint unto them, and they shall be called stakes, for the curtains or the strength of Zion."

Pr. 39. This is what the Lord says he will do if the President doesn't listen to the saints: v.90-91. "And in his hot displeasure, and in his fierce anger, in his time, will cut off those wicked, unfaithful, and unjust stewards, and appoint them their portion among hypocrites, and unbelievers; Even in outer darkness, where there is weeping, and wailing, and gnashing of teeth."

Pr. 40. v.100-1. "Nevertheless, I do not say they shall not dwell thereon; for inasmuch as they bring forth fruit and works meet for my kingdom they shall dwell thereon. They shall build, and another shall not inherit it; they shall plant vineyards, and they shall eat the fruit thereof. Even so. Amen."

Results:

Pr. 37. The promises made here have been repeated several times and were never fulfilled. All the people of that generation have long since departed this world and so have all their children.

Pr. 38. Zion was a specific place with "none other place appointed", and only when that was full would the Lord appoint "other places" for the saints which "shall be called "stakes". Today, there are over two-thousand-seven-hundred stakes worldwide, none of which should have existed before Zion was built and fully occupied.

Pr. 39. In 1839, Joseph Smith himself visited President Van Buren to plead for the government to help around 20,000 Mormon settlers who had been forced from the state during the 1838 so-called 'Mormon War'. The request was refused and the Mormon God did nothing about it.

Pr. 40. The fact is that they never built anything there and others did inherit it. They did not plant any "vineyards" – regardless of what "fruit" they might have eaten thereof.

Section 102
17 February 1834. Kirtland, Ohio.

History.

1835 D&C Sec. V. 2010 D&C Sec. 102.

Section 102 comprises minutes of a meeting at which the 'high council' of the Church in Kirtland is established for hearing "important difficulties" that arose. The structure is claimed as having been "appointed by revelation". The system described is essentially the same as used today in Mormon Stake High Council disciplinary council proceedings. I personally participated in many such types of council during the fifteen years or more that I served as a member of one.

When this section was recorded, there was to be only one 'high council' at that time and Smith of course was voted to preside, along with Rigdon and Williams as counsellors. Twelve others were chosen to fill the council and the system of operation is described. Smith added v.30-32 the following year, in 1835, to make it clear this was different to the travelling high council of twelve apostles. There can be an appeal from the decision of the high council but not from the Quorum of Twelve Apostles whose decision is final.

> **30.** There is a distinction between the high council or traveling high priests abroad, and the traveling high council composed of the twelve apostles, in their decisions.
> **31.** From the decision of the former there can be an appeal; but from the decision of the latter there cannot.

32. The latter can only be called in question by the general authorities of the church in case of transgression.

These verses, which were added in 1835, completely violated the Lord's *previous* declaration as detailed in the part of Section 107 that had been recorded back in 1831.

> **D&C 107:78.** Again, verily, I say unto you, *the most important business* of the church, and *the most difficult cases* of the church, inasmuch as there is not satisfaction upon the decision of the bishop or judges, it *shall be handed over and carried up unto the council* of the church, before the *Presidency of the High Priesthood.*
> 79. And *the Presidency of the council of the High Priesthood* shall have power to call other high priests, even twelve, to assist as counselors; and thus the Presidency of the High Priesthood and its counselors shall have power to decide upon testimony according to the laws of the church.
> 80. And after this decision it shall be had in remembrance no more before the Lord; for *this is the highest council of the church of God, and a final decision upon controversies in spiritual matters.*
> 81. *There is not any person belonging to the church who is exempt from this council of the church.*
> 82. And inasmuch as a President of the High Priesthood shall transgress, he shall be had in remembrance before the common council of the church, who shall be assisted by twelve counselors of the High Priesthood;
> 83. And *their decision upon his head shall be an end* of controversy concerning him.
> 84. Thus, *none shall be exempted* from the justice and the laws of God, that all things may be done in order and in solemnity before him, according to truth and righteousness. (Emphasis added).

In 1834, Smith established a high council. In 1835, he added verses confirming an appeal was available following high council decisions but not Quorum of Twelve decisions which were final. Yet in 1831, the Lord had already declared otherwise. The high council was the highest in the Church; their decision was final – and no one was exempt *(See pp. 257-8)*.

THE MORMON DELUSION
Section 103
24 February 1834. Kirtland, Ohio.

History.

1844 D&C Sec. CI. 2010 D&C Sec. 103.

Parley P. Pratt and Lyman Wight turned up in Kirtland to ask Smith about the "relief and restoration of the saints to their lands in Jackson County" (italics in original) according to the Section header. Naturally, Smith feels he first has to make some excuses. The Lord has "suffered them thus far" (allowed it to happen) for two reasons.

Firstly, it is so those who drove the saints out "might fill up the measure of their iniquities, that their cup might be full" (v.3), which is always the excuse given in any religion for anything that goes wrong for followers. Those who are against them need to build up enough bad acts to condemn themselves – usually at the expense of the faithful. That is never a satisfactory explanation any more than it is fair on followers. A real God *could* protect them and still condemn the perpetrators for their intentions – after all, he knows them all. It is just an excuse for things that cannot otherwise be explained away. Be patient in affliction and God will one day make it right – or not, as the case may be. There are records of many such promises but *none* of any verifiable retribution; just the promises.

Smith usually added "in mine own due time" to escape being called on non-fulfilment; it is going to happen – one day; the Lord said so. He does so here *(see next paragraph)*. There is no questioning that for a believer. It all started with biblical events that went very wrong for the Israelites but as those were just handed down myths, the stories could also contain records of the Lord's actual retribution. A classic example is the plagues in Egypt, which in reality were all part of the same myth, none of which actually happened at all. The Israelites never were in Egypt as slaves in such numbers. Later Jews would not know the truth as the stories were ancient. When all else fails, the Lord always says he will make retribution; but only after perpetrators have built up enough sin "that their cup might be full". Meanwhile, the saints just have to suffer.

Secondly, the reason is; "that those who call themselves after my name might be chastened for a little season with a sore and grievous chastisement, because they did not hearken altogether unto the precepts and commandments which I gave unto them" (v.4). If that really were the case, it is harsh to say the least. Clearly, Smith was just reiterating excuses he had mentioned in earlier Sections. Smith also has the Lord confirm that the saints were "smitten by the hands of mine enemies, on whom I will pour out my wrath without measure in mine own time" (v.2). The Lord's "own due time" – there's that well worn phrase again.

Nevertheless, Smith now becomes quite bold. He has the Lord state that from that very hour they will begin to prevail against their enemies and "they shall never cease to prevail until the kingdoms of the world are subdued under my feet, and the earth is given unto the saints, to possess it forever and ever" (v.7). That is quite a promise, but conveniently, it is based on their obedience, or the kingdoms will prevail against *them*. To date, it seems the saints are still not worthy of the promise being fulfilled as no kingdoms have been overcome.

The Mormon Church remains a small and somewhat insignificant minor cult within the extremely overcrowded religious category of Christianity which contains well over thirty-four-thousand different sects – and that is before even considering other religions.

But, says the Lord "I have decreed that your brethren which have been scattered shall return to the lands of their inheritances, and shall build up the waste places of Zion. For after much tribulation, as I have said unto you in a former commandment, cometh the blessing" (v.11-12). Now the Lord explains how they will get their own back – in both senses; on their enemies, and regain their property. This is very specific and cannot be misunderstood.

> 13. Behold, this is the ***blessing which I have promised*** after your tribulations, and the tribulations of your brethren—***your redemption***, and the redemption of your brethren, even their ***restoration to the land of Zion, to be established, no more to be thrown down.*** (Emphasis added).

The Lord adds that if they subsequently "pollute their inheritances" then they *will* be thrown down, but considering they never 'inherited' it in the first place, that never came into question. The Lord confirms that the redemption of Zion "needs come by power"; Smith will lead them to war against the enemy and they *will* take the lands back.

> 15. Behold, I say unto you, *the redemption of Zion must needs come by power*;
> 16. Therefore, *I will raise up unto my people a man*, who shall lead them like as Moses led the children of Israel.
> 17. For ye are the children of Israel, and of the seed of Abraham, and *ye must needs be led out of bondage by power, and with a stretched-out arm.*

18. And as your fathers were led at the first, even so shall the redemption of Zion be.

19. Therefore, let not your hearts faint, for *I say not unto you as I said unto your fathers: Mine angel shall go up before you, but not my presence.*

20. But I say unto you: Mine *angels shall go up before you, and also my presence*, and *in time ye shall possess the goodly land*.

21. Verily, verily I say unto you, that my servant *Joseph Smith, Jun., is the man to whom I likened the servant to whom the Lord of the vineyard* spake in the parable which I have given unto you.

22. Therefore let my servant Joseph Smith, Jun., say unto the strength of my house, my *young men and the middle aged—Gather yourselves together unto the land of Zion*, upon the land which I have bought with money that has been consecrated unto me.

23. And let all the churches send up wise men with their moneys, and purchase lands even as I have commanded them.

24. And *inasmuch as mine enemies come against you to drive you from my goodly land,* which I have consecrated to be the land of Zion, even from your own lands after these testimonies, which ye have brought before me against them, *ye shall curse them;*

25. And *whomsoever ye curse, I will curse, and ye shall avenge me of mine enemies.*

26. *And my presence shall be with you even in avenging me of mine enemies*, unto the third and fourth generation of them that hate me.

27. *Let no man be afraid to lay down his life* for my sake; for whoso layeth down his life for my sake shall find it again.

28. And *whoso is not willing to lay down his life for my sake is not my disciple*. (Emphasis added).

So, there's the plan; yet in August of 1833 (Section 98:16) the Lord had specifically commanded: "Therefore, renounce war and proclaim peace." Here, in February 1834, just six months later, the Lord is 'raising Smith up' as a man to lead the saints to war against their enemies. Sidney Rigdon is to talk to the eastern county congregations about the "restoration and redemption of Zion". Parley P. Pratt and Lyman Wight are to "obtain companies" of tens, twenties, fifties and hundreds until they have got five hundred people to go up to Zion.

Then he adds that if they can't find five hundred, to make do with three hundred. If they can't find three hundred, and if not very many, make do with one hundred, but they shouldn't go up with fewer than one hundred. Surely the Lord would have a better idea of how many people they could muster, and if not, why would he go through such rigmarole as that? As ever, it is perfectly clear where this was coming from – and it certainly wasn't the Lord.

Parley P. Pratt can go up with Smith, and Lyman Wight can go off with Rigdon; Hyrum Smith is paired with Williams; Orson Hyde with Orson Pratt; Smith can decide where they should go and the Lord leaves the rest up to them.

So much detail for the Lord to get involved with, and yet there is so much contradiction and lack of methodology imparted. We will come back to it again later but for now suffice it to say that no army ever redeemed Zion.

Section 103 – Summary

Prophecies made:	2
Prophecies fulfilled:	0

Prophecies made:

Pr. 41. The persecution was allowed "that those who call themselves after my name might be chastened for a little season with a sore and grievous chastisement, because they did not hearken altogether unto the precepts and commandments which I gave unto them" (v.4). Smith also has the Lord confirm that the saints were "smitten by the hands of mine enemies, on whom I will pour out my wrath without measure in mine own time" (v.2).

Pr. 42. But, says the Lord "I have decreed that your brethren which have been scattered shall return to the lands of their inheritances, and shall build up the waste places of Zion. For after much tribulation, as I have said unto you in a former commandment, cometh the blessing (v.11-12). Now the Lord explains how they will get their own back – in both senses; against their enemies and get their property back. This is very specific and cannot be misunderstood.

> **13.** Behold, this is the ***blessing which I have promised*** after your tribulations, and the tribulations of your brethren—***your redemption***, and the redemption of your brethren, even their ***restoration to the land of Zion, to be established, no more to be thrown down.*** (Emphasis added).

The Lord confirms the redemption of Zion "needs come by power"; Smith will lead them to war against the enemy and they will take the lands back.

Results:

Pr. 41. If that really were the case, it is harsh, to say the least. Clearly, Smith was just reiterating excuses he mentioned in earlier Sections. The Lord's *"own due time"* was one of Smith's pet phrases he had the Lord use *(see: The Final Analysis, Part 2)*. The fact is that no such retribution was ever meted out – in anyone's due time.

Pr. 42. The army, Zion's Camp, eventually marched almost nine-hundred miles in order to 'redeem' Zion, but succeeded only in encountering some dire circumstances along the way, often with little or bad food, and then cholera decimating the party. They were entirely unsuccessful in asking for their lands back and rather than stay and fight for them, they turned tail and went home with absolutely nothing to show for their efforts. *(See Section 105, p. 361 on).*

Section 104
23 April 1834. Kirtland, Ohio.

History.

1835 D&C Sec. XCVIII. 2010 D&C Sec. 104.

Despite the fact that more than one attempt at establishing a 'united order' failed miserably, Smith had had his God declare in no uncertain terms that it was a *commandment* and an *everlasting* order.

> **1.** Verily I say unto you, my friends, I give unto you counsel, and a commandment, concerning all the properties which belong to the order which I commanded to be organized and established, to be a united order, and an everlasting order for the benefit of my church, and for the salvation of men until I come—

Verses 2-3 confirm that obedience promises a "multiplicity of blessings" and that promise is *immutable* and *unchangeable*. However, if they are not faithful they will be "nigh unto cursing". They were recently cursed "with a very sore and grievous curse" (v.4) for not obeying the commandants – they were driven out of Zion. If anyone in the order is found to be out of line, they are to be turned over to the buffetings of Satan. That meant they were to be thrown out of course. Everything is to be done the Lord's way (v.16) in order that the poor may be "exalted" and "the rich made low". The Earth contains plenty for everyone and if anyone takes an "abundance" but doesn't give of their "portion", they will end up in hell.

Smith then has the Lord decide who is to get which properties. The list includes several now familiar names such as Rigdon, Harris, Williams and Cowdery. The Lord says that he will "multiply blessings" upon various people, seven or eight times, and for good measure, four times he adds that he will "multiply" a "multiplicity of blessings" on them. This strange turn of phrase was also used previously, in Section 97:28. *(See also: The Final Analysis, Part 3).* In view of what later transpired, it should be noted that the allotted property was for them *and* their seed after them (v.32). This was just the start of a long term project, set to last until the second coming. There is now to be one "United Order of the Stake of Zion, the City of Kirtland", and then once they are organised, another separate "United Order of the City of Zion" (v.48).

After some detail about the treasury of the order, there follows one of Smith's classic "in other words" sequences, wherein the Lord repeats exactly the same thing twice, this time in reverse order – and it is hardly chiasmus.

> **68.** And all moneys that you receive ...*shall be cast into the treasury as fast as you receive moneys, by hundreds, or by fifties, or by twenties, or by tens, or by fives.*
> **69.** *Or in other words,* if any man among you obtain *five dollars let him cast them into the treasury; or if he obtain ten, or twenty, or fifty, or an hundred, let him do likewise;* (Emphasis added).

Usually, when Smith had the Lord use the phrase "in other words", he simply repeated the very same thing again – not actually *in* 'other words', but generally using very same words a second time. This typifies Smith's lack of vocabulary, rather than it being evidence of further explanation by deity *(see analysis on p. 93 and summary in The Final Analysis, Part 2).*

In the final few verses, the Lord declares that they should pay their debts and write "speedily to New York", which again doesn't sound much like the Lord speaking, but he will soften the hearts of people they owe money to, so they won't come after them for immediate payment. This once, they can put up the properties in the 'order' as security "to loan enough to deliver yourselves from bondage" (v.84-6).

As v.1 confirms the United Order a commandment, and an everlasting one at that, and as v.48 confirms two United Order groups should be established, in addition to all the earlier promises made by the Lord that we have already identified, the Church now faces criticism that the idea shortly fell into disarray and did not survive. Such is the obvious non-fulfilment of this prophecy, there was even an Ensign article dedicated to an explanation as to why the Lord could, and apparently did, rescind the whole idea *(See: June 1986 Ensign – I have a question).* An unchangeable God can apparently change His mind after all, and somehow make an 'everlasting commandment' last next to no time.

In order to recover from the problem, in the Ensign article, the writer first explains the Lord's ways are not the ways of man and that he looks upon things from an eternal perspective. Previously, we have seen excuses for apparent '*eternal* damnation' and '*endless* torment' being rationalised away as to being for a lesser timescale by Smith himself having the Lord relate the designations to some of the 'names' of the Lord *(See pp. 135-7)*.

The writer of the Ensign article uses the very same tactic here:

> These statements suggest that God may have something else in mind when he uses words like *everlasting, eternal, Endless, or forever.* "Endless torment" and "eternal damnation," for example, do not mean there is no end to punishment, only that such punishment is God's punishment. "The punishment which is given from my hand is endless punishment, for Endless is my name. (Emphasis in original).

The writer then claims "a number of scriptures in the Bible sustain this principle". The article goes on to cite examples which are supposed to support the concept that the Lord can and does change his mind about what he himself once considered an 'everlasting' covenant, commandment or promise.

The first example is drawn from Exodus 12:14 where the Lord instigates the Passover: "And this day shall be unto you for a memorial; and ye shall keep it a feast to the Lord throughout your generations; ye shall keep it a feast by an ordinance for ever." He then cites Leviticus 16:34, referencing the Day of Atonement which was to be "an everlasting statute unto you." Then, assuming members will be satisfied with it without even considering the almost insane connotation, the writer has the audacity to claim that the Lord changed his mind about the need for that:

> Today, we celebrate neither the Passover nor the Day of Atonement. We understand that both were in similitude of the everlasting release of God's children from the bondage of sin and death through our great High Priest, Jesus Christ.

Completely ignoring the fact his so-called 'evidence' for that is drawn from the New Testament *(Hebrews 6:20 and Hebrews 8)*, which is Christian material not associated in any way with Judaism, the writer also ignores the fact that the Old Testament *belongs* to the Jews and was hijacked and rationalised into Christianity to suit the new religion. The Jews didn't just cease to exist when Christianity came along. To state that "we" no longer celebrate the Passover or the Day of Atonement obfuscates the truth and does not remotely equate to God rescinding the commandment that He gave to the *Jews*.

Obviously *Mormons* don't celebrate the Passover or the Day of Atonement these days – but a Christian-style Day of Atonement does actually model itself on the Jewish Holiday of Yom Kippur (Day of Atonement). The Jews were God's chosen race and those 'days' most certainly were, and still are, dutifully observed by Jews in fulfilment of the commandment to do so. In actual fact, the Day of Atonement also has deep significance in the New Testament.

The same is true of the 'Feast of the Passover' that the article mentions; God's chosen race, the Jews, still celebrate it today. To them, God never rescinded that law (or any other *eternal* law). It was and is 'forever'. Some Christian groups also celebrate elements of that feast.

Moving on to yet another supposed rescinded 'everlasting covenant'; the writer now turns to circumcision, citing Genesis 17:9-14. This, he claims, is also no longer observed. It may not be in Mormonism, any more than in mainstream Christianity, but these religions came along long after God gave the commandment – which was, once again, to the Jews. Ask any Jew about that. These commandments were for the *Jews* and they still observe them *all* today. Yet the writer claims:

> In the first century A.D., this practice created problems when gentiles were converted to Christianity. Consequently, an apostolic council pronounced that this "everlasting" rite ended when Christ restored the fulness of the gospel. (See Acts 15:6–31.)

Acts is traditionally considered to have been written by the author of Luke – but no one knows who wrote Luke. Whist it was 'ascribed' to Luke, it almost certainly was not written by that biblical character. Did that council of apostles and elders, if it ever did convene and consider such a thing (long after Jesus lived and never commented on), have any right to pronounce the rite ended?

God had declared it *everlasting* to the Jews and it still is. Just because gentile converts to Christianity didn't like the idea and a 'council' or committee decided to do away with the tradition, didn't mean *God* rescinded circumcision any more than the feast days. The Mormon Church claims the early Christian church quickly fell into apostasy and yet here seems to accept a committee decision to discontinue circumcision as being the will of God. They can't have it both ways. Was that a God-inspired decision or an apostate one?

It reminds me very much of the way the Mormon Church today eventually bows to the tide of popular opinion, changing 'everlasting covenants' in order to retain members and gain converts. The Lord had pronounced that no one of black African origin would *ever* hold the Priesthood until the Millennium, and even then, only after all the white people and the rest had received it. The same applied to the 'never to be changed' temple endowment – which has changed beyond all recognition. Because the Lord (at least, the Mormon version) supposedly changed his mind about all that, it can then be applied to everything else. It simply does not work, and in fact it makes a liar of the Mormon God.

Having run out of ideas, the article then claims that three years after giving the 'everlasting' commandment to live the 'Law of Consecration' as it also became known, it was 'suspended', "although some aspects remained". Those 'aspects' turn out to be "tithing, fast offerings, welfare projects, storehouses, and other principles and practices. Through these programs we should, as individuals, implement in our own lives the bases of the united order." *(c. Ensign, May 1977, pp. 94–95. Marion G. Romney: The Purpose of Church Welfare Services.)*

Happy that the point has been adequately made, the article concludes:

> Although the united order was placed in abeyance, it is part of the everlasting gospel of Jesus Christ. The principle is clear in the scriptures: The Lord is everlasting and eternal; hence, everything he commands is everlasting and eternal, although a particular commandment may not be practiced all the time, but only for the period the Lord wills. So it is with the united order—it will be lived in full when the Lord commands. It is his law, which is everlasting.

So, whilst 'eternal suffering' is rationalised not to actually *be* eternal, as it only relates to a *name* the Lord goes by, the United Order *is* an eternal principle which must one day be lived again. It is an inconsistent and flawed supposition.

In any event, it didn't work in mortal life, and by all accounts of things reportedly 'eternal' in nature – such an order should not even be required as part of such an existence. There would be no need for it in an environment where people are creating and populating their own worlds. Everyone would have everything and the concept of a United Order becomes entirely obsolete. It is yet another man made idea based on Smith's communistic idealism and it simply did not work.

At best, this is one of the most ignorant of articles I have ever read; and at worst, it is one of the most arrogant and deceitful. Rank and file Mormons will most probably not even question the rationale and just accept it as the way things are. Rarely will someone say, hang on a minute, if it really was the case that all these words, such as "everlasting, eternal, Endless, or forever" did *not* actually mean those things, why didn't the Lord clarify that in each case, and just say – "until I say otherwise". That would have been clearer – and also a lot more honest. If He is real, the Mormon God is *not* honest. He is devious in His ways and very unclear in His intent, and that is not good enough to rely on for anyone with a grain of common sense or the ability to reason. Faith doesn't enter into it, honesty and integrity do – and a God should be the prime example of such things.

This is the real question: Why should there *ever* be a need to second guess God?

Section 104 – Summary

Prophecies made: 1
Prophecies fulfilled: 0

Prophecies made:

Pr. 43.   v.1: ...the order which I commanded to be organized and established, to be a united order, and an everlasting order...

Results.

Pr. 43. This prophecy has been repeated many times, yet within three years, the United Order had fallen apart. God would have known that would happen.

Section 105
22 June 1834. Fishing River, Missouri.

History.

1844 D&C Sec. CII. 2010 D&C Sec. 105.

In Smith's December 1833 revelation *(D&C 101)*, regarding the loss of land and property at 'Zion', the Lord had instructed the saints to obtain redress through the courts and political process before military action was considered. But, it also predicted the time would come when Smith would have to drum up an army to reclaim the lands by force *(Sec. 101:43, 56-60)*.

    On 4 May 1834, the outcome of the Lord's earlier instruction through Smith *(in Section 103)*, to have five-hundred men located, or if not, three-hundred – or at least one hundred, was realised when one-hundred and thirty men plus a few women and children assembled to become part of 'Zion's Camp'. By the time they had joined forces with volunteers in other locations, just over two-hundred men formed Smith's little army. They were ready to march almost nine-hundred miles to redeem Zion, first by asking nicely and then taking the lands by force if necessary. They even enacted a mock battle near Decatur in order to test their military ability. *(Google: April 1979 Ensign, 'Zion's Camp March')*.

    Those familiar with Smith's claim that an unearthed skeleton from a burial mound was an ancient and famous Lamanite warrior named Zelph who died in battle, may be interested to learn that this 'find' occurred along the march, on 3 June 1834, when Smith and a few others climbed a bluff and dug into the mound which lies a mile south of Valley City *(See: HC. Vol. 2:79, 80n)*. Smith would have been in his element; such digging was reminiscent of his money-digging days. In his early life, he had no luck with it but now there was a 'find'.

This is not an obscure and unknown location. The above mentioned Ensign article indicates that 'tourism' by Mormons is not encouraged as the site is now privately owned. So, here's an idea; why doesn't the Mormon Church put its money where its mouth is (well, Joseph Smith's mouth) and take DNA samples from the bones of Native Americans buried in that mound and determine their age and origin? We know they never will because they already know what the results would be. Nevertheless, it's a challenge worth making.

Of course, if anyone ever did verify the DNA, the Mormon Church would then assert the tests may not have included Zelph's bones (perhaps an angel took them away); or DNA is an unreliable science – they still seem to be fond of that one; Smith's claim was just an opinion; he wasn't speaking as a prophet at that moment; and of course – he was after all, only human. Pick an excuse.

Regardless of the above challenge, which undoubtedly will never be taken up, the fact remains that Smith's *claim* is enough to yet again question the Mormon Church concerning the whereabouts of Lamanites. Whilst the Church now turns to other implausible suppositions, from the time of Smith and his followers, right up until I was a young enthusiastic believer, we all *knew* who the Lamanites were and *where* they could be located. Even the prophets of the twentieth century knew. Now, they have no idea and don't like to talk about it.

The following day, on 4 June, they entered Missouri and by the end of that month they had crossed most of the state, but news of their approach had already reached the settlers who got themselves organised and raised their own militia which far outnumbered the Mormon group. That action resulted in a quick and easy decision for Joseph Smith. There was absolutely no success in negotiating a return of the lands. Rather than stay and fight a militia that far outnumbered Smith's contingent, he disbanded Zion's Camp and they started their long and weary journey home.

It wasn't just a matter of enjoying a casual trip. Most had to walk and it was more than an arduous time for them. Many became ill and fourteen people died from cholera. Food was often in short supply and such as was located was not always fresh or even edible. Smith did not have enough resources to provide properly for the group and many were not happy at all. Not only were they suffering from the physical toll that such a long walk presented, along with the trauma of the accompanying illnesses and the several deaths, but the prophecy had *not* been fulfilled. Many members believed they should have fought for their lands as Smith's God had predicted they would. There was dissension and criticism which Smith was to face even more of when they eventually reached Kirtland and members there learned of the failure and the deaths. Zion's Camp was discharged on 3 July and they finally disbanded on 25 July 1834.

D&C - SECTIONS 100-108, OLD 101, 134 & GENERAL ASSEMBLY

Two years later, in 1836, the Missouri legislature was to set aside the new 'Caldwell County' for Mormons as a compromise, but they were soon driven from there, across the Mississippi and into Illinois.

Whilst many Zion's Camp travellers were critical of Smith and his failed expedition, others stood firm with him and were solid in their support. It was from this group that many later Mormon leaders were drawn, including all of the first twelve apostles.

It was on 22 June 1834 at Fishing River, when Smith, faced with failure, dissension and criticism, recorded Section 105 in order to diffuse the situation. He had been somewhat helped when a mob gathered on the opposite side of the river and a heavy storm swelled the river by about thirty feet, forcing the mob to disperse rather than cross the river and attack them. Smith claimed 'God was in that storm' and some said it was a miracle. In Smith's new revelation, he tried to excuse the problems and make promises for the future.

Naturally, and predictably, the first thing the Lord has to say is that were it not for the transgressions of the saints (as a group, rather than any individuals being named) things would have been far different. They have not been faithful to the commandments. The Lord actually declares they are "full of all manner of evil, and do not impart of their substance, as becometh saints, to the poor and afflicted among them" and that they "are not united according to the union required by the law of the celestial kingdom; And Zion cannot be built up unless it is by the principles of the law of the celestial kingdom; otherwise I cannot receive her unto myself" (v.3-5).

The Lord cannot receive them *unless* they live the United Order, yet all the early attempts at it soon fell into disarray and it has never been reinstated. If it is an eternal law which has to be lived *before* the Lord can 'receive' the saints, and no one now lives it, the Lord still can't receive them. Ergo, all is now lost for the Mormon Church and its faithless members. There will be excuses found for that, pulled out of thin air and recorded somewhere no doubt.

They must meanwhile be chastened and learn obedience, which is why they must suffer. Smith is obviously having a very hard time of it and has the Lord specifically say they must "speak not concerning those who are appointed to lead my people, who are the first elders of my church, for they are not all under this condemnation" (v.7). To diffuse the situation, the Lord doesn't even blame the local saints directly, but says "I speak concerning my churches abroad—there are many who will say: Where is their God? Behold, he will deliver them in time of trouble, otherwise we will not go up unto Zion, and will keep our moneys." Therefore, says the Lord, they must wait awhile. Smith has the Lord get him off the hook but he clearly has no idea what to do next. He just wants people to give up their money and land to the united order.

Not enough young men and middle aged men volunteered to join Zion's Camp (v.16-17), but there is a 'teaser'; for those who did go, something good is in store. "For behold, I have prepared a great endowment and blessing to be poured out upon them, inasmuch as they are faithful and continue in humility before me. Therefore it is expedient in me that mine elders should wait for a little season, for the redemption of Zion" (v.12-13). Zion can wait, but the Kirtland endowment will be an interim blessing for those who have showed faith. They have to learn more and obey more (v.18-19). Smith was trying to retain control and regain some lost credibility. Today, we would call it damage limitation. However, Smith then takes things more than a step too far, exposing complete lack of consistency in his own already established concepts, forgoing all logic and reason – even for his imaginative mind.

What Smith has the Lord say next is quite incredible. In v.14, the Lord says, look, I don't require you to "fight the battles of Zion"; I have told you before – "*I* will fight your battles". The question then is why on earth did the Lord send them on a pointless trip, ostensibly to do just that; a venture that cost several lives and achieved absolutely nothing? It then gets very strange, as having said *he* will fight their battles, the Lord sends *Satan* to do the job.

> **15.** Behold, the destroyer I have sent forth to destroy and lay waste mine enemies; and not many years hence they shall not be left to pollute mine heritage, and to blaspheme my name upon the lands which I have consecrated for the gathering together of my saints.

Among many other references, Smith's own D&C 61:19 and 101:51-54, as well as the Mormon 'Guide to the Scriptures', confirm "Satan is the destroyer" in no uncertain terms. In Judaism, the idea of God sending HaSaTan to do such a thing would work well as he is not an evil character and sits on God's council as an adversary. He can only act with permission and under the direction of God. However, in Christianity, and most certainly within Mormonism, that is not the case at all. Satan is positively evil and works *only* in opposition to God. God has absolutely no control over Satan in that sense and he is hardly likely to assist God by laying waste to God's enemies; indeed, God's enemies are surely Satan's natural allies. The claim conflicts with Mormon doctrine.

Nevertheless, this verse contains a direct commitment from the Lord that he has already sent "the destroyer" who will redeem Zion and in not many years none of the 'enemies' will be left upon the land consecrated for the saints. This is not only an entirely unfulfilled prophecy; it is a contradiction from Smith's God, as Satan could never be sent by God to do any such thing. It is perfectly clear that this is pure nonsense, whichever way you look at it.

The Lord tells the saints not to be judgmental and to use judgment and justice according to the law – until the "army of Israel becomes very great". Had he not just said *he* will fight their battles and had sent Satan to take care of the enemies? Smith got himself in a real muddle over this so-called revelation.

In v.27, Smith has the Lord quote a Bible myth, saying he will soften the hearts of the people just like he did "from time to time" with Pharaoh. Smith had no idea that no such thing really happened and that it was just another old Hebrew legend with no basis in reality. The Lord is still insisting wise men must go to Jackson County and the surrounding areas to buy up land ready for their inheritance. Once that has been achieved, despite the fact he has just promised them (again) that *he* will take care of matters, even sending Satan to take care of things once and for all, the Lord says:

> 30. And after these lands are purchased, I will hold the armies of Israel guiltless in taking possession of their own lands, which they have previously purchased with their moneys, and of throwing down the towers of mine enemies that may be upon them, and scattering their watchmen, and avenging me of mine enemies unto the third and fourth generation of them that hate me.

Far from really taking care of things himself, "First let my army become great" says the Lord (v.31). He wants their "banners" to become "terrible unto all nations", showing far more optimism than befits God. Smith makes matters even worse, in a complete abandonment of sanity, presumably because he felt that if he had the Lord say it, there would be no argument. This is how bizarre things got. The Lord himself declares "That the kingdoms of this world may be constrained to acknowledge that the kingdom of Zion is in very deed the kingdom of our God and his Christ; therefore, let us become subject unto her laws" (v.32). This silly idea was never realised and of course it never will be.

Finally, the Lord reminds them yet again to first "lift up an ensign for peace" (v.39) "and all things shall work together for your good" (v.40). They did – and things didn't.

Section 105 – Summary

Prophecies made:	3
Prophecies fulfilled:	0

Prophecies made:

Pr. 44. The time would come when Smith would have to drum up an army to reclaim the lands by force *(Section 101:43, 56-60).* Over two-hundred men formed Smith's army. They marched almost nine-hundred miles to redeem Zion, first by asking nicely and then taking the lands by force if necessary.

Pr. 45. They "are not united according to the union required by the law of the celestial kingdom; And Zion cannot be built up unless it is by the principles of the law of the celestial kingdom; otherwise I cannot receive her unto myself" (v.3-5).

Pr. 46. Verse 15 contains a direct commitment from the Lord that he has already sent "the destroyer" who will redeem Zion and in not many years, none of the 'enemies' will be left upon the land consecrated for the saints.

Results.

Pr. 44. Smith's 'Zion's Camp' consisted of over two-hundred men who were prepared to fight in order to reclaim their lands and property, just as the prophecy had foretold. They even enacted a mock battle near Decatur in order to test their military ability. When negotiations failed, instead of resorting to force, Smith disbanded his army, turned around and went home. The prophecy remained unfulfilled.

Pr. 45. The Lord cannot receive them *unless* they live the United Order, yet all the early attempts to do so soon fell into disarray and it has never been reinstated. Ergo, all is lost for the Mormon Church which cannot be 'received unto the Lord' as they don't live that 'eternal' law.

Pr. 46. This is not only an entirely unfulfilled prophecy; it is a contradiction from Smith's God, as Satan could not be *sent* by God to do any such thing. Satan works in opposition to God and would never be disposed to assist Him in any way. It makes no (Mormon) theological sense.

****

History of the Church Vol. 2:145.
16 August 1834

History

Letter from Joseph Smith – not included in the D&C.

Joseph Smith wrote to "Lyman Wight, Edward Partridge, John Corrill, Isaac Morley, and others of the High Council of Zion". The following prophecy concerning 'Zion' was included in his letter which was not canonised. Some of Smith's later letters were canonised *(see Sections 121-123, 127, 128)*.

> You will recollect that *the first Elders are to receive their endowment in Kirtland*, before *the redemption of Zion*…
>
> But, in case the excitement continues to be allayed, and peace prevails, use every effort to prevail on the churches to gather to those regions and locate themselves, to be in readiness to move into Jackson county In *two years from the eleventh of September next*, which is *the appointed time for the redemption of Zion*. (Emphasis added).

There are two points regarding this. Firstly, the so-called 'endowment' experienced at Kirtland was nothing like the eventual ceremony performed in Nauvoo, as Smith had yet to invent the more complex rituals – with the help of Masonic signs, tokens and penalties which he was yet to discover and utilise.

Secondly, 11 September 1836 – the day appointed for the 'redemption of Zion' – passed without incident, or at least without Zion being redeemed. It is a tragic irony that 11 September was selected. Whilst it remained meaningless in the year 1836, that date twenty-one years later, in 1857, saw the murder of over one-hundred-and-thirty innocent men, women and children by Mormons at Mountain Meadows, and of course 9/11 in 2001 needs no comment at all.

This was prophecy unfulfilled, but it is mentioned out of historical interest rather than for inclusion in Smith's list of failures, as the Mormon Church will claim that as it was never canonised, it cannot be considered actual prophecy.

****

Section 106
25 November 1834. Kirtland, Ohio.

History.

1835 D&C Sec. XCIX. 2010 D&C Sec. 106.

Five months have passed since the disastrous Zion's Camp expedition and this is the first time further revelation has been recorded since then. Section 106 comprises a few verses calling Oliver Cowdery's older brother, Warren, to be a presiding high priest over the area. Such verses are designed purely and simply to encourage the person named to do Smith's bidding. Warren will be blessed and he has a crown awaiting him – of course, that reward will come – hereafter.

Smith adds that "the coming of the Lord draweth nigh" and it "overtaketh the world as a thief in the night". That sentiment appears a couple of times in the New Testament of course so Smith would have felt safe in having the Lord use those words here. The trouble is, and Smith often got this aspect entirely wrong, they were not words that the Lord used himself; it was others describing their concept of how the Lord would return. Luke mentions the idea and Paul told the Thessalonians they knew very well the Lord would return "as a thief in the night". The concept is human and the Lord did not use the term, so why would he do so now?

Section 107 (Part)
(v. 1-58, 70, 73, 76-77, 88, 90, 93-98).
Circa April 1835. Kirtland, Ohio.

History.

1833 BOC LXXI (unpublished). 1835 D&C Sec. III. 2010 D&C Sec. 107. (The balance of Section 107 was recorded on 11 November 1831 in Hiram, Ohio).
(See pp. 255-8).

Around April of 1835 is when Smith added a number of verses to a revelation originally recorded in November 1831. In the additional verses, Smith has the Lord define Aaronic and Melchizedek Priesthood offices and provide details of what each office entails.

The thing is that Smith got so embroiled in making up all his new ideas that he forgot what he previously recorded. Within the original verses of Section 107, which had been written in 1831, Smith had had the Lord explain that the high council (over which Smith himself presided) was the "highest council of the church of God, and a final decision upon controversies in spiritual matters. There is not any person belonging to the church who is exempt from this council of the church" (v.80-81). The decision of the high council was final.

When Smith wrote the minutes of a meeting that established such a council in February of 1834 *(See Sec. 102, p. 350)*, he recorded that the travelling high council could organise such a council wherever they went and it was possible for someone to "appeal to the high council of the seat of the First Presidency of the Church, and have a re-hearing" *(Sec. 102:26)*. Other than that, decisions were still final. In 1835, Smith added three verses to Section 102, explaining there *could* be an appeal from the high council, but *not* from the Quorum of Twelve Apostles.

Within the verses that were added to Section 107, Smith also had the Lord confirm:

> 23. The twelve traveling councilors are called to be the Twelve Apostles, or special witnesses of the name of Christ in all the world— thus differing from other officers in the church in the duties of their calling.
> 24. And they form a quorum, equal in authority and power to the three presidents previously mentioned.

Although, in another added verse we find these words:

> 37. The high council in Zion form a quorum equal in authority in the affairs of the church, in all their decisions, to the councils of the Twelve at the stakes of Zion.

All three groups now appear equal in authority. It is no wonder confusion and dissension abounded just a few years later following the death of Joseph Smith in 1844.

From new verses 42-58, Smith once more gets into some detail about who handed down the priesthood from the time of Adam. He did this previously within Section 84, which is analysed in *TMD Vol. 4:202-5 (S76-9)*. Section 84:6-16 lists the Priesthood being conferred from *father to son* in this order, although there are obvious gaps in the sequence. Adam → Abel → **Enoch** → Noah → Melchizedek → Abraham; then, God → Esaias, who *"lived in the days of Abraham"* according to Smith (Section 84:13) → Gad → Jeremy → Elihu → Caleb → Jethro → Moses.

It is an interesting list, as some of the people mentioned as personally ordaining the next person in the sequence after God ordained 'Esaias', lived in entirely the wrong timeframe and Esaias wasn't even a real person; it is Greek for Isaiah. *(See TMD Vol. 4:205)*. Abraham was probably born between 2100-1800 BCE and purportedly lived for 175 years. Isaiah (Greek: Esaias) lived 775-701 BCE. Smith's mythical Esaias lived over a thousand years earlier.

Section 84 confirms each person received the priesthood from the hand of his *father* – "And Jethro received it under the hand of Caleb" (v.7) etc., through their lineage, back to *Abel* who received it from Adam.

> **D&C 84:14.** Which Abraham received the priesthood from Melchizedek, who received it through the lineage of his fathers, even till Noah;
> 15. And from ***Noah till Enoch***, through the lineage of their fathers;

16. And *from Enoch to Abel*, who was slain by the conspiracy of his brother, who received the priesthood by the commandments of God, by the hand of his father Adam, who was the first man— (Emphasis added).

In Section 107:40-52, among other details, Smith has the Lord declare the Priesthood was "confirmed to be handed down *from father to son*" (v.40) (Italics added) from the days of Adam. Yet the Lord then notes seven men to whom the Priesthood was given directly *by* Adam. Most names do not appear in the above list which is incomplete. The men that the Lord tells Smith *Adam* ordained includes:

According to Smith, **Adam** ordained these seven men:	Take Adam's 'mortality' as year 1 for the sake of this analysis.
Seth – ordained at age 69.	Adam ordained Seth in year 199.
Enos – ordained at age 134.	– Enos in year 369.
Cainan – ordained at age 87.	– Cainan in year 412.
Mahalaleel – ordained at age 496.	– Mahalaleel in year 891.
Jared – ordained at age 200.	– Jared in year 660.
Enoch – ordained **at age 25.**	– Enoch in year 647.
Methuselah – ordained at age 100.	– Methuselah in year 787.

This list of seven is lifted straight from Genesis 5 and presents a number of problems. Firstly, Smith's sequence in *Section 84:16* continues with *Abel* to Enoch after Adam. Conversely, the Bible lists Abel's brother, *Seth*, as next in that sequence. Abel was of course killed by his brother Cain according to the Bible. Enoch cannot have come through the lineage of both Abel, as Smith claims in Section 84:16 *and* Seth which the Bible records. The fact that it is all just fiction, confirmed simply due to the ages people supposedly lived to be, when the worldwide average age of death in that era was less than thirty *(see pp. 271-2)*, does not excuse Smith getting details entirely wrong that his Church and the rest of Christianity accept as true in the Bible.

The other obvious question is, if Adam *did* ordain these seven characters, why at such different ages? Smith says Adam ordained Methuselah before his great-grandfather, Mahalaleel, who was ordained over one-hundred years later.

Genesis 5:5-32 gives the direct line from Adam to Noah.

Adam begat Seth at age 130 and lived to be 930.
Seth begat Enos at age 105 and lived to be 912.
Enos begat Cainan at age 90 and lived to be 905.
Cainan begat Mahalaleel at age 70 and lived to be 910.

Mahalaleel begat Jared at age 65 and lived to be 895.
Jared begat Enoch at age 162 and lived to be 962.
Enoch begat Methuselah at age 65 and lived to be 365.
Methuselah begat Lamech at age 187 and lived to be 969.
Lamech begat Noah at age 182 and lived to be 777.
Noah was 500 when he begat Shem, Ham and Japheth.

Smith's 'Inspired Revision' of the Bible confirms exactly the same details as recorded in the Genesis list. Smith did not alter the genealogy from the way it appears in Genesis; although he obviously thought some information must be lacking where the Bible just says Noah was 500 when he had his three boys, as Smith added some pointless detail.

IR. Gen. 7:85. And Noah was four hundred and fifty years old, and begat Japheth, and forty-two years afterwards, he begat Shem, of her who was the mother of Japheth, and when he was five hundred years old, he begat Ham.

Of all the things the Lord could have 'inspired' Smith to add, this is not exactly important or enlightening information and clearly just plucked out of Smith's own imagination. He doesn't even confirm the mother's name.

But one name *does* appear in both lists. Note that Smith has the Lord claim *Enoch* was given the high priesthood by *Adam*. There are two Enoch's listed in the Bible, the second being the son of Cain, who hardly qualifies for the high priesthood in Mormon theology, so we know it has to be the same character in Sections 84 and 107. In Section 84, the Lord said Enoch (and everyone else), was ordained by his *father* and confirms it *again* in 107:40. Then he declares that Enoch and six others were ordained by Adam, in complete contradiction to what he had previously said and again just confirmed. Would the Lord make such a mistake as that?

Incidentally, historically, we know for a fact that Genesis mainly consists of fiction and that humans had been around for a very long time by BCE 4000 or so. Not only were there around five million humans alive at that time, the longevity spoken of in the Bible is yet another example of Hebrews magnifying their position in their known world. Genesis was written down thousands of years after claimed events took place and the people in the stories supposedly existed. Handed down oral legends eventually became their history, just as was the case in many other cultures that existed then or even long predated the Hebrews. Many of their own legends, including the Adam and Eve story, the exodus, and the flood, were borrowed from earlier recorded myths and legends.

The famous Shakespearian 'three-score-years-and-ten' idea, originating from Psalm 90:10 was not an average, it was the exception at the higher end of the scale. Only relatively recently has longevity really started to climb. Today, the *average* age of death in the UK is higher than ever, at 77.4 years. That is still well short of the hundreds of years attributed to early patriarchs. We *know* such longevity to have been utterly impossible and yet we were raised on the idea, if we were taught to accept the Bible as factual – on faith.

Common sense and reason suggest we should accept the science first – and then see what's left of the Bible that may still be worth considering. But many people seem to just accept it without *thinking*. The same is true of those who accept the Hindu Vedas; the Qur'an of Islam; Tipitaka of Buddhism; Shinto's Kojiki; or Guru Granth Sahib of Sikhism – or other religious works, such as the Book of Mormon, and of course the Doctrine and Covenants. They should each be considered in conjunction with what we actually scientifically *know* is true and/or remotely possible, before accepting what they say purely on faith.

Verse 57 confirms that details of Adam's predictions about what would befall later generations are to be found in the book of Enoch and "are to be testified in due time." The Mormon Bible Dictionary claims "There are at least three apocalyptic works purporting to be books of Enoch; these are included in the category usually called "pseudepigrapha," meaning writings under assumed names, compiled long after the time of the supposed author."

A lot of the Bible as we know it today also consists of pseudepigrapha. In particular, the four gospels, which were written long after the time of Christ; and yet the Mormon Church ignores the evidence of this and prefers to view them as the original words of those to whom they are ascribed 'according to' in each case, despite many contradictions between them and impossible claims in them.

Smith never did have the Lord reveal the location of the lost book of Enoch and it is hardly going to be recognised by the Mormon Church now as one of the early books that was discarded when the Bible was formulated by several committees over the first few centuries of the Common Era. Nevertheless, the Mormon Bible Dictionary concludes: "On the basis of latter-day revelation it appears there are some truths contained in the apocalyptic Enoch books."

They are available, so why doesn't the Church reveal which one it is? Then members could benefit from the hidden knowledge. The reason is that all the material rejected when the Bible was compiled (as well as some that actually got included, such as the book of Revelation), did not make much of any sense and some of it was sheer and obvious nonsense to the compilers, which is why they were discarded. Smith had the Lord declare the book of Enoch would be *"testified in due time."* I venture to suggest that it never will be.

Mormon prophet Gordon B. Hinckley self-confessed they no longer receive direct revelation *(see p. xiv)*. They have to ask questions and they get 'feelings' for answers. Can you imagine the current prophet asking the Lord for the book of Enoch to be revealed? Of course not; "we have a great body of revelation" according to Hinckley. It's an excellent excuse for not having anything new to say.

From what we have observed so far in the D&C, if that is revelation, it isn't exactly very good revelation, is it? If the Lord doesn't care to explain (for example) what happened to all the Lamanites, which when I was young, we all *knew* for a fact consisted of all Native North Americans and the peoples in the rest of the Americas as well as many of the islands of the sea because prophets constantly declared it, he is hardly likely to reveal the location of the book of Enoch. It doesn't exist any more than Lamanites do.

Section 107 (Part) – Summary

Prophecies made:	1
Prophecies fulfilled:	0
Other non-prophetic revelation:	2

Prophecies made:

Pr. 47. v.57: "These things were all written in the book of Enoch, and are to be testified of in due time."

Results:

Pr. 47. There has been no further mention of the whereabouts of such a book. Joseph Smith invented the idea, and I venture to suggest it will never be mentioned again, let alone identified and revealed.

Non-prophetic revelation.

1. The high council (over which Smith presided) was the "highest council of the church of God, and a final decision upon controversies in spiritual matters. There is not any person belonging to the church who is exempt from this council of the church" (v.80-81). The decision of the high council was *final*.

In 1835, Smith added three verses to Section 102 explaining there *could* be an appeal from the high council, but *not* from the Quorum of Twelve Apostles, thus contradicting his earlier pronouncement. These were all supposedly the Lord's directions regarding such matters.

2. In Section 84:6-16, the Lord lists the Priesthood being conferred in order, from father to son. In Section 107:40-52, among other details listed, Smith has

the Lord declare that the Priesthood was "confirmed to be handed down from father to son" (v.40) from the days of Adam.

The Lord then lists seven people that Adam ordained *directly*. One of these, Enoch, was previously listed as being ordained by his father; also, that he came through the lineage of *Abel* (84:16). Genesis 5 lists Enoch as from the lineage of *Seth*. The Lord apparently forgot father-son ordinations had been initiated and subsequently violated – by Adam. He also forgot the correct lineage.

BOC Chapter 101 (Marriage)
Circa August 1835. Kirtland, Ohio.

History.

1835 D&C Sec. CI. Discarded in 1876. (Replaced with Section 132).

Some Mormon writers have suggested that this Section may have been inserted into the D&C while Smith was 'out of town' and he may not have approved it, but that is provably not the case at all; the fact is that it remained throughout every edition until it was replaced by Section 132 in 1876.

Smith had every opportunity to either alter or delete it before the 1844 edition was published but he didn't and there is nothing in any additional Section that did enter the 1844 edition which conflicts with Section 101. Smith appeared quite happy with the lie that had been published and canonised. That should tell people something. It was in fact accepted by the Church in 1835 as scripture in quite a unique way.

In the *JS Papers Vol 2:561-2*, we find a scanned copy of the original Section 101. I have provided a transcript in *TMD Vol. 1, Apx. G. (See also Vol. 1:33, 72-3). (S97-8)*. Things are actually far worse for the Church in respect of whether Smith and the general membership were 'aware' of Section 101 in 1835 than many may imagine. Far from it being surreptitiously included as some have asserted, in fact, as it was a new 'article', it was actually read out to the entire membership before the vote was taken to sustain it as part of the D&C. That action was recorded in the "General Assembly" minutes which were also originally included in the 1835 edition of the D&C *(see p. 378)*.

> President W. W. Phelps then read an article on Marriage, which was accepted and adopted, and ordered to be printed in said book, by a unanimous vote.

D&C - SECTIONS 100-108, OLD 101, 134 & GENERAL ASSEMBLY

In fact, there was no reason for Smith to have done anything other than approve of such a statement in 1835, as he was yet to embark on his journey into polygamy. He had entered a lengthy adulterous relationship with Fanny Alger during 1833, but everyone knew (and some recorded) that it was no more than an affair and Smith never refuted that *(See TMD Vol. 1. Ch.4)*. Smith got caught in the act and begged forgiveness. There was never any mention of it being anything other than adultery. The Church *assumes* there *must* have been a marriage of some sort because the affair is so well documented and they simply cannot admit their first prophet was adulterous.

But there is absolutely *no* evidence Smith and Fanny Alger were anything other than lovers. When Smith's wife Emma threw Fanny out of the house, that was the end of the affair – and it had been just that, an affair. Smith's first real (recorded) foray into polygamy as such, did not occur until 1838, with Lucinda Pendleton Morgan Harris, some three years *after* Section 101 was written and canonised. In light of these facts, there was no reason for Smith *not* to have approved Section 101 which at the time exactly reflected Mormon theology.

Somewhat influenced by the Church's claim that Smith had *married* Fanny Alger, I concluded in *TMD Volume 1* that Smith had invented polygyny as a 'post-affair' cover for his relationship shortly after that event. Upon further reflection, I realised that there is no *evidence* to suggest that at all. Polygyny amongst themselves was not actually considered quite that early, though there is some indication that already married missionaries were instructed to marry Lamanite women also.

It seems polygyny was not invented until quite some time *after* Smith's confessed adultery with Fanny. Their affair is dated to 1833, although there is some suggestion that it had lasted for quite some time, possibly two or three years. Section 101 was published in 1835; Smith's 'recorded' polygyny and polyandry started in 1838. That possibly establishes the reason why Section 101 was acceptable to Smith when it was published in 1835; polygamy came later. Whatever the case, it is not really important; what *is* important is what Smith *later* did with Section 101, when true details concerning the past dwindle into insignificance.

Joseph Smith became more than culpable when he and Dr. Bennett were both prolifically adding wives to their collections in 1842. Word was getting out; rumour and gossip were spreading; Smith had married a dozen women in that year alone, before Section 101 was republished in *Times and Seasons* and Smith made Bennett the fall guy in order to protect himself. The following affidavit was added to D&C 101 by Smith when it was republished in the Church newspaper on 1 October 1842.

> We have given the above rule of marriage as the only one practiced in this church, to show that Dr. J. C. Bennett's "secret wife system"

is a matter of his own manufacture; and further to disabuse the public ear, and shew [show] that the said Bennett and his misanthropic friend Origen Bachelor, are perpetrating a foul and infamous slander upon an innocent people, and need but be known to be hated and despise. In support of this position, we present the following certificates:-

We the undersigned members of the church of Jesus Christ of Latter-Day Saints and residents of the city of Nauvoo, persons of families do hereby certify and declare that *we know of no other rule or system of marriage than the one published from the Book of Doctrine and Covenants*, and we give this certificate to show that Dr. J. C. Bennett's "secret wife system" is a creature of his own make as we know of no such society in this place nor never did.

S. Bennett,	Reynolds Cahoon,
N. K. Whitney,	John Taylor,
George Miller,	Wilson Law,
Albert Pettey,	E. Robinson,
Alpheus Cutler,	W. Woodruff,
Elias Higbee,	Aaron Johnson.

We the undersigned members of the ladies' relief society, and married females do certify and declare that *we know of no system of marriage being practised [practiced] in the church of Jesus Christ of Latter Day Saints save the one contained in the Book of Doctrine and Covenants*, and we give this certificate to the public to show that J. C. Bennett's "secret wife system" is a disclosure of his own make.

Emma Smith, President,	Thirza Cahoon,
Elizabeth Ann Whitney, Counsellor,	Phebe Woodruff
Sarah M. Cleveland, Counsellor,	Ann Hunter,
Eliza R. Snow, Secretary,	Leonora Taylor,
Mary C. Miller,	Jane Law,
Catharine Pettey,	Sarah Hillman,
Lois Cutler,	Sophia R. Marks,
Sarah Higbee,	Rosannah Marks.

(Times and Seasons 1 Oct 1842. Vol 3. No. 23:939). (Emphasis added).

Although I referred to it, I did not include the above detail or list in *TMD Vol. 1*, hence including it here. I did make the following comment which is worth repeating, just to clarify how devious and reprehensible Joseph Smith's tactics were, and how he could and did manipulate people to do his bidding.

This is the type of man Mormons believe represented God on Earth.

Many of the people signing the affidavit knew polygamy was being practiced. They included two Apostles, John Taylor and Wilford Woodruff, who were aware of polygamy, Bishop Whitney who had personally married his young daughter Sarah to Smith as a plural wife, Whitney's wife Elizabeth who had witnessed the ceremony, Sarah M. Cleveland and Eliza R. Snow, who were already Smith wives. They openly and knowingly *lied* in their statement. How then could there be any credence to Smith's *Book of Mormon* witnesses who were all close family and friends, when such obvious 'lying for the Lord' was so firmly established in the way he operated. There can be no trusting anyone who signed their name to anything on behalf of Joseph Smith. *(TMD Vol. 1:34).*

Section 134
Circa August 1835. Kirtland, Ohio.

History.

1835 D&C Sec. CII. 2010 D&C Sec. 134.

"Of Governments and Laws in General" (1835 Header).

Section 134 is represented as *"a declaration of belief regarding governments and laws in general, adopted by unanimous vote at a general assembly of the Church..."* (Italics in original header). It declares "governments were *instituted of God*" (v.1). It is hard to accept that statement of 'belief' in light of the later attitude toward the American Government and the Mormon temple "Oath of Vengeance" against the United States *(See: TMD Vol. 3:167-8). (S99).*

Governments are seen as there "for the good and safety of society" (v.1). Obviously they were not familiar with some other governments of the world which ranged from their 'American' experience and other democratic systems, to kings, queens, corrupt leaders, extremist rulers and military dictatorships – I doubt they had any experience of North Korea for example.

Today, we are seeing dictatorships questioned and challenged by various uprisings where discontent has been brewing for years. God didn't *"institute"* governments of any description; men did. They were often initiated by invasion or military coup. Rather than institute governments, surely a God would have established a reliable and sustainable theocracy? America was not that different either, having fought the British to obtain independence not that long before Smith's own time. Governments are to be "upheld by the voice of the people if a republic, or the will of the sovereign" (v.3). A simplistic view coupled with much naiveté methinks – and not remotely part of a message from the Lord.

I had never noticed v.4 previously which claims "We believe that religion is instituted of God" when the Mormon Church denounces every religion outside its own, all of which are considered part of the "Great and Abominable Church" – which surely God did not then institute. It goes on to claim that men are obliged to "sustain and uphold" governments; "sedition" and "rebellion" are unbecoming and should be punished. That's rich, coming from a group that wanted to overthrow the United States government and had the Lord prophesy that it would happen. *(See TMD Vol. 3:167-8. S.99)*.

Following several meaningless verses giving opinions about crime and punishment, there are a few (equally meaningless) verses essentially suggesting separation of Church and State. Finally, Smith turns to the treatment of slaves in v.12. Make of it what you will.

> **12.** We believe it just to preach the gospel to the nations of the earth, and warn the righteous to save themselves from the corruption of the world; but we do not believe it right to interfere with bond-servants, neither preach the gospel to, nor baptize them contrary to the will and wish of their masters, nor to meddle with or influence them in the least to cause them to be dissatisfied with their situations in this life, thereby jeopardizing the lives of men; such interference we believe to be unlawful and unjust, and dangerous to the peace of every government allowing human beings to be held in servitude.

This Section, then an 'article', was also read out to the congregation for approval, this time by Oliver Cowdery. It was voted on and unanimously "accepted and adopted" to be included in the 1835 D&C. Today it is listed as Section 134.

General Assembly
17 August 1835. Kirtland, Ohio.

History.

1835 D&C pp. 255-7 (No Section Number). Deleted after 1835.

Included in the 1835 D&C is an abridged version of the minutes of the meeting at which the D&C was formally adopted and canonised as scripture. In respect of canonising the D&C, the minutes record that leaders of various groups and quorums stood in turn and bore testimony of the truthfulness of the work and had their respective groups vote on whether to accept it as the 'doctrine'

(Lectures) and the 'covenants' (Sections) of the Church. In each case the voting was recorded as unanimous.

Each act was recorded in a similar way. An example is "Acting President, John Gould, gave his testimony in favour of the book, and with the travelling Elders, accepted and acknowledged it as the doctrine and covenants of their faith, by a unanimous vote."

The minutes conclude with notes that the "article on Marriage" (old Section 101) and the "article on governments and laws in general" (now Section 134) were read and accepted by a unanimous vote and thus "ordered to be printed in said book".

Section 108
26 December 1835. Kirtland, Ohio.

History.

First Published in the Deseret News 10 July 1852.
Added to the D&C in 1876. 2010 D&C Sec. 108.

Section 108 is yet another short Section initiated by someone asking Smith what their duties were. It was hardly worth printing in the Deseret News, let alone including in canonised scripture, as it really did not include anything of merit. The reader can no doubt by now quickly and easily predict what Smith had the Lord include for Lyman Sherman who had approached him.

The Lord speaks and forgives Sherman's sins, telling him his soul should be at rest concerning his spiritual standing; but as ever in such messages from the lord, Sherman is to be more careful in observing his vows and then he will be "blessed with exceeding great blessings." He is to be patient and wait for the solemn assembly when he will receive a calling.

Meanwhile, what is he to do? That's right; preach the gospel and strengthen people. Did it really need a revelation from the Lord to say that? Could Smith not have just told him that, without the Lord having to placate Sherman?

Sherman was a close friend of Smith's and he had been a faithful follower throughout the disastrous Zion's Camp expedition. He was later called and he served as a President in the First Quorum of Seventy from 1835-1837.

According to several sources, while Joseph Smith was in Liberty Jail, in January 1839, he wrote to Brigham Young and Heber C. Kimball informing them that Sherman should be called as an Apostle. However, Sherman's health was failing and he was never told of his new calling. He died in February 1839, in Far West, without ever knowing anything about it. Mormons may consider it wonderful that Sherman was offered such a calling even though he never knew

THE MORMON DELUSION

of it. Sceptics will no doubt conclude that the Lord could not possibly have been involved with such nonsense as calling someone who was to die before they could accept.

Chapter 21

**Doctrine and Covenants
Sections 109 – 120 & 137**

Section 137
21 January 1836. Kirtland Temple, Ohio.

History.

Added in 1981. 2010 D&C Sec. 137.

Retrieved from the pages of Church History, this Section was not added to the D&C until the 1981 edition. Smith claims he saw "the celestial kingdom of God" which is quite a claim. In reviewing Smith's description of the place and also the people he saw there, he inadvertently exposes his claim as fraudulent in several ways. It could not have been more than a fanciful idea. Smith declares that he could not tell whether it was "in the body or out" which means it was an event experienced (indeed, if actually experienced at all), entirely in the imagination.

Naturally, in keeping with traditional biblical ideas, there is a 'gate' to this kingdom. This alone gives the game away, as Smith's 'celestial kingdom' is supposedly a *planet* and the Earth itself will one day become 'celestialised'.

Where would there be a *gate* to a planet? Early concepts were akin to a city rather than a planet and Smith repeated the tradition without thinking. He *imagined* a gate. In true Smith style, he had been seduced by such as Genesis 28:17 "this is the gate of heaven" and he even incorporated the concept into his Book of Mormon, Helaman 3:28, which includes, "the gate of heaven" idea. In the Book of Mormon there is absolutely no mention of any kingdoms *other* than 'heaven'.

It is actually interesting to note Smith's 'Book of Mormon' theology (of 1829) when he wrote it. Helaman 3:28, which Smith's book asserts was written some forty to fifty years BCE, actually says: "Yea, thus we see that the gate of heaven is open to all, even to those who will believe on the name of Jesus Christ, who is the Son of God." In this sentence, we see Smith's 1829 concept that there is indeed a 'gate' to heaven. Although here it could be construed as figurative, in the D&C, Smith claims to *see* it. There is just *one* heaven, and anyone who 'believes on Jesus' can enter, confirming the traditional Christian concept that all we have to do is believe, in order to be saved. He uses the *name* of Jesus and *title* of Christ (supposedly) several decades before Christ was born, and centuries before the name and title were invented and then combined.

The 'gate' Smith claims to see is like a circle of flames. Smith doesn't describe the place or how far into the kingdom he had to go to see it, but next, the 'throne' on which God and Jesus are sitting is also ablaze. The streets now get a mention and as expected, they look like they are paved with gold. Isn't it always the case in such 'vision' claims that *anyone* makes, that they invariably include flames and gold? And that is all we learn about the place; fire and gold.

Smith quickly turns to whom he saw there. The list includes Adam, Abraham, Smith's parents (who were still alive at the time) and brother Alvin (who had died). Smith was surprised Alvin was there as he died before the restoration and had not been baptised. Thus Smith claims the Lord told him that anyone who would have received the truth will be saved in the "celestial kingdom of God", as will children who die before the age of accountability, defined in Section 68 as the age of eight. This is not the only Section that we will review where there are claims to have seen people such as Adam and Abraham. We will be looking at another prophet's even wilder claims later.

Interestingly, in Joseph Smith's journal, which is the origin of this Section, between what is now v.9 and v.10 there is a statement the Church does not include today. Smith wrote "And again, I also beheld the Terrestrial Kingdom" but then he crossed it through. Either he did see it or he didn't. If he did *not* see it, he should not have written that he did (whether crossed out or not). If he *did* see it, he should have left it in and perhaps described more of what he saw. Such a retracted entry smacks not of a man who was about to add more detail of a real vision, but rather someone about to construct some more imaginative storyline to pad out the short summary he had so far dreamed up.

DOCTRINE & COVENANTS – SECTIONS 109-120 & 137

How would Smith have ever known he was seeing Adam or Abraham particularly? How would he have even known what they looked like compared with other deceased people? Did the Lord introduce them to Smith? There are no details, but considering we know for a scientific fact the character 'Adam' is entirely mythological without any doubt whatsoever, Joseph Smith has a lot of explaining to do.

Other than handed down oral stories that eventually got written down, there is equally no tangible evidence that an individual character named Abraham ever existed either. It is accepted purely on unauthenticated writings that are believed simply because they are old and were accepted by our ancestors who rejected all the other gods and settled on the God of Abraham. Smith's claimed vision has no basis in reality and if not a complete concoction, it is at best just an imaginative day dream. There are suggestions that sometimes they used cannabis which farmers were encouraged to grow. That would explain a lot.

Section 109
27 March 1836. Kirtland Temple, Ohio.

History.

Added in 1876. 2010 D&C Sec. 109.

This is the prayer that Joseph Smith offered at the dedication of the Kirtland Temple. *"According to the Prophet's written statement, this prayer was given to him by revelation."* (Italics in original header). In other words, Smith claimed the Lord told him all the nice things he wanted said about him rather than let Smith offer up his own thanks and thoughts. In point of fact, the prayer had been constructed by *committee* the day before the dedication, on Saturday 26th – and recorded by Oliver Cowdery.

> This day our school did not keep, we prepared for the dedication of the Lord's house. I met in the president's room, pres. J. Smith, jr. S. Rigdon, my brother W. A. Cowdery & Elder W. Parrish, and assisted in writing a prayer for the dedication of the house. *(Oliver Cowdery's Kirtland, Ohio Sketch Book, reprinted in BYU Studies 12:4 (1972).*

The prime purpose of the temple is designated to be so "the Son of Man might have a place to come and manifest himself to his people" (v.5). Two years *later*, Smith would write a story in which God and Jesus had been happy enough to appear to Smith in the woods – back in 1820.

Amid all the nice words that he wants said, the Lord has Smith ask "that no unclean thing shall be permitted to come into thy house to pollute it" (v.20). But even that is not enough; the Lord has Smith also ask:

> **25.** That no weapon formed against them shall prosper; that he who diggeth a pit for them shall fall into the same himself;
> **26.** That no combination of wickedness shall have power to rise up and prevail over thy people upon whom thy name shall be put in this house;
> **27.** And if any people shall rise against this people, that thine anger be kindled against them;
> **28.** And if they shall smite this people thou wilt smite them; thou wilt fight for thy people as thou didst in the day of battle, that they may be delivered from the hands of all their enemies.

Having asked the Lord to get angry and fight their battles for them, Smith goes on to ask for a lot of other 'deliverances' before v.32: "Therefore we plead before thee for a full and complete deliverance from under this yoke."

There follows a lengthy and entirely meaningless diatribe in which the Lord seems to repeat himself several times, but then he does that throughout the D&C so we should not be too surprised. Of course, such a remark would be criticised by the Church as coming from someone who is not reading 'by the spirit'. However, reading this Section, it is hard to see how the Lord would ever have required such awful material to be read back to him, with or without a committee writing it and with or without a sympathetic approach to it.

It may be prudent just to check and see how the Lord responded to all this supplication that he had revealed to Smith and instructed him to repeat – and which was somehow also written by a committee. Did the Lord come through on promises he had Smith ask for? Did no unclean thing ever enter the house? Are cows and sheep considered unclean? They later occupied part of the temple. Or does it just refer to bad people? The very next year, following Smith's Kirtland Bank fraud, when many members lost all they had, a new schism formed in Kirtland (there had been some before and there were more to come) when so-called 'dissenters', led by Warren Parrish, took control of the temple and other church property. After that, the temple was used by the Western Reserve Teacher's Seminary. Eventually, a probate court in Ohio sold the temple, which had reportedly cost somewhere around $40,000 to build (about $967,000 in purchasing power today), to pay off just some of the outstanding debt owed by Joseph Smith's estate *(See p. 333).*

DOCTRINE & COVENANTS – SECTIONS 109-120 & 137

Section 110
3 April 1836. Kirtland, Ohio.

History.

Added in 1876. 2010 D&C Sec. 110.

The D&C 'Introduction' refers to this Section; "Other ordinations followed in which priesthood keys were conferred upon them by Moses, Elijah, Elias, and many ancient prophets" *(see p. 9)*. I comment there that of course Elias is the Greek form of Elijah and they are in fact one and the same person. Section 110 is also discussed at length in Chapter 9 in conjunction with Section 2 *(See pp. 90-95)*.

In this Section, Smith claims that he and Oliver Cowdery both experienced a 'vision' of "Jehovah" who, according to the subheading for verses 1-10, *"accepts the Kirtland Temple as his house"* (Italics in original). Unfortunately, he didn't give them any idea that within a couple of years it would be out of Smith's Mormon Church hands forever, and that cows and sheep would later occupy it instead of people. Perhaps that would have been too demoralising and Jehovah decided against it.

So, in order to get some perspective, what does Smith claim they saw and heard? The Lord was standing on something that looked like gold. His eyes were like fire, he had white hair and his 'countenance' shone brightly. This description is somewhat consistent with some published ethereal experiences of other *white* people. *(See examples on pp. 5-6)*. Such claimed experiences and the subsequent descriptions appear to depend on the culture people live in and what they *expect* to see to suit their own ideas of deity.

In a letter, purported to be from Pontius Pilate to Tiberius Caesar, Pilate described Jesus as having golden hair. Publius Lentulus (who may have been a fictional character), President of Judea, apparently wrote the following in an epistle to the Senate concerning the 'Nazarene called Jesus'. There are various versions of this letter and I don't take it too seriously. However, it does at least provide someone's idea of the appearance of a man claimed to be Jesus.

> ...his hair of (the colour of) the chestnut, full ripe, plain to His ears, whence downwards it is more orient and curling and wavering about His shoulders. In the midst of His head is a seam or partition in His hair, after the manner of the Nazarenes. His forehead plain and very delicate; His face without spot or wrinkle, beautified with a lovely red; His nose and mouth so formed as nothing can be reprehended; His beard thickish, in colour like His hair, not very long, but forked; His look innocent and mature; His eyes grey, clear, and quick...

THE MORMON DELUSION

One person claiming to have seen Jesus in a vision said he was astonished that the portrait painted from the imprint on the Turin shroud was exactly like Jesus as he saw him in vision. The Turin shroud has since been dated to many centuries *after* Christ so clearly the portrait was not akin to whatever Jesus may have looked like. However, other people contacted the person to say they too had experienced visions or dreams of Jesus, and that was exactly how he had appeared to them. (The painting depicts a character with long dark brown hair with a central parting and a full beard). Others claiming to have seen Jesus in vision generally go with long reddish-brown locks of hair to the shoulders.

There were many assertions and forged early descriptions of Jesus and by the 19th century there were theories that Jesus was European, and in particular Aryan. Other theories preferred a Jesus of black African descent. All claimed descriptions have been subjective of course but most people who claim to have *seen* Jesus describe what they saw as a child in pictures depicting him. The reality is that if he ever lived at all as one individual being, he was in all likelihood an Arab Jew and Lentulus's description (whether it is real or not) is therefore probably about right as it could describe any number of such people.

From light skinned with blond hair and blue eyes to dark skinned with red hair and grey eyes to black skinned with dark hair, Jesus generally looks the way people *expect* him to look if they claim to have experienced a visitation.

One thing is certain; Joseph Smith is not alone in such claims. In Smith's case, not surprisingly, his description is not dissimilar to the published claims of several others of his era who thought they had experienced similar visions.

Smith describes Jehovah's voice as "the sound of the rushing of great waters" but does he say anything important or useful with his 'rushing of great waters' voice or is it the same old nonsense we have become accustomed to?

Firstly, he announces himself – so they can be sure who he is; "I am the first and the last; I am he who liveth, I am he who was slain; I am your advocate with the Father" (v.4). Their sins are forgiven (as always) and so are the sins of all those who helped to build his house. He accepts the house and promises to appear to people there. The temple was not in the hands of the Church long enough for that actually to happen.

Tens of thousands will rejoice because of the endowment his servants have received in that house. But what they experienced in Kirtland wasn't much of anything at all and not remotely anything like the endowment many Mormons today may imagine it was. The modern endowment bears little resemblance to the Nauvoo endowment; and before that, what was *called* an endowment at Kirtland was nothing more than washing and perfuming their bodies, anointing with oil, a glorified set of prayers and laying on of hands. Tens of thousands did *not* rejoice over servants receiving it at all. Smith himself recorded it thus. (In the following, the "loft of the printing office" was the loft of the temple).

At about 3 o'clock P.M. I dismissed the school. The presidency retired to the loft of the printing office, where we attended the ordinance of washing our bodies in pure water. We also perfumed our bodies and our heads, in the name of the Lord.

At early candlelight, I meet with the presidency at the west school room in the Chapel [Kirtland Temple] to attend to the ordinance of annointing our heads with holy oil. Also the councils of Kirtland and Zion meet in the two adjoining rooms, who waited in prayer while we attended to the ordinance.

I took the oil in my right / left hand, father Smith being seated before me and the rest of the presidency encircled him round about. We then stretched our right hands to heaven and blessed the oil and consecrated it in the name of Jesus Christ. We then laid our hands on our aged fath[er] Smith, and invoked, the blessings of heaven. I then annointed his head with the consecrated oil, and sealed many blessings upon his/m/ [him] head.

The presidency then in turn, laid their hands upon his head, beginning at the eldest, untill they had all laid their hands on him, and pronounced such blessings, upon his head as the Lord put into their hearts. All blessing him to be our patraark [patriarch] and /to/ annoint our heads, and attend to all duties that pertain to that office.

I then took the seat, and [my] father annoint[ed] my head, and sealed upon me the blessings of Moses to lead Israel in the latter days, even as Moses led him in days of old. Also the blessings of Abraham, Isaac and Jacob. All of the presidency laid their hands upon me and pronounced upon my head many prophecies, and blessings... (Joseph Smith's Diary, 21 January 1836). *(Faulring, 1989:118.)*

Following the above details in Smith's journal, we find what is now included in Section 137. The above was all that Smith could dream up for an endowment experience in Kirtland. What became the endowment in Nauvoo was of course entirely new and completely different, thanks to Smith's recent encounter with Freemasonry a few weeks earlier which formed more than just the basis of his new endowment ideas *(See TMD Vol. 3: Sec. 3)*.

The Lord then appears to deliberately lie to Smith in v.10, claiming: "And the fame of this house shall spread to foreign lands; and this is the beginning of the blessing which shall be poured out upon the heads of my people. Even so. Amen." It most certainly did not become famous in foreign lands and it wasn't a blessing to them; they almost immediately lost control of the temple and it later effectively became no more than a cow shed for a period before falling into the hands of a schism which still owns it today. That wasn't much of a blessing for the Lord's supposed chosen people – unless it relates to the RLDS

Church (Community of Christ) who will quite naturally claim it relates to them.

Smith claims the vision then closed, whereupon Moses appeared and "committed unto us the keys of the gathering of Israel from the four parts of the earth, and the leading of the ten tribes from the land of the north." Once again, there is a real lack of information provided; this time by Moses, who failed to mention the 'lost tribes' are not actually *in* a "land of the north". Naturally, there is no record from that day to this of any 'Mormon' gathering of the tribes occurring. That is because the groups comprising these tribes were scattered and interspersed with various other nations.

The ten tribes, traditionally of the Northern Kingdom of Israel, are considered to be those of Reuben, Simeon, Dan, Naphtali, Gad, Asher, Issachar, Zebulun, Ephraim, and Manasseh. Those not included are Judah, Levi, and Benjamin. These ten tribes vanished from Hebrew records (scripture) after they had been invaded, conquered, enslaved, and deported numerous times by the Neo-Assyrian Empire between 740 and 722 BCE. It is suggested some may have fled voluntarily to European and African countries before they could be caught and deported.

Medieval Rabbinic fable led to the 'ten lost tribes' *myth* which Smith, and therefore the Mormon Church, seemed to embrace; but nevertheless, the idea remains mythical and conflicts with recorded history. Although Wikipedia is known to be unreliable, the following summary is accurate enough on this:

> The recorded history differs from this fable: no record exists of the Assyrians having exiled people from Dan, Asher, Issachar, Zebulun or western Manasseh. Descriptions of the deportation of people from Reuben, Gad, Manasseh in Gilead, Ephraim and Naphtali indicate that only a portion of these tribes were deported and the places to which they were deported are known locations given in the accounts. The deported communities are mentioned as still existing at the time of the composition of the books of Kings and Chronicles and did not wholly disappear by assimilation into the Assyrian populace, although a portion may have.
>
> This is a subject based upon written religious tradition and partially upon speculation. There is a vast amount of literature on the Lost Tribes and no specific source can be relied upon for a complete answer. *(Ten Lost Tribes; Wikipedia).*
> See: http://en.wikipedia.org/wiki/Ten_Lost_Tribes

The idea that Moses committed keys of leading ten lost tribes from the "land of the north" is as fanciful as Smith being given a key to the wardrobe that leads to Narnia. Smith told good stories but unfortunately for him, we now know more than he did and his ideas generally fall apart due to modern-day knowledge and understanding. Ten lost tribes waiting to be gathered from a land in the north, is just as fictional as Native Americans being Lamanites of Jewish ancestry; it is all historically provable nonsense. Once it is discovered that Smith's claims are historically *impossible*, the game is up; Moses could not possibly have appeared and said that. Smith's hoax is exposed. This happened so often that only a deluded mind that will *not* consider *evidence* can remain true to a belief in Smith's absurd claims.

Section 111
6 August 1836. Salem, Massachusetts.

History.

Added in 1876. 2010 D&C Sec. 111.

Judging by the story behind this Section, Joseph Smith must have had his passion for treasure hunting rekindled upon learning from a 'William Burgess' that a large amount of treasure was hidden in the cellar of a house at Salem. In any event, Smith jumped at the chance to at least go and look for it and travelled some six-hundred miles to do so. Once Smith, accompanied by his brother Hyrum, Sidney Rigdon and Oliver Cowdery arrived in Salem, he naturally had the Lord more than endorse their trip. Unfortunately, in his enthusiasm, Smith went too far and had the Lord make some specific promises about it, none of which materialised.

Considering the fact that in all his earlier treasure-seeking exploits which had covered the best part of a decade, Smith never once located anything of worth, you would think by now that he would have learned, and common sense alone should have told him the claim might not pan out. However, Smith and his pals were heavily in debt and desperate for money so *any* idea must have seemed like a good one.

This Section is more fully covered in *TMD Vol. 3:306-9. (S100-3)*, and in a nutshell, these are the details. The Lord tells Smith he is not displeased they went to Salem. Moreover, he says, he has much treasure for them in Salem. Apologists who claim this refers to 'spiritual' treasure and 'conversions' don't seem to notice that the Lord says he is referring to "wealth pertaining to gold and silver" which seems pretty clear to everyone except Mormon apologists. Smith was convinced anyway and boldly has the Lord declare he will give Salem over to them and they will have power over it. They can forget about their debts, the Lord will give them power to pay them.

Regarding where they should stay, the Lord says something quite strange really "where it is my will that you should tarry, for the main, shall be signalized unto you by the peace and power of my Spirit, that shall flow unto you". "Signalized" – would the Lord say that? "For the main" – would he also say that? What about the rest of the time, which was not 'for the main'? Did the Lord have other ideas for them? Apparently not; they had to arrange their lodgings by feelings which of course can be, and very often are, very misleading indeed, especially when you *want* something to be true.

Naturally, the Lord couldn't actually give them an address in advance as that would have been too close to potential evidence of a *real* revelation and prophecy and we have yet to discover a single one of those. As the Lord has more than one treasure for them in Salem, they should seek out some of the older inhabitants who may be able to assist them. Such optimism from Smith; the Lord says he will "order things for their good" – but he didn't.

The upshot of the story is that they never found anything and had to travel back the six-hundred miles empty handed. The Lord failed to give them any "wealth pertaining to gold and silver" as promised and they still couldn't pay their debts – at a time when things were pretty desperate for them. Not only that, they hadn't even converted anyone as the revelation had promised would be the case; "and many people in this city, whom I will gather out in due time for the benefit of Zion, through *your* instrumentality" (v.2). (Italics added).

The situation became such an embarrassment for the early Church that six years later, in 1842, Hyrum Smith gave Erastus Snow (who was later ordained an apostle, in 1849), and Benjamin Winchester, a copy of the revelation and asked them to go to Salem to *fulfil* the prophecy. They had to *make* the prophecy *appear* to be fulfilled in order to at least recover something from the disastrous failure. Yet the prophecy had stated conversions would be "through *your* instrumentality" referring to Smith and company. *(See TMD Vol. 3:308; or S102 for more information).*

Section 111 – Summary

Prophecies made: 3
Prophecies fulfilled: 0

Prophecies made:

Pr. 48. "I have much treasure in this city for you" (v.2). "wealth pertaining to gold and silver shall be yours" (v.4). "there are more treasures than one for you in this city." (v.10).

DOCTRINE & COVENANTS – SECTIONS 109-120 & 137

Pr. 49. "and many people in this city, whom I will gather out in due time for the benefit of Zion, through your instrumentality" (v.2).

Pr. 50. "I will give this city into your hands, that you shall have power over it" (v.4).

Results:

Pr. 48. Smith and company located no treasure of any description at Salem and they eventually returned to Kirtland empty-handed. The Lord's promised treasure never materialised.

Pr. 49. In 1842 Hyrum Smith gave Erastus Snow, who was later ordained an apostle in 1849, and Benjamin Winchester, a copy of the revelation and asked them to go to Salem to *fulfil* the prophecy. They had to somehow *make* the prophecy *appear* to be fulfilled in order to at least recover something from the failure.

Pr. 50. The city of Salem did not fall into Smith's hands and he did not have any power over it. Hardly anyone knew they were even there.

****

The Kirtland Safety Society Bank
becomes
The Kirtland Safety Society *Anti* Bank*ing* Co.

In order to give some perspective as to how desperate things were financially and what may have sparked Smith's disastrous attempt to locate the claimed treasure at Salem, it is worth inserting a note here. Following the complete failure of the aborted Salem venture, there was no more revelation that made its way into the D&C for almost a year, during which time things went from bad to worse as Smith desperately tried to think of ways out of his ever increasing financial problems.

Ultimately, he and Sidney Rigdon decided to float their own bank, which Smith claimed was set up by *revelation* and that "like Aaron's rod would swallow up all other banks" Unfortunately, Smith didn't know anything at all about banks or banking. *(See TMD Vol. 3:42-44 & 52.n.39). (S103-5).*

Notwithstanding his lack of experience and ability, Smith sent Apostle Orson Hyde to the Ohio legislature to obtain a bank charter, and in anticipation, at the same time, he sent Oliver Cowdery to Philadelphia to obtain the plates to print money. Cowdery duly returned with the plates but Hyde failed to obtain a charter. Undeterred, Smith opened an *illegal* bank anyway, on 2 January 1837, as a joint stock company to serve as a quasi-bank. He then added words to the banknotes so the title now read *The Kirtland Safety Society* **Anti** *Banking* **Co**. The worthless banknotes were as *illegal* as the bank itself. Nevertheless, they started issuing them in abundance, regardless of the fact there never were any assets remotely close to the claimed $4 million capitalisation. The bank was doomed before it even opened for business. It was an impossible venture.

I have somewhat covered the Kirtland Bank debacle in *TMD Volume 3 (see reference above)* in conjunction with the lies about the story that were included by the Mormon Church in their 2008 Priesthood Manual. This is how Fawn Brodie described the events that transpired following the collapse of the bank.

> If the bank needed a final blow to shatter what little prestige it still held among the faithful, it received it when Warren Parrish resigned as cashier, left the church, and began openly to describe the banking methods of the prophet. Parrish was later accused of absconding with $25,000, but if he took the sum it must have been in WORTHLESS BANK NOTES, since that amount of specie in the vaults would have saved the bank, at least during Joseph's term as cashier.
>
> The toppling of the Kirtland bank loosed a hornets' nest. Creditors swarmed in upon Joseph armed with threats and warrants. He was terribly in debt. There is no way of knowing exactly how much he and his leading elders had borrowed, since the loyal Mormons left no itemized account of their own claims. But the local non-Mormon creditors whom he could not repay brought a series of suits against the prophet which the Geauga county court duly recorded. These records tell a story of trouble that would have demolished the prestige and broken the spirit of a lesser man.
>
> Thirteen suits were brought against him between June 1837 and April 1839, to collect sums totaling nearly $25,000. The damages asked amounted to almost $35,000. He was arrested seven times in four months, and his followers managed heroically to raise the $38,428 required for bail. Of the thirteen suits only six were settled out of court-about $12,000 out of the $25,000. In the other seven the creditors either were awarded damages or won them by default.
>
> Joseph had many additional debts that never resulted in court action. Some years later he compiled a list of still outstanding Kirtland loans, which amounted to more than $33,000. If one adds to these the two great loans of $30,000 and $60,000 borrowed in New York and Buffalo in 1836, it would seem that the Mormon leaders owed to non-Mormon individuals and firms well over $150,000. *(Brodie, 1963: 198-202).*

DOCTRINE & COVENANTS – SECTIONS 109-120 & 137

If $150,000 was the total claim on Smith by 1839 with the various suits and outstanding claims added together, then in today's money that would amount to around $3.63 million. Of course, that would not include losses of members who remained faithful and did not follow the mass exodus out of the Church that occurred in Kirtland in 1837 due to Smith's fraud. Such people would never have dared make a claim for their money and property. It went without saying that they would never get it back and their faith had to sustain them.

Joseph Smith never did satisfy all his creditors and following his death in 1844, Smith's wife Emma refused to pay *any* of her husband's debts, including the inheritance of $8,000 in gold (over $200,000 today) of two teenage foster daughters, Maria & Sarah Lawrence, which Smith had spent. He also groomed and married both of them, either on or about the same day (11 May 1843) for good measure, when they were sixteen and nineteen years old respectively.

Emma claimed the debts were all her husband's and they had nothing to do with her. Eventually, the sisters' inheritance was paid by William Law who had absolutely no financial responsibility whatsoever toward the girls. *(See TMD Vol. 1:77-80).*

Joseph Smith had always put any property he owned into Emma's name immediately he obtained it and was personally always either broke or seriously in debt. He died as penniless as he had lived, at least on paper, but Emma remained quite wealthy, owning several valuable properties and plots of land.

We noted, regarding the Kirtland Temple *(on p. 333 and p. 384)*, that the temple was later sold off in order to pay some of Smith's estate debts that were still outstanding. It wasn't exactly the outcome that Smith had had the Lord prophesy about for the temple he had 'accepted'.

Section 112
23 July 1837. Kirtland, Ohio.

History.

1844 D&C Sec. CIV. 2010 D&C Sec. 112.

This Section is directed to Thomas B. Marsh. The Lord hasn't been too happy with Marsh but now that he has "abased" himself, his sins are forgiven and apparently he will preach, not only to the gentiles but also to the Jews (v.4). In what I will term typical 'Smithology', that could equally refer to Native North Americans (Lamanites) or to the people of Israel. The Lord has a great work for Marsh to do and his path lies among the mountains and many nations. He is to lead the Quorum of Twelve. Apparently he will be able to "unlock the kingdom" in places where 'Joseph, Sidney and Hyrum' cannot come (v.17). An "effectual door" will be opened for him.

Smith had the Lord use the expression, "an effectual door" in section 100:3 *(see p. 340)*, also here in v.19, and then again in Section 118:3 *(see p. 413)*. 'Effectual' is an adjective, meaning capable of, or successful in producing an intended result; meaning effective, or effectively. It is of course quite obvious what the word means, even though less commonly used these days.

'Effectual' is a late 14th century word and in the way Smith had the Lord use it, it actually implies: 'I have opened an effective door for you'. Smith obviously did not mean the Lord would provide an actual *door* that would be an effective or well working door, and more probably meant, 'I have opened the way and the *result* of that will be effective for you'. 'Effectual' is a less usual word today, but it does work in sentences such as "It was astonishing that such a remedy could prove so effectual" or "Taking aspirin is an effectual way to soothe a headache", although these days we would more commonly see the word 'effective' rather than 'effectual' in such instances.

However, it is perfectly correct and you may see it now and then. The question is not so much why did Smith *use* the word, but why did he use it in the *way* that he did? The verses in question do not use the word in a manner that made the best of sense in Smith's day any more than they do now. It was meant to *sound* biblical, especially as the Lord was supposedly using it; so had Smith, as is usually the case in such instances, seen it somewhere before?

The word was used a handful of times in the Bible by seventeenth-century scholars, but only *once* in connection with a *door*. Smith's source for his use of the word in a Jacobean 'style' of writing was probably 1 Corinthians 16:9. "For a great door and effectual is opened unto me, and there are many adversaries." Although archaic to us now, the logic behind the expression is clear. This was not the Lord speaking; it was Paul (or someone claimed to be Paul) writing the words.

These are the three instances where Smith has the Lord use 'effectual' and 'door'.

> **D&C 100:3.** Behold, and lo, I have much people in this place, in the regions round about; and **an effectual door** shall be opened in the regions round about in this eastern land.
>
> **D&C 112:19.** Wherefore, whithersoever they shall send you, go ye, and I will be with you; and in whatsoever place ye shall proclaim my name **an effectual door** shall be opened unto you, that they may receive my word.

D&C 118:3. ...I, the Lord, give unto them a promise that I will provide for their families; and *an effectual door* shall be opened for them, from henceforth. (Emphasis added to all the above).

The three identical phrases actually read as if the Lord will provide a door that worked; it was the door that would be effective, rather than him providing help once it had opened. Had he really been speaking, would the Lord not have chosen something akin to the language used in the Common English Bible, where the somewhat awkward wording in the KJV of 1 Corinthians 16:9 is translated as: "In spite of the fact that there are many opponents, a big and productive opportunity has opened up for my mission here." There is an 'Easy to Read' version of the Bible which translates: "I will stay here, because a good opportunity for a great and growing work has been given to me now. And there are many people working against it." Smith's Lord preferred "an effectual door" and used the expression three separate times. None of them sit very well.

Why would Smith pretend the Lord used such an expression? He found it in the Bible and it sounded good (to him). He reversed the words into a sequence that could (and, I venture to suggest, most certainly would) have been much better phrased had the Lord really been speaking. Smith ascribed it to the Lord who used it on three different occasions. Historically, the Lord had only ever spoken in Hebrew prior to his supposed communications with Smith; not that we should expect Hebrew now, but why a hopeless, usually incorrect, Jacobean style of speaking rather than clear and unambiguous modern English?

Smith used such tactics so his claimed revelations *sounded* like scripture and he often turned to the Bible for ideas. To Smith, it would not have sounded as authentic, had the Lord said '...wherever you declare my name, I will open up the way for you and people will receive my word' (my composition); he preferred the archaic terminology "...whatsoever place ye shall proclaim my name an effectual door shall be opened unto you, that they may receive my word." It works for Mormons who already believe the Lord was speaking, but for the objective observer, it is simply evidence that Smith was the voice – and the Lord, as ever, was not involved. The language structure doesn't work at all.

In any event, the Lord says wherever the twelve send anyone; they will have "power to open the door of my kingdom unto any nation" (v.21). Then, as if this 'effectual door' was not enough, we get yet another description of how things are in the world. We should remember that God created the mess that he is never happy with, when Smith has Him speak. In reality, most people were, and are, much better than Smith's God claims. Coincidentally, as I write this, last night was the annual 'Children in Need' appeal here in the U.K. with a TV show dedicated to raising money throughout the evening. Despite the economic crisis that the world in general is currently facing, the good people of Britain donated a record amount of money to help children in need. There are many millions of good and decent people who do not deserve to be branded as evil in the manner that Smith's God constantly ascribes to *everyone*. You and I know of many people, religious and otherwise, who deserve more credit than that.

A real God would not speak that way. Smith copied Old Testament ideas that may have frightened the ancients into obedience but it doesn't work now. According to the OT, God was a mass murderer – among other nasty things. The Lord (Jesus Christ) does not appear quite as bad in the NT. Times had already changed and new ideas were created which were more acceptable to the people looking for a saviour.

The Lord tells Smith that "darkness covereth the earth, and gross darkness the minds of the people, and all flesh has become corrupt before my face" (v.23). Please forgive this departure, especially if it sounds unprofessional, but I just have to stop there for a moment, and with tears in my eyes, silently shout 'No, no it does not.' And 'no, no they are not.' It was Smith who was corrupt and most people of the Earth deserve much better consideration from Smith's supposed God who showed 'effectual' neglect for so many centuries. Enough!

God continues to decry his own creations thus: "vengeance cometh speedily upon the inhabitants of the earth, a day of wrath, a day of burning, a day of desolation, of weeping, of mourning, and of lamentation" (v.24). Give it a rest God; *God* had got everyone into this situation – everyone but Smith's little crowd; left them holding the bag and had the nerve to say He wasn't pleased with *them*. It begs the question, why did God bother to create everyone in the first place if things were destined to end up like this? But there is more…

Verse 25 claims that it will begin "upon my house" and from my house go forth. At that time, that would have been the Kirtland Temple no doubt – the one that virtually became a cow shed and later sold off to pay some of Smith's outstanding debts. If he still wants to start there, the temple is now in good order, but unfortunately owned and operated by the RLDS Church (Community of Christ), considered an apostate group by the Mormon (LDS) faction which God supposedly favours; quite a dilemma for the Lord really. Alternatively, it may have meant the temple in Zion – which of course was never built. Perhaps he won't come now that he doesn't have a starting point.

He is not finished yet; when that time comes, first he is going to deal with those who have professed to know his name but who don't know him and have blasphemed his name in the midst of his house – so they had better behave. As ever, Smith is trying to retain tight control over his followers through fear. To end on a positive note, of course those who repent and are baptised will be saved – oh, but those who don't believe and are not baptised? They "shall be damned". No change there.

Nice things are then said about the twelve before the Lord ends by saying he will come quickly – which of course he didn't. The Church already has its excuses lined up – our time is not the Lord's time; no one knows when it will be; and 'quickly' doesn't equate to 'soon'. My question is simple; why didn't the Mormon 'Lord' ever say what he *meant* so people knew where they were? He seemed to talk in riddles; nothing he said ever materialised when and how the saints expected it, and that has to be explained somehow. I firmly believe it is actually very easily explained – and this book is doing it.

Verse 34 contains another occurrence of "and my reward is with me to recompense every man according as his work shall be" *(See pp. 219-21 & The Final Analysis Part 2)*. Verse 1 contained "nations, kindreds, tongues and people" – again *(See pp. 180-1 & The Final Analysis Part 2)*.

So, what of Thomas B. Marsh; so highly favoured of the Lord that he is called to lead the Quorum of Twelve? Not only was he told that he would preach to "the ends of the earth", to "the gentiles" and "the Jews" (v.4); he was promised that he would be *exalted*. This is yet another occasion where Smith's all-knowing Mormon God hadn't a clue what would happen next. Yet God declared He *did* know what would happen; He told Marsh (v.11) "I know thy heart" when He really didn't know much of anything at all.

Of course, the apologetic response would immediately be that it was all based on obedience, but after a while that just doesn't wash. So many promises were made and so many simply did not pan out. Why would any God make so many predictions such as this; a) when He already knew that the outcome would be bad, and b) when that outcome would come so soon as to become yet another embarrassment? It makes no sense whatsoever. But then, what else can a floundering church say today, when everything is so heavily stacked against the remotest possibility of a God ever having been involved with it?

In Marsh's case, less than two years after his call and magnificent promises, he went the way of the world and left the Church. He returned to membership in 1857 and wrote an autobiography in 1867 in which he recanted some things he had said, but that didn't change history or the recorded facts surrounding the events of 1838. In fact, Marsh didn't just 'fall away' from the Church through sin or a lack of faith. He was excommunicated in absentia after he, Orson Hyde and others signed an affidavit against Joseph Smith regarding the burning of Gallatin. We discussed details when reviewing Section 31 *(See pp. 161-2)*.

Section 113
March 1838. Far West, Missouri.

History.

Added in 1876. 2010 D&C Sec. 113.

In this Section, Joseph Smith has the Lord 'explain' some of Isaiah. Regarding the "stem of Jesse" – "Thus saith the Lord; it is Christ". Should he not have said 'that is me' rather than refer to himself in the third person? It actually is – and also it isn't – Christ. It all depends on how you view it, but it doesn't take a genius to work out the general idea. It is a fundamental concept in all of Christianity that the Messiah would come *from* the stem of Jesse – that would be the *lineage* rather than actually Christ, but it can also be taken *as* the Christ; although we should note, that as the Hebrew text was written by Jews, to them it does *not* relate to the person who Christians take it to be and of course they are still awaiting such a character to arrive.

The next questions are what are the "rod of Jesse" and the "root of Jesse" (Isaiah 11:1 and 11:10). Smith claims the "rod" is a *servant* in the hands of Christ; partly a descendant of Jesse and party of Ephraim (the house of Joseph), and the "root" is someone who will have the keys of gathering in the last days. There are no prizes for guessing who that was supposed to represent.

Smith of course used Isaiah to his own advantage. In the real world, the "stem of Jesse" was used to denote the family of David (son of Jesse, who was a commoner) – representing a more humble ancestry than a King (David). The line would ultimately include Jesus of course, and the "root of Jesse" was the Messiah – *not* Joseph Smith. That understanding is also evident in the book of Revelation (5:5). "And one of the elders saith unto me, Weep not: behold, the Lion of the tribe of Juda, the Root of David, hath prevailed to open the book, and to loose the seven seals thereof." There is no mistaking who that referred to. Smith had his own agenda and always twisted things to suit it. Revelation was certainly *not* talking about Joseph Smith. That was, as ever, just a figment of Smith's overactive imagination, powered by his overreaching ego. It was his enormous ego combined with his imagination that made him the unabashed braggart, narcissist, and maniacal fraud that he was.

Elias Higbee then asks some questions about Isaiah to which Smith gives equally ludicrous answers in order to make everything fit their own time and promote what Smith was going to do to redeem the world. His questions and the answers are not even worth mentioning.

Section 114
17 April 1838. Far West, Missouri.

History.

Added in 1876. 2010 D&C Sec. 114.

This is the text of Section 114:

DOCTRINE & COVENANTS – SECTIONS 109-120 & 137

1. Verily thus saith the Lord: It is wisdom in my servant David W. Patten, that he settle up all his business as soon as he possibly can, and make a disposition of his merchandise, that he may perform a mission unto me next spring, in company with others, even twelve including himself, to testify of my name and bear glad tidings unto all the world.
2. For verily thus saith the Lord, that inasmuch as there are those among you who deny my name, others shall be planted in their stead and receive their bishopric. Amen.

Joseph Smith had been having a run of bad luck, both financially and with the people he thought would do well for him. In August of 1836, Smith had been excited about treasure he thought would be found in Salem. The illegal Kirtland Bank then failed completely, almost as soon as it had opened for business. In July 1837, Thomas B. Marsh had been called to head up the Quorum of Twelve Apostles. The Lord promised Marsh he would be exalted, yet he was excommunicated in absentia less than two years later after writing and then co-signing a damning affidavit against Smith following the burning of Gallatin.

Smith had the Lord say "as there are those among you who deny my name, others shall be planted in their stead" as he had lost several apostles since the original twelve had been called on 15 February 1835. Luke Johnson, Lyman Johnson and William McLellin had already been excommunicated, and in 1839 Smith would excommunicate Marsh, John Boynton and also Orson Hyde who had been out of favour. Hyde was restored to the twelve a few weeks later.

Now Smith has confidence in David W. Patten, one of the original twelve apostles. Patten was loyal and surely he would do Smith's bidding. He must have seemed a safe bet for Smith to have the Lord prophesy about. Smith's luck would surely change now. The Lord says Patten should prepare to serve a mission in the spring. Nothing could be simpler and Patten did remain faithful – that is, until the thirty-eight year old was killed, on 25 October 1838, at the Battle of Crooked River. Smith's God just couldn't get anything right at all. Surely, God would have known Patten would be killed six months later and not have been silly enough to predict an event that was never going to happen? Or does the Lord *not* know everything past, present and future after all?

Section 114 – Summary

Prophecies made:	1
Prophecies fulfilled:	0

Prophecies made:

Pr. 51. "Thus saith the Lord" – David W. Patten was to "perform a mission unto me next spring" in company with the rest of the twelve apostles.

Results:

Pr. 51. Patten was killed at the Battle of Crooked River on 25 October 1838 just six months after the Lord prophesied that Patten would serve a mission the following spring.

Section 115
26 April 1838. Far West, Missouri.

History.

Added in 1876. 2010 D&C Sec. 115.

After *eight* years and at least *one-hundred-and-fifteen* 'revelations' plus several claimed visions since the Lord supposedly re-established his true Church – he finally makes up his mind what to call it. "For thus shall my church be called in the last days, even The Church of Jesus Christ of Latter-day Saints" (v.4). Mormons are taught to believe that the Church should be named after Christ – or else it is not *his* church. This is one sign of it truly being the Lord's Church.

The truth is that Joseph Smith didn't seem able to decide what he wanted to call his new Church and his God certainly didn't tell him what to name it when it was first inaugurated in 1830 – or any time during the following *eight* years. The organisation was informally known as the 'Church of Christ' during 1829, compatible with the name of the church in the Book of Mormon, which Smith had just written.

The new Church was legally instituted with that name on 6 April 1830. It became the 'Church of the Latter Day Saints' in 1834, so it no longer contained the all important name of Christ. Later, it was to change to the 'Church of Jesus Christ' and next to the 'Church of God' – once again losing 'Christ' from the title. Now, God finally gets round to saying it should be called "The Church of Jesus Christ of Latter Day Saints" *(See Section 21, pp. 139-40 and TMD Vol. 4:120-1).*

Why did God not reveal that in 1830 and get things right from the start? If God *had* been in control of Smith's marvellous restoration, surely one of the very first things He would have attended to would be to reveal the *name* that

He wanted for His Church? Yet God waited eight years and gave Smith well over one-hundred revelations before revealing the correct name. Smith was human and making things up as he went along, but if this was truly a restored Church, among all the early 'revelations', would God not have given this name in time for the legal institution of his Church in April of 1830. Of course he would, and the fact he not only didn't, but that it had *five* different names over an *eight year* period gives a very clear picture of what was really going on.

To suggest the Lord would *not* have given his chosen name to the restored Church from day one is simply absurd. Far from the ultimate name *now* being an evidence of its truth, the history behind the name provides evidence of the hoax and it condemns Smith and his Church as fraudulent – right from the start.

As Church members had been driven out of the Lord's proposed 'Zion' and Smith had had to flee Kirtland, then naturally, Far West, where Smith now is, suddenly becomes the focus of the Lord's attention. Not surprisingly, it is now here that he wants yet another house (temple) built. They must begin work in the summer; in fact 4th July would be a good day to start; but they must build it just the way *he* wants it or it will not be accepted. If they do build it the way he wants it, the Lord will accept it. What nonsense is this from deity? But that is exactly what Smith claims the Lord told him. It is worth a look:

> **14.** But let a house be built unto my name according to the pattern which I will show unto them.
> **15.** And if my people build it not according to the pattern which I shall show unto their presidency, I will not accept it at their hands.
> **16.** But if my people do build it according to the pattern which I shall show unto their presidency, even my servant Joseph and his counselors, then I will accept it at the hands of my people.

Really?

Smith and Rigdon shouldn't get into any more debt over this project. That would be a sensible idea and it didn't need the Lord to tell them that; they were already in enough of a financial mess. Brigham Young dedicated the temple site on 4 July 1838. That was the day Sidney Rigdon delivered his infamous Independence Day Oration (not to be confused with his equally infamous 'Salt Sermon'), neither of which did the Church any favours at all. In his so-called Salt Sermon, given just a few weeks earlier, on 17 June, Rigdon had frightened many 'dissenters' and a number of members fled the area in fear of their lives.

Now Rigdon turns on locals and tells them what will happen if they don't leave the Mormons alone. His speech was (and is) considered by many to have been a contributing factor in sparking the 'Mormon War'. This extract from the end of Rigdon's speech may explain why:

> We take God and all the holy angels to witness this day, that we warn all men in the name of Jesus Christ, to come on us no more forever, for from this hour, we will bear it no more, our rights shall no more be trampled on with impunity. The man or the set of men, who attempts it, does it at the expense of their lives. And that mob that comes on us to disturb us; it shall be between us and them a war of extermination, for we will follow them, till the last drop of their blood is spilled, or else they will have to exterminate us: for we will carry the seat of war to their own houses, and their own families, and one party or the other shall be utterly destroyed. -- Remember it then all MEN.
>
> We will never be the aggressors, we will infringe on the rights of no people; but shall stand for our own until death. We claim our own rights, and are willing that all others shall enjoy theirs.
>
> No man shall be at liberty to come into our streets, to threaten us with mobs, for if he does, he shall atone for it before he leaves the place, neither shall he be at liberty, to villify and slander any of us, for suffer it we will not in this place.
>
> We therefore, take all men to record this day, that we proclaim our liberty on this day, as did our fathers. And we pledge this day to one another, our fortunes, our lives, and our sacred honors, to be delivered from the persecutions which we have had to endure, for the last nine years, or nearly that. Neither will we indulge any man, or set of men, in instituting vexatious law suits against us, to cheat us out of our just rights, if they attempt it we say we be unto them.
>
> We this day then proclaim ourselves free, with a purpose and a determination, that never can be broken, "no never! *no never!!* **NO NEVER**"!!! *(Sidney Rigdon Speech, 4 July 1838. The entire oration is available at this link:* http://sidneyrigdon.com/rigd1838.htm*).*

A year from today, which will be 26 April 1839, they should re-commence laying the foundation and then there is to be *no* stopping until the temple is finished. "Thus let them from that time forth labor diligently until it shall be finished, from the cornerstone thereof unto the top thereof, until there shall not anything remain that is not finished" (v.12).

The Lord really needn't have bothered with all that detail – what a fuss-pot, dictating what he would and would not accept. He should have known very well that once again, it would never get built; Smith and his crew would upset the locals and they would, as ever, get driven out before they even got started.

Notwithstanding the fact that *we* know what happened next, the Lord seems to have no idea about it and instructs Smith that Far West should be built up as quickly as possible, along with other stakes 'in the regions round about' – as will be revealed to Smith. The Lord closes with "For behold, I will be with him, and I will sanctify him before the people; for unto him have I given the keys of this kingdom and ministry. Even so. Amen" (v.19). Far West failed and a few months later they were driven out, just as 'Zion' had previously failed and they had been driven from there. Six years later, Smith would be shot to death and a squabble for the keys of the kingdom would ensue. The Lord didn't exactly plan very well for all of that and the Church was once again decimated.

Section 115 – Summary

Prophecies made:	1
Prophecies fulfilled:	0
Other non-prophetic revelation:	1

Prophecies made:

Pr. 52. The Lord gives instructions for a temple to be built at Far West. He will only accept it if it is built the way *he* wants it built. That really meant Smith could plan it out the way he would like it and as he claimed it came from the Lord, the ideas of others would not be valid. Smith often used the Lord in order to get his own way. A year from today (on 26 April 1839) they should re-commence laying the foundation and then there is to be *no stopping* until the temple is *finished*.

Results:

Pr. 52. The temple was never built and the saints were driven out the following spring (1839). The Mormon Church repurchased the site in 1909 and the original cornerstones are now under glass cases for tourists to view. *(See* http://www.ldschurchtemples.com/farwest/ *for details and photo)*. This link includes an assertion, using typical Mormon propaganda, that five apostles and others (at great risk to themselves) visited the site a year later 'in fulfilment of prophecy', on 26 April 1839. They actually secretly crept in just after midnight and didn't hang around very long. The prophecy claimed all twelve would start a mission from that spot on that day. Less than half turned out – in the middle of the night *(See p.413)*.

Note that the Church had to somehow try to 'make' the prophecy come true. The same thing happened when Erastus Snow and Benjamin Winchester were asked to go to Salem *(See p. 390)*, among other equally strange examples of 'making' prophecy come true in order to cover Smith's otherwise entirely unfulfilled predictions. In this case, the Church neglects to include the fact that the prophecy was *specifically* that from 26 April 1839 on, they should "…labor diligently until it shall be *finished*, from the cornerstone thereof unto the top thereof, until there shall not anything remain that is not finished." Other than placing a stone on top of one of the cornerstones, the apostles did nothing on that day (or rather, night) and nothing has been done since. Other than the original corner stones, now encased in glass, all there is on the site today – is grass. That is prophecy most definitely *unfulfilled*.

Non-prophetic Revelation:

1. "For thus shall my church be called in the last days, even The Church of Jesus Christ of Latter-day Saints" (v.4). Mormons believe the Church should be named after Christ – or it is not *his* church. This is one sign of it truly being the Lord's Church.

The Mormon Church was informally known as the 'Church of Christ' during 1829. It was legally instituted with that name on 6 April 1830. It became the 'Church of the Latter Day Saints' in 1834, so no longer contained the all important name of Christ. Later, it was to change to the 'Church of Jesus Christ' and then the 'Church of God' – once again losing 'Christ' from the title. Now, God eventually gets round to saying it should be called "The Church of Jesus Christ of Latter Day Saints." Five different names in eight years equates to anything *but* divine revelation.

Section 116

9 May 1838. Near Wight's Ferry, Spring Hill, Daviess County, Missouri.

History.

Added in 1876. 2010 D&C Sec. 116.

This is the full text of Section 116:

> 1. Spring Hill is named by the Lord Adam-ondi-Ahman, because, said he, it is the place where Adam shall come to visit his people, or the Ancient of Days shall sit, as spoken of by Daniel the prophet.

In Mormonism, this little gem is the basis for a belief that this is where Adam and Eve lived and raised their family after being driven from the Garden of Eden. This would mean that everything from Adam until the time of the biblical flood transpired in North America.

Whatever beliefs we may or may not individually hold, one thing is for certain; the Adam and Eve story, as well as the global flood idea (and probably almost everything in between), are purely mythological. Joseph Smith assumed the Bible to be historically accurate. We now know with absolute certainty that much is anything but correct. The Mormon Church is stuck with concepts long since overturned by indisputable scientific evidence. We *know* for an absolute fact that there was a worldwide population of around five million humans by 4000 BCE and we also *know*, in addition to the fact that a biblical global flood was an impossible occurrence on every imaginable scientific level, that there was *no* flood 'gap', in a biblical timeframe, of the many civilisations that have been documented as having existed for many thousands of years, from long before, during and after the flood date. Even occurrences of localised flooding, from which earlier 'ark' stories arose, and from which Bible mythology may well have been drawn, are inconsistent with the biblical timeframe.

The idea that Spring Hill was where God placed Adam as a 'first' human being is today so absurd a concept that no one other than faithful and believing Mormons could or would ever even begin to consider the idea as a remotely plausible supposition. We now *know* the general origin and distribution of humankind across the globe, both in terms of species and time frame, beyond reasonable doubt – and no amount of faith can overcome the truth of the data which spans tens, if not hundreds of thousands of years.

Adam-Ondi-Ahman was yet another location where the Lord wanted his saints to organise a Stake and build him a temple. He seemed to like beautiful temples being built for him before the people arriving were even settled and making a proper living for themselves. Smith recorded the following:

> Adam-ondi-Ahman, Missouri, Daviess county, June 25, 1838. A conference of Elders and members of the Church of Jesus Christ of Latter-day Saints was held in this place this day, for the purpose of organizing this Stake of Zion, called Adam-ondi-Ahman. *(HC. Vol. 3 Ch. IV)*.

A 'temple square' site was chosen and dedicated in October of 1838 by Brigham Young, accompanied by Smith, Heber C. Kimball and others. Once again, the temple was never built. This time, they never even managed to lay cornerstones. This was the third temple to be prophesied and planned but never constructed; it was certainly not a case of 'third time lucky'; the saints were ordered out of the settlement within days of the temple square dedication. *(See http://www.ldschurchtemples.com/adamondiahman/ for details and photo)*. In the detail, the Church claims the temple would have been at the centre of a new city named after the son of Adam, the 'City of Seth' – it was never built.

THE MORMON DELUSION

On 7 November 1838, the saints were given just ten days to leave the area and they moved to Far West, Missouri; a move that turned out to be equally as disastrous as trying to settle at Spring Hill had been – regardless of what name Smith said the Lord gave it.

Many saints were almost constantly on the move during this year, driven from pillar to post, but Smith always seemed to know where they should go next – until they were moved on again by the locals. He was even particular about where they settled in relation to the locations he selected. They had to do as they were told – or they were thrown out.

> Monday, 6 August 1838: This morning my council met me at my house, to consider the conduct of certain Canada brethren, who had settled on the forks of Grand river, contrary to counsel. On investigation, it was resolved that they must return to Adam-ondi-Ahman, according to counsel, or they would not be considered one with us. *(HC Vol. III. Ch. VI)*.

The Smith brothers continued to show their lack of financial prowess in many ways. One classic example of their complete failure to comprehend the needs of a group of travellers they had had embark on a five-hundred mile trip is exposed in a letter from Smith's young brother Don Carlos. It is reminiscent of Smith's 'Zion's Camp' shortfall in finance and essential provisions.

NINE MILES FROM TERRE HAUTE, INDIANA.

> Brother Joseph:--I sit down to inform you of our situation at the present time. I started from Norton, Ohio, the 7th of May, in company with father, William, Wilkins Jenkins Salisbury, William McClary and Lewis Robbins, and families, also Sister Singly. We started with fifteen horses, seven wagons, and two cows. We have left two horses by the way sick, and a third horse (our main dependence) was taken lame last evening, and is not able to travel, and we have stopped to doctor him. We were disappointed on every hand before we started in getting money. We got no assistance whatever, only as we have taken in Sister Singly, and she has assisted us as far as her means extended. We had, when we started, $75 in money. We sold the two cows for $13.50 per cow. We have sold of your goods to the amount of $45.74, and now we have only $25 to carry twenty-eight souls and thirteen horses five hundred miles.
>
> We have lived very close and camped out at night, notwithstanding the rain and cold, and my baby only two weeks old when we started. Agnes is very feeble; father and mother are not well and very much fatigued; mother has a severe cold, and in fact it is

nothing but the prayer of faith and the power of God, that will sustain them and bring them through. Our courage is good, and I think we shall be brought through. I leave it with you and Hyrum to devise some way to assist us to some more expense money. We have unaccountably bad roads, had our horses down in the mud, and broke one wagon tongue and thills, and broke down the carriage twice, and yet we are all alive and encamped on a dry place for almost the first time. Poverty is a heavy load, but we are all obliged to welter under it.

It is now dark and I close. May the Lord bless you all, and bring us together, is my prayer. Amen. All the arrangements that brother Hyrum left for getting money failed; they did not gain us one cent. DON C. SMITH. *(HC. Vol 3. Ch. V, 6 Jul, 1838).*

Mormons looking at this sympathetically may consider the circumstances and trials to be faith-promoting and evidence of devotion to the Lord. In reality, Smith once again failed completely in providing properly organised facilities, this time for Don Carlos and his fellow travellers, including providing not nearly enough money or provisions for such a long and arduous trip. Hyrum's 'arrangements' raised nothing at all and the Lord did not venture to 'reveal' to Smith what problems would occur so they could be avoided. Had he done so, perhaps things would have fared better for Don Carlos and his little company. Having to sell the two cows would have meant sacrificing the milk they would have otherwise had each day. Circumstances must have been grim and they had five-hundred miles to go. They barely managed to survive the trip.

In any event, the letter seemed to prompt Smith to record Section 119 *(see pp. 413-4)* in which he devised a new way of raising money. Not satisfied with having asked the saints to consecrate everything they could upon joining the Church, he now wants ongoing tithing in addition. That would give Smith a regular income to support his ventures within Mormonism. Having seemingly learned a lesson from his mistakes with Don Carlos, Smith first makes sure that he and his pals are well looked after when they travel. On 26 July 1838, he called a council to agree on funding and this was the result:

> Thursday, 26. The First Presidency, High Council, and Bishop's court assembled at Far West to dispose of the public properties of the Church in the hands of the Bishop, many of the brethren having consecrated their surplus property according to the revelations.
>
> It was agreed that the First Presidency should keep all their properties that they could dispose of to advantage, for their support, and the remainder be put into the hands of the Bishop or Bishops, according to the commandments.

Moved, seconded, and carried unanimously:

First--That the First Presidency shall have their expenses defrayed in going to, and returning from Adam ondi-Ahman; equally by the Bishop of each place.

Second--That all the traveling expenses of the First Presidency shall be defrayed.

Third--That the Bishop be authorized to pay orders coming from the east, inasmuch as they will consecrate liberally, but this is to be done under the inspection of the First Presidency.

Fourth--That the First Presidency shall have the prerogative to direct the Bishop as to whose orders shall or may be paid by him in this place, or in his jurisdiction... *(HC. Vol. III, CH. VI).*

During 1838, Mormons took the offensive against settlers who were bent on driving them out and on both sides there were burnings and lootings when several people were killed. On 1 November 1838, Joseph and Hyrum Smith, Lyman Wight, Alexander McRae, Caleb Baldwin, and Sidney Rigdon were all arrested on charges of high treason against the state, murder, burglary, arson, robbery, and larceny. Preliminary court hearings in Richmond held from 12-29 November, found there were charges to be answered. The men were transferred to the jail in Liberty where all except Sidney Rigdon, who was released after an investigation, remained incarcerated until April the following year (1839).

Smith recorded an incident that occurred while he was held at Richmond which he determined to be fulfilment of a prophecy. If this was the best he could do about fulfilling prophecy, he was not much of a prophet and Smith was just clutching at straws to cover silly things he had predicted. This little conversation was really of no consequence but became a convenient cover for something that otherwise would have remained 'unfulfilled'. You could hardly call having a chat with a lady whilst in a prison, fulfilment of a prophecy that a 'sermon' would be preached by 'one of our Elders' in Jackson County before the end of 1838. Yet Smith claimed it – and that was that.

> Sunday, 4.--We were visited by some ladies and gentlemen. One of the women came up, and very candidly inquired of the troops which of the prisoners was the Lord whom the "Mormons" worshiped. One of the guard pointed to me with a significant smile, and said, "This is he." The woman then turning to me inquired whether I professed to be the Lord and Savior? I replied, that I professed to be nothing but a man, and a minister of salvation, sent by Jesus Christ to preach the Gospel.

DOCTRINE & COVENANTS – SECTIONS 109-120 & 137

This answer so surprised the woman that she began to inquire into our doctrine, and I preached a discourse, both to her and her companions, and to the wondering soldiers, who listened with almost breathless attention while I set forth the doctrine of faith in Jesus Christ, and repentance, and baptism for remission of sins, with the promise of the Holy Ghost, as recorded in the second chapter of the Acts of the Apostles.

The woman was satisfied, and praised God in the hearing of the soldiers, and went away, praying that God would protect and deliver us. Thus was fulfilled a prophecy which had been spoken publicly by me, a few months previous--that a sermon should be preached in Jackson county by one of our Elders, before the close of 1838. *(HC. Vol. III, Ch. XIV)*.

Section 116 – Summary

Prophecies made:	1 *(From HC, related to Spring Hill)*.
Prophecies fulfilled:	0
Non-prophetic revelation:	1

Prophecies made:

Pr. 53. A 'temple square' site was chosen and dedicated in October of 1838 by Brigham Young, accompanied by Smith, Heber C. Kimball and others *(see pp. 405-6 for related references)*.

Results:

Pr. 53. This was the third temple to be prophesied and planned but never constructed. This time, they never even managed to lay cornerstones. It was certainly not a case of 'third time lucky'; the saints were ordered out of the settlement within days of the dedication.

Non-prophetic revelation:

1. Adam and Eve lived and raised their family in Spring Hill (Adam-Ondi-Ahman) after being driven from the Garden of Eden. This would mean that everything from then until the time of the biblical flood transpired in North America.

Whatever beliefs we may or may not individually hold, one thing is for certain; the Adam and Eve story, as well as the global flood idea (and probably everything in between), are pure mythology. We *know* there was a worldwide population of around five million humans by 4000 BCE and we also *know*, in addition to the fact that a global flood was an impossible occurrence on every imaginable scientific level, that there was *no* flood 'gap', in a biblical timeframe, of many civilisations that have been documented as having existed for many thousands of years.

Section 117
8 July 1838. Far West, Missouri.

History.

Added in 1876. 2010 D&C Sec. 117.

Sections 117, 118, 119 and 120 were all given on the same day. Only Section 119 appeared in the 1844 D&C and the rest were added in 1876. In Section 117, which has all of sixteen verses, Smith has the Lord use the expression "saith the Lord" *fifteen* times. Was the Lord so unsure that his audience would know who the 'voice' was in this Section, or was Smith getting desperate and adding the Lord's command to every little requirement?

William Marks and Newel K. Whitney are now to sell up and get out of Kirtland as quickly as possible. They must not hang about or it will not be well for them; and as always, they are to repent – for good measure. They should not be covetous "for what is property unto me? saith the Lord" (v.4), meaning they would likely lose a lot of money by selling quickly, if they could sell at all. However, the Lord doesn't much care about all that. They are to let the Kirtland properties go in order to pay off debts.

The Lord then makes his excuses for that being necessary, by talking about birds and fish and beasts, then saying he holds the destinies of all the armies of the nations of the earth, for some reason; none of which was of any help to the saints whatsoever. Then the Lord declares:

> **8.** Is there not room enough on the mountains of Adam-ondi-Ahman, and on the plains of Olaha Shinehah, or the land where Adam dwelt, that you should covet that which is but the drop, and neglect the more weighty matters?
> **9.** Therefore, come up hither unto the land of my people, even Zion.

The Lord still thinks Adam and Eve lived at Spring Hill and moreover, in July 1838, he seems convinced there is plenty of room there for everyone. Smith made up the name "Olaha Shinehah" for effect. It has not been heard of before or since. In v.9, the Lord even calls it Zion; yet he failed to mention the fact that they would be driven from there four months later. Why hide the truth;

and more importantly, why not reveal a place they *could* gather, where they would actually be able to *stay*, whether he mistakenly thought Adam had lived there or not? Ignoring the problems ahead, the Lord says Whitney should go to Adam-Ondi-Ahman and be Bishop there. That idea wasn't to last long.

Next, the Lord says he remembers 'Oliver Granger' who's "name will be had in sacred remembrance from generation to generation, forever and ever" (v.12). Granger was assigned to stay in Kirtland, sell off property and pay creditors. Granger's assignment was managed very well, but most property was never sold and it fell into the hands of people who never did pay for it. Granger died in Kirtland in 1841 at age forty-seven. No one really knows who he was now, but apologists claim that as long as we *have* the D&C, his name will be known, as prophesied, *in* it. As previously mentioned, Mormons had to 'make' Smith prophecy come true – it *never* happened of its own accord.

In any event, that 'prophecy' isn't the one that critics or apologists should worry about; it is of no significance at all. It's the next part that takes some explaining and yet no one seems to notice it. Remember, the *Lord* is saying this about Granger:

> **13.** Therefore, let him contend earnestly for the redemption of the First Presidency of my Church, saith the Lord; and when he falls he shall rise again, for his sacrifice shall be more sacred unto me than his increase, saith the Lord.
> **14.** Therefore, **let him come up hither speedily, unto the land of Zion**; and in the due time **he shall be made a merchant unto my name, saith the Lord**, for the benefit of my people.
> **15.** Therefore let no man despise my servant Oliver Granger, but let the blessings of my people be on him forever and ever. (Emphasis added).

Forget whether anyone *remembers* Oliver Granger or not; here "thus saith the Lord", he will go up to Zion, which at that time meant Spring Hill (Adam-Ondi-Ahman), and "be made a merchant unto my name". That was a prophecy which failed on two counts. Firstly, the saints were driven out of Spring Hill well before the end of the same year; and secondly, Granger never left Kirtland and he died there in 1841.

The Lord often finishes his revelations to Smith with some odd statements. This one is very strange indeed. The Lord closes by saying his servants in the land of Kirtland should remember the "Lord their God" and his "house also" in Kirtland, "keep and preserve it holy" – "and to overthrow the moneychangers in mine own due time, saith the Lord. Even so. Amen" (v.16). So, in the Lord's "own due time" – one of his favourite phrases *(see p.214 & The Final Analysis, Part 2)* – they are to overthrow the moneychangers in the Kirtland temple.

There never were any moneychangers to overthrow but they soon lost control of the temple. It was not even 'kept' let alone 'preserved holy' – unless there were such things as holy cows...

Section 117 – Summary

Prophecies made: 3
Prophecies fulfilled: 0

Prophecies made:

Pr. 54. v.8-9. "Is there not room enough on the mountains of Adam-ondi-Ahman, and on the plains of Olaha Shinehah, or the land where Adam dwelt, that you should covet that which is but the drop, and neglect the more weighty matters? Therefore, come up hither unto the land of my people, even Zion."

Pr. 55. Lord says Newel K. Whitney should go to Adam-Ondi-Ahman and be Bishop there.

Pr. 56. "Thus saith the Lord", Oliver Granger will go up to Zion (at that time, Adam-Ondi-Ahman) and be made a merchant to the Lord.

Results:

Pr. 54. The Lord still thinks Adam lived at Spring Hill and moreover, in July 1838, he seems convinced there is plenty of room there for everyone. In v.9 the Lord even calls it Zion; yet he failed to mention the fact that they would be driven from there four months later.

Pr. 55. The 'Whitney' prophecy of July 1838 failed because the saints were driven from Spring Hill by November of that year and they never returned.

Pr. 56. The 'Granger' prophecy was a prophecy which failed on two counts. Firstly, the saints were driven out of Spring Hill well before the end of the same year; and secondly, Granger never left Kirtland and he died there in 1841.

Section 118
8 July 1838. Far West, Missouri.

History.

Added in 1876. 2010 D&C Sec. 118.

This short Section concerns the twelve apostles. Thomas B. Marsh should stay in Zion to "publish my word" and the rest should go off and preach. This is where the Lord says they needn't worry about their families as he "will provide for their families, and an *effectual door* shall be opened for them, from henceforth" (italics added), whatever he meant by that *(see pp. 393-6)*.

The Lord then instructs the twelve to go "over the great waters" in the spring. "Let them take leave of my saints in the city of Far West." The trouble was that there were no saints left in Far West to "take leave of" by the following spring. Nevertheless, they are to start from the temple spot at Far West on the day prophesied to be when construction would commence, on 26 April 1839 *(see Section 115)*. At this time Smith clearly imagined a glorious day of celebration at the start of building the temple, coupled with seeing the twelve apostles off on a great mission abroad. Unfortunately, in order to ultimately *make* this come true, as they had been driven from Far West long before then, the twelve had to creep in to the site in the dead of night. It was not much of a celebration but it was claimed as prophecy fulfilled. They put one stone on top of a cornerstone while they were there as a symbol of construction commencement. To this day, that's all that has ever been done *(See pp. 403-4)*.

John Taylor, John E. Page, Wilford Woodruff and Willard Richards are called to the twelve to replace several who have "fallen".

Section 119
8 July 1838. Far West, Missouri.

History.

1844 D&C Sec. CVII. 2010 D&C Sec. 119.

This Section is taught to investigators during missionary lessons. I commented on it in *TMD Vol. 4:345-6*. The Mormon Church explains the reason for this Section in the header. Note that it says the covenant to consecrate every surplus thing is just the start; then they must tithe. It was supposed to be "a standing law unto them forever" (v.4). Tithing is still operated today but no one gives up anything on joining the Church; consecration is *agreed* to in temple covenants.

> Revelation given through Joseph Smith the Prophet, at Far West, Missouri, 8 July 1838, in answer to his supplication: "O Lord! Show unto thy servant how much thou requirest of the properties of thy people for a tithing" (History of the Church,3:44). The law of tithing, as understood today, had not been given to the Church previous to this revelation. The term tithing in the prayer just quoted and in previous

> *revelations (64:23; 85:3; 97:11) had meant not just one-tenth, but all free-will offerings, or contributions, to the Church funds. The Lord had previously given to the Church the law of consecration and stewardship of property, which members (chiefly the leading elders) entered into by a covenant that was to be everlasting. Because of failure on the part of many to abide by this covenant, the Lord withdrew it for a time and gave instead the law of tithing to the whole Church. The Prophet asked the Lord how much of their property he required for sacred purposes. The answer was this revelation.* (Italics in original).

In the first two verses, Smith jumps right in and says all surplus property is to be handed over to the Church. What is it for? "For the building of mine house, and for the laying of the foundation of Zion and for the priesthood, and *for the debts of the Presidency* of my Church" (Italics added), but "that is just the beginning of the tithing of my people" (v.2).

"And after that, those who have thus been tithed shall pay one-tenth of all their interest annually; and this shall be a standing law unto them forever" (v.3). Anyone who does not do all this will be thrown out – "shall not be found worthy to abide among you" (v.5). This is to be "an ensample" to all the stakes of Zion. Smith was constantly inventing ways to get people to part with money.

Section 120
8 July 1838. Far West, Missouri.

History.

Added in 1876. 2010 D&C Sec. 120.

Revelation given through Joseph Smith the Prophet, at Far West, Missouri, 8 July 1838, making known the disposition of the properties tithed as named in the preceding revelation, section 119 (see *History of the Church,* 3:44).

> 1. Verily, thus saith the Lord, the time is now come, that it shall be disposed of by a council, composed of the First Presidency of my Church, and of the bishop and his council, and by my high council; and by mine own voice unto them, saith the Lord. Even so. Amen.

That speaks for itself; Smith was desperately trying to pay off his debts and anything they could sell would go toward getting him out of trouble. The Lord says that is what they should do, so that makes it alright in order to pay off "the debts of the presidency", as recorded the same day in Section 119:2.

Chapter 22

**Doctrine and Covenants
Sections 121 – 131**

After Section 120, there were no further D&C entries for the next two years and eight months, when Section 124 was written. In March of 1839, what later became D&C 121-123 (long after Smith's death) was written in letter form while Smith was in Liberty Jail. These three Sections comprise extracts from two of several letters Smith wrote during his incarceration. Section 121 is taken from various parts of the first letter plus the first part of the second. Sections 122 and 123 are from the middle and end of the second of the two letters.

However, the 'letter' Sections were originally a great deal longer and much has subsequently been deleted. What is left has been altered a great deal from the original text since first published in Times and Seasons.

The following link to 'Eye on Apologetics' provides a complete transcript of the original Smith letters from which the current Sections 121-123 have been extracted, identifying exactly what was and was not published in 'Times and Seasons', including additions and deletions from the original parts that were included – compared with the later 'Sections' as they appeared in the 1876 D&C – and with what we read today. There is absolutely *no* comparison. The transition is complex to describe and I consider this link an absolute *must* for the serious reader.
http://eyeonapologetics.com/800/changes-made-to-doctrine-and-covenants-sections-121-122-and-123

The above link includes relevant scanned original pages from *Times and Seasons* Vol. 1, No. 7 and No. 9 where the letters were published. It is quite amazing to see what was and what was not originally included and the extent to which details were changed, added to and deleted from Smith's original letters.

For example, the author (Glenn Hendrickson) comments that some words were *later altered* from the original for the D&C, in order to make them *sound* more like early modern English, so it would appear the Lord was involved.

> **D&C 121:12.** "And also that God **hath** set his hand..." (Originally, "has")
>
> **D&C 122:4.** "...thou **shalt** be had in honor" (Originally, "shall")
>
> D&C 122:8 "The Son of Man **hath** descended below..." (Originally, "has")
>
> **D&C 123:7.** "...that spirit which **hath** so strongly riveted..." (Originally, "has")
>
> **D&C 123:15.** "...there is much **which lieth** in futurity..." (Originally, "that lies")

As Glenn comments "Why are these phrases being altered to sound like they had been translated by an Englishman from the 1600s? This is an odd phenomenon considering the primary goal of a translator is to translate a document into the language and dialect spoken by the receiving audience, not one which had been dead for 200 years."

It is very difficult to argue with that. There is no mention in the D&C today of the fact these three sections originally comprised two far larger documents from which various paragraphs have been selected, any more than there is any annotation that they have also been completely altered in the process.

I will provide one final citation with grateful thanks to Glenn for publishing the details, and once again refer readers to the above link for more information.

> The letter in *Times and Seasons* Vol. 1, No. 7, pp 99-104 is comprised of 3569 words. In today's D&C this document stands behind D&C 121:1-33, which totals 945 words. The second letter in *Times and Seasons* Vol. 1, No, 9, pp. 131-134 is comprised of 2496 words. This document stands behind the current D&C 121:34-123:17 which is made up of 1475 words. The raw difference in word number is as follows.
>
> First Letter: 3569 – 945 = **2624**
> Second Letter: 2496 – 1475 = **1021**

DOCTRINE & COVENANTS – SECTIONS 121-131

> This does not tell us the whole story, as many words which were removed from the original document would be supplemented by the sections which were added from (seemingly) nowhere. It is, however, worth recognizing due the large number of words lost. This can not be accounted for due to words which may have legitimately been lost in translation from a non-English language. Joseph originally wrote in English!

As an aside, one of the other letters Smith wrote while he was in jail was to "Mrs. Norman Bull", who was in fact Norman Buell's wife. This is just a snippet of what Smith included:

> LIBERTY JAIL, March 15, 1839.

> ...I am your true friend. I was glad to see you. No tongue can tell what inexpressible joy it gives a man, after having been enclosed in the walls of a prison for five months, to see the face of one who has been a friend. It seems to me that my heart will always be more tender after this than ever it was before.

> ...There will be a short work on the earth. It has now commenced. I suppose there will soon be perplexity all over the earth. Do not let our hearts faint when these things come upon us, for they must come, or the word cannot be fulfilled.

> ...I wanted to communicate something, and I wrote this. Write to us if you can.

Obviously, Pres(c)endia Buell had visited Smith while he was incarcerated. The middle extract I have included above has Smith claiming the end would not be that long in coming. It didn't come, and we are of course still awaiting the predicted event. As this letter has not been claimed revelation or included in the D&C, I am not counting it as prophecy. It is however, quite clear what Smith intended to convey.

In comparison, the first and third extracts are somewhat personal, bordering on romantic. This may not be far from the truth, as Smith was to polyandrously marry Pres(c)endia Lathrop Huntington Buell as his approximate sixth plural wife a couple of years later, on 11 Dec 1841, and they had clearly become very close prior to that event.

Section 121
20 [25] March 1839. Liberty Jail, Clay County, Missouri.

History.

Added in 1876. 2010 D&C Sec. 121.

Regarding Sections 121-123, Smith himself did not extract the details from his letters, nor did he personally declare them to be revelations which should be included in the D&C. The 1844 edition was published with no mention of them at all. Section 124 came almost two years after the Smith letters and Section 124 *was* included in the 1844 D&C.

Although Section 121 is today dated 20 March 1839, at least part of one letter from which it is derived is dated 25 March. This is the first of three Sections extracted from letters penned by Smith in the March of 1839 while in Liberty Jail. The header says this Section contains "prayer and prophecies" – so will we find anything prophesied that was actually fulfilled? If we do, it will certainly be a first.

In the first six verses, Smith is complaining bitterly to God and begs Him to get angry with his enemies and "with thy sword avenge us of our wrongs" (v.5). Smith himself had become quite aggressive toward locals when any existing populations objected to the saints wherever he tried to settle them and that was what had landed him in jail. He would later often parade on horseback as 'Lieutenant-General Joseph Smith', complete with a magnificent uniform and sword to match his self-proclaimed 'station' with the Nauvoo Legion (a private army) following behind. No wonder original settlers in the area became afraid and wanted none of it. But we will come to all that in due course.

The Lord then responds to Smith (from v.7), but today's Mormons will have no idea that in the original letter, there were seven and a half paragraphs between what is now v.6 and v.7. Verse 7 starts half way though paragraph eight and hardly reflects an immediate response from God regarding v.1-6. Reading the missing paragraphs, it is easy to understand why the Church left them out of the D&C as they don't exactly make compelling reading.

There are also five and a half paragraphs missing between v.25 and v.26; one paragraph missing between v.32 and v.33; and following v.33, there are a further six paragraphs missing which take us to end of the letter; then we are missing the first seven paragraphs of the second letter before the Section picks up again at v.34. That hardly provides a continuous narrative, but there is no mention in the D&C that Section 121 consists of four separate chunks of text 'cut and pasted' together from two different letters Smith wrote while he was in jail. Without any such reference, the Church is pretending it is one revelation.

DOCTRINE & COVENANTS – SECTIONS 121-131

As pointed out by Glenn Hendrickson in his article, v.12 was later changed from reading "has" to "hath" to make it sound more like God than Smith.

It is easy to guess what the Lord will say (from v.7). In a nutshell (as Smith pads this out for several verses – and this is clearly just in his imagination), God tells Smith he must bear it; everything will work out; Smith's adversaries will pay for what they have done. How will that be? "…not many years hence …they and their posterity shall be swept from under heaven, saith God, that not one of them is left to stand by the wall" (v.15). What on earth had their children ever done to deserve such judgment? In any event, there is no record that the Lord ever "swept" anyone from "under heaven" and it was, as ever, just Smith rhetoric. The Section header calls it prophecy; if it was, it was an extremely cruel one. It was also yet another that was entirely and quite rightly unfulfilled.

Nevertheless, Smith has the Lord say "wo unto them" and "Their baskets shall not be full, their houses and their barns shall perish, and they themselves shall be despised by those that flattered them" (v.20). Why would the Lord talk about 'baskets' and use the expression "their houses and barns shall perish" – and why would they be despised by "those who flattered them"? It makes no sense whatsoever – unless it was Smith just playing with words; then it makes perfect sense.

Smith then has the Lord add "It had been better for them that a millstone had been hanged about their necks, and they drowned in the depth of the sea" (v.22). Smith stole that line from the NT where it is recorded in the first three gospels. He had used the "drowned in the depth of the sea" idea in Section 54:5 but didn't include a millstone on that occasion. The Lord continues to rant, calling locals a generation of vipers and condemning them to hell. Judgment is going to be swift – but of course there never actually was any judgment. In any event, *why* were they a generation of vipers? They had been just fine until Mormons invaded the territory and Smith tried to take over anything he could, controlling everything in the immediate area. It is notable that in *every* location where the 'saints' tried to settle, Smith almost immediately upset the locals to the extent that they soon wanted the Mormons out. It is interesting to note that a number of other religious groups in those areas did not have that problem; including several Mormon schisms *(see p.432)*.

God just rambles on for several more verses and then says the working of the sun, moon and stars, along with everything else, "was ordained in the midst of the Council of the Eternal **God of all other gods** before this world was" (emphasis added) in v.32, identifying Smith's *later* concept of plural gods. This could be considered to imply that 'our' God was "the God of all other gods", yet Smith later taught that God had a father, in his 'King Follett Sermon', so surely this verse must mean that some earlier or even original 'god' headed this 'council'? Not really; Smith was just making things up again.

Just before that, in v.28, Smith had claimed "A time to come in the which nothing shall be withheld, *whether there be one God or many gods*, they shall be manifest" (emphasis added). Was he not sure if there was more than one? We know the 'plural gods' concept was *new* because the words about 'gods' were added *later*; the original text didn't include the idea at all when first written – or even when first published. It is hard to discover whether they were even added by Smith. As the Sections were not published until 1876, perhaps it was Brigham Young who adapted them to include the later theology. Whoever it was, it all came *after* the original event. Let's compare the texts.

When the letters, from which this Section was derived, were first published in 'Times and Seasons' the words were somewhat different to those we see in the D&C today. Originally, what was later to become v.28-29 and 31 were published thus:

> ...until a time when nothing shall be withheld, when all the glories of earth and heaven, time and eternity shall be manifest to all those, who have endured valiantly for the gospel of Jesus Christ.

> ...according to that which was ordained in the midst of the council of heaven in the presence of the eternal God, before this world was. *(Times and Seasons, Vol. 1. No. 7. May 1840. pp. 99b-104a).*

There is no mention of more than one God in those lines and this is supposedly *revelation*. What they later became in the 1876 D&C, included changes to the original text and inserted words identifying *later* theology on the plurality of gods. History of the Church Volume III (1902) also contains the *later* D&C falsifications, placed *directly* into Smith's letters, just as if they had originally appeared that way. It is this kind of duplicity that proves time and again that Mormon Church leaders care nothing for the truth and are perfectly happy to deceive their members. God was *not* involved in any of this; He couldn't be – or He would not *be* God.

The added words regarding plural gods are once again emphasised below in the equivalent current D&C verses for comparison. The several other changes to the original text (above) are obvious but not significant – other that is, than to say whatever it was the Lord was really supposed to have 'revealed', it should have been written down correctly in the first place. The completely altered text comprising these D&C verses, along with 'History of the Church' which was falsified to match the D&C additions, comprise a conspiracy to deceive the faithful. It is more than shameful; it is completely reprehensible.

> **121:28-9.** ...a time to come in the which nothing shall be withheld, ***whether there be one God or many gods***, they shall be manifest. All thrones and dominions, principalities and powers, shall be revealed and set forth upon all who have endured valiantly for the gospel of Jesus Christ.
>
> **31.** ...according to that which was ordained in the midst of the Council of the ***Eternal God of all other gods*** before this world was...

God says no one can "hinder the Almighty from pouring down knowledge from heaven upon the heads of the Latter-day Saints" (v.33). If that is so, by my reckoning at least, He had yet to say a single thing worth mentioning or of any practical use. There was no 'pouring down knowledge' to *be* hindered.

There is a line in v.34 that is well known in Mormonism; "Many are called but few are chosen". Smith had used it before in Section 95:5 *(see p.328)*, and as stated there, he stole it from Matthew 20:16 and 22:14. The Church will claim they are the words of Jesus, and God can of course use them if He wants to. However, coupled with everything else that Smith has God say, the entire conversation is not exactly conducive to something that could realistically be attributed to a God, unless you are captured in a religious delusion. Everything about His speech, as well as the content, is positively dreadful.

But then, does the Church claim God is actually speaking at this point? As the text is drawn from two different letters, and by this point, from a section that appears to be Smith grumbling again, perhaps the Church will concede that they are just the words of Smith, as in reality, that is precisely what they are.

In v.38, assuming this is Smith rather than God, he says when man tries to cover his sins, he is left to himself "to kick against the pricks", which again Smith plagiarised; this time, from Acts 9:5 and 26:14. If God said that, he was in fact using more words originally attributed to Jesus. The year before this was written (1838), Smith had decided God and Jesus were two separate beings when he wrote his final version of the first vision story. Still, Smith having called on God, and God having answered, perhaps we could forgive Him for using words attributed to His son; except that the likelihood of Jesus having actually spoken the two phrases in those exact words is historically extremely remote. Smith next says the following; making it clear Smith is speaking rather than God, as God would obviously not have to learn about the "nature and disposition of almost all men" by "sad experience".

> **39.** We have learned by sad experience that it is the nature and disposition of almost all men, as soon as they get a little authority, as they suppose, they will immediately begin to exercise unrighteous dominion.
>
> 40. Hence many are called, but few are chosen.

This clearly could not be God lacking experience of men. God had created and populated many worlds, according to Smith in his Book of Moses. He is depicted, even in Mormonism, as 'all knowing', and would have been perfectly well aware of the disposition of humans long before this world was created and He placed us here. The fact that Smith even mentions this, confirms God was *not* speaking at this point.

Speaking of the Book of Moses; as an aside, it is worth mentioning that in establishing God's vast experience of creating "worlds without number" and thus already knowing men well enough, Smith inadvertently makes yet another serious error.

> **Moses 5: 33.** And ***worlds without number have I created***; and I also created them for mine own purpose; and by the Son I created them, which is mine Only Begotten.
> **34.** And the first man of all men have ***I called Adam, which is many.***
> **35.** But ***only an account of this earth, and the inhabitants thereof, give I unto you.*** For behold, there are many worlds that have passed away by the word of my power. And there are many that now stand, and ***innumerable are they unto man***; but ***all things are numbered unto me, for they are mine and I know them***. (Emphasis added).

If God has created and populated worlds without number and all are known to Him, he will not be learning from experience, sad or otherwise – so that was Smith. But here, Smith has God declare 'Adam' means 'many' *(v.34 above)*.

Adam is a word derived from Hebrew which actually means exactly what you might imagine: from Heb. Adam "man" lit. "(the one formed from the) ground" (Heb. Adamah "ground"); cf. L. homo "man." Humanus "human," humus "earth, ground, soil." What 'Adam' does *not* mean at all, is 'many', irrespective of what Smith and his God claim. Smith (or his God) seemed to get everything wrong. The meaning of 'Adam' was no exception.

Section 121 – Summary

Prophecies made:	1
Prophecies fulfilled:	0

DOCTRINE & COVENANTS – SECTIONS 121-131

Non-prophetic revelation: 1

Prophecies made:

    Pr. 57. The Section header claims this is *"Prayer and **prophecies** written by Joseph Smith the Prophet"* (Italics in original, bold added); v.15: "And not many years hence, that they and their posterity shall be swept from under heaven, saith God, that not one of them is left to stand by the wall." v.18: "And those who swear falsely against my servants, that they might bring them into bondage and death—" v.20: "Their basket shall not be full, their houses and their barns shall perish, and they themselves shall be despised by those that flattered them." v.23: "Wo unto all those that discomfort my people, and drive, and murder, and testify against them, saith the Lord of Hosts; a generation of vipers shall not escape the damnation of hell."

    Results:

    Pr. 57. No recorded retribution by the Lord has ever been established. No baskets have been emptied, no houses or barns have perished by the hand or sword of God; and no one, along with their posterity, has mysteriously been swept from the earth by the *Lord*. The only time people had their property burned or they got killed was at the hands of Mormons when they went on the offensive. Divine intervention has never been recorded, established or claimed. Whether they will "escape the damnation of hell" or not remains to be seen.

    Non-prophetic revelation:

1. Original text read "...until a time when nothing shall be withheld, when all the glories of earth and heaven, time and eternity shall be manifest to all those, who have endured valiantly for the gospel of Jesus Christ ...according to that which was ordained in the midst of the council of heaven in the presence of the eternal God, before this world was. *(Times and Seasons, Vol. 1. No. 7. May 1840. pp. 99b-104a).*

    Revised text later included words that are claimed as revelation, with no indication that they were added *after* the event. 121:28-9, 31. "...a time to come in the which nothing shall be withheld, **whether there be one God or many gods**, they shall be manifest. All thrones and dominions, principalities and powers, shall be revealed and set forth upon all who have endured valiantly for the gospel of Jesus Christ. ...according to that which was ordained in the midst of the Council of the ***Eternal God of all other gods*** before this world was..."

Section 122
March 1839. Liberty Jail, Clay County, Missouri.

History.

Added in 1876. 2010 D&C Sec. 122.

Section 122 continues from where Section 121 left off in the letter. There is no explanation as to why it continues in a new Section any more than there is mention of the fact that it is a continuation of the same letter. There are only nine verses and again, as noted by Glenn Hendrickson, v.4 and v.8 later had "shall" altered to read "shalt" and "has" altered to read "hath" respectively, to make them sound more like God.

Smith has the Lord declare that fools will hold Smith in derision while the wise and noble will seek him. What Smith has God say next is so ridiculous I cannot believe I missed it in all my years as a Mormon. I am including it below so the reader can carefully consider whether they think God would really speak this way. I have no further comment on it other than to say that naturally it didn't read that way when first written or published. As ever, there were a number of changes, amounting to over forty words added, deleted or altered from the original text. This simply was *not* God speaking, before or after all the changes that were made.

> **5.** If thou art called to pass through tribulation; if thou art in perils among false brethren; if thou art in perils among robbers; if thou art in perils by land or by sea;
> **6.** If thou art accused with all manner of false accusations; if thine enemies fall upon thee; if they tear thee from the society of thy father and mother and brethren and sisters; and if with a drawn sword thine enemies tear thee from the bosom of thy wife, and of thine offspring, and thine elder son, although but six years of age, shall cling to thy garments, and shall say, My father, my father, why can't you stay with us? O, my father, what are the men going to do with you? and if then he shall be thrust from thee by the sword, and thou be dragged to prison, and thine enemies prowl around thee like wolves for the blood of the lamb;
> **7.** And if thou shouldst be cast into the pit, or into the hands of murderers, and the sentence of death passed upon thee; if thou be cast into the deep; if the billowing surge conspire against thee; if fierce winds become thine enemy; if the heavens gather blackness, and all the elements combine to hedge up the way; and above all, if

DOCTRINE & COVENANTS – SECTIONS 121-131

the very jaws of hell shall gape open the mouth wide after thee, know thou, my son, that all these things shall give thee experience, and shall be for thy good.

Finally, Smith has the Lord prophesy that his life will *not* be shortened – "Thy days are known, and thy years shall not be numbered less; therefore, fear not what man can do, for God shall be with you forever and ever" (v.9). A little over five years later, Smith was shot dead at the age of thirty-eight. Smith's days *were* cut short, in complete contradiction to this prophecy. It is no good the Church claiming those were the number of his days or that for some reason he had to seal his testimony with his blood. The Smith brothers had spent hours persuading the town council to destroy William Law's printing press in what was considered an act of treason *(see TMD Vol. 1:97-100)* which is why they were arrested and ultimately got killed by a mob whilst in jail awaiting trial.

Smith's illegal actions were not in any way godly and he was not a martyr. Smith was a violent criminal who had a price on his head following his alleged conspiracy in the attempted murder of Governor Boggs; he had been in and out of jail, and was finally killed whilst once again in jail facing charges of treason.

Smith and his cohorts were to escape their captors on this occasion, on 16 April 1839, and never did face the treason and other charges in court. This time, Smith escaped and evaded the law and was lucky, but he always pushed his luck and ultimately it simply ran out – and his life *was* cut short. Had it not been, he would almost certainly have been found guilty of treason, and if not hanged or shot, would probably have spent the rest of his life in prison.

Section 122 – Summary

Prophecies made:	1
Prophecies fulfilled:	0

Prophecies made:

Pr. 58. "Thy days are known, and thy years shall not be numbered less; therefore, fear not what man can do, for God shall be with you forever and ever" (v.9).

Results:

Pr. 58. A little over five years later, Joseph Smith was shot dead at the age of thirty-eight. His days *were* cut well short of a normal life-span, in complete contradiction to this prophecy.

Section 123
March 1839. Liberty Jail, Clay County, Missouri.

History.

Added in 1876. 2010 D&C Sec. 123.

Section 123 does not follow on from Section 122; there are four missing paragraphs between the two Sections. This Section contains notes from Smith, suggesting members list all their grievances – the "facts and sufferings and abuses" (v.1). He suggests a committee be formed to collate all the losses and damages listed in the resulting affidavits. Then, in suggesting they also collate all the libellous publications, Smith added in a statement which he probably considered profound but in reality sounds like he ate a dictionary for breakfast.

> **5.** And all that are in the magazines, and in the encyclopedias, and all the libelous histories that are published, and are writing, and by whom, and present the whole concatenation of diabolical rascality and nefarious and murderous impositions that have been practised upon this people—

Once again, two words have been changed to an older English style by altering "has" to "hath" in v.7 and "that lies" to "lieth" in v.15, for no obvious reason – as God is clearly not intended to be identified as the one speaking. Old habits die hard it seems.

Smith spends the rest of the Section repeating in several different ways, and giving several different reasons why, it is "an imperative duty" (v.11) to collate all the information. Smith wasn't one to be succinct and use just a few words when close to five-hundred could be used to make the point. To say he made a meal of this is more than an understatement.

It includes a verse which is regularly used in the missionary discussions today:

> **12.** For there are many yet on the earth among all sects, parties, and denominations, who are blinded by the subtle craftiness of men, whereby they lie in wait to deceive, and who are only kept from the truth because they know not where to find it—

Of course, although the header mentions Smith was in Liberty jail, Mormon missionaries do not apprise their investigators of the fact that Joseph Smith and his friends were in jail, quite rightly charged with high treason against the state, murder, burglary, arson, robbery, and larceny – when he wrote that.

DOCTRINE & COVENANTS – SECTIONS 121-131

Section 124
19 January 1841. Nauvoo, Illinois.

History.

1844 D&C Sec. CIII (unnumbered). 2010 D&C Sec. 124.

This Section came almost two years after the letters that were used in the last three sections. Apart from the rambling letters, it was actually close to three years since Smith had claimed any new revelation as such. He makes up for it with this lengthy Section containing one-hundred-and-forty-five verses; but do they have any real merit? Well, we shall see.

By this time, the action had moved to Nauvoo, Illinois. 'The Lord' declares he is speaking in this Section on numerous occasions, and in nine instances confirms it is actually *God* doing the talking rather than the Lord Jesus. A summary of various names God/Jesus calls Himself in each Section is available in *The Final Analysis, Part 4: Who am I?* We are back to the more traditional style of Smith revelations where he has God dictate what he (Smith) wants to have happen, so there can be no complaints from his followers.

God is pleased with Smith and his prayers are "acceptable". Smith has God command him to make a proclamation to the President of the United Sates and to all the kings and other leaders of the world. The problem is, as is always the case with such things, what Smith's God wants them told is not going to go down well and of course they are not going to listen. Smith appears to be entering a deeper delusional state and not thinking clearly at all.

Smith will have a "crown" and "blessings and great glory" if he does this. Robert B. Thompson and John C. Bennett are assigned to help Smith write the proclamation which appears to need things like this included in it:

> **8.** And that I may visit them in the day of visitation, when I shall unveil the face of my covering, to appoint the portion of the oppressor among hypocrites, **where there is gnashing of teeth, if they reject my servants and my testimony** which I have revealed unto them.
>
> **9.** And again, *I will visit and soften their hearts, many of them for your good, that ye may find grace in their eyes, that they may come to the light of truth*, and the Gentiles *to the exaltation or lifting up of Zion*.
>
> **10.** For *the day of my visitation cometh speedily, in an hour when ye think not* of; and where shall be the safety of my people, and refuge for those who shall be left of them?

11. *Awake, O kings of the earth! Come ye, O, come ye, with your gold and your silver, to the help of my people*, to the house of the daughters of Zion. (Emphasis added).

Smith has God sandwich a prophecy that he will soften many national leaders' hearts, between two threats, and ends with a plea for them to provide riches for the saints. It was clearly not a good idea and if God really did want such a document sent, His strategy wasn't exactly thought through. It must be obvious to anyone who stops to think, that if God exists, He would not use such silly tactics to achieve His aims as they would clearly only ever incite ridicule and scorn rather than receive a listening ear. However, God prophesies that he will soften their hearts in v.9 and claims many of them will come to the light of truth. Naturally – they didn't.

Having got that out of the way, God next instructs several individuals on what he requires of them and then says they need to build a boarding house for Smith – just the way Smith will show them it should be built.

23. ...a house that strangers may come from afar to lodge therein; therefore let it be a good house, worthy of all acceptation, that the weary traveler may find health and safety while he shall contemplate the word of the Lord; and the cornerstone I have appointed for Zion.
24. This house shall be a healthful habitation if it be built unto my name, and if the governor which shall be appointed unto it shall not suffer any pollution to come upon it. It shall be holy, or the Lord your God will not dwell therein.

Smith is to be provided with a large property with numerous rooms. So far, Smith had only had a couple of polygamous relationships, although there is no evidence of him actually marrying either Fanny Alger or Lucinda Pendleton Morgan Harris with whom he had affairs. Smith was soon to enter a phase where several teenage housemaids and adopted daughters would live in the Smith household. Invariably, he would end up marrying them.

The new boarding house would have suited Smith well but it was never completed. After the saints had been driven out of Nauvoo in the late 1840s, Smith's first wife Emma retained ownership and later, she, along with her second husband, Lewis C. Bidamon, made a smaller home of it and lived there from 1871 until they died. In 1909, The RLDS Church acquired the property and they still own it today.

Next, God wants yet another temple built.

> **25.** And again, verily I say unto you, let all my saints come from afar.
>
> **26.** And send ye swift messengers, yea, chosen messengers, and say unto them: Come ye, with all your gold, and your silver, and your precious stones, and with all your antiquities; and with all who have knowledge of antiquities, that will come, may come, and bring the box-tree, and the fir-tree, and the pine-tree, together with all the precious trees of the earth;
>
> **27.** And with iron, with copper, and with brass, and with zinc, and with all your precious things of the earth; and build a house to my name, for the Most High to dwell therein.
>
> **28.** For there is not a place found on earth that he may come to and restore again that which was lost unto you, or which he hath taken away, even the fulness of the priesthood.

This was the *fourth* temple that the Lord had wanted built which was never completed. God had wanted a temple in Zion (Independence) *(pp.224-5)*; Far West *(p.401)*; Spring Hill (Adam-ondi-Ahman) *(pp.405-6)*; and now – Nauvoo. Although this time it was *nearly* finished before it was destroyed. The basement and ground floor levels were completed and used for a few weeks before the saints started moving west. In 1999, the Mormon Church built a modern temple on the site which, inside, is nothing like the one God instructed Smith to build, although the outside is similar. It was completed in 2002. Why was the interior not the same as the original? Times change and things had moved on in Mormonism. But why did God ask for temples to be built differently at Kirtland and in Nauvoo? The new 'endowment' was introduced in Nauvoo. It was not performed in Kirtland because it was yet to be invented so naturally that temple was not designed to accommodate it. Smith *invented* it in the Nauvoo period; thus the interior of the new temple was entirely different.

For the very first time, God tells Smith there is no baptismal font on the earth where the saints can be baptised for the *dead*. There was no mention of that in Kirtland – or for that matter, for any of the other temples that were prophesied and planned yet never constructed. This is a *new* idea. Why did God *not* have a font included in the Kirtland Temple or the other planned temples?

Whatever Smith's God had previously been thinking, He now suddenly and out of nowhere requires a baptismal font. It is also interesting that God repeats Himself several times in typical 'Smith revelation' fashion.

> **29.** For a baptismal font there is not upon the earth, that they, my saints, may be baptized for those who are dead—

30. For this ordinance belongeth to my house, ***and cannot be acceptable to me, only in the days of your poverty, wherein ye are not able to build a house unto me.***

31. But I command you, all ye my saints, to build a house unto me; and I grant unto you a ***sufficient time to build a house unto me; and during this time your baptisms shall be acceptable unto me.***

32. But behold, ***at the end of this appointment your baptisms for your dead shall not be acceptable unto me***; and if you do not these things at the end of the appointment ***ye shall be rejected as a church, with your dead***, saith the Lord your God.

33. For verily I say unto you, that after you have had sufficient time to build a house to me, wherein the ordinance of baptizing for the dead belongeth, and for which the same was instituted from before the foundation of the world, ***your baptisms for your dead cannot be acceptable unto me;***

34. For therein are the keys of the holy priesthood ordained, that you may receive honor and glory.

35. And ***after this time, your baptisms for the dead***, by those who are scattered abroad, ***are not acceptable unto me***, saith the Lord.

36. For it is ordained that in Zion, and in her stakes, and in Jerusalem, those places which I have appointed for refuge, shall be the places for your baptisms for your dead. (Emphasis added).

Surely they would have got the message the first, or even the second time, but Smith was very repetitive so his God became so too. Three times, God says that after the time allotted to build the temple, baptisms for the dead outside the temple will not be acceptable. He actually states that if they do *not* do these things by the end of the appointed time, "ye shall be rejected as a church, with your dead" (v.32). What better way for Smith to put the pressure on to get the temple built. But would a real God actually say such a thing? Work progressed so slowly that eventually funds and labour were diverted from the Smith boarding house project to focus on completing the temple. Smith died well over a year before the temple was completed sufficiently to be even partially usable.

When I published *TMD Volume 3*, which includes a section describing the evolution of the endowment ceremony, I was careful to only use information accepted by the Church, along with my own personal experiences, to construct details of what actually went on *inside* the temple. I avoided reference to any descriptions written by anyone not considered 'reliable' by the Church. Now we are past that stage, although it is somewhat of an aside, I thought readers may be interested in what transpired during the first ceremonies, as recorded by one of the early couples who attended. Although the account is incomplete and invariably will not be entirely accurate, several aspects are quite interesting and certainly very different to what members experience today.

For example, as I was able to identify elsewhere, it confirms there were at first only two marks or 'emblems' on the garment rather than four; a square over the breast and a compass over the knee. It also confirms that the 'Oath of Vengeance' against the United States was included from the very start. I am therefore including *Appendix C* – but only out of general interest.

God then explains they need a temple so their washings and anointings will be acceptable to Him and He (or Smith, take your pick) fills several verses with what is really just very badly worded and grammatically disastrous 'waffle' – such as verse 39.

Question: would a God *really* speak as badly as this?

> **39.** Therefore, verily I say unto you, that your anointings, and your washings, and your baptisms for the dead, and your solemn assemblies, and your memorials for your sacrifices by the sons of Levi, and for your oracles in your most holy places wherein you receive conversations, and your statutes and judgments, for the beginning of the revelations and foundation of Zion, and for the glory, honor, and endowment of all her municipals, are ordained by the ordinance of my holy house, which my people are always commanded to build unto my holy name.

Despite everything God wanted and promised, Smith was killed when the temple was only half complete. Following the succession crisis, when Brigham Young succeeded in gaining the most followers, mob violence increased and the saints were forced to prepare to leave the city. Young encouraged members to finish the temple and although it never was fully completed, part of it was used for three months, from December 1845 to February 1846. It was dedicated once the interior of the first floor was completed, on 30 April and 1 May 1846.

When the saints left the area in September 1846, vigilantes vandalised the temple. Various attempts at leasing or selling (asking up to $200,000) failed, until it was finally sold for a pittance ($5,000) in 1848 by Church agents – to a Mormon. That may sound like a good investment but later he sold it at a loss. It was soon to be gutted by fire and then hit by a tornado in 1850 before being demolished completely a few years later.

Is it just coincidence that Smith has God say this? – "And ye shall build it on the place where you have contemplated building it, for that is the spot which I have chosen for you to build it. If ye labor with all your might, I will consecrate that spot that it shall be made holy" (v.43-4). God chose the very spot that Smith had selected. Holy 'spot' or not – the temple was destroyed.

God goes on to say that if they hearken to His voice, they will not be moved out of their place (v.45). If they don't listen to God, or to Smith and his men, they will not be "blest". The saints certainly appeared to try hard to accomplish what was required of them but they were driven out anyway. Did that mean they had *not* listened? God actually says that even if they build His house but do not do the things He says, "instead of blessings, ye, by your own works, bring cursings, wrath, indignation, and judgments upon your own heads, by your follies, and by all your abominations, which you practise before me, saith the Lord" (v.48). Were they really that bad? Of course not, but Smith was; the suffering and persecution of the saints can be traced directly back to the way he personally behaved and how he treated and tried to control people, not just in his Church but also the local community and government.

It is interesting to note that whilst Mormons were constantly driven from place to place, many of the other cults and minor sects of the day did not seem to have such severe problems and were mostly happily settled and accepted, or at least tolerated, by local communities.

Mormonism itself spawned quite a number of schisms, almost from the start. By the time Smith was killed in 1844, about nine splinter groups had already formed. Following the confusion which resulted after Smith's demise, coupled with Brigham Young's later creation of further strange and new doctrines, by 1863, over a dozen further schisms had formed. Although many did not survive due to lack of organisation or interest, most were not persecuted and driven from state after state as was the case with Joseph Smith's group.

The Whitmerites and Gladdenites for example weren't persecuted or driven out of Kirtland; the Church of Christ (Temple Lot) survived in Independence. They all peacefully coexisted with the locals. The Strangites were eventually rounded up and thrown off Beaver Island by residents of Makinac Island, due to antagonism – not over religion, but competition with commercial lake ports. That appears to be an exception rather than the rule, even for Mormon schisms.

The largest schism, the 'New Organisation', later incorporated as the RLDS Church (now Community of Christ), was not driven from Smith's 'Zion', of Independence, Missouri, when formally organised in 1860. Smith's son, Joseph Smith III accepted leadership of the church, and its headquarters, along with a beautiful temple, are still there today. The Mormons had been driven out and their temple was destroyed. That should tell us something, if not everything, we need to know about *why* Smith's Mormons in particular were singled out for so-called 'persecution'. What you give is often what you get.

God goes on to say that if enemies 'hinder' the work, what they were able to accomplish will be accepted, and as for those who hindered it; "the iniquity and transgression of my holy laws and commandments I will visit upon the heads of those who hindered my work, unto the third and fourth generation, so long as they repent not, and hate me, saith the Lord God" (v.50). They didn't hate God; many worshipped Him; they just hated what Smith was doing to their community. I am driven to ask – yet again, what on earth had great-great-grandchildren, who were yet to be born, ever done to deserve such a curse? For good measure, God then repeats all that again, in almost the same words – and then he does so yet again. Having done that, He then commands them to build the temple – again.

While He is in a repetitive mood, God turns back to Smith's boarding house and makes a prophecy.

> **56.** And now I say unto you, as pertaining to my boarding house which I have commanded you to build for the boarding of strangers, let it be built unto my name, and let my name be named upon it, and let my servant Joseph and his house have place therein, from generation to generation.
> **57.** For this anointing have I put upon his head, that his blessing shall also be put upon the head of his posterity after him.

God should have known better. It was decades after Smith's death before his wife Emma and her second husband Lewis C. Bidamon lived there. She had not followed Brigham Young and for a time associated with the Methodists, later affiliating with the RLDS Church when the Smith's son, Joseph III, was finally persuaded to lead it in 1860. As mentioned on *p.428*, in 1909, the RLDS Church acquired the property and they own it today. Beyond that, Smith's posterity most certainly did not "have place therein, from generation to generation" and such blessing was not "put upon the head of his posterity after him". God got it all wrong – again. Not only that, but he repeated it all again so we could be absolutely sure about what it was He was going to get so very wrong. He even names it – "Nauvoo House". Notwithstanding God's revealed choice of name, Emma had her own ideas and when she later moved in, she named it 'Riverside Mansion' – not exactly God's chosen name. The prophecy was not fulfilled.

What Smith has God say next has to be one of the silliest things that I have ever seen claimed to have come from God. Once again, I cannot even begin to imagine how I didn't notice or question this once in all my years as a Mormon. It is positively embarrassing to admit that I do not remember all this. God names several men who are to form a committee to oversee the financing and building of Smith's proposed house. This is what God Himself then says to Smith and the saints:

63. And they shall form a constitution, whereby they may receive stock for the building of that house.

64. And they shall not receive less than fifty dollars for a share of stock in that house, and they shall be permitted to receive fifteen thousand dollars from any one man for stock in that house.

65. But they shall not be permitted to receive over fifteen thousand dollars stock from any one man.

66. And they shall not be permitted to receive under fifty dollars for a share of stock from any one man in that house.

67. And they shall not be permitted to receive any man, as a stockholder in this house, except the same shall pay his stock into their hands at the time he receives stock;

68. And in proportion to the amount of stock he pays into their hands he shall receive stock in that house; but if he pays nothing into their hands he shall not receive any stock in that house.

69. And if any pay stock into their hands it shall be for stock in that house, for himself, and for his generation after him, from generation to generation, so long as he and his heirs shall hold that stock, and do not sell or convey the stock away out of their hands by their own free will and act, if you will do my will, saith the Lord your God.

Yes, that really does say "saith the Lord your God" at the end of that. I am speechless. It gets even worse – God isn't finished:

70. And again, verily I say unto you, if my servant George Miller, and my servant Lyman Wight, and my servant John Snider, and my servant Peter Haws, receive any stock into their hands, in moneys, or in properties wherein they receive the real value of moneys, they shall not appropriate any portion of that stock to any other purpose, only in that house.

71. And if they do appropriate any portion of that stock anywhere else, only in that house, without the consent of the stockholder, and do not repay fourfold for the stock which they appropriate anywhere else, only in that house, they shall be accursed, and shall be moved out of their place, saith the Lord God; for I, the Lord, am God, and cannot be mocked in any of these things.

God is *still* speaking – and He will "not be mocked in any of these things". I can't help feeling Smith was doing just that; mocking everyone's intelligence with all these concoctions that he attributed to God for his own benefit. I will not bore the reader with more details, but God is *still* not finished. He goes on for a further twelve verses, citing names of people who can put minimum and maximum stock into the house, promising that it will be "for himself and his generation after him, from generation to generation", to *seven* different people (v.69, 74, 77, 78, 80, 81, 82), even coming back to it yet again, for an *eighth* time in v.117 as He still wasn't finished with the subject and started adding even more names. No one received anything "from generation to generation".

Finally, God runs out of steam and He turns to other matters. He has a rant against Almon Babbitt with whom He is not at all pleased at the moment. William Law is to replace Hyrum Smith as a counsellor in the First Presidency. It seems ironic that (in 1836) Babbitt, along with John Taylor, had converted Law who was now to join the First Presidency, while Babbitt gets a dressing down from God.

Despite debating any and every issue, and getting himself disfellowshipped four separate times (1839, 1841, 1843, and 1851), Babbitt was always quickly restored to full fellowship and he survived in the Church until his death. He found fault with everything that Brigham Young did and having entered the political arena, made several trips to Washington. On one such trip, in 1856, Babbitt was shot to death by arrows, allegedly by Cheyenne Native Americans.

William Law, on the other hand, was to leave the Church and publish the Nauvoo Expositor; an act that frightened Smith into having the press destroyed before a second, even more damaging edition could be published. Manipulating the town council to agree to the action over extended meetings which lasted some thirteen hours, it got the Smith brothers arrested on charges of treason and ultimately led to their deaths at Carthage jail. The Laws' established a short lived schism, 'The True Church of Jesus Christ of Latter Day Saints' or the 'Reformed Mormon Church'.

Hyrum Smith is to become Church patriarch in place of his father. It is determined to be a 'right'. The father-son *right* to be Church patriarch seemed to be held for a period but it was not to last. Eventually the Church 'patriarch' was not always a direct father-son lineage and ultimately, once Stake patriarchs started to be established across the world, no more were called. It really all fell apart in 1946 upon the discovery that serving Church patriarch Joseph Fielding Smith was gay. The great-grandson of Hyrum Smith (not to be confused with two Church Presidents of the same name) was released on 'health' grounds and his sexual orientation suppressed. No one replaced him. *(See TMD Vol. 4:381-4 for a complete chronology of Mormon Church patriarchs).*

God tells Law that he will not only be able to heal the sick and cast out devils, but he will be delivered from those who would administer him deadly poison. Considering how much talking God did with Smith, which amounted to nothing useful whatsoever, it may have been better to tell Law who was going to poison him, if ever anyone actually intended to. Why anyone would want to poison Law, God doesn't explain. But not only will Law be able to withstand that, he will be led down paths where poisonous serpents can't get to him – and he might even raise the dead (v.100). Three and a half years later, Smith and his brother could have done with Law raising them from the dead – but by then Law was running a new schism.

William Law and Hyrum Smith are to go off on a mission together but Joseph Smith can stay at home. Rigdon is to move his family to Nauvoo and not skulk off to safety in the east – if he wants to remain in the Presidency. God puts the pressure on people for Smith and gets into so much detail for so many people it is incredible, yet He never considers the bigger picture by helping the millions who could have done with revelations on such simple things as health issues, as I have previously commented.

As mentioned above, Smith eventually has God return yet again to list even more people who should buy stock in the "Nauvoo House". This God does for several verses before finally moving on to other things – which He had also already covered earlier. Hyrum becoming patriarch gets another mention. Then, in v.125, God says "I give unto you my servant Joseph to be a presiding elder over all my church, to be a translator, a revelator, a seer, and prophet."

This was in 1841, and if that had not been firmly established before then, something was alarmingly wrong. Why would Smith's God 'announce' such a thing when Smith had pronounced himself a prophet over a decade previously when the Church was inaugurated? As ever, Smith's leadership was constantly in question; his character and everything he did was highly questionable and people *did* question and they often left his Church in droves – sometimes even setting up their own version of the church. 'Dissenters' were quickly replaced with new converts that missionaries were constantly adding to the fold.

God then lists the names of those in the First Presidency, the Quorum of Twelve apostles, High Council and other quorum presidencies, the Seventy and Bishopric, to be considered for a sustaining vote at the upcoming conference. In those days, it was never certain that everyone would actually be accepted by the congregation. The membership really did have a say in such matters.

Finally, God says to make sure all the different quorums have rooms in his house (temple) when it is built. That included the Presidencies of the Priests, Teachers and Deacons. In those days, they were all adult men. Today, they are teenage boys who don't get near a temple other than if performing baptisms for the dead, when they are restricted to the basement. In establishing the gospel in this 'dispensation', why did God not explain those offices were for youngsters who should not be in the temple? Obviously Smith thought priesthood holders should all be adults. Young men holding such positions came much later.

DOCTRINE & COVENANTS – SECTIONS 121-131

Section 124 – Summary

Prophecies made: 5
Prophecies fulfilled: 0
Non-prophetic Revelation: 2

Prophecies made:

Pr. 59. "And again, *I will visit and soften their hearts, many of them for your good, that ye may find grace in their eyes, that they may come to the light of truth*, and the Gentiles to the exaltation or lifting up of Zion (v.9).

Pr. 60. This was the *fourth* temple the Lord prophesied would be built and which was not completed. God had wanted a temple in Zion (Independence); Far West; Spring Hill (Adam-ondi-Ahman); and now – Nauvoo.

Pr. 61. Three times, God says that after the time allotted to build the temple, baptisms for the dead outside the temple will not be acceptable. He actually states that if they do *not* do these things by the end of the appointed time, "ye shall be rejected as a church, with your dead" (v.32).

Pr. 62. God says that if they hearken to His voice, they will not be moved out of their place (v.45). If they don't listen to God or Smith and his men, they will not be "blest". God actually says that even if they build His house but do not do the things He says "instead of blessings, ye, by your own works, bring cursings, wrath, indignation, and judgments upon your own heads, by your follies, and by all your abominations, which you practise before me, saith the Lord" (v.48).

Pr. 63. God says that if enemies 'hinder' the work, what they were able to accomplish will be accepted and as for those who hindered it; "the iniquity and transgression of my holy laws and commandments I will visit upon the heads of those who hindered my work, unto the third and fourth generation, so long as they repent not, and hate me, saith the Lord God" (v.50). For good measure, God then repeats all that, in almost the same words – and then he does so yet again.

Pr. 64. "And now I say unto you, as pertaining to my boarding house which I have commanded you to build for the boarding of strangers, let it be built unto my name, and let my name be named upon it, and let my servant Joseph and his house have place therein, from generation to generation. For this anointing have I put upon his head, that his blessing shall also be put upon the head of his posterity after him" (v.56-7). God names it "Nauvoo House".

Results:

Pr. 59. Gentile leaders did not do anything for "the exaltation or lifting up of Zion" (v.9) and no "kings of the earth" came with any "gold and your silver, to the help of my people" (v.11).

Pr. 60. Although used and later dedicated, the Nauvoo Temple was never completed. It was burned out, later hit by a tornado and finally demolished.

Pr. 61. The Nauvoo Temple was never completed, let alone in any allotted time, yet God did not reject the Mormon Church along with their dead. At least they claim He didn't.

Pr. 62. The saints certainly appeared to try hard to accomplish what was required of them but they were driven out anyway. Did that mean they had *not* listened? Were they really that bad?

Pr. 63. They didn't hate God; many worshipped Him; they just hated what Smith was doing to their community. I am driven to ask – yet again, what on earth had any of their great-great-grandchildren, who were yet to be born, done to deserve such a curse. There is no record of any such retribution by God on any generation.

Pr. 64. Smith and his posterity most certainly did not "have place therein, from generation to generation" and such blessing was not "put upon the head of his posterity after him". Emma later named it "Riverside Mansion".

Non-prophetic Revelation:

1. For the very first time, God tells Smith there is no baptismal font on the earth where the saints can be baptised for the dead. The Nauvoo Temple must contain a font.

There was no mention of that for the Kirtland Temple – or for that matter, any of the other temples prophesied and planned yet never constructed. This is a *new* idea. Why did God *not* have a font included in the Kirtland Temple or the other planned temples? Whatever God had previously been thinking, He now suddenly requires a baptismal font.

2. This is the way God speaks: v.39. "Therefore, verily I say unto you, that your anointings, and your washings, and your baptisms for the dead, and your solemn assemblies, and your memorials for your sacrifices by the sons of Levi, and for your oracles in your most holy places wherein you receive conversations, and your statutes and judgments, for the beginning of the revelations and foundation of Zion, and for the glory, honor, and endowment of all her municipals, are ordained by the ordinance of my holy house, which my people are always commanded to build unto my holy name."

I don't understand how anyone could possibly rationalise that as coming from God. If the Mormon Church wishes to assert the only alternative, in that they have to agree, because the structure is so awful; that it just reflects Smith's 'understanding' of what the Lord wanted to say and was how Smith reflected the Lord's desires through his own words – then we are back to 'feelings' and 'impressions' rather than God actually speaking his own mind – and that is too unreliable to accept. This however has not been claimed to date. God *says* He is speaking and thus He is responsible. Smith's revelations invariably include "thus saith the Lord" and this one is no exception. The above nonsense is *God*.

Section 125
March 1841. Nauvoo, Illinois.

History.

Added in 1876. 2010 D&C Sec. 125.

Not only are the saints to build up Nauvoo; they are to build other cities, starting with one to be named 'Zarahemla', which should be built on the land across the Mississippi River, opposite the city of Nauvoo. They are to also build up Nashville (Lee County, Iowa). Both locations already had some saints living there. This is what the Lord wants.

> **3.** Let them build up a city unto my name upon the land opposite the city of Nauvoo, and let the name of Zarahemla be named upon it.
> **4.** And let all those who come from the east, and the west, and the north, and the south, that have desires to dwell therein, take up their inheritance in the same, as well as in the city of Nashville, or in the city of Nauvoo, and in all the stakes which I have appointed, saith the Lord.

Is that what the Lord got? Did great cities develop and grow in those areas any more than Nauvoo did? Of course not; when Nauvoo failed and the saints were driven out, the other cities that the Lord had prophesied about had already dwindled into insignificance.

> ...during January 1842, the Zarahemla Stake was discontinued and reduced to branch status. Thus the whole life of this eastern Iowa stake was but 27 months. The dissolution of the Zarahemla Stake and the subsequent decline of the Church in eastern Iowa was caused by the continuing in-gathering to Nauvoo. Thereafter little is heard of Church activities in Iowa, although a few branches struggled on for a period. *(Brown, Cannon & Jackson. 1994:58).*

Section 125 – Summary

Prophecies made: 1
Prophecies fulfilled: 0

Prophecies made:

Pr. 65. The saints are to develop Nauvoo and also to build up cities called Zarahemla and Nashville.

Results:

Pr. 65. Zarahemla and Nashville did not develop into cities full of saints any more than Nauvoo did. By the time the saints were leaving Nauvoo, it was over as far as any other cities were concerned.

Section 126
9 July 1841. Brigham Young's House, Nauvoo, Illinois.

History.

Added in 1876. 2010 D&C Sec. 126.

Smith goes to all the trouble of having the Lord thank Brigham Young for his work and say he can now stay home. Considering all that was going on and with people coming and going from missions, it is difficult to see how this is worthy of inclusion in the D&C; but then that could be said of everything else in it, so such trivia is only to be expected. This is the whole of Section 126.

DOCTRINE & COVENANTS – SECTIONS 121-131

1. Dear and well-beloved brother, Brigham Young, verily thus saith the Lord unto you: My servant Brigham, it is no more required at your hand to leave your family as in times past, for your offering is acceptable to me.
2. I have seen your labor and toil in journeyings for my name.
3. I therefore command you to send my word abroad, and take especial care of your family from this time, henceforth and forever. Amen.

It is worth mentioning that the above, for once, apart from "thus *saith* the Lord", is particularly bereft of the attempted Jacobean English we have come to expect from Smith's Lord – who misses over half a dozen opportunities here. The Lord should be consistent, even if his Jacobean is consistently wrong. Here the Lord reverts to modern English – so why does he not use it all the time?

Section 127
1 September 1841. Nauvoo, Illinois.

History.

1844 D&C Sec. CV. 2010 D&C Sec. 127.

Section 127 consists of a letter from Smith to the saints in Nauvoo regarding baptism for the dead, although he then doesn't say much about it. He starts by grumbling that he is still being pursued by the law for reasons unknown to him. He was constantly on the run from the law and was well aware of the validity of the charges against him, most of which were not answered in court. Smith claims the Lord told him his enemies were after him. The fact that he had evaded justice previously by escaping did not mean there were no warrants outstanding. He did not voluntarily submit to the law until he really had no choice due to pressure from his own followers mid 1844 and that led to his death. The fact is that he now had to once again go on the run and hide.

The Mormon Church claims Smith was a prophet but never acknowledges he was actually little more than an outlaw – and this time with a price on his head. A warrant had been issued for his arrest as a suspected accomplice in the failed assassination attempt of Missouri Governor Lilburn Boggs. Meanwhile, Orrin Porter Rockwell was caught and incarcerated for almost a year awaiting trial for the attempted murder while Smith did nothing to help him.

Despite the fact that Rockwell had been seen, not only in the area, but in the very store from which the gun used to shoot Boggs was stolen later the same day, there was insufficient evidence to ultimately convict Rockwell and he was eventually released. This also then let Smith off the hook.

This is the way Smith describes his situation in September of 1841.

> 1. Forasmuch as the Lord has revealed unto me that my enemies, both in Missouri and this State, were again in the pursuit of me; and inasmuch as they pursue me without a cause, and have not the least shadow or coloring of justice or right on their side in the getting up of their prosecutions against me; and inasmuch as their pretensions are all founded in falsehood of the blackest dye, I have thought it expedient and wisdom in me to leave the place for a short season, for my own safety and the safety of this people. I would say to all those with whom I have business, that I have left my affairs with agents and clerks who will transact all business in a prompt and proper manner, and will see that all my debts are canceled in due time, by turning out property, or otherwise, as the case may require, or as the circumstances may admit of. When I learn that the storm is fully blown over, then I will return to you again.

If the warrants that had been issued for Smith's arrest were "all founded in falsehood of the blackest dye" then why did he not give himself up, go to court and prove it? Perhaps Rockwell would have been released sooner – if Smith was telling the truth; but he didn't exactly honour or obey the law in any way and often took the law into his own hands. So, he ran away and hid – and not for the first time. Meanwhile, Rockwell languished in jail.

Smith then makes a prophecy that was to fall flat in less than three years; "I shall triumph over all my enemies, for the Lord God hath spoken it" (v.2). This is quickly followed in v.3 with yet another (repeat) prophecy that the Lord will avenge them; but he never did. "Let all the saints rejoice, therefore, and be exceedingly glad; for Israel's God is their God, and he will mete out a just recompense of reward upon the heads of all their oppressors." The reward they got was the Mormons were driven out and the locals were finally left in peace.

They are to get on with building the temple and their reward for that will (conveniently) be in heaven. So far as baptisms for the dead are concerned, Smith just says they should be recorded. He had wanted to speak about it from the stand the next Sunday, but as he has had to run away and hide, a letter will have to do instead. (I am slightly paraphrasing of course).

Section 127 – Summary

Prophecies made: 2
Prophecies fulfilled: 0

Prophecies made:

Pr. 66. 1 September 1841. "I shall triumph over all my enemies, for the Lord God hath spoken it" (v.2).

Pr. 67. "Let all the saints rejoice, therefore, and be exceedingly glad; for Israel's God is their God, and he will mete out a just recompense of reward upon the heads of all their oppressors."

Results:

Pr. 66. 27 June 1844. Joseph and Hyrum Smith are shot to death by a mob.

Pr. 67. There is no record of any such "just recompense" ever meted out on the heads of any "oppressors" by God. The saints were driven out and local residents just got on with life.

Section 128
6 September 1841. Nauvoo, Illinois.

History.

1844 D&C Sec. CVI. 2010 D&C Sec. 128.

A few days after Smith's letter that became Section 127, he again wrote to the saints at Nauvoo while hiding from the long arm of the law. He talks some more about baptism for the dead and who should record such events, justifying the practice from the Bible. He also feels compelled to mention being chased by his enemies – perhaps justifying his absence; maybe even looking for a sympathy vote.

In v.17, Smith solicits the help of Elijah; "for Malachi says, last chapter, verses 5th and 6th: *Behold, I will send you Elijah the prophet before the coming of the great and dreadful day of the Lord: And he shall turn the heart of the fathers to the children, and the heart of the children to their fathers, lest I come and smite the earth with a curse.*" (Italics in original).

We looked at this in Chapter 9 *(see pp. 89-92)*. The 'Introduction' to the D&C also references Section 128:18, 21. Detail regarding priesthood keys is otherwise very sparse. Smith claims that "turn the heart of the fathers to their children" etc., means baptism for the dead, yet in Section 2 he had related it only to the priesthood. The Bible mentions *neither*. If Smith claimed Moroni *altered* Malachi back in 1823, how is it that baptism for the dead was not explained at that time? Why is it only now being 'revealed' the best part of two decades later and long after the planning of several previous temples with no provision for a font? The answer is too obvious to require further comment.

****

History of the Church Vol. 4: 550-1; Vol. 5: 1-2.
15 March and 4 May 1842

History

Joseph Smith revelation – not included in the D&C.

This concerns claimed revelation rather than prophecy but is included as part of the timeline and out of historical interest. On 15 March 1842, Joseph Smith became a Freemason. The very next day Smith rose to the 'sublime degree' and became a Master Mason *(See: TMD Vol. 3:141-3)*.

The Mormon endowment, modelled on Masonic ritual, was introduced into Mormonism seven weeks later. Records confirm Smith's own endowment took place on 4 May 1842, although one record dates it to 5 May, not that it matters *(See TMD Vol. 3:172 n.1&2)*. Endowments took place in the same upper office used as a Masonic Lodge room. It is interesting that initially, as with Masonry, the endowment was *only* available to men. Emma Smith eventually became the first female to be allowed the endowment. In a trade off, Emma (temporarily) agreed to her husband taking two new wives, in exchange for her receiving the endowment and becoming the first 'Elect Lady'. She was soon to change her mind about Smith's new wives and threw them out *(See TMD Vol. 1:86-90)*.

When Smith introduced his Masonic based ceremony as the 'Endowment' to be received in Mormon temples, he claimed it was "received as a revelation from God." *(HC 5:1-2)*. For a complete coverage of Mormonism and Masonry, including word by word comparison of the endowment, see *TMD Vol. 3, Sec. 3*.

****

Section 129
9 February 1843. Nauvoo, Illinois.

History.

Added in 1876. 2010 D&C Sec. 129.

DOCTRINE & COVENANTS – SECTIONS 121-131

The year is now 1843; Smith is somewhat back in circulation, and here he is giving instructions. Smith explains "there are two kinds of beings in heaven". What happened to all the different kingdoms he invented? There are angels, who are resurrected and have bodies; then there are the *spirits* of just men made perfect who are still spirits and yet "inherit the same glory".

Theologically, in Mormonism, there is no way of progressing from the 'Spirit World' to any 'degree' of glory (or heaven) until the resurrection, and the Mormon Spirit World is *not* heaven; so the question arises, how could spirits *be* in heaven – regardless of which kingdom you pick? Smith doesn't even begin to explain any of the inconsistencies he has just introduced.

He just makes up a method of determining who has come to see you if ever you receive a visitation. Smith had already told the saints long since that all revelations and visitations, other than ones he receives, are not of God *(See Sections 28 & 50).*

Smith failed to mention anywhere in his earlier writings that *he* had ever personally employed such techniques to determine whether the angel Moroni, God, Jesus, or any other claimed visitor was 'real'. Had he 'tested' any of them in this, or any other manner? Apparently, Smith himself just accepted what he saw until now. Thus Smith's claimed 'apparitions' could have been deceptions sent from Satan and he would have been none the wiser. Smith had no way of determining otherwise, unless he personally tested each visitor – based on his own teachings revealed here. The fact is, he had only just thought of the idea.

> **4.** When a messenger comes saying he has a message from God, offer him your hand and request him to shake hands with you.
> **5.** If he be an angel he will do so, and you will feel his hand.
> **6.** If he be the spirit of a just man made perfect he will come in his glory; for that is the only way he can appear—
> **7.** Ask him to shake hands with you, but he will not move, because it is contrary to the order of heaven for a just man to deceive; but he will still deliver his message.
> **8.** If it be the devil as an angel of light, when you ask him to shake hands he will offer you his hand, and you will not feel anything; you may therefore detect him.
> **9.** These are three grand keys whereby you may know whether any administration is from God.

For three "grand keys" they are not really very grand at all. Imagine if the devil really appeared to someone as an "angel of light" and one offered him one's hand. Would he really be stupid enough to try to shake hands, knowing he was just a spirit and the person wouldn't feel it and thus discover him to be the devil? It is simply absurd. The devil is supposed to be cunning – not stupid. Obviously there is no such being, but if there were, this idea would never work.

We can therefore confidently conclude that this was nothing more than yet another piece of outrageous 'Smithology' designed to sound clever but never plausibly testable. Angels shaking hands indeed – that is an entirely human concept; and even then, only certain humans use that as a greeting and many more do not. To Smith, all angels were the equivalent of white Americans.

Imagine Inuit, Polynesian or Maori angels wondering why someone didn't want to rub noses, or many Europeans or Latin American angels expecting cheek kissing in order to test them. Depending on etiquette and culture it could require, one, two, three, four or even more kisses to observe greeting rituals. In fact kissing is the most prolific form of greeting there is. Hand shaking would not do at all in many instances. Many cultures use forms of greeting which involve no contact at all; bows and nods are all you will get. Many Native Americans would have just raised an arm in greeting. In Kenya there is a two handed wave. As always, Smith didn't think it through. All angels are restricted to hand-shakers apparently.

The other thing to ask is why did Smith's God *not* reveal these simple tests when Smith was struggling to come up with ideas for determining spirits in Section 50, which is pathetic by comparison? *(See pp. 207-9)*. Smith had yet to invent the idea or he most certainly would have included it there. There is absolutely no doubt whatsoever about that.

Section 130
2 April 1843. Ramus, Illinois.

History.

Added in 1876. 2010 D&C Sec. 130.

Parts of this Section are discussed in *TMD Vol. 3:313 (v.14-15); Vol. 4:267-8 (v.20-21) & also Vol. 4:27 (v.22). (S105-8)*. Joseph Smith is once again making up ideas that cannot be tested. First he declares that when we see Jesus, he will appear as a man. He then declares that John 14:23, regarding the appearance of the Father and the Son, is a personal appearance and that the idea of the Father and Son dwelling in our hearts is an old and false "sectarian notion".

Did Smith select the right word to use there? The concept is practically universal within Christianity outside of Mormonism, yet Smith uses a word that relates to adhering to a particular sect, faction, or a doctrine; narrow minded, especially as a result of rigid adherence to a particular sect. That sounds more like Mormonism than a wide ranging Christian concept.

DOCTRINE & COVENANTS – SECTIONS 121-131

> 6. The angels do not reside on a planet like this earth;
> 7. But they reside in the presence of God, on a globe like a sea of glass and fire, where all things for their glory are manifest, past, present, and future, and are continually before the Lord.

Naturally, Smith claims angels live on a "globe" with God and of course it will be like "glass and fire". His imaginative ideas were revealed earlier. The concept is consistent with Revelation 15:2 and Smith 'explained' John 4:6 in D&C 77:1 *(see pp. 278-80)*. He does confirm in such circumstances, everything is "manifest, past, present and future, and are continually before the Lord" which immediately lands him in deep water and confirms many questions raised throughout this work. If God always knew exactly what was going to happen next, why did he get so much, and so many people, so wrong? Time is different there. That is about all Smith got right, as time can indeed be different elsewhere and the perception of 'time' depends on a number of varying factors, not that it has anything to do with a globe of glass on which angels live in fire with God.

Smith confirms his theology that the Earth will become like crystal and be a giant Urim and Thummim to those who live there. He does not understand what will really happen to our planet in due time. That's not 'the Lord's own due time' of course, that's in the due time of the law of entropy (the second law of thermodynamics), which anyone who has studied a little science will readily understand as the determining factor in the ultimate fate of *everything*. If the reader does happen to be unfamiliar, I recommend a little time researching that.

It beats Smith's ideas because it is based exclusively on science and reason. It also happens to be very exciting to be able to predict what will happen in the future with a great degree of accuracy. Faith isn't required. Scientific data and evidence evaluated with common sense and reason will do nicely.

I mentioned entropy on p. 282 *(and on p. 314, regarding time)*. Professor Brian Cox's explanation of it in his wonderful BBC TV series and book of the same name, 'The Wonders of the Universe', is very easy to understand and also most fascinating. I would highly recommend the book – see Bibliography *(Cox & Cohen 2011)*.

Smith surrounds his ideas with nonsense about stones with names on them. Professor Cox, on the other hand, explains in the simplest of terms why science is correct. It is not opinion or conjecture; it is simply *discovery*, as a result of searching for evidence of the truth and a willingness to accept it, regardless of what that truth may be. Whatever conclusion is reached, it does not derive from any preconceived notion, simply from enquiry; which means regardless of what anyone *believes*. Smith has to be wrong – like it or not.

Smith then gets into prophetic mode.

> **12.** I prophesy, in the name of the Lord God, that the commencement of the difficulties which will cause much bloodshed previous to the coming of the Son of Man will be in South Carolina.
> **13.** It may probably arise through the slave question. This a voice declared to me, while I was praying earnestly on the subject, December 25th, 1832.

Smith's imagination is now running riot. This is additional detail regarding prophecy of the Civil War covered in Section 87 *(see pp. 307-9)*, which Smith considered to be imminent. Here, Smith claims it will be the "commencement of the difficulties" previous to "the coming of the Son of Man". Clearly, the Civil War (1861-1865) was over and done with almost one-hundred-and-fifty years ago. It did not lead to other bloodshed ushering in the second coming – and if such a happening *does* occur at some future date, it will be completely unconnected and entirely unrelated to those earlier events. This was another *false* prophecy.

> **14.** I was once praying very earnestly to know the time of the coming of the Son of Man, when I heard a voice repeat the following:
> **15.** Joseph, my son, if thou livest until thou art eighty-five years old, thou shalt see the face of the Son of Man; therefore let this suffice, and trouble me no more on this matter.

Smith went on to say that he had no idea whether that meant the Saviour would return then, or just visit Smith, or if he would die and see him. However, alongside other Smith comments about when a return might be, it all seemed to fit, at least as far as the saints of the day were concerned; and many, including apostles, embraced the idea that the second coming would be around 1891. *(See: TMD Vol 3:313 or S106).* As ever, whatever we (or apologists) *think*, is entirely irrelevant; what the saints of the day considered it to mean is the *only* important factor in such matters.

If converts are obedient to the commandments, they will be blessed. The last that thing any of the early saints were, was blessed. They had an awful time of things and would have fared far better without Smith, his God, and his Church.

> **20.** There is a law, irrevocably decreed in heaven before the foundations of this world, upon which all blessings are predicated—
> **21.** And when we obtain any blessing from God, it is by obedience to that law upon which it is predicated.

DOCTRINE & COVENANTS – SECTIONS 121-131

As faithful Mormons, we all fall for this and firmly believe we are 'blessed' by God for our efforts, when nothing could be further from the truth. It keeps families apart, costs a fortune and tires us out. And where does that get us? No 'blessings' are actually received at all; just a life filled with things of little or no consequence, achieving next to nothing. I lost count of the thousands of hours wasted in pointless travel and meetings as well as the small fortune I spent on 'living the gospel'. As an ex-member, why then is life no less 'blessed'? Well, it is actually easier and slower, so you could consider it a life *more* blessed.

We feel neither blessed nor cursed for 'turning our backs on the truth', or even that we are no longer blessed at all. We feel the same. All the studies that have ever been undertaken in this area, just as is the case regarding answers to prayer, indicate that it makes absolutely *no* difference what you believe or join; life is what it is and remains unaffected by those choices. Any concept of being 'blessed' is purely in the mind of the believer – a psychological effect of belief; but it is a powerful thing and minds can be trained to believe almost anything – if we are not careful *(See TMD Vol. 4:267-8 or S106-7)*.

Finally, Smith's famous theology about God having a body surfaces for the first and *only* time. It is short, sharp, and to the point – but it leaves questions unanswered – indeed, completely unanswerable.

> **22.** The Father has a body of flesh and bones as tangible as man's; the Son also; but the Holy Ghost has not a body of flesh and bones, but is a personage of Spirit. Were it not so, the Holy Ghost could not dwell in us.

As this is an important so-called revelation, I will include an extract from a booklet I published which includes a comment on this concept. *(See also TMD Vol. 4:27 or S107-8)*.

The Mormon God

> Regarding the Mormon claim that their God has a body; Smith did not state such in his 1838 story (of 1820), so other than the assumption that is attached to Smith's 1838 version of his First Vision, when and where did God (or Joseph Smith) ever confirm that He actually does have a body?
>
> The one and only place the concept of God having a physical body is ever mentioned anywhere in supposed scripture is the Mormon book *Doctrine and Covenants,* in Section 130:22 which Smith wrote on 2 April 1843. Smith says "The Father has a body of flesh and bones as tangible as man's; the Son also;" When did **God** ever declare that He was anything other than an omnipresent spirit? The answer to the question is **never.**

Nothing Smith ever wrote prior to that confirmed a *physical* God. Even then, it does not say "Thus saith the Lord" and is simply buried at the end of some "items of instruction given by Joseph Smith."

Not once in six-thousand years did God ever declare any such thing. In just one single phrase taken from one single sentence which is placed at the end of "items of instruction", Joseph Smith would have us believe that *he* captured the very essence of the character of God in a manner that God Himself had been entirely incapable of conveying during the previous six-thousand years.

If God does have a physical body, it was incumbent upon Him to explain that from the very beginning and thus it would be mentioned in Genesis. It is *unthinkable* that not only would God not mention that He has a body but that He would explicitly declare instead that He is a spirit – even in Joseph Smith's own *Book of Mormon*.

If God exists, He may move in mysterious ways, but they are not that mysterious, they are not that devious, and certainly not that misleading.

Not once does God mention that he has a body in the *Old Testament*; not once in the *New Testament*; not in the *Book of Mormon*; not in earlier *D&C* revelations; not in the *Book of Moses* or the rest of Smith's *Inspired Revision* of the Bible; not in the *Book of Abraham*. Not anywhere did God *ever* previously declare Himself to have a physical body – until Joseph Smith's late change in theology which completely contradicted everything that he (and everyone else) had ever previously written. Smith then just mentions his latest theology, almost in passing, in the D&C – and that changes **everything.** *(Whitefield 2011b: 41-2).*

Section 130 – Summary

Prophecies made: 1
Prophecies fulfilled: 0

Prophecies made:

Pr. 68, I prophesy, in the name of the Lord God, that the commencement of the difficulties which will cause much bloodshed previous to the coming of the Son of Man will be in South Carolina (v.12).

Results:

Pr. 68. "This a voice declared to me, while I was praying earnestly…" Smith was hearing voices, but the Civil War was three decades later and was over in four years or so; it did *not* usher in the second coming.

DOCTRINE & COVENANTS – SECTIONS 121-131

History of the Church Vol. 5:336.
6 April 1843

History

Joseph Smith prophecy – not included in the D&C.

Were I going to prophesy, I would say the end [of the world] would not come in 1844, 5, or 6, or in forty years. There are those of the rising generation who shall not taste death till Christ comes.

This statement comes just before Smith's comment about seeing Jesus if he lives to be eighty-five years old and confirms his belief that the Saviour would return in that "rising generation".

I was once praying earnestly upon this subject, and a voice said unto me, "My son, if thou livest until thou art eighty-five years of age, thou shalt see the face of the Son of Man." I was left to draw my own conclusions concerning this; and I took the liberty to conclude that if I did live to that time, He would make His appearance.

The prophecy about the rising generation seeing Jesus return before they die was not canonised, so it is now (conveniently) simply ignored. As it was not canonised I have not listed it; nevertheless, it remains unfulfilled prophecy. It is noted here out of historical interest.

Section 131
16 & 17 May 1843. Ramus, Illinois.

History.

Added in 1876. 2010 D&C Sec. 131.

On 16 May 1843, Smith wrote the first four short verses of Section 131 which declared there are three kingdoms within the highest of the three degrees of glory and that to enter the highest of those kingdoms (known as exaltation), man must enter "this order of the priesthood [meaning the new and everlasting covenant of marriage];" (v.2). Whether that meant polygyny or not is open to debate, but Section 132 comes next, and it was pretty clear what was on Smith's mind when he wrote that.

THE MORMON DELUSION

During May of 1843, just prior to this revelation, Smith had married Lucy Walker (age 17) Maria and Sarah Lawrence (aged 16 and 19) and Helen Mar Kimball (age 14). Smith had married Emily and Eliza Partridge in March 1843.

When Emma was temporarily persuaded to let him marry more wives, she agreed, as long as she could choose them for him. She unwittingly selected the Partridge sisters, and to keep things peaceful, Smith did not tell his wife that he had already married the girls and married them a second time in front of Emma on 11 May. They were 19 and 22 years old respectively. Honesty was not part of Joseph Smith's character. Emily described the events very clearly.

> ...Joseph and his wife Emma offered us a home in their family, and they treated us with great kindness... I was married to Joseph Smith on the 4th of March 1843... My sister Eliza was also married to Joseph a few days later. This was done without the knowledge of Emma Smith. Two months afterward she consented to give her husband two wives, providing he would give her the privilege of choosing them. She accordingly chose my sister Eliza and myself and to save family trouble Brother Joseph thought it best to have another ceremony performed. Accordingly on the 11th of May, 1843, we were sealed to Joseph Smith a second time, in Emma's presence... From that very hour, however, Emma was our bitter enemy. We remained in the family several months after this, but things went from bad to worse until we were obligated to leave the house and find another home. *(Baskin 1914:95).*

Smith wrote the rest of Section 131 the following day (17 May), adding four more short verses; this time saying that "The more sure word of prophecy means a man's knowing that he is sealed up unto eternal life, by revelation and the spirit of prophecy, through the power of the Holy Priesthood." This alluded to what is now known as the 'Second Endowment' or 'Second Anointing' or ones 'calling and election made sure' *(See TMD Vol. 3:126-130). (S108-11).*

****

History of the Church Vol. 5:394, Vol. 6:116.
18 May 1843, 16 December 1843

History

Joseph Smith prophecy – not included in the D&C.

DOCTRINE & COVENANTS – SECTIONS 121-131

In concert with Smith's assertion made over a decade earlier on 4 January 1833 *(See pp. 319-20)*, in May of 1843, he is once again prophesying against his own country.

> I prophecy in the name of the Lord God of Israel, unless the United States redress the wrongs committed upon the Saints in the state of Missouri and punish the crimes committed by her officers that in a few years the government will be utterly overthrown and wasted, and there will not be so much as a potsherd left for their wickedness in permitting the murder of men, women and children, and the wholesale plunder and extermination of thousands of her citizens to go unpunished, thereby perpetrating a foul and corroding blot upon the fair fame of this great republic, the very thought of which would have caused the high-minded and patriotic framers of the Constitution of the United States to hide their faces with shame. *(HC 5:394)*.

Smith had paid a visit to President Van Buren on 29 November 1839 and again in February of 1840, begging him to assist some 20,000 saints, following Governor Boggs' extermination order. Van Buren refused to help the saints.

In December 1843, Smith made a further prophecy.

> While discussing the petition to Congress, I prophesied, by virtue of the holy Priesthood vested in me, and in the name of the Lord Jesus Christ, that, if Congress will not hear our petition and grant us protection, they shall be broken up as a government, **and god shall damn them. And there shall nothing be left of them - not even a grease spot.** (Emphasis added).

The above appeared in the Mormon British magazine, Millennial Star *(Vol. 22:455)*. However, in *HC Vol 6:116*, the emphasised text has been omitted.

Congress was not broken up and the government has continued unaffected. The Mormon Church tried to rationalise the failure of this prophecy in *HC*, suggesting it referred to the party in power at the time; the word 'government' meaning the present 'administration'. At that time, it would have referred to the Democrats. However, it is specifically 'congress' that is going to be broken up, according to the revelation, and congress constitutes members of *both* parties.

Chapter 23

Doctrine and Covenants
Sections 132, 135–136, 138, OD1, OD2

Section 132
12 July 1843. Nauvoo, Illinois.

History.

Added in 1876. 2010 D&C Sec. 132.

This Section is known as the 'polygamy section' and it replaced 'old Section 101' *(see pp. 374-6)*. Section 132 has been fully covered in *TMD Vol. 1:26-32, 52-67 (S111-32)* & in *Vol. 4:301-3,318-9, 372*. It is full of "thus saith the Lord" statements from the start and several confirm God is speaking, but some refer to Jesus and 'Alpha and Omega'. The Church will of course claim that Jesus is a God and will attribute it all to him. Throughout the D&C, no differentiation seems to have been made between God the Father and Jesus Christ, with all the terminology appearing to have been interchangeable *(see The Final Analysis, Part 4)*.

As this Section has been fully covered in earlier work, I will just briefly summarise the details here rather than go through them again in depth. It starts with God confirming to Smith that He "justified my servants Abraham, Isaac, and Jacob, as also Moses, David and Solomon, my servants, as touching the principle and doctrine of their having many wives and concubines".

In Smith's Book of Mormon, plural marriage is strictly forbidden. Smith even reinforces the 'forbidden' position in the Book of Mormon, and here in Section 132, he claims it was 'justified', citing the very same characters (David and Solomon) and the very same scripture, and he also reinforces his *new* take on the subject. He now says they had the Lord's blessing. Smith used the very same people and the very same scriptures, first to forbid and then to justify the very same acts. Smith also *reinforced* each opposing position, fully evidencing the fact that he was just manipulating scripture to suit his own carnal desires. As this is a crucial testimony against Smith, the following is extracted from *TMD Vol. 4:302*.

> **Jacob 2: 23-24.** For behold, ***thus saith the Lord***: ... Behold ***David and Solomon*** truly had ***many wives*** and concubines, which thing was ***abominable before me***, saith the Lord. *(Book of Mormon – written in 1828-29).* (Emphasis added).

> Some years later, when Smith had taken several women as plural wives – some young and single and others who were already married, he needed to somehow justify his actions. He invented revelation permitting his activities and in his defence he called on none other than *God* to now *justify* David and Solomon's very same actions that the *Book of Mormon* declared *abominable*.

> **D&C 132:1.** Verily, ***thus saith the Lord*** ... I, the Lord, ***justified*** my servants Abraham, Isaac, and Jacob, as also Moses, ***David and Solomon***, my servants, as touching the principle and doctrine of their having ***many wives*** and concubines— *(Written in 1843).* (Emphasis added).

> If that was not enough to question Smith as a prophet and/or his God as authentic, he – God or Smith, take your pick – went on in both the *Book of Mormon* and the *D&C* to *reinforce* the contradictory position established in each book.

> **Jacob 1:15.** The people of Nephi ... began to ... indulge themselves somewhat in ***wicked practices***, such as like unto ***David*** of old desiring ***many wives*** and concubines, and also ***Solomon***, his son. (Emphasis added).

D&C 132:38-39. *David* also received *many wives* and concubines, and also *Solomon* and Moses my servants ... *in nothing did they sin* ...David's wives and concubines *were given unto him of me*... (Emphasis added).

The *Book of Mormon* confirms the practice "abominable" and the *D&C* states that the practice was "justified". *Both* refer to the wives of David and Solomon and *both* are preceded by *"Thus saith the Lord"*. There is *nowhere* to go on this but admit to the truth.

"I am afraid I can't adequately reconcile these two statements... If the one in Doctrine and Covenants 132:1 had omitted the names of David and Solomon, then I think I could reconcile the two statements." *(Apostle LeGrand Richards letter to Morris L. Reynolds dated 14 July 1966. Tanner 1987:205). (Extract: TMD Vol. 4:302).*

Today, In Mormonism, the 'New and Everlasting Covenant' is determined as the fullness of the gospel – all of it, and marriage is just one part; but Smith referred to it specifically as plural marriage. This may well have been what was on his mind when he wrote Section 131 *(see p. 451)*, marrying several teenage girls during the same period. He spells it out in Section 132 anyway:

> 4. For behold, I reveal unto you a new and an everlasting covenant; and if ye abide not that covenant, then are ye damned; for no one can reject this covenant and be permitted to enter into my glory.
> 5. For all who will have a blessing at my hands shall abide the law which was appointed for that blessing, and the conditions thereof, as were instituted from before the foundation of the world.
> 6. And as pertaining to the new and everlasting covenant, it was instituted for the fulness of my glory; and he that receiveth a fulness thereof must and shall abide the law, or he shall be damned, saith the Lord God.

The header to this Section claims *"the doctrines and principles involved in this revelation had been known by the Prophet since 1831"* (italics in original) but neglects to confirm that is because Smith had documented affairs with Fanny Alger and Lucinda Pendleton Morgan Harris during the 1830s *(See TMD Vol. 1, Apx A)*, but as no marriages were recorded, the Church just makes an assumption that Smith knew all about "the doctrines and principles" and that he must have had unrecorded ceremonies of some description.

The "historical records" mentioned in the header do not refer to any known earlier revelation concerning polygyny, unless it is supposed to allude to the controversial and *suppressed* revelation concerning marrying Native American Indians. They were known as *Lamanites* to Mormons, and an 1831 revelation had the Lord requiring marriages to Native Americans so they would become "white" and "delightsome" *(Tanner 1980b:207-8)*.

The 'New and Everlasting Covenant' which Smith claimed would get you damned if you did not live it, was indeed polygyny. When I was a member, I was given to understand that one feature of such a marriage was that the first wife had to give her consent. I was shocked to discover that this was not actually the case and under the 'Law of Sarah', if a first wife did not consent, she would be damned and the husband could take another wife anyway *(see TMD Vol. 1:26-32 [or S111-8], & Vol. 4:318-9)*. Even in the twentieth century, the sixth prophet, President Joseph Fielding Smith, understood the 'Law of Sarah' and explained it during the Reed Smoot Senate hearings. This short extract is from *TMD Vol. 1:31*.

Senator Pettus:	Have there been in the past plural marriages without the consent of the first wife?
Mr. Smith:	I do not know of any, unless it may have been Joseph Smith himself.
Senator Pettus:	Is the language that you have read construed to mean that she is bound to consent?
Mr. Smith:	The condition is that if she does not consent the Lord will destroy her, but I do not know how He will do it.
Senator Bailey:	Is it not true that in the very next verse, if she refuses her consent her husband is exempt from the law which requires her consent?
Mr. Smith:	Yes; he is exempt from the law which requires her consent.
Senator Bailey:	She is commanded to consent, but if she does not, then he is exempt from the requirement?
Mr. Smith:	Then he is at liberty to proceed without her consent, under the law.
Sen. Beveridge:	In other words, her consent amounts to nothing?
Mr. Smith:	It amounts to nothing but her consent.
	(Reed Smoot Case 1907: Vol. 1:201).

The verses directed at Smith's wife Emma were anything but ambiguous. Either she permitted him more wives or she would be *damned* – and Smith would be given more wives anyway. The 'first wives' could not win – and according to Smith's revelations, it was *God* who invented the misogynistic system that treated them that way. Women in Mormonism today generally have no idea about the 'rules' of Mormon polygyny.

52. And let mine handmaid, *Emma Smith, receive all those that have been given unto my servant Joseph,* and who are virtuous and pure before me; and those who are not pure, and have said they were pure, shall be destroyed, saith the Lord God.

53. For I am the Lord thy God, and *ye shall obey my voice*; and I give unto my servant Joseph that he shall be made ruler over many things; for he hath been faithful over a few things, and from henceforth I will strengthen him.

54. And I command mine handmaid, Emma Smith, to abide and cleave unto my servant Joseph, and to none else. But *if she will not abide this commandment she shall be destroyed*, saith the Lord; for I am the Lord thy God, and will destroy her if she abide not in my law. (Emphasis added).

In v.7, the Lord tells everyone "I have appointed unto my servant Joseph to hold this power in the last days, and there is never but one on the earth at a time on whom this power and the keys of this priesthood are conferred" but he fails to explain why in Genesis, quite a number of people who held the priesthood and the keys were all alive at the very same time, as they supposedly lived for many hundreds of years *(see one example on p. 370).*

60. Let no one, therefore, *set on my servant* Joseph; for I will justify him; for *he shall do the sacrifice* which I require at his hands for his transgressions, saith the Lord your God. (Emphasis added).

Can you imagine a God actually saying "Let no one, therefore, *set on my servant* Joseph" or "he shall *do* the sacrifice I require"? It is hardly 'heavenly' language to say the very least, and just reflects nineteenth century wording that Smith himself would have used. God would be more dignified – if ever He bothered to speak at all.

Section 132 was the last revelation written by Joseph Smith and recorded in the D&C.

Section 135
27 June 1844. Carthage, Illinois.

History.

1844 D&C Sec. CXI. (John Taylor). 2010 D&C Sec. 135.

John Taylor and Willard Richards were at Carthage with Joseph and Hyrum Smith when the latter were killed. This Section comprises John Taylor's account of what happened.

Whilst the details provided appear to be accurate enough, a lot is missing, and a great deal of bias is attached to the way the situation is portrayed. Taylor neglects to mention that guns had been smuggled into the jail and the brothers effectively died in a shoot-out when Joseph Smith shot and wounded three men himself before getting killed.

In v.4, Taylor speaks of the "pretended requirements of the law" when the requirements were not pretended at all; the Smith brothers were both arrested on charges of treason following the destruction of the printing press owned by the Law brothers. Taylor claims they went as lambs to the slaughter and they were martyrs for their religion. He fails to mention they were criminals arrested for treason, which is an entirely different thing. They were *not* falsely accused.

There is no denying the fact that the Smiths had the press destroyed and it was that which had led to their arrests. In v.7, Taylor claims the brothers were "innocent of any crime" but that was far from the truth. He claims they were "only confined in jail by the conspiracy of traitors and wicked men" which again was not the case at all. The fact is that Smith had tried to seduce William Law's wife Jane. She refused Smith's advances and then Law exposed Smith in print, promising more details of polygamous relationships in the next edition.

Smith desperately wanted to stop the truth getting out and he had the press destroyed before that could happen. Smith's problem was that it was not just an illegal act; stifling the freedom of the press was considered treason. Taylor of course ignored all this when reporting on the deaths of Joseph and Hyrum Smith. I covered the underlying story in *TMD Vol. 1*. This is a short extract:

> Following such embarrassing exposure, Smith was frantic and he became desperate to put a stop to matters, before more damning evidence could be published in the next issue. The City Council met in two sessions for over six hours on a Saturday and again for seven hours the following Monday, before arriving at a decision to destroy the press. Apologists argue that the length of these meetings proves that the Smiths did not try to convince or manipulate the Council, each individual deciding and voting as he chose. They are **wrong**.
>
> The basis of initial debate concerning the character of the Laws, which lasted for several hours, came *directly* from the Smiths. The Laws were accused of: "oppressing the poor, counterfeiting, theft, conspiracy to murder, seduction and adultery." This is ignored by apologists. These allegations were all unfounded and were actually the things that Joseph Smith was guilty of himself.
>
> Also ignored by apologists, are outright lies by Hyrum and Joseph Smith who declared to the Council that the revelation that had been read (now Section 132) about a multiplicity of wives was, according to Hyrum: "…in answer to a question concerning things which transpired in former days, and had no reference to the present time." Joseph said: "They make it a criminality for a man to have a

wife on the earth while he has one in heaven... the order [was] in ancient days, having nothing to do with [t]he present times." *(Van Wagoner 1989:68).* Both brothers individually, knowingly and deliberately lied to the Council in order to get the action they required. It took a total of thirteen hours to win the Council over to the Smiths' way of thinking. For apologists to argue otherwise in the face of such evidence is proof only of their own delusional state and they cannot be taken seriously.

As Mayor, Joseph Smith had a strong voice in the City Council. It was Hyrum Smith who introduced the idea of destroying the Law's printing press rather than issuing legal proceedings for the claimed libel. The statements made in the Expositor were actually true, a fact that also seems to have escaped the notice of apologists. The Smiths, knowing the truth, had the legal and moral responsibility to *dissuade* the Council from the action finally decided upon.

Nevertheless, Hyrum proposed that the press be destroyed and eventually almost everyone went along with the idea. The Smiths controlled the decision. They manipulated the Council for thirteen hours with lies and deception.

The coerced vote instigated not only an illegal act but one which violated the very constitution. It was therefore viewed as treason, for which the Smith brothers were arrested and charged. The brothers paid very dearly for it before they could be tried in court. The root cause of the problem lay in Smith's inability to control his insatiable obsession with women. Had Smith not made advances towards Jane Law, perhaps the sequence of events which followed would never have happened and he may have lived a little longer. His eventual downfall and death were the result of his lust for women, his extravagant lies to conceal the facts and his unlawful action against people who exposed the truth. *(TMD Vol. 1:98-9)*

Section 136

14 January 1847. Winter Quarters, near Council Bluffs, Iowa.

History.

Added in 1876. (Brigham Young). 2010 D&C Sec. 136.

This is the one and only 'revelation' recorded in the D&C by Brigham Young. If he was continuing in the footsteps of Smith we should ask why this was not just the first of many revelations to be added to the D&C by Young – or any of the later prophets. Young claimed all his speeches could be taken as revelation. Most are recorded in the Journal of Discourses but the Church now shies away from much of what Young had to say as it is awkward and embarrassing for the Church. Times change and Young's ideas are no longer popular or acceptable.

This Section concerns organisation of the journey west. Under the direction of the Quorum of Twelve, companies are to be organized "with captains of hundreds, captains of fifties, and captains of tens, with a president and his two counselors at their head." Each company must bear an equal share of widows, orphans and families of men who had joined the army. The Lord then lists some people he wants to lead each company.

There is a reminder that this is all just temporary and that "Zion shall be redeemed in mine own due time" in v.18. The Lord tells them he is the God of Israel, the God of Abraham and of Isaac and of Jacob. "I am he who led the children of Israel out of the land of Egypt; and my arm is stretched out in the last days, to save my people Israel" (v.22). The only thing is, as previously discussed, we now know from Egyptian history and extensive archaeological evidence that the Israelite exodus was a Hebrew fictional legend *(see p.118)*.

While explaining the rules they are to observe when travelling, the Lord says not to worry about their enemies; he will take care of them "Fear not thine enemies, for they are in mine hands and I will do my pleasure with them" (v.30). His "pleasure" was apparently to leave them in peace, as peace is what they enjoyed once the Mormons left. Nevertheless, the Lord says those who drove them out will be sorry; "now cometh the day of their calamity, even the days of sorrow" as they "killed the prophets and …shed innocent blood" (v.36).

Official Declaration 1 (1890 Manifesto)
6 October 1890. Salt Lake City, Utah.

History.

Added in 1908. (Wilford Woodruff). 2010 D&C OD1.

Canonising the Manifesto meant that later Mormons (such as myself) assumed polygyny ceased *in* 1890, in obedience to agreement reached with the United States government. Nothing could be further from the truth. Church assets had been seized and financially the Church was about to fold. Woodruff issued the Manifesto to get the Church off the hook when most apostles were out of town and the first many knew of it was when they read about it in the newspaper.

The Church claims that this was revelation from God but in reality, it was constructed by lawyers and finished off by Woodruff for publication. Woodruff makes several mistakes in what he says in the Manifesto which sets him up as a fraud and a liar of the most devious nature.

In the Manifesto, Woodruff claimed that reports of recent plural marriages were all lies. He declared as President of the Church that the charges were false when he knew they were true.

> President Lorenzo Snow offered the following:
>
> "I move that, recognizing Wilford Woodruff as the President of The Church of Jesus Christ of Latter-day Saints, and the only man on the earth at the present time who holds the keys of the sealing ordinances, we consider him fully authorized by virtue of his position to issue the Manifesto which has been read in our hearing, and which is dated September 24th, 1890, and that as a Church in General Conference assembled, we accept his declaration concerning plural marriages as authoritative and binding."
>
> The vote to sustain the foregoing motion was unanimous.
> Salt Lake City, Utah, October 6, 1890.

In fact, the vote was not unanimous at all as numerous saints and several of the apostles *abstained* from voting on the Manifesto when it was presented at conference.

In the D&C, we find extracts from three sermons that Woodruff later gave wherein he emphasises the reasoning behind Manifesto.

> The Lord will never permit me or any other man who stands as President of this Church to lead you astray. It is not in the programme. It is not in the mind of God. If I were to attempt that, the Lord would remove me out of my place, and so He will any other man who attempts to lead the children of men astray from the oracles of God and from their duty.
>
> The Lord showed me by vision and revelation exactly what would take place if we did not stop this practice. If we had not stopped it, you would have had no use for ... any of the men in this temple at Logan; for all ordinances would be stopped throughout the land of Zion. Confusion would reign throughout Israel, and many men would be made prisoners.
>
> I saw exactly what would come to pass if there was not something done. I have had this spirit upon me for a long time. But I want to say this: I should have let all the temples go out of our hands; I should have gone to prison myself, and let every other man go there, had not the God of heaven commanded me to do what I did do; and when the hour came that I was commanded to do that, it was all clear to me. I went before the Lord, and I wrote what the Lord told me to write.

These are no obscure or rarely seen quotes. They are appended to *Official Declaration 1* in the D&C. Note that Woodruff claims, in canonised scripture no less, that the "charges are false", they were "not teaching polygamy", "not permitting any person to enter into its practice", it was "my intention to submit to those laws", "the God of heaven commanded me to do what I did", and "I went before the Lord, and I wrote what the Lord told me to write". The Church agreed to end polygamy and that from that time each Mormon man would only cohabit with *one* wife. The only apostle to do so was Lorenzo Snow who selected his youngest wife Minnie whom he had married when he was fifty-seven and she was sixteen. The rest took no notice of the agreement at all.

On 24 November the previous year, following a discussion about promising there would be *no* more plural marriages in the Utah territory, Woodruff had dictated a *revelation* which instructed the First Presidency to make *no* promises to end plural marriage. This was accepted by the First Presidency and Quorum of Twelve but never officially published or canonised. Today, it is ignored.

Now Woodruff relented. That being the case, perhaps he (or in his absence, his God, though the current prophet) would like to explain why the following all happened *after* 1890 when everyone was supposed to be dutifully obeying their God, the Manifesto and the Church agreement with the government.

A number of the apostles and other general authorities entered into further polygynous marriages after 1891, several occurring in the following century *(see TMD Vol. 1:23 for full details)*.

One of those was Wilford Woodruff himself, who married his sixth wife, Lydia Mountford on 19 August 1897 when he was ninety and she was thirty-nine years old, fifty-one years his junior. Woodruff completely ignored what he himself had declared in no uncertain terms – was the word of the *Lord*.

Heber J. Grant, who later became prophet, was fined $100 for cohabitation in 1899 *(See TMD Vol. 1:222-3)*.

The sixth Mormon prophet, Joseph Fielding Smith, was as guilty as Wilford Woodruff, issuing an endorsement of the Manifesto to make it look as though they were obeying the law. He was responsible for the 1904 official statement, categorically confirming he did: "affirm and declare that no such marriages have been solemnized with the sanction, consent or knowledge of the Church of Jesus Christ of Latter-day Saints." Yet he had authorized many such unions.

Joseph F. Smith was arrested in 1906. The charge could have been much worse but was reduced to that of unlawful cohabitation with four women in addition to his lawful wife. When the case went to trial on 23 November 1906, Smith pleaded *guilty* and was fined $300 which was the maximum penalty permitted under the law. *(Deseret Evening News, 23 Nov 1906; Salt Lake Tribune, 24 Nov 1906)*. A *Prophet* of God admitted being guilty of knowingly and wilfully breaking the agreed law of the land, the Articles of Faith, and violating the laws of the God he represented. Smith had thirteen children by five polygamous wives post Manifesto, the last being in 1906. *(See TMD Vol. 1:224 for full list)*.

When listing post-Manifesto children conceived and born to polygamous (not first) wives of Mormon leaders, I located at least one-hundred-and-twenty children. Mormons leaders continued to violate the very law they had publicly declared on several different occasions *God* had commanded, whilst claiming they and their followers were abiding by it. This included the 1890 Manifesto; the declaration of 1900 reaffirming the ban on polygamy; and the 1904 official statement upholding the Manifesto. *(See TMD Vol. 1. Chs. 14, 15, & Apx K, pp. 376-9)*. Some members refused to discontinue the practice and ultimately, when abandoned by the mainstream Mormon Church, they formed schisms which continue to practice polygamy to this day. Research indicates there are probably more polygamists now than there were in 1890. *(See TMD Vol. 1. Ch. 16)*. (Whilst 'polygamy' was the term used, it referred exclusively to *polygyny* rather than also including polyandry by the time of the Manifesto).

Section 138
3 October 1918. Salt Lake City, Utah.

History.

Added in 1981. (Joseph F. Smith). 2010 D&C Sec. 138.

I covered this Section in *TMD Vol. 4:192-5, 202. (S132-6)*. In a nutshell, Smith claims to have seen things that were impossible, thus negating it as a plausible reality. At best it was imagined and at worst it was made up, in the same way Joseph Smith concocted his visions.

I will just review who Joseph F. Smith claims to have seen, and refer the reader to *TMD 4 or S132-8* for more details. "I saw the hosts of the dead, both small and great. And there were gathered together in one place an innumerable company" (v.11-12). This is how Smith 'saw' things:

> 17. Their sleeping dust was to be restored unto its perfect frame, bone to his bone, and the sinews and the flesh upon them, the spirit and the body to be united never again to be divided, that they might receive a fulness of joy.
> 18. While this vast multitude waited and conversed, rejoicing in the hour of their deliverance from the chains of death, the Son of God appeared, declaring liberty to the captives who had been faithful;

> **19.** And there he preached to them the everlasting gospel, the doctrine of the resurrection and the redemption of mankind from the fall, and from individual sins on conditions of repentance.

What Smith claimed to see was a brief interlude between Christ's death and resurrection. Christ did not go to the wicked; he organised others to do that. Then Smith gets down to defining the people he actually *saw*. Considering the countless number of people the "innumerable company" would have to include, Smith does not explain how he actually knew who some of them were or how he identified them. However, that it was simply imagined (at best) becomes perfectly clear when he sees people who never even existed.

Smith lists Adam and Eve (who we scientifically *know* to be mythological beings), Abel, Seth, Noah, Shem, Abraham, Isaac, Jacob, Moses, Isaiah, Ezekiel and Daniel. So far, so good (for believers) – if he could actually somehow identify them. Then he claims to see *Elias*, making the same mistake Joseph Smith made in Section 110 *(see p.386)*. I also commented on this in detail on *p.9*. Section 110 was discussed at length in Chapter 9, in conjunction with Section 2 *(See pp. 90-91, 92-4)*.

The fact that Smith now claims to see Elias, someone who never actually existed, exposes the claimed vision as nothing more than delusional imaginings – if not outright lies. It was certainly not a reality. Smith goes on to say he saw many more people, including prophets of the Nephites, but he neglects to say which ones he actually saw.

In an apparent switch in timeframe (without reference) from the time of Jesus to the present, Smith next claims to see Joseph and Hyrum Smith, Brigham Young, John Taylor, Wilford Woodruff and "other choice spirits".

This introduces a problem which is ignored by the Church as they do not admit the truth. Firstly, Smith and Young participated in polyandry which the Church has admitted to me personally was and is contrary to doctrine; therefore in Mormon theological terms, they both forfeit their eternal salvation. In which case, they would not have been there; they would have been found among the wicked. Likewise, as we discussed regarding OD1, Wilford Woodruff violated his own declared revelation from God regarding the Manifesto, so he would also have ended up among the wicked. Nevertheless, Smith claims he 'saw' that they were chosen in the beginning to be "rulers in the Church of God".

D&C – SECTIONS 132, 135–136, 138, OD1, OD2

Official Declaration 2
30 September 1978. Salt Lake City, Utah. (Issued 9 June 1978).

History.
Added in 1981. (Spencer W. Kimball). 2010 D&C OD2.

OD2 is a supposed 'revelation' concerning the Priesthood being made available to all men. It was issued on 9 June 1978 and canonised following the vote at conference on 30 September 1978. I have covered this as the 'black and cursed' issue in *TMD Vol. 2:250-60. (S136-46)* and would refer readers to that analysis.

Meanwhile, I will just mention that this is the one item added to the D&C during my lifetime and explain how it affected me and my wife at the time.

There have been a couple of occasions when my first wife Jan and I had to sit down and seriously consider our membership in the Church – and this was one of them. When we first learned of this, it was completely unexpected and a total shock. We, like most Mormons, were never racist; quite the opposite in fact. It was just that God had 'marked' black Africans, due to something that had, or perhaps had not (it was all a little vague), happened in the pre-existence and we knew for certain that doctrinally they could *never* hold the Priesthood until the millennium when every white person had first had the opportunity. It was known *doctrine*.

When the announcement came in 1978, we were devastated that established doctrine was being violated. This surely could not be. We assumed, and at first concluded, that it may have come about through intense pressure from outside the Church regarding what must have appeared extreme racism. But we *knew* the Church leaders would obey God and never violate His dictates in favour of the tide of popular public opinion.

We were told that it was *direct revelation* from the Lord. The time had come for change. At the time, we lived in a small Branch and at Church there were lengthy discussions after which everyone concluded that all they could do was to go home and pray about it. Jan and I discussed the situation well into the night, going back and forth from thinking this must mean the Church was not true, as God could not go back on His word – to accepting that it must still be true as surely He would never allow a prophet to lead us astray; considering yet another Mormon doctrine. Perhaps He hadn't changed his mind; perhaps all those who had been so cursed had now come to the Earth. He could hardly just change the colour or bloodline of children being born now. Perhaps the second coming had been delayed and the time was right. Perhaps...

In the end, we were strongly leaning toward the conclusion that the Church could not possibly be true if such a revelation was claimed, as it surely could *never* be so, regardless of how unpopular the concept was. Then we panicked and questioned what we would do if we left the Church. We would lose all our friends and our children would have no direction at all. Then we remembered what our old Mission President (Marion 'Duff' Hanks) had once said in 1962. "You know, even if the Church was not true, I know of no finer way to live life."

We had never forgotten that counsel and now we clung to it. We decided to say no more about it and stay – for the sake of the family. We *wanted* the Church to be true so we *decided* it was true. Inside, we were in turmoil but eventually everything settled and we forgot about how the change had affected us. It was never mentioned again. We felt 'faithful' in the face of trial. It also made it easier not to have to 'explain' the doctrine when non-members faced us with the *problem* of 'blacks and the priesthood'. We could declare 'it's behind us' just as recent prophet Hinckley proclaimed about 'polygamy' (polygyny).

We should have known better and left the Church there and then. We both knew the truth in our hearts but we couldn't bring ourselves to accept it so we effectively ignored it when we could still have saved our children. Now it is a generation too late and grandchildren are serving missions for the Church.

Since leaving the Church in 2003, among all the devastating truths I have uncovered is the fact that the 1978 declaration was not a direct revelation from God after all. The prophet of the day, Spencer W. Kimball, had wanted to get away from the criticism and accusations of racism for years but several apostles had argued the 'doctrine' case so strongly that it didn't make much headway. Gradually, the twelve had either died and been replaced or had been persuaded, until the final remaining dissenters capitulated one evening and the decision was made. Prior to the 1978 decision, some of the 'big fifteen' had died, including such men as Richard L. Evans (1971); Joseph Fielding Smith (1972); and Harold B. Lee (1973). New callings were extended to Boyd K Packer (1970); Marvin J. Ashton (1971); Bruce R. McConkie (1972) and David B. Haight (1976).

The new blood may have been easier to persuade than old die-hards. The closest it ever got to revelation was that after the usual discussions, they had a prayer after which they all (finally) agreed it was time, following many years of dissent. It finally 'felt' right to all of them. The pressure on the final one or two apostles who had been holding out must have been immense. God didn't actually have a say in the matter; at least He never *said* anything about it, which amounts to the same thing. I can't help wondering if new apostles were asked how they felt about it before they were called.

Once again, I was devastated. I was devastated it had not been unsolicited revelation and devastated because we had been lied to in 1978. If Jan and I had known the 'method' that the so-called revelation took, there would have been no discussion and we would have left the Church there and then in 1978. It is always easy to be wise after the event.

D&C – SECTIONS 132, 135–136, 138, OD1, OD2

****

Our journey has taken us through five volumes.

Determining the truth behind Mormonism is *not* akin
to completing a complex 5000 piece jigsaw puzzle,
comparing each piece to see what fits where
until you can see the complete picture
and determine the truth.

There is just a two piece puzzle
to any and every aspect of Mormonism.

One piece is called a 'claim';
the other – 'evidence' or established 'facts'.

We have examined each claim and compared it with the evidence;
none of them are compatible and *none* of them fit.

It is not actually a puzzle at all;
it is just a box of tricks – confidence tricks.
None of Smith's concoctions fit with the evidence,
the truth, common sense or reason.

May the reader take comfort in knowing the truth
and in being free from 'The Mormon Delusion'.

****

THE FINAL ANALYSIS

PART 1

Joseph Smith's Prophecies

**In the final analysis, what does each Section
of the Doctrine and Covenants contain
that could be considered proven
as true and fulfilled prophecy?**

**In the following summary, Sections not containing
any of Joseph Smith's prophecies are excluded.**

Section & Prophecy.	Joseph Smith's Prophecies. Sections in current sequence; prophesies in original sequence.
Sec. 2 Pr. 1	"I will reveal unto you the Priesthood, by the hand of Elijah." (p.95)
Sec 2 Pr. 2	"...before the coming of the great and dreadful day of the Lord", which according to the referenced D&C 110:16, was "at the doors". (pp.95-6)
Sec. 3 Pr. 3	God knew Smith would lose the 116 pages and provided an alternative BCE version on the gold plates in order to resolve the problem. (p.104)
Sec. 3 Pr. 4	Residual Lamanites are Native North Americans whom the Book of Mormon will convert. Missionaries sent *to* the 'Lamanites'. (p.104)
Sec. 5 Pr. 7	Joseph Smith was to have one and only one gift and that was to translate the Book of Mormon. He was explicitly to have *no* other gift. (p.112)
Sec. 5 Pr. 8	There would be three witnesses to the Book of Mormon. No one else would be granted that power. (p.112)
Sec. 5 Pr. 9	If that generation did not accept Smith's words they would be destroyed. (p.112)
Sec. 6 Pr. 10	Oliver Cowdery was promised he would translate records that had thus far been kept back because of the wickedness of the people. (p.116)
Sec. 7 Pr. 11	Apostle John would live until Christ returns, bring souls to him and prophesy before nations, kindreds, tongues and people. (p.117)
Sec. 8 Pr. 12	Cowdery is again promised that he will "translate and receive knowledge from all those ancient records which have been hid up." (pp.119-20)
Sec. 9 Pr. 13	Cowdery is promised for the third time "other records have I, that I will give unto you power that you may assist to translate." (p.122)
Sec. 10 Pr. 5.	Repeat of Section 3, prophecy 3. (p.104)
Sec. 10 Pr. 6.	Repeat of Section 3, prophecy 4. (p.104)
Sec. 17 Pr. 15	The three witnesses were promised that they would physically see the gold plates – even as Joseph Smith had seen them. (p.133)
Sec. 17 Pr. 16	Joseph Smith was not to be destroyed if the three witnesses had faith and testified that they had seen the gold plates. (p.133)
Sec. 18 Pr. 14	Cowdery, and ... David Whitmer ... search out the Twelve ... And when you have found them you shall show these things unto them." (pp.130-31)
Sec. 29 Pr. 17	To be "gathered in unto *one place* on the face of this land" to "be prepared ... tribulation and desolation [to be] sent upon the wicked". (p.157)
Sec. 42 Pr. 18	In v.62 the Lord explains that "...it shall be revealed unto you in mine own due time where the New Jerusalem shall be built". (p.186)
Sec. 45 Pr. 19	"...when ye think not the summer shall be past, and the harvest ended, and your souls not saved." Jesus was expected *in their* generation. (p.199)
Sec. 45 Pr. 20	Verse 31 claims that *in* the generation when the gospel is restored, a desolating sickness will cover the land. (p.199)
Sec. 45 Pr. 21	Saints are commanded to gather riches and people from across the world and build New Jerusalem; no one will dare do battle with them. (p.199)

THE FINAL ANALYSIS – PART 1. JOSEPH SMITH'S PROPHECIES

Results of Joseph Smith's Prophecies, all of which completely failed – without exception.

The prophecy was written (1838) *after* the supposed but unquantifiable fulfilment (in 1836).
Smith claimed in the D&C that a voice told him the Saviour would return by 1891. One-hundred-and-twenty years after Smith's deadline, we find ourselves still waiting.
Smith wrote Sections 3 and 10 in 1828 *before* he wrote the *Book of Mormon* in which he then included the required prophecy and story.
DNA evidence has conclusively proven Native North Americans are *not* of Israelite descent. Mormon apologists are still searching in vain to find such people–*somewhere*.
Smith later falsified the original account to make it read that translation was just the first of his gifts, making a liar out of God.
Smith managed to convince eight close family and friends to be further witnesses to the Book of Mormon in direct contradiction to God's words.
A very small percentage of people approached join the Mormon Church. No verifiable evidence exists to confirm God has ever done anything about those who reject it.
No records of any kind were ever translated by Oliver Cowdery.
The apostle, John, has never been recorded and evidenced as having survived beyond his own time period nor has he prophesied before anyone, anywhere, ever.
No records of any kind were ever translated by Oliver Cowdery.
No records of any kind were ever translated by Oliver Cowdery.
Smith wrote Sections 3 and 10 in 1828 *before* he wrote the Book of Mormon in which he then included the required prophecy and story.
DNA evidence has conclusively proven Native North Americans are *not* of Israelite descent. Mormon apologists are still searching in vain to find such people–*somewhere*.
If the gold plates existed, Smith physically saw and handled them. The three witnesses confirmed that they only ever *imagined* them in their minds.
In spite of the witnesses testifying, Joseph Smith *was* destroyed. He was shot dead in June 1844, leaving the Church in disarray and confusion, creating a succession crisis.
Oliver Cowdery and David Whitmer did not search out, or show the prophecy to, or convert a single one of the original twelve apostles.
They 'gathered' in Kirtland; then in Nauvoo; then in Salt Lake; later the Church instructed members to *stop* gathering and build the kingdom where they lived.
The location for Zion, the New Jerusalem, and the temple "to which all nations should come" was explicitly to be Independence, Missouri (Sec. 57). It has never been built.
Almost two centuries have passed and Jesus still hasn't returned. If he wasn't going to return during their lifetime, Jesus should have ensured they didn't *expect* him to do so.
In that generation and several that followed, the prophecy remained unfulfilled. No *desolating* sickness occurred that *covered the land*.
Zion, the New Jerusalem, never was built and Mormon conflicts in Missouri resulted in an Extermination Order which ultimately drove the Mormons out.

THE MORMON DELUSION

Section & Prophecy.   **Joseph Smith's Prophecies.**
Sections in current sequence; prophesies in original sequence.

Section & Prophecy	
Sec. 52 Pr. 22	v.2: …Missouri … I will consecrate unto my people, which are a remnant of Jacob, and those who are heirs according to the covenant. (p.217)
Sec. 54 Pr. 23	Newel Knight is told he must be "patient in tribulation until I come; and, behold, I come quickly, and my reward is with me." (p.221)
Sec. 57 Pr. 24	Wherefore, this is the land of promise, and the place for the city of Zion … Independence is the center place … for an everlasting inheritance. (p.227)
Sec. 58 Pr. 25	v.7: "…and in bearing record of the land upon which the Zion of God shall stand." v.12: "Behold, I, the Lord, have spoken it." (p.231)
Sec. 64 Pr. 26	…inhabitants of Zion shall judge all things … shall flourish … come out of every nation under heaven … nations shall tremble. (p.239)
Sec. 70 Pr. 27	The law of consecration is reaffirmed. None are exempt. The 'generations' shall enter into the joy of these things. Even so. Amen. (v.18). (pp.260-1)
Sec. 77 Pr. 28	Smith prophesied "concerning this earth during the seven thousand years of its continuance, or its temporal existence." (p.288)
Sec. 78 Pr. 29	"regulating and establishing … the storehouse for the poor … *permanent* and *everlasting* establishment and order unto my church." (p.291)
Sec. 82 Pr. 30	Similar details as Section 78 are repeated. They are to enter the covenant and have equal claims, and that is to be "an *everlasting* order". (p.297)
Sec. 84 Pr. 31	v.2-3: "…the city of New Jerusalem … shall be built, beginning at the temple lot…" v.4: "in this generation." (p.303)
Sec. 84 Pr. 32	Whitney is to preach in New York, Albany and Boston. If they don't listen "desolation and utter abolishment" and "judgment is nigh." (p.303)
Sec. 87 Pr. 33	Smith predicted an imminent Civil War. Slaves would be marshalled for war. The south would call on Great Britain and other nations. (p.309)
Sec. 90 Pr. 34	The Lord declared that: "Zion will not be removed out of her place. I, the Lord, have spoken it." (v.37). (p.325)
Sec. 97 Pr. 35	"…nations of the earth …shall say …Zion is the city of our God …Zion cannot fall, neither be moved out of her place, for God is there." (p.332)
Sec. 98 Pr. 36	An "immutable covenant" will be fulfilled; "all things wherewith you have been afflicted …work together for your good …saith the Lord." (pp.337-8)
Sec. 101 Pr. 37	"Zion shall not be moved out of her place. They …shall return, and come to their inheritances, they and their children." (p.349)
Sec. 101 Pr. 38	"…there is none other place appointed …for …gathering of my saints … when there is …no more room …then I have other …stakes." (pp.349-50)
Sec. 101 Pr. 39	If the President doesn't listen to the saints: "…in his hot displeasure [he will] cut off those wicked, unfaithful, and unjust stewards." (pp.349-50)
Sec. 101 Pr. 40	"…they shall dwell thereon. They shall build, and another shall not inherit it; they shall plant vineyards, and …eat the fruit thereof." (pp.349-50)
Sec. 103 Pr. 41	The persecution was permitted by the Lord so as to condemn the perpetrators. He promised retribution "in mine own due time." (pp.355-6)
Sec. 103 Pr. 42	"…your brethren which have been scattered shall return to the lands of their inheritances, and shall build up the waste places of Zion." (pp.355-6)

THE FINAL ANALYSIS – PART 1. JOSEPH SMITH'S PROPHECIES

Results of Joseph Smith's Prophecies, all of which completely failed.

This prophecy referred to the local Native North Americans – Lamanites, inheriting the land. Today, the Mormon Church has no idea where any Lamanites actually are.
Newel Knight died 11 January 1847 at age 46. Jesus did not return as promised during the lifetime of Knight.
The Church never did build the City of Zion – the New Jerusalem or a temple at Independence, Missouri. Two Mormon schisms now occupy some of that area.
It didn't – and still doesn't stand there. According to Smith's revelation, "Who am I, saith the Lord, that have promised and have not fulfilled?" (v.31). Who indeed.
Zion did not 'flourish'; the Church does not have a viable presence in the location specified by the Lord. It remains unfulfilled prophecy and "The Lord hath spoken it."
The system quickly failed. Rather than rekindle it in Salt Lake, Young used tithing to develop his own empire, so much so that the Church had to sue his estate for over $1m.
The Earth has been around for some 4.54 billion years and that is an indisputable scientific fact. That is already a little over seven thousand; isn't it?
The system failed completely and was ultimately abandoned. In Salt Lake it could have been re-established. Young preferred to use tithing to make himself into a millionaire.
The system failed completely and was ultimately abandoned. In Salt Lake it could have been re-established. Young preferred to use tithing to make himself into a millionaire.
There never was a temple or city of Zion built as prophesied. Today there is still no Mormon temple or city of Zion – the New Jerusalem at Independence, Missouri.
The gospel was no more 'received' in those places than anywhere else, but no such judgment as Smith predicted has ever befallen any of the cities mentioned.
The war *everyone* predicted did not occur until three decades later. Slaves did not vex gentiles. The south did not call on Great Britain. There was no "full end to all nations".
A few short years later, having unsuccessfully tried to establish Zion, the saints were driven from the territory, never to return. Zion does not exist in Independence.
The saints never did build a temple in Zion as commanded. They were subsequently driven out of Missouri following the Extermination Order.
The Lord promised everything would be all right – but it wasn't, things turned out to be anything *but* all right. Two months later, in October 1833, the saints were evicted.
Promises made had been repeated several times and were never fulfilled. All the people of that generation have long since departed this world and so have all their children.
Today, there are over two-thousand-seven-hundred stakes worldwide, none of which should have existed before Zion was built and fully occupied.
In 1839, Joseph Smith himself visited President Van Buren to plead for the government to help around 20,000 Mormon settlers. The request was refused and God did nothing.
The fact is that they never built anything there and others did inherit it. They did not plant any "vineyards" – regardless of what "fruit" they might have eaten thereof.
There is no record of any such retribution by the Lord concerning the locals. The Lord's "own due time" is still awaited – yet everyone involved is long since dead.
Eventually, when Zion's Camp did march nine-hundred miles to 'redeem' Zion, having achieved nothing, they turned around and went home, suffering cholera and 14 deaths.

THE MORMON DELUSION

Section & Prophecy. Joseph Smith's Prophecies.
Sections in current sequence; prophesies in original sequence.

Sec. 104 Pr. 43	…the order which I commanded to be organized and established, to be a united order, and an everlasting order… (v.1). (p.361)
Sec. 105 Pr. 44	The time would come when Smith would have to drum up an army to reclaim the lands by force. (Sec. 101:43, 56-60). (p.366)
Sec. 105 Pr. 45	They "are not united according to the union required by the law of the celestial kingdom; …I cannot receive her unto myself." (v.3-5). (p.366)
Sec. 105 Pr. 46	The Lord has already sent "the destroyer" (v.15) to redeem Zion; none of the 'enemies' will be left upon land consecrated for the saints. (p.366)
Sec. 107 Pr. 47	v.57: "These things were all written in the book of Enoch, and are to be testified of in due time." (p.373)
Sec. 111 Pr. 48	"much treasure in this city for you …wealth pertaining to gold and silver shall be yours …more treasures than one for you in this city." (pp.390-91)
Sec. 111 Pr. 49	"and many people in this city, whom I will gather out in due time for the benefit of Zion, through your instrumentality." (v.2). (p.391)
Sec. 111 Pr. 50	"I will give this city into your hands, that you shall have power over it." (v.4). (p.391)
Sec. 114 Pr. 51	"Thus saith the Lord" – David W. Patten was to "perform a mission unto me next spring" in company with the rest of the twelve apostles. (p.400)
Sec. 115 Pr. 52	Lord instructs temple to be built at Far West. On 26 April 1839 they should lay the foundation and not stop until the temple is finished. (pp.403-4)
Sec. 117 Pr. 53	A 'temple square' site was chosen and dedicated in October of 1838 by Brigham Young, accompanied by Smith, Kimball and others. (p.409)
Sec. 117 Pr. 54	Is there not room enough on the mountains of Adam-ondi-Ahman, …come up hither unto the land of my people, even Zion. (p.412)
Sec. 117 Pr. 55	The Lord says Newel K. Whitney should go to Adam-Ondi-Ahman and be Bishop there. (p.412)
Sec. 117 Pr. 56	"Thus saith the Lord", Oliver Granger will go up to Zion (at that time, Adam-Ondi-Ahman) and be made a merchant to the Lord. (p.412)
Sec. 121 Pr. 57	Smith's accusers: "they and their posterity shall be swept from under heaven, saith God, that not one of them is left to stand by the wall." (p.423)
Sec. 122 Pr. 58	v.9. "Thy days are known, and thy years shall not be numbered less; …fear not what man can do, for God shall be with you forever and ever" (p.425)
Sec. 124 Pr. 59	"I will visit and soften their hearts, many of them for your good …ye may find grace in their eyes … they may come to the light of truth." (pp.437-8)
Sec. 124 Pr. 60	The Lord prophesied for a *fourth* time, a temple that was not completed, Zion (Independence); Far West; Spring Hill and now – Nauvoo. (pp.437-8)
Sec. 124 Pr. 61	Three times, God says if they do not do these things by the end of the time appointed, "ye shall be rejected as a church, with your dead." (pp.437-8)
Sec. 124 Pr. 62	God says that if they hearken to His voice, they will not be moved out of their place (v.45). (pp.437-8)
Sec. 124 Pr. 63	If enemies 'hinder' the work, "I will visit upon the heads of those who hindered my work, unto the third and fourth generation" (pp.437-8)

THE FINAL ANALYSIS – PART 1. JOSEPH SMITH'S PROPHECIES

Results of Joseph Smith's Prophecies, all of which completely failed.

This prophecy had been repeated many times, yet within three years the United Order had fallen apart. The Mormon God should have known that would happen.
When negotiations failed, instead of resorting to force, Smith disbanded his army, turned around and went home. The prophecy remained unfulfilled.
The Lord cannot receive the Church *unless* they live the United Order; all is lost for the Mormon Church which cannot be 'received unto the Lord' as they don't live that law.
This is not only an entirely unfulfilled prophecy; it is a contradiction from Smith's God; Satan could not be *sent* by God to do any such thing. Satan works in opposition.
There has been no further mention of the whereabouts of such a book. Smith invented the idea and I venture to suggest it never will be mentioned again, let alone identified.
Smith and company located no treasure of any description at Salem and eventually returned to Kirtland empty-handed. The Lord's promised treasure never materialised.
In 1842, Erastus Snow and Benjamin Winchester were asked to go to Salem to *fulfil* the prophecy. They had to *make* the prophecy appear fulfilled to recover from the failure.
The city of Salem did not fall into Smith's hands and he had no power over it. Hardly anyone knew they were even there.
David W. Patten was killed at the Battle of Crooked River on 25 October 1838 just six months after the Lord prophesied Patten would serve a mission the following spring.
The temple was never built and the saints were driven out the following spring (1839). The Mormon Church repurchased the site in 1909 but a temple has never been built.
This was the third temple to be prophesied and planned but never constructed; yet again, it was never built. The saints were ordered out of the settlement within days.
Smith had a conference and duly organised a Stake at Spring Hill (Adam-Ondi-Ahman) in July 1838. By November, the saints were driven from Spring Hill, never to return.
The 'Whitney' prophecy of July 1838 failed because the saints were driven from Spring Hill by November of that year and they never returned.
The 'Granger' prophecy failed on two counts. 1. The saints were driven out of Spring Hill in November 1838. 2. Granger never left Kirtland, he died there in 1841.
No retribution by the Lord has ever been established. Divine intervention has never been recorded. The only recorded burnings and killings were perpetrated by Mormons.
A little over five years later, Smith was shot dead at the age of thirty-eight. His days *were* cut short of a normal lifespan, in complete contradiction to this prophecy.
Gentile leaders did not do anything for "the exaltation or lifting up of Zion" and no "kings of the earth" came with any "gold and your silver, to the help of my people."
Although part of it was used and it was dedicated, the Nauvoo Temple was never completed. It was burned out, later hit by a tornado and finally demolished.
The Nauvoo Temple was never completed, let alone in any allotted time, yet God did not reject the Church and their dead. At least they claim He didn't.
The saints certainly appeared to try hard to accomplish what was required of them but they were driven out of Nauvoo anyway.
They didn't hate God; many worshipped Him; they just hated what Smith was doing to their community. There is no record of any retribution by God on any generation.

Section & Prophecy.	Joseph Smith's Prophecies. Sections in current sequence; prophesies in original sequence.
Sec. 124 Pr. 64	"…pertaining to my boarding house … let my servant Joseph and his house have place therein, from generation to generation." (pp.437-8).
Sec. 125 Pr. 65	The saints are to develop Nauvoo and also build up cities called Zarahemla and Nashville. (p.440)
Sec. 127 Pr. 66	1 September 1841. "I shall triumph over all my enemies, for the Lord God hath spoken it." (v.2). (p.443)
Sec. 127 Pr. 67	"Let all the saints rejoice …Israel's God is their God, and he will mete out a just recompense …upon the heads of all their oppressors." (p.443)
Sec. 130 Pr. 68	I prophesy …the commencement of the difficulties which will cause much bloodshed previous to the coming of the Son of Man. (v.12). (p.450)

The Final Analysis.

Doctrine and Covenants: 68 prophecies – 68 failures.

In the final analysis – God and Smith were not connected.

D&C Introductory Section 1:37-38.

Search these commandments, for they are true and faithful, and *the prophecies and promises which are in them shall all be fulfilled*. What I the Lord have spoken, I have spoken, and *I excuse not myself*; and though the heavens and earth pass away, my word shall not pass away, but shall be fulfilled, whether *by mine own voice or by the voice of my servants, it is the same*. (Emphasis added).

THE FINAL ANALYSIS – PART 1. JOSEPH SMITH'S PROPHECIES

Results of Joseph Smith's Prophecies, all of which completely failed.

Smith and his posterity did not "have place therein, from generation to generation" and such blessing was not "put upon the head of his posterity after him."
Zarahemla and Nashville did not get developed any more than Nauvoo did. By the time the saints were leaving Nauvoo, it was over as far as any cities were concerned.
27 June 1844. Joseph and Hyrum Smith were shot to death by a mob.
There is no record of any "just recompense" ever meted out on heads of "oppressors" by God. The saints were driven out and local residents just got on with life.
"This a voice declared to me, while I was praying earnestly…" Smith was hearing voices. The Civil War was three decades later and did not usher in the second coming.

For those who believe in the Bible.

Deuteronomy 18:20-22

18:20. But the prophet, which shall presume to speak a word in my name, which I have not commanded him to speak, or that shall speak in the name of other gods, even *that prophet shall die*.
21. And if thou say in thine heart, *How shall we know* the word which the LORD hath not spoken?
22. When a prophet speaketh in the name of the LORD, *if the thing follow not, nor come to pass, that is the thing which the LORD hath not spoken, but the prophet hath spoken it presumptuously: thou shalt not be afraid of him.* (Emphasis added).

"When a prophet speaketh in the name of the Lord, if the thing followeth not, nor come to pass" he has "spoken it presumptuously." It doesn't even say if *some* things work out but some don't, then that's okay. If any *one* single prophetic pronouncement made in the name of the Lord does *not* come to pass then the person who made that prophecy is a *false* prophet and he shall *die*.

All Joseph Smith's prophecies were made in the name of the Lord and *none* of them ever materialised. Joseph Smith was killed by a mob on 27 June 1844.

(See also: Matthew 7:15; 2 Corinthians 11:4-15; Galatians 1:6-9; 1 Timothy 4:1; 2 Peter 2:1-3).

THE MORMON DELUSION
For those who believe in science

> The whole world is made of incredibly tiny things, much too small to be visible to the naked eye – and yet none of the myths or so-called holy books that some people, even now, think were given to us by an all-knowing god, mentions them at all! In fact, when you look at those myths and stories, you can see that they don't contain any of the knowledge that science has patiently worked out. They don't tell us how big or how old the universe is; they don't tell us how to treat cancer; they don't explain gravity or the internal combustion engine; they don't tell us about germs, or nuclear fusion, or electricity, or anaesthetics. In fact, unsurprisingly, the stories in holy books don't contain any more information about the world than was known to the primitive peoples who first started telling them! If these holy books really were written, or dictated, or inspired, by all-knowing gods, don't you think it's odd that those gods said nothing about any of these important and useful things?"

Richard Dawkins 'The Magic of Reality' 2011. p. 95.

In line with Richard Dawkins' observations, Joseph Smith continued the same tradition as every other so-called 'holy man'. Among all his revelations and prophecies, not only is there absolutely no evidence that anything ever became properly 'fulfilled', there is plenty of evidence confirming they did not.

In addition, Joseph Smith's God gave absolutely no useful or worthwhile information to Smith that would have benefited his followers. This is where knowledge of Dawkins' "incredibly tiny things" would have come in useful. God didn't even need to reveal the details to Smith – just what to do to avoid disease and death resulting from lack of knowledge. There was no advice about cholera or malaria which would have been simple enough to give and to follow.

Subsequently, hundreds of people died entirely unnecessarily. Likewise, Smith was not given achievable instructions about where Zion should be built as God's location was never a viable proposition for such a settlement. Things did not improve under Young and instead of revealing to Young more sensible detail regarding suitable times of the year and modes of transport to use when travelling west, thousands lost their lives along the way or shortly after arriving in the valley. Using cheap handcarts through winter months was suicidal.

God did not give any revelations at any time that were of actual benefit or merit whatsoever. Early Mormons would actually have fared far better without God, had they simply ignored everything that Smith claimed God conveyed to him and lived in peace and harmony in the areas they were in.

Smith just wanted to take over the world and everything he said and did was for his own purpose and not for the consideration of his followers who did

THE FINAL ANALYSIS – PART 1. JOSEPH SMITH'S PROPHECIES

not benefit from anything Smith ever 'revealed'. The 'small' things God didn't ever divulge have all, without exception, come to our knowledge through science rather than God who was of no help to anyone whatsoever at any time – especially Joseph Smith's time.

> There is much that remains deeply mysterious, and it is not likely that we will ever uncover all the secrets of a universe as vast as ours; but, armed with science, we can at least ask sensible, meaningful questions about it and recognise credible answers when we find them. We don't have to invent wildly implausible stories: we have the joy and excitement of real, scientific investigation and discovery to keep our imaginations in line. And in the end that is more exciting than fantasy. *Richard Dawkins 'The Magic of Reality' 2011. p. 202.*

THE FINAL ANALYSIS

PART 2

Pet Phrases used by Smith's God/Jesus

Joseph Smith created a number of 'pet phrases' that he attributed to God/Jesus and other characters.

The following is a summary, extracted from the main text, of the repetitive use of impossible phrases, along with their origins, that Smith included in the Doctrine and Covenants and other works he was responsible for producing.

"In other words" *(p. 93)*.

Origin:

This is not a biblical phrase; it appears nowhere in accepted scripture. It was something Smith often wrote himself, as recorded numerous times in 'History of the Church', especially Volume 1, where it appears *eighteen* times. Joseph Smith was the originator of the use of the phrase in *all* of the material he was responsible for writing. Many people use the phrase when writing of course – but *never* the Lord or the ancients in the Bible. I have used it myself a number of times to explain an underlying reason for something Smith says or does. For example, on p. 179: " '...that which he has consecrated unto the poor and the needy of my church, or in other words, unto me—' *(D&C 42:37)*. **Or in other words**, unto Smith & co—." Smith's use of the expression is attempted further explanation rather than irony or sarcasm but it rarely adds anything worthwhile.

Smith's usage:

Smith often used the phrase on behalf of God/Jesus and other characters; it appears in the *D&C*, his *Inspired Revision* of the Bible and also in the *Book of Mormon*, where Smith has several different people re-explain things they have just said. This is because that is *exactly* the way Smith himself wrote; he would write something, then think of a better way of expressing it, and add it after saying "in other words" so he fell into the habit of having his 'characters' use the very same technique and thus the same expression. As with Smith's own recorded use of it, many of the second explanations by Smith's characters were often so similar to the first, that rephrasing was hardly necessary or helpful.

Smith has the Lord rephrase, or sometimes even almost *repeat*, the exact same thing, using the phrase "in other words" on no less than **twenty-two** occasions in the D&C.

In addition, Smith has several different characters use "in other words" a *dozen* times in the Book of Mormon, where it appears **three times by Nephi**, some 600 years BCE; **once by Mosiah** in 121 BCE; **six times by Alma, the Son of Alma**, 82-72 BCE; **once by Nephi, son of Nephi the son of Helaman**, CE 26-30; and also once by him quoting a **letter from Gaddianhi** (leader of the Gadianton robbers), to Lachonius, asking him to surrender.

Conclusion:

Smith often wrote something and then rephrased it, trying to make it clearer, using "in other words" when he did so. It appears regularly in his 'History of the Church' but much less so after Volume 1. It is interesting that it doesn't

THE FINAL ANALYSIS – PART 2. PET PHRASES OF GOD/JESUS

appear at all in Volume 7. The reason for that is Smith didn't write it. Volume 7 mainly covers the period following Smith's death. Smith wrote *some* of the text in earlier volumes after Volume 1, but much of 'History of the Church', despite it being written in the first person, was not actually penned by Smith at all; it was drawn from various historical records and written after his death in a style made to look as though Smith wrote it himself, in more Mormon duplicity that the Church actually now admits. Thus "in other words" only appears four or five times at most in volumes 2-6. "In other words" was a regular feature in Smith's writing, so it is not surprising that his fictional characters follow suit, including the Lord, who would hardly have needed to clarify his own words; they would have been perfect and correctly stated the first time. What are the chances of so many different characters using *that* same phrase so many times to re-explain themselves, in words *always* emanating from Joseph Smith?

Richard Packham lists about a hundred references where Smith rephrased what was supposedly not clearly stated the first time by the ancients engraving on metal plates, at this link: http://packham.n4m.org/inotherwords.htm

Smith's "nation, kindred, tongue and people" fetish. *(pp. 180-81).*

Origin:

Smith plagiarised this sequence of words directly from Revelation 14:6 which reads "every nation, kindred, tongue and people." It appears nowhere else in the Bible and the Lord did not say it.

Smith's usage:

Smith used it in that *exact* sequence, sometimes singular and sometimes plural, no less than *nine* times in the D&C, once in JS–History, and *fifteen* times, by *eight* different characters in his Book of Mormon, in *addition* to using several other quite *similar* expressions.

In D&C 7:3, Smith claims the apostle **John** wrote that exact sequence on parchment that he (Smith) saw (presumably in his imagination) and translated. In six Sections the **Lord** is repeating the sequence and **Smith** himself uses the exact expression twice in the D&C.

In *addition* to my own count, in speaking of locals going to war against the saints, in D&C 98:34-36, Smith has the Lord use it twice more, just omitting the word 'kindred', as clearly the saints would not go to war against their own.

In JS–History 1:33, ***Moroni*** is speaking. Smith has him say "…my name should be had for good and evil among all ***nations***, ***kindreds***, and ***tongues***, or that it should be both good and evil spoken of among all *people*" – in the same sequence.

From the Book of Mormon, we have exactly the same sequence of words from **Lehi**; five times from **Nephi**; from **Zenos**; from **King Benjamin**; twice from **Abinadi**; three times from *Alma the son of Alma*; from Alma the Younger quoting *the Lord*; and from **Mormon**. Additionally, in the Book of Mormon, we get several other *similar* occurrences. Smith used quite a number of other similar phrases in his writing, but he clearly remembered "nation, kindred, tongue and people" best.

The 'Testimony of Three Witnesses' and 'Testimony of Eight Witnesses' in the Book of Mormon both start with: "Be it known unto all nations, kindreds, tongues, and people…" so it doesn't take a genius to work out who wrote that for the witnesses to sign.

Conclusion:

In chronological order, the first person ever to have said those words would have been Smith's fictional Old Testament prophet 'Zenos' whom Nephi claims said it some time before 600 BCE. The Book of Mormon was written in 1829 and instances of the use of that phrase in it were backdated to anything from over 600 BCE through to the early CE period.

Smith simply used the expression he located in the KJV of Revelation 14:6 on no less than *twenty-six* separate occasions, attributing the words to several different characters and also many times to the Lord, who was not recorded in the Bible as having ever used such an expression at all.

Smith found the phrase and used it numerous times by multiple characters in his Book of Mormon. He had the Lord use it several times in his D&C revelations between 1828 and 1837, yet the Lord *never* used it before or since then. He liked it so much that Smith also used it for the testimonies of 'three' and then 'eight' witnesses, and in 1838 he recorded Moroni using it during his claimed visit to Smith, which Smith then backdated to 1823. *Every* reference that Smith made, from his Moroni claim, the Book of Mormon, for the witness statements, and D&C revelations, was *written* between 1828 and 1837 – all twenty-six, plus several others that closely match the sequence, which I have not included.

For that *exact* sequence of words to appear even once or twice in ancient America in the same format as used in the Book of Revelation in the CE, it could be considered very suspicious and more than just mere coincidence – but *twenty-four* occasions (plus two by Smith), by so many different characters, some in different locations, over such a timescale, including several times by the Lord, who was not even the originator of the phrase? There is *no* other explanation for this other than the obvious. Joseph Smith had to be the one to

THE FINAL ANALYSIS – PART 2. PET PHRASES OF GOD/JESUS

concoct every single instance of the use of that expression outside of the book of Revelation, along with inventing every single character who ever used it – including Smith's version of the Lord.

"As seemeth me good" *(pp. 213-14).*

Origin:

The expression "as seemeth me good" is not a phrase attributed to the Lord **anywhere** other than in Smith's own writings. This is another very suspicious aspect regarding Smith; even more so because he doesn't *only* have the Lord use the phrase, he also has Moroni use it in the Book of Mormon where Moroni (10:1) says he will "…write somewhat *as seemeth me good"*. The origin of this expression lies in Joseph Smith's own imagination.

Smith's usage:

If they are *not* faithful "they shall be cut off, even as I will, as seemeth me good" (D&C 52:6). Not only is that statement slightly nonsensical and unnecessarily repetitive, the last phrase, "as seemeth me good" seems quite a strange turn of phrase for the Lord to use about Smith – or about anyone else for that matter. It smacks of being a human term used to *sound* like the Lord; moreover, Smith often has the Lord use it. Does it really sound like something a God would say even once, let alone quite a number of times?

In the D&C, it appears several times in addition to the above. Section 40:3 "…it remaineth with me to do with him *as seemeth me good*"; 42:16 "…ye shall speak and prophesy *as seemeth me good*"; 56:4 "I the Lord, command and revoke, *as it seemeth me good*"; 84:103 the "Lord shall direct them, for thus *it seemeth me good*". In D&C 60:5 and also 62:5 the Lord says "…*as seemeth you good*, it mattereth not unto me";* in 100:1 the Lord says to "…my friends Sidney and Joseph" that their families are well "and I will do with them *as seemeth me good*". In 124:72 and also 124:77 Hyrum can put stock into 'Nauvoo House' "*as seemeth him good*". God had **never** said it before Smith put the words into His mouth – numerous times. In Smith's Moses 6:32, he has God say "I will do *as seemeth me good*" to Enoch. In **eleven** instances, Smith has the Lord introduce a phrase *never* seen elsewhere.

* The Lords expression "it mattereth not unto *me*" or "it mattereth not unto *thee*" also appears several times in the Book of Mormon and in the Doctrine and Covenants. Once again, it is not an expression the Lord *ever* used – other

than in Smith's own writings. Essentially, here (above), it is coupled with "as seemeth you good", meaning 'do what you like, I really don't care'. Smith used it several times as if the Lord said it. If something didn't really matter to the Lord, why would he even bother to mention it? Clearly, he wouldn't.

Conclusion:

"As seemeth me good" is a Smith concoction put into the mouth of the Lord on a number of occasions. In the Bible, the Lord is not recorded as having spoken that way. It only occurs in material that Smith was responsible for writing. The author of those words is clearly and obviously Joseph Smith and not the Lord.

"In mine own due time" *(p. 214)*.

Origin:

This is another expression invented by Joseph Smith. The Lord is not recorded as having ever said such a thing outside of Smith's writings.

Smith's usage:

Smith often put "in mine own due time" into the mouth of the Lord when something went wrong or if someone didn't perform in the way Smith had the Lord predict they would. Smith then has the Lord say that he is going to deal with that person – in his own due time. My research into such instances reveals *no* recorded retribution coming upon anyone in that category. "In mine own due time" appears *twelve* times in the D&C. All were written by Smith, except Section 136, which was recorded in 1847 by Brigham Young who copied Smith's style. The expression also appears three times in the Book of Mormon. The Lord is speaking on every occasion.

Conclusion:

The Lord was *never* recorded as saying "in mine own due time" *other* than in material written by Joseph Smith and once by Brigham Young. Smith used the expression, pretending the Lord was saying it when something went wrong or when someone didn't perform, or when so-called 'enemies' got the better of them. There was nothing Smith could do, so the Lord would deal with such people in his "own due time" – just leave it with me, so to speak. It was Smith's method of letting himself off the hook.

THE FINAL ANALYSIS – PART 2. PET PHRASES OF GOD/JESUS

Unfortunately for Smith, from all of the evidence available, it appears the Lord never actually did anything at all about any of these people. Had the Lord really been speaking, we would expect to see at least some results of people subsequently being 'dealt' with. Some authors have tried to find such evidence concerning those responsible for the death of Joseph Smith. A few decades ago, a book was published by N. B. Lundwall under the title of "The Fate of the Persecutors of the Prophet Joseph Smith" which I read and blindly accepted as a member. It contained some gory detail but turned out to be full of nonsense and the claimed 'evidence' just speculative. The book has just been republished (May 2011) with Lundwall as 'editor' and a foreword by John A. Widtsoe.

Obviously, the concept of the Lord's retribution is still popular. However, no matter what is claimed or argued, such a thing as the Lord ever 'dealing' with people 'in his own due time' has *never* demonstrably happened. There is no documented or substantiated record of *any* such retribution *by the Lord* regarding anyone that Smith ever claimed the Lord would deal with in his own due time.

"Behold, I come quickly" – "and my reward is with me" – "to give to every man according as his work shall be." *(pp. 219-21).*

Origin:

"…behold, I come quickly, and my reward is with me" is direct plagiarism from the book of Revelation (22:12). "I come quickly" – "and my reward is with me" – "to give to every man according as his work shall be" are all taken from verses in Revelation.

Smith's usage:

The expression "I come quickly" appears *eleven* times in the D&C. The Lord is not personally recorded as having said that anywhere else at all. On two occasions, Smith also adds "and my reward is with me" for good measure and even paraphrases "to give every man according as his work shall be" – all from Revelation, and clearly identifying pure unadulterated plagiarism.

Conclusion:

The exact sequence of translated words is *impossible* for Jesus to have ever spoken in the first place, let alone to Smith in the 1800s. At best, Revelation consists of handed down stories, or memories combined with imagination or dreams rather than any exact words ever spoken by the Saviour. The exact sequence of translated words is *impossible* for Jesus to have ever spoken in the first place, let alone to Smith in the 1800s.

> **D&C 112:34.** Be faithful until I come, for *I come quickly; and my reward is with me to recompense every man according as his work shall be.* I am Alpha and Omega. Amen.

> **Revelation 22:12.** And, behold, *I come quickly; and my reward is with me, to give every man according as his work shall be.*

The above sequence of *nineteen words* in D&C 112 and Revelation 22 is *identical* with the exception of one word Smith replaced (give = recompense). The chances of that sequence happening twice in real life are so infinitesimal as to be rendered not just implausible but entirely ***impossible*** – and that is before even considering the fact that the KJV is just *one* version of a translation.

"Even so. Amen." *(p. 227).*

Origin:

Revelation 1:7. Words of the author of Revelation – not the Lord.

Smith's usage:

D&C Section 33, written in October 1830, was the first time Smith attributed these three words to the Lord – who had *never* been recorded as having used them together before. After that, they became a regular feature in the Doctrine and Covenants, appearing some *fifty-five* times.

Smith also included it in Moses 1:42, as if God had used the expression when speaking to Moses. Interestingly, in 1918, Joseph F. Smith copied Joseph Smith's wording, ending his own claimed vision *(Section 138)* with the same three words, but in his case they are not attributed to deity.

Conclusion:

The Lord did not use such an expression anywhere in the Old Testament, New Testament or even the Book of Mormon. Smith created it, or plagiarised it from Revelation, pretending it was the Lord speaking in the D&C. Had Smith found it *before* 1830, undoubtedly it would also appear in the Book of Mormon.

THE FINAL ANALYSIS – PART 2. PET PHRASES OF GOD/JESUS

"Weeping and Wailing and Gnashing of Teeth" *(p. 253)*.

Origin:

Smith picked up the idea of "weeping and wailing and gnashing of teeth" from the New Testament where there are several references to either "weeping and gnashing of teeth" or "wailing and gnashing of teeth" – but never "weeping *and* wailing and gnashing of teeth." There are also two or three instances of "weeping and wailing" in the Old Testament, but no gnashing of teeth in the same references (although that idea is found elsewhere in the OT).

Smith's usage:

Smith combined New Testament expressions and used "weeping *and* wailing and gnashing of teeth" a couple of times in the Book of Mormon by *different* characters, once in his Book of Moses, and three times in the D&C. Smith also used "wailing, and anguish, and gnashing of teeth", "wailing and gnashing of teeth", and "gnashing of teeth" in the D&C pretending the Lord was the voice.

Conclusion:

Smith plagiarised the expression and put it into the mouth of his characters and in particular in the D&C, directly into the mouth of the Lord who would be unlikely to copy and combine expressions of writers of the New Testament.

This was clearly just Smith trying to make his work sound more like the Bible and therefore more 'believable'. It doesn't – and it isn't.

THE FINAL ANALYSIS

PART 3

God may move in mysterious ways
but the Mormon God *speaks* in mysterious ways.

The Mormon God says the Strangest of Things.

Humans may often quite naturally say some odd things
but would God or Jesus Christ really speak like this?

Joseph Smith would have us believe that the following
statements all came directly from the mouth of deity.

Question each one – would God/Jesus *really* speak this way?

This is just a very small, almost random, selection of strange ways for deity to speak. There are many more to be found in the *D&C, Book of Mormon, Book of Moses* and *Book of Abraham*. Words that Smith put into the mouth of deity are often far from correctly structured, sometimes completely unreasonable, rarely plausible and they never really sound sensible; something bad enough for a human carefully writing down his or her thoughts, but deity speaking? Smith's deity also often repeats himself.

"These words are not of men nor of man, but of me" *(D&C 18:34).*

If this is the best that deity can do – God help us (to coin a phrase).

D&C 1:10. …the Lord shall come to recompense unto every man according to his work, and measure to every man according to the measure which he has measured to his fellow man.

D&C 3:9. Behold, thou art Joseph, and thou wast chosen to do the work of the Lord, but because of transgression, if thou art not aware thou wilt fall.

D&C 8:1. …you shall receive a knowledge concerning the engravings of old records, which are ancient, which contain those parts of my scripture of which has been spoken…

D&C 12:9. Behold, I am the light and the life of the world, that speak these words, therefore give heed with your might, and then you are called. Amen.

D&C 18:8. And now, marvel not that I have called him unto mine own purpose, which purpose is known in me; wherefore, if he shall be diligent in keeping my commandments he shall be blessed unto eternal life; and his name is Joseph.

D&C 20:41-43. And to confirm those who are baptized into the church, by the laying on of hands for the baptism of fire and the Holy Ghost, according to the scriptures; And to teach, expound, exhort, baptize, and watch over the church; And to confirm the church by the laying on of the hands, and the giving of the Holy Ghost; *(Example of repetition. There are dozens more).*

D&C 29:13. …the dead which died in me, to receive a crown of righteousness, and to be clothed upon, even as I am, to be with me, that we may be one.

D&C 38:34. And now, I give unto the church *in these parts* a commandment…

THE FINAL ANALYSIS – PART 3. GOD SAYS STRANGE THINGS

D&C 88:32. And they who remain shall also be quickened; nevertheless, they shall return again to their own place, to enjoy that which they are willing to receive, because they were not willing to enjoy that which they might have received.

D&C 90:25. Let your families be small, especially mine aged servant Joseph Smith's, Sen., as pertaining to those who do not belong to your families;

D&C 97:1. I speak unto you with my voice, even the voice of my Spirit…

D&C 97:28. …I will bless her with blessings, and multiply a multiplicity of blessings upon her. *(The Lord became obsessed with this idea in Section 104).*

D&C 104:2. …blessed with a multiplicity of blessings / 23. I will multiply blessings upon him / 25. I will multiply blessings upon him / 31 …and multiply blessings upon them / 33. I will multiply blessings upon them and their seed after them, even a multiplicity of blessings / 35. I will multiply blessings upon him / 38. I will multiply a multiplicity of blessings upon him / 42. I will multiply blessings upon him and his seed after him, even a multiplicity of blessings / 46. And I will multiply blessings upon the house of my servant Joseph Smith, Jun., inasmuch as he is faithful, even a multiplicity of blessings.

D&C 98:33-36. …this is the law that I gave unto mine ancients, that they should not go out unto battle against any nation, kindred, tongue, or people, save I, the Lord, commanded them. And if any nation, tongue, or people should proclaim war against them, they should first lift a standard of peace unto that people, nation, or tongue; And if that people did not accept the offering of peace, neither the second nor the third time, they should bring these testimonies before the Lord; Then I, the Lord, would give unto them a commandment, and justify them in going out to battle against that nation, tongue, or people.

D&C 100:3. Behold, and lo, I have much people in this place, in the regions round about; and an effectual door shall be opened in the regions round about in this eastern land.

D&C 117. The section begins "Thus saith the Lord" which is not startling in itself, except that the Lord repeats "saith the Lord" fifteen times in the sixteen verses of this Section. Would the Lord really want or need to do that? If so, why didn't he use the expression as prolifically as this in all the other Sections? See example below.

D&C 117:5. Let the properties of Kirtland be turned out for debts, *saith the Lord*. Let them go, *saith the Lord*, and whatsoever remaineth, let it remain in your hands, *saith the Lord*.

D&C 124:3. "…and to all the nations of the earth scattered abroad." As all the other nations were abroad; "scattered abroad" is a non sequitur and God would hardly make such a mistake as to unnecessarily add it.

D&C 104:39. This is *God* speaking about why He wants a temple to be built at Nauvoo: "Therefore, verily I say unto you, that your anointings, and your washings, and your baptisms for the dead, and your solemn assemblies, and your memorials for your sacrifices by the sons of Levi, and for your oracles in your most holy places wherein you receive conversations, and your statutes and judgments, for the beginning of the revelations and foundation of Zion, and for the glory, honor, and endowment of all her municipals, are ordained by the ordinance of my holy house, which my people are always commanded to build unto my holy name." This single sentence is far from grammatically correct and it makes no sense whatsoever.

These are just a few examples of ludicrous statements for Smith to claim came directly from deity. It is perfectly clear that this was just Smith's hopeless attempt at a Jacobean style of writing and not God or Jesus speaking at all.

I have not even begun to mention the fact that in addition to the absurdity of the things Smith has God *say* and the manner of speech he generally uses, he has God/Jesus continue to use the same archaic early modern form of speech that he used for the Book of Mormon and other works. There is a consistency between all of Smith's writings where he has the Lord use such language. It is invariably consistently entirely incorrect in every imaginable way. The author of everything Smith wrote in (poorly attempted) early modern English is easily determined by the very fact that all of it is consistently *wrong*. There are no excuses either as Smith has the Lord himself declare the words are not of man or men, but of him *(D&C 18:34. See p. 494).*

I am not a linguist, although it appears quite obvious in so many instances that there is something very wrong with the grammar and manner of speech Smith has God use compared with the KJV. Luckily, I know someone who is a linguist, who has explained where and why Smith got everything wrong and I would refer the reader to a more professional analysis of this area than I could ever provide. The following is a link to my friend, Richard Packham's work on this area. It is highly recommended. http://packham.n4m.org/linguist.htm

THE FINAL ANALYSIS

PART 4

WHO AM I; GOD, JESUS – OR BOTH?

In the Mormon Church, theologically, God and Jesus Christ are two separate and distinct beings, both with bodies of flesh and bone.

Joseph Smith was monotheistic until about 1835-1836.

In many sections of the D&C, Smith's 'voice of deity' switches *between* being God, God the redeemer, the Lord, Jesus Christ, and several other descriptions; sometimes they are even combined and represented as one and the same being.

So… who *is* actually speaking in each case?
This is the voice of Smith's deity…

If God and Jesus are two separate and distinct personages, then whoever is the 'voice' – one or the other, should make it very clear and specific in each D&C Section as it is 'revealed'. If they are one and the same, it doesn't much matter.

All the following descriptions refer to one 'being' who is actually speaking. There is no noted change of speaker in any D&C Section. Included, is every *different* description from each Section listed; many of which appear more than once. Possible *third party* references such as "the Lord is God" have been excluded. Some, such as "the Lord will utter his voice" are included where they may allude to another 'being' in context of defining the speaker. The 'voice' often appears to speak in the *third person*; thus some are included for reference and comparison. Other than for clarity, only first person declarations are included. In particular, it is not always easy to determine who "I, the Lord" is in each Section as the phrase appears to be interchangeable. The terminology of the 'voice' often appears entirely monotheistic, or at least very ambiguous.

In Mormonism, 'Alpha and Omega' refers to Jesus Christ. In the main, that seems to follow in the D&C, but Sections 35 and 76 suggest it is God; "your God, even Alpha and Omega" (35:1) "Alpha and Omega, your Lord and your God" (75:1).

So, who is actually speaking in each Section? D&C 6* is perfectly clear; it states the speaker is God and that God is also Jesus Christ; one and the same. D&C 86** also confirms the monotheistic concept "with Christ in God—".

D&C 1: the voice of Him who dwells on high / the Lord / God the Lord, even the Savior of the world / I am God / Lord of Hosts / I the Lord.

D&C 5: I, the Lord, am God / I the Lord.

***D&C 6:** I am God / I am Jesus Christ, the Son of God.

D&C 8: This has the third party statement "as the Lord liveth, who is your God and your Redeemer", confirming Smith's monotheism, but who is it that is speaking? "I am the same that spake unto you from the beginning."

D&C 10: Behold, I am Jesus Christ, the Son of God / your Redeemer, your Lord and your God.

D&C 11: I am God / believing in the power of Jesus Christ ... For, behold, it is I that speak / I am Jesus Christ, the Son of God.

D&C 12: I am God / I am the light and the life of the world. (Jesus Christ is recognised in Mormonism and also mainstream Christianity as being the light and life of the world).

D&C 14: I am God / ask the Father in my name / I am Jesus Christ, the Son of the Living God.

D&C 17: I, Jesus Christ, your Lord and your God.

D&C 18: I, Jesus Christ, your Lord and your God / I, Jesus Christ, your Lord and your God, and your Redeemer.

THE FINAL ANALYSIS – PART 4. WHO AM I; GOD OR JESUS?

D&C 19: I am Alpha and Omega, Christ the Lord ... the beginning and the end, the Redeemer of the world / for I, God, am endless / I am endless / Endless is my name / I God / myself, even God / I am Jesus Christ / me thy Savior.

D&C 20:28. Smith confirms his monotheism: "Which Father, Son, and Holy Ghost are one God, infinite and eternal, without end. Amen."

D&C 21: thus saith the Lord God / this church of Christ, bearing my name— / saith the Lord God.

D&C 27: Listen to the voice of Jesus Christ, your Lord, your God, and your Redeemer.

D&C 29: Listen to the voice of Jesus Christ, your Redeemer, the Great I AM / the Lord of Hosts / I the Lord God / the wicked... will I be ashamed to own before the Father / by the power of my Spirit created I them; yea, all things both spiritual and temporal / my works have no end, neither beginning / I, the Lord God (four consecutive occasions).

D&C 34: ...hear and behold what I, the Lord God, shall say unto you, even Jesus Christ your Redeemer / I am your Lord and your Redeemer.

D&C 35: This is one continuous statement by the Lord God; v.1-2: "Listen to the voice of the Lord your God, even Alpha and Omega, the beginning and the end, whose course is one eternal round, the same today as yesterday, and forever. I am Jesus Christ, the Son of God, who was crucified for the sins of the world." / I am one in the Father, as the Father is one in me / For I am God / the day of my coming / Behold, I come quickly.

D&C 36: Thus saith the Lord God, the Mighty One of Israel / I am Jesus Christ, the Son of God.

D&C 38: This is one continuous statement by the Lord God; v.1-3: "Thus saith the Lord your God, even Jesus Christ, the Great I AM, Alpha and Omega, the beginning and the end, the same which looked upon the wide expanse of eternity, and all the seraphic hosts of heaven, before the world was made; The same which knoweth all things, for all things are present before mine eyes; I am the same which spake, and the world was made, and all things came by me" / I am Christ.

D&C 39: listen to the voice of him who is from all eternity to all eternity, the Great I AM, even Jesus Christ—

D&C 41: saith the Lord and your God / I come quickly.

D&C 42: in my name, even Jesus Christ the Son of the living God, the Savior of the world / I will be your God / I spake by the mouths of my prophets.

D&C 43: these are the words of the Lord your God / Behold, I am Jesus Christ, the Savior of the world.

D&C 45: give ear to him who laid the foundation of the earth, who made the heavens and all the hosts thereof, and by whom all things were made which live, and move, and have a being / Listen to him who is the advocate with the Father / I am Alpha and Omega, the beginning and the end, the light and the life of the world / I the Lord / behold, I will come; and they shall see me in the clouds of heaven, clothed with power and great glory / the Lord shall utter his voice / the Jews look upon me and say: What are these wounds in thine hands and in thy feet? / I am Jesus that was crucified. I am the Son of God / the Lord shall be in their midst / I, the Lord / when the Lord shall appear he shall be terrible unto them.

D&C 49: Thus saith the Lord; for I am God, and have sent mine Only Begotten Son into the world / Behold, I am Jesus Christ.

D&C 50: give ear to the voice of the living God / I, the Lord / thus saith the Lord /them that my Father hath given me / the Father and I are one. I am in the Father and the Father in me / I am the good shepherd.

D&C 51: saith the Lord your God / I am Jesus Christ.

D&C 52: thus saith the Lord / I, the Lord / I am Jesus Christ, the Son of God.

D&C 53: thus saith the Lord, even Alpha and Omega, the beginning and the end, even he who was crucified for the sins of the world—

D&C 56: the Lord your God / I, the Lord / the Lord God of hosts / thus saith the Lord / the Lord shall come.

D&C 58: I, the Lord / my law shall be kept / let God rule him / laws which ye have received from my hand / Who am I that made man / Who am I, saith the Lord / behold the Son of Man cometh.

D&C 59: saith the Lord / the mansions of my Father / I, the Lord.

D&C 60: thus saith the Lord / I, the Lord, rule in the heavens above …when I shall make up my jewels, all men shall know what it is that bespeaketh the power of God.

D&C 61: hearken unto the voice of him who has all power, who is from everlasting to everlasting, even Alpha and Omega, the beginning and the end / thus saith the Lord / I, the Lord / I suffered it that ye might bear record / that you may abide the day of his coming.

D&C 62: saith the Lord your God, even Jesus Christ / I, the Lord.

D&C 63: hear the word of the Lord / I, the Lord / I am God / the Lord your God / when the Lord shall come / I am Alpha and Omega, even Jesus Christ.

D&C 64: thus saith the Lord your God / I, the Lord / My disciples, in days of old / that God may be glorified / The Lord hath spoken it.

D&C 65: (This Section is classed as revelation but designated as a prayer) a voice as of one sent down from on high / Pray unto the Lord (that would be God, as Mormons are forbidden to pray to Jesus) / the Son of Man shall come.

D&C 66: thus saith the Lord / saith the Lord your Redeemer, the Savior of the world / I, the Lord / my Father / thus saith the Lord your God, your Redeemer, even Jesus Christ.

THE FINAL ANALYSIS – PART 4. WHO AM I; GOD OR JESUS?

D&C 67: whose prayers I have heard (Mormons pray exclusively to God the Father) / I, the Lord / that which is righteous cometh down from above, from the Father of lights / you shall see me and know that I am—not with the carnal neither natural mind, but with the spiritual / Neither can any natural man abide the presence of God.

D&C 68: this is the promise of the Lord unto you / I, the Lord…even Jesus Christ, that I am the Son of the living God / I, the Lord / I am Alpha and Omega.

D&C 69: saith the Lord your God / I, the Lord.

D&C 72: listen to the voice of the Lord / thus saith the Lord / for him of my Father / the Lord your God, your Redeemer.

D&C 75: I who speak even by the voice of my Spirit, even Alpha and Omega, your Lord and your God— / I, the Lord / this is the will of the Lord your God concerning you / thus saith the Lord.

D&C 78: the Lord your God / saith the Lord God / thus saith the Lord / the Lord God, the Holy One of Zion / saith your Redeemer, even the Son Ahman / For ye are the church of the Firstborn, and he will take you up in a cloud.

D&C 81: Listen to the voice of him who speaketh, to the word of the Lord your God / the house of my Father / Alpha and Omega, even Jesus Christ.

D&C 82: I, the Lord / Ye call upon my name / what I say unto one I say unto all …the anger of God kindleth / I, the Lord / saith the Lord your God / it shall be done according to the laws of the Lord / with an eye single to the glory of God / according to the laws of my church (The Church of Jesus Christ…).

D&C 84: A revelation of Jesus Christ / the word of the Lord / the Lord confirmed a priesthood also upon Aaron …which is after the holiest order of God / ordained by the angel of God / whatsoever is light is Spirit, even the Spirit of Jesus Christ / And the Father teacheth him / you are mine apostles, even God's high priests; ye are they whom my Father hath given me / where my Father and I am / For your Father, who is in heaven / For I, the Almighty / as the Lord shall direct them / saith the Lord Almighty / I, the Lord / I am Alpha and Omega, the beginning and the end. (Note third party references.)

**D&C 86: thus saith the Lord / the angels are crying unto the Lord day and night / but the Lord saith unto them / have been hid from the world with Christ in God— / through this priesthood, a savior unto my people Israel. The Lord hath said it. (Note the monotheistic statement "with Christ in God".)

D&C 88: thus saith the Lord / This is the light of Christ. As also he is in the sun, and the light of the sun / Which light proceedeth forth from the presence of God / the power of God who sitteth upon his throne / even with the presence of God the Father / even the law of Christ / all things are by him, and of him, even God / the power of God / the decree which God hath made / Whatsoever ye ask the Father in my name / That I may testify unto your Father, and your God, and my God / and the face of the Lord shall be unveiled / They are Christ's, the first fruits / those who are Christ's at his coming / until I come. (Try to determine which are third *party* and which are third *person* statements).

D&C 93: thus saith the Lord / I am in the Father, and the Father in me, and the Father and I are one— / The Father because he gave me of his fulness, and the Son because I was in the world and made flesh my tabernacle, and dwelt among the sons of men / be glorified in me as I am in the Father / I was in the beginning with the Father, and am the Firstborn.

D&C 95: thus saith the Lord / into the ears of the Lord of Saboath, which is by interpretation, the creator of the first day, the beginning and the end / this is the promise of the Father unto you / saith your Lord / saith Son Ahman; or, in other words, Alphus; or, in other words, Omegus; even Jesus Christ your Lord.

D&C 97: I, the Lord / a house should be built unto me in the land of Zion / build a house unto me in the name of the Lord / my presence shall be there, for I will come into it, and all the pure in heart that shall come into it shall see God / thus saith the Lord / saith the Lord your God.

D&C 98: saith the Lord your God / I, the Lord / I, the Lord God / live by every word which proceedeth forth out of the mouth of God. For he will give unto the faithful line upon line / saith the Lord / in my Father's house are many mansions / where my Father and I am / the Lord your God.

D&C 101: I, the Lord / I am God / when the Lord shall come (third party).

D&C 112: Verily thus saith the Lord / I, the Lord / the Lord thy God / saith the Lord.

D&C 124: thus saith the Lord / for I, the Lord / saith the Lord / saith the Lord God / saith the Lord your God / saith the Lord God; for I, the Lord, am God / I, the Lord your God.

D&C 132: thus saith the Lord / I am the Lord thy God / saith the Lord God / saith the Lord / I am the Lord thy God ... no man shall come unto the Father but by me / the only wise and true God, and Jesus Christ, whom he hath sent. I am he / saith the Lord; for I, the Lord, am thy God / saith the Lord your God / by my Father / the work of my Father / I, the Lord his God / I am Alpha and Omega.

THE FINAL ANALYSIS

PART 5

Smith and his Lamanites

Due to conclusive DNA evidence proving
Native Americans are not of Israelite descent,
the Mormon Church has watered down its previous
declaration in the 'Introduction' to the Book of Mormon.

It originally stated "After thousands of years, all were destroyed except the Lamanites, and they are *the principal* ancestors of the American Indians." In the 'Doubleday' edition of 2007 and later, in the online version of 2010, that statement was altered to read "…and they are *among the* ancestors of the American Indians."
http://lds.org/scriptures/bofm/introduction?lang=eng

From "principal" to "among" in one *unannounced* slick change.

Regarding the D&C, what did the *Lord* say directly to Joseph Smith and his associates regarding the Lamanites?

Surely, if anyone knows the truth, it should be the Lord…

This is what the Lord told Joseph Smith about the Lamanites.

D&C 3.16. Nevertheless, my work shall go forth, for inasmuch as the knowledge of a Savior has come unto the world, through the testimony of the Jews, even so shall the knowledge of a Savior come unto my people—

17. And to the Nephites, and the Jacobites, and the Josephites, and the Zoramites, through the testimony of their fathers—

18. And this testimony shall come to the knowledge of the Lamanites, and the Lemuelites, and the Ishmaelites, who dwindled in unbelief because of the iniquity of their fathers, whom the Lord has suffered to destroy their brethren the Nephites, because of their iniquities and their abominations.

19. And for this very purpose are these plates preserved which contain these records—that the promises of the Lord might be fulfilled, which he made to his people;

20. And that the Lamanites might come to the knowledge of their fathers, and that they might know the promises of the Lord, and that they may believe the gospel and rely upon the merits of Jesus Christ, and be glorified through faith in his name, and that through their repentance they might be saved. Amen.

D&C 10:48. Yea, and this was their faith—that my gospel, which I gave unto them that they might preach in their days, might come unto their brethren the Lamanites, and also all that had become Lamanites because of their dissensions.

D&C 19:27. Which is my word to the Gentile, that soon it may go to the Jew, of whom the Lamanites are a remnant, that they may believe the gospel, and look not for a Messiah to come who has already come.

D&C 28:8. And now, behold, I say unto you that you shall go unto the Lamanites and preach my gospel unto them; and inasmuch as they receive thy teachings thou shalt cause my church to be established among them; and thou shalt have revelations, but write them not by way of commandment.

9. And now, behold, I say unto you that it is not revealed, and no man knoweth where the city Zion shall be built, but it shall be given hereafter. Behold, I say unto you that it shall be on the borders by the Lamanites.

D&C 28:14. And thou shalt assist to settle all these things, according to the covenants of the church, before thou shalt take thy journey among the Lamanites.

D&C 30:6. And be you afflicted in all his afflictions, ever lifting up your heart unto me in prayer and faith, for his and your deliverance; for I have given unto him power to build up my church among the Lamanites;

THE FINAL ANALYSIS - PART 5. SMITH AND HIS LAMANITES

D&C 32:1. And now concerning my servant Parley P. Pratt, behold, I say unto him that as I live I will that he shall declare my gospel and learn of me, and be meek and lowly of heart.
2. And that which I have appointed unto him is that he shall go with my servants, Oliver Cowdery and Peter Whitmer, Jun., into the wilderness among the Lamanites.
3. And Ziba Peterson also shall go with them; and I myself will go with them and be in their midst; and I am their advocate with the Father, and nothing shall prevail against them.

D&C 49:24. But before the great day of the Lord shall come, Jacob shall flourish in the wilderness, and the Lamanites shall blossom as the rose.

D&C 54:8. And thus you shall take your journey into the regions westward, unto the land of Missouri, unto the borders of the Lamanites.

Not only did the early saints know exactly *who* and *where* the Lamanites were, the Lord actually sent men such as Parley P. Pratt, Oliver Cowdery, Peter Whitmer and Ziba Peterson to *teach* them the gospel *(D&C 32:1-3 above)*.

The Section 32 header confirms who the Lamanites were. *"supplication was made that the Lord would indicate his will as to whether elders should be sent at that time to* **the Indian tribes in the West***"* and the sub-heading for v.1-3 confirms *"Parley P. Pratt and Ziba Peterson are called to* **preach to the Lamanites** *and to accompany Oliver Cowdery and Peter Whitmer, Jr.* (Italics in original, bold added).

The following extract from an article appearing in the Salt Lake Tribune includes comment from my good friend and fellow author Simon Southerton.

> Many Mormons, including several church presidents, have taught that the Americas were largely inhabited by Book of Mormon peoples. In 1971, Church President Spencer W. Kimball said that Lehi, the family patriarch, was "the ancestor of all of the Indian and Mestizo tribes in North and South and Central America and in the islands of the sea."
>
> After testing the DNA of more than 12,000 Indians, though, most researchers have concluded that the continent's early inhabitants came from Asia across the Bering Strait.
>
> With this change, the LDS Church is "conceding that mainstream scientific theories about the colonization of the Americas have significant elements of truth in them," said Simon Southerton, a former Mormon and author of Losing a Lost Tribe: Native Americans, DNA and the Mormon Church.

> "DNA has revealed very clearly how closely related American Indians are to their Siberian ancestors," Southerton said in an e-mail from his home in Canberra, Australia. "The Lamanites are invisible, not principal ancestors." *(Salt Lake Tribune 8 Nov, 2007).*
> *(Currently available here:* http://www.sltrib.com/faith/ci_7403990*).*

The term Lamanite includes all Indians and Indian mixtures, such as the Polynesians, the Guatemalans, the Peruvians, as well as the Sioux, the Apache, the Mohawk, the Navajo, and others. It is a large group of great people. *(Of Royal Blood, Spencer W. Kimball, Ensign, July 1971, p. 7).*

Appendix A

In 1831. Joseph Smith became disturbed by the publication of a series of letters written by Ezra Booth, following Booth's 'apostasy' from the Church. *(See pp. 260-62).*

The following extracts will provide a flavour of the content of Ezra Booth's published letters. I hope they will also provide an incentive for the reader to take time at some stage to review all Booth's letters in full, in conjunction with D&C Sections 61 and 71 (and perhaps some in between). The letters provide insight into the underlying psychology of Smith's actions and his so-called revelations which can then be more fully appreciated. It quickly becomes clear what was really going on. The underhand methods employed by Smith and his closest associates get an airing in a rare first hand account by someone who was there and experienced a sequence of real events and false revelations.

Part 1.

Referenced from *p. 234* regarding D&C Section 61 *(see also TMD Vol. 4:284-92 or S45-53)*. This is Ezra Booth's account of the Missouri River experience.

Extract from Letter VII.

> The commandment we received to purchase, or make a water craft, directed us to proceed down the river in it as far as St. Louis, and from thence, with the exception of Joseph and his two scribes, we were to proceed on our journey home two by two. The means of conveyance being procured, we embarked for St. Louis, but unpropitious events rolled on, superceded the commandment, frustrated our plans, and we had separated before we had accomplished one half of the voyage. The cause which produced this disastrous result, was a spirit of animosity and discord, which made its appearance on board, the morning after we left Independence. The conduct of the Elders became very displeasing to Oliver, who, in the greatness of his power, uttered this malediction: "as the Lord God liveth, if you do not behave better, some accident will befall you." The manner in which this was handed out, evinced it to be the ebullition of a spirit, similar to that which influenced Joseph in the school-house. No accident, however, befell them, until Joseph, in the afternoon of the third day, assumed the direction of affairs on board that canoe, which, with other matters of difference, together with Oliver's curse, increased the irritation of the crew, who, in time of danger, refused to exert their physical powers, in consequence of which they ran foul of a sawyer, and were in danger of upsetting.

This was sufficient to flutter the timid spirit of the Prophet and his scribe, who had accompanied him on board of that canoe, and like the sea-tossed mariner, when threatened with a watery grave, they unanimously desired to set their feet once more upon something more firm than a liquid surface; therefore, by the persuasion of Joseph, we landed before sunset, to pass the night upon the bank of the river. Preparations were made to spend the night as comfortably as existing circumstances would admit, and then an attempt was made to effect a reconciliation between the contending parties. The business of settlement elicited much conversation, and excited considerable feeling on both sides. Oliver's denunciation was brought into view; his conduct and equipage were compared to "a fop of a sportsman;" he and Joseph were represented as highly imperious, and quite dictatorial; and Joseph and Sidney were reprimanded for their excessive cowardice. Joseph seemed inclined to arm himself, according to his usual custom, in case of opposition, with the judgments of God, for the purpose of pouring them, like a thunder bolt, upon the rebellious elders; but one or two retorted, "None of your threats;" which completely disarmed him, and he reserved his judgments for a more suitable occasion. Finding myself but little interested in the settlement, believing the principles of discord too deeply rooted to be easily eradicated, I laid myself down upon the ground, and in silence contemplated awhile the events of the evening, as they passed before me. These are the men to whom the Lord has intrusted the mysteries, and the keys of his kingdom; whom he has authorized to bind or loose on earth, and their decision shall be ratified in Heaven. These are the men sent forth, to promulgate a new revelation, and to usher in a new dispensation -- at whose presence the "Heavens are to shake, the hills tremble, the mountains quake, and the earth open and swallow up their enemies." -- These are the leaders of the church, and the only church on earth the Lord beholds with approbation. Surely, I never witnessed so much confusion and discord, among the Elders of any other church; nevertheless they are all doomed to be a perpetual curse; except they receive the doctrines and precepts which Mormonism [allocates], and place themselves under the tuition of men, more ignorant and unholy than themselves. In the midst of meditations like these, I sunk into the arms of sleep, but was awakened at a late hour, to witness and consent to a reconciliation between the parties. The next morning Joseph manifested an aversion to risk his person any more upon the rough and angry current of the Missouri, and, in fact, upon any other river; and he again had recourse to his usual method of freeing himself from the embarrassments of a former commandment, by obtaining another in opposition to it. A new commandment was issued, in which a great curse was pronounced against the waters: navigating them was to be attended with extreme danger; and all the

APPENDIX A – THE EZRA BOOTH LETTERS

saints, in general, were prohibited in journeying upon them, to the promised land. From this circumstance, the Missouri river was named the river of Destruction. It was decreed that we should proceed on our journey by land, and preach by the way as we passed along. Joseph, Sidney, and Oliver were to press their way forward with all possible speed, and to preach only in Cincinnati; and there they were to lift up their voices, and proclaim against the whole of that wicked city. The method by which Joseph and Co. designed to proceed home, it was discovered, would be very expensive. "The Lord don't care how much money it takes to get us home," said Sidney. Not satisfied with the money they received from the bishop, they used their best endeavours to exact money from others, who had but little, compared with what they had; telling them, in substance "You can beg your passage on foot, but as we are to travel in the stage we must have money." You will find, sir, that the expense of these three men was one hundred dollars more than three of our company expended, while on our journey home; and, for the sake of truth and honesty, let these men never again open their mouths, to insult the common sense of mankind, by contending for equality, and the community of goods in society, until there is a thorough alteration in their method of proceeding. It seems, however, they had drained their pockets, when they arrived at Cincinnati, for there they were under the necessity of pawning their trunk, in order to continue their journey home. Here they violated the commandment, by not preaching; and when an inquiry was made respecting the cause of that neglect, at one time they said they could get no house to preach in; at another time they stated that they could have had the court-house, had they stayed a day or two longer, but the Lord made it known to them that they should go on; and other similar excuses, involving like contradictions. Thus they turn and twist the commandments to suit their whims, and they violate them when they please with perfect impunity. They can any time obtain a commandment suited to their desires, and as their desires fluctuate and become reversed, they get a new one to supercede the other, and hence the contradictions which abound in this species of revelation. The next day after we were cast upon the shore, and had commenced our journey by land, myself and three others went on board of a canoe, and recommenced our voyage down the river. From this time a constant gale of prosperity wafted us forward, and not an event transpired, but what tended to our advancement, until we arrived at our much desired homes. At St. Louis, we took passage in a steam-boat, and came to Wellsville; and from thence in the stage home. We travelled afloat eight hundred miles further than the three who took their passage in the stage, and arrived at our homes but a few days later. -- It is true, we violated the commandment by not preaching by the way, and so did they by not preaching at Cincinnati. But it seems that none of us considered the commandment worthy of much notice. In this voyage upon the waters, we demonstrated that the great dangers existed only in imagination, and the commandment to be the offspring of a pusillanimous spirit.

When I wrote *TMD Volume 4*, I included an analysis *(on pp. 284-92)* of D&C Section 61. Within it I noted the following verses.

> **61:3.** But verily I say unto you, that it is not needful for this whole company of mine elders to be moving swiftly upon the waters, whilst the inhabitants on either side are perishing in unbelief.
> **4.** Nevertheless, I suffered it that ye might bear record; behold, there are many dangers upon the waters, and more especially hereafter;
> **5.** For I, the Lord, have decreed in mine anger many destructions upon the waters; yea, and especially upon these waters.

And I also made the following comment:

> As Smith seems to have *accepted* Phelps's daylight vision of the destroyer, which was not always a given, Smith reinforces God's curse by having God say "I, the Lord, have decreed, and the destroyer rideth upon the face thereof, and I revoke not the decree". The whole 'revelation' would never have been given were it not for Phelps and his vivid imagination.

I should now add that of course from the perspective provided by Ezra Booth, if Smith *was* afraid to continue travelling by canoe because the arguing men had almost upset it, then he would have welcomed the opportunity to not have to do so. In which case, Phelps' 'vision' would have been a very welcome scapegoat, so naturally Smith exploited rather than rejected it. Perhaps Joseph Smith could not swim. Perhaps Smith even prompted Phelps to say he had seen such a vision. It is also possible Phelps was somewhat disinclined to continue on with the canoe trip, thus imagining the story.

Whatever the case, it is interesting background information, as the history the Church portrays is always written as they would like it to have been and anything that detracts from Smith's position as a 'prophet, seer and revelator' is carefully excluded. Booth explains some of them ultimately went on in a canoe without incident – despite Smith's revelation that the waters were dangerous.

Something obvious, that I did not consider when writing *Volume 4*, is that if Smith's revelation was real and the Lord was right, why did he not 'reveal' all that before they even started to return by river? Why not give the revelation *before* they set off? In fact, in Section 60, the Lord didn't seem to mind what they did. In v.5-6 they are to make or buy a craft to actually go **by river**. Why

APPENDIX A – THE EZRA BOOTH LETTERS

was the Lord placing his servants in such danger – undisclosed until mid-way through the trip – when Smith got cold feet and wanted out of the canoe?

> **60:5.** But, verily, I will speak unto you concerning your journey unto the land from whence you came. *Let there be a craft made, or bought, as seemeth you good, it mattereth not unto me*, and take your *journey speedily for the place which is called St. Louis.*
> **6.** And from thence let my servants, **Sidney Rigdon, Joseph Smith, Jun., and Oliver Cowdery, take their journey for Cincinnati;**
> (Emphasis added).

I think the answer to the above question is quite obvious. They got less than half way to St. Louis before Smith and his pals bailed out, and despite Smith saying they should all continue by land, Booth and others continued peacefully in a canoe for several more days. From the above extract:

> The next day after we were cast upon the shore, and had commenced our journey by land, myself and three others went on board of a canoe, and recommenced our voyage down the river. From this time a constant gale of prosperity wafted us forward, and not an event transpired, but what tended to our advancement, until we arrived at our much desired homes.

The Lord says it doesn't matter to him whether they buy or make a craft, in Section 60, but they are to go by river; and yet in Section 61:18 he declares:

> **61:18.** And now I give unto you a commandment that what I say unto one I say unto all, that you shall forewarn your brethren concerning these waters, that they come not in journeying upon them, lest their faith fail and they are caught in snares;

Also in Section 60, the Lord says that from St. Louis, they are to preach along the way home, but "not in haste".

> **60:8.** And let the residue take their journey from St. Louis, two by two, *and preach the word, not in haste*, among the congregations of the wicked, until they return to the churches from whence they came. (Emphasis added).

Yet in Section 61:8, Gilbert and Phelps are to "be in haste upon their errand and mission", and in v.9, the two are to "take their journey in haste that they may fill their mission". New revelations sometimes contradicted earlier ones.

THE MORMON DELUSION
Part 2.

Referenced from *p. 262* regarding D&C Section 71.

Smith sent a number of men, including Ezra Booth, to Missouri, claiming the Lord had given him a revelation that a large branch of the Church had been established there by Oliver Cowdery. The reality, quickly discovered upon their arrival, was that there were just three or four families, as we later learn in letter seven, an extract from which I have placed first to give better perspective. This is followed by a brief selection of other interesting extracts.

Letter VII:

The first thing that materially affected my mind, so as to weaken my confidence, was the falsehood of Joseph's vision. You know perfectly well, that Joseph had, or said he had, a vision, or revelation, in which it was made known to him by the spirit, that Oliver had raised up a large church in Missouri. This was so confidently believed, previous to our leaving Ohio, that while calculating the number of the church, several hundred were added, supposed to be in Missouri. The great church was found to consist of three or four families...

When you complained that he had abused you, you observed to him, "I wish you not to tell us any more, that you know these by the spirit when you do not; you told us, that Oliver had raised up a large church here, and there is no such thing;" he replied, "I see it, and it will be so." This appeared to me, to be a shift, better suited to an impostor, than to a true Prophet of the Lord.

Letter I:

At times I was much elated; but generally, things in prospect were the greatest stimulants to action. On our arrival in the western part of the State of Missouri the place of our destination, we discovered that prophecy and vision had failed, or rather had proved false. -- The fact was so notorious, and the evidence so clear, that no one could mistake it -- so much so, that Mr. Rigdon himself said that "Joseph's vision was a bad thing." This was glossed over, apparently, to the satisfaction of most persons present; but not fully to my own...

APPENDIX A – THE EZRA BOOTH LETTERS
Other Selected Extracts:

Letter I:

Since my return, I have had several interviews with Messrs. Smith, Rigdon and Cowdery, and the various shifts and turns, to which they resorted in order to obviate objectors and difficulties, produced in my mind additional evidence, that there was nothing else than a deeply laid plan of craft and deception...

The scenes of the past few months, are so different from all others in my life, that they are in truth to me "as a dream when one awaketh." Had my fall affected only myself, my reflections would be far less painful than they now are. But to know -- that whatever influence I may have possessed, has been exerted to draw others into a delusion, from which they may not soon be extricated, is to me a source of sorrow and deep regret. They are at this moment the object of my greatest anxiety and commiseration. I crave their forgiveness...

Letter II:

Judgments are denounced against the sinners of this generation; or in other words, all who reject the Book of Mormon, are threatened with eternal damnation. Great promises are made to such as embrace it, signs and wonders are to attend them, such as healing the sick, the blind made to see, the lame to walk, &c; and they are to receive an everlasting inheritance in "the land of Missouri," where the Savior will make his second appearance; at which place the foundation of the temple of God, and the City of Zion, have been laid, and are soon to be built. It is also to be a city of Refuge, and a safe asylum when the storms of vengeance shall pour upon the earth, and those who reject the Book of Mormon, shall be swept off as with the besom of destruction. Then shall the riches of the Gentiles be consecrated to the Mormonites; they shall have lands and cattle in abundance, and shall possess the gold and silver, and all the treasures of their enemies...

Every thing in the church is done by commandment: and yet it is said to be done by the voice of the church. For instance, Smith gets a commandment that he shall be the "head of the church," or that he "shall rule the Conference," or that the Church shall build him an elegant house, and give him 1000 dollars. For this the members of the church must vote, or they will be cast off for revelling against the commandments of the Lord...

Joseph Smith, Jun., Sidney Rigdon, Oliver Cowdery and Martin Harris, may be considered as the principals in this work; and let Martin Harris tell the story, and he is the most conspicuous of the four. – He informed me, that he went to the place where Joseph resided, and Joseph had given it up, on account of the opposition of his wife and others; but he told Joseph. "I have not come down here for nothing, and we will go on with it." Martin Harris is what may be called a great talker, and extravagant boaster; so much so, that he renders himself disagreeable to many of his society…

Letter III:

Smith is the only one at present, to my knowledge, who pretends to hold converse with the inhabitants of the celestial world. It seems, from his statements, that he can have access to them when and where he pleases. He does not pretend that he sees them with his natural, but with his spiritual, eyes; and he says he can see them as well with his eyes shut, as with them open. So also in the translating. The subject stands before his eyes in print, but it matters not whether his eyes are open or shut; he can see as well one way as the other. You have probably read the testimony of the three witnesses appended to the Book of Mormon. These witnesses testify that an angel appeared to them, and presented them the golden plates, and the voice of God declared it to be a divine record. To this they frequently testify, in the presence of large congregations. When in Missouri, I had an opportunity to examine a commandment given to these witnesses, previous to their seeing the plates. They were informed that they should see and hear these things by faith, and then they should testify to the world, as though they had seen and heard, as I see a man, and hear his voice: but after all, it amounts simply to this – that by faith or imagination, they saw the plates and the angel, and by faith or imagination they heard the voice of the Lord.

In the last paragraph, Booth is referring to what is now Section 17. The full text of Ezra Booth's letters is available in *Howe, 1834*; currently available to read online at the following link:

http://www.truthnet.org/mormon/mormonismunveiled/15_1831Ezrabooth.htm

Appendix B

Extracts from 'Mormonism Unvailed' [sic]. E. D. Howe. 1834.

In my work, I have endeavoured to avoid speculation, personal opinion and supposition, sticking to evidence and facts in order to establish the truth. There are many external accounts concerning how the Smith family were seen from the 'outside' which the Church ignores, claiming them biased and unreliable.

Indeed, I am sure some of them are speculative or hearsay rather than from first hand experience. However, it is perfectly clear from all the available evidence that in turn, the Church, both historically and today, also manipulated and rewrote its own history with extreme bias and that it too is more than unreliable. Proof of that lies in almost every page of my work.

I thought I would add to this volume, just a few words from one 'outside' account which gives some perspective otherwise unavailable to those studying Mormon Church history. It is not included in any way as evidence of the truth. It is simply a view from outside which is included here simply out of historical interest. In part, perhaps it balances the scales and the reader may recognise a little of what may really have happened at the very beginning in the following short extracts.

> **Page11.** We find them in the town of Manchester, Ontario county, N.Y. which was the principal scene of their operations, till the year 1830. All who became intimate with them during this period, unite in representing the general character of old Joseph and wife, the parents of the pretended Prophet, as lazy, indolent, ignorant and superstitious -- having a firm belief in ghosts and witches; the telling of fortunes; pretending to believe that the earth was filled with hidden treasures, buried there by Kid or the Spaniards. Being miserably poor, and not much disposed to obtain an honorable livlihood by labor, the energies of their minds seemed to be mostly directed towards finding where these treasures were concealed, and the best mode of acquiring their possession.
>
> **Page 12.** Joseph. Jun. in the mean time, had become very expert in the arts of necromancy, jugling, the use of the divining rod, and looking into what they termed a "peep-stone," by which means he soon collected about him a gang of idle, credulous young men, to perform the labor of digging into the hills and mountains, and other lonly places, in that vicinity, in search of gold. In process of time many pits were dug in the neighborhood, which were afterwards pointed out as the place from whence the plates were excavated. But we do not learn that the young impostor ever entered these

excavations for the purpose of assisting his sturdy dupes in their labors. His business was to point out the locations of the treasures, which he did by looking at a stone placed in a hat. Whenever the diggers became dissatisfied at not finding the object of their desires, his inventive and fertile genius would generally contrive a story to satisfy them. For instance, he would tell them that the treasure was removed by a spirit just before they came to it, or that it sunk down deeper into the earth.

Pp. 14-15. He [Martin Harris] engaged in the new Bible business with a view of making a handsome sum of money from the sale of the books, as he was frequently heard to say. The whole expense of publishing an edition of 5000 copies, which was borne by Martin, to secure the payment of which, he mortgaged his farm for $3000. Having failed in his anticipations about the sale of the books, (the retail price of which they said was fixed by an Angel at $1.75, but afterwards reduced to $1.25, and from that down to any price they could obtain) he adopted Smith as his Prophet, Priest and King. Since that time, the frequent demands upon Martin's purse have reduced it to a very low state.

Page17. ...various verbal accounts, all contradictory, vague, and inconsistent ... were given out by the Smith family respecting the finding of certain Gold or brazen plates... They say that some two years previous to the event taking place, Joseph, Jun., began his interviews with Angels, or spirits, who informed him of the wonderful plates, and the manner and time of obtaining them. This was to be done in the presence of his wife and first child, which was to be a son. In the month of September, 1827, Joseph got possession of the plates, after a considerable struggle with a spirit. The remarkable event was soon noised abroad, and the Smith family commenced making proselytes among the credulous, and lovers of the marvelous, to the belief that Joseph had found a record of the first settlers in America. Many profound calculations were made about the amount of their profits on the sale of such a book. A. religious speculation does not seem to have seriously entered into their heads at that time. The plates in the mean time were concealed from human view, the prophet declaring that no man could look upon them and live. They at the same time gave out that, along with the plates, was found a huge pair of silver spectacles, altogether too large for the present race of men, but which were to be used, nevertheless, in translating the plates.

Page 18. Instead of looking at the characters inscribed upon the plates, the prophet was obliged to resort to the old "peep stone," which he formerly used in money-digging. This he placed in a hat, or

APPENDIX B – EXTRACTS FROM MORMONISM UNVAILED

box, into which he also thrust his face. Through the stone he could then discover a single word at a time, which he repeated aloud to his amanuensis, who committed it to paper, when another word would immediately appear, and thus the performance continued to the end of the book.

Another account they give of the translation, is, that it was performed with the big spectacles before mentioned, and which were in fact, the identical *Urim and Thumim* mentioned in Exodus 28 -- 30, and were brought away from Jerusalem by the heroes of the book, handed down from one generation to another, and finally buried up in Ontario county, some fifteen centuries since, to enable Smith to translate the plates *without looking at them!*

Page 19. The Golden Bible was finally got ready for the press, and issued in the summer of 1830, nearly three years from the time of its being dug up. It is a book of nearly six hundred pages, and is unquestionably one of the meanest in the English, or any other language. It is more devoid of interest than any we have ever seen. It must have been written by an atheist, to make an experiment upon the human understanding and credulity. The author, although evidently a man of learning, studied barrenness of style and expression, without an equal. It carries condemnation on every page. The God of Heaven, that all-wise Being, could never have delivered such a farrago of nonsense to the world. *(Howe, 1834).*

I find it quite fascinating to read of how others saw the Smith family and the commencement of Mormonism. The view of Mormons today is moulded by the Church and its publications to fit a perception that is provably far from the truth. Whether books such this one by E. D. Howe are entirely accurate or not doesn't much matter and I do not reference them as evidence in my work. The fact is that no matter what the ultimate truth is, it is *not* what Smith claimed and not what the Church teaches today. That is the only fact that really matters.

For those who are interested, Howe's book is available (along with others) to read or download free from the internet. Just use a search engine to find the current locations. This is one presently available link: http://www.truthnet.org/mormon/mormonismunveiled/

Appendix C

When the Nauvoo Temple was opened for business, Brigham Young was still formulating ideas for the new ceremony which Joseph Smith had asked Young to complete. This would continue for several decades *(See TMD Vol. 3: Sec. 3)*.

The following entry from the 'Nauvoo Temple Journal' gives an idea as to how far Young had got at the time. The following was *new* detail on that day.

> Last evening an arrangement was made establishing better order in conducting the endowment. Under this order it is the province of Eloheem, Jehovah and Michael to create the world, plant the Garden and create the man and give his help meet. Eloheem gives the charge to Adam in the Garden and thrust them into the telestial kingdom or the world. Then Peter assisted by James and john conducts them through the Telestial and Terrestrial kingdom administering the charges and tokens in each and conducts them to the vail where they are received by the Eloheem and after talking with him by words and tokens are admitted by him into the Celestial Kingdom.... *(Nauvoo Temple Journal, 13 December 1845).*

An account of the Nauvoo Temple Ceremony, as held in February of 1846 was recorded by Increase Van Deusen and his wife Maria; it gives an idea of how things were at first in the new Mormon temple. Their record is not entirely accurate of course, but these extracts will give some idea of what went on. The extracts are somewhat reformatted for ease of reading; original words retained.

> The following is what myself and wife were taken through personally in the Temple, in 1846, in the month of February, said to be our reward from God for four years' labor on the Temple. The Drama, (as I call it) runs thus: We have a notice to appear at the Temple at five in the morning. I am instructed to wear drawers; they are to be white. My wife is to bring her night clothes with her. –
>
> We are first conducted through a narrow temporary hall, where we meet a man stationed; he says to us, "you must here separate" - directs me through a door to the right, my wife through one at the left, in an opposite direction:
>
> I am here ordered by a conductor to lay off my clothes, all but shirt and drawers...
>
> We are taken from this into another room: In this room is a temporary bath of water on the floor. We are now ordered by the conductor to divest our selves of the remaining part of our clothing.

THE MORMON DELUSION

They now put us in this bath and wash us all over, from head to foot, accompanied with the following ceremony: "I wash you that you may be clean to perform the work assigned you; your eyes, that you may see the glory of God; your ears, that you may hear His voice: your mouth, that you may speak forth His praise; your arms and breast, that you may be strong to perform His work; and so down to our feet, that we may be swift to run the race," &c. We are, all this time, rolled and tumbled about in the bath, - at last, the priest lays his hands on our heads and pronounces us clean, in the name of the Lord. –

We are then taken by another priest, who turns oil on our heads, from a horn, until it runs partly over the body. We are thus annointed all over - even to the soles of the feet. After this, we are placed on a stool, and ordained to power and authority, for time and eternity. I was ordained to be King in time and eternity, and my wife to be Queen. After being ordained King, I am presented with, and have put on, what they call an under garment. This is a tight fit, made of white cotton cloth, with two marks in it; a square on the breast, and a compass on the knee.

We are told this garment represents the white stone in scripture, in which was a new name given. We here have a new name given us. We are told, also, that we are always to wear this garment under our clothes, while we are in the world. God has ordered this; and we can receive no harm while we have it on. The name I received was Lehi, one of the names of the Book of Mormon. This name I was forbidden to reveal to any but the one at the door of the Celestial Kingdom. What this meant, I found our afterwards. The compass on the knee signifies our willingness to now always; the square, God's protection, &c. We now have put on us, over this under garment, a common shirt.

In this dress, after so much ceremony, we are conducted into a third room, where a lesson commences, as the reader will see by attention. We are now seated - all is silent for a while; the silence is at length broken by a rumbling noise, as from a distance; the noise terminates in a voice, as follows: "Let the light be divided from the darkness; let the light be called day, and the darkness night: Let there be a firmament in the midst of the waters; let the firmament be called heaven; let the waters under the firmament be gathered together into one place, and let the dry land appear; let the dry land be called earth; and the gathering together of the waters, seas; let the earth bring forth grass, the herb yielding seed, and the fruit-tree yielding fruit, after his kind, whose seed is in itself upon the earth; let the earth bring forth the living creature after his kind, cattle and creeping things and beasts of the earth, after their kind."

APPENDIX C – EARLY TEMPLE EXPERIENCES

After the individual thus representing the Lord behind the curtain, (as in the act of creation) is supposed to have created the heavens and the earth, cattle, beasts, creeping things, fowls of the air, fish of the sea, &c., he continues his work further, and says, "Now let us go down and make man in our image, after our likeness." All this time we are seated in silence, hearing, but not seeing anything, and knowing not what is to take place the next moment; for all is new and unexpected, from first to last, of this whole drama. When he says, "Let us go down and make man," we hear his footsteps approaching the room where we are seated; he comes in - comes to where we are - puts his hand to the floor, and then on us, as if fulfilling this scripture: "And the Lord God formed man of the dust of the ground and breathed into his nostrils the breath of life; and man became a living soul."

After going on, as if forming us newly of the dust of the ground, he stoops down and breathes on us, and now we are supposed to first spring into life. We are next ordered to change our position from sitting to a sleeping one, as if fulfilling, "And the Lord God caused a deep sleep to fall upon Adam, and he slept." We are now ordered to put our heads down low, and feign ourselves in a deep sleep. The individual representing the Almighty, continues his work as if fulfilling, "And he took a rib, and the rib which the Lord God had taken from man made he a woman, and brought her unto the man."

After he has taken the rib, he passes out of the room and is supposed to have formed the woman of the rib; he soon returns with a woman and places her directly before us, as we are sitting, heads down, as if in deep sleep. We are now saluted with a loud voice, "Adam, here is thy companion. I give her to be with thee - what wilt thou call her?" He awaked out of sleep and answers, "This is now bone of my bone and flesh of my flesh, she shall be called woman, because she was taken out of man." This was my wife whom I parted with on first entering the Temple; she has passed through two rooms, in the same ceremony that I have gone through, precisely, only conducted by the females exclusively.

We are now brought together in the third room; she is brought in her night clothes. We are now supposed to be Adam and Eve, and the reason of my shirt's being out side, and she having on night clothes, is, to represent nature. I now am ordered to take Eve and follow our conductor out through a partition door into another apartment; and what should you suppose we there behold? A large room, the floor all nicely covered with green trees, shrubbery, flowers, &c. Representing the garden of Eden. We follow a conductor about this temporary garden, beholding the strange and unexpected scenery that has just presented itself to our view. He says, "This is a beautiful place, every thing delightful for the eye and taste - of all these things you may freely eat; but of the tree of the knowledge of good and evil, thou shalt not eat; neither shalt thou touch it, for in the day thou eatest thereof thou shalt surely die."

He leaves the garden, and in a few moments another individual comes in, representing the Devil. He walks round between the trees and peaks and skulks, as if intent on some mischief, and coming to the tree which we have been forbidden to partake of, he says to Eve: "This is the best of all the fruit of the garden," and solicits her to partake. She takes, eats, and gives to Adam. While we are amu[s]ing ourselves with the delicious taste of the fruit, (which is raisins tied on a small tree on the floor) the conductor starts up all of a sudden, and says, "Hark! The Lord is coming; let us hide!" We are ordered to squ[at] down behind the shrubbery on the floor.

The supposed Lord's foot steps are now heard - coming in, he walks about on the floor, at last calls out, "Adam! where art thou?" We answer, "we heard thy voice and footsteps in the garden, and were afraid, and hid ourselves." And he says, "Who told thee that thou was naked? Hast thou eaten of the tree whereof I command thee not to eat?" The answer is, "The woman whom thou gavest to be with me, she gave me of the tree and I did eat."

He then turns to the woman, and says, "What is this that thou hast done?" She answers, "The Serpent beguiled me and I did eat." He now turns to the individual representing the Devil, and says, "Because thou hast done this, thou art cursed above all cattle, and above every beast of the field; upon thy belly shalt thou go, and dust shalt eat all the days of thy life."

The Devil is now supposed to have on him the curse, and he gets down on his belly and crawls out of the room or garden. To the woman he now adds, "I will greatly multiply thy sorrow and thy conception; in sorrow thou shalt bring forth children," &c. And unto the man he says, "Because thou hast hearkened unto the voice of thy wife, and hast eaten of the tree of which I commanded thee, saying, thou shalt not eat of it; cursed is the ground for thy sake: in sorrow shalt thou eat of it all the days of thy life. Thorns and thistles shall it bring forth to thee; in the sweat of thy face shalt thou eat bread, till thou return unto the ground; for dust thou art, and unto the dust shalt thou return." He adds, "the man is now as one of us, knowing good and evil. Thou shalt now be sent forth to till the ground from whence thou wast taken."

APPENDIX C – EARLY TEMPLE EXPERIENCES

We now have aprons put on of white cloth, about eighteen inches square with green silk leaves pasted on. We are ordered to kneel down to an altar that stands on the centre [center] of the floor. We are now instructed in many things with regard to the fall, the law of God, &c.

We have also certain signs and tokens given. One of the grips, is, the two right hands clasped with the end of the thumbs on the upper joint of the fore fingers; second, the end of the thumbs directly between the upper two joints of the first and second fingers. One of the key-words is the Sun [Son]. We are particularly instructed in these signs, key-words, grips, &c., three of each.

After some more ceremony of not much consequence, we are conducted into another, a fifth room, which is a representation of the present Religious world, or Adam and Eve, six thousand years old, having been engaged for eighteen hundred years in promulgating the sectarian religion, except the Mormon, (for this is what is represented in this room.) Our attention is now attracted by an individual coming in from an adjoining room, representing the Devil. He comes in great glee, hopping and skipping about the floor, holding in his hand a long-handled wooden noggin, which holds about a pint. He says, "Good morning brother Methodist, Presbyterian, Roman Catholic, Baptist, Universalist, Shaking-Quaker, Millerite, Campbellite," &c., enumerating all the sects of the day, except the Mormons: "Come, let us drink the cup of fellowship this morning." He now drinks, and hands the noggin to us; we drink, and hand it back.

He then goes on with a long ceremony, as follows: "Wel[l], brethren, you have done well - had a great many revivals - gained a numerous host of converts, and would have succeeded in getting the whole world into some of our churches, had it not been for that Joe Smith and the Mormons. They are round every where, preaching that we are all wrong - not organized according to Scri[ptu]re, and say we (Protestants) have no authority to preach, except what we have got from the Catholics, and all the world agrees that is good for nothing.

And now, brethren of the sects, I tell you that Mormon plan is an almighty one, and much to be dreaded - it strikes at the very root and foundation of all our holy religion, and will eventually become the prevailing religion, unless something can be done to stop it. It has been supposed a humbug, and would soon come to naught. But this supposition is founded altogether in ignorance. Now, who can not but see his (Joe's [Joseph Smith's]) plan is well calculated to undermine all of us."

THE MORMON DELUSION

He says, "God has nothing to do with our churches - he has never sent us to preach; and they have the impudence to ask us to show our authority, and this we cannot do, of course. It is true, we read in the Bible, 'Go ye into all the world, and preach the Gospel to every creature;' but they say that commission is not to us, but to men of that generation in which it was given. (And is not this true?) Now, the world has been long wondering how so many ways could be right, and differing one from the other; and Mormonism is calculated to unravel all this mystery; and they come right out and say we have all been preaching men's precepts for the commandments of God. And now, I tell you there is much truth in their sayings. We might as well know the truth, and then prepare ourselves accordingly. We could do well when our authoirty was not questioned; but when they come with the evidence they bring, and say, 'They are sent by Revelation;' I tell you it is not easy to withstand them. And finally, brethren, I am satisfied that it will not do to undertake to hold an argument with them, and we had better let them entirely alone, and neither hear nor read any of their books, but keep up the popular cry, 'Oh, how great is the delusion of Joe Smith and Mormonism! Oh, how great!' and as long as we can keep the people ignorant of their real principles, we shall do well. Now, brethren, of all sects, we are talking over things this morning among ourselves - and it must not go to the world." &c.

After a long ceremony of this kind in favor of the Mormon Fraternity, we are interrupted by another individual coming in, supposed to have been sent directly from Heaven, with authority and great power. He commands the Devil to depart and let these deceived people (the sects,) alone, and trouble them no longer; for the time has come when they shall be delivered from your Satanic influence and power, by which they have been bound since the Apostolic age of the world.

The Devil now reluctantly withdraws, and makes towards the door, looking back over his shoulder at the heavenly messenger, and halts, as if at a loss to leave or stay. He is now commanded again, in the name of the Lord, to leave, and let the sects alone. He now drops his noggin and flees out of the room with great haste and fury; we, Adam in his shirt-tail and Eve in her night-gown, are left standing.

After hearing all this conversation, supposed to be contaminated with some one of the religions of the day, except Mormonism, we are taken by the heavenly messenger and instructed in Mormon doctrine, exclusively, and supposed to be converted to that faith; in token whereof, we have our clothing changed, and are dressed in white linen, exactly alike.

APPENDIX C – EARLY TEMPLE EXPERIENCES

We are now conducted into another secret room, in the centre of which is an altar with three books on it - the Bible, Book of Mormon, and Doctrine and Covenants, (or Joseph's Revelations.) We are required to kneel at this altar, where we have an oath administered to us to this effect; that we will avenge the blood of Joseph Smith on this Nation, and teach our children the same. They tell us that the nation has winked at the abuse and persecution of the Mormons, and the murder of the Prophet in particular; Therefore the Lord is displeased with the nation, and means to destroy it; and this is the excuse for forming this league or conspiracy.

We are also sworn by a solemn oath, that we will never divulge what we here see, and do, and agree to, &c. in this Holy Temple. The penalty is, if we do, we agree to let them take our lives, and the manner of taking them is described: Our bowels are to be taken out, throats cut across, tongues taken out by the roots, &c. We now have signs, tokens, key-words, &c. given, of a higher order than those given in the garden, the particulars of which we do not distinctly recollect.

After this, we are conducted to a veil, behind which stands a man - we converse with him awhile through this veil, which is composed of very thin cloth. We here give the signs, new name, &c. which are the conditions of our entrance. A door is now knocked at, a few feet to the left of this veil, by our conductor. One from within asks, "who is there?" Our conductor says, one having kept all the commandments of God, (referring to this ceremony) desires to enter the kingdom and be forever with the Lord." We now pass through this door into a large room, representing the celestial kingdom of God. Here we are clothed in white robes, and have crowns put on our heads, and are really King and Queen, according Mormon theory.

(Increase Van Deusen. 1847. The Mormon Endowment; A Secret Drama, or Conspiracy, in the Nauvoo Temple, in 1846. pp. 3-9. Syracuse, NY: N.M.D. Lathrop).

Bibliography, Recommended Books & Web Sites
(The following relate to Volumes 1, 2, 3, 4 & 5 of this work).

Anderson, Lavina F. (ed.). 2001. *Lucy's Book. A Critical Edition of Lucy Mack Smith's Family Memoir*. Salt Lake City, UT: Signature Books.
Anderson, Rodger I. 1990. *Joseph Smith's New York Reputation Re-examined*. Salt Lake City, UT: Signature Books.
Andrus, Hyrum Leslie. 1968. *God, Man, and the Universe*. Salt Lake City, UT: Bookcraft.
Baer, Dick & Robertson, Jim. (Comp.). 2002. *False Prophecies of Joseph Smith*. Mesa, AZ: Concerned Christians.
Bagley, Will. 2004. *Blood of the Prophets: Brigham Young and the Massacre at Mountain Meadows*. Oklahoma, OK: University of Oklahoma Press.
Bancroft, Hubert Howe. 1889. *History of Utah*. San Francisco, CA: The History Company. †
Barrett, David B; Kurian, George Thomas; Johnson, Todd M. 2001. *World Christian Encyclopaedia*. New York, NY: Oxford University Press.
Baskin. R.N. 1914. *Reminiscences of Early Utah*. Salt Lake City, UT: Tribune. †
Bauder, Peter. 1834. *The Kingdom and the Gospel of Jesus Christ: Contrasted with That of Anti-Christ. A Brief Review of Some of the Most Interesting Circumstances, Which Have Transpired Since the Institution of the Gospel of Christ, from the Days of the Apostles*. Canajoharie, New York, NY: A. H. Calhoun.
Beadle, J. H. 1872. See: Hickman, Bill.
Bennett, John C. 1842. *Mormonism Exposed - History of the Saints*. Boston, MA: Leland & Whiting. †
Bergera, Gary James. (ed.). 1989. *Line upon Line. Essays on Mormon Doctrine*. Salt Lake City, UT: Signature Books.
— 2002. *Conflict in the Quorum*. Salt Lake City, UT: Signature Books.
A Book of Commandments, for the Government of the Church of Christ, organised According to Law, on the 6th April, 1830. 1833. Reprinted 1972. Independence, MO: Herald House. †
The Book of Mormon, (BOM) 1830. Joseph Smith Jr. New York, NY: Egbert B. Grandin. †
— 1981 Edition. Joseph Smith Jr. Salt Lake City, UT: LDS Church. †
Brodie, Fawn M. 1963. *No Man Knows My History: The Life of Joseph Smith, the Mormon Prophet*. Great Britain 1st Edition. London: Eyre & Spottiswoode. (First U.S. Edition 1945. New York, NY: Alfred A. Knopf). §
Brooks, Juanita. 2003. *The Mountain Meadows Massacre*. Oklahoma, OK: University of Oklahoma Press.
Brown, Hugh B. 1965. *The Abundant Life*. Salt Lake City, UT: Bookcraft.
Brown, S. Kent; Cannon, Donald Q; Jackson, Richard H. (eds.). 1994. *Historical Atlas of Mormonism*, New York: Simon and Schuster.
Budge, E.A. Wallis. 1989. (First published 1893). *The Mummy, A Handbook of Egyptian Funerary Archaeology*. New York, NY: Dover Publications Inc.

Buerger, David John. 2002. *The Mysteries of Godliness: A History of Mormon Temple Worship*. Salt Lake City, UT: Signature Books.
Campbell, Alexander. 1832. *Delusions: An Analysis of The Book of Mormon*. Boston, MA: Benjamin H. Greene. †
Campbell, Eugene E. 1988. *Establishing Zion*. Salt Lake City, UT: Signature Books. †
— (ed.). 1992. *The Essential Brigham Young*. Salt Lake City, UT: Signature. †
Cannon, Frank J. & Harvey J. 1911. *Under the Prophet in Utah; the National Menace of a Political Priestcraft*. Boston, MA: C.M. Clark Publishing. †
Cannon, George Q. 1907. *The Life of Joseph Smith, the Prophet*. Salt Lake City, UT: Deseret News.
The Catholic Encyclopedia. 1907-1912. New York, NY: Appleton. † Online version of original print publication: 2003. Kevin Knight. Located at: www.newadvent.org
Christensen, Culley K. 1981. *The Adam-God Maze*. Independent Publishers.
Church Almanac. (Published annually as *Deseret Morning News Church Almanac*). 2006 & 2007 editions cited. Salt Lake City, UT: Deseret Morning News.
Clark, Rev. John Alonzo. 1842. *Gleanings by the Way*. Philadelphia, PA: W.J. & J.K. Simon; New York, NY: Robert Carter.*
Collier, Fred C. & Harwell, William S. (eds.). 2002. *Kirtland Council Minute Book*. Salt Lake City, UT: Collier's Publishing Co.
Collier, Fred C. 1979. *Unpublished Revelations of the Prophets and Presidents of The Church of Jesus Christ of Latter-Day Saints*. 3 Vols. Salt Lake City, UT: Collier's Publishing Co.
— 2005. (ed.). *Nauvoo High Council Minute Books of The Church of Jesus Christ of Latter Day Saints*. Salt Lake City, UT: Collier's Publishing Co.
Comprehensive History of the Church. See: Roberts, B. H. 1978.
Compton, Todd. 1997. *In Sacred Loneliness: The Plural Wives of Joseph Smith*. Salt Lake City, UT: Signature Books. §
Cowan, Marvin W. 1997. *Mormon Claims Answered*. Salt Lake City, UT: UTLM. †
Cowley, Matthias F. 1964. *Wilford Woodruff: History of his Life and Labors*. Salt Lake City, UT: Bookcraft.
Cox, Brian & Cohen, Andrew. 2011. *Wonders of the Universe*. London: Harper Collins Publishers Ltd.
Cox, Brian & Forshaw, Jeff. 2011. *The Quantum Universe: Everything that can happen does happen*. London: Allen Lane; Penguin Books Ltd.
Davies, Glynn. 2002. *A History of Money from Ancient Times to the Present Day*. Cardiff: University of Wales.
Dawkins, Richard. 2003. *The Devil's Chaplain*. London: Weidenfeld & Nicolson.
— 2006. *The God Delusion*. London: Bantam Press. (Transworld). §
— 2009. *The Greatest Show on Earth: The Evidence for Evolution*. London: Bantam Press. §
— 2011. *The Magic of Reality: How we Know what's Really True*. London: Random House Group (Transworld). §
Daynes, Kathryn M. 2001. *More Wives than One, Transformation of the Mormon Marriage System 1840 - 1910*. Urbana & Chicago, IL: University of Illinois Press. †

BIBLIOGRAPHY, RECOMMENDED BOOKS & WEB SITES

Dialogue, A Journal of Mormon Thought. An ongoing series of articles concerning the Church, available online www.dialoguejournal.com or www.lib.utah.edu/digital

A Dictionary of the Bible. (10 Vols). 1900. Hastings, James (1852-1922). New York, NY: C. Scribner's sons. (Referenced: Vol 2: Part 1. 2004. Hastings, James. (ed.). University Press of the Pacific).

Doctrine and Covenants (D&C). 1981. Salt Lake City, UT: LDS Church. †

Duncan, Malcolm A. 1866. *Duncan's Masonic Ritual and Monitor. (Duncan's Ritual of Freemasonry:* 2007). New York, NY: Dover Publications. Complete 1866 original work available online at: www.sacred-texts.com/mas/dun/

The Elders' Journal of The Church of Jesus Christ of Latter Day Saints. (Elders' Journal). 4 Issues. (Vol.1:1-4): Oct & Nov 1837 (Kirtland, OH), Jul & Aug 1838 (Far West, MO).

Encyclopædia Britannica. 2007. Online version also available at www.britannica.com

Encyclopedia of Mormonism. (EM) 1992. Online Version. New York, NY: Macmillan. Available at: www.lib.byu.rdu/Macmillan/

Evans, Arza. 2003. *The Keystone of Mormonism.* St. George, UT: Keystone Books. §

Evans, Richard C. 1920. *Forty Years in the Mormon Church: Why I Left It!* Toronto, Canada: Bishop R. C. Evans (Self Published). †

FAIR — *The Foundation for Apologetic Information and Research.* (Mormon Apologetics). Available online at: www.fairlds.org/

FARMS — *The Foundation for Ancient Research and Mormon Studies.* Now renamed: *The Neal A. Maxwell Institute for Religious Scholarship.* (Mormon Apologetics). Available online at: http://farms.byu.edu/

Faulring, Scott H. (ed.). 1989. *An American Prophet's Record: The Diaries and Journals of Joseph Smith.* Salt Lake City, UT: Signature Books.

Fielding, Robert Kent. 1992. *The Unsolicited Chronicler.* New Mexico: Paradigm.

Froiseth, Jennie Anderson. (ed.). 1881. *The Women of Mormonism: Or The Story of Polygamy as Told by the Victims Themselves.* Detroit, MI: C.G.G. Paine. † §

Gibbs, Josiah F. 1910. *Mountain Meadows Massacre.* Salt Lake City, UT: Salt Lake Tribune. †

Hall, William. 1852. *The Abominations of Mormonism Exposed.* Cincinnati, OH: I. Hart & Co.

Hawthornthwaite, Samuel. 1857. *Mr. Hawthornthwaite's Adventures among the Mormons as an Elder, During the Last Eight Years.* Manchester, England. Published by author. Currently available: http://www.jstor.org/pss/60238014 §

Hardy, B. Carmon. 1992. *Solemn Covenant, the Mormon Polygamous Passage.* Illinois: University of Illinois Press.

Hickman, Bill. (The Danite Chief of Utah). 1872. *Brigham's Destroying Angel.* Salt Lake City, UT: Shepard Publishing Co. 1904 edition online at UTLM. †

Hill, Donna. 1977. *Joseph Smith: The First Mormon.* New York, NY: Doubleday.

History of the RLDS Church. 1951. RLDS Church. Independence, MO: Herald House.

History of the Church of Jesus Christ of Latter-day Saints. (HC) 1902 on. 7 Vols. Salt Lake City, UT: LDS Church.

History of the (Reorganised) Church of Jesus Christ of Latter-day Saints. 1897-1908. 4 Vols. Smith, Joseph III & Smith, Heman Conoman. (Vol 2:1897 cited). Lamoni, IA: RLDS. Herald Publishing House.

Hoth, Hans Peter Emanuel. 1853-1857. *Hoth Diary.* Translation from original German. Berkeley, CA: University of California, Berkeley: Bancroft Library. († UTLM).
Howe, E.D. 1834. *Mormonism Unvailed. [sic].* Painesville, OH: Howe. †
Hyde, John Jr. 1857. *Mormonism, Its Leaders and Designs.* New York, NY: W. P. Fetridge & Co.†
Hyde, Orson. 1842. *Ein Ruf aus der Wüste, eine Stimme aus dem Erhoofe der Erbe.* Frankfurt. (A Cry from the Wilderness, a Voice from the Dust of the Earth). Translated 1962 and available in English. Google 'Orson Hyde First Vision'.
An Inspired Revision of the Authorised Version. (IR). *(The Holy Scriptures: Inspired Version),* Joseph Smith. 1980. Independence, MO: Herald House. RLDS. †
The International Standard Bible Encyclopedia. 1995. (4 Vols. Fully Revised) by Geoffrey W. Bromiley. Grand Rapids, MI: William B. Eerdman Publishing.
Jenson, Andrew. (comp.). 1887. *The Historical Record.* 9 Vols. Salt Lake City, UT: Jenson.
— 1899. *Church Chronology.* Salt Lake City, UT: Deseret News.
Jessee, Dean. (comp.). 1984. *The Personal Writings of Joseph Smith.* Salt Lake City, UT: Deseret Book.
Jessee, Dean C; Esplin, Ronald K; Bushman, Richard L. (comp). 2011. *Joseph Smith Papers: Revelations and Translations, Vol. 2: Published Revelations.* Salt Lake City, UT: Deseret Book.
Joseph Smith Begins His Work. 1833, 1835. Salt Lake City, UT; Wilford C. Wood – via UTLM.
Joseph Smith Papers: Revelations and Translations, Vol. 2. See: Jesse, Dean C. et al.
Journal of Discourses (JD) 1854-1884 by Brigham young, President of the Church of Jesus Christ of Latter Day Saints, His Two Counsellors, The Twelve Apostles and Others. 26 Volumes. Liverpool: R. James. †
Kenney, Scott. (ed.). 1984. *Wilford Woodruff's Journal 1833-1898.* Salt Lake City, UT: Signature Books.
Kimball, Spencer W. 1976. *Marriage and Divorce.* Salt Lake City, UT: Deseret Book.
Kirkham, Francis W. 1942. *A New Witness for Christ in America.* Independence, MO: Zion Printing & Publishing Co.
— 1951. *A New Witness for Christ in America.* Vol. 2. Independence, MO: Zion Printing & Publishing Co.
Kirtland Elder's Quorum Record 1836-1841. 1985. Cook, Lyndon W. & Backman, Milton V. Jr., (eds.). RLDS Church Archives. Provo, UT: Grandin Book Co. †
Kirtland Revelation Book. 1831-1839. Salt Lake City, UT: LDS Church Archives.
Lamb, Rev. M. T. 1887. *The Golden Bible.* (Reprint of Original). Salt Lake City, UT: UTLM.
Larsen, Charles M. 1992. *By His Own Hand Upon Papyrus: A New Look at the Joseph Smith Papyri.* Grand Rapids, MI: Institute for Religious Research. † (Part).
Larson, Stan. (ed.). 1993. *A Ministry of Meetings: The Apostolic Diaries of Rudger Clawson.* Salt Lake City, UT: Signature Books, in association with Smith Research Associates.
— 1997. *Quest for the Gold Plates: Thomas Stuart Ferguson's Archaeological Search for the Book of Mormon.* Salt Lake City, UT: Freethinker Press, in

BIBLIOGRAPHY, RECOMMENDED BOOKS & WEB SITES

association with Smith Research Associates.

Lauritzen, Bill. 2011. *The Invention of God: The Natural Origins of Mythology and Religion.* Lexington, KY: StreetWrite.

Lee, John D. 1877. *Mormonism Unveiled.* 2001. Albuquerque, NM: Fierra Blanca Publications, facsimile 1891 reprint, St. Louis, MO: D.M. Vanderwalker & Co.

Lewis, Catherine. 1848. *Narrative of Some of the Proceedings of the Mormons.* Lynn, MA: C. Lewis.

Linn, Alexander. 2001. *The Story of the Mormons.* Seattle, WA: The World Wide School. †

Lyman, Edward Leo. 1986. *Political Deliverance: The Quest for Utah Statehood.* Chicago, IL: University of Illinois Press.

Marquardt, H. Michael. 2005 *The Rise of Mormonism: 1816-1844. Fairfax, VA: Xulon Press.

Marquardt, H. Michael & Walters, Wesley P. 1994. *Inventing Mormonism.* Salt Lake City, UT: Signature Books.

McConkie, Bruce R. 1958. *Mormon Doctrine.* Salt Lake City, UT: Bookcraft.

Morgan, Dale. 1986. *Early Mormonism: Correspondence and A New History*, Salt Lake City, UT: Signature Books.

Morgan, William. 1827. *Illustrations of Masonry by One of the Fraternity Who has Devoted Thirty Years to the Subject.* Batavia, NY: David C. Miller. †

Naifeh, Steven & Smith, Gregory White. 1988. *The Mormon Murders - A True Story of Greed, Forgery, Deceit and Death.* New York, NY: New America Library, division of Penguin.

The Neal A. Maxwell Institute for Religious Scholarship. See FARMS.

Nelson, Leland R. (comp.). 1979. *The Journal of Joseph Smith.* Provo, UT: Council Press.

Newell, Linda King & Avery, Valeen Tippetts. 1994. 2nd Edition. *Mormon Enigma: Emma Hale Smith.* Chicago, IL: University of Illinois Press.

Nibley, Hugh W. 1957. *An Approach to the Book of Mormon.* Salt Lake City, UT: Deseret Book & FARMS.

O'Bryan, Aileen. 1956. *The Dîné: Origin Myths of the Navaho Indians.* Washington, D.C: Bulletin 163 of the Bureau of American Ethnology of the Smithsonian Institution.

The Pearl of Great Price. (PoGP). A selection from the revelations, translations, and narrations of Joseph Smith. 1981. Salt Lake City, UT: LDS Church. †

Pratt, Orson. 1840. *An Interesting Account of Several Remarkable Visions, and of the Late Discovery of Ancient American Records.* Edinburgh: Ballantyne & Hughes. †

— 1850. *Divine Authenticity of the Book of Mormon.* Liverpool. †

Pratt, Parley P. 1837. *A Voice of Warning.* New York, NY: W Sanford. †

Quinn, D. Michael (ed.). 1992. *The New Mormon History.* Salt Lake City, UT: Signature Books.

— 1994. *The Mormon Hierarchy: Origins of Power.* Salt Lake City, UT: Signature Books.

— 1997. *The Mormon Hierarchy: Extensions of Power.* Salt Lake City, UT: Signature Books.

— 1998. *Early Mormonism and the Magic World View.* Salt Lake City, UT: Signature Books.

Reed Smoot Case. 1907. *Proceedings Before the Committee on Privileges and Elections of the United States Senate in the Matter of the Protests Against the Right of Hon. Reed Smoot, a Senator from the State of Utah, to Hold his Seat.* Comprises 4 Volumes covering the 1904-1906 hearings. Washington, D.C: Govt. Printing Office.

Reimherr, Otto. (ed.). 1987. *Quest for Faith, Quest for Freedom.* Susquehanna, PA: Susquehanna University Press.

The Revised Laws of Illinois. 1833. Vandalia, IL: Greiner & Sherman.

Roberts, B.H. 1895. *New Witnesses for God.* (V.3 cited) Salt Lake City, UT: George Q. Cannon & Sons Co.

— 1978. *Comprehensive History of the Church.* (CHC) Salt Lake City, UT: BYU.

Robinson, John J. 1993. *A Pilgrim's Path: Freemasonry and the Religious Right.* New York, NY: M. Evans & Co.

Robinson, Stephen E. 1993. *Are Mormons Christians?* Salt Lake City, UT: Deseret Book.

Rupp, I. Daniel. (ed.). 1844. *An Original History of the Religious Denominations at Present Existing in the United States.* Philadelphia, PA: J. Y. Humphreys.*

Schele, Linda & Freidel, David. 1990. *A Forest of Kings: The Untold Story of the Ancient Maya.* NY: Quill. William Morrow.

Schindler, Harold. 1993. *Orrin Porter Rockwell: Man of God/Son of Thunder.* Salt Lake City, UT: University of Utah Press.

Schwartz, Marion. 1998. *A History of Dogs in the Early Americas.* New Haven, CT. & London: Yale University Press.

Senate Document 189. (Danite Treason Trial). 1841. 26th Congress, 2nd session. Available as a photo Reprint: Salt Lake City, UT: UTLM.

Senate Hearings - See: Reed Smoot Case 1907.

SHIELDS — *Scholarly & Historical Information Exchange for Latter-Day Saints.* (Mormon Apologetics). Available online at: www.shields-research.org

Smith, Lucy Mack. 1853. *Biographical Sketches of Joseph Smith the Prophet, and his progenitors for many generations.* Liverpool: S. W. Richards. (Photo reprint of the original 1853 edition: Tanner. *Joseph Smith's History by his Mother.* Salt Lake City, UT: UTLM).

Smith, Ethan. 1825. *View of the Hebrews.* Poultney, VT: Smith & Shute. Available as a Photo reproduction (including *The Parallels Between the Book of Mormon and the View of the Hebrews,* by the Mormon Historian B. H. Roberts): Salt Lake City, UT: UTLM.

Smith, Joseph Fielding (Jr). 1905. *Blood Atonement and the Origin of Plural Marriage.* Salt Lake City, UT: Deseret News Press.

— 1938. (Comp). *Teachings of the Prophet Joseph Smith by Joseph Smith.* Salt Lake City, UT: Deseret News Press.

— 1954. *Doctrines of Salvation.* 3 Vols. Salt Lake City, UT: Bookcraft.

— 1972. *Essentials in Church History.* Salt Lake City, UT: Deseret Book.

Smith, William B. 1883. *William Smith on Mormonism.* Lamoni, Iowa: RLDS. †

Smoot, Reed. *Senate Hearings.* See: Reed Smoot Case 1907.

BIBLIOGRAPHY, RECOMMENDED BOOKS & WEB SITES

Sorenson, John L. 1985. *An Ancient American Setting for the Book of Mormon.* Salt Lake City, UT: Deseret Book & FARMS.

Southerton, Simon G. 2004. *Losing a Lost Tribe: Native Americans, DNA and the Mormon Church.* Salt Lake City, UT: Signature Books.

Sperry, Sidney B. 1964. *The Problems of the Book of Mormon.* Salt Lake City, UT: Bookcraft.

Staker, Susan. (Ed.). 1993. *Waiting for World's End.* Salt Lake City, UT: Signature Books.

Stenhouse, Fanny. (Mrs. T.B.H). 1874. *Tell It All, the Story of a Life's Experience in Mormonism.* Hartford, CT: A. D. Worthington. † §

Stenhouse, T.B.H. 1873. *The Rocky Mountain Saints - A Full and Complete History of The Mormons.* New York, NY: D. Appleton & Co. Available as a Photo reproduction: UTLM. §

Stewart, John J. 1966. *Joseph Smith: The Mormon Prophet.* Salt Lake City, UT: Mercury.

Stout, Hosea. 1844-1869 Diary. Available at: http://robandsusanpages.com (Histories page).

Tanner, Jerald. 1988. *Tracking the White Salamander.* Salt Lake City, UT: UTLM. †

Tanner, Jerald & Sandra. 1968 The Case Against Mormonism. (Vol 2 referenced). There are 3 Vols, published 1967, 1968 & 1971. Salt Lake City, UT: UTLM. §

— 1970a. *Mormon Scriptures and the Bible.* Salt Lake City, UT: UTLM.

— 1970b. *Joseph Smith and Money Digging.* Salt Lake City, UT: UTLM.

— 1971. *Falsification of Joseph Smith's History.* Salt Lake City, UT: UTLM.

— 1980a. *Following the Brethren (Benson & McConkie)* Salt Lake City, UT: UTLM. †

— 1980b. *The Changing World of Mormonism.* Chicago, IL: Moody Press. †

— 1982. *Clayton's Secret Writings Uncovered: Extracts from the Diaries of Joseph Smith's Secretary William Clayton.* Salt Lake City, UT: Modern Microfilm.

— 1987. *Mormonism - Shadow or Reality?* 5th Edition. Salt Lake City, UT: UTLM §

— 1991. Flaws in the Pearl of Great Price. Salt Lake City, UT: UTLM. §

— 1996. *3,913 Changes in The Book of Mormon.* Salt Lake City, UT: UTLM. §

Taylor, Samuel Woolley. 1974. *Family Kingdom.* Salt Lake City, UT: Zion Book.

The Temple Lot Case. 1893. The RLDS Church, complainant, vs. the LDS Church at Independence, Missouri. Complainant's abstract of pleading and evidence. United States Circuit Court. (8th Circuit). Lamoni, IA: Herald Publishing. Available as a Photo reproduction: Salt Lake City, UT: UTLM.

Tullige, Edward Wheelock. 1877. *The Women of Mormondom.* New York, NY: Tullige & Crandall.

Van Waggoner, Richard S. 1989. *Mormon Polygamy: A History.* Salt Lake City, UT: Signature Books. §

— 1994. *Sidney Rigdon: A Portrait of Religious Excess.* Salt Lake City, UT: Signature Books.

Vlachos, Chris A. 1979. *Adam is God???* Salt Lake City, UT: UTLM.

Vogel, Dan. 1986. *Indian Origins and the Book of Mormon.* Salt Lake City, UT: Signature. †

— (ed.). 1996-2003. *Early Mormon Documents.* 5 Vols. Salt Lake City, UT: Signature.
Wallace, Irving. 1961. *The Twenty Seventh Wife.* New York, NY: Simon & Schuster.
Walters, Wesley P. 1990. *The Use of the Old Testament in the Book of Mormon.* Salt Lake City, UT: UTLM.
Werner, M.R. 1925. *Brigham Young.* New York, NY: Harcourt, Brace & Co. Available as a photo reproduction: Salt Lake City, UT: UTLM.
Whitefield, Jim. 2009a. *The Mormon Delusion. (TMD) Volume 1. The Truth Behind Polygamy and Secret Polyandry.* Raleigh, NC: Lulu Press Inc.
— 2009b. *The Mormon Delusion. (TMD) Volume 2. The Secret Truth Withheld From 13 Million Mormons.* Raleigh, NC: Lulu Press Inc.
— 2009c. *The Mormon Delusion. (TMD) Volume 3. Discarded Doctrines and Nonsense Revelations.* Raleigh, NC: Lulu Press Inc.
— 2011a. *The Mormon Delusion. (TMD) Volume 4. The Mormon Missionary Lessons – A Conspiracy to Deceive.* Raleigh, NC: Lulu Press Inc.
— 2011b. The First Vision: The Joseph Smith Story. Raleigh, NC: Lulu Press Inc.
Whitmer, David. 1887. *An Address to All Believer's In Christ.* Richmond, MO: D. Whitmer. † §
Whitney, Orson F. 1888. 2nd ed. 1945. *Life of Heber C. Kimball.* Salt Lake City, UT: Stevens & Wallace Inc.
Widtsoe, John A. 1960. *Evidences and Reconciliations.* Salt Lake City, UT: Bookcraft.
The World Christian Encyclopaedia. 2001. Barrett, David B; Kurian, George T; Johnson, Todd M. Oxford: Oxford University Press.
Wyl, Wilhelm. (Wilhelm Ritter von Wymetal). 1886. *Joseph Smith the Prophet, His Family and Friends.* Salt Lake City, UT: Tribune Printing & Publishing Co.
Young, Ann Eliza. 1876. *Wife No. 19, Or the Story of a Life in Bondage, being a Complete Exposé of Mormonism and Revealing the Sorrows, Sacrifices and Sufferings of Women in Polygamy.* Hartford, CT: Dustin, Gilman & Co.†

Bibliography Notes.

§ A dozen or so selected books, recommended initial reading.

* Complete book available to read online at *Google Book Search.*

† Fully downloadable, readable (or excerpts available) online via an internet search on the title. Sometimes, a search on an author's name brings up locations where you can read part, if not all of a book which may not show as available to read via *Google Book Search.*

Many books are available to read online at *The Anti-Mormon Preservation Society*, located at http://antimormon.8m.com and also the *Utah Lighthouse Ministry* (UTLM) at www.utlm.org. Books annotated above with † *and* UTLM, are currently available to read there.

BIBLIOGRAPHY, RECOMMENDED BOOKS & WEB SITES

A user friendly source of information is now available under the title *The Mormon Handbook* which is a guide to many false claims, along with references and also links to quite a number of online resources that are now available. It is well worth a browse and is available at: http://www.mormonhandbook.com/home/sources.html

Mormon (LDS) Scriptures, including the *King James Version* of the Bible, *Book of Mormon, Doctrine and Covenants* and the *Pearl of Great Price* are all available to research at: http://scriptures.lds.org

Various versions of complete Bible texts are available for comparison and research, including *Young's Literal Translation* (which I have referenced in these volumes) at: www.biblegateway.com

Many of the early newspapers cited in my work, such as *Messenger and Advocate, Times & Seasons* and others, are now available to read online via a search on the name and year of the publication.

Various Church manuals and magazines (such as the *Ensign*) can be researched via the Mormon online library at: www.lds.org/gospellibrary

If I had to recommend *one* book in which to locate clinically written evidence (as a reference book) against the Mormon Church, it would resoundingly be *Mormonism - Shadow or Reality?*, by Jerald & Sandra Tanner, whose research and findings are painstakingly detailed and highly accurate, not to mention easily readable and well indexed. It is a veritable encyclopaedia of the real truth. A beautifully written favourite account of the truth in more flowing book form is by Fawn Brodie (niece of David O. McKay), *No Man Knows My History. (Brodie 1945). (Brodie 1963 for the U.K.).*

Likewise, if I had to choose *one* book that eloquently relates the experience of the British (and European) Saints concerning early lies about polygamy, emigration to Salt Lake and the real underlying and heartbreaking polygamy story, blood atonement and more, *Tell It All*, by Fanny Stenhouse is heartfelt and revealing, enthralling and yet devastating. It will break your heart. You can feel her torment, anguish and confusion. You simply *cannot* put it down. It places period drama into an entirely new dimension. And yet it is unfortunately a true and accurate account of what actually happened.

Books written by early English saints are rare, so I also enthusiastically recommend Samuel Hawthornthwaite's book, written in 1857: *Mr. Hawthornthwaite's Adventures among the Mormons as an Elder, During the Last Eight Years.* It was only brought to my attention as I was putting the finishing touches to volume five, and I have to say it is the most remarkable little book I have ever encountered regarding how the Church operated in England (and also somewhat in Utah) in the early years. It contains first hand experiences and accounts of corruption and duplicity of apostles and other leaders during the eighteen-fifties and I thus consider it to be a *'must read'* book. Personal experiences, letters and sworn statements are written in a nineteenth century English writing style that is quaint and endearing. The content is profound and devastating.

THE MORMON DELUSION

There are many Mormon and ex-Mormon websites. A good starting point for anyone who is questioning Mormonism and its beliefs, or needs help in their recovery from Mormonism is www.exmormon.org which provides hundreds of stories, articles and a debating forum, plus links to several other sites at the bottom of the home page. I would also recommend Richard Packham's web site for succinct and accurate answers to questions. His home page and many other useful links can be located by searching his name, directly from the *exmormon* link or at: http://home.teleport.com/~packham/ or from www.salamandersociety.com/links/ which is another very useful web site.

There are dozens of links available to various web sites (many Christian), and some excellent source material on Mormonism, further resources, scriptures, documents, information, books, newspapers and periodicals through UTLM. The direct link to the page for these resources is: www.utlm.org/navotherwebsites.htm

Mountain Meadows Massacre - movie: *September Dawn* (released 2008). This film weaves a fictional love story into the history of the massacre. Whilst it is not entirely accurate according to historical evidence, it is close and depicts the general details well.

A documentary one hour video evidencing the *Book of Abraham* fraud is available online, courtesy of The *Institute for Religious Research* - www.irr.org. This excellent and highly recommended programme can be purchased as a video or DVD or viewed free online. The detail is accurate and the evidence is conclusive. *The Lost Book of Abraham: Investigating a Remarkable Mormon Claim* can be viewed free of charge at the following direct link: www.irr.org/mit/lboa-video.html

Similarly, a documentary film regarding DNA and the *Book of Mormon* can be viewed free, courtesy of Living Hope Ministries: www.lvhm.org/vid_dna_med.htm

The Mormon Church manipulated votes, financially and organisationally, against gay rights during the 'Proposition 8' campaign in California in 2008. A DVD of the documentary movie '8: The Mormon Proposition' is available from Amazon et al.

INDEX

116 lost pages (See: Book of Lehi)
Aaron, firstborn descendants – right to be Bishops; 243-4, 257
Aaronic Priesthood; 126, 302
Abel; 466
Abraham; 24, 275, 341, 369
Abraham, Isaac and Jacob; 455, 462, 466
Adam – meaning of name; 422
Adam and Eve; 21, 34, 156, 404, 410, 466
Adam-ondi-Ahman (Adam-on-diahmon), aka Spring Hill; 162, 223, 292
  - temple square dedicated; 405
Adam's altar; 21
Adamic language; 31
adulterers to be cast out: 186
Africans, black; 36, 273
age for baptism; 244
Ahman; 291, 329
Ain Ghazal, Jordan; 38
Aitkin Party; 177
Alexander, Thomas G; 64
Alger, Fanny; 178, 187, 204, 235, 374, 428, 457
Almighty, the; 302
Alpha and Omega; 194, 218
Alphus and Omegus; 329
American Civil War; 307, 448
angels, origin; 197
Apocrypha; 325
Apollos; 275
apostles, testimony of; 11
appointed unto death; 179
archaeology; 24
Article of Faith 10; 185
Ashley, Major N; 266
Avars, Sampson; 162
Babbitt, Almon; 435
Babylon; 249
Baldwin, Caleb – arrested for treason; 408
baptism; 144, 244
baptismal font required in Nauvoo temple; 429
Basset, Heman; 215
Belial, sons of; 214
Bennett, Dr. John C; 375, 427
Bidamon, Lewis C; 428
bishops; 10, 243
black skin; 36
Boggs, Governor Lilburn; 92
Bonian culture; 38

Book of Abraham; 115, 167
Book of Commandments; 8, 10, 11
Book of Lehi; 97, 99-102, 132
Book of Mormon –
  - contains the gospel; 103, 127
  - contains fullness of the gospel; 142, 177
  - failed copyright sale; 157-8
  - for Lamanites; 103
  - written, rather than translated; 145
Book of Moses; 167, 184, 422
Booth, Ezra; 234, 237, 261
Boynton, John; 399
bread; 33, 34
Brodie, Fawn; 392
Buell, Pres(c)endia Lathrop Huntington; 417
Burgess, William; 389
Burnett, Stephen; 292
Cahoon, Reynolds; 333
Cain and Abel; 36
Caldwell County compromise; 362
calling and election made sure; 310, 452
Cannon, George Q; 64
Carter, Jared; 293, 333
casting dust from feet; 145-6, 266, 298, 301
Çatalhöyük, Turkey; 38
Celestial kingdom; 273, 310, 301
Cephas; 275
cereals and grasses; 32-33
changing name of the Church; 140
chariots; 234
chickens, as a hen gathereth; 188, 189
children cannot sin; 156
cholera; 155, 217
Christ, Jesus (see: Jesus Christ)
Church of Christ (Joseph Smith); 10, 139, 400
Church of Christ (Temple Lot); 226, 432
Church of Christ (Warren Parrish); 108, 333
Church of God; 140, 400
Church of Jesus Christ; 140, 400
Church of the Latter-Day Saints (The); 15
Church of the Latter Day Saints; 140, 400
circumcision; 359
Cishan culture; 38
Clark, Wycam; 108
code names in the D&C; 290
Coe, Joseph; 221
Community of Christ; 223, 299, 322, 333, 388, 396, 432
concoctions; 7
consecration, law of; 179, 212, 259, 326
  - permanent and everlasting; 290, 356-7
  - suspended; 359
Constantine; 175

continental drift; 250
Copley, Leman; 204, 218
Corrill, John; 162, 215, 366
Council of Fifty; 223
Council of Laodicea; 278
Council of the twelve; 10
Covill, James; 172-3, 295
Cowdery, Oliver; 113, 115, 118, 121, 127, 129, 132, 137, 141, 150, 158, 163, 166, 203, 221, 258, 296, 378, 383, 389, 392
Cowdery, Warren; 367, 383
Cox, Professor Brian; 282, 214, 447
creation; 33-34
Creationism; 285
Cucuteni-Trypillian culture; 38
Dane, William H; 47
Daniel; 466
Danites; 162, 293
David and Solomon; 456
Dawkins, Richard; 56
Day of Atonement (Yom Kippur); 358
daystarre; 270
deacons; 256, 302
Dionysis; 142
discerning false spirits; 207-9, 445-6
dispensation of the fullness of times; 9
dissenters; 174
divining rod; 118, 119
DNA; 47, 159, 161, 190, 243
DNA challenge; 361-2
doctrines change over time; 177-8
Dodds, Asa; 266
domesticated animals; 31-32
dust from feet (see: casting dust from feet)
dysentery; 155
early cultures; 38
Earth – age of; 311
    - hangs upon nothing; 66
    - seven thousand year existence; 156, 285, 311
    - to become celestialised; 312
    - will eventually be obliterated; 312
effectual door; 340, 393-5, 413
Egypt; 21, 24, 118, 184
Egyptian culture; 38
Egyptus; 21, 250
Elam, farming region; 38
elders; 256
Elias; 9, 90-91, 92-93, 94-5, 126, 149, 275, 385, 466
Elijah; 9, 90-91, 126, 275, 335, 385
endless is not always endless; 136-7

endowment; 45
endowment at Kirtland temple; 363, 367
enmity; 343-4
Enoch; 184, 194, 372
ensample; 318-9
entropy; 172
Esaias; 275
eternal is not always eternal; 136-7
evangelists; 83
evidence overrides faith; 17, 22, 23
evolution; 21, 193, 268, 274
exaltation; 451
extermination order (Missouri Executive Order 44); 198, 341, 348
Eye on Apologetics; 415-6
Ezaias; 300
Ezekiel; 466
faith – degree of, saves a person; 80
    - first principle of religion; 17, 27
    - first principle of revealed science; 22
    - God works by; 20-21
    - principle of action; 24
    - principle of power; 25, 26
false spirits; 206
falsified wording in D&C 39; 173
Far West; 155, 158, 333
    - temple prophesied to be built at; 401
Father of Lights; 247
fear, the prime motivator; 305
First and Second Elder; 10
First Presidency; 10
First Vision; 8-9, 61, 85-86, 248
firstlings of flocks; 35
fish, to die of thirst; 252-3
Fishing River; 362
flood; 21, 38, 184
flood-gap; 38, 405
Fort Sumner; 161
Gabriel; 149
Gallatin; 162
gate of heaven; 381-2
gathering – 168-9
    - from the four winds; 249
Gause, Jesse; 294
Gibeah; 214
gift of Aaron; 119
Gilbert, Algernon Sidney; 217, 226-7, 296,
    - 324, 348
Gladdenites; 432
glossolalia; 83, 202
God –
    - anger of; 46

INDEX

- attributes; 55
- characteristics; 44
- contradictory; 55
- has a body; 30
- has faith in Himself; 39
- invisible spirit; 68, 71
- is a spirit; 39, 62, 63, 66
- is called the Son because of the flesh; 68
- is evil; 52
- is homophobic; 52
- mind is the holy spirit; 63, 68, 69
- monotheistic; 39, 56
- omnipotent; 29-30
- omnipresent; 29-30, 39
- omniscient; 29-30
- says men are to rule over women; 32
- without beginning of days; 29-30, 39

Godhead; 61
   - Holy Ghost not a member; 62
   - two personages; 62, 65
Gould, John; 340
Granger, Oliver; 410-11
Grant, Heber J; 84, 464
Grant, Jedediah M; 223
gravity (space-time curvature); 314
Great Britain to assist in Civil War; 308
great deep to be driven back; 250
Griffin, Selah J; 223
Guru Granth Sahib (Sikhism); 372
Haight, Isaac C; 47
Hanks, Marion Duff; 467
Harris, Lucinda Pendleton Morgan; 375, 428, 457
Harris, Martin; 99, 107, 111, 129, 132, 137, 138, 229-30, 258, 292, 296, 333
HaSatan; 269-70
Heaven; 276
   - is paradise; 283, 285
Hell; 272-3
Helminths; 345
Hendrickson, Glenn; 416, 419, 424
Higbee, Elias; 398
High Council; 256, 350, 351
High Priests; 243, 256
Hinckle, George M; 162
Hinckley, Gordon B; xiv, 30, 182, 316
Holy Ghost – 310, 311
   - doctrine reconstructed; 64
   - exclusive to Mormons; 311
Holy Spirit – mind of God; 63, 68, 69
Holy Spirit of Promise; 310
homicide, might be forgiven; 177

homosexuality; 52
honesty; 164
Houli culture; 38
Hyde, Orson; 243, 249, 266, 340, 354, 391-2, 399
idolatry; 215-6
'Indians' are Lamanites; 190-1
Inspired Revision of the Bible: 30-31, 214, 252, 263, 278
interpretation of tongues; 83
Isaiah; 275, 300, 466
Israelites; 184
Jackson County; 364
Jackson, President Andrew; 308
Jaques, Vienna; 324
Jehovah; 385
Jerusalem; 183, 249
Jesus Christ –
   - a saved being; 81
   - birth date; 142
   - God of the Old Testament; 153
   - is God manifest in the flesh; 63, 153
   - in the bosom of the Father; 63
   - name mis-transliterated; 128
   - name used by Smith BCE; 382
   - named Yeshua; 128
   - possesses the fullness of the Father; 68
   - possesses same mind with Father; 63, 69
   - quotes Malachi; 252
   - will burn people when he comes; 154
Joel; 196
John (apostle) – 233
   - parchment; 116
John the Baptist; 300
Johnson, John; 299, 330
Johnson, Luke S; 243, 266, 399
Johnson, Lyman E; 243, 399
Jones, Miles H; 294
Israelites; 24
Katich, Samuel; 209
Kimball, Helen Mar; 452
Kimball, Spencer W; 159-61, 189-90
King Follett sermon; 201
Kirtland; 154-5, 158, 296, 332, 351, 401
Kirtland endowment; 363, 367
Kirtland (Safety Society) Bank; 108, 129, 158, 203, 333, 391-3
Kirtland Temperance Society; 321
Kirtland temple; 332-3, 396
   - dedicatory prayer; 383-4
   - sold to pay Smith's estate debts; 333, 384
Knight, Joseph Sr; 125, 141

Knight, Newel; 218, 219, 223
Kojiki (Shinto); 372
Lamanites – 97, 102, 158, 159-61, 163, 195, 205, 213, 225, 458
  - 'Indians' are L; 190-1
  - to blossom as the rose; 205
  - to be gathered; 189
land of promise; 172
Lauritzen, Bill; 196-7, 205
law of apostolic succession; 129
Law of Sarah; 458
law of the land, obey; 229
Law, William; 229, 231, 393, 435, 436
Law brothers – printing press destroyed; 460
Law of Sarah; 48
Lawrence, Maria & Sarah; 393, 452
Lectures of Faith = 'Doctrine' part of D&C; 8
  - are doctrine; 17, 84
  - deleted from D&C (1921); 12, 17
  - voted on as doctrine twice; 11-12, 84-85
Lectures *on* Faith or Lectures *of* Faith; 15
Lee, Ann; 204
Lee, John D; 47
Liahona; 132
Liberty Jail; 415, 417, 418
Light of Christ; 311
longevity; 371
Lord – coming soon; 187
  - coming in that generation; 208
  - coming suddenly to his temple; 248
  - coming with a curse and judgment; 248
  - excuses not himself; 246
  - of Sabaoth; 328-9, 340
Lost tribes myth (see: ten lost tribes myth)
Lucifer; 269-70
Lyman, Amasa M; 323
Malachi; 251-2, 335
malaria: 155
Manifesto (1890); 462-5, 466
Marks, William; 256, 410
Marsh, Thomas B; 161-2, 222-3, 393, 397, 399, 412
Matthew 1; 200
McConkie, Bruce R; 85
McLellin, William; 158, 241-2, 243, 266, 324, 399
McRae, Alexander – arrested for treason; 408
Melchizedek Priesthood; 126, 150, 203, 300
Mestizo tribes; 160
milk –
  - and honey (land of promise); 172
  - before meat; 30, 138

  - in the human diet; 33
Millennial Star; 453
millstone; 419
moon – light of; 311
  - turned to blood; 154
Morley, Isaac; 237, 261, 366
Morning star; 271
Moses; 9, 24, 91, 118, 126, 300, 385, 456, 466
Mountain Meadows massacre; 46-47, 177
murder, might be forgiven; 177
Murdock, John; 215, 298
Murdock, Julia Clapp; 299
name of the Lord's Church; 10, 400
Nashville (Lee County, Iowa); 439
nation, kindred, tongue and people; 180-1
Native Americans – legends; 36
  - marriage to; 458
natural selection; 344
Nauvoo Expositer; 435
Nauvoo House; 433, 436
Nauvoo, Illinois; 155, 439
  - temple prophesied to be built at; 429
Navajo; 161
Neo-Assyrian Empire; 388
Neolithic period; 38
Neolithic settlement at Mehrgarh; 38
New and everlasting covenant; 457, 458
New Jerusalem; 177, 183, 184, 185, 198, 299
Nicea, Council of; 175
Noah; 24, 38, 149, 466
Nullification process; 308
Oath of Vengeance; 57
Olaha Shinehah; 410
Ottoman Turks; 249
Packer, Boyd K; 315-6
Page, Hiram; 157, 158
Page, John E; 413
paid ministry; 185
Palaeolithic period; 38
Palestine; 249
Papuan people; 38
parable – of 12 workers in a field; 314-5
  - of nobleman and vineyard; 345-6
  - of wheat and tares; 346
  - of the woman and unjust judge; 347
Paradise; 283, 285
parchment (of apostle John); 116
Parish, Warren; 108, 333, 383, 384
Partridge, Edward; 167, 175, 207, 211, 226, 296, 366
Partridge, Emily & Eliza; 352
Passover (feast of); 358

INDEX

Pastors; 83
patriarchs; 435
Patten, David W; 399
Paul (apostle); 128, 275
Peck, Reed; 162
Peiligang culture: 38
Perdition; 271
persecution; 73
Peter, James and John; 126; 149
Peterson, Ziba; 163, 230
Phelps, W.W; 129, 158, 162, 221, 227, 230, 233, 258, 296, 304
pioneer deaths; 57
plagues; 184
plural gods; 30, 419-20
polyandry; 209
polygamy (polygyny); 455-9
polytheistic Judaism; 35
Pontius Pilate; 385
Pope John I; 142
Pratt, Orson; 164, 354
Pratt, Parley P; 163, 204, 330, 351, 354
prayer; 26
pre-existence, a twentieth century idea; 65-66
preach to gentiles, then Jews; 249
presidency; 203
presidents; 256
priesthood, passed father to son; 369-70
priests; 256, 302
proclamation to the US President; 427-8
prophecies and promises will be fulfilled; 246
pseudepigrapha; 372
Publius Lentulus; 385
Pure Church of Christ; 108
purse or scrip, go without; 301
Quorum of Twelve Apostles; 257, 350, 351
Qur'an (Islam); 372
rainbow; 38
Red Sea; 24, 118
Reed Smoot Senate Hearings; 458
Reformed Mormon Church (The True Church of Jesus Christ of Latter Day Saints); 435
Reorganised Church of Jesus Christ of Latter Day Saints (See: Community of Christ)
revelation –
  - can be changed; 111
  - formed in the mind; 118
  - no longer received; xiv
Revelation, Book of; 219, 278
Revelation 1:6; 200-1
Richards, Willard; 413, 459
riches of gentiles for the saints; 179

Richmond; 408
Rigdon, Sidney; 166, 167, 175, 203, 204, 236, 256, 258, 260, 267, 296, 323, 327, 333, 339, 350, 354, 383, 389, 391, 436
  - arrested for treason; 408
  - Independence Day Oration; 401
  - Salt Sermon; 401
Riggs, Burr; 162, 266
Riverside Mansion; 433
RLDS Church (see Community of Christ)
Roberts; Brigham H; 64, 70
Rockwell, Orrin Porter; 441-2
rod of Jesse; 398
rod of nature; 119
root of Jesse; 398
Rodinia; 250
Ryder, Simonds; 215
Sabaoth (see: Lord of Sabaoth)
sacrament 148-9
sacrifice; 74-75
safe conduct pass; 46
Salem; 389-90
Satan; 36, 156, 269-70
  - sent to fight Mormon enemies; 364
saved, because God is saved; 79
School of the Elders; 16, 321
School of the Prophets; 16
science; 22
  - is theology; 78
sea of glass; 278-9
second anointing (see second endowment)
second coming –
  - no one knows when; 315, 316
  - not before 2060-2080; 316
  - won't be for a long time; 315
second endowment; 319, 452
second law of thermodynamics; 314
Sesklo culture; 38
Seth; 466
Seth, City of; 405
seven thousand years existence of earth; 21
Seventy; 10
Shakers; 204, 205
shaking dust from feet (see: casting dust...)
sheaves; 165, 293
Sherman, Lyman; 379
Shilo; 183-4
sickle; 293
sickness, desolating; 194-5
Sinai; 24, 184
Smith, Don Carlos; 406-7
Smith, Eden; 292

541

Smith, Emma; 147-8, 256, 299, 428
Smith, Ethan; 113
Smith, George A; 223
Smith, Hyrum; 123, 141, 215, 333, 354, 383, 389, 390, 435, 436, 459
- arrested for treason; 408
- seen in vision by Joseph F. Smith; 466
Smith, Joseph –
- arrested for treason; 408
- becomes a Freemason; 444
- boarding house to be built for; 428
- Carthage account by John Taylor; 459-60
- debts on his estate; 333, 384
- house to be built for; 175
- Melchizedek Priesthood (no record); 150
- monotheistic; 62, 115, 127, 130, 133, 143
- needs to repent; 327
- one gift or many; 107
- outlaw; 74
- prophecy against United States; 453
- seen in vision by Joseph F. Smith; 466
- sins forgiven, 323
- to be financially supported; 187
- translation by inspiration; 142
- treason; 231
- vision of Celestial kingdom; 382
- vision of God and Christ; 268
- vision of Jehovah; 385
Smith, Joseph III; 147
Smith, Joseph F. (sixth prophet); 9, 84, 458, 464, 465-6
Smith, Joseph Fielding (patriarch); 435
Smith, Joseph Sr; 105, 141
Smith, Lucy Mack; 9
Smith, Samuel H; 141, 242, 266
Smoot, Reed (see: Reed Smoot Senate Hearings)
Snow, Erastus; 390
Snow, Lorenzo; 84, 464
Son of Ahman; 291, 329
song, new; 302
Sons of Perdition; 271
soul; 312
Spanish flu pandemic; 284
spirit (of humans); 312
Spring Hill (Adam-ondi-Ahman); 404-6, 409, 410
- temple prophesied to be built at; 405-6
stakes, to be formed *after* Zion built; 343
stem of Jesse; 398
Strangites; 432
sun and moon stand still; 20, 26

sun – life span of; 282
- shall be darkened; 154
- will become a white dwarf; 312
Sweet, Northrop; 108
sword of Laban; 132
Syarthola cave, Norway; 38
taken over the rim of the basin; 46
taking a wife and her mother is wickedness; 52
Talmage, James E; 64, 70
Taylor, John; 84, 413, 435, 459
- seen in vision by Joseph F. Smith; 466
teachers; 256, 302
Telestial kingdom; 274, 310
temple lecture; 82
ten lost tribes myth; 388
Terrestrial kingdom; 273, 310, 382
testimony of the apostles; 11
Thayre, Ezra; 222-3
The Church of Jesus Christ of Latter-day Saints; - first named; 400
The Church of the Latter-Day Saints; 15
The True Church of Jesus Christ of Latter Day Saints (Reformed Mormon Church); 435
thermodynamics, second law of; 314
theology is revealed science; 21
Thompson, Robert B; 427
three witnesses (only); 108-9
thunder and lightening; 188
time is relative; 313
Times and Seasons; 415-6
Tipitaka (Buddhism); 372
tithing; 259, 330, 407, 413, 414
tongues; 83
translation process; 121
Turin shroud; 386
twelve apostles: Cowdery and Whitmer to locate and convert; 128
united order (see consecration, law of)
Urim and Thummim; 98, 132, 281
used up (in the pocket of the Lord); 46
Van Buren, President; 453
Varna Culture; 38
Vedas (Hindu); 372
View of the Hebrews; 113
Vinča culture; 38
volcanoes; 196-7
Vučedol culture; 38
Walker, Lucy; 452
war in heaven; 273
washing of feet; 145-6, 319
weeping, wailing and gnashing of teeth; 253
Wentworth letter; 185

INDEX

Western Reserve Teacher's Seminary; 384
wheat; 33
wheat and tares parable; 305
Whitmer, David; 125, 132, 133, 159
Whitmer family; 158
Whitmer, John; 125, 159, 166, 203, 258, 296
Whitmer, Peter Jr; 125, 159, 163
Whitmerites; 432
Whitney, Newel K; 263, 296, 327, 330, 410
Widtsoe, John A; 64, 70
Wight, Lyman; 215, 261, 351, 354, 366,
    - arrested for treason; 408
Williams, Frederick G; 162, 237, 294, 323,
    326, 327, 350, 354
Wilson, Calvers; 266
Winchester, Benjamin; 390
witnesses, testimony of; 11
Woodruff, Wilford; 84, 223, 413, 462, 464
    - seen in vision by Joseph F. Smith; 466
women must obey husbands; 48
Xinglongwa culture; 38
Yeshua (salvation); 128
Young, Brigham; 46, 84, 137, 223, 256, 308
    - above the law; 74
    - dedicates Far West temple site; 401
    - D&C Section 136 written by; 461-2
    - ordained teenage sons apostles; 302
    - plural gods; 419
    - seen in vision by Joseph F. Smith; 466
    - used Cowdery's divining rod; 118
    - used tithing to become rich; 259, 290
Zacharias; 149
Zarahemla (new city by Mississippi); 439
    - Stake discontinued; 440
Zelph; 361
Zenos; 181
Zion; 183, 184, 324, 331, 340, 341-2, 345
Zion (city of Enoch); 194
Zion (Independence, Missouri); 154, 185, 224-5, 226, 228, 234, 238, 249, 290, 299, 331, 348, 352-3, 401
    - restoration and redemption; 354
    - temple prophesied to be built at; 224-5
Zion's Camp; 154-5, 217, 298, 361-2